1 MONTH OF
FREE
READING

at
www.ForgottenBooks.com

By purchasing this book you are
eligible for one month membership to
ForgottenBooks.com, giving you
unlimited access to our entire
collection of over 1,000,000 titles via
our web site and mobile apps.

To claim your free month visit:
www.forgottenbooks.com/free1012916

ISBN 978-0-331-08910-3
PIBN 11012916

REPORTS OF CASES

ARGUED AND DETERMINED

IN THE

Courts of Exchequer & Exchequer Chamber,

FROM

MICHAELMAS TERM, 5 VICT.

TO

EASTER TERM, 5 VICT., BOTH INCLUSIVE;

WITH

TABLES OF THE CASES AND PRINCIPAL MATTERS.

BY

R. MEESON, Esq., AND W. N. WELSBY, Esq.,

OF THE MIDDLE TEMPLE, BARRISTERS AT LAW.

VOL. IX.

LONDON:
S. SWEET, CHANCERY LANE; A. MAXWELL, BELL YARD;
AND V. & R. STEVENS & G. S. NORTON, BELL YARD, LINCOLN'S INN;
Law Booksellers & Publishers:
AND ANDREW MILLIKEN, GRAFTON STREET, DUBLIN.

1843.

LONDON :
W. M'DOWALL, PRINTER, PEMBERTON-ROW,
GOUGH-SQUARE.

JUDGES

OF THE

COURT OF EXCHEQUER,

DURING THE PERIOD COMPRISED IN THIS VOLUME.

The Right Honourable JAMES, Lord ABINGER, Chief Baron.

· BARONS.

The Right Honourable Sir JAMES PARKE, Knt.
Sir EDWARD HALL ALDERSON, Knt.
Sir JOHN GURNEY, Knt.
Sir ROBERT MONSEY ROLFE, Knt.

ATTORNEY-GENERAL.
Sir FREDERICK POLLOCK, Knt.

SOLICITOR-GENERAL.
Sir WILLIAM WEBB FOLLETT, Knt.

TABLE

OF THE

NAMES OF THE CASES REPORTED
IN THIS VOLUME.

———

REPORTS OF CASES

ARGUED AND DETERMINED

IN

The Courts of Exchequer

AND

Exchequer Chamber.

MICHAELMAS TERM, 5 VICTORIÆ.

Exch. of Pleas,
1841.

Nov. 3.

HAZLEWOOD v. BACK.

WHITEHURST had obtained a rule, calling on the plaintiff to shew cause why the Master should not review his taxation. The declaration contained one count, for removing the defendant's son from the plaintiff's school without a quarter's notice. The defendant pleaded the general issue, and two special pleas of justification. A verdict was found for the plaintiff on the first and third pleas, and for the defendant on the second, which was an answer to the whole cause of action.

The Master, on taxation, allowed the plaintiff one half of his counsel's fees, a consultation fee upon the first issue, a portion of the costs of drawing and copying the briefs, and also the costs of subpœnaing a witness to prove the prospectus of the plaintiff's terms.

Knowles shewed cause.—The defendant having denied

Where several pleas are pleaded, and one of them, which amounts to an answer to the whole cause of action, is found for the defendant, and others for the plaintiff, the latter is entitled to the costs of the issues found for him, including a portion of the briefs and counsel's fees.

the contract by the general issue, and that plea having been found against him, the Master is right in allowing the plaintiff the costs occasioned by that issue. In *Hart* v. *Cutbush* (a), it was held, that if a defendant pleads the general issue, and several special pleas, and the jury find for him on the general issue, and for the plaintiff on the special pleas, the latter is entitled to the costs of the pleadings, and witnesses on those pleas. That decision was recognized in *Spencer* v. *Hamerton* (b), where, on consideration, the Court held, that where several pleas are pleaded, and one party obtains a verdict on some of the pleas, entitling him to the general costs of the cause, he is liable to pay the opposite party on the issues found for him, not only his costs of the pleadings, but also his costs of preparing evidence on those issues; and that the law has not been altered by the general rule, 1 Reg. Gen. H. T. 2 Will. 4, s. 74. By that rule it is ordered, that "no costs shall be allowed on taxation to the plaintiff, upon any count or issues upon which he has not succeeded, and the costs of all issues found for the defendant shall be deducted from the plaintiff's costs." *Othir* v. *Calvert* (c) is relied upon by the other side; but *Parke*, B., in *Hart* v. *Cutbush*, expresses doubt as to the correctness of that decision. Some difficulty may exist in the apportionment of the costs, but the principle is clear, that the plaintiff is entitled to be reimbursed the expense to which he has been put by the defendant's pleading an unfounded plea, although the latter may be entitled to the general costs of the cause.

Whitehurst, in support of the rule.—Admitting that the plaintiff is entitled to the costs of the pleadings and evidence, there is no authority to shew that he is also entitled to a portion of the briefs. *Othir* v. *Calvert* decided, that where costs in the cause are adjudged to the defendant,

(a) 2 Dowl. P. C. 456.   & M. 22.
(b) 4 Ad. & Ell. 413; 6 Nev.   (c) 1 Bing. 275; 8 Moore, 239.

and to the plaintiff costs on the issues found for him, the costs of the issues include only the costs of the pleadings. It is true that since that time a different practice has prevailed, but the subject has never been under the consideration of this Court. At all events, the Master ought not to have allowed any portion of the counsel's fees, or the consultation fee. They are not costs of the *pleas* or *evidence*, within the rule of H. T., 4 Will. 4, s. 7; and how is it practicable to apportion part of a fee to a particular plea?

Exch. of Pleas, 1841.

HAZLEWOOD v. BACK.

PARKE, B.—We think the Master is right in his taxation, and that the rule must be discharged. There is nothing in the language of the stat. 4 Ann. c. 16, s. 5, to confine the costs to those of the pleadings only. If the defendant, by his pleading, occasions the necessity of larger briefs and fees to counsel, he ought to pay the expense he occasions thereby.

The rest of the Court concurred.

Rule discharged.

JORDEN v. BERWICK.

HUGH HILL had obtained a rule, calling upon the plaintiff to shew cause why the defendant should not be at liberty to enter a suggestion on the roll to deprive the plaintiff of costs, under an act of 47 Geo. 3, c. 78, intituled, "An act for the more speedy recovery of small debts in the sokes of Bolingbroke, Horncastle, and other places in the county of Lincoln." The action was in debt, to recover the sum of 5*l.* 12*s.* for wages. The defendant pleaded,

Nov. 3.

Where an action was brought for a sum of 5*l.* 12*s.*, and the defendant paid into Court the sum of 4*l.* 18*s.* 6*d.*, which the plaintiff took out in full satisfaction of his demand, and entered a nolle prosequi as to the residue:—*Held*, that the acceptance by the plaintiff of the smaller sum was not of itself sufficient evidence that no more was due, so as to entitle the defendant to enter a suggestion under a Court of Requests Act, giving jurisdiction over debts to the amount of £5.

The form of the plea of payment of money into Court does not preclude a defendant from applying to enter a suggestion to deprive the plaintiff of costs.

except as to 4*l.* 18*s.* 6*d.*, nunquam indebitatus, and payment into Court of that sum, in satisfaction of the plaintiff's demand. The plaintiff, by his replication, accepted in full satisfaction the sum so paid in, and entered a nolle prosequi as to the residue.

The 18th section of the act enables any person, having any debt not exceeding £5 due to him from a person inhabiting within the places mentioned, to summon the debtor, &c. By the 40th section it is enacted, " that if any action or suit for any debt or damages, recoverable by virtue of this act in the said Court of Requests, shall be commenced in any other Court whatsoever, or elsewhere than in the said Court of Requests, (other than and except in the Courts Baron for holding pleas of debt within the manor and soke of Bolingbroke aforesaid, belonging to his Majesty in right of his duchy of Lancaster, and other than and except in all such other Courts Baron, for holding pleas of debt within the soke of Horncastle, &c. &c.,) then and in every such case, the plaintiff or plaintiffs in such action or suit shall not, by reason of a verdict for him, her, or them, or otherwise, have or be entitled to any costs whatsoever." The defendant stated in his affidavit, that at and since the commencement of the suit, he had been residing within the jurisdiction of the Court of Requests; but it was not stated that the debt in question was less than the sum of £5.

Baines shewed cause.—There is a material difference between money taken out of Court in full satisfaction, and money recovered by the verdict of a jury. This Court of Requests Act applies to the latter case only, for it enacts, that the plaintiff, improperly bringing his action in another Court, shall not, " by reason of a verdict for him, her, or them, or otherwise," be entitled to any costs. Here no verdict has been recovered, and it does not appear that more is not due than the sum paid into Court. The plaintiff is entitled to tax his costs by virtue of the rule of Court of Trinity Term, 1 Vict., which directs, that he shall be at liberty to accept the sum so paid into Court, in full satisfaction and discharge of the cause of action in which it has been paid in; and he " shall be at liberty in that case to tax his costs of suit." In *Tarrant* v. *Morgan* (a), where the defendant pleaded payment of 1*l.* 18*s.* into Court in satisfaction of the cause of action, and the plaintiff took the money out of Court, it was held, that the defendant was not entitled to enter a suggestion on the roll to deprive the plaintiff of costs, on the ground that the action was brought to recover a less sum than 40*s.*, and therefore recoverable in the county court. Here it is neither admitted in the pleadings, nor does it appear to the satisfaction of the Court, that the action was brought for a smaller sum than £5. It would be a great hardship if, in an action for 5*l.* 1*s.*, a plaintiff could not accept 4*l.* 19*s.* in full satisfaction, without losing his costs. If that were so, he would be compelled to continue the action for the recovery of the remaining 2*s.* In *Davey* v. *Renton* (b), on the construction of the statute 43 Geo. 3, c. 46, s. 8, by which costs are to be allowed to a defendant who has been arrested without probable cause, it was held that the statute does not extend to cases where the defendant pays money into Court, and the plaintiff takes it out, although it be a much smaller sum than that for which the defendant is holden to bail.

Hugh Hill, in support of the rule.—The case of *Tarrant* v. *Morgan* is not applicable, because that was a case in the county court, where no suggestion is allowed to be made on the roll, the proper course being to apply to the Court to stay the proceedings. *Bernard* v. *Turner* (c) is in point. It was there held that the Court of Requests Acts are not

(a) 2 C. M. & R. 252. (b) 2 B. & C. 711; 4 D. & R. 186.
(c) 1 M. & W. 580.

Exch. of Pleas,
1841.

JORDAN
v.
BERWICK.

affected by the statute under which the rules relating to payment of money into Court were made, which do not alter the law of payment, but merely the mode. In *Jordan* v. *Strong* (a), it was held that a plea of tender did not preclude the defendant from entering a suggestion on the roll. In the construction of the 43 Geo. 3, c. 46, the word "recover" has been held to mean, recover by the verdict of a jury; but here, the language of the Court of Requests act is more ample, namely, that a party recovering less than £5 shall not be entitled to costs, by reason of a verdict, "or otherwise." *Baildon* v. *Pitter* (b), *Graham* v. *Browne* (c), *Drew* v. *Coles* (d), are in point. In ascertaining the amount of the debt, affidavits ought not to be regarded; the inconvenience would be great, if the Court were to depend upon affidavits; the record alone should be looked at to see what is due. A nolle prosequi is a confession that the plaintiff cannot recover beyond the amount paid into Court. The plaintiff may, if he pleases, demur to or traverse the suggestion. *Barney* v. *Tubb* (e), *Jordan* v. *Strong*. [*Parke*, B.—The Courts are not in the habit of ordering suggestions to be made, with a view to their being traversed or demurred to; we usually decide the matter on motion, to save expense.]

PARKE, B.—The case of *Turner* v. *Bernard*, which was decided by this Court, shews that payment of money into Court does not deprive the defendant of the benefit of a suggestion on the roll, if he is entitled to it by law. But there the question had been decided by a jury; and it is a just principle to lay down, that we should consider their finding conclusive, and not inquire further into the amount of the debt. Here, however, we are called upon to give to a nolle prosequi the same effect as to a verdict. I think we are not bound to do so. If the plaintiff brings his

(a) 5 M. & Sel. 196.   (d) 2 Cr. & J. 505.
(b) 3 B. & Ald. 210.   (e) 2 H. Bl. 354.
(c) 2 Cr. & J. 327.

action for more than £5, and is content to take less, there
is no reason why he should proceed, and incur risk and
trouble in recovering the whole of his demand. I think,
too, that he may explain the amount of his demand by affidavit; and as he has shewn that he sued the defendant
for more than £5, and the defendant has not shewn that the
subject-matter of the action is less than that sum, I think
the defendant is not entitled to enter a suggestion.

GURNEY, B.—I am of the same opinion. If the defendant wished to succeed in his application, he should
have laid before the Court some ground for believing that
the sum sought to be recovered was less than £5. This
he has not done; and therefore I think this rule must be
discharged.

ROLFE, B., concurred.

Rule discharged, with costs.

———◆———

SHARP and Others *v.* THE GREAT WESTERN RAILWAY
COMPANY.

ASSUMPSIT for goods sold and delivered, work and
labour and materials, money paid, and on an account
stated.

The plaintiffs
agreed with the
defendants to
manufacture for
them certain
locomotive engines, under the following contract: " Each engine and tender to be subject to a
performance of a distance of 1,000 miles, with proper loads; during which trial Messrs. S. & Co.
(the plaintiffs) are to be liable to any breakage which may occur, if arising from defective materials or workmanship; but they are not to be responsible for nor liable to the repair of any
breakage or damage, whether resulting from collision, neglect, or mismanagement of any of the
Company's servants, or any other circumstances, save and except defective materials or workmanship. The performance to which each engine is to be subjected, to take place within one
month from the day on which the engine is reported ready to start; in default of which, Messrs.
S. & Co. shall forthwith be released from any responsibility in respect of the said engine; the
balance to be paid on the satisfactory completion of the trial, and release of Messrs. S. & Co. from
further responsibility in respect of such engine." It was also agreed, that the fire boxes should
be made of copper, of the thickness of 7-16ths of an inch (and they were accordingly so made);
and that the best materials and workmanship were to be used. The engines were accordingly
delivered to the defendants, and performed the distance of 1,000 miles within the month of trial,
but nine months afterwards the fire box of one of them burst, when it was discovered that the
copper had been considerably reduced in thickness:—*Held,* in an action against the defendants
for the balance due from them, that they could not give evidence of an inherent defect in the
copper, (no fraud being alleged), since, by the terms of the contract, the month's trial, if satisfactory, was to release the plaintiffs from all responsibility in respect of bad materials and bad
workmanship.

Exch. of Pleas,
1841.

SHARP
v.
GREAT
WESTERN
RAILWAY Co.

Plea, non assumpsit; on which issue was joined; with two other pleas, which became immaterial.

At the trial before *Wightman*, J., at the last Liverpool Assizes, it appeared that the plaintiffs, who were engine makers at Manchester, agreed with the defendants to make, at a certain price, ten locomotive engines and tenders, for the use of the railway. It appeared by the written contract, that the engines and tenders were to be made according to the specification and drawings furnished by the directors, and were to be delivered at certain specified periods, at the Company's station at Paddington; the copper composing the fire boxes was to be of the thickness of 7-16ths of an inch. The third article of the contract was in these terms:—" Each engine and tender to be subject to the performance of a distance of 1,000 miles, with proper loads; during which trial, Messrs. Sharp, Roberts, & Co. are to be liable to any breakage which may occur, if arising from defective materials or workmanship; but they are not to be responsible for nor liable to the repair of any breakage or damage whatever resulting from collision, neglect, or mismanagement of any of the Company's servants or any other circumstance, save and except defective materials or workmanship." The fourth was—" The said performance to which each engine is to be subjected, to take place within one month from the day on which the engine is reported ready to start; in default of which, Messrs. Sharp, Roberts, & Co. shall forthwith be released from any responsibility in respect of the said engine." The sixth article provided for the payment, and stipulated, that the balance was " to be paid on the satisfactory completion of the trial, and release of Messrs. Sharp, Roberts, & Co. from further responsibility in respect of each engine." A printed specification, delivered by the defendants to the plaintiffs, contained the following " general stipulation :"—" The manufacturer is to deliver, put together, and start the engines, in complete working order, upon the line of the Great

Western Railway Company, either at London or Bristol, as may be directed by the Company, and shall be held liable for any breakages that may occur, either from bad materials or bad workmanship, until each engine has performed a distance of 1,000 miles, with proper loads; at the end of which time, should the engine be perfect, the manufacturer will be relieved from any further responsibility. No deviation from the drawings and specification will be allowed without the consent of the company; and throughout the whole, the best materials and workmanship shall be used." The engines were delivered at the Company's station, and performed the distance of 1,000 miles within the month, as specified in the contract, during which time no defect was discovered in them. Nine months afterwards, the inside fire box of one engine having burst, it was found that the copper of which it was made had been reduced from 7-16ths to 3-16ths of an inch in thickness; and that the fire boxes of the other engines had also been reduced in thickness. The plaintiffs refused to replace or repair the fire boxes, alleging that the trial of the engines had released them from all further responsibility; and upon the defendants refusing to pay the balance due to them, brought the present action. The plaintiffs' case having closed, the defendants' counsel admitted that the copper composing the fire boxes had originally been of the requisite thickness, and that no fraud was to be imputed to the plaintiffs; but he proposed to prove, that it was defective in quality, and that this was the cause of its thickness having been reduced. He also proposed to prove that the plaintiffs had departed from the contract, by inserting iron instead of copper rivets in the fire boxes. This evidence being objected to on the part of the plaintiffs, on the ground that after the trial of the engines it was too late to object to defects in the workmanship, the learned Judge refused to receive it. The objection to the admissibility of the evidence relating to the rivets was subse-

Exch. of Pleas,
1841.

SHARP
v.
GREAT
WESTERN
RAILWAY Co.

quently withdrawn by the plaintiffs' counsel; but the defendants' counselrefusing to rest his case on that ground alone, the jury, under the direction of the learned Judge, returned a verdict for the plaintiffs, damages £662, the amount of the balance claimed.

Wortley now moved for a rule to shew cause why a new trial should not be granted, on the ground of the improper rejection of the evidence, and of misdirection.—It is conceded that there is no fraud in this case, and that the copper originally was of the thickness required by the contract; but the defendants are at liberty to shew that it was owing to an inherent defect in its quality that it became reduced in thickness, and eventually burst. They may shew this in reduction of damages: *Basten* v. *Butler* (a). Formerly the remedy would have been by a cross-action; but the Courts now hold that it is unnecessary to resort to that mode of proceeding. Even where goods are delivered according to positive contract or sample, original defects, which reduce the value, may be shewn as an answer to the demand. It is consequential and subsequent damage and loss only, that must be the subject of a cross-action. This was decided by the recent case of *Mondel* v. *Steel* (b); see also *Jones* v. *Bright* (c) and *Shepherd* v. *Kain* (d). The trial of 1,000 miles was intended by the parties to this contract to be conclusive as to those defects only which could be discovered by such an experiment. It does not preclude the defendants from insisting on latent defects, which could be discovered only by time and use of the engine. It is clear, from the use of the word " breakage," that the object of the trial was only to test the mechanism and power of the engines, and not such defects as were inherent in the materials themselves. If a horse is warranted thorough-bred, and sound wind and limb, the purchaser to be at liberty to

(a) 7 East, 479.   (c) 5 Bing. 533; 3 M. & P. 155.
(b) 8 M. & W. 858.   (d) 5 B. & Ald. 240.

Exch. of Pleas,
1841.

SHARP
v.
GREAT
WESTERN
RAILWAY Co.

make trial of him, and he proves, on being galloped, to be sound, but turns out not to be thorough-bred, can it be said that a purchaser is concluded by a trial which, though it tested his speed, could prove nothing as to his pedigree? [*Parke*, B.—It all depends on the construction of the contract.] The meaning of it was, that for all latent defects that could not be discovered by a trial, the plaintiffs should be answerable.

PARKE, B.—The true construction of this contract is, that the trial of a month was to be conclusive as to defective materials and workmanship; but that if the defendants could shew that iron rivets were substituted for copper, or that the copper originally was less than 7-16ths in thickness, they might avail themselves of this deviation from the agreement. Look at the contract itself. It must have been the opinion of both parties to it, that the period of a month would determine the sufficiency of the materials and workmanship. The question does not depend on the third section only of the contract; but coupling that with the fourth section, which is not unimportant, it appears, that the distance of 1,000 miles is to be performed within one month; and in default of such performance taking place within that time, the plaintiffs "shall forthwith be released from any responsibility in respect of the said engine;" that is, if the trial which takes place within that period proves satisfactory, the plaintiffs are to be released from any responsibility arising from defective materials and workmanship. The "general stipulation" at the end of the specification confirms this conclusion: "The manufacturer is to deliver, put together, and start the engines, in complete working order, upon the line of the Great Western Railway Company, and shall be liable for any breakages that may occur either from bad materials or bad workmanship, until such engine has performed a distance of 1,000 miles, with proper loads: at the end of which

Exch. of Pleas,
1841.

SHARP
v.
GREAT
WESTERN
RAILWAY Co.

time, should the engines be perfect, the manufacturer will be relieved from any further responsibility;" that is, if no breakage is found to have occurred. That being so, there seems to be an end of the question. What amounts to bad materials and bad workmanship, will always be a matter of dispute; and it is plain that the parties intended, by the trial, to put an end to such questions. If the defendants wished to insist upon their present objections, they should have made their contract in different terms. The intention was that all disputes of this kind should for ever be set at rest; and that if the defendants did not avail themselves of the trial, or the trial proved satisfactory, all inquiry as to defective materials or workmanship should thenceforth be determined. The learned Judge was therefore right in the view he took of the case. It would have been a different thing, if a distinct breach of the terms of the contract had been shewn: but no evidence was given of any violation of the contract, nor did the defendants shew, as it seems they had at first intended, that iron rivets had been substituted for copper.

GURNEY, B., concurred.

ROLFE, B.—I agree with the rest of the Court in thinking that this rule must be refused. The defendants' argument amounts to this, that although there was to be a trial of the sufficiency of the engines during a month, yet the manufacturers' responsibility was to endure till the end of time. In that case, the trial would have been altogether superfluous.

Rule refused.

Exch. of Pleas,
1841.

BURDEKIN, Public Officer, &c., *v.* POTTER and Others.

Nov. 4.

ERLE moved for a rule to shew cause why the judgment signed upon a warrant of attorney given by the defendants in this cause, for £20,000, and the execution thereon, should not be set aside. One of the objections on which he relied was, that the jurat of the affidavit of the execution of the warrant of attorney described it as "sworn before ——, a *commissioner* &c.," without stating that he was a commissioner for taking affidavits in this Court. The affidavit was duly entitled in the cause in this Court. He referred to *Rex* v. *Hare* (a), *Howard* v. *Brown* (b), and a case of *Tarte* v. *Barnett*, decided in this Court on the last day of last Trinity term (c).

An affidavit, entitled in the proper Court, and purporting to be sworn before A. B., "a commissioner, &c.," is sufficient: the jurat need not state that he is a commissioner for taking affidavits in that Court.

Lord ABINGER, C. B.—I think this objection cannot prevail. If you go upon any principle, it would seem that if the party be named at all, the Court may examine to see whether he is one of its commissioners. I doubt whether any thing at all need be added to his name.

PARKE, B.—I am also of opinion that no rule ought to be granted. If an affidavit be entitled in the Court, the description in the jurat of the person before whom it is sworn as "a commissioner &c.," is quite sufficient. In *Rex* v. *Hare*, the affidavit was not entitled in any Court; in *Howard* v. *Brown*, the party was not described as a commissioner at all. And it was expressly held in *Kennet* v. *Jones* (d), that it was no objection to an affidavit to hold to bail, that it was not entitled in the King's Bench, or that it appeared to have been taken before a commissioner, who was not stated to be a commissioner of that Court.

The other Barons concurred.

Rule refused (e).

(a) 13 East, 189.
(b) 4 Bing. 393; 1 M.&P. 22.
(c) Not reported.
(d) 7 T. R. 451.

(e) See *White* v. *Irving*, 2 M. & W. 127; *Daly* v. *Mahon*, 6 Dowl. P. C. 192.

Nov. 12.

Where in an
action by hus-
band and wife,
in right of the
wife as execu-
trix, a peremp-
tory undertak-
ing was given
to try at a spe-
cified time;
and the hus-
band afterwards
died:—*Held,*
that the under-
taking was not
binding on the
wife.

Lee and Wife, Executrix, *v.* Armstrong.

IN this action, which was brought by the husband and
wife in right of the wife as executrix, the defendant had
obtained a rule for judgment as in case of a nonsuit, which
was discharged on a peremptory undertaking to try at a
specified time. After the rule was discharged the husband
died, and the wife not having proceeded to trial according to the undertaking,

Sir *John Bayley* now moved for a rule absolute for judgment as in case of a nonsuit, for not proceeding to trial
pursuant to the peremptory undertaking, and contended
that as the action, being in right of the wife as executrix
did not abate by the death of the husband, the wife was
bound to go to trial pursuant to the undertaking.

Sed per Curiam.—The wife never entered into this
peremptory undertaking at all, and therefore cannot be
bound by it. The undertaking was altogether the act of
the husband, who was a necessary party to the action, and
under whose control the wife must be supposed to be in
the conduct of it. She clearly is not bound by it.

Rule refused.

Nov. 15.

An application
to the Court to
amend plead-
ings does not
fall within the
rule respecting
the setting
aside proceed-
ings for irregu-
larity, with re-
gard to the
promptness of
the application.

Welsh *v.* Hall.

ATKINSON, on the 10th of November, obtained a rule
calling upon the plaintiff to shew cause why the plea
pleaded on the 2nd of November should not be amended.
The cause of the delay in applying to this Court, although
not stated in the affidavit, was that a similar application
had been made to a Judge at chambers, and had been refused by him.

Humfrey shewed cause.—The application is too late.

There has been great delay; and the Court will not take notice, without affidavit, that the delay arose from an application to amend having been made to a Judge at chambers: *Goren v. Tute (a)*. That being so, the present rule must be discharged, as the defendant has given no explanation of the lateness of his present motion.

PARKE, B.—A party complaining of an irregularity must come to the Court at an early period, or explain the reason why he has not done so. But this is an application to amend the pleadings, and we do not hold applications of that nature to such strict rules as applications relating to matters of practice. I think, therefore, the objection as to the lateness of the application ought not to prevail.

The other Barons concurred.

The rule was then argued on the merits, but was ultimately discharged on terms.

BROOKS and Others, Assignees of CHARLES EVANS, a Bankrupt, *v.* MITCHELL.

TROVER, to recover a promissory note for £1000, dated 24th December, 1824, made by one Lens, payable on demand, with interest, to the bankrupt, Charles Evans, or his order. The first count was upon the possession of the bankrupt, the second on the possession of the plaintiffs as assignees.—Pleas, 1st, not guilty; 2ndly, that the bankrupt was not possessed of the note, modo et formâ; 3rdly, that the note was not the property of the plaintiffs as assignees, modo et formâ; 4thly, that before the supposed conversion, and before the bankruptcy, to wit, on the 12th

Nov. 8.

A promissory note, payable on demand, cannot be treated as over-due, so as to affect an indorsee with any equities against the indorser, merely because it is indorsed a number of years after its date, and no interest had been paid on it for several years before such indorsement.

(a) 7 M. & W. 142.

of March, 1836, the said Charles Evans indorsed and delivered the said note to one Royle, who afterwards, to wit, on the 16th of January, 1838, indorsed and delivered the same to the defendant, bonâ fide, and for a good and valuable consideration, and without notice of any right or title in the plaintiffs as assignees of the said Charles Evans. Verification.—The plaintiff joined issue on the first three pleas, and for replication to the last, admitting the indorsement and delivery in fact by Evans to Royle, and by Royle to the defendant, traversed the allegation that the indorsement and delivery by Royle to the defendant was bonâ fide, and for a valuable consideration, and without notice of any right or title of the plaintiffs as assignees. Issue thereon.

At the trial, before *Wightman,* J., at the last Liverpool assizes, the following facts appeared. The bankrupt, Evans, who had been a banker in Manchester, having advanced to Lens, who was his foster brother, the sum of £1000, received from him, as a security for its repayment, the promissory note in question, which bore date the 24th of December, 1824. Evans had debited Lens in account with the interest half-yearly, down to the 25th of December, 1835. On the 12th of March, 1836, Evans indorsed the note to Royle, and, as the plaintiffs alleged and endeavoured to prove, without any consideration. In August of the same year, Evans became a bankrupt. On the 16th January, 1838, Royle indorsed and delivered the note to the defendant, and in the March following himself became bankrupt. A dividend of 5s. 6d. in the pound was paid under the fiat against Evans, and of 4s. 6d. in the pound under that against Royle; but no mention was made of the note in question until June, 1839, when the defendant made application to Lens, the maker, for payment of interest upon it; and, on Lens's death in the following August, the defendant commenced an action against his widow, to recover the amount of it. Upon these facts, the learned judge directed the jury to consider, whether the note was indorsed by Evans to Royle before the bankruptcy of Evans; and if it was so indorsed, whether Royle gave a valuable consideration for the indorsement; and if he did not, whether the defendant gave value for the note to Royle, without knowledge that Royle had given no value to Evans. The jury found, that the note was indorsed to Royle by Evans before his bankruptcy, and that the defendant gave value for it to Royle; and as to the question whether Royle gave value for it, they said there was no sufficient evidence to the contrary. The learned judge thereupon directed a verdict for the defendant.

Wortley now moved for a new trial, on the ground of misdirection.—The finding of the jury is incomplete, for they have not found in terms that Royle gave any consideration for the note; and all the evidence given in the cause went to shew that he gave none. That being assumed to be the case, if the note was overdue when it came to the hands of the defendant, he could have no better title than Royle, and no right to retain the note as against the assignees of Evans. Now, the note was overdue when it came to the hands of the defendant, for it was a note made in the year 1824, payable on demand, on which it appeared no interest had been paid for three years; and under these circumstances, the demand of payment by the defendant was not made within a reasonable time. The rule is laid down in Bayley on Bills, p. 232, (5th edit.), that "a bill or note, payable on demand, must not be kept locked up; if it be, the loss will fall upon the holder." [*Parke*, B.—The author is speaking there of the liability of collateral parties. The case of a *cheque* is quite different from that of a promissory note. A cheque ought to be presented speedily; but a promissory note payable on demand circulates for years.] The foundation of the rule just referred to is, that the delay in presentment raises an inference of fraud, which ought, therefore, to put the party who takes the instrument under such circumstances upon his guard; Bayley on Bills, 157; *Taylor* v. *Mather* (a). That applies equally to a note payable on demand as to any other negotiable instrument. A party taking a note under such circumstances, takes it subject to the same consequences as a party who takes an overdue note payable after date. [*Parke*, B.—The non-payment of interest for three years was the only circumstance tending to have put the defendant upon his guard, because a promissory note payable on demand is current for any length of time.] It is settled law, that a note payable on demand is payable immediately; and therefore that the Statute of Limitations runs upon it from the date of the note, and not from the time of the demand; *Christie* v. *Fonsick* (b). *Barough* v. *White* (c) shews, indeed, that a note payable on demand cannot be considered as overdue at the time of the *indorsement* of it; but this case goes much further, since here the note was made in 1824, and no demand of interest, or of payment of the principal, was made by any party from 1835 till 1839.

PARKE, B.—I cannot assent to the arguments urged on behalf of the plaintiffs. If a promissory note payable on demand is, after a certain time, to be treated as overdue, although payment has not been demanded, it is no longer a negotiable instrument. But a promissory note payable on demand is intended to be a continuing security. It is quite unlike the case of a cheque, which is intended to be presented speedily.

The rest of the Court concurred, and on this ground the rule was, therefore,

Refused.

(a) 3 T. R. 83, n.   (b) 1 Selw. N. P. 141.
                (c) 4 B. & C. 325; 6 D. & R. 379.

Exch. of Pleas,
1841.

JONES *v.* DOWLE.

Nov. 8.

DETINUE for a picture. Pleas: first, that the chattel in the declaration mentioned was not the property of the plaintiff; secondly, non detinet.

At the trial before Lord *Abinger*, C. B., at the Middlesex sittings after last term, it appeared that the plaintiff had bought the picture in question at a sale by auction, at which the defendant was the auctioneer, and had paid down a deposit to the defendant's clerk, who took down his name as the purchaser. The defendant, however, understood that he had sold it to one Clift; and accordingly entered Clift's name as the purchaser, and delivered the picture to him on payment of the price. The plaintiff demanded it from Clift, who refused to give it up; whereupon this action was brought. It was objected for the defendant, that the action could not be maintained, the picture not being in the possession or control of the defendant. The Lord Chief Baron overruled the objection; and having left it to the jury to say whether the plaintiff was really the purchaser, they found a verdict for the plaintiff, damages £3, leave being reserved to the defendant to move to enter a nonsuit.

Petersdorff now moved accordingly. In order to maintain this action, the plaintiff was bound to shew that the chattel in question was in the possession or custody of the defendant, or of an agent over whom he could exercise control, at the time of action brought. Here it had been delivered to a third party, in pursuance of a supposed contract of sale. The *detention* necessary to support an action of detinue is not to be interpreted in the same sense as a *conversion* in trover. [*Parke*, B.—The evidence of the detention is, that the defendant does not return the chattel when demanded.] That is because he has parted with

Under the plea of non detinet, the plaintiff is entitled to a verdict on proof that the defendant has not returned the chattel to the plaintiff on demand, having previously delivered it, under a supposed contract of sale, to a third party.

Exch. of Pleas,
1841.

JONES
v.
DOWLE.

it to another, over whom he had no control. [*Parke*, B.— That was his own fault. It is laid down in Comyns' Digest, Detinue (A), that the action of detinue lies, "though the defendant quitted the possession before the action brought, by delivery of the goods to another;" and Brooke's Abridgment, Detinue, 1, 2, 33, 34, 40, is cited in support of the position.] That may mean where he has merely parted with the physical custody of the goods.

PARKE, B.—There will be no rule in this case. Detinue does not lie against him who *never had* possession of the chattel, but it does against him who once had, but has improperly parted with the possession of it.

The other Barons concurred.

Rule refused.

———•———

Nov. 11.

In an action of debt, in which the writ of summons was indorsed for £57, the defendant pleaded, as to all but £19, payment; as to the £19, payment into Court. At the trial he proved payment to the plaintiff of all the debt beyond the £19; but it appeared that a sum of £13 was paid after action brought. The

FEWSTER *v.* BOGGETT.

KNOWLES moved for a rule to shew cause why the Master's taxation in this case should not be reviewed. It was an action of debt. The writ of summons was indorsed for 57*l.* 2*s.* 7*d.* The defendant pleaded, as to all but 19*l.* 12*s.* 8*d.*, payment; as to that sum, payment into Court. At the trial before Lord *Denman*, C. J., at the last York Assizes, the defendant proved payment of the difference between the above sums; but it appearing that a sum of £13 had been paid after the commencement of the action, the learned judge directed a verdict to be entered for the plaintiff for nominal damages. The plaintiff's counsel then applied to his lordship to certify that it was a fit

verdict was thereupon entered for £13, the plaintiff undertaking to sue out execution for the costs only:—*Held*, that the plaintiff was entitled to costs to be taxed on the scale applicable to a recovery of a sum above £20.

cause to be tried at the Assizes, but he refused the application. On the following day, the plaintiff's counsel applied to have the verdict entered for £13, undertaking not to issue execution for the debt, but only for the costs. This was done, and the plaintiff's undertaking was indorsed on the Nisi Prius record. The Master, on taxation, taxed the plaintiff his costs on the scale applicable to verdicts for a sum above £20.

Knowles now contended, that although in strictness the plaintiff might be entitled to a verdict for the £13, yet as he was bound by his undertaking not to issue execution for any part of that sum, but for the costs only, the sum really recovered in the action was only the £19 paid into Court, and the costs ought, therefore, to be taxed on the reduced scale. He referred to *Savage* v. *Lipscome* (a), and *Wallen* v. *Smith* (b).

PARKE, B.—This is not a case within the meaning of the directions to the ófficers to tax the costs on the reduced scale applicable where the verdict recovered is under £20. In the present case, the sum really recovered is the £13 paid after the commencement of the action, and the £19 paid into Court. The plaintiff, therefore, recovers £32.

Knowles then urged that the Judge had no power to cause the verdict to be altered after it had once been recorded and the jury discharged.

PARKE, B.—Then you will only put the other side to a cross motion; for the Court would take care that justice should be done. You had better take no rule.

Rule refused.

(a) 5 Dowl. P. C. 385.   (b) 3 M. & W. 138.

Esch. of Pleas,
1841.

Nov. 11.

KENRICK *v.* DAVIES.

An affidavit to
hold to bail,
stating the de-
fendant to be
indebted to the
plaintiff in £22
"on the balance
of an account
for goods sold
and delivered
by the plaintiff
to the defend-
ant:"—*Held*
sufficient, with-
out stating that
it was an ac-
count stated
between the
parties.

LUSH moved for a rule to shew cause why the Judge's
order obtained in this cause for the issuing of a capias
against the defendant should not be set aside, on the
ground of the alleged insufficiency of the affidavit on which
it was obtained.   The affidavit stated, that the defendant
was indebted to the plaintiff in the sum of £22, " on the
balance of an account for goods sold and delivered by the
plaintiff to the defendant." He contended, that it ought to
have stated that it was an account stated between the parties, and cited *Jones* v. *Collins* (a), where an affidavit, stating
that the defendant was indebted "upon and for the balance of an account between [not saying " *stated* between"] the plaintiff and defendant," was held insufficient.
[*Parke*, B.—That is not necessary here, because the affidavit states that the balance of the account was for goods
sold and delivered. Lord *Abinger*, C. B.—In the case you
cite, no consideration was stated; here the affidavit states
the consideration to have been goods sold and delivered.]

PER CURIAM,

                                                    Rule refused.

(a) 6 Dowl. P. C. 526.

Exch. of Pleas,
1841.

Nov. 11.

ELLIOTT and Others, Executrix and Executors, *v.* ELLIOTT and Another.

ASSUMPSIT for money had and received by the defendants to the use of the plaintiffs as executrix and executors, and on an account stated with them as such. Plea, non assumpserunt. At the trial before Lord *Denman*, C. J., at the last Spring Assizes for Surrey, the following facts appeared:—

The plaintiffs' testator, who was a coach-maker in the Westminster Road, had received an order for a chariot, which, at the time of his death, on the 13th January 1838, was on his premises, and was still, as the defendants alleged, in an unfinished state. By his will, he bequeathed to his two sons, the defendants, his two carriage manufactories, " with all fixtures, implements, tools, *stock*, job-carriages, harness, and every thing appertaining to his trade or business in the said manufactories, excepting book debts;" and the residue of his effects he divided equally amongst his five children. On the 7th February, 1838, the plaintiffs took out probate of his will; and a difference arising between them and the defendants, as to whether the chariot in question could be considered " stock," within the terms of the above bequest, the plaintiffs made the following entries in the legacy receipt:—" Stephen Frederick Elliott and Joseph Elliott, sons;"—" Stock in trade, and part residue, in which five children are interested, 2833*l.* 10*s.*"—" A disagreement arising between the said Stephen Frederick and Joseph, and the executors, as to whether the whole of this item belongs to the said sons, or part to the residue, the executors desire to pay the duty on

A testator bequeathed to his two sons his two carriage manufactories, with all fixtures, implements, tools, *stock*, job-carriages, harness, and every thing appertaining to his trade in the said manufactories. At the time of his death, a carriage was in one of the manufactories, unfinished, which was being built to the order of a purchaser. A question arose between the executors and the sons, whether this carriage fell within the above bequest; and the executors paid the legacy duty on the whole, but annexed the following memorandum to the legacy receipt:—"A disagreement arising between the sons S. and T. and the executors, as to whether the whole of this item belongs to the said sons, or

part to the residue, the executors desire to pay the duty on the whole, leaving it for them to settle with the legatees the proportion of duty, when the matter in dispute shall be determined." The sons retained possession of and finished the carriage, delivered it to the purchaser, and received the price. In an action by the executors against them for money had and received, commenced two years afterwards:—*Held,* that there was no evidence to go to the jury of assent by the executors to the legacy of the carriage to the defendants.

the whole, leaving it for them to settle with the legatees the proportion of duty, when the matter in dispute shall be determined." The defendants continued to carry on the business on the same premises, and retained the carriage in question, and (according to their evidence) finished it at their own expense, delivered it to the purchaser in March or April 1838, and received the price. The question to which the evidence on both sides, at the trial, was mainly directed, was whether the carriage was in fact in such an unfinished state, at the time of the testator's death, as to fall within the description of " stock," in the bequest to the defendants; but at the close of the defendants' case, the plaintiffs' counsel contended that they were at all events entitled to recover, there being no evidence of the assent of the plaintiffs to the bequest of the carriage to the defendants; and the Lord Chief Justice, in summing up the case, addressed the jury in these words:—" Gentlemen, do you see any assent on the part of the executors? I do not." The jury found for the plaintiffs, damages £240.

In Easter Term, *Channell,* Serjt., obtained a rule nisi for a new trial, on the ground of misdirection; against which

Thesiger and *Gurney* shewed cause.—The direction of the learned Judge was correct, for there was no evidence of assent to the bequest of this particular carriage. It is clear, from the memorandum on the legacy receipt, that the executors thought it formed no part of the stock in trade, but was in such a state at the time of the testator's death, that the property in it had passed to the purchaser. That memorandum proves non-assent, because it shews that the plaintiffs disputed the defendants' title. [Lord *Abinger,* C. B.—It shews that their assent was withheld for the present.] The Court then called on

Montagu Chambers, in support of the rule.—The learned

Judge misdirected the jury, in stating to them broadly, that there was no evidence of assent. He ought to have informed them what constituted, in point of law, an assent by an executor to a bequest, and to have left it to them to say whether there was not evidence of such assent in the present case. It is quite clear there was an assent to the specific bequest of the stock in trade to the defendants, and the question is, whether there was not a conditional assent to their taking the carriage in question as part of that specific bequest, if it should turn out to be stock in trade, which it clearly was. If there be an assent to a specific bequest, then, if an article come fairly within the description in the bequest, that binds the executor as to the whole. The law is thus laid down in Comyns' Digest, Administration (C. 6) :—" So an assent to take part as residuary legatee, is an assent to take the whole residue as legatee." That would equally apply to a residue consisting of many chattels as of one. [Lord *Abinger*, C. B.—The meaning of that is, that thereby the executor admits a residue; therefore the legatee is entitled to the whole. *Parke*, B.—It is an assent to his taking it *as part of the residue*.] Again, the conduct of the executors, in permitting the defendants to retain possession of the carriage and receive payment for it, was strong evidence of an assent by them to the bequest of it. In Shep. Touch. 456, it is said, —" Any agreement in word or deed will suffice to make an assent, and execute a devise. Let executors take heed, therefore; for if an executor do but agree that the legatee of a term of years of land shall take the profits thereof, and that but for a time only; or say to the legatee, ' God send you joy of it;' or, ' I intend you shall have it according to the devise,' or the like; this is a good assent to the legacy." And in p. 457, it is said—" If a term be devised to A. for life, the remainder to B., and the executor assent to the devise of A.; in this case, this is a good assent to the devise of B., and shall execute the same also,

whether the executor have assets or not." And again—
" If a man devise the occupation of a book or any other
chattel personal to J. S., or that J. S. shall have the occupation of any such like thing during his life, and that after
his decease it shall go to J. D. for ever, and the executor
deliver the thing to J. S.; it seems this is a good execution
of the legacy to the second devisee, J. D." In *Noel* v. *Robinson* (a), where the defendant, an executor, had let for a
term of years an estate devised to the plaintiff, and reserved rent in trust for him; it being objected that there was
no assent, Lord *Nottingham* said, " It did tantamount to an
assent, and being a lawful act, a little matter will be taken
for an assent." The law is laid down in similar terms in
Cray v. *Willis* (b). In the present case, it was not disputed
that there were assets, and the circumstances shewed that it
was a rightful and proper act for the executors to assent to
this bequest.

Lord ABINGER, C. B.—It appears to me that the direction of the Lord Chief Justice was right. I see no evidence of assent to the taking of this particular chattel by
the defendants. Putting the case in the strongest way for
them, that the executors had assented to the bequest of
the stock, they yet expressly withheld their assent as to
this carriage, supposing that it did not form part of the
stock in trade, or at least wishing for time to make up
their minds whether it came within that description of
property or not. And we have no right to consider whether they were right in thus withholding their assent or
not; that is a question for the consideration of a Court of
Equity, on a bill filed; but the legatee can maintain no
action at law until the executor *has* assented to the bequest.
Here, for some reason, good or bad, it appears that the
executors had withheld their assent; and they had a right

(a) 1 Vern. 90; 2 Ventr. 358.   (b) 3 P. Wms. 531.

to do so until compelled by a competent authority. It was at least a matter of some doubt, upon the evidence, whether this carriage was part of the stock in trade or not, and upon that doubt the executors had a right to withhold their assent. Whether there has been an assent or not may involve matter of law, but it is generally a question of fact. The cases cited by Mr. *Chambers* are of the former kind: as where an executor assents to a taking by one of several legatees of one specific thing, that being a parting with his interest in the chattel altogether. But this is the case of a bequest consisting of a number of chattels, and the executors have a right to determine, before giving their assent, whether any particular chattel falls within the same class or not. I think, therefore, that the jury were right in the conclusion to which they came under the direction of the Lord Chief Justice, and that this rule ought to be discharged.

PARKE, B.—I entirely concur in thinking that the Lord Chief Justice was right in saying that there was no evidence of assent in this case; for the facts, when rightly understood, so far from proving assent, clearly prove dissent on the part of the executors. If the only question were whether this carriage was stock in trade, I am strongly disposed to think it was. But an assent to one article falling within the description of stock in trade was not necessarily an assent as to all; and the executors were not likely to have given their assent to the bequest of this particular chattel, when they entertained a doubt whether it proved part of the testator's stock in trade. The case of the bequest of a term of years, or of one specific chattel, is altogether different. In that case, no doubt, an assent to the estate of a legatee for life is an assent to him in remainder. So, an assent to take part as residuary legatee is an assent to take the whole, because it admits that there is a residue, and that the debts and legacies, which alone

Exch. of Pleas,
1841.

ELLIOTT
v.
ELLIOTT.

could entitle the executor to withhold his assent, are paid.
The position which has been cited from Sheppard's Touchstone requires some qualification. The law is correctly
stated in Williams on Executors (*a*), that a *conditional*
assent is sufficient only where it is the case of a condition
subsequent, or such a one as the executor had no authority
to annex for his own benefit. It is unnecessary, however,
to give any opinion on that point: the only question here
is, whether the executors, who have assented to the bequest
of stock in trade, have therefore assented to the bequest of
this particular chattel, not as a part of one entire thing,
but on the ground of its being one of numerous chattels
constituting stock in trade. Undoubtedly they are not
obliged to assent as to all, but may withhold their assent
as to part: and here it is clear that, doubting whether this
carriage was part of the stock, they refused to assent as to
it. They are therefore entitled to recover it in trover,
seeing that it never vested in the legatees.

GURNEY, B., concurred.

ROLFE, B.—I am of the same opinion. There is a clear
distinction between the effect of an assent by an executor
as to one out of several chattels, and an assent to the
bequest of a term of years. If he assent to the tenant for
life taking, it would be manifestly unjust that it should
not be an assent to him in remainder; that the executor
should have it in his power afterwards to take and sell the
reversion for payment of the testator's debts, would be an
act of great injustice. But the case is totally different as
to the bequest of a number of articles, as stock in trade, or
plate: there an executor may properly withhold his assent
as to some, because he may want them, and want them
rightfully, for payment of the debts of the testator.

Rule discharged.

(*a*) Vol. 2, pp. 1089, 1090, 3rd edit.

Exch. of Pleas,
1841.

Nov. 11.

BRADSHAW *v.* BRADSHAW.

ASSUMPSIT for money paid, money had and received, and on an account stated. Plea, non assumpsit. At the trial before Lord *Abinger*, C. B., at the London Sittings after Easter Term, the following facts appeared :—

The plaintiff, being in embarrassed circumstances, proposed to his creditors to pay them a composition of 10*s.* in the pound, to be secured by his acceptances, payable in three instalments. All the creditors agreed to sign a composition agreement to this effect, except the defendant, who was a creditor for the sum of 559*l.* 16*s.* 8*d.*, and he refused to execute the agreement, unless he were paid the additional sum of 2*s.* in the pound upon the amount of his debt. The party who conducted the negotiation on behalf of the plaintiff thereupon gave the defendant a cheque for 55*l.* 19*s.* 8*d.* (the amount of 2*s.* in the pound on his debt), drawn by one Waite, the father-in-law of the plaintiff, without the plaintiff's knowledge : and the defendant then signed the agreement, and received from the plaintiff three bills of exchange for 91*l.* 11*s.* 10*d.* each, for the amount of his composition; after which he executed an unconditional release to the plaintiff. It was opened for the plaintiff at the trial, that the bills given to the defendant were, at the time of their maturity, outstanding in the hands of third parties as indorsees, and that the plaintiff had paid the amount of them to the holders out of his own funds. The plaintiff brought this action to recover back the sum of 55*l.* 19*s.* 8*d.*, and rested his claim on two grounds; first, that the advance of that sum by Waite, on behalf of the plaintiff, to the defendant, was without consideration; and secondly, that as the defendant had received not only that money from Waite, but also the value of the composition

The plaintiff, being insolvent, proposed to his creditors to pay them a composition of 10*s.* in the pound, to be secured by his acceptances. All the creditors agreed to the arrangement except the defendant, who refused to execute the agreement unless he were paid the additional sum of 2*s.* in the pound on his debt. A cheque for that amount was accordingly given him by a relation of the plaintiff, without the plaintiff's knowledge, and he then signed the agreement, and received from the plaintiff his acceptances for the 10*s.* compositi°n. *Semble,* that, under these circumstances, the plaintiff, if he were compelled to pay the bills at maturity to boná fide indorsees, to whom they had been transferred by the defendant for value, might recover back from the defendant the

excess received by him beyond the amount of the composition.

negotiated by him, and paid when due by the plaintiff, he had thus received more than the amount of the agreed composition, and the overplus might be recovered back by the plaintiff. The Lord Chief Baron, adverting to the first point, (which had been most prominently made), thought that, as the money had been paid by Waite to the defendant without the privity of the plaintiff, the latter had no right to recover it back, and accordingly directed a nonsuit.

In Trinity Term, *Erle* obtained a rule to shew cause why the nonsuit should not be set aside, and a new trial had; against which

Thesiger now shewed cause.—The case on the part of the plaintiff is put in two ways: first, that the payment of the 55*l.* 19*s.* 8*d.* by Waite to the defendant was in fact a payment by the plaintiff, and that the agreement whereon it was paid being fraudulent, he is entitled to recover it back: or secondly, that the surplus received by the defendant beyond the composition of 10*s.* is, under the circumstances, recoverable as money had and received to the plaintiff's use. With respect to the first ground, it is clear that the money was paid by Waite without the plaintiff's knowledge; it was in fact Waite's money and not the plaintiff's: and as Waite could not have recovered it back, it being a voluntary payment by him, and he being in pari delicto with the defendant, so neither could the plaintiff, by assuming himself to be the debtor of the defendant, give himself a title to recover which Waite had not. With regard to the second ground of objection, it is not necessary on the present occasion to question the cases which have established that any private arrangement, whereby one creditor is to receive a greater benefit than the others, as an inducement to sign a composition deed, is a fraud on the other creditors, and void: *Cockshott* v. *Ben-*

nett (a), *Steinman* v. *Magnus* (b), *Lewis* v. *Jones* (c). But here the debtor is attempting to recover back money which has been actually paid to the creditor. In *Knight* v. *Hunt* (d), the creditor was seeking to enforce the composition, after receiving the surplus under the fraudulent agreement; which distinguishes that case from the present. The case of *Ward* v. *Bird* (e) appears most to resemble the present. There the defendant, who was a creditor of the plaintiff, stipulated, by a composition deed, that his debt should be paid at 6s. in the pound by promissory notes; and after the execution of the deed, obtained payment from the plaintiff in full : and it was held, that the plaintiff could not recover back the difference between the full amount of the defendant's debt and the composition, without proving that the composition notes had been paid, or giving some evidence equivalent to such proof. [*Parke*, B.—That case is very inaccurately reported. The money sought to be recovered back had been paid in settlement of an action by the plaintiff himself.] The case of *Turner* v. *Hoole* (f) is there referred to as an authority. There a creditor, after having signed a composition deed, induced the debtor to give him bills of exchange for the full amount of his debt, bearing date the day before the composition deed; and, after receiving one instalment, sued the debtor on the bills, and recovered the amount, minus the instalment paid. Lord *Tenterden* ruled, that the debtor might maintain an action for money had and received against the creditor, to recover back the difference between the full amount of the debt and the amount of the composition. That case would certainly appear to be an authority against the present defendant, but for the circumstance that the report cannot be relied on, since it states the

Exch. of Pleas, 1841.

BRADSHAW
v.
BRADSHAW.

(a) 2 T. R. 763.
(b) 11 East, 390.
(c) 4 B. & C. 506; 6 D. & R. 567.

(d) 5 Bing. 432; 3 M. & P. 18.
(e) 5 C. & P. 229.
(f) Dowl. & Ry. N. P. C. 27.

agreement for payment in full to the defendant to have been made *after* the signing of the composition deed, in which case it would not be fraudulent at all. And in *Wilson* v. *Ray* (a), Lord *Denman*, C. J., remarking on the case of *Turner* v. *Hoole*, says, " Lord *Tenterden*, in deciding that case, was not reminded of another principle of at least equal importance, which was established in *Marriot* v. *Hampton* (b), that what a party recovers from another by legal process, without fraud, the loser shall never recover back by virtue of any facts which could have availed him in the former proceeding." *Smith* v. *Cuff* (c) will no doubt be relied on for the plaintiff. But there one of the promissory notes given by the plaintiff, the debtor, had been negotiated by the defendant, and payment had been enforced against the plaintiff by the holder. That, therefore, was a payment by compulsion, and it was not a case of par delictum. [*Parke*, B.—It is most probable that *Turner* v. *Hoole* was a case of the same description, and that the defendant had enforced payment of the bills against the plaintiff, by putting them into the hands of an indorsee.] In *Alsager* v. *Spalding* (d), which was a decision on the same ground, it is admitted arguendo that *Smith* v. *Cuff* is not distinguishable from *Turner* v. *Hoole*. But *Wilson* v. *Ray* is an authority for the defendant. In that case, a creditor refused to sign the composition deed without receiving a bill of exchange for the remainder of his debt, which the debtor gave him, and he then signed the deed; and the debtor having afterwards paid the amount of the bill to the creditor, it was held that this was a voluntary payment, and that the amount could not be recovered back as money had and received. In the present case, it is not the *creditor* who is seeking to enforce the

(a) 10 Ad. & Ell. 82; 2 P. & D.   (c) 6 M. & Sel. 160.
253.   (d) 4 Bing. N. C. 407; 6 Scott,
     (b) 7 T. R. 269.   204.

illegal agreement, but the *debtor*, after a voluntary payment according to the agreement, is seeking to recover back the money so paid. [Lord *Abinger*, C. B.—But suppose it turns out that the plaintiff was compelled to pay the amount of the bills to the holders?] He has not been compelled to pay, nor has he ever paid, *this money*, which he now seeks to recover back. In *Smith* v. *Cuff*, and *Alsager* v. *Spalding*, the money was that of the debtor himself. [*Rolfe*, B., referred to *Howden* v. *Haigh* (a).] That also was the case of a creditor seeking to enforce the illegal agreement. Here the debtor, who is the party suing, has only paid the composition, and the money paid beyond it was that of a third person. [*Rolfe*, B.—Suppose, after Waite paid the £55 to the defendant, and before the plaintiff paid any thing, he had discovered the transaction, could he have resisted payment of his acceptances?] No doubt *Knight* v. *Hunt* and *Howden* v. *Haigh* are authorities that he might. But how can the payment of the bills give the plaintiff a right of action for this money? He has paid no more than he ought to pay, and, if he recovers in this action, he will have paid nothing.

Erle and *Bramwell*, contrà.—[*Parke*, B.—There can be no question as to the first point, because there was no payment to the defendant on the part of the plaintiff, but directly the reverse, and no ratification by the plaintiff could adopt it.] Then as to the other point. The only distinction between this case and that of *Smith* v. *Cuff* is, that there the plaintiff himself, here his relative, paid the surplus amount beyond the composition. But the foundation of that case is, that the notes given by the debtor were *void*, and could not be enforced by a creditor; and if the creditor puts them into circulation, and enables a third party thereby to extort from the debtor the money, the

Exch. of Pleas,
1841.

BRADSHAW
v.
BRADSHAW.

(a) 11 Ad. & Ell. 1033; 3 P. & D. 661.

payment of which could have been resisted if they had remained in the hands of the creditor, as against him the negotiation of them is void, and the money received by him is money had and received to the plaintiff's use. The cases of *Knight* v. *Hunt,* and *Leicester* v. *Rose,* are clear authorities to shew that it makes no difference whether the money be obtained from the debtor, or from a third person: in either case, the favoured creditor is guilty of an extorsive and oppressive fraud. The question really is, whether the agreement between the plaintiff and the defendant was void altogether, or only as against the defendant. It is said the plaintiff has paid no more than he was bound to pay; but if the agreement was illegal and void, he was not bound to pay anything. [*Parke,* B.— Must he not pay the original debt?] No; as to that, the creditor would be met by the deed of release; and if he alleges that it is void as being in pursuance of the fraudulent agreement, he is met by the answer, that he cannot take advantage of his own fraud. A creditor would be no loser by insisting on an undue preference, if, on being unable to retain it, he were remitted to his original rights. This is not a case of par delictum: the debtor is under oppression, and the payment by him upon the bills is not voluntary. No doubt, however void the transaction were, if the money were paid by the debtor at a time when he might have resisted the payment, he cannot recover it back; but here the payment was made because the plaintiff had no defence against the holder of the bills.

Lord ABINGER, C. B.—If I were satisfied that the whole of the points essential to constitute the case of the plaintiff, upon the second ground which has been taken on his behalf, had been made at the trial, I should have been sorry to expose him to the payment of any costs. But, to enable him to recover, it was essential for him to shew, first, that the bills were paid by him, otherwise non constat

that the defendant had received more than the amount of his
composition; and secondly, that when they were so paid,
they were not in the hands of the defendant; because, if
they were, they were paid voluntarily, and the case would
fall within the authority of *Wilson* v. *Ray*. And further,
he must have shewn also that they were paid *by him;* if
they were paid by his surety, I do not see how he could
convert the defendant's supposed fraud into the means of
getting into his own pocket money which he could not
otherwise have got. It must be *his* money—money had
and received to his use. He must, therefore, prove that
the bills were in the hands of third persons, so that he had
no defence to their claim; and that they were paid out of
his own funds. If either of these facts failed in proof, then
he would not be entitled to recover. I think, therefore,
that the cause must go down to a new trial, to give an opportunity to the plaintiff of ascertaining these facts, and
to the defendant of setting up any case he may have to
meet them. With regard to the costs, we think that if the
defendant succeeds, he should have the costs of both trials,
but that if the plaintiff succeeds, he should not have the
costs of the first trial. The rule will therefore be absolute for a new trial—the costs to abide the event. I may
add, that it forms a part of my consideration of the case,
that the release given by the defendant is not in the ordinary form, a conditional one, but an absolute one, in consideration of the composition being secured to the creditors
by the sureties.

PARKE, B.—It is clear that the plaintiff could not have
recovered on the first ground taken at the trial, because
the money paid by Waite to the defendant was not money
had and received to his use; the payment was not with the
plaintiff's money, but on the contrary, was to be kept
secret from him. As to the other point, the question is, in
what situation the plaintiff will be, if it turn out that the

Exch. of Pleas,
1841.

BRADSHAW
v.
BRADSHAW.

payment was made by him involuntarily, out of his own funds, and in discharge of a bonâ fide claim. That raises a very important question, on which it will probably become necessary to take the opinion of the Court; but the case is not yet ripe for that decision.

GURNEY, B., and ROLFE, B., concurred.

Rule absolute.

———◆———

Nov. 11.

BILL *v.* BAMENT.

The defendant ordered goods of H., the del credere agent of the plaintiff, at a stipulated price, to be paid for on delivery; and on receiving notice that the goods had arrived at H.'s warehouse, went there, and directed a boy whom he saw there to put a certain mark on the goods. On the defendant's refusal to receive the goods by reason of a dispute about the price, an action was commenced against him by the plaintiff; after which, at H.'s request, the defendant

ASSUMPSIT for goods sold and delivered, and on an account stated. Plea, non assumpsit. At the trial before Lord *Abinger*, C. B., at the London sittings after Trinity Term, the following facts appeared:—

The defendant ordered of one Harvey, who was an agent of the plaintiff under a del credere commission, a quantity of goods, including twenty dozen hair-brushes and twelve dozen clothes-brushes, to be paid for on delivery, at a stipulated price; but no memorandum in writing of the bargain was made at the time. On receiving notice from Harvey that the brushes had arrived at his warehouse, the defendant, on the 22nd of March last, went there, and directed a boy, whom he saw there, to alter the mark " No. 1," upon one of the packages, to " No. 12," and to send the whole of the goods to the St. Catharine's Docks. The next day, an invoice was delivered to the defendant, charging the brushes respectively at the rate of 8*s.* and 12*s. each.* The defendant objected to this

wrote in H.'s ledger, at the bottom of a page, containing the statement of the goods in question and headed with the plaintiff's name, the words " Received the above," which he signed: —*Held,* that there was no evidence to go to the jury of a delivery and acceptance, sufficient to satisfy the Statute of Frauds.

A memorandum in writing of a contract, to satisfy the Statute of Frauds, must have been made before action brought.

price, alleging that by the contract, as he had understood it, the above were to be the prices of the brushes
per dozen; and refused to pay for them. On the 24th of
March, the plaintiff commenced the present action for the
price. On the 27th, the defendant, at Harvey's request,
wrote in Harvey's ledger, at the bottom of the page which
contained the statement of the articles ordered by the defendant, and which page was headed "Bill & Co.," the following words:— "Received the above, John Bament."
The rest of the goods were sent to and received by the
defendant. It was objected for the defendant, that there
was no evidence of any contract in writing, or of any acceptance of the brushes, sufficient to satisfy the 17th section of the Statute of Frauds. The Lord Chief Baron
reserved the point, and the plaintiff had a verdict for the
amount claimed, leave being reserved to the defendant to
move to enter a nonsuit.

Erle having obtained a rule nisi accordingly,

Thesiger and *Martin* now shewed cause.—First, the defendant's receipt in the ledger, although written after the
commencement of the action, amounts to a memorandum
in writing sufficient to satisfy the statute, or, at all events,
is evidence of a previous acceptance of the goods within
the 17th section. That section requires that one of three
matters—part acceptance of the goods, earnest or part
payment, or a memorandum in writing of the bargain, shall
occur, in order to shew a reality in the contract, beyond
that which parol evidence would establish; but there is
nothing in the statute to shew that these must all have
existed before action brought. The statute does not make
the contract in itself illegal and void, but only says that
no contract shall be allowed (that is, by the Court on the
trial) to be good, except one of these three things shall
appear. It has been decided that the memorandum need

not be signed *with the intent* of attesting the bargain. *Coles* v. *Trecothick* (a). But, at all events, the acknowledgment, " Received the above," was evidence to go to the jury of a previous acceptance. There is nothing in it to confine its operation to the particular moment at which it was signed. All that is prohibited by the statute is, that such a contract as is mentioned therein shall not be imposed on a party without a particular species of proof; but if the plaintiff produces in evidence a document which goes to prove a good contract anterior to the commencement of the action, that is sufficient. Secondly, there was besides independent evidence of acceptance. The defendant was allowed to deal with the goods as his own, and had possession of them, although Harvey might still retain a lien on them for the price. The present case is distinguishable from all those which will be relied upon for the defendant. In *Tempest* v. *Fitzgerald* (b), the horse, although ridden by the vendee for the purpose of trial, remained throughout in the possession of the vendor as the owner. So, in *Carter* v. *Toussaint* (c), the horse was sent to grass in the vendor's name, by the vendee's direction. So also, in *Maberley* v. *Sheppard* (d), the waggon remained, unfinished, in the possession of the maker. *Baldey* v. *Parker* (e) only decides that the mere marking of goods by the vendee in the vendor's shop does not constitute an acceptance; but here more was done. The order for the marking may be coupled with the subsequent acknowledgment by the receipt in the ledger.

Erle (with whom was *Whateley*), contrà.—It is now said that there was evidence for the jury of an acceptance; but at the trial the point was left for the Court to determine, whether the undisputed facts amounted in law to an ac-

(a) 9 Ves. 250.
(b) 3 B. & Ald. 680.
(c) 5 B. & Ald. 855; 1 D. & R. 515.

(d) 10 Bing. 99; 3 Moo. & Sc. 436.
(e) 2 B. & Cr. 37; 3 D. & R. 220.

ceptance; and such has been the course in all the cases on this subject. There is nothing in the terms of the receipt to shew that it was meant to be an acknowledgment of a previous actual acceptance; nor could an act, done after the repudiation of the contract, and after action brought to enforce it, operate as such. Neither was there any acceptance before action brought. This was a ready money bargain; so that the delivery of the goods and the payment of the price were to be concurrent acts. The goods remained in the corporal possession of Harvey, as the plaintiff's agent; and no *act* was done by the defendant, but merely a verbal direction given by him as to the marking. It is clear that the vendor retained his lien for the price; and that, according to *Carter* v. *Toussaint* and *Tempest* v. *Fitzgerald*, is the test whereby to determine whether there has been an acceptance within the statute. *Tempest* v. *Fitzgerald* was a stronger case than the present, for there the horse was dealt with between the parties as if the bargain was complete. In *Maberley* v. *Sheppard*, the waggon was completed before action brought, and what the defendant did to it made it complete; yet, the plaintiff never having parted with his lien for the price, that was held insufficient to amount to an acceptance. The same principle is applied in *Baldey* v. *Parker*.

Secondly, there was not any memorandum in writing sufficient to satisfy the statute. The point now taken for the plaintiff, that it may be a writing subsequent to the commencement of the action, has never before been applied to the Statute of Frauds. The statute declares, that no contract for the sale of goods above the value of £10 shall be allowed to be good, except it be accompanied with certain requisites. That must mean requisites existing when the contract comes in esse: or, at all events, they are necessary ingredients in the cause of action, which must be in existence, so as to make it complete, when the action is brought.—He was then stopped by the Court.

Lord ABINGER, C. B.—If the question at the trial had turned altogether upon the acceptance, I should then have formed the same opinion as I do now. In order to make it such an acceptance as to satisfy the statute, it should appear that there was a *delivery.* Here Harvey was the plaintiff's agent, and sold for ready money, and he was not bound to deliver the goods until payment of the price. Now all that takes place is a direction by the defendant to alter the mark on the goods, and to send them to the docks: but the question is, whether this was done under such circumstances, and Harvey stood in such a situation, as that he was *bound* to send them to the docks. The acceptance, to be effectual under the statute, should be such as to devest the property in the goods out of the seller. Here the defendant probably meant to accept them, and to make Harvey his agent for shipping them. But can it be said that he was his agent to deliver at all events? I think clearly not. He was at liberty to say that he would not deliver to or ship for the defendant until the goods were paid for. There is nothing to shew that he contracted to hold them as the defendant's agent, or by implication to make him his agent. Therefore, for want of a *delivery,* there was no sufficient *acceptance* of these goods. The rule will be absolute, but not for a nonsuit, as it appears that some goods were received by the defendant, but for a new trial on payment of costs by the plaintiff.

PARKE, B.—I concur in thinking that there was no evidence to go to the jury to satisfy the Statute of Frauds. With regard to the point which has been made by Mr. *Martin,* that a memorandum in writing after action brought is sufficient, it is certainly quite a new point, but I am clearly of opinion that it is untenable. There must, in order to sustain the action, be a *good contract* in existence at the time of action brought; and to make it a good contract under the statute, there must be one of the three requisites therein mentioned. I think, therefore, that a written memorandum, or part payment, after action brought, is not sufficient to satisfy the statute. Then, to take the case out of the 17th section, there must be both *delivery* and *acceptance;* and the question is, whether they have been proved in the present case. I think they have not. I agree that there was evidence for the jury of acceptance, or rather of intended acceptance. The direction to mark the goods was evidence to go to the jury quo animo the defendant took possession of them: so also, the receipt was some evidence of an acceptance. But there must also be a *delivery;* and to constitute that, the possession must have been parted with by the owner, so as to deprive him of the right of lien. Harvey might have agreed to hold the goods as the warehouseman of the defendant, so as to deprive himself of the right to refuse to deliver them without payment of the price; but of that there was no proof. There was no evidence of actual marking of the goods, or that the order to mark was assented to by Harvey. I am of opinion, therefore, that there was no sufficient proof of acceptance to satisfy the statute, and that the case falls within the 17th section.

GURNEY, B., and ROLFE, B., concurred.

Rule absolute accordingly.

A Judge at chambers only, and not the Court, has authority, under the stat. 1 & 2 Vict. c. 110, s. 14, to make an order to charge a fund with the payment of money recovered by a judgment: if he makes an absolute order, the Court has jurisdiction to set it aside if wrongly made; but if he only makes an order nisi, the Court has no authority to entertain the question, although the Judge expresses his desire to refer it to the Court.

BROWN, Public Officer, &c. *v.* BAMFORD.

IN this case a rule had been obtained, calling upon the defendant to shew cause why a third part of certain stock in the public funds, standing in the name of a trustee to the defendant's use, should not be charged with the payment of the sum of £750 recovered against her by the judgment in this action, pursuant to the stat. 1 & 2 Vict. c. 110, s. 14. It appeared from the affidavits, that on the 8th of October last, a Judge at chambers made an order nisi for charging the stock with the sum in question. This order was not made absolute, but the learned Judge directed the parties to make the application to the Court. The order had been served on the Bank of England. On the 9th of October a writ of error coram vobis was allowed, and on the 15th of the same month notice of the allowance thereof was served on the plaintiff's attorney.

Erle (*Wallinger* with him) shewed cause.—First, the proceedings on the Judge's order were altogether stayed by the writ of error, which operated as a supersedeas from the time of service of the allowance of it: *Levy* v. *Price* (a), *Birch* v. *Triste* (b). But, secondly, the order of the Judge could not operate as a valid execution until it was made absolute. By the statute, the authority to order the fund to stand charged with the amount of the judgment, is vested in a Judge, not in the Court, and he ought, therefore, to have made an absolute order, if he thought it a case within the statute; the mere order nisi is only to bring the parties before him.

Cresswell, contrà.—There is at least an inchoate execution, for the 15th section of the statute expressly provides

(a) 2 M. & W. 533.   (b) 8 East, 412.

that the order to shew cause shall operate as a distringas on the Bank, so as to restrain them from permitting any transfer of the stock in the mean time. Then the Court, to whom the matter has been referred by the Judge, has the power of making the rule absolute; and when that is done, it will have the effect of a valid and perfect execution.

Lord ABINGER, C. B.—I think that the Court has no power to interfere in this case. The statute expressly gives to the Judge, and not to the Court, the power of making orders of this nature; if he thinks fit to make an order, the Court has authority to set it aside; but we have no original jurisdiction to make such an order.

PARKE, B.—I am of the same opinion. It is clear that the original jurisdiction in this case belongs to the Judge, and not to the Court. If the Judge is desirous of referring the question to the Court, his course is to make the rule absolute, and then the party against whom it is made may apply to the Court to set it aside.

Rule discharged.

———◆———

SWINBURN *v.* TAYLOR and Another.

TRESPASS for entering the plaintiff's house, and seizing and imprisoning him; to which the defendants pleaded a justification under a ca. sa., founded on a judgment of the Court of Common Pleas, in a suit in which the now defendants were plaintiffs, and the now plaintiff defendant. The plaintiff replied nul tiel record, and served a notice upon the defendants to produce the record in this Court; and on their omitting to do so, signed judgment.

Nov. 13.

Where, on an issue on nul tiel record, the record is to be produced by the defendant, a four day side-bar rule to produce it is necessary, and a notice to the defendant to produce it is not sufficient.

Kelly, for the defendants, now moved to set aside this

judgment, and all subsequent proceedings, for irregularity, with costs, contending that although, when it is incumbent on a plaintiff to produce the record, a notice to the defendant that he would produce it was sufficient, yet where it is to be produced by the defendant, a four day rule to produce it was necessary: *Begbie* v. *Grenville* (a).

Erle shewed cause in the first instance, and produced an affidavit stating that the plaintiff had applied to the officers of the Court for a rule of the kind now said to be necessary, but was informed by them that the practice was to serve a notice only. Although Mr. Tidd (2 Tidd. Pr. 743, 9th ed.) states that a four day rule is necessary for this purpose, the practical direction given in a more recent work, Chit. Archb. Vol. ii. p. 678, is—" Give notice of your bringing in the record, or rule the other party to bring it in and proceed to trial," &c., without stating any distinction as to whether the burden of proof lies on the plaintiff or the defendant. The delivery of the issue, in which the defendant is commanded to produce the record in Court on a given day, renders a rule superfluous for any practical purposes.

Lord ABINGER, C. B.—The question simply is, what is the real practice of the Court in the present case, for on principle there is no difference between the one cause and the other; common sense suggests that a notice to produce the record is as good as a four day rule. According to the practice, however, it appears that the latter course is the proper one, where the defendant is to produce the record. This rule must therefore be absolute, and, as the last decision, in *Begbie* v. *Grenville*, is against the plaintiff, with costs.

PARKE, B.—There is a discrepancy in this respect be-

(a) 3 Dowl. P. C. 502.

tween the practice of this Court and that of the Common Pleas, which has not been provided against by the Rule of H. T. 4 Will. 4, s. 8.

GURNEY, B., and ROLFE, B., concurred.

Rule absolute, with costs.

———◆———

WELLS *v.* BENSKIN.

THIS cause was referred to arbitration, by an order of nisi prius, with power to the arbitrator to settle all matters in difference between the parties, and to order and determine what he should think fit to be done by either party respecting the matters in dispute; and the order provided, " that the parties respectively are to be examined on oath, to be sworn in Court or before the said arbitrator, if thought necessary by him, and to produce before the said arbitrator all such books, papers, &c., relating to the matters in difference between them, as the said arbitrator should think fit," &c. The arbitrator examined both parties as to the whole of their respective cases upon all the matters referred; and subsequently made his award in favour of the plaintiff.

Where a cause is referred to arbitration, with power to the arbitrator to settle all matters in difference between the parties, the submission providing also that the parties respectively are to be examined on oath, if thought necessary by him, it is in the discretion of the arbitrator to examine the parties, each in support of his own case, if he think fit.

Humfrey now moved for a rule to shew cause why the award should not be set aside.—The arbitrator was only entitled, so far as the cause is concerned, to examine the plaintiff in support of the defendant's case, or the defendant in support of the plaintiff's. To examine the parties in support of their own case is in violation of the ordinary rules of evidence, and is not warranted by the order of reference; the general authority to examine either of the parties applies only to the other matters in difference. The course taken in this case was indeed allowed in *Warne* v.

Bryant (a), but there the reference was of all matters in difference *in the cause.* And in *Morgan* v. *Williams* (b), the Court held that the arbitrator had done right in not examining a plaintiff in support of his own case.

Lord ABINGER, C. B.—All that the Court said in that case was, that the arbitrator had, under the peculiar circumstances, exercised a sound discretion in not examining the plaintiff; but his authority to do so was not questioned.

PARKE, B.—The order of reference in this case leaves it entirely to the discretion of the arbitrator to examine the plaintiff and defendant, when and to which of the matters referred he thinks fit.

ALDERSON, B.—I always considered, when acting as an arbitrator, that I had a general discretion given me as to which of the parties I should examine, and to what parts of the case; my practice certainly was to exercise it in the manner suggested by Mr. *Humfrey;* so as, in effect, to render the reference a substitute for a bill of discovery.

Rule refused.

(a) 3 B. & Cr. 590; 5 D. & R. 301.   (b) 2 Dowl. P. C. 123.

Exch. of Pleas,
1841.

Nov. 8.

SIMPSON *v.* DISMORE.

INDEBITATUS ASSUMPSIT for medicines and attendances by the plaintiff as a surgeon and apothecary.

Plea, non assumpsit.

At the trial before the under-sheriff of Middlesex, the plaintiff proved the attendances and supply of medicines, &c.; and for the purpose of shewing that he had been duly admitted to practise as an apothecary, put in evidence a license under the seal of the Apothecaries' Company, (which seal was proved to be genuine), in which a right to practise and dispense medicines as an apothecary was granted to a person bearing the christian and surname of the plaintiff. It was objected for the defendant, that some further evidence ought to be given to identify the plaintiff as the person named in the license; but the sheriff was of opinion that the evidence adduced was sufficient, and a verdict was found for the plaintiff for the amount claimed, leave being reserved to the defendant to move to enter a nonsuit on the above ground.

In an action for medicines and attendances by the plaintiff as an apothecary, the plaintiff put in evidence a license from the Apothecaries' Company to practise as such, granted to a person bearing the same christian and sur-name:—Held, that this was sufficient primâ facie evidence to shew the identity of the plaintiff with the person named in the license.

Pearson now moved accordingly.—Evidence ought to have been given to identify the plaintiff with the person named in the license. In *Whitelock* v. *Musgrove* (a), it was held, that in an action against the obligor of a bond, some evidence must be given of the identity of the obligor with the party sued; and that where the subscribing witness is dead, or residing abroad, proof of his hand-writing was insufficient, without some evidence to shew the identity of the party sued with the party named in the instrument.—He cited also *Dartnall* v. *Howard* (b).

PARKE, B.—I am of opinion that no rule ought to be

(a) 1 C. & M. 511.   (b) Ry. & M. 169.

granted in this case. There was ample evidence to go to the jury of the identity of the plaintiff with the person named in the license. We find him acting as an apothecary, prescribing and dispensing medicines to his patients, and then producing a certificate or license for that purpose in his name, from the body empowered by law to grant it. That is quite sufficient evidence of identity to go to the jury.

GURNEY, B.—It is certainly sufficient evidence of identity to call on the defendant for an answer to it.

ROLFE, B., concurred.

Rule refused.

———◆———

DOE d. DAVIES and Others v. EVANS.

Lands being held by G. as tenant from year to year to D., D., who died in 1837, devised the same to trustees for the term of 140 years, upon trust (inter alia) to permit his wife E. D. to take the rents and profits thereof during her life. G. paid the rent to E. D. the widow, after D.'s death, from 1837 to 1840, and on receiving a notice to quit from her in March 1840, stated that he did not think she would turn him out of possession, as she had promised he should continue on as tenant from year to year:—*Held*, in an action of ejectment brought by the trustees for the recovery of the premises, that this was sufficient evidence of a disclaimer by G. of the title of the trustees, to warrant the jury in finding a verdict for the plaintiff.

EJECTMENT to recover the possession of a messuage and lands in the county of Carmarthen. There had been a former ejectment brought by the same parties, in which a verdict had been found for the defendant, on the ground that there was no determination of the tenancy of one Thomas Griffith in the premises in question; and that was the principal point in the present case. This cause was tried before *Erskine*, J., at the last Summer Assizes for the county of Carmarthen, when it appeared that, prior to and during the year 1837, Griffiths had been and continued tenant to one John Davies of the premises sought to be recovered, and had paid him rent for the same; and that John Davies, who died in that year, devised the property in question to certain persons, who were the lessors of the plaintiff in this action for the term of 140 years, upon trust (inter alia) to permit his wife, Elizabeth Davies, to take the rents and profits thereof during her life. The widow received rent from Thomas Griffiths from 1837 to 1840, and in March in that year she sent him a notice to quit the premises. Evidence was given at the trial, and not objected to, that Thomas Griffiths, on receiving the notice to quit, said he did not think Mrs. Davies would turn him out of possession, as she had said that he should not be removed, but continue on as tenant from year to year. It was objected for the defendant, that as the legal estate was in the trustees of the will of John Davies, they alone were the lessors of Griffiths, and as such entitled to give notice to quit, and as they had not given any notice, there was no proof of the determination of Griffiths's tenancy. The learned Judge refused to stop the case, but directed the jury to consider whether Griffiths held the premises as the tenant of the trustees or of the widow, Mrs. Davies; telling them, that if he was not tenant to Mrs. Davies, he had disclaimed the title of the trustees, and therefore no notice to quit by them was necessary to entitle them to recover. The jury thereupon found their verdict for the plaintiff, the learned Judge giving leave to the defendant to move to enter a verdict for him, if the Court should be of opinion that there was no evidence of the determination of the tenancy of Griffiths.

E. V. Williams now moved accordingly.—There ought to have been a notice to quit given by the trustees, in order to determine the tenancy of Griffiths. What was said by him on receiving notice to quit from Mrs. Davies, could not amount to a disclaimer of the title of the trustees; neither would the payment of rent to a cestui que trust be any proof of disclaimer of their title. They and they only had the legal estate, and had power to determine the tenancy.

PARKE, B.—I think no rule ought to be granted in this

case. The statement of Griffiths, not being objected to, was admissible in evidence, and that was, that Mrs Davies had promised him that he should not be removed, but continue as tenant from year to year; that affords some evidence of his having agreed to hold under the tenant for life, whereby he disclaimed the title of the trustees. And that, accompanied by his having paid rent to her, is evidence to go to the jury of attornment to the tenant for life, and of repudiation of the title of the trustees. In a case like the present, slight evidence would be sufficient to remove a mere technical objection.

The rest of the Court concurred.

Rule refused.

Wigden and Another *v.* Birt.

On an application under the stat, 4 & 5 Will. 4, c. 62, s. 31, for leave to issue execution on a judgment in the Court of Common Pleas at Lancaster, the affidavit must state distinctly that the defendant was a resident within the jurisdiction of that Court at the time of the judgment or of action brought, and then had goods and chattels there, which he has since removed out of the jurisdiction. It is not sufficient to state that he is not now a resident in the county of Lancaster, and has not any goods or chattels within the jurisdiction; or, that he is not now a resident there, and has removed all his goods and chattels out of the jurisdiction since the judgment.

The affidavit must be entitled in the superior Court.

ON the first day of this term, *Cowling* applied in this case, under the stat. 4 & 5 Will. 4, c. 62, s. 31, for leave to issue execution upon a judgment obtained in the Court of Common Pleas at Lancaster. The affidavit on which he moved (which was entitled in the Court of Common Pleas at Lancaster) stated, that "the defendant is not now a resident in the county of Lancaster, but resides in the county of Middlesex, and hath not any goods or chattels within the jurisdiction of the said Court of Common Pleas at Lancaster." He admitted that this affidavit did not in terms follow the language of the statute, which enables the superior Courts to issue execution on a judgment in that Court, where the party against whom it has been recovered "shall remove his person or goods or chattels from and out of the jurisdiction of the said Court of

Exch. of Pleas,
1841.

Wigden
v.
Birt.

Common Pleas at Lancaster," but urged that substantially it was the same, and shewed sufficiently that the defendant must have removed within the meaning of the statute, since the writ must have been directed to him as of the county, and he must have been served within the county. He stated also, that some of the officers of this Court differed in opinion as to whether the affidavit should be entitled in the Court below or in this Court.

The Court, however, held the affidavit to be defective, inasmuch as it did not state that the defendant had ever been a resident within the county of Lancaster, or that he had *removed* any goods or chattels out of the jurisdiction. He might have been there by accident. It was better to adhere to the language of the statute. They held also that the affidavit ought to have been entitled in this Court.

Cowling afterwards (Nov. 11) renewed his application on an affidavit (entitled in this Court) in the following terms :—" that the defendant is not now a resident in the county of Lancaster, but resides in the county of Middlesex, and has removed, since the judgment in this action, all his goods and chattels from and out of the jurisdiction of the said Court, &c., and has not now any goods or chattels within the jurisdiction of the said Court, whereon the plaintiff can levy the amount of his said judgment," &c.

The Court thought the affidavit still defective, in not stating expressly, that at the time of the commencement of the suit, or before judgment, the defendant was resident within the jurisdiction of the Court of Common Pleas at Lancaster, and then had goods there which he had subsequently removed.

And now, the affidavit being amended by stating, that " at the time of the commencement of the action, and at the time of the judgment, the defendant was a resident in the county of Lancaster, and then had goods and chattels within the jurisdiction of the Court, and that he had since removed all his said goods and chattels out of the jurisdiction of the said Court," &c., &c.

The rule was granted.

———◆———

HOWITT *v.* RICKABY.

Nov. 18.

A plaintiff does not waive his right to an attachment against the sheriff for not duly returning a writ of fi. fa., by directing him, after the expiration of the rule to return the writ, to proceed with the execution, which had been suspended by an adverse claim.

W. H. WATSON moved for a rule calling upon the defendant to shew cause why an attachment against the sheriff, for not returning a writ of fieri facias, should not be set aside, with costs. His affidavits stated, that the writ was delivered to the sheriff on the 22nd of June, and on the 28th he was required, by a judge's order, to return it. On that day, a claim was made by a third party to the goods; but that claim being afterwards barred, the plaintiff's attorney, on the 8th of July, directed the sheriff to proceed with the execution. The writ was returned by the sheriff on the 21st of September. It was now contended, that by the direction, on the 8th of July, to proceed with the execution, the plaintiff had waived his right to attach the sheriff for not returning the writ pursuant to the order of the 28th of June.

PARKE, B.—In a case of this kind, subsequent obedience to the rule to return a writ is no answer to an application for an attachment. The sheriff ought to have returned the writ at the expiration of the rule. The plaintiff, wishing to assist him, afterwards directs him to go on with the execution; but that is no waiver of his right to have an attachment. The attachment may be set aside on payment of costs.

Per CURIAM,

Rule accordingly.

Exch. of Pleas,
1841.

Nov. 18.

THOMAS *v.* HAWKES and Another.

THE plaintiff having obtained a verdict on the trial of this cause, a rule for a new trial was made absolute in last Trinity Term, no mention being made of costs (*a*). This rule was afterwards abandoned, both parties agreeing to a reference, and it being stipulated in the order of reference that the costs were "to abide the event." The arbitrator found in favour of the defendants on all the issues, and the Master allowed them, on taxation, the costs of the trial. *Hugh Hill* having obtained a rule to shew cause why the taxation should not be reviewed,

J. Henderson now shewed cause.—It must be admitted that, according to the authorities on this subject, if the cause had been tried again, and the defendants had succeeded on that trial, they would not have been entitled to the costs of the first trial; but the rule is different in the case of a reference after the first trial; the parties have thereby waived any benefit they might have claimed under the rule for a new trial, and have submitted the question of costs to the arbitrator.

PARKE, B.—It is clear that if the cause had gone down to a second trial, and the defendants had succeeded, neither party would have had the costs of the first trial. The case of *Jolliffe* v. *Mundy* (*b*) is an authority in favour of the plaintiff; for though it was not the case of a reference to arbitration after a rule for a new trial, and therefore not precisely in point, this case falls clearly within its principle.

Rule absolute (*c*).

After a verdict for the plaintiff, the defendant obtained a rule for a new trial, which was made absolute, no mention being made of costs. The parties then agreed to a reference, and the order of reference stipulated that the costs were to abide the event. The arbitrator having decided the cause in favour of the defendant:—Held, that the defendant was not entitled to the costs of the trial.

(*a*) See 8 M. & W. 140.   (*b*) 4 M. & W. 502.
(*c*) See *Rigby* v. *Okell*, 7 B. & C. 57.

KELLY *v.* SOLARI.

Nov. 18.

Money paid by the plaintiff to the defendant under a bonâ fide *forgetfulness* of facts which disentitled the defendant to receive it, may be recovered back in an action for money had and received.

It is not sufficient to preclude a party from recovering money paid by him under a mistake of fact, that he had the *means of knowledge of the fact, unless he* paid it intentionally, not choosing to investigate the fact.

ASSUMPSIT for money paid, money had and received, and on an account stated. Plea, non assumpsit. At the trial before Lord *Abinger*, C. B., at the London sittings after Trinity Term, it appeared that this was an action brought by the plaintiff, as one of the directors of the Argus Life Assurance Company, to recover from the defendant, Madame Solari, the sum of 197*l.* 10*s.* alleged to have been paid to her by the company under a mistake of fact, under the following circumstances.

Mr. Angelo Solari, the late husband of the defendant, in the year 1836, effected a policy on his life with the Argus Assurance Company for £200. He died on the 18th of October, 1840, leaving the defendant his executrix, not having (by mistake) paid the quarterly premium on the policy, which became due on the 3rd of September preceding. In November, the actuary of the office informed two of the directors, Mr. Bates and Mr. Clift, that the policy had lapsed by reason of the non-payment of the premium, and Mr. Clift thereupon wrote on the policy, in pencil, the word "lapsed." On the 6th of February, 1841, the defendant proved her husband's will; and on the 13th, applied at the Argus office for the payment of the sum of £1000, secured upon the policy in question and two others. Messrs. Bates and Clift, and a third director, accordingly drew a cheque for 987*l.* 10*s.*, which they handed to the defendant's agent, the discount being deducted in consideration of the payment being made three months earlier than by the rules of the office it was payable. Messrs. Bates and Clift stated in evidence, that they had, at the time of so paying the money, entirely forgotten that the policy in question had lapsed. Under these circumstances, the Lord Chief Baron expressed his opinion, that if the directors had had knowledge, or the *means of knowledge*, of the policy having lapsed, the plaintiff could not recover, and that their afterwards forgetting it would make no difference; and he accordingly directed a nonsuit, reserving leave to the plaintiff to move to enter a verdict for him for the amount claimed.

Thesiger, in the former part of this term, obtained a rule nisi accordingly, or for a new trial; against which,

Platt and *Butt* now shewed cause.—It has long been a settled principle of law, that a party cannot recover back money which he has paid with full knowledge, or means of knowledge, of all the circumstances, although he was not legally liable to the payment of it, if it be not unconscientious in the other party to retain it. That is expressly laid down by *Bayley*, J., in *Milnes* v. *Duncan* (a); and the same rule of law had been previously recognized in *Bilbie* v. *Lumley* (b). [*Parke*, B.—All that that case decides is, that money paid with full knowledge of all the facts cannot be recovered back by reason of its having been paid in ignorance of the law. But in the case of *Lucas* v. *Worswick* (c), it was held that money may be recovered back which was paid under a *forgetfulness* of facts within the plaintiff's knowledge.] That was not the case of money which, being paid, could in equity or conscience be retained, since it was a second payment of the same debt. But here it was admitted that the omission to pay the premium was a mere mistake. [*Parke*, B.—The important bearing of that case is, that it shews that although the mistake be of facts within the party's knowledge, if the money be paid under the influence of that mistake, it may be recovered back.] This being also added, that it is not retainable in equity or conscience. Here the defendant was an executrix; she made the demand bonâ fide;

(a) 6 B. & C. 671; 9 D. & R. 731.　　(b) 2 East, 469.

(c) 1 M. & Rob. 293.

when received, the money became assets; and if she have distributed it, she must herself, if the plaintiff succeeds, be at the loss of it, for no fault of hers. It was paid with full means of knowledge throughout all the stages of the transaction. *Brisbane* v. *Dacres* (a) is a strong authority in favour of the defendant.

Thesiger and *Whateley*, contrà.—The real question in such cases as the present has been, not whether the party had or has used the means of knowledge within his reach, but whether the money was paid under a mistake of *fact* or of *law*. If under a mistake of fact, then, if nothing has subsequently occurred to render it unconscientious to recover it, it may be recovered back. Such is stated to be the general rule of law in *Wilkinson* v. *Johnston* (b); and there is no authority that the possession of the *means of knowledge*, simply, is sufficientto disentitle the party to recover back money paid by him under immediate ignorance of the facts. Now *forgetfulness* is immediate ignorance of the facts. The question is, was the payment *a voluntary payment, with knowledge at the time.* The doctrine, that means of knowledge are equivalent to knowledge, rests altogether on the dictum of *Bayley*, J., in *Milnes* v. *Duncan*, and is not supported either by the former or subsequent authorities. *Bilbie* v. *Lumley* proceeded entirely on the ground of the payment having been made in ignorance of the *law.* In *Chatfield* v. *Paxton* (c), *Ashhurst*, J., said, that "where a payment had been made, not with full knowledge of the facts, but only under a *blind suspicion* of the case, and it was found to have been paid unjustly, the party might recover it back again." That is an expression which implies that full knowledge was obtainable by further investigation. So, in *Cox* v. *Prentice* (a), the plaintiff had the fullest means of knowledge, had he chosen to avail himself of

(a) 5 Taunt. 143.   (c) 2 East, 471, n.
(b) 2 B. & Cr. 429; 5 D.& R. 403. (d) 3 M. & Selw. 344.

them. In *Lucas* v. *Worswick,* the plaintiff was held entitled
to recover, because the money was paid by him under a
mistake of fact *at the time:* and that is the real test. [Lord
Abinger, C. B.—This appears to be like the case of a payment on a balance of accounts, when it is always taken
" errors excepted;" in such a case, money paid on a mis-
calculation of the items may be recovered back.] Yet the
party there has full *means of knowledge,* since, with a little
more care, the items might have been calculated correctly;
and the same rule of law must apply to all cases of payment by mistake. And it is in every case unconscientious
to retain money paid under a mistake of fact, where the
receiver knows that it was not meant to be paid knowingly.
—They cited also *Bize* v. *Dickason* (a), and *Cripps* v.
Reade (b), and were then stopped by the Court.

Lord ABINGER, C. B.—I think the defendant ought to
have had the opportunity of taking the opinion of the jury
on the question whether in reality the directors had a
knowledge of the facts, and therefore that there should be
a new trial, and not a verdict for the plaintiff; although I
am now prepared to say that I laid down the rule too
broadly at the trial, as to the effect of their having had
means of knowledge. That is a very vague expression, and
it is difficult to say with precision what it amounts to; for
example, it may be that the party may have the means of
knowledge on a particular subject, only by sending to and
obtaining information from a correspondent abroad. In
the case of *Bilbie* v. *Lumley,* the argument as to the party
having *means of* knowledge was used by counsel, and
adopted by some of the judges; but that was a peculiar
case, and there can be no question that if the point had
been left to the jury, they would have found that the plaintiff had actual knowledge. The safest rule however is,

(a) 1 T. R. 285.   (b) 6 T. R. 606.

that if the party makes the payment with full knowledge of the facts, although under ignorance of the law, there being no fraud on the other side, he cannot recover it back again. There may also be cases in which, although he might by investigation learn the state of facts more accurately, he declines to do so, and chooses to pay the money notwithstanding; in that case there can be no doubt that he is equally bound. Then there is a third case, and the most difficult one,—where the party had once a full knowledge of the facts, but has since forgotten them. I certainly laid down the rule too widely to the jury, when I told them that if the directors once knew the facts they must be taken still to know them, and could not recover by saying that they had since forgotten them. I think the knowledge of the facts which disentitles the party from recovering, must mean a knowledge existing in the mind at the time of payment. I have little doubt in this case that the directors had forgotten the fact, otherwise I do not believe they would have brought the action; but as Mr. *Platt* certainly has a right to have that question submitted to the jury, there must be a new trial.

PARKE, B.—I entirely agree in the opinion just pronounced by my Lord Chief Baron, that there ought to be a new trial. I think that where money is paid to another under the influence of a mistake, that is, upon the supposition that a specific fact is true, which would entitle the other to the money, but which fact is untrue, and the money would not have been paid if it had been known to the payer that the fact was untrue, an action will lie to recover it back, and it is against conscience to retain it; though a demand may be necessary in those cases in which the party receiving may have been ignorant of the mistake. The position that a person so paying is precluded from recovering by laches, in not availing himself of the means of knowledge in his power, seems, from the cases cited, to have been founded on the dictum of Mr. Justice *Bayley*, in the case of *Milnes* v. *Duncan;* and with all respect to that authority, I do not think it can be sustained in point of law.   If, indeed, the money is intentionally paid, without reference to the truth or falsehood of the fact, the plaintiff meaning to waive all inquiry into it, and that the person receiving shall have the money at all events, whether the fact be true or false, the latter is certainly entitled to retain it; but if it is paid under the impression of the truth of a fact which is untrue, it may, generally speaking, be recovered back, however careless the party paying may have been, in omitting to use due diligence to inquire into the fact.   In such a case the receiver was not entitled to it, nor intended to have it.

Exch. of Pleas,
1841.

KELLY
v.
SOLARI.

GURNEY, B., concurred.

ROLFE, B.—I am of the same opinion.   With respect to the argument, that money cannot be recovered back except where it is unconscientious to retain it, it seems to me, that wherever it is paid under a mistake of fact, and the party would not have paid it if the fact had been known to him, it cannot be otherwise than unconscientious to retain it.   But I agree that Mr. *Platt* has a right to go to the jury again, upon two grounds: first, that the jury may possibly find that the directors had not in truth forgotten the fact; and secondly, they may also come to the conclusion, that they had determined that they would not expose the office to unpopularity, and would therefore pay the money at all events; in which case I quite agree that they could not recover it back.

Rule absolute for a new trial.

as,

1841.

Nov. 19.

Assumpsit on an agreement to build a house according to certain drawings, plans, and specifications, and to the satisfaction of the plaintiff, and with the best materials; alleging as breaches that the defendant did not build the house to the satisfaction of the plaintiff; and that he did not perform the work with the best materials. Pleas, 1st, non assumpsit; 2ndly, that the defendant did the works to the satisfaction of the plaintiff; 3rd, that before the breach the contract was rescinded; 4th, leave and license; 5th, that the defendant deviated from the drawings by the direction of the plaintiff's architect; 6th, a plea stating an agreement between plaintiff and defendant to build a stone wall in lieu of the wall mentioned in the original agreement; 7th, that the defendant, by command of the plaintiff, erected a stone wall instead of a brick wall. The plaintiff took issue on the two first pleas, traversed the 3rd, 6th, and 7th, replied de injuriâ to the 4th, and demurred to the 5th. The cause was at the assizes referred to an arbitrator, the costs of the cause and reference to abide the event; and he awarded a general verdict to be entered for the defendant.

Held, that the award was not uncertain, inconsistent, or repugnant, and that it was not necessary for the arbitrator to assess contingent damages on the demurrer, neither party having requested him to do so, but acted as if the matter had not been submitted to him.

Held, also, that the 5th plea was bad on general demurrer, the architect not being shewn to be the plaintiff's agent to bind him by any deviation from the drawings.

ASSUMPSIT on an agreement to build a house for the plaintiff, according to certain drawings, plans, and specifications, and to the satisfaction of the plaintiff, and also that the work should be performed with the best materials. Breach; first, that the defendant did not do the works to the reasonable satisfaction of the plaintiff, but on the contrary thereof, wholly deceived the plaintiff therein, and the same works were done in a manner wholly and reasonably unsatisfactory to the plaintiff, in this, to wit, that the defendant did, in building the said house and completing the said several works, erect a certain wall there, being parcel of the said house and works, in so unsatisfactory and improper a manner, and in a way contrary to the said drawings, that the said wall stood and projected into and upon the shop of the plaintiff, and thereby, contrary to the said agreement and promise of the defendant, did deprive the plaintiff of the use of a part of his said shop, and the same shop then was and still is, by reason of the premises, of far less use to the plaintiff for the purpose of carrying on his trade therein. The second breach alleged was, that the defendant did not perform the work with the best materials, but on the contrary, performed the same with bad and improper materials, and such as were unfit for the purposes to which the same were applied, and which did not in any way correspond with the drawings in the agreement mentioned.

Pleas: first, non assumpsit: secondly, that the defendant

did do the said works to the reasonable satisfaction of the *Exch. of Pleas*, plaintiff: thirdly, that after the making of the contract and 1841. before any breach, it was mutually agreed by and between the plaintiff and defendant that the contract and promise should then be and the same then were wholly rescinded and abandoned, and the plaintiff was thereby wholly discharged from the performance thereof: fourthly, as to so much of the declaration as relates to the erecting of the wall, that the defendant, at the request of the plaintiff, and by his leave and license, committed the supposed breach of contract, so far as the same relates to the erecting of the said wall: fifthly, as to so much of the declaration as charges the defendant with a deviation from the said drawings, that he the defendant did deviate from the said drawings at the instance and request of, and by the direction and authority of the architect of the plaintiff: sixthly, that after the committing of the breaches of contract, it was agreed by and between the plaintiff and defendant, at the request of the plaintiff, that the defendant should build for the plaintiff a certain other wall of stone, in lieu of the wall before agreed to be built by the defendant, and mentioned in the plans and specifications, and that the plaintiff should accept such agreement and the performance thereof, in full satisfaction and discharge of the causes of action in the introductory part of that plea mentioned; that defendant built the stone wall in all respects according to the last-mentioned agreement, which performance the plaintiff accepted in full satisfaction, &c.: seventhly, as to the causes of action "as to the projection of the said wall, that during the performance of the works, it was discovered by the defendant and by the architect of the plaintiff, that the wall by the plans and specifications proposed to be built of brick, was insufficient for the purposes by the plans and specifications proposed and intended, and thereupon the defendant, at the request of the architect of the plaintiff, and also by the command and autho-

COOPER
v.
LANGDON.

rity of the plaintiff, did, in the place and stead of the brick wall, erect and build the said wall of stone, and did thereby necessarily and unavoidably encroach a little on the shop of the plaintiff, and the said stone wall did, by reason of the same being much wider and thicker than the brick wall in the plans and specifications mentioned, necessarily and unavoidably a little stand and project into and upon the shop of the plaintiff, without any default whatever of the defendant.

The plaintiff joined issue on the two first pleas: to the third he replied, by denying that the contract was rescinded or abandoned; to the fourth, de injuriâ; to the fifth, a general demurrer; to the sixth, that he did not accept the agreement in that plea mentioned, or the performance thereof, in satisfaction or discharge; to the last plea, that the wall of stone built in the place of the brick wall, was not built by the command or authority of the plaintiff.

The cause, so far as related to the issues in fact, came on for trial at the last Summer Assizes for the county of Hants, when a verdict was entered for the plaintiff by consent, subject to the award of a gentleman at the bar; the costs of the cause and of the reference to abide the event. The arbitrator having proceeded and held the reference, afterwards made his award, by which he ordered that the verdict entered for the plaintiff should be set aside, and a verdict entered for the defendant.

Erle had obtained a rule to shew cause why the award should not be set aside, on the ground that it was uncertain and inconsistent; that the pleas were inconsistent and repugnant to each other, and yet the arbitrator had ordered a general verdict for the defendant, without saying whether it was to be entered on some or all of the issues; and that the award was not final, in omitting to assess contingent damages on the demurrer.

Crowder shewed cause.—First, the award is not uncertain; it determines the whole cause in favour of the defendant. If the plaintiff wished the arbitrator to find specifically on each issue, he ought to have requested him to do so. [Lord *Abinger*, C. B.—You need not trouble yourself upon that point]. Then it is said that the award is inconsistent and repugnant in itself, inasmuch as the arbitrator, by ordering a general verdict to be entered for the defendant, determines by the first issue that there was no such agreement between the parties as that alleged in the declaration, while by the second and subsequent pleas such agreement is admitted to exist. But the award is not necessarily inconsistent; the effect of the pleas merely is, that there was no such agreement, but if there was, the defendant has performed it, or is excused from doing so. The plaintiff under the first issue is called upon to make out his case, and if he fails in doing so, there is no inconsistency in awarding a general verdict for the defendant. In *The Duke of Beaufort* v. *Welsh* (a), which was assumpsit on a retainer to project certain works, and to examine certain bills with care, skill, and diligence, the defendant pleaded first, non assumpsit; secondly, no retainer; thirdly, that the defendant did use care &c. in projecting the works; fourthly, that he did use care &c. in examining the bills. The cause and all matters in difference were referred by order of Nisi Prius, the costs of the cause to abide the event. The arbitrator by his award found for the defendant on the first, second, and fourth issues, and for the plaintiff on the third; and it was held that the award was good, and not repugnant, for that the finding on the third and fourth issues must be regarded as hypothetical, and only for the purpose of determining the costs of them. That decision is strongly in point. [*Parke*, B.—Another question here is, whether the award is final, the arbitrator having omitted to assess contingent damages on the

(a) 10 Ad. & Ell. 527.

demurrer.]   Neither of the parties brought that matter
before the arbitrator, but acted as if it was not submitted
to him.

Erle and *Rawlinson*, in support of the rule.—The arbitrator ought to have assessed contingent damages on the
demurrer: *In re Robson & Railston* (a).   In that case, on a
ference of all matters in difference, a demand on one side
was laid before the arbitrators, and immediately admitted
by the other party; no evidence was in consequence given
concerning it, nor any adjudication upon it requested.
The arbitrators published their award of and concerning
the matters referred to them, directing payment of a sum
of money (without saying on what account) to the party
against whom the above claim had been made, with costs;
and it was proved that they left that claim out of consideration in making their award, as a matter not in dispute.   It
was held that the award was bad, as the arbitrator ought to
have taken notice of the admitted demand.   Lord *Tenterden*, in delivering the judgment of the Court, said, " There
would be no end of disputes, if the practice were to prevail, that whenever, on a meeting before arbitrators, one
party gave up items one, two, and three of his demands,
and the other four, five, and six; these were all to be laid
out of consideration in making the award." [Lord *Abinger*,
C. B.—In that case the effect of the finding was to render it necessary that the arbitrators should have adjudicated
upon the claim; but here, as the arbitrator finds for the
defendant on all the issues, there can be no necessity for
him to assess contingent damages upon the demurrer].
Then the award is inconsistent and repugnant.   The pleas
are inconsistent with each other, and if the arbitrator
must be taken to have found all the facts stated in them to
be true, such a state of things could not exist.   An arbi-

(a) 1 B. & Adol. 723.

trator stands in the same situation as a jury, and no more intendment can be made in favour of his finding than of that of a jury. A verdict which is inconsistent or repugnant is void; Com. Dig., Pleader (S. 23). They cited also *Marler* v. *Ayliffe* (a), and *England* v. *Davison* (b).

Exch. of Pleas, 1841.

COOPER *v.* LANGDON.

Lord ABINGER, C. B.—I am of opinion that this rule ought to be discharged. I think the award is neither inconsistent nor repugnant. If the cause had been tried at Nisi Prius, the circumstances of the case might have been such, and it might have taken such a course, that a verdict might have been found for the defendant on every one of the issues. Suppose the plaintiff failed in proving his case under the general issue, the defendant might go on and give evidence in support of the issues, the proof of which rests upon him; and if he succeeded in establishing them, then the general verdict would be for him. There would have been no necessary inconsistency, if the jury had found for the defendant on the general issue and also on all the other issues.

PARKE, B.—I am of the same opinion. The first objection is, that the award is uncertain, inasmuch as it does not determine whether the verdict is to be entered for the defendant on some or all of the issues; but I think the meaning of the award is, that a verdict shall be entered for the defendant upon each issue which could be found for him. In *England* v. *Davison*, the award was uncertain, because the arbitrator had not disposed of the issues; but in the present case, the arbitrator directs a general verdict to be entered for the defendant. Then comes the question, whether the issues may not all consistently be found for the defendant. I have no doubt they may. Suppose the plaintiff to fail in proving the agreement, as for instance, or want of a stamp, and that the defendant were to prove

(a) Cro. Jac. 134.   (b) 9 Dowl. P. C. 1052.

the other issues, there would be no inconsistency in finding them all for him. Under the statute of Anne, each issue is to be disposed of as if it stood alone upon the record. With respect to the matter arising upon the demurrer, it may be that, according to the true construction of the submission, the arbitrator ought to have disposed of it; but, as both parties have in effect agreed that he should not, that amounts to a new agreement by parol to abide by the award; and all the issues in fact being found for the defendant, it became unnecessary to assess contingent damages on the demurrer.

GURNEY, B., and ROLFE, B., concurred.

Rule discharged.

In Hilary Term, 1842 (Jan. 24), the demurrer came on for argument.

Kelly, who appeared to support it, was stopped by the Court, who called upon

Crowder to support the plea.—The plea amounts in substance to an averment, that the deviation from the drawings was by the direction of an agent of the plaintiff. The defendant has a right to assume, on this demurrer, that the *drawings* did not altogether agree with the plans and specifications, and that therefore the architect directed a deviation from them: supposing that to be the case, can such deviation furnish a ground of action?

Lord ABINGER, C. B.—We cannot surmise that. The plea is clearly bad: the declaration does not state the architect to have been the agent of the plaintiff, neither does the plea allege that he was.

ALDERSON, B.—The defendant undertook to do the works according to the drawings. He has not done so; but he says he deviated from them by the authority of the architect of the plaintiff. He does not aver that he did them according to the plans and specifications: and no authority is shewn on the part of the architect to bind the plaintiff by any deviation from the drawings.

GURNEY, B., concurred.

Judgment for the plaintiff.

Exch. of Pleas,
1841.

COOPER
v.
LANGDON.

SINGLETON *v.* JOHNSON.

PASHLEY had obtained a rule for judgment as in case of a nonsuit, upon affidavits which were intitled " Between John Singleton, plaintiff, and George Johnson, defendant." The affidavits in answer to the rule stated that there were two persons of the name of George Johnson, and that all the proceedings in the cause hitherto had been intitled " Between John Singleton and George Johnson the elder."

Heaton shewed cause.—The affidavit on which the rule was obtained is improperly intitled. It is an established rule that where there is a cause in Court, all affidavits used in Court must in their title follow the title of the cause. In *Shrimpton* v. *Carter* (a), an affidavit intitled " G. Shrimpton *v.* W. Carter the elder, sued as W. Carter," the cause being G. Shrimpton *v.* W. Carter, was rejected as being improperly intitled.—He cited also *Borthwick* v. *Ravenscroft* (b).

Pashley, in support of the rule.—All that is required in

Nov. 19.

An affidavit on which a rule for judgment as in case of a nonsuit was founded, was intitled " Between J. S., plaintiff, and G. J., defendant." The affidavit in answer to the rule stated, that there were two G. J.s, and that all former proceedings in the cause were intitled " J. S. v. G. J. *the elder :"—Held,* that the affidavit was sufficient.

(a) 3 Dowl. P. C. 648.　　　(b) 5 M. & W. 31.

F 2

Exch. of Pleas,
1841.

SINGLETON
v.
JOHNSON.

intitling an affidavit is to state correctly the Christian and surnames of the parties in the cause, which has been done in the present case. It is no objection that the word "elder" is omitted. Where the name of a party is given without any description of "elder" or "younger," the former is always presumed.

Lord ABINGER, C. B.—We think the affidavit is sufficient. In the case of *Shrimpton* v. *Carter*, the affidavit, by describing "W. Carter" as "W. Carter the elder," gave an addition to the name of the party, which might not have been true; but, in the present case, George Johnson means George Johnson the elder, unless the contrary is expressed.

PARKE, B.—The case of *Shrimpton* v. *Carter* was the converse of the present; and there the title of the affidavit contained more than the title of the cause.

Rule discharged on a peremptory undertaking.

———————

Nov. 19.   THOMAS *v.* JOHN BIRD and THOMAS BIRD.

In an action against an administrator for taking the plaintiff's goods, to which he pleaded that they were his goods as administrator:—
Held, that one of the next of kin of the intestate was a competent witness for the defendant, without a release.

TRESPASS for imprisoning the plaintiff, and seizing and taking away her goods; to wit, sovereigns, guineas, &c. Pleas: 1st, not guilty; 2ndly, that the goods and chattels in the declaration mentioned were not the goods of the plaintiff; 3rdly, that they were the goods of the defendant John Bird, and W. Maddocks, as administrators of William Bird, deceased; 4thly, leave and license. The plaintiff joined issue on the two first pleas, traversed the allegation

Quære, whether a release by *two* of the next of kin to the administrator, of their respective interests in the goods the subject of the action, required more than one stamp?

Such a release (if necessary) would have been sufficient, without extending also to the costs of the action; inasmuch as they would not necessarily be allowed to the administrator as a charge on the estate, in case of a verdict for the plaintiff.

in the third plea of their being the goods of the adminis-

trators, and to the fourth plea replied de injuriâ. Issues thereon.—At the trial before *Tindal*, C. J., at the last Assizes for Surrey, the defendants called as a witness, in support of the issue on the third plea, one Frances Monckton, who was a niece of the intestate William Bird, and entitled to a distributive share of his property. Her competency being objected to on the part of the plaintiff, the defendants put in a deed of release, whereby the witness and her husband, Stephen Monckton, and Elizabeth Hayward (another niece and next of kin of the intestate, who also was a witness) and her husband released to the administrators all their interest in or arising out of the goods, the subject of this action. This deed bore one 35s. stamp only. It was contended for the defendants, that this deed was not sufficient to restore the witness to competency, on two grounds : first, that the release applied only to the goods in question, and not to the costs of this action, which would constitute a burthen on the estate ; and secondly, that, the interests of the two releasing parties being several, two stamps were necessary. The learned judge was of opinion that the release was sufficient in both these respects ; and the plaintiff had a verdict, leave being given to the defendants to move to enter a nonsuit. On an early day in this term,

Platt moved for a rule pursuant to the leave reserved, or for a new trial, and renewed the objections taken at Nisi Prius.—First, the costs of the cause would form a burthen on the estate, in case the plaintiff succeeded, and the witness was interested in relieving it of that burthen : the release should, therefore, have extended to the costs also. The witness had a direct interest in making out the property to be part of the intestate's estate. [*Parke*, B.— The damages for false imprisonment could not, *certainly* would not, and the costs of the cause would not necessarily, be allowed to the administrator as a charge on the estate. Lord *Abinger*, C. B.—It is not a direct consequence of the verdict.] Secondly, one stamp was not sufficient. The interests of the two nieces were several, and required several acts and deeds of release. They were not joint tenants. The deed ought, therefore, to have borne a stamp in respect of each of those interests.

Cur. adv. vult.

The judgment of the Court was now delivered by

Lord ABINGER, C. B.—In this case the question was, whether one of the next of kin, who was examined on behalf of the defendants, one of whom was an administrator, was a competent witness. The witness had joined with another next of kin, also a witness, in a release of their interest in or arising out of the goods, part of the subject of this action. The release was in one instrument, with one stamp; and the objection was that, the interests of the two witnesses being separate, there ought to have been two stamps. The Lord Chief Justice was of opinion that the release of both was one joint transaction, and admissible on the same principle that a release by all creditors under a composition deed has been received. We do not say that this opinion was not right, though possibly we might have thought it fit to receive further consideration. But we are of opinion that the witness was competent without any release, as the verdict was not admissible in evidence for or against her, and she was not interested in the event of the trial. To support the objection on account of interest in the event, the legal consequence of the verdict must be such as *necessarily* to affect the interests of the witness; and that was not the case in this action. The verdict might practically affect them, and probably would; but it would not necessarily follow that it would.

Nothing would be legally determined by it, so as to affect the rights of the next of kin, as to the goods, the subject of the action, being part of the effects of the deceased, to be accounted for by the administrators. There will therefore be no rule.

Rule refused.

Exch. of Pleas,
1841.

THOMAS
v.
BIRD.

POOLE v. PALMER.

Nov. 13 & 16.

DEBT for work and labour, money paid, and on an account stated. Plea, nunquam indebitatus. At the trial before Lord *Abinger*, C. B., at the London sittings after Trinity Term, it appeared that the action was brought by the plaintiff, an auctioneer and estate agent, to recover compensation for business done by him relative to an intended sale of an estate in the county of Surrey, which he had undertaken in pursuance of a written authority to sell the property, dated 10th of August, 1840, signed by the defendant and several other persons. One of these persons being called as a witness for the defendant, was objected to as being a co-contractor with him, and therefore incompetent. The Lord Chief Baron allowed the objection, and the plaintiff obtained a verdict.

In an action against one of several joint contractors, the other co-contractors are competent witnesses for the defendant, since the stat. 3 & 4 Will. 4, c. 42, ss. 26, 27.

In this term, *Thesiger* obtained a rule to shew cause why there should not be a new trial, on the ground that the witness was improperly rejected relying on *Russell* v. *Blake* (a).

Platt (with whom was *James*) now shewed cause.—The witness was rightly rejected, because he had a direct interest to defeat the plaintiff's claim, and so to prevent himself from becoming liable to the defendant for contribution. In *Jones* v. *Pritchard* (b), this Court held that a part-owner of

(a) 2 Scott, N. R. 574.   (b) 2 M. & W. 199.

a ship was a competent witness for another part-owner sued for work done to the ship, but *after a release.* Here no release was given. In *Jackson* v. *Galloway* (a), a part-owner was rejected as incompetent under similar circumstances, notwithstanding cross releases. In *Planchè* v. *Braham* (b), and *Steers* v. *Carwardine* (c), also, joint contractors were held incompetent witnesses for their co-contractor. In *Green* v. *Warburton* (d), where a defendant justified a trespass to chattels by a plea alleging them to be the property of J. S., and that he committed the trespass by the command of J. S., *Patteson,* J., held that J. S. was not a competent witness for the defendant, and that he could not be made so by the indorsement of his name on the postea, under the stat. 3 & 4 Will. 4, c. 42, s. 26. Could a co-obligor in a bond be called to defeat that bond? It was conceded that this was a joint contract, and the witness clearly came to exonerate himself from liability under it. If the defendant succeeds in this action, then, in case of a second action being brought against the witness, he could plead in bar the judgment in this. [*Parke,* B.—This point has been decided against you in *Russell* v. *Blake,* after a full consideration of all the cases. Lord *Abinger,* C. B.—Suppose the defendant had paid the money without an action being brought, he might still bring his action for contribution; the verdict, therefore, would only be evidence to charge him with the costs of the action, for which he would not be liable, because he might say the defendant ought to have paid without an action.] Therefore it is that his incompetency is not removed by the recent statute; he is not affected by the record, but by the act of payment, to prevent which he has a direct interest.

Thesiger (with whom was *Creasy*), contrà.—The witness

(a) 8 C. & P. 480.
(b) Id. 68.
(c) Id. 570.
(d) 2 M. & Rob. 105.

was clearly competent, if not at common law, at all events by the operation of the stat. 3 & 4 Will. 4, c. 42, s. 26. If, indeed, the nature of his interest were such that he was directly interested in the event of the suit, his incompetency would not be removed by the statute: *Bailiffs of Godmanchester* v. *Phillips* (a). But if he was no further interested than because the verdict or judgment could be used as evidence against it, he becomes competent by the express provision of the statute. [He referred to the cases of *Burgess* v. *Cuthill* (b), *Faith* v. *M'Intyre* (c), *Pickles* v. *Hollings* (d), and *Creevey* v. *Bowman* (e).] The cases cited on the other side do not apply. In *Jones* v. *Pritchard*, the witness had received a release, and the present question, therefore, was never raised. In *Jackson* v. *Galloway*, and *Steers* v. *Carwardine*, the witness was called for the plaintiff. The statute cannot apply to such a case as that, because the verdict and judgment in the action cannot be evidence for or against the witness; if therefore he be interested at all, it is in the event of the suit. *Green* v. *Warburton*, and *Stanley* v. *Jobson* (f), decided by the same learned judge, must be considered to have been overruled by *Russell* v. *Blake*, which directly governs the present case. In *Stanley* v. *Jobson*, a co-maker of a promissory note, for whom the defendant had signed it as a surety, was held to be an incompetent witness for the defendant, on the ground that he might, on a verdict for the plaintiff, be liable to the costs of the action, including the defendant's own costs; and that as to the latter, the statute did not apply. In such a case the witness is under two distinct liabilities; there is a liability to an indemnity against payment of the note by his surety, independent of the result of the suit, arising out of the original suretyship; and there is a liability to pay-

(a) 4 Ad. & Ell. 550; 6 Nev. & M. 211.

(b) 1 M. & Rob. 315; 6 C. & P. 282.

(c) 7 C. & P. 44.

(d) 1 M. & Rob. 468.

(e) Id. 496.

(f) 2 M. & Rob. 103.

ment of the costs. But as to the latter, the only proof of that liability would be by means of the record in the action. *Russell* v. *Blake,* however, is an express authority for the defendant: the witness in the present case stands in precisely the same situation as the joint maker of the note in that case. It is said that the witness has a direct interest in the result of the suit, because, in a fresh action against him, he could plead the judgment for the defendant in this action. It may be doubtful whether, if he pleaded in abatement the non-joinder of the present defendant and his other co-contractors, and the plaintiff, accordingly, under the provisions of the statute, discontinued, and brought a fresh action against them all, the first defendant could plead his former judgment; but even if he could, the witness is precluded from doing so, by the express terms of the 26th section. [He was then stopped by the Court.]

Lord ABINGER, C. B.—It would be quite sufficient to say, that the last decision, in the Court of Common Pleas, is directly in point, and ought to govern us. But I go further, and think that I was wrong in principle, and that in reality the witness stood indifferent between the parties. If the plaintiff failed, the witness could not use the judgment except by means of the record, and that the statute prevents him from doing. Then how does the case stand? If the plaintiff recovers, the witness is liable to contribution; if he fails, the witness is still liable to the whole debt, because he cannot use the judgment in his favour. He is therefore indifferent.

PARKE, B.—I entirely concur in the judgment delivered by the Court of Common Pleas, in the case of *Russell* v. *Blake.* This question was very much considered in that case, and the decision is quite satisfactory to my mind. I quite concur, also, in the doubts expressed by that Court, whether the cases which have been decided on this subject were right, independently of the statute. For, as it appears to me, the witness is altogether indifferent; if the plaintiff succeeds, the witness is liable for contribution; if the plaintiff fails, he is liable for the whole debt; and as to the costs, he is not liable for them at all. However, it is unnecessary to consider that question : it is enough to say that this case is clearly within the authority of *Russell* v. *Blake.*

Exch. of Pleas,
1841.

POOLE
v.
PALMER.

ALDERSON, B.—I quite agree that we are concluded by the decision in *Russell* v. *Blake,* looking at it as a question of authority; besides which, I quite agree with that decision, if it be considered as a question of principle.

ROLFE, B., concurred.

Rule absolute.

———◆———

THOMAS JONES v. HUGH JONES.

Nov. 16.

ASSUMPSIT by indorsee against maker of a promissory note for £50. Pleas: first, that the defendant did not make the note in the declaration mentioned, on which issue was joined; secondly, that the defendant made the note at the request and for the accommodation of the plaintiff, to which there was a replication de injuriâ, and issue thereon. At the trial before Lord *Abinger,* C. B., at the Middlesex sittings after Trinity Term, the plaintiff's counsel called a person whose name appeared on the note as attesting witness, and he proved the signature "Hugh Jones" to the note to have been written in his presence, and that the Hugh Jones whose signature he so attested kept a public-house, the Glasgow Tavern, at Llangefni, in the county of

In an action by indorsee against maker of a promissory note, the defendant pleaded, 1. that he did not make the note; 2. that he made it for the accommodation of the plaintiff. There was an attesting witness to the note, who, on being called at the trial, stated that he saw the signature (Hugh Jones) to the note written by a party whose occupation and

residence he described, but that he had had no communication with him since, and that this was a common name in the neighbourhood where the note was made:—*Held,* that there was no evidence to go to the jury of the identity of the defendant with the maker of the note, and that the second plea could not be called in aid for that purpose.

Anglesey. On cross-examination, he admitted that he had not seen or had any communication with that Hugh Jones since the date of the note; and that the name was a very common one in Anglesey. This being all the evidence adduced by the plaintiff, *Atherton,* for the defendant, objected that the plaintiff ought to be nonsuited, on the ground that there was no evidence to go to the jury of the identity of the Hugh Jones, whose subscription to the note had been proved, with the defendant on this record. The Lord Chief Baron reserved the point; and under his direction a verdict was taken for the plaintiff for the amount of the note and interest, with leave to the defendant to move to enter a nonsuit.

Atherton having obtained a rule nisi accordingly,

Jervis and *Crompton* now shewed cause.—If there was any evidence at all to go to the jury of the identity of the defendant as the party to the note, there cannot be a nonsuit. Now, although there be several Hugh Jones's, it will be assumed, until the contrary appears, that only one note, such as that declared on, was signed by a Hugh Jones. Then the Hugh Jones who has been served with the writ, having notice by the declaration of the purport of that note, and having had an opportunity of inspecting it, comes in and appears by counsel, and pleads that he made it for the plaintiff's accommodation; that is, he admits that he knows something of the note declared on. True, one plea cannot be called in aid of another issue; but it may be used as some evidence of the identity of the party; and very little evidence is sufficient. [*Parke,* B.— That argument would dispense with any proof of the handwriting.] If the strictness now contended for is to prevail, the identity can only be proved by employing a person to serve the writ who is acquainted with the handwriting of the party. If the defendant is not the real

maker of the note, he may come and set all the proceedings aside. [Lord *Abinger,* C. B.—The burthen is not
thrown on him.] The same difficulty will occur in ordinary cases of goods sold and delivered. [*Parke,* B.—So
it often does.] There are several cases in which it has
been ruled by Lord *Tenterden* and other judges at Nisi
Prius, that proof of the handwriting of the subscribing
witness to an instrument, he being dead or not to be found,
is sufficient to charge the party to the instrument, without
any further proof of his identity, except the identity of
name and description: *Page* v. *Mann* (a), *Mitchell* v. *Johnson* (b), *Kay* v. *Brookman* (c). [*Parke,* B., referred to
Whitelocke v. *Musgrove* (d), as establishing the rule on this
subject.] In *Hennell* v. *Lyon* (e), the copy of a bill and
answer, the latter purporting to be an answer by a person
of the same name as the defendant, in the character of
administrator, was held, without more, sufficient primâ facie
evidence of identity in order to prove assets, upon an issue
on plene administravit. So, in *Bulkeley* v. *Butler* (f), in
an action by indorsee against acceptor of a bill, of which
E. S. was the payee, proof that a person calling himself
E. S. came to the place of the plaintiff's residence with the
bill in question and other genuine documents, and indorsed
it to the plaintiff, was held sufficient primâ facie evidence of
his identity with E. S. the payee. [*Rolfe,* B.—There he
was in possession of the same bill.] *Whitelocke* v. *Musgrove* was the case of a note signed by a marksman. *Cor-
field* v. *Parsons* (g) is distinguishable; that was merely
the case of a declaration supposed to be made to the witness by the plaintiff, who might easily be personated, and
who had no power to deny or disprove the witness's statement, which he, being imposed upon by another person,

(a) Moo. & M. 79.
(b) Id. 176.
(c) Id. 286.
(d) 1 C. & M. 511.

(e) 1 B. & Ald. 182.
(f) 2 B. & Cr. 434 ; 3 D. & R. 625.
(g) 1 C. & M. 730.

might honestly make.　Here the Hugh Jones served with the writ has had notice of all the proceedings, and has the means of disproving the conclusion that he is the party to the note.

Atherton, contrà, was not called upon.

Lord ABINGER, C. B.—The argument for the plaintiff might be correct, if the case had not introduced the existence of many Hugh Jones's in the neighbourhood where the note was made.　As it was, I think there was no sufficient evidence of the identity.　I am aware that Lord *Tenterden* had a different practice, but I believe it never became necessary to raise the question before the Court.

PARKE, B.—This point must be considered as settled by the case of *Whitelocke* v. *Musgrove.*　All the authorities are cited in Phillipps on Evidence, vol. ii., p. 661, and the rule of law on this subject is there laid down correctly.　The plaintiff might have called the defendant's attorney to say whether the person who employed him in the case was the Hugh Jones who lived at the Glasgow Tavern, Llangefni.

ROLFE, B., concurred.

The rule was made absolute, not for a nonsuit, but for a new trial on payment of costs by the plaintiff (*a*).

(*a*) The cause was re-tried at the London Sittings after Michaelmas Term (the venue having been changed), when the attesting witness was again called, and stated that, since the former trial, he had seen the Hugh Jones whose signature he had attested; and described his occupation and residence; and the clerk to the plaintiff's attorney produced the writ of summons and other proceedings in the action, and identified the person spoken to by the other witness as the individual upon whom those proceedings had been served: and the verdict was thereupon again found for the plaintiff.

Exch. of Pleas,
1841.

BECKHAM *v.* DRAKE, KNIGHT, and SURGEY.

Nov. 19.

ASSUMPSIT. The declaration stated, that the defendants were united in co-partnership, and used and exercised the trade and business of type-founders, stereotype founders, and letter-press printers; and that the said W. M. Knight and J. Surgey were the ostensible partners in the said partnership, and the said W. W. Drake was a secret partner in the said co-partnership: that at the time of making the memorandum of agreement thereinafter mentioned, the plaintiff was in the service and employment of the defendants, so being such partners as aforesaid, as their foreman, in carrying on their trade and business of type-founders, stereotype founders, &c., but without any permanent engagement, and he the plaintiff, and the defendants, as such partners as aforesaid, were desirous of continuing their connexion together for a certain period or term, to wit, the period or term of seven years from the 20th of October, 1834; and thereupon theretofore, to wit, on the said 20th of October, 1834, they the said W. M. Knight and J. Surgey, on behalf of themselves and the said W. W. Drake, as such partners as aforesaid, made and entered into a certain memorandum of agreement with the plaintiff, which said memorandum of agreement was and is in writing, and was and is in the words and figures following, viz:—

"Memorandum of an agreement made and entered into this 23rd day of October, 1834, between William Moxey Knight and John Surgey, of Bishop's Court, Old Bailey, in the city of London, type-founders, stereotye founders, and letter-press printers, and co-partners, of the one part, and

A., B., & C. being in partnership together as type-founders (C. as a dormant partner), an agreement was entered into between A. and B. of the one part, and the plaintiff of the other part, by which, after reciting that the plaintiff had been in the employment of A. and B. as foreman in carrying on the said trade of type-founders, the plaintiff covenanted and agreed with A. and B. and the survivor of them, to serve them and the survivor of them in their said trade for the term of seven years; and they covenanted and agreed to employ him as their foreman for the term of seven years, if they or either of them should so long live, and to pay him three guineas per week; and it was mutually agreed, that if

either party should not perform the covenants on their respective parts, the party so failing or making default should pay to the other £500, by way of specific damages. At the time the agreement was entered into it was unknown to the plaintiff that C. was a partner in the business:—*Held,* that an action was maintainable by the plaintiff against A., B., & C., for a breach of this agreement, although C. was not a party named in it or signing it.

Daniel Beckham, of the same place, of the other part, as follows: Whereas the said D. Beckham hath been for some time in the employment of the said W. M. Knight and J. Surgey, as their foreman, in carrying on their said trades of type-founders, &c.; and the said parties to these presents are mutually desirous of continuing their connexion together for the term of seven years from the date of these presents: Now these presents witness, that the said D. Beckham, for the considerations hereinafter mentioned, doth hereby covenant and agree to and with the said W. M. Knight and J. Surgey, and the survivor of them, in manner following, (that is to say), that he the said D. Beckham shall and will well and faithfully serve the said W. M. Knight & J. Surgey, and the survivor of them, for and during the term of seven years, to commence and be computed from the day of the date of these presents, as their foreman, in the management and carrying on of their said trades of type-founders, &c., and shall and will, to the best of his power, promote and advance the success and prosperity of the said W. M. Knight and J. Surgey, in the said trades; and also that he the said D. Beckham shall not nor will, during the said term of seven years, be engaged or concerned in the same or any other trade or business, either on his own account, or on account of, or for the benefit of, any other person whatsoever, other than the said W. M. Knight and J. Surgey, and the survivor of them, without the consent of the said W. M. Knight nd J. Surgey, or one of them, in writing, first had and obtained for that purpose; and the said W. M. Knight and J. Surgey, for the considerations aforesaid, do hereby, for themselves and the survivor of them, covenant and agree to and with the said D. Beckham, that they the said W. M. Knight and J. Surgey, or the survivor of them, shall and will employ the said D. Beckham as their foreman, in carrying on, managing, and conducting the said trades of type-founders, &c., during the said term of seven years, if the said W. M.

Knight and J. Surgey, or either of them, shall so long live, *Exch. of Pleas,* and the said D. Beckham shall well and faithfully observe 1841. and keep the covenants and agreements hereinbefore on his part contained; and that they the said W. M. Knight and J. Surgey, or the survivor of them, shall and will pay to the said D. Beckham wages after the rate of 3*l.* 3*s.* of lawful money weekly. And it is hereby mutually agreed and declared by and between the said parties hereto, that in case either of the said parties shall not well and truly observe, perform, and keep the covenants and agreements herein on their respective parts contained, then and in such case the party so failing or making default shall and will pay to the other of them the sum of 500*l.* by way or in the nature of specific damages. In witness whereof the said parties to these presents have hereunto set their hand the day and year first above written. W. M. Knight, John Surgey, Daniel Beckham. Witness, J. R. Barrett."

The declaration then averred performance of the agreement by the plaintiff during the time he remained in the service of the defendants, and that the plaintiff was ready and willing to have continued in the service of the defendants, and to have performed the agreement, but that the defendants, before the expiration of the seven years, without reasonable or sufficient cause, dismissed and discharged him from their service, &c.

The defendant Knight allowed judgment to go by default. The two other defendants severally pleaded, first, non assumpsit; secondly, the bankruptcy of the plaintiff. To the latter plea the plaintiff demurred generally, on the ground that the contract set out in the declaration being a contract for the personal labour of the plaintiff, his cause of action did not pass to the assignees. The demurrer was argued in Trinity Term, and judgment was given for the plaintiff (*a*).

(*a*) See the case reported, 8 M. & W. 846.

At the London Sittings after Trinity Term, the cause was tried before Lord *Abinger*, C. B., on the issue raised on the plea of non assumpsit; when the agreement set out verbatim in the declaration was given in evidence, and it was proved that Drake was a dormant partner with the other defendants, and that the plaintiff continued to serve them under the agreement for the space of two years, when the partnership was dissolved and the business stopped, and the plaintiff was dismissed by Drake. At the conclusion of the plaintiff's case several objections were taken: 1st. that it was a contract inter partes, and not binding on Drake, who did not sign it; 2ndly. that the contract was in its terms personal to the parties signing it, and the survivor of them, and that there was no mutuality, and therefore Drake could not sue or be sued upon it; 3rdly. that it was a contract not to be executed within a year, and was not signed by the party charged, or his lawful agent, at least not in the name of the firm, as required by the Statute of Frauds. The Lord Chief Baron overruled the objections, but gave the defendant leave to move to enter a nonsuit on the above grounds, leaving to the jury only the question of damages, which they estimated at 100*l.*, and for which amount a verdict was entered for the plaintiff.

Thesiger having accordingly obtained a rule to enter a nonsuit,

Erle and *Stammers* shewed cause.—The first objection is, that the contract on which the action is brought is a contract inter partes, which is binding only on the parties between whom it is made, and excludes the idea of making any one liable but those parties; and therefore that the defendant Drake is not liable. But there is no such principle of law, even as applicable to the case of a deed, and à fortiori, none such in the case of an agreement not under seal. A person is bound who seals a deed, although he is no party to it: *Salter* v. *Kidgley* (a). In that case *Holt*, C. J., said, "Why cannot a man oblige himself by deed, if there be express words for it, and the deed is sealed by him?—And he made a distinction in this case, that one party to a deed could not covenant with another who was no party, but a mere stranger to it; but one who is not a party to a deed may covenant with another that is a party, and thereby be bound by sealing the deed." That authority shews that a person not a party to a deed may be made liable to the covenants contained in it. In Mr. Butler's note to Co. Litt. s. 874, n. 141 (b), it is said, "Where three were enfeoffed by deed, and there were several covenants in the deed on the part of the feoffees, and only two of the feoffees sealed the deed, the third entered and agreed to the estate conveyed by the deed, he was bound in a writ of covenant by the sealing of his companions: 2 Roll. Rep. 63. In 38 Ed. 3, p. 9, it is said, 'That if land is leased to two for years, and only one puts his seal, but the other agrees to the lease, and enters and takes the profits with him, he shall be charged to pay the rent, though he has not put his seal to the deed.'" *Brett* v. *Cumberland* is the case there referred to from 2 Rolle's Rep. 63. The next objection is, that on the face of this contract Drake was excluded from liability, as it was a personal contract with Knight and Surgey only, and the survivor of them. But there is no express or implied exclusion of Drake from the contract, and as he was in partnership with the other two, although merely a dormant partner, he is jointly liable with them. There are many cases to shew that a dormant partner may sue and be sued on contracts entered into by his co-partners for the benefit of the firm; and any person really interested in a contract, although unknown to the other contracting party, is liable. The contract not being under seal, and

Exch. of Pleas,
1841.

BECKHAM
v.
DRAKE.

(a) Holt's Rep. 211; 1 Shower, 58; Carthew, 76.   (b) 230 b.

G 2

consequently in law a parol contract, it is competent to the plaintiff to shew who were the real parties who entered into it. In *Skinner* v. *Stocks* (a), it was held that the joint owners of a vessel engaged in the whale fishery might sue a purchaser for the price of whale oil, although the contract of sale was made by one only of the part owners, and the purchaser did not know that other persons had any interest in the transaction. So, in *Cothay* v. *Fennell* (b), where three parties agreed to be jointly interested in certain goods, but that they should be bought by one of them in his own name only, and he made a contract for the purchase accordingly; it was held that all might join in suing the vendor for a breach of that contract. There the Court laid it down as " a general rule, that whenever an express contract is made, an action is maintainable upon it, either in the name of the person with whom it was actually made, or in the name of the person with whom in point of law it was made." That was an express decision that a dormant partner not named in the agreement may sue for a breach of it. In the present case, therefore, Drake might have sued with Knight and Surgey, if the plaintiff had broken the contract in the lifetime of Knight or Surgey. In *Robson* v. *Drummond* (c), *Littledale*, J., says —" I am disposed to think there was no objection to Robson and Sharpe suing on a contract made by Sharpe only on behalf of himself and his partner." It is not stated that the contract in that case was in writing, but from the specific nature of the agreement it must have been so. In *Alexander* v. *Barker* (d), where A. applied to B., a member of a banking establishment, for a loan of money, which B. advanced out of funds in which he and his partners were jointly interested; it was held that the firm might sue A. for money lent. There the contract was in writing. The

(a) 4 B. & Ald. 437.   (c) 2 B. & Adol. 303.
(b) 10 B. & Cr. 671.   (d) 2 Cr. & J. 133.

question always is, who are the parties to the contract; and Exch. of Pleas, 1841. parol evidence is admissible to shew who were the real parties. The case of a dormant partner is in this respect BECKHAM v. DRAKE. analogous to that of an undisclosed principal who contracts by his agent. In *Wilson* v. *Hart* (a), it was held that the Statute of Frauds did not exclude parol evidence that a written contract for the sale of goods, purporting to be made between A. the seller, and B. the buyer, was on B.'s part made by him only as agent. In *Trueman* v. *Loder* (b), there was a written contract, which was only signed by Higginbotham, the agent employed by the defendant Loder, yet the latter was held liable. Lord *Denman*, C. J., in delivering the judgment of the Court, distinguishes the case from some which had been cited, wherein the question, "whether an agent or a partner bound himself only, or his principal or firm, had been held to depend on his intention to deal for himself, or for the principal or partnership:" and says,—"On examining all those cases, it will be found that the contracting party was carrying on two different concerns, one for himself, the other for his principal or his firm. The world would know him in two different characters, and each party dealing with him was bound to inquire in which he appeared on any particular occasion. But here is the case of one exclusively an agent for another, and in that light only regarded by the customer." In the present case there is no evidence of any trade carried on under two different firms, nor of any trade carried on except under the name of Knight & Surgey. If a person, by becoming a dormant partner in a firm, chooses to give an implied authority to the ostensible partners to contract for him, it does not lie in his mouth to say that he has given no such authority. Who is to hire the servants in such a case, but the ostensible partners?—

(a) 7 Taunt. 295. As to this case, see Smith's Leading Cases, Vol. 2, p. 224; and *Higgins* v. *Senior*, ante, Vol. 8, pp. 840—45.

(b) 3 Per. & D. 267; 11 Ad. & Ell. 589.

Lord *Denman* further says—" Parol evidence is always necessary to shew that the party sued is the person making the contract, and bound by it. Whether he does so in his own name, or in that of another, or in a feigned name, and whether the contract be signed by his own hand or by that of an agent, are inquiries not different in their nature from the question, who is the person who has just ordered goods in a shop. If he is sued for the price, and his identity made out, the contract is not varied by appearing to have been made by him in a name not his own." So here, the contract is not varied by shewing it to be made in the name of Knight and Surgey. *Emly* v. *Lye* (a), and *Siffkin* v. *Walker* (b), may be cited on the other side; but those were cases on bills of exchange, and are therefore distinguishable; and on the former case being cited in *Vere* v. *Ashby* (c), *Parke*, J., said,—" The case of the *South Carolina Bank* v. *Case* (d), shews, that if a firm, consisting of several, carry on business in the name of one of the partners, the whole firm will be bound by the acts done by him, as representing the firm."

Another objection here is, that there is no mutuality; but that doctrine has been broken in upon, and there are various instances in which an action may lie, notwithstanding a want of mutuality between the parties. A great number of cases were cited on the argument in *Beckham* v. *Knight* (e), but *Cothay* v. *Fennell* is a decisive authority on this subject; and according to the rule there laid down, the action is maintainable upon the contract, either against the person who actually makes the contract, or against the person who in point of law makes it: and whether the contract be express or implied makes no difference. But in truth, there is no want of mutuality, for Drake might

(a) 15 East, 7.

(b) 2 Camp. 308.

(c) 10 B. & Cr. 288.

(d) 8 B. & Cr. 427; 2 Man. & R. 459.

(e) 5 Scott, 619; 4 Bing. N.C. 243.

have joined in an action against the plaintiff for non-per-formance of the contract by him.

Thesiger and *E. V. Williams*, contrà.—The Court cannot come to a conclusion in favour of the plaintiff, without over-ruling the decision of the Court of Common Pleas in *Beck-ham* v. *Knight.* It was there expressly held that, Knight and Surgey having entered into a written engagement to employ the plaintiff in their service for seven years, the plaintiff could not sue Drake, a dormant partner with them, but no party to the agreement. *Tindal,* C. J., there says, —"The action is brought on an express contract between Knight and Surgey of the one part, and the plaintiff of the other part. It appears by the plea, that three persons were carrying on business under the firm of Knight & Surgey, and that the defendant Drake was a dormant partner. The agreement is in writing, and inter partes; and it contains no intimation that Knight and Surgey were carrying on business as members of a more extensive firm. I know of no authority for introducing a dormant partner into such a contract. In implied contracts, where the benefit is equal, and the liability not limited, a dormant partner may be included; but there is no authority which extends the principle to express contracts. The only authorities in point are rather the other way." And *Bosanquet,* J., says, —"The plaintiff is precluded, by the form of the contract, from saying that any other person entered into it besides himself and Knight and Surgey." That case has been im-ported as an authority into Chitty on Contracts; and it is there said, (p. 242),—"Nor is a dormant partner liable to be sued, where an express contract in writing is entered into with the known and apparent partners. As where K. and S. entered into a written agreement with the plaintiff to employ him as their foreman for a term of seven years; it was held that D., a dormant partner, not a party to the agreement, could not be made a co-defendant with K. and

S. in an action on such agreement." And again, (p. 250),
—"With respect to dormant partners, they are bound by
the acts of their co-partners as to all implied contracts, but
are not liable on express contracts with the known and acting partners." No doubt there are numerous authorities
to shew, that where a contract is entered into in a particular name, it may be shewn that the party in point of fact
entered into it for another person, so as to charge the principal; but here there was no evidence of that kind, and
nothing was left to the jury as to the character in which
Knight and Surgey entered into the contract. If that was
a question which ought to have been left to the jury, it was
not so left. Although it is competent to one partner to
bind another in matters relating to the partnership concerns, yet that is only when it is done in the partnership
name: there is no implied authority to do so in the partner's own individual name. Where goods are sold to a
firm, it is matter of inquiry who are the persons who constitute the firm; but where the contract is a written one,
you can see by the paper itself who it is that has entered
into it. [Lord *Abinger*, C. B.—Except where the statute
law requires the contract to be in writing, there is no difference between contracts written and oral.] Where goods are
supplied to a firm, the seller must shew that they were so
supplied, and that the defendants are the members of it;
but where the contract is written, you look to the contract
itself to see who are the parties to it. In *Myers* v. *Edge* (a),
it was held that a promise in writing, directed to A., B.
& C., a house in trade, to pay for goods to be furnished to
another, could not be enforced in an action by B. and C. to
recover the value of goods furnished after A. had withdrawn
from the partnership. That decision was on the ground that
the Court must adjudicate upon the express contract that
the parties had made, and ought not to substitute another

(a) 7 T. R. 254.

in lieu of it. *Robson* v. *Drummond* is very far from being a
strong authority for the plaintiff. Lord *Tenterden*, C. J., there says (a)—"It is unnecessary to decide whether, if Sharpe had continued in the partnership till the expiration of the five years during which the contract made by him was to continue in force, the action in the joint names of him and his partner might not have been maintained." And *Parke*, J., says,—"The defendant had a right to have the benefit of the judgment and taste of Sharpe to the end of the contract, and which in effect he has declined to supply." [*Parke*, B., (after reading his judgment in *Robson* v. *Drummond*).—That is an authority, as far as my opinion goes, that the action could be maintained by Robson and Sharpe.] That point did not necessarily arise. In this case it will be seen, on reference to the contract, that it is a mere personal contract to serve these two individual partners; and the plaintiff cannot import into it another party, unless he shews that it was made by them as agents for him. The case of *Alexander* v. *Barker* (b) turned on the fact of the money lent being the money of the firm, in which event the Court held that they might maintain the action. It is clear, also, that there the action was not founded on a written contract; and the case is therefore inapplicable. *Emly* v. *Lye* and *Siffkin* v. *Walker* are express authorities in favour of the defendant, and are not distinguishable from the present case. In the latter case Lord *Ellenborough* said,—"The import and legal effect of a written instrument must be gathered from the terms in which it is expressed." A party cannot be sued on a contract because he has had the benefit of it, but only where he is a party to it. The plaintiff must make out that Drake gave his partners an implied authority to enter into this contract for him, and that they have exercised that authority; but neither has been shewn. On the contrary, it is a per-

(a) 2 B. & Adol. 307.   (b) 2 Cr. & J. 133.

sonal contract with Knight and Surgey; they are to have the benefit only during their lives; and it would not survive to Drake. The law will not imply a contract from a partial benefit. There are many cases in which it might be advantageous to a party to enter into a several contract with one or two members of a firm, so as to be able to follow his or their estate in the hands of executors. But even assuming these parties to have had authority to bind the other partner, it must be collected from the instrument itself whether they have exercised that authority. In cases of bills of exchange, where one partner may bind his co-partners by drawing bills in the name of the partnership firm, yet if he does not use the name of the firm, he does not bind them: that is because the instrument does not shew that he has exercised his authority. Suppose in this case that the parties who in point of fact made this contract were to die, there having been a breach of contract in their lifetime; the Court would say that the plaintiff had a right to sue the executor of the survivor, because he has expressly made a contract personally with them and the survivor of them. The general doctrine is correctly stated by *Tindal*, C. J., in *Beckham v. Knight :* " In implied contracts, where the benefit is equal, and the liability not limited, a dormant partner may be included, but there is no authority which extends the principle to express contracts."

Lord ABINGER, C. B.—I quite agree with the statement of the counsel for the defendant, that in giving our judgment for the plaintiff, we must be taken to disagree entirely from the opinion expressed by the Court of Common Pleas in the action between the same parties, and which was afterwards brought before the Court of Error. Perhaps it is unfortunate that in every case each particular point mooted at the bar is not decided by the Court; much litigation would probably be avoided by it. It was formerly very much the practice of courts of justice to go out of the particular question, and determine every point which had arisen in the case. But in modern times it has been the usage of judges, not to go out of the way to decide every point that arises, but .to adjudicate only upon the point necessary for the disposal of the cause. Had the old practice continued, it is probable that this point would never have arisen in this Court, as I do not believe there was, when this case was before the Court of Error, any difference of opinion with respect to the judgment of the Court of Common Pleas, on the point upon which they had decided the case; but there was ground to support the decision on a point of pleading, and upon that we gave our opinion (a). We must have affirmed the judgment, whatever we might have thought of the points raised in argument to-day, and nothing was then said by the Court of Error negativing the opinion we are about to express.

I am of the same opinion that I was then, that the doctrine stated by the Court of Common Pleas—that where a contract is in writing between parties signing their names to it, it cannot be used against other parties than those who signed their names to it—cannot be supported either on principle or authority. That position, indeed, is contradicted by the whole series of authorities bearing on the subject.

There is no question that a contract in writing by an agent, signed by himself, will bind his principal, when the other contracting party discovers the principal, although the contract was made without his knowing who the principal is: as, for instance, in the case of a bill of lading signed by the master, where the action is brought against the owners. It is also the case of every charter-party which is signed by the owner, where the owner is rendered

(a) See 1 Scott, N. R. 675; 1 Man. & G. 738.

liable by the act of the master, because the master is his agent. So it is in a vast variety of other cases which frequently occur, all establishing the principle, that the parties really contracting are the parties to sue in a court of justice, although the contract be in the name of another. I say the parties *really* contracting, because it is possible that an agent, meaning to contract in his own name, is the party to sue. An agent may say to the person with whom he is dealing, " I am the person responsible in this particular transaction," or the other party may say, " I hold you responsible to me, though I know your principal;" and that is not an uncommon case, where the party so contracting has been held responsible. These principles, which are sanctioned as well by the authorities as by common sense, are quite consistent with those cases where the party really meant a different thing, and intended to bind the principal.

Now the contrary of this doctrine is stated as the ground of the decision in the Court of Common Pleas; and the only cases cited by the Judges who follow the Lord Chief Justice are cases of bills of exchange, which are quite different in principle from those which ought to govern this case, and in which, by the law merchant, a chose in action is passed by indorsement, and each party who receives the bill is making a contract with the parties upon the face of it, and with no other party whatever. That is a class of cases quite distinct in its nature from the present. But the law makes no distinction in contracts, except between contracts which are and contracts which are not under seal. I recollect one of the most learned judges who ever sat upon this or any other bench being very angry when a distinction was attempted to be taken between parol and written contracts, and saying " they are all parol unless under seal." If they are written, they may indeed require to be stamped; but it is the act of Parliament which makes that distinction; the common law makes none. A con-

tract under seal can bind none but those who sign and
seal it. A contract not under seal is open to all the common-law requirements and incidents of a contract, whether in writing or not. Suppose these two partners
Knight and Surgey had made a contract verbally, not having said a word about Drake; no question could then have arisen, that Drake might nevertheless be made liable upon it. How then does the fact of its being in writing, and of their having put their names to it, alter the case? The parties are just in the same situation, and there can be no difference. There is nothing affirmative on the face of the contract to shew an intention to exclude every body but themselves. It is open to the defendant Drake to shew such an intention, but unless it be shewn, the objection does not arise. When goods are ordered to be sent to a particular house by name, and they are so sent, the parties sending them are entitled to sue the real principal, whenever they discover who the real principal is; and they are at liberty to proceed against him upon the contract, whether written or not, if signed only by an agent.

Now in the present case the record states, that the defendant Drake, and Knight and Surgey, were connected in partnership together in the business of type-founders; that is admitted by the pleadings; and then it is stated that the defendants entered into this contract with the plaintiff, the object of which was a permanent engagement.

What is the evidence?—That they formed a partnership on the 1st of January, 1834, and in the month of August of the same year the plaintiff was by a verbal contract engaged in the service of the concern. In whose service was he? It is admitted he was in the service of the firm. It is true he was hired by a contract to which Drake was personally no party; but he was hired to serve the partnership, in a business from which Drake derived an immediate benefit. Then the parties were desirous of fixing him by a permanent engagement, he being a very skilful person; upon which the plaintiff enters into this contract with Knight and Surgey, on behalf of themselves and Drake, by which he is to serve the partnership, consisting of themselves and Drake, for seven years; and he continues to serve them accordingly for two years, from 1834 to 1836, when the partnership and business stopped. He was, therefore, in the service of the partnership of which Drake was the principal partner; he was working the whole time for Drake's benefit; he was working under a contract, not to serve them separately or conjointly in any other concern, but in the very concern in which they were in partnership with Drake. What profits were made were equally for Drake's benefit as for the rest of the firm, and the wages paid were equally Drake's money. Then in the month of June, 1836, the business not being very profitable, Drake thinks fit to stop the concern, and discharges all the workmen, and the plaintiff amongst the rest. What right had he to discharge the plaintiff, except he was a party to the agreement? Knight and Surgey were alive, but the service was put an end to by Drake; he, assuming the right to act as he did under the circumstances, discharges the plaintiff with the other workmen. It appears to me, upon the whole, that it cannot be denied that this was a contract made by these persons, in the terms of the declaration,—on behalf of themselves and Drake; being made by the two other partners with his implied assent, and being necessary in order to carry on the joint trade in which all three were engaged. It seems to me to be opposed to every rule of law to say, that a man who has by his partners entered into a contract, he himself being afterwards allowed to carry on the business, is not bound by that contract. All the partners in the concern, as it appears to me, were equally bound by this contract. I think, therefore, the declaration is sufficiently proved, and that there is no more objection in point of law than in point of pleading to the form of the contract.

Upon these grounds, I am of opinion that the judgment

of the Court of Common Pleas was wrong; and it is more than probable that the Judges who formed the Court of Error were also of that opinion, though we did not think it necessary to give any judgment upon that ground, there being another clear ground to support the judgment.

Exch. of Pleas,
1841.

BECKHAM
v.
DRAKE.

PARKE, B.—The main point to be considered in this case is, whether the principle laid down by the Court of Common Pleas, in the case of *Beckham* v. *Knight,* as to the distinction between contracts by parol, or implied contracts, and express contracts in writing not under seal, and the liability of an undisclosed principal or dormant partner to be sued thereon, is correct in point of law. Had it not been for the statement made by the Lord Chief Baron, I should have certainly wished for a little time, not so much for the purpose of considering this case, as of consulting the other Judges who sat in the Court of Error, whether their judgment was clear against the opinion which the Court of Common Pleas entertained upon this point. I was one of the Judges who considered that case with a view to the discussion in the Exchequer Chamber, but happened not to be present at the time it was argued; and speaking for myself, I should certainly have concurred in that which is suggested to have been the opinion, on this point, of the Judges who were present. The case of *Beckham* v. *Knight* for the first time discloses an intimation of there being any difference between such contracts; and I cannot help thinking that there has been a mistake, in applying to contracts which are, in point of law, parol, although reduced into writing, the doctrine which is applicable exclusively to deeds,—regularly framed instruments between certain parties. Those parties only can sue or be sued upon an indenture, who are named or described in it as parties; but this doctrine is applicable to deeds only, and I was not aware of any opinion being entertained, before this case occurred, that the same rule extended to all written contracts. With regard to the practice on this subject, it must be familiar to every one that there are innumerable mercantile contracts in writing, where the real principal, when disclosed, is made liable, though the contract is entered into by another; and many cases have been cited to the Court in the course of the argument, to shew that where a contract is made in another name than that of the real principal, the real principal can sue and be sued. In the cases of *Cothay* v. *Fennell*, and *Robson* v. *Drummond*, the contract was in writing; and in *Wilson* v. *Hart*, and *Trueman* v. *Loder*, the undisclosed principal was held liable upon a written contract for the purchase of goods, although the contract was executed in the name of the agent. The doctrine rests upon this principle, that the act of the agent was the act of the principal, and the subscription of the agent was the subscription of the principal; and I am not aware of the existence of any cases in which a distinction has been suggested between a contract which has been entered into by one individual for another, or by two individuals for themselves and another, as to the liability of the principal to be sued. The case of bills of exchange is an exception, which stands upon the law merchant; and promissory notes another, for they are placed on the same footing by the statute of Anne. In neither of these can any but the parties named in the instrument, by their name or firm, be made liable to an action upon it.

My opinion, therefore, clearly is, after a good deal of consideration of the case when it was in the Court of Error, and that opinion has been confirmed by the present argument, that the decision of the Court of Common Pleas cannot be supported, and consequently that there is no ground for the rule to enter a nonsuit.

There were some other minor questions in this case discussed at the bar. I think Mr. *Williams* has fairly stated the law upon the subject. In the first place, I agree that

inasmuch as the defendant Drake has not subscribed this
instrument with his own hand, it must be made out that
he is a party to it in point of law, and that he authorized
Knight and Surgey to sign it on his behalf. I think that is
shewn by the fact of his being a partner in the trade, and
sharing the profits of it. Being a dormant partner, he
authorizes the ostensible partners to enter into such contracts as are usually entered into in the course of such
a business. Then the question will be, whether this contract is of that description. I see no reason to doubt
that it is, being a contract fairly and reasonably entered
into for the purpose of employing and retaining the workmen necessary to carry on such a concern. Then it is said
it would be a hardship on this party to be made liable upon
a contract of which he cannot have the benefit; but he *had*
the benefit of it, and 'had a right to sue upon it, if the
plaintiff withheld his services for the period of time stipulated, provided Knight and Surgey should so long live.
Again, it is said that this is not a contract in the ordinary
course of mercantile transactions, because there is a penalty attached to it; but no authority has been cited,
either here or by the counsel in the Court of Common
Pleas, for the position, that a party cannot bind another
by an agreement in which there is a penalty. I am not
aware that there is any authority for it, and I do not see
any reason for it in principle : I see no objection to a
partner entering into an agreement with workmen, or into
a covenant, to which there is a penalty attached. On the
whole, therefore, I quite agree with the opinion of my
Lord in this case, that there was an implied authority
communicated by the defendant to his partners to enter
into this agreement. But I agree, also, that it is necessary to make out that the partners meant to pursue that
authority, and meant to make a contract on behalf of their
co-partner Drake and themselves, in order to make the partnership liable. That is rather a question of fact than of law;

Exch. of Pleas,
1841.

BECKHAM
v.
DRAKE.

and the facts which are submitted for the consideration of the Court, from which to draw that inference, are sufficient, in my opinion, to enable us to come to the conclusion that the contract was for the benefit of the partnership. The defendant is bound as a partner to know what contracts have been made, and it is incumbent upon him to shew, in order to get rid of his liability, that it was the intention of the parties to the contract that he, Drake, should not be bound, but Knight and Surgey only: that is a matter of fact for the jury, but I do not find that any evidence was laid before them tending to such a conclusion. It seems to me, therefore, that all those propositions which are necessary in point of law to be proved, in order to render the defendant Drake liable, are made out in the present case; and judging from the whole evidence taken together, I think Drake was bound, and that the result is that he is liable upon this contract.

If the plaintiff entered into the contract in ignorance of Drake being a real partner, the case would be within the same principle of law which applies to the introduction of a principal before unknown, where the party who contracted upon the supposition that the agent was the principal, is entitled to all the same benefits and rights, and stands precisely in the same situation, as he would have been if he had been aware of the real principal. For all questions between partners are no more than illustrations of the same questions as between principal and agent.

In this case, therefore, it seems to me, entertaining the greatest respect for the decision of the Court of Common Pleas, that they were in error in supposing there was a difference in this respect between written and parol contracts. I apprehend that an undisclosed principal may be made liable as soon as disclosed, subject to all the equities between the parties; and that the distinction which is to be found in the authorities applies to deeds only; and that therefore our judgment ought to be for the plaintiff.

GURNEY, B.—I agree entirely in the opinion expressed
by my Lord and my Brother *Parke*, that this was a contract made with two of the partners, by whom the business was conducted, for the benefit of all the partners,
and that the circumstance of the defendant being a dormant partner accounts for his not being named in the contract; but it is a contract for the benefit of all the partners, as well those known to the world as the one remaining unseen, and it seems to me to be clear that there
was an implied authority to them to enter into the contract
with the plaintiff for the benefit of the whole firm. I am
of opinion, therefore, that the defendant Drake is liable
in this case.

ROLFE, B.—I am of the same opinion. The only
doubt I had in the case was, how far we could decide in
the face of the judgment of the Court of Common Pleas;
but for the reasons stated by my Lord, and from my own
recollection of what passed in the Court of Error, I am
fully prepared to concur in the opinion expressed by the
rest of the Court; and I think that the decision in *Beckham*
v. *Knight* must be considered as being virtually overruled,
quoad the reasoning applicable to the present case, attributed, and I have no doubt correctly attributed, to the
learned Judges who gave their opinion on that occasion.

The question resolves itself into a very short point;
whether or not Knight and Surgey, under all the circumstances of this case, entered into the contract on their
own account, or for themselves and Drake. Perhaps Mr.
Erle has stated the proposition of law applicable to the
case somewhat too broadly against himself. I do not know
that in every case it is necessary, where you enter into a
contract with partners, to shew, in order to charge them all,
that benefit will necessarily result to the firm. There may
be cases in which the partnership would be bound, although
that might not be the case; but it must always be a strong

Exch. of Pleas, fact to shew that the partners acted for the firm, if it be es-
1841.   tablished that the contract was for the benefit of the firm.

BECKHAM   The point to be considered in each case is, is the party act-
v.   ing for himself alone, or on account of the firm? That the
DRAKE.   parties were acting in this case on behalf of the firm, is
abundantly clear: they were making all the arrangements
necessary to carry on the business, and it may therefore
fairly be assumed that the defendant gave authority for
this contract to be entered into, which was one of the arrangements necessary for carrying on the business. In
pursuance of that authority the contract was entered into;
or at least it would naturally flow from such an authority. I think it is perfectly obvious that it was made on
behalf of the firm, and that the plaintiff is entitled to
retain the verdict. The rule must therefore be discharged.

Rule discharged.

Nov. 20.   FARMER *v.* MOUNTFORT.

A writ of trial   IN this case, a Judge's order having been obtained for the
was directed to   trial of this cause before the Recorder of Northampton on
the recorder of
a borough, di-   the 28th of October, a writ of trial issued, directed to the
recting him to   learned Recorder, directing him to summon twelve men of
summon a jury
of the borough,   the town and borough of Northampton, duly qualified ac-
duly qualified   cording to law, who should be sworn truly to try the said
according to
law:—*Held*   cause. On the 18th of October, the plaintiff's attorney
regular, and   served upon the defendant's attorney the following notice
that it was not
necessary, un-   of trial:—"Take notice, that the issue joined in this cause
der the stat.   will be tried at the next borough Court of Record, before
3 & 4 Will. 4,
c. 42, s. 17,   the Recorder of the town and borough of Northampton,
that the jury   pursuant to the statute in that case made and provided.
should be taken
from the coun-
ty.
    A notice of
trial in an inferior court of record is insufficient, unless it specify the day of trial. Such defect
is waived by the defendant's taking out a summons to set aside the notice, and insisting, on the
hearing of the summons, on a different objection only, which is overruled by the Judge.

Dated this 18th day of October, 1841." The defendant's *Exch. of Pleas,* attorney, on the receipt of this notice, took out a summons 1841. to shew cause why the notice of trial should not be set FARMER aside for irregularity, on the ground that such notice had *v.* MOUNTFORT. been given to try before the Recorder of Northampton, who had no authority to try causes. This was the only objection made to the notice on the hearing of the summons, and the Judge refused to make any order. The trial took place accordingly on the 28th of October, when a verdict was found for the plaintiff.

On a former day in this term, *Humfrey* obtained a rule to shew cause why the notice of trial, and the trial had before the Recorder of Northampton, and all subsequent proceedings thereon, should not be set aside with costs, or why the judgment should not be arrested; on the grounds, first, that the notice of trial was bad, as containing no mention of the day of trial; secondly, that the writ was irregular in directing the Recorder to summon a jury from the town and borough, instead of from the county of Northampton.

Flood now shewed cause.—There are two answers to the first objection. First, the notice of trial is sufficient, in the same way that a recognisance, in general terms, to appear at the next sessions, is good, without specifying the day on which they are to be held. It is as much the defendant's duty to inform himself of the day of holding the sessions, as it is the plaintiff's to apprise him of it. [Lord *Abinger*, C. B.—Every one is bound to know the time of holding the county sessions, because they are fixed by act of Parliament; but a party is not eqally bound to take notice of the day of holding a borough sessions. *Parke*, B.—The plaintiff might have applied to the Recorder to fix a day for the trial of the cause, and then have given a notice of trial for that day. A notice of trial before the sheriff states the time and place of trial (*a*), and the same rule must apply

(*a*) Tidd's Pr. 468.

to trials before a Recorder. This notice is certainly insufficient.] If so, the defect has been waived by the
defendant's attorney appearing before the Judge at chambers, and omitting to take the objection. If he had then
made it, the plaintiff was in time to have abandoned his
notice, and to have given a new one.—The Court then
called on

Humfrey, in support of the rule.—The defect in the notice was not waived by the proceedings at chambers. If a
plaintiff gives a defective notice of trial, he goes on at his
peril, and the defendant is not bound to take any objection
to it before the trial; he may refuse to appear and try,
and may afterwards set aside the proceedings for the irregularity. [*Parke,* B.—Here the defendant goes before
the Judge with one ground of objection expressly stated in
writing, and makes no other at that time; had he then
stated both objections, the plaintiff would not have gone
on upon the defective notice. He has no right, therefore,
to come after the trial, and seek to set aside all the previous proceedings, by urging another objection which he
never hinted at before the Judge.]

Secondly, the writ is irregular. The stat 3 & 4 Will. 4,
c. 112, s. 16, never contemplated that a party should be
deprived of the privilege of trying his cause before a jury
of the county, and should be compelled to try it by jurors
chosen from a limited district. On the former discussion
of this case, *Alderson,* B. said (*a*),—" The provision in the
statute, which authorizes the issuing of writs of trial to be
tried before any judge of any court of record, looks as if
it was meant that he should have the power of summoning
a jury for that particular occasion, from those who, under
the general Jury Act, may be compelled to try ordinary
cases."

(*a*) 8 M. & W. 268.

Lord ABINGER, C. B.—I think this writ of trial is not void, on the ground that it directs the Recorder to summon a jury from the borough. It appears to me that the right construction of the statute is, that the inferior judge to whom a writ of trial is directed, shall summon for the trial such a jury as by law and usage he is entitled to summon. The Recorder, therefore, was right in summoning a borough jury, and was not bound to try the cause before a jury of the county. The rule must be discharged.

Exch. of Pleas,
1841.

FARMER
v.
MOUNTFORT.

PARKE, B.—I am of the same opinion. I cannot think that a party loses any benefit by having his cause tried by a town instead of a county jury. The act of Parliament does not permit any causes to be tried before these inferior tribunals, except such as, in the opinion of the superior judge, are not likely to involve any difficult question of fact or law. It seems to me that the meaning of the act is, that writs of trial shall be tried by the inferior judge in the same manner as causes arising in his own court; that is, by the jury he is empowered to summon for that purpose. I should have thought the writ good, if it had directed the Recorder to summon a jury generally, without naming the district from which they were to be summoned.

GURNEY, B., and ROLFE, B., concurred.

Rule discharged.

Where one of several defendants, having been arrested on a ca. sa., has been discharged under the Insolvent Debtors' Act, his goods cannot be afterwards seized under a fi. fa. issued against him and the other defendants.

RAYNES and Another *v.* JONES and Three Others.

JERVIS had obtained a rule calling upon the plaintiffs to shew cause why the fieri facias issued in this cause, and tested the 11th of August, 1841, should not be set aside for irregularity, with costs. The following facts appeared upon the affidavits :—In November 1839, a writ of fi. fa. issued against the four defendants, on a judgment against them for a joint debt. It did not appear that anything had been done upon this writ. On the 1st August, 1840, a ca. sa. was sued out against the four, under which, on the 10th of August, the defendant Jones was arrested by the sheriff of Carnarvonshire. He thereupon filed his petition for relief in the Insolvent Debtors' Court, and on the 22nd of August was discharged out of custody by order of that Court, on giving bail for his appearance at the hearing of the petition ; and on the 13th of November he was finally discharged under the Insolvent Act. On the 9th October, 1841, the sheriff seized a horse belonging to the defendant Jones, under a second writ of fieri facias issued against all the defendants, dated the 11th August preceding, which was the writ now sought to be set aside.

J. Henderson shewed cause.—The writ of fi. fa. is regular, inasmuch as it pursues the judgment ; and the plaintiffs were not bound to confine it to the other three defendants. Where one defendant is discharged by the voluntary consent of the plaintiff, no doubt that operates as a discharge of the others, *Clarke* v. *Clement* (a) ; but here the discharge of the defendant Jones was by act of law. It may be admitted, that after the issuing of the ca. sa., and until the discharge of the defendant Jones under the Insolvent Act, the plaintiffs' remedy against the other defendants was suspended ; but it was not absolutely lost.

(a) 6 T. R. 525.

It will be said that the stat. 1 & 2 Vict. c. 110, s. 91,

applies to this case; but that has reference only to process
against a single individual after his discharge under the
act, and leaves the law in its former state as to the issuing
of execution against joint defendants. The plaintiff has a
right to the same remedies as before against those defendants to whom the discharge does not apply.

Jervis, contrà.—The writ in question is irregular on several grounds. In the first place, the taking of one defendant under a ca. sa. is a taking for all purposes: the sheriff
thereby becomes responsible; the plaintiff thereby makes
his election, and cannot afterwards have a fi. fa. against the
same defendant; and a discharge of such defendant from the
ca. sa. is a discharge of all the others: Tidd's Pr. 996. Where
a writ of fi. fa. issues, and there is a return of nulla bona, if
a ca. sa. is afterwards sued out, it must issue against all the
defendants, although it may be executed against one only;
and a discharge of that one from the execution will be a
discharge of all the others. But at all events, the issuing
of a fi. fa. against the defendant Jones, after his discharge
under the Insolvent Act, was clearly irregular, since the
1 & 2 Vict. c. 110, s. 91, expressly provides, that after any
person has become entitled to the benefit of the act, no
writ of fieri facias or elegit shall issue against him on any
judgment obtained for any debt with respect to which he
has so become entitled.

Lord ABINGER, C. B.—I am disposed to think this rule
might be made absolute on more grounds than one; but it
is sufficient to state one. The statute 1 & 2 Vict. c. 110,
s. 91, enacts, that " after any person shall have become entitled to the benefit of this act by any such adjudication as
aforesaid, no writ of fieri facias or elegit shall issue on any
judgment obtained against such prisoner, for any debt or
sum of money to which such person shall have so become

entitled." The obvious intention of the Insolvent Act was, to discharge out of custody all persons who came within the sphere of its operation, not only from all debts contracted by them solely, but also from all joint debts. Then we have an express clause in the same act of Parliament, declaring that when once a party has been discharged under the act, *no* writ of fieri facias shall issue against him on any judgment for any debt with respect to which he was entitled to the benefit of the act. Here the very course thus prohibited has been pursued; a writ of fi. fa. has been issued against a party so entitled, which therefore is a proceeding contrary to law, and must be set aside. It seems to me that it would have been possible, without any inconsistency, to have made such a return to the writ, or had such a suggestion entered on the record, as would have warranted the issuing of a fi. fa. against the three other defendants; for I cannot think that the discharge of one defendant under the Insolvent Act is a discharge of all the rest from their debt. It is equally consistent with law and common sense, that if one of four defendants be discharged from legal liability, the plaintiff may suggest that as a reason for confining his execution to the other three. But the positive words of the act, that no fieri facias shall issue against any person discharged under it from the debt, afford sufficient ground for us to say that this writ is irregular. The rule will therefore be absolute for setting aside the writ and execution thereon, the defendant undertaking not to bring any action.

PARKE, B.—I entertain some doubt whether this writ should be set aside as irregular, although, upon the whole, I am inclined to think that it is so, and that the proper course for the plaintiff to pursue would have been to take out fresh process against the other three defendants, with a suggestion on the face of it of the discharge of the other, and giving that as a reason for the variance between the writ and the judgment. If, however, in order to dispose of this rule, it were absolutely necessary to decide that point, I should wish to have an opportunity of giving the question further consideration. But either this writ is positively irregular for having issued against all the defendants, or at least it was improperly executed against the goods of the party who had obtained the benefit of the Insolvent Debtors' Act, and ought to have issued with a special direction to the sheriff not to execute it against him. The 1 & 2 Vict. c. 110, s. 91, applies in its terms to the case of a single debtor only, and makes no mention of the mode of proceeding against him when sued jointly with others: but it is quite clear that the legislature meant that his person and goods at least should not be liable to be taken in execution after his discharge; and there ought therefore to have been either the suggestion or the special direction to which I have referred, and in default of which the writ ought to be set aside as against him. I am not prepared to say that I entirely agree that the writ itself is absolutely irregular, because the notion hitherto has undoubtedly been, that it is sufficient if the writ pursues the judgment, provided always that care be taken to prevent injustice, by directing the sheriff not to execute it against any party who may have become exempt from its operation.

GURNEY, B., and ROLFE, B., concurred.

Rule absolute, with costs.

EMERY and Another *v.* HOWARD.

Where the issue
and writ of
trial were in-
formal in the
following re-
spects:—1.
that the date
of the writ of
summons did
not appear in
the writ of
trial; 2. that
the issue did
not recite any
writ of sum-
mons or award
of venire; 3.
that the award
of venire, in
the writ of trial,
stated the debt
to be above
£20; 4. that
the writ of trial
bore no date;
and 5. that it
did not recite
when and out
of what Court
it issued : the
defendant hav-
ing appeared at
the trial with-
out objection,
and a verdict
having been
found for the
plaintiff, the
Court refused to
set aside the
proceedings,
but directed
that the writ of
trial should be
amended, the
plaintiff paying
the costs of the
amendment and
of the applica-
tion to set aside
the proceed-
ings.

IN this case *Pearson* had obtained a rule, calling upon the plaintiffs to shew cause why the issue, writ of trial, and verdict thereon, should not be set aside for irregularity, with costs, and why the sum of £20, which had been paid into Court, should not be paid out to the defendant. The following were the grounds of irregularity alleged on the part of the defendant:—first, that the date of the writ of summons did not appear in the writ of trial; second, that the issue did not recite any writ of summons or award of venire; third, that the award of venire, in the writ of trial, stated the debt to be *above* £20; fourth, that the writ of trial did not recite when and out of what Court it issued; and lastly, that the writ of trial bore no date, the conclusion being thus :—" Witness ourself, at Westminster, the day of in the fourth year of our reign." The defendant had appeared at the trial by counsel, without taking any objection on the ground of irregularity, and a verdict was found for the plaintiffs.

Lee now shewed cause.—The defendant is too late to make these objections, after having appeared at the trial and taken his chance of a verdict there. [*Parke,* B.— There appears to be some difference in the practice upon this point, between this Court and the Court of Common Pleas.] The cases, when examined, are quite reconcileable. In *Worthington* v. *Wigley* (a), there was an omission to transcribe the dates of the pleadings into the issue as delivered, and the Court of Common Pleas set aside the proceedings. So, in *White* v. *Farrer* (b), where the date of the writ of summons was untruly stated in the writ of trial, this Court set aside the proceedings. But in both those

(a) 3 Scott, 555; 5 Dowl. P. C. 209.　　(b) 2 M. & W. 288.

cases, the defendant had not appeared at the trial, and so had done nothing to waive the irregularity. In the latter case, *Parke*, B., says expressly, "The writ is void, and all the proceedings under it are therefore irregular; and the irregularity *has not been waived.*" In *Lycett* v. *Tenant* (a), where the date of the writ of summons was omitted in the issue, but was supplied in the writ of trial, the Court set aside the writ; but there also the defendant's attorney had objected to the proceedings, and conducted the case at the trial under protest. On the other hand, in *Ikin* v. *Plevin* (b), where the date of the writ of summons was wrongly stated in the issue, and the word "defendant" was used instead of "defendants," and the award of the venire was to the *then* sheriff, this Court refused to set aside the issue, saying that the proper course was to apply to a Judge for an amendment at the plaintiff's costs. Again, in *Farwig* v. *Cockerton* (c), where there was a variance in date between the issue and the writ of trial, and *Parke*, B., had amended the issue after verdict, the Court refused to set it aside.

Pearson, contrà.—In the cases cited on the other side in which amendments were allowed, such amendments were of the *issue* only. But here the date of the writ of summons is omitted in the writ of trial. Now, the writ of trial is conclusive as to the date of the writ of summons, and its omission might therefore materially affect the defendant's situation, in case the Statute of Limitations were pleaded: *Whipple* v. *Manley* (d). But further, the writ of trial is void for being itself without date. In *Quilters* v. *Neely* (e), where the objection was that a copy of a distringas was undated, *Patteson*, J., says, "If it had appeared that the defect existed in the writ itself, I should have said that it

(a) 4 Bing. N. C. 168.
(b) 5 Dowl. P. C. 594.
(c) 3 M. & W. 169.

(d) 1 M. & W. 432.
(e) 9 Dowl. P. C. 139.

was no writ at all." *White* v. *Farrer* is an authority for the defendant on this point. Again, the issue, which does not recite the writ of summons, is at variance with the rule of H. T. 4 W. 4, r. 1: *Hiam* v. *Smith* (a). Lastly, the writ of trial is bad, in stating the sum sought to be recovered to be *above* £20.—He referred also to *Peel* v. *Ward* (b), and *Handford* v. *Handford* (c).

PARKE, B.—The decision of this Court in *White* v. *Farrer* might appear to clash with a subsequent one of *Percival* v. *Connell* (d), but that is not really so. The party does not, by appearing to defend, waive any defect in the *writ of trial*, because until the time of trial he does not know what the writ will contain. In the present case, the best course is that the rule should be discharged, and the issue and writ of trial amended at once, the plaintiffs paying the costs of the amendment and of this application. The plaintiffs will then retain their verdict, and will have the costs of the cause.

The other Barons concurred.

Rule discharged.

(*a*) 6 Dowl. P. C. 710.   (*c*) 6 Dowl. P. C. 473.
(*b*) 5 Dowl. P. C. 169.   (*d*) Id. 68.

———◆———

SHEPHERD *v.* THOMPSON.

A defendant
who has be-
come bankrupt
and obtained
his certificate
after trial and
verdict against
him, has a right
to set it aside
for the want of
a sufficient notice of trial, although his estate is insolvent, and his assignees are no parties to the
application.

A RULE had been obtained, calling upon the plaintiff to shew cause why the verdict obtained by him should not be set aside for irregularity, on the ground that no sufficient notice of trial had been given. The cause was tried in July last: in August a fiat in bankruptcy was issued

against the defendant, under which, before the commencement of the present term, he had obtained his certificate.
It was sworn that the estate was wholly insolvent, and it
did not appear that the assignees had assented to this application.

J. Henderson shewed cause, and contended that, admitting no good notice of trial to have been given, the
defendant was not entitled to take advantage of it, inasmuch as, having been discharged by his certificate from
the debt and costs in the action, and his estate being
insolvent, he had no longer any possible interest in the
verdict.

PARKE, B.—I think the bankrupt is at liberty to make
this application. He has still an interest in the question,
for although the debt may be barred by his certificate,
he may reasonably object to its being said that it was
discharged thereby, when perhaps he might be able to
shew, upon the trial, that no debt at all was due from
him.

The rest of the Court concurred.

Rule absolute.

Cowling appeared in support of the rule.

BROKENSHIR *v.* MONGER.

Nov. 23.

THIS was an action of assumpsit for money lent, to which
the defendant, having obtained an order for leave to plead
several matters, pleaded (inter alia), that in an action in

To an action of
assumpsit for
money lent, the
defendant
pleaded, that in
an action in
which the now

defendant was plaintiff, and the now plaintiff was defendant, the now plaintiff set off the same
debt for which the present action was brought, and in that action the now defendant obtained
a verdict:—*Held*, that this was not a plea of judgment recovered, within the meaning of the
rule of H. T. 4 Will. 4, r. 8, and that the plaintiff could not sign judgment as for want of a
plea.

Exch. of Pleas,
1841.
BROKENSHIR
v.
MONGER.

which the now defendant was plaintiff, and the now plaintiff was defendant, the now plaintiff then set off the same debt for which the present action was brought, and that in that action the now defendant obtained a verdict. The defendant also pleaded a set-off. The plaintiff took out a summons for particulars of set-off, and afterwards signed judgment as for want of a plea, on the ground that the above was in substance a plea of judgment recovered, and that the defendant had not stated the date of the judgment, and the number of the roll, in compliance with the rule of H. T. 4 Will. 4, r. 8.

Butt now moved for a rule to shew cause why this judgment should be set aside for irregularity, with costs: and contended, first, that the rule did not apply to such a plea as this, but only to the ordinary plea of a judgment recovered by the plaintiff for the same debt, its object being to get rid of the old sham plea of judgment recovered; and secondly, that, the plea not being a nullity, but good on the face of it, the omission to state the date &c. in the margin, even if that were necessary, was an irregularity only, which had been waived by the plaintiff's applying for particulars of set-off: *Margerem* v. *Makilwaine* (a).

Martin shewed cause in the first instance, and insisted that this was in substance nothing more than the ordinary sham plea of judgment recovered, and that being a nullity, there was no waiver.

PARKE, B.—This appears to be the first time that the Court has been called upon to put a construction upon this rule of Court; and I certainly think that it was intended to apply only to the well-known and usual sham plea of a former judgment recovered by the plaintiff against the de-

(a) 2 N. R. 509.

fendant for the same demand. Besides, the plaintiff, by taking out a summons for particulars of the defendant's set-off, has admitted that the only question between him and the defendant now relates to that set-off, and therefore has waived his present objection. The rule must therefore be absolute, with costs.

The other Barons concurred.

Rule absolute, with costs.

. GRANT *v.* ELLIS.

REPLEVIN.—Cognisance by the defendant, as the bailiff of William Pexton, for rent in arrear due from one Harriet Stuart Smetham, under a demise at a yearly rent.

2nd cognisance, for rent in arrear due from Nugent Kirkland and Thomas Gould, under a similar demise.

3rd cognisance, that one David Burnsall, before and at the time of the making of the indenture hereinafter next mentioned, was seised in his demesne as of fee of and in a certain piece of ground, on part whereof the said dwelling-house in which &c., at the said time &c., had been erected and stood, with the appurtenances, situate &c.; and being so seised as aforesaid, to wit, on the 6th July, 1764, by a certain indenture of lease then made &c., the said David Burnsall demised unto Jacob Leroux, his executors, administrators, and assigns, all the said piece of ground &c., from Michaelmas then last past for ninety-nine years, at the yearly rent of £25, payable quarterly on the usual days; and the said Jacob Leroux covenanted for the payment of such rent accordingly; by virtue of which said demise the said Jacob Leroux thereupon, to wit &c., en-

Nov. 9.

The stat. 3 & 4 Will. 4, c. 27, s. 2, does not apply to rent reserved on a demise.

tered &c.—The title to the reversion in fee immediately expectant on the determination of the said term, was then deduced through various conveyances &c. down to William Pexton, under whom the defendant made cognisance for the same amount of rent as that mentioned in the other cognisance.

To the first cognisance the plaintiff pleaded in bar, that the demise in that cognisance mentioned was made by an indenture of lease theretofore, to wit, on the 6th day of July, 1764, made between one David Burnsall, who was then seised in his demesne as of fee of and in the premises hereinafter mentioned to have been demised, of the one part, and Jacob Leroux of the other part; and whereby the said David Burnsall demised a certain piece of ground, on part whereof the said dwelling-house in which &c., and at the said time when &c., had been erected and stood, and on which the said dwelling-house was afterwards erected, to have and to hold the same unto the said Jacob Leroux, his executors, administrators, and assigns, from Michaelmas day then last for ninety-nine years, at the yearly rent of £25, payable quarterly, &c.: and that the reversion of the said David Burnsall of and in the said demised premises, expectant on the end or other sooner determination of the said demise, and all his estate and interest therein, more than twenty years before the right to distrain for the said arrears of rent in the said first cognisance mentioned, or any part of those arrears, first accrued, by divers mesne assignments thereof before then made, legally came to and vested in divers persons, and amongst others eventually to John Taylor, Robert Stubbing, and James Iveson, who then became and were seised as joint-tenants in their demesne as of fee of and in the said reversion of and in the said demised premises. And the plaintiff further says, that the said John Taylor afterwards, to wit, on the 13th June, 1836, died, and afterwards the said reversion of and in the said demised premises, expectant on

the end or other sooner determination of the said demise, to wit, on the 2nd August, 1836, by assignment
thereof then made, came from the said Robert Stubbing
and James Iveson, and legally vested in the said William
Pexton : And that for and during a long period of time,
exceeding twenty years, to wit, for twenty-five years next
preceding the time when the right to make the distress in
the said first cognisance mentioned first accrued, and for
respective periods exceeding twenty years, to wit, of twenty-
five years each, next preceding the time when the right to
make a distress for any of the said respective arrears of
rent in the said first cognisance mentioned first accrued,
none of the said rent reserved by the said indenture had
ever been paid or received: And the persons who were entitled to the same rent, and in the receipt thereof, hereafter
mentioned, to wit, the said John Taylor, Robert Stubbing,
and James Iveson, more than twenty-five years before the
time when the right of making the said distress in the said
first cognisance mentioned for the first quarter of the rent
therein mentioned to have been distrained for accrued,
to wit, on the 25th December, 1806, became and were out
of the receipt of the said rents so reserved as aforesaid,
and then wholly discontinued such receipt, or any receipt
of the same rent or any part thereof; and the right of distraining for certain arrears of the said rent, to wit, for one
quarter of a year of the said rent which then became and
was due, then accrued to the said John Taylor, Robert
Stubbing, and James Iveson : And that the said John Taylor, Robert Stubbing, and James Iveson, and the said
William Pexton have always, since the said time when the
said John Taylor, Robert Stubbing, and James Iveson so
became out of the receipt of the said rent as aforesaid, in
the said first cognisance mentioned, and so discontinued
the receipt of the same as aforesaid, remained and been
out of the receipt of the said rent or of any part thereof,

and none of the same has ever since been paid, received, or distrained for or sued for until the time of the making of the said distress in the said first cognisance, and for the arrears of rent therein mentioned; and that the right of making a distress for any of the said arrears of rent in the said first cognisance mentioned to have been distrained for, arose and accrued to the said William Pexton more than twenty years since the time when the said John Taylor, Robert Stubbing, and James Iveson, first became and were out of the receipt of the said rent as aforesaid, and when their right to distrain for any part of the same first accrued as aforesaid. Verification.

To the second and third cognisance the plaintiff pleaded pleas in bar, similar in substance to the plea in bar to the first cognisance.

. General demurrer to the pleas in bar respectively, and joinders in demurrer.

J. Henderson, in Trinity Vacation (June 26), argued in support of the demurrer.—William Pexton, the landlord under whom the defendant makes cognisance, being seised of the reversion immediately expectant on the determination of the tenant's term, was entitled to the rent as incident to that reversion, and the pleas in bar shew nothing in derogation of that title. It is clear, that unless this case be affected by the late stat. 3 & 4 Will. 4, c. 27, the mere discontinuance of the receipt of rent would not bar the landlord's rights: *Doe* d. *Cook* v. *Danvers* (a). There is no question here as to disseisin. The act of a stranger in taking rent by distress or otherwise would be a disseisin only by the option of the landlord: Littleton, ss. 588, 589. It will be contended for the plaintiff, that Pexton's right to the rent distrained for is barred by the 2nd section of the stat. 3 & 4 Will. 4, c. 27. By that section it is

(a) 7 East, 299.

enacted, that "no person shall make an entry or distress, or bring an action to recover any land or rent, but within twenty years next after the time at which the right to make such entry or distress, or to bring such action, shall have first accrued to some person through whom he claims; or if such right shall not have accrued to any person through whom he claims, then within twenty years next after the time at which the right to make such entry or distress, or to bring such action, shall have first accrued to the person making or bringing the same." The word "rent" in that section does not apply to rent reserved on a lease, as in this case, but to rent which is a charge upon land—rent for which an assise would lie. Such is the opinion expressed by *Tindal*, C. J., in *Paget* v. *Foley* (a). Thus an annuity charged on land was, in *James* v. *Salter* (b), considered to be a case within the act. So, in a rent-charge there may be an estate: *Rivis* v. *Watson* (c). These are instances of the class of rents to which the enactment in question applies—rents in which there is a legal estate, and not incident to, but having a legal existence distinct from, the legal estate in the lands out of which they issue. The person entitled to rent reserved on a demise has no estate in the *rent: Prescott* v. *Boucher* (d). The only estate which Pexton had was in the *land*, as reversioner in fee; and on the determination of the tenant's estate, Pexton's right to maintain ejectment would not be affected by the act, under the circumstances disclosed in these pleadings: *Doe* d. *Davy* v. *Oxenham* (e). The rent in question in this case would not have been affected by the former act of limitation as to rent, viz. the 32 Hen. 8, c. 37 : see *Foster's case* (f), and Co. Litt. 115. a.

But if the second clause of the 3 & 4 Will. 4, c. 27, were

(a) 2 Bing. N. C. 688; 3 Scott, 135.

(b) 3 Bing. N.C. 544; 4 Scott, 168.

(c) 5 M. & W. 255.

(d) 3 B. & Adol. 849.

(e) 7 M. & W. 131.

(f) 8 Rep. 64, b.

construed as prohibiting an *action* for rent reserved by lease, under the circumstances stated, it was repealed pro tanto, within a few weeks, by the 3 & 4 Will. 4, c. 42, s. 8, which allows an action of debt or covenant for such rent within ten years after the passing of the act, or twenty years after the cause of action accrued.

The construction to be contended for by the plaintiff would deprive the landlord of his rent, while it leaves untouched his rights to the land on which it is reserved, and to the benefit of all covenants except for rent, and his responsibility to the tenant on all landlords' covenants. There is nothing in this clause of the 3 & 4 Will. 4, c. 27, to require or justify such a construction. It plainly contemplates an *estate* in rent, and an *estate* in land. The other clauses of the act shew or confirm the meaning of the legislature to be, that the rent mentioned in the second clause is only such rent as that in which there could be an estate. Where rent on a demise is contemplated, other language is used, as in the 42nd section, which speaks of *arrears* of rent. The third section limits the operation of the second to cases in which there is an " estate or interest" in the rent. The subsequent clauses all indicate a similar meaning, and the ninth in particular strongly illustrates it. The present case, therefore, is not affected by the act, and the defendant is entitled to judgment.

Erle, contrà.—The question is, whether the Limitation Act, 3 & 4 Will. 4, c. 27, applies to a rent incident to a reversion expectant on the determination of a lease for years; it is submitted that it clearly does. The words are general—" any land or rent;" which are applicable to rents of every kind. If rents of this description had been meant to be excluded, there should have been an exception at the end of the clause, that the act should not be deemed or taken to extend to rents incident to a reversion.

The first or interpretation clause expressly declares that the word "rent" shall extend to all rents, and to all services and suits for which a distress might be made. The effect of the statute is, that after cessation of payment of rent for more than twenty years, no distress can be made for the rent, or action maintained to recover it, during the continuance of the term. Although at the end of the term the person entitled to the reversion may maintain ejectment to recover the land, yet during the continuance of the term he cannot distrain for the rent, after a cessation to receive it for twenty years. This may properly be described as rent-service, for which a distress might be made. The second is the governing section, and shews the meaning of the act, and to what rents it is intended to apply, and that is " all rents." Here there was a rent which first accrued more than twenty years before the distress was attempted to be made; and Pexton, and those under whom he claimed, having discontinued the receipt of that rent for more than twenty years, the remedy by distress is gone. If a rent had been granted out of the estate, it must be admitted to have been within the act; *James* v. *Salter* clearly shews that. It is said that the second section is applicable only to rents for which an assise would lie—freehold rents; but, because there are sections which are applicable to those rents only, it does not follow that there is to be any restriction or exception as to other rents. By the ninth section, rent created by a lease for years is treated as coming within the rents mentioned in the prior part of the act. The statute in its terms is equally applicable to rents incident to a reversion expectant on the determination of a term of years, as to freehold rents; and there is nothing to shew, either by express terms or necessary implication, that the latter only were intended. The enactments contained in it which are applicable only to freehold rents must be applied to them, and those which are applicable to rents under an ordinary lease

Exch. of Pleas,
1841.

GRANT
v.
ELLIS.

should be applied to the latter only. [*Parke,* B.—The 42nd section shews that the legislature intended to distinguish "rent" from "arrears of rent." According to that section, parties must sue or distrain for arrears of rent within six years, but according to the second section they might do so at any time within twenty years.] There certainly appears to be an inconsistency in those two clauses; but it will not be necessary for the Court to decide that the one overrules or repeals the other, or that the 42nd section applies to freehold as well as to other rents. It has been said that if the plaintiff's construction be correct, the reversioner could not maintain an ejectment to recover the premises at the end of the term; but that cannot affect the present question.

J. Henderson, in reply.—As this is a case of a " service for which a distress may be made," the words cited from the interpretation clause might occasion some difficulty, if unqualified. But they are subject to the general exception in the previous part of the clause, viz. " except where the nature of the provision or the context of the act shall exclude such construction." Here the nature of the provision in the second clause, and the whole context of the act, are hostile to the construction of the word " rent," in that clause, as including rent incident to a reversion.

Cur. adv. vult.

The judgment of the Court was now delivered by

ROLFE, B.—This was an action of replevin for taking the goods of the plaintiff in his dwelling-house at Kensington.

It appears by the pleadings, that, in the year 1764, David Burnsall, being seised in fee of the land on which the house in question was afterwards built, demised the

same on a building lease for a term of ninety-nine years,
at an annual rent of £25, payable on the four usual days
of payment; and it further appears, that on the 13th day
of June, 1836, the reversion expectant on the determination of the term became, after various mesne assignments,
vested in William Pexton in fee. The defendant in replevin made cognisance as the bailiff of William Pexton, and
justified the taking, as a distress for three years and three
quarters of a year's rent due at Lady-day, 1840; being
the rent accrued due subsequently to the time when William Pexton had acquired the reversion.

To this cognisance the plaintiff pleaded in bar, that, for
a period of more than twenty years before any of the rent
in question had become due, the parties entitled to the
reversion, and through whom the said William Pexton
claimed, had discontinued the receipt of the rent reserved
by the original lease, and that during that period no rent
had been paid or received. To this plea there was a demurrer; and the question for our decision is, whether the
plea in bar does or does not disclose a good defence to
the claim of rent on the part of William Pexton. The
question turns entirely on the construction of the Real
Property Limitation Act, 3 & 4 Will. 4, c. 27.

By the second section of that act it is enacted, "that no
person shall make an entry or distress, or bring an action
to recover any land or rent, but within twenty years next
after the time at which the right to make such entry or
distress, or to bring such action, first accrued to the person through whom he claims." And by the third section
it is, amongst other things, enacted, "that when the person
claiming such land or rent, or some person through whom
he claims, shall, in respect of the estate or interest claimed,
have been in possession or in receipt of the profits of such
land, or in receipt of such rent, and shall, while entitled
thereto, have been dispossessed or have discontinued such
possession or receipt, then such right shall be deemed to

have first accrued at the time of such dispossession, or discontinuance of possession, or at the last time at which such profits or rent were or was so received." It is on these two enactments that the question mainly turns.

On the part of the plaintiff it is contended, that his case comes expressly within the provisions of the act. William Pexton, he says, derives title to the rent claimed through several persons named in the third cognisance of the defendant, who were successively the owners in fee of the reversion expectant on the termination of the lease; and those persons, being so entitled to the reversion, discontinued the receipt of the rent for a period of more than twenty years next before the time when any of the rent distrained for became due, during which period no rent has been paid or received; and this, the plaintiff contends, is precisely within the letter and spirit of the statute.

The defendant, on the other hand, contends, that this is not a case within the statute at all. He contends, that the word "rent," in the second section of the statute, cannot be taken as having any reference to rents such as that now in question, namely, rents reserved on leases for years by contract between the parties, as the conventional equivalent for the right of occupation; but must be confined to rents existing as an inheritance distinct from the land, and for which before the statute the party entitled might have had an assise, such as ancient rent-service, fee-farm rents, or the like. We accede to this latter view of the case.

In order to come to a just conclusion as to the meaning of the word "rent," as used in the two sections to which we have referred, it is important first to consider what is the meaning of the word "recover," as used in the second section. The enactment is, that no person shall make an entry or distress, or bring an action to "recover" any land or rent, but within twenty years &c. Now, so far as relates to land, the word "recover," in this passage, clearly means the same thing as "*obtain possession or seisin of.*" The clause assumes one party to be in wrongful seisin or possession of land to which another has the right, and then limits the time within which the right must be asserted.

If such be the meaning of the word "recover," when used with reference to one of its objects—"land," it is very reasonable to suppose that the legislature intended it to have the same meaning in respect to the other object—"rent." It is true, indeed, that with respect to an incorporeal hereditament like rent there cannot be strictly any wrongful adverse seisin or possession by another. If A. claims and receives the rent due to B., B. has still the same right against the terre-tenant as if no payment had been made to A. The receipt of rent by A. is not inconsistent with a similar receipt by B., as the possession of land by A. is necessarily inconsistent with possession of the same land by B. But still, before the passing of this act, a party seised of rents, whether rents-service, rent-charges, or rents-seck, might, in case the rent was paid to another or withheld from him, consider himself, if he thought fit, as being disseised of such rent. And a party electing to consider himself so disseised, might have the same remedy by an assize to recover seisin of his rent, as a party disseised of land might have to recover seisin of his land. The judgment in each case was the same, "quod recuperet seisinam;" and in each case the party was entitled to a writ of habere facias seisinam, which, in case of a recovery of rent, was executed by the sheriff delivering to the plaintiff an ox or other chattel on the land, in lieu of execution; and in case of a subsequent withholding of rent, the party aggrieved might have his writ of re-disseisin, with all its consequences, as in the case of a subsequent disseisin of lands or houses.

Now we are of opinion, that it is to this sort of recovery only that the second section of the statute has reference; for such is clearly the meaning of the word "recover," when used with reference to land; and the plain grammatical construction requires us to give it the same meaning when applied to rent, unless, which is not the case here, some manifest absurdity or inconvenience should result from our so doing. It follows from hence, as a matter of course, that the word "*rent,*" in the second section, must necessarily be confined to rent which might in its nature have been the object of such a recovery; and this certainly does not include the rent reserved on common leases for years.

According to our view of this case, therefore, even if the second section had stood alone, we should have been of opinion that the pleas in bar afforded no answer to the defendant's cognisance, and consequently that he was entitled to judgment in his favour. But we think it right to add, that the correctness of the construction we put on the second section appears to us to be strongly confirmed by the subsequent parts of the statute.

In the third and some other sections the act proceeds to define the time, in most, though (as is noticed by Lord Chief Justice *Tindal* in the case of *James* v. *Salter* (a)) not in all possible cases, at which the right to make a distress, for the purpose of recovering any rent, shall be deemed to have first accrued to the party making the same. The first case put is that of a party who has himself, *in respect of the estate or interest claimed,* been in possession of the rent, and who afterwards has been dispossessed, or has discontinued the receipt of the rent. *The estate or interest claimed* must, according to the context, mean the estate or interest claimed *in the rent,* and not in the lands out of which the rent issues. Now, a person entitled to the rent reserved on a common lease for years has no estate in the rent at all; *Prescott* v. *Boucher* (b); he is entitled to the rent, when it from time to time becomes due, as being an incident to his

(a) 3 Bing. N. C. 553.   (b) 3 B. & Adol. 849.

reversion, and not because he has any estate in the rent itself. He is himself the freeholder of the land, and can therefore have no estate in rent issuing out of the land. The word "interest," indeed, is of so large and comprehensive a nature, as perhaps to embrace the right which the reversioner has in the rent as incident to his reversion; still that interest can in no fair sense be described as *the interest claimed*. What is claimed by a landlord, distraining for rent on a common lease for years, is the amount of the arrears, wholly irrespective of the extent of his estate or interest in the reversion, as an incident to which the right to those arrears has accrued: what he "*recovers*" by his distress is the amount due for arrears of rent, and will be the same whether he is tenant in fee simple, tenant for life, or tenant for years. The statute, in this branch of section 3, clearly looks to the party recovering *the same estate or interest* of which he was previously possessed, and of which he had been dispossessed; and this is altogether inapplicable to a distress for rent incident to a reversion expectant on a common lease for years. Indeed, this very distinction appears to have been contemplated by the legislature in this act; for by the 42nd section a limit is imposed as to the number of years' arrears for which a party entitled to rent may distrain, and there the subject-matter to be recovered by the distress is described, not as "rent," but as "arrears of rent."

It must further be observed in the present case, that at the end of the ninety-nine years the reversioner will clearly be entitled to the possession of the land; for by one of the express provisions of section 3, the right to the reversion is to be deemed to have first accrued when the estate falls into possession, unless, which is not the case here, some third person shall in the mean time have got into wrongful receipt of the rents; this being in certain cases treated by the act as analogous to an actual disseisin. As, therefore, the rights of the reversioner, which are to be enforced when the particular estate is determined, are certainly preserved, it seems impossible to imagine that those rights which exist as incidents to the reversion during the subsistence of that particular estate, could have been intended to be extinguished. The reason why, at the end of the ninety-nine years, the reversioner will be entitled to recover the land, is, that during that term the party in possession has been holding under the lease in question, one of the terms of which is, that he is to pay the rent reserved. The argument of the plaintiff goes to this, that, though the tenant is most undoubtedly holding under the lease, yet that lease is to be treated as if all that concerns the reservation of rent were struck out, and all the other provisions remained. The landlord will be bound by his covenants for title (unless made conditional on payment of rent by the tenant); he will also be bound by his covenants, if such there are, to build or repair, or furnish materials for building or repairing, and by all collateral engagements. The tenant, on the other hand, will be bound by his covenants as to cultivation, repairing, and the like; and this appears to us altogether inconsistent with the notion, that the legislature meant to bar the reversioner of his right to recover the rent when due. A strong argument in favour of the construction which we have put on this act may be drawn from the 9th section. It is there provided, that, where a party is in possession of land under a lease, on which a yearly rent not exceeding 20*s.* is reserved, and the rent shall have been received by some person wrongfully claiming the reversion, *and no payment of rent shall have been afterwards made to the person rightfully entitled;* there the right to distrain for rent, or after the termination of the term to bring an action to recover the land, shall be deemed to have first accrued when the rent was first received by the wrongful claimant, and no such right shall be deemed to have first accrued on the determination of the term. It was strongly argued on the part of the defendant, that this amounts to a virtual recognition by the

legislature of the accuracy of the proposition for which he
contends, namely, that where there is no receipt of rent by
a party wrongfully claiming the reversion, there the right
to the reversion, and to the rent as incident to it, remains
unaffected. We think there is great force in this argument; and its weight may be much increased by considering what, upon the plaintiff's construction of the statute,
would be the position of the reversioner if no rent should
be paid for twenty years, and after that time a wrongful claim should be set up by some party not entitled.
Mere non-payment of rent will certainly not bar the
reversioner's right to recover the land at the end of the
term. When, therefore, no rent has been paid for twenty
years, the condition of the reversioner, according to the
plaintiff's view of the law, is, that he has no possibility of
obtaining payment of any further rent; but when the term
is expired he will be entitled to recover the land. Suppose,
then, that in this state of things a wrongful claimant
should succeed in getting the tenant to pay rent to him,
and that then, after twenty years, the term should expire;
it is clear that, by the express provision of the 9th section,
the right of the reversioner to the land would be barred;
so that by the act of a party wrongfully obtaining rent to
which he was not entitled, and which act the reversioner
had, according to the plaintiff's argument, no possible
means of contesting, the reversioner is at the end of the
term deprived of what, but for such wrongful act, he would
have been clearly entitled to, namely, his right to the possession of the land. On the view which we take of the
law, no such anomaly exists; for the reversioner, by distraining for or otherwise obtaining his rent, within twenty
years after the first wrongful receipt of it by the adverse
claimant, effectually prevents his being, by the wrongful
act of another, deprived of the estate at the expiration of
the term.

It is not unworthy of notice, that throughout the act the receipt of rent is constantly mentioned in a mode which appears as if studiously designed to mark that the rent contemplated is not the ordinary rent reserved on leases for years—not that which is usually spoken of as *the rents and profits,* but something distinct from both. For instance, in the second section the language is—" *When the person claiming such land or rent shall have been in possession or in receipt of the profits of such land, or in receipt of such rent;*" and the same, or nearly the same, mode of expression is used throughout the act. This is certainly not the ordinary mode of speaking of a person in actual possession of land, or in receipt of the rents reserved on leases for years. We do not rely very much on this argument, but the circumstance is worth adverting to.

It was pressed on the part of the plaintiff, that whatever question might have been raised as to the meaning of the word " *rent,*" deducing that meaning from the second and subsequent section of the statute, yet that it was not competent to the Court to give to the word any but its most extended meaning, by reason of the express enactment in the first section—the interpretation clause. But we do not feel pressed by that argument, inasmuch as that clause expressly excludes from its operation all cases in which the context requires a less extended signification.

On the whole, therefore, we are of opinion, that the limitation by the 2nd section of the statute does not apply to the present case, and consequently that there must be judgment for the defendant.

Judgment for the defendant.

PROHIBITION. — The declaration recited, that the
plaintiff, before and at the time of the passing of the Tithe
Commutation Act, 6 & 7 Will. 4, c. 71, and from thence
hitherto, was and still is patron and rector of the parish of
Shipdham in the county of Norfolk, and that no agreement for the commutation of tithes within the limits of the
parish had been before made; that the Tithe Commissioners afterwards, and after the 1st of October, 1838, to wit,
on the 1st of May, 1839, did proceed in the manner in the
act mentioned, and under the powers thereby given, by a
certain assistant commissioner in that behalf duly appointed, to wit, John Mee Mathew, Esq., to ascertain and
award the total sum to be paid by way of rent-charge, instead of the tithes of the said parish; that the plaintiff, as
such rector, claimed to be entitled to all the tithes arising
in, upon, and out of all and singular the lands situate
within the bounds of the said parish, except certain allotments before then made to the trustees of the poor of the
parish, under a certain act, 47 Geo. 3, for inclosing lands in
the said parish. It then recited, that the defendant Wyrley
Birch was the lessee of certain lands in the said parish,
and being such lessee, he the said W. B. afterwards, to
wit, on the day and year last aforesaid, made and preferred
a claim in writing before the assistant commissioner (setting it out), that there was payable by the occupiers of the
said lands called Shipdham Park, for the time being, to
the rector of the said parish for the time being, at Lammas-
day in every year, or as soon afterwards as demanded, the
yearly sum of 6*s.* 8*d.* as a modus, in lieu of all tithes, as
well great as small, yearly arising &c. in and upon the
said lands; that the plaintiff then disputed the said claim
of the said Wyrley Birch, and thereby there then was a

*Where a claim
of a modus or
other exemp-
tion from tithe
is preferred be-
fore the tithe
commissioners
appointed un-
der 6 & 7 Will.
4, c. 71, who
decide against
the claim set
up, the party is
not precluded
from setting up
a claim to a dif-
ferent modus
on the same
lands, unless
the commis-
sioners have
made their
final award un-
der the act;
even though a
feigned issue,
delivered under
the 46th sec-
tion, be pending
to try the valid-
ity of the first
modus.*

Exch. of Pleas,
1841.

BARKER
v.
THE TITHE
COMMISSION-
ERS.

question as to the existence of the said alleged modus,
whereby the making of the award by the said J. M. W., as
such assistant commissioner, was then hindered; whereupon
he the assistant commissioner appointed a day to hear and
determine the said claim, and did hear and determine the
said question by a certain instrument in writing, (which
was set out), and thereby awarded and determined that the
modus had not been sufficiently established, and could
not be sustained, and that the plaintiff and his successors
for the time being, rectors of Shipdham, is and are entitled to all manner of tithes, as well great as small, arising
&c. in, upon, and out of the said lands called Shipdham
Park; which decision was in due manner, according to the
said statute, notified to the plaintiff and the said Wyrley
Birch. The plaintiff then averred, that the yearly value
of the payment to be made by the said Wyrley Birch,
as and for the tithes of the said several lands in respect of which the said modus was so claimed by the said
W. B. as thereinbefore mentioned, exceeded the sum of
£20; and that the said W. B. being dissatisfied with the
said decision, did afterwards, and within three calendar
months after it had been notified, cause an action on promises to be brought in the Court of Exchequer, in which
the said W. B. was the plaintiff and the now plaintiff defendant, and did afterwards, to wit, on &c., deliver to the
now plaintiff a feigned issue in the said action, whereby
the said disputed right might be tried; that the now plaintiff caused an appearance to be entered, and the feigned
issue was afterwards, pursuant to the provisions of the
said statute, in due manner settled by the Right Hon.
T. Erskine, one &c., in which said feigned issue the question to be tried was [setting it out verbatim] whether
there was a modus of 6s. 8d. payable in respect of the said
lands, &c. That afterwards, at the Assizes held for the
county of Norfolk, on the 3rd of April, 1841, it was ordered by the Right Hon. Sir N. C. Tindal, Knt., C. J., &c.
that the time for the trial of the issue should be extended

Exch. of Pleas,
1841.

BARKER
v.
THE TITHE
COMMISSION-
ERS.

to the then next Assizes, upon payment of all costs by the
said Wyrley Birch, to be taxed by the Master; that the
said order was still in full force, and that the time therein
appointed for the trial of the issue is not yet elapsed, and
that the said action is still pending and undetermined, of
all which premises the defendants had notice. The declaration then alleged, that whilst the said action was so pending, to wit, on the 10th of February, 1841, the said Wyrley
Birch caused a memorial to be presented to the said Tithe
Commissioners, praying that they would receive from him
a new claim, and appoint a time and place for hearing and
determining the question as to the existence of the modus
therein alleged to be due and payable: that he the plaintiff caused a memorial to be presented to the said tithe
commissioners, in which he insisted that the said Wyrley
Birch was not entitled, on the merits, to prefer any new
or further claim, and denied that the said Tithe Commissioners had any power or authority to grant the prayer of
the said Wyrley Birch, and prayed them not to receive any
new or other claim in respect of any other alleged modus:
that the said Tithe Commissioners did afterwards, on the
10th of March in the year last aforesaid, take the said
memorial of the said W. B. into their consideration, and
did by a certain order in writing, bearing date &c., decide
that the said W. B. should be permitted to raise the question of a different modus on certain conditions; and that
although he, the plaintiff, had always objected that they
had not power to receive or entertain any such new or
further claim, and the said issue was still pending, yet the
said defendant W. B. did afterwards, to wit, on &c. present, and the commissioners received from him, a certain
other claim in writing, [which was set out, and was a claim
of exemption from tithe for a portion of the lands in question, in consideration of a modus of 6s.; and in respect of
the residue, claiming an exemption from tithe altogether,
under the provisions of the Inclosure Act]. It then alleged,

Exch. of Pleas,
1841.

BARKER
v.
THE TITHE
COMMISSION-
ERS.

that the lands and allotments in the last-mentioned claim and those in the first-mentioned claim were the same, and that he, the plaintiff, objected before the commissioners that they had no power to receive the last-mentioned claim; yet the said Tithe Commissioners caused a certain notice [which was set out] to be issued and sent to the said now plaintiff, appointing the 18th of May, 1841, for hearing the said claim for a modus of 6*s.*, which time was, by an order of the 14th of May, postponed to the 11th of June in the same year: and so the now plaintiff says, that the said Tithe Commissioners have proceeded and are proceeding in the said last-mentioned claim, &c., wherefore the now plaintiff prays that a writ of our said Lady the Queen of prohibition, from the Court of our said Lady the Queen before the Barons &c., do issue to the said Tithe Commissioners and to the said Wyrley Birch, that they do not proceed further in the hearing or determining of the said last-mentioned claim.

Demurrer by the Tithe Commissioners, assigning for causes, that it does not appear by the declaration that the Tithe Commissioners have not jurisdiction over the matters in the declaration mentioned, or that they will improperly exercise such jurisdiction, or that they have improperly or at all exercised their jurisdiction as to the said matters, or that the said instrument signed by the said J. M. Mathew, and therein set out, had been confirmed under the hands and seals of the commissioners, or that the fact of such confirmation had been published in the parish of Shipdham by the said commissiouers, or that it had any effect or validity, or was in any way binding on the persons interested in the said lands and tithes, nor does it appear that the said matters have by any means been removed or taken out of their jurisdiction.

The defendant Birch also demurred, assigning similar causes.

Joinders in demurrer.

The following were the points marked for argument on behalf of the Tithe Commissioners :—That they are not precluded, by the matters alleged in the declaration, from hearing evidence of another modus in lieu of the tithes of the land in question. That none of those matters made it obligatory on them to confirm their assistant commissioner's finding mentioned in the declaration. That until they have confirmed and published it as their award, they have the power, subject to the control of the Court of Queen's Bench, of receiving all evidence necessary for their information, before giving a decision which is to be final and irreversible. And all or any of the other grounds mentioned in the demurrer will be relied upon.

The Solicitor-General, for the Tithe Commissioners.— The principal question in this case is, whether, the assistant commissioner having decided that the claim to a modus of 6s. 8d. was not well established, and could not be sustained, it is not open to the commissioners to inquire whether there was a valid claim to a modus of 6s., or even a total exemption from tithes, in respect of the lands in question, they not having yet made their award, or had, as they think, the means of proceeding to do so without investigating the validity of this claim. The commissioners contend that they are bound to investigate any claim bonâ fide made pursuant to the provisions of the act.

The commissioners are first directed, by the 36th section of the act 6 & 7 Will. 4, c. 71, to ascertain and award the total sum to be paid by way of rent-charge, instead of the tithes of every parish in England and Wales, in which no agreement binding upon the whole parish shall have been made and confirmed in the manner pointed out by the previous sections. And the 37th section provides, that in every case in which the commissioners shall intend making an award, notice thereof shall be given in such manner as to them shall seem fit; and after the expiration of twenty-one days after such notice shall have been given, the commis-

Exch. of Pleas,
1841.

BARKER
v.
THE TITHE
COMMISSION-
ERS.

sioners or assistant commissioner shall proceed to ascertain the clear average value of the tithes of the parish. Then the 44th section enacts, " that if any modus or composition real or prescriptive, or customary payment, shall be payable instead of the tithes of any of the lands or produce thereof in the said parish, the commissioners or assistant commissioner shall, in such case, estimate the amount of such modus, composition, or payment as the value of the tithes payable in respect of such lands or produce respectively, and shall add the amount thereof to the value of the other tithes of the parish ascertained as aforesaid; and shall also make due allowance for all exemption from or non-liability to tithes of any lands, or any part of the produce of such lands."

Then comes the 45th section, which is important. It enacts, " that if any suit shall be pending touching the right to any tithes, or if there shall be any question as to the existence of any modus or composition real, or prescriptive or customary payment, or any claim of exemption from or non-liability under any circumstances to the payment of any tithes in respect of any lands or any kind of produce, or touching the situation or boundary of any lands, or if *any difference shall arise whereby the making of any such award by the commissioners or assistant commissioner shall be hindered,* it shall be lawful for the commissioners or assistant commissioner to appoint a time and place, in or near the parish, for hearing and determining the same; and the decision of the commissioners and assistant commissioner shall be final and conclusive on all persons, subject to the provisions hereinafter contained." Here a difference has arisen whereby the making of an award by the commissioners is hindered, and therefore it was their duty to appoint a time and place to hear and determine that difference. There is nothing in that section to prevent a party, having put forward a claim to a particular modus which turns out to be incorrectly stated, from afterwards setting up another; or to shew that the commissioners are to bind him to that original claim. If a party is dissatisfied with the decision of the commissioners or assistant commissioner, he may, by the 46th section, appeal, by bringing an action and trying the matter upon a feigned issue, or if there is no dispute about the facts, the commissioners or assistant commissioner are empowered to state, at the request of the parties dissatisfied, a special case for the opinion of a court of law; and the clause concludes with a proviso, that after such verdict given and not set aside by the Court, or after such decision of the Court, the said commissioners or assistant commissioner shall be bound by such verdict or decision; and the costs of every such action, or of stating such case and obtaining a decision thereon, shall be in the discretion of the Court in or by which the same shall be decided, &c.

There is nothing in the 45th section respecting an award to be made by the assistant commissioner, but if there be a matter of difference he is to decide it; the party however is at liberty to attack his decision before any of the courts of law in Westminster Hall. It is not like the case of an arbitrator, who is finally to award upon every matter in difference between the parties.

The 50th section provides, that as soon as all such suits and differences shall have been decided, or, if none, then as soon as the commissioners or assistant commissioner shall have ascertained the total value of all the tithes of the parish, the commissioners or assistant commissioner shall frame the draft of an award, declaring that the sum ascertained shall be the amount of the rent-charge to be paid in respect of the tithes of the parish. And the 51st enacts, that as soon as the said draft shall have been made by the commissioners or assistant commissioner, they or he shall deposit a copy of the same, and of any special report thereunto annexed, at some convenient place within the parish, for the inspection of all persons interested in

Exch. of Pleas,
1841.

BARKER
v
THE TITHE
COMMISSION-
ERS.

the lands or tithes, and shall forthwith give notice where the said copy may be inspected; and shall also in such notice appoint some convenient place and time for holding a meeting to hear objections to such intended award by any person interested therein; and the said commissioners &c. at such meeting shall hear and determine any objection which may be then and there made to the said intended award, or adjourn the further hearing thereof, if they or he shall think proper, to a future meeting; and may, if they or he shall see occasion, direct any further valuation of the lands or tithes: and then it provides, that when the commissioners or assistant commissioner shall have heard and determined all such objections, they shall amend the draft of such award accordingly, if they shall see occasion.   Then the 52nd section enacts, that as soon as the commissioners or assistant commissioner shall have made such amendments in the draft of the award, they shall cause the same to be fairly written, and shall sign and send it to the office of the commissioners, and the commissioners shall satisfy themselves that all the proceedings incident to the making of such award have been duly performed; and if they shall think the award ought to be confirmed, shall confirm the same under their hands and seal, and shall add to the award the date of such confirmation, and shall publish the fact of such confirmation, and the date thereof, in the parish, in such manner as to them shall seem fit; and every such confirmed award shall be binding on all persons interested in the said lands or tithes. The decision in this case, therefore, of the assistant commissioner, was not an *award*, but merely a decision incidental to the inquiry upon the matter submitted to him, viz. whether there was a modus of 6*s*. 8*d*. upon this farm; and he has decided that there was not. That was a decision upon that question, but nothing else, and it was upon that question only that such decision was binding.   There is nothing in the act to prevent Mr. Birch from setting up

any other claim before the commissioners. [Lord *Abin-*
the party set up a modus of 6*s*. 8*d*., and the decree of the
Court of Equity was against that particular modus, that
would not be a bar to the party subsequently setting up
a modus of 6*s*.]   The decision of the commissioners or
assistant commissioner is to be final and conclusive upon
the matter in difference before them, but upon that only.
If any other difference afterwards arises which shall hinder
the making of the award, the commissioners are to examine
the documents touching the claim, and to appoint a time
for hearing and determining it.   If a bonâ fide claim is
made, and a real matter in difference arises, there is nothing in the act to prevent their adjudicating upon it at
any time before they make their final award.

So also with respect to the apportionment. The commissioners having found what the value of the tithes payable
in any particular parish is, it is then to be apportioned
upon the lands of the parish, but that apportionment is
not to take place until after the commissioners have confirmed the award.   The 53rd section enacts, that as soon
as the commissioners shall have confirmed any such award,
the commissioners or some assistant commissioner shall
call a parochial meeting of the owners of land, subject to
tithes in the said parish, for the purpose of choosing valuers to apportion the amount so awarded among the
lands of the parish.   And by the 54th section, if upon the
expiration of six calendar months after the day of the date
of the confirmation of any agreement or award no valuer
or valuers shall have been appointed, or the apportionment
by such valuers or valuer shall not have been made and
sent to the office of the commissioners as thereinafter
provided, it shall be lawful for the commissioners or some
assistant commissioner to apportion the rent-charge previously agreed or awarded to be paid, among the lands of
the said parish, having regard to the average titheable.

Exch. of Pleas,
1841.

BARKER
v.
THE TITHE
COMMISSION-
ERS.

produce and productive quality of the said lands, according to the discretion and judgment of the commissioners or assistant commissioner, but subject to the provisions thereinafter contained, and so that the several lands may have the full benefit in each case of every modus, composition real, prescriptive and customary payment, and of every exemption from or non-liability to tithes relating to the · said lands respectively, and having regard to the several tithes to which the said lands are severally liable. So that the intention of the legislature is, that the amount of the rent-charge payable by the whole parish shall depend upon whether the lands are or are not covered by a modus or composition; and then, in apportioning the rent-charge, to make up the gross amount, among the lands of the several tithe-payers, they are to pay the rent-charge so assessed only in respect of land liable to pay tithe in kind.

The 55th section points out the form of the apportionment; the 59th provides that, for the purpose of making any such apportionment, as well as for the purpose of making any award, the commissioners and assistant commissioner may employ land surveyors and tithe valuers; and the 60th provides, that the draft of the apportionment shall be signed by the person making it, and sent to the commissioners. Then the 61st enacts, that as soon as such draft shall have been sent to the commissioners, they shall cause a copy of it to be deposited at some convenient place in the parish for the inspection of persons interested in the lands or tithes, and shall give notice where the said copy may be inspected, and also in such notice appoint some convenient place and time for holding a meeting to hear objections to the intended apportionment by any person interested therein, and the commissioners or assistant commissioner at such meetings shall hear and determine any objections which may be made, or adjourn the further hearing to a future meeting, and may direct a fur-

Exch. of Pleas,
1841.

BARKER
v.
THE TITHE
COMMISSION-
ERS.

ther valuation, &c.; and when the said commissioners or assistant commissioner shall have heard and determined all such objections, they are required to cause such apportionment to be amended, if they shall see occasion. Then, by section 68, after such proceedings shall have been had, and all such objections shall have been finally disposed of, the commissioners or assistant commissioner shall cause the instrument of apportionment to be engrossed on parchment, and shall annex the map or plan thereunto belonging to the engrossed instrument of apportionment, and shall sign the instrument and map, and shall send both to the office of the commissioners, and if the commissioners shall approve the apportionment, they shall confirm the instrument of apportionment under their hands and seal, and shall add thereunto the date of such confirmation. Then the 66th section enacts,—" that no confirmed agreement, award, or apportionment, shall be impeached after the confirmation thereof, by reason of any mistake or informality therein, or in any proceeding relating thereunto." Therefore, in the first place, previous to the making of the award by which a rent-charge is to be fixed upon the parish generally, the commissioners have full power to decide upon any bonâ fide claim brought before them, and to inquire into any bonâ fide difference relating to that claim; and they are to satisfy themselves what the sum really is that is to be paid by the parish before they make their award, which is to be binding upon all persons whatever. There are two clauses, the 73rd and 74th, which give power to the commissioners to direct the costs of proceedings before them in relation to any matter in difference to be paid in any proportion they shall think reasonable; so that it is not likely that any person would bring forward a claim vexatiously or for the purpose of annoyance.

Such being the provisions and such the manifest intent of the act of Parliament, the Court will not interfere by prohibition. The act having imposed upon the Tithe Commis-

Exch. of Pleas,
1841.

BARKER
v.
THE TITHE
COMMISSION-
ERS.

sioners the duty of making this award and apportionment, they were proceeding in the best way they could for the purpose of satisfying themselves how the award ought justly to be made, and there is nothing in the act to preclude them from taking the steps they have taken to satisfy themselves of the justice of this claim.

There is another point raised upon the pleadings, with respect to the pendency of the feigned issue, which was set down for trial at the Spring Assizes, then ordered to stand over to the Summer Assizes, but was not then tried, and is still undetermined. By section 46, the parties are bound to try within a limited time, unless the Court or a Judge shall extend the time for going to trial; and the learned Judge having made an order that this issue should stand over till the Summer Assizes, unless another order be made that it shall be continued, it cannot be proceeded with, the time having gone by in which the plaintiff was allowed to try it. But the Court may impose a condition that the issue should not be any further proceeded with. That issue, however, does not relate to this question but to another, namely, whether a modus of 6s. 8d. is payable in lieu of tithes. The question here is, whether a modus of 6s. is payable, which is a different question from that which the assistant commissioner has decided upon; that is a matter within the jurisdiction of the Tithe Commissioners, and it is their duty to hear and investigate that claim before making their final award.

Kelly appeared in support of the demurrer by the defendant Wyrley Birch.

The Attorney-General, contrà.—The writ of prohibition ought to issue. There are, under this act of Parliament, several matters which are to be disposed of as preliminaries, which when disposed of are final. The question of modus or no modus is one of them; and the commissioners having decided this question, they are as much bound by it as if they had made their final award. But even if they could have such power under the act as is contended for on the other side, they cannot exercise it pending another claim not yet disposed of. By the 44th section of the act it is provided, "that if it shall appear to the commissioners or assistant commissioner, that any question concerning any modus or composition real &c., relating to the lands in question shall have been decided by competent authority before the making of the said award, the commissioners or assistant commissioner shall act on the principle established by such decision, and shall make their award as if such decision had been made at the beginning of the said period of seven years" mentioned in the act. Now suppose there had been a suit by the plaintiff for tithes in kind, and the defendant Birch had set up a modus of 6s. 8d., and there had been an issue thereon, and subsequently a decree by a Court of Equity that the rector was entitled to the tithes in kind, and that that decree had been made at the beginning of the seven years mentioned in the act; would not the commissioners be bound to act upon the principle of such decision? [Lord *Abinger*, C. B.—When the decision of a Court of Equity overrules a specific modus, it necessarily involves a decree for the party to account for the tithes in kind; but it is not a final decree that tithes in kind are due; it is only a decree that prevents that particular modus being set up; it does not prevent a party from setting up another modus.] The commissioners are to act upon the principle established by the decision made by a court of competent authority. [Lord *Abinger*, C. B.—And if the decision is in favour of the modus, they are bound by it, because that would be conclusive against the claim for tithes in kind; but if the decision is against the modus, another might be set up.] It would depend upon the form of the decree, whether it would bind the right. [He cited Bacon's Abr., Tit. " Suits in Equity for Tithes," vol. 8, p. 88,

Exch. of Pleas,
1841.

BARKER
v.
THE TITHE
COMMISSION-
ERS.

Exch. of Pleas,
1841.

BARKER
v.
THE TITHE
COMMISSION-
ERS.

7th edit.] If a defendant sets up a particular modus, and an issue is directed, which is found against him, and a decree is made, whether that binds the right permanently or not in equity, it would bind the right for the purpose of this clause, which says " they shall act upon the principle of that decision." [Lord *Abinger*, C. B.—That is, that they shall act as if there were no such modus as the ·particular modus decided against. It does not say that another modus might not be established.] The object was to put an end to litigation upon these subjects. Then the 45th section provides, that if any suit shall be pending touching the right to any tithes, or if there be any question as to the existence of any modus &c., or if any difference shall arise whereby the making of any award shall be hindered, it shall be lawful for the commissioners or assistant commissioner to appoint a time and place for hearing and determining the same, and the decision of the commissioners or assistant commissioner shall be final and conclusive, " subject to the provisions hereinafter contained." It is manifest that those provisions are, an appeal to a jury by an issue or an appeal to the Court by a case, which are mentioned in the following section. The first is the appeal by an issue at law. Now, it is said that this issue has been dropped; but that is not so, for although the parties are bound to proceed within a certain time, yet if the Judge finds it impossible to try it, he may postpone it to some future time. The other branch of the appeal is taking the opinion of a court of law upon a case; and there is a provision that the proceedings are not to abate by the death of the parties, but may still be carried on. On the construction of the 50th & 51st sections, it is insisted on the other side, that up to the time that the award is made, and certainly on the occasions where the commissioners meet to hear objections, a party having previously set up one modus might still come forward and set up a different one: but that is not so. That is an objection which the legislature did not intend should be then raised. It is clear upon the construction of those sections, that it would not be competent to a party then for the first time to claim an exemption from tithes. He cannot then dispute the basis and the principle of the award; all he can then bring under the review of the commissioners are the details or matters of arrangement as to value. He could not then for the first time object to the award because, since the former meetings under the act, he had discovered that he could set up a modus with every prospect of success. The commissioners, under the 61st section, have power to make a fresh valuation if they think fit; but they have no power under that section to grant an issue or to direct a case for the opinion of the Court. All those powers are gone. If a person has not set up a modus before, it is then too late. If a party had a doubtful case, he should set it up in the alternative, and not set up first one modus, without suggesting that there was any other. The proceedings mentioned in the 50th & 51st sections are not to take place " until all such suits and differences shall have been decided." As soon as all those suits and differences shall have been decided, the commissioners are to make the draft of the award, and then to hear the objections. It is clear, therefore, that the objections which they are then to hear are objections which do not relate to those suits or differences. [Lord *Abinger*, C. B.—In this case they have not made any draft of an award.] Although they have not made the draft of an award, the parties were before the commissioners for the purpose of stating what were the differences, and what were the questions to be decided. Any questions or differences which are not *then* stated, are not impediments to the making of the award, within the meaning of the act, and it is too late afterwards to set them up. The 45th section, when it says that " it *shall be lawful* for the commissioners to hear and determine the same," is imperative, those words being applied to the discharge of a public duty; and if the Court decide that they *may* enter-

Exch. of Pleas,
1841.

BARKER
v.
THE TITHE
COMMISSION-
ERS.

tain another claim afterwards set up, they will be compellable by mandamus to do so; the result of which might be,
that they might go on ad infinitum.   If the commissioners
have the right to hear, the parties have a right to be heard;
and if the commissioners had refused to hear Mr. Birch,
he might have applied to the Court of Queen's Bench to
compel them.   But that cannot be the intention of the
act; while, on the other hand, it cannot be in the option
of the commissioners whether a second claim such as this
shall be set up or not. [*Rolfe*, B.—The party can have
no interest in multiplying suits and trying questions,
when he will have to pay the costs.]   Many instances
have occurred where that has been done, when a party
may have taken a strong view of the merits of his own case.
There could be no hardship in calling upon a person who
disputes the title to tithes, to say in the first instance on
what ground he makes his claim. [Lord *Abinger*, C. B.—
It has very often happened that persons claiming exemption from the payment of tithes in kind, have found great
difficulty in so shaping the pleadings as to accommodate
them to the proof, and nothing is more common than for
such matters to go through one or more ordeals of litigation before the real and precise modus is pleaded.   The
act of Parliament has substituted a new tribunal for settling these questions, and has given to that tribunal, with
some modification, the same powers as the Courts had
before.   It is not to be presumed, unless there are strong
words to induce us to come to that conclusion, that the
act meant to preclude a party from litigating a bonâ fide
claim by a bar of this sort.   If the act had intended to
confine the party to the claim stated in the first instance,
I should have expected to find words expressive of that intention,—as " that if a party shall make a claim for a modus
in a particular way, he shall not be allowed to make it in
any other."]   The words used in the commencement of
the 45th section, "if any suit shall be pending touching

the right to any tithes," mean any suit pending at the time the commissioners enter upon the investigation, and if any suit were brought afterwards, it clearly would not be within the clause, because the suit must be pending in order that the commissioners may deal with it. It excludes future suits as effectually as if they had been in terms excluded. The same meaning is applicable to the words which follow—"if there shall be any question as to the existence of any modus." There was no question as to the existence of a 6*s.* modus, and the commissioners are as incompetent to entertain that question as to entertain the subject of a new suit : both rest on the same foundation. If the case was doubtful as to what the exact modus was, which the parties must know, they might have brought any number of moduses before the commissioner, so as to have his decision upon the question, subject to their right to try by an issue at law all the questions that might be necessary : but when the party has finished his claim, and has stated all the questions which he alleges to exist, and has obtained the issue, he cannot afterwards apply to the commissioners to entertain another question, in order that another issue may be directed.

But in this case there is a suit now pending, in which the party claims a modus of 6*s.* 8*d.*; and before that suit is terminated, even assuming that, under other circumstances, he might set up another claim, he cannot now do so. That question must be disposed of first. It is said that other suit is terminated, but there is nothing on this record to shew that it is, and the Court cannot know anything on this demurrer except from the statement on the record. The Court would not allow two issues to be going on simultaneously to try two different questions of modus, both of which cannot be right. Two counts on different claims of modus might be put upon the same record, because the jury could not find both. But in this case, until

Exch. of Pleas,
1841.

BARKER
v.
THE TITHE
COMMISSION-
ERS.

one issue is terminated or abandoned, the parties cannot go on with another. If anything has occurred to make it desirable to alter the issue, an application should be made to the Court for that purpose.

The *Solicitor-General*, in reply, was directed to confine himself to the question, whether the commissioners could entertain a new claim before the other was disposed of. [*Parke*, B.—There is nothing in the act which says that the commissioners shall have a discretion,—they must either receive one claim and dispose of it, or every claim that is made.] There is a power in that as in other courts, to say when they will investigate the matter. There is nothing in the act to prevent the commissioners from saying that they will not adjudicate upon a second claim before the first is determined. They have a certain discretion over the proceedings,—they are by the act to appoint a time to hear and determine any question in difference,—and they may so direct their proceedings that one claim shall not clash with another. It is said that inconvenience may arise from having a number of different issues to try the different moduses; but that is not likely to occur, and even if it should, that cannot deprive the Court of jurisdiction. The pendency of a suit cannot take away the jurisdiction of the Court; for suppose a claim is made, and the commissioners decide against it, then another claim for a different modus is made, which the commissioners are bound to receive, and after that the party appeals against the first decision; that could not deprive the Court of jurisdiction until after the appeal had been decided. The Court cannot be ousted temporarily of its jurisdiction. If it could, the consequence would be, that the Superior Courts might issue a prohibition to deprive the Court below of its jurisdiction whilst the appeal was being decided, and the day after it was terminated, that Court might go on as it did before. That shews that there cannot be a temporary want of jurisdiction arising from the appeal. But in this case the other suit is at an end by effluxion of time; the suit terminates at the end of the second Assizes, if it is not continued by a judge's order. [*Rolfe,* B.—Must we not proceed as if this case were argued on the 27th of May last, when the declaration was filed?] Not in a case of prohibition. The Court must be satisfied that the inferior Court is exceeding its jurisdiction. It does not follow, that because the suit was pending when the declaration was filed, it is pending now. The inference is that it is not; because by the provisions of the act it could not be kept alive except by the authority of a judge.

Lord ABINGER, C. B.—If this question were to be considered on the mere ordinary principles of justice and equity, nobody, I apprehend, could doubt that a man who made one claim which turned out to be imperfect, ought not to be precluded from making another of a different sort, in the same manner as he might have done before the act. There is no doubt that a man might formerly have set up, in opposition to a claim of tithe in kind, a modus, and if that were decreed against him, he might set up in another suit another modus. From my own experience, I know there is often very great difficulty, and much nicety is required in stating a modus correctly. I have known instances where there has been litigation for above a hundred years upon the subject of a modus in a particular parish, which the party has not been able to set out in such a manner as to make the evidence precisely support it, until very considerable litigation has taken place, and investigations and decisions in courts of justice have been repeatedly had. The legislature intended to put an end to all controversy about tithes, by providing a summary and conclusive jurisdiction, and to give to that jurisdiction the same powers to decide

Exch. of Pleas,
1841.

BARKER
v.
THE TITHE
COMMISSION-
ERS.

Exch. of Pleas,
1841.

BARKER
v.
THE TITHE
COMMISSION-
ERS.

litigated questions which courts of law had before. Would
not one suppose that they would make some provision that
a party should not be barred by the mere form of a claim
in the first instance, when he had a substantial claim be-
hind? Would it not be reasonable that the commissioners
should have power to adjudicate upon a bonâ fide claim, if
the party had one? If so, we ought to construe the act of
Parliament in the way we should suppose it was intended
to operate, if the words will allow it ; if the words bind us
to do an act of injustice, we are bound by those words ; but
we must be fully satisfied there are such words, before we
put such a severe construction upon the act.

Now what are the words of the clause in question?—
" That if any suit shall be pending touching the right to
any tithes, or if there shall be any question as to the existence of any modus or composition real, or prescriptive or
customary payment, or any claim of exemption from, or
non-liability, under any circumstances, to the payment of
any tithes in respect of any lands or any kind of produce,
or touching the situation or boundary of any lands, or if
any difference shall arise whereby the making of any such
award by the commissioners or assistant commissioners
shall be hindered, it shall be lawful for the commissioners
or assistant commissioner to appoint a time and place in
or near the parish, for hearing and determining the same."
Now suppose that a suit was, at the time of the passing of
the act of Parliament, depending, in which a particular
modus was put in issue, but was not decided; the commissioners would, by this clause, have precisely the same power
to determine that suit, as the Court would in which the suit
was instituted. Then if they take the determination upon
themselves, and decide against the modus, would it not be
most unjust to say that the party, notwithstanding that
determination, should not have the same power before them
as he would have before the Court of Chancery or the Court
of Exchequer, to set up another modus? And where is

the difference between the two cases? In the case before us, we may say the suit is brought before the commissioners, and that they have determined it; and we look no further than that. The same party says, I now claim another modus:—may that not come under these words—" If any difference shall arise whereby the making of any such award by the commissioners, or assistant commissioners, shall be hindered, it shall be lawful, &c."? That means, if any difference shall arise before they have made their award, which, in their judgment, hinders their making a satisfactory and just award. The act of Parliament has not defined the difference; but it must be such a difference as in their judgment, as reasonable men, would hinder them from making a just award. Then if, at any time before they can make a proper award, a difference has arisen which induces them to think they cannot make a satisfactory award without adjusting it, they are bound to appoint a time to hear it. It appears to me that there is no limitation in point of time, except the limitation of that period which, though not defined by time, is defined by circumstances;—when they have adjusted all differences, and when they have actually made their award in writing. Even then, it is still not binding and final in certain cases which are provided for, and as to which they have still a power of hearing and determining, before the award is made upon parchment, and deposited in the proper custody. But during the time the award is making, if any difference occurs which induces them to think they cannot satisfactorily adjust it without hearing it, it appears to me that they have the power of doing so, and ought to do so. Now here is a question between the rector and an owner of land as to a modus. The latter has claimed one modus—that has been decided against him. He now claims another, before the commissioners have made their award, and they apprehend that they cannot make a satisfactory award without determining the second claim. That is what they propose to do,

Exch. of Pleas,
1841.

BARKER
v.
THE TITHE
COMMISSION-
ERS.

Exch. of Pleas,
1841.

BARKER
v.
THE TITHE
COMMISSION-
ERS.

and I think they have jurisdiction to do it; and unless we find in the act of Parliament some precise words to preclude their exercising that jurisdiction, we ought to endeavour to find words to give it to them, in order to do justice to the parties. For these reasons, it appears to me that there is no ground for this prohibition.

PARKE, B.—When this matter was before the Court in the first instance, upon the application for the rule for a prohibition, and afterwards on shewing cause (*a*), I certainly entertained doubts whether the commissioners had any jurisdiction to entertain a second application for the purpose of trying a second question of modus for the same land; and I believe those doubts were felt, and perhaps still more strongly, by other members of the Court; which made it proper and desirable that the case should be brought forward in a shape in which it might be taken before a Court of Error.

After the argument that has now taken place, I am satisfied that those doubts ought not to have been entertained. I think, upon the true construction of this clause of the act of Parliament, there is nothing to prevent the commissioners from entertaining a new claim of modus until they have made their final award, when, by the express terms of the act of Parliament, and not till then, their jurisdiction ceases. They are bound to inquire what is the proper sum to be paid by the entire parish by way of commutation, and by the 66th section, that award, even though there should be any mistake or informality in it, is still made binding; but, according to the provisions of the statute, there is nothing else which necessarily makes the act of the commissioners final and binding for all purposes.

The question turns upon the interpretation of the 45th

(*a*) In Hilary Term, 1841.

section; and it seems to me, according to the ordinary grammatical construction of that section, it has not the effect of concluding the question whether *any* modus existed upon these lands, but only of concluding the question as to *each particular* modus. The words of the section are—" If any suit shall be pending touching the right to any tithes, or if there shall be any question as to the existence of any modus or composition real, or prescriptive or customary payment, or any claim of exemption from, or non-liability under any circumstances to, the payment of any tithes in respect of any lands, or any kind of produce, or touching the situation or boundary of any lands, or if any difference shall arise whereby the making of any such award by the commissioners or assistant commissioner shall be hindered :"—That I interpret to mean, if any question shall arise before the making of the final award (which I think is to be conclusive), then the commissioners are to put that question in a course of inquiry, and it is to be decided by the commissioners or the assistant commissioner, and the decision of the commissioners is to be " final and conclusive on all persons, subject to the provisions hereinafter contained ;" but it is to be final and conclusive only as to the question so submitted to the assistant commissioner. Now according to the ordinary meaning of these words, if it should happen that *any* question as to modus, or any question as to boundaries, should arise before the making of the award, the commissioner shall have power to determine it : and according to the ordinary construction of the words so we ought to decide, unless it lead to some manifest repugnance to the intention of the legislature, or some incongruity to be collected from other sections of the act. But this view of the case is certainly consistent with strict justice on the one hand; and on the other, the only consequence is, that there might be some possible though not probable, inconvenience in a person bringing forward first one description of modus and then another; that, however,

Exch. of Pleas,
1841.

BARKER
v.
THE TITHE
COMMISSION-
ERS.

is not likely to happen, because if it does, there is a power in the commissioners to mulct the party bringing forward such claims in the payment of costs; but on the other hand, if the modus be shut out for ever, the greatest possible injustice would be committed. We have, therefore, the justice of the case clearly in favour of the ordinary construction of the 45th section.

Now if the intention of the legislature had been that all claims should be brought forward, and all disputes with respect to the liability of lands to any modus, or any exemption from tithe, should be finally disposed of once for all in the first instance, and that no other claim for a modus should afterwards be made, all I can say is, they ought so to have said. If they had, we should have been bound to yield to that enactment, although it might have worked hardships, and placed the parties in difficulties. But the legislature has used no language of that sort, but it has said, in language consistent with the ordinary construction of words, that there shall be a power from time to time of bringing forward claims of exemption, and that each claim shall be disposed of, till such time as the final award is made by the commissioners. That being the meaning of the 45th section, there does not appear to be anything in the context to contract that meaning; no doubt it is liable to some inconvenience, but it is much more speculative than probable, because it is not very probable that a person would bring forward a modus which he was not likely to be able to support, when he would have to pay the costs occasioned by it, if unsuccessful.

It appears to me, therefore, on the whole, that the commissioners have jurisdiction to entertain a separate claim, for a distinct modus from the claim which has been decided upon before. They have no discretion upon the subject; they are bound to admit the claim; but they have a discretion in fixing a time and place, and they would not adjudicate on a second claim of modus till the first was dis-

MICHAELMAS TERM, 5 VICT.

posed of. They would fix a time when the original claim was entirely disposed of, or impose a condition upon the parties, that they should abandon their claim to the modus of 6s. 8d. But the existence of that claim does not appear to me to be any bar to the power of the commissioners to entertain the present claim: therefore it seems to me, upon the whole, that the defendants are entitled to our judgment.

Exch. of Pleas,
1841.

BARKER
v.
THE TITHE
COMMISSION-
ERS.

GURNEY, B.—When this case was before the Court upon the former occasion, I was strongly inclined to think that, under the 45th section of the act, the party was concluded by the award of the assistant commissioner, but upon hearing the argument of to-day, I am satisfied that that is not the correct construction of the act, and I agree with my Lord and Brother *Parke* that the commissioners are bound to receive this claim, and therefore that the judgment must be for the defendants.

ROLFE, B.—I am entirely of the same opinion. The object of this act is to provide a rent-charge, to be paid for all time hereafter as a substitute for the tithe; and as a preliminary to doing that, I quite concur with the observations of the *Attorney-General*, in the opening of his argument, that the object of the act was in the first place to ascertain conclusively the existence or non-existence of all moduses and exemptions as speedily as possible, consistently with giving to the parties the opportunity of trying whether such exemptions did or did not exist. But surely, when the legislature is concluding parties for ever, it must be very strong language that could lead us to suppose that they meant to give less time and less facilities to the parties to raise those questions than they had before by the common law, when they were only to be concluded pro hâc vice in each particular suit. Now it is well known that if a rector claimed tithes, and the defendant, the land-owner, set up a modus, and it was found that he had set it up in-

Exch. of Pleas,
1841.

BARKER
v.
THE TITHE
COMMISSION-
ERS.

correctly, it was the good fortune of the tithe-owner that he got his tithes for a certain number of years, when it was quite consistent with the fact that there might have been a valid modus existing, the nature of which was disclosed by the proceedings; and when the rector claimed the tithes again, the land-owner set up the proper modus. Unless we see language of the very strongest nature in this act to force us to the determination that the rights of parties are more restricted by it, we ought not so to decide. But so far from finding any such language, it appears to me that, construing the 45th section according to its plain natural import, there is no doubt upon the subject; for it says—" if there shall be any question as to the existence of *any* modus or composition real, or prescriptive or customary payment," and so on, " it shall be lawful for the commissioners to hear," and so on; which certainly I take to mean that the commissioners *shall* do it. Then is there not a question in this case? No doubt there is; a claim has been delivered in of a modus of 6*s.*; therefore the question exists, and why are we to suppose that the legislature meant, that because originally the parties had not stated the question correctly, but had stated another question, this claim is not to be adjudicated upon? I never can imagine that such was the intention of the legislature. It certainly seems to me, the language being such as to give the commissioners jurisdiction, and the injustice of a contrary construction being so very glaring, that there can be no doubt they have this power, and consequently that the plaintiff must fail, and the writ of prohibition cannot issue.

Judgment for the defendants.

Exch. of Pleas,
1842.

HINCHLIFFE *v.* ARMITSTEAD, Clerk (a).

DEBT for work and labour and materials, and on an account stated. Plea, nunquam indebitatus. At the trial before Lord *Abinger*, C. B., at the last assizes for Cheshire, it appeared that the action was brought by the plaintiff, an attorney at Nantwich in that county, to recover from the defendant, who was the most considerable landowner within the township of Moston, in the parish of Warmingham, in the same county, a certain proportion of the plaintiff's bill for business done by him as solicitor to the landowners, in the course of the proceedings towards effecting a commutation of the tithes of the above township, under the stat. 6 & 7 Will. 4, c. 71. It appeared that the plaintiff was, in the first instance, employed by the Rev. George Clayton, the rector of Warmingham and owner of the tithes, to take the necessary steps for carrying into effect an agreement for the commutation. The plaintiff accordingly, on behalf of Mr. Clayton, called a parochial meeting of the landowners, pursuant to the 17th section of the act, which was held on the 15th of December, 1837. At that meeting (at which the defendant was not present) it was proposed by one of the landowners present, and unanimously resolved, that the plaintiff should be appointed their secretary and legal adviser. The plaintiff accordingly took minutes of the proceedings of the meeting, which, in consequence of the interest of the parties present in the lands of the township being less than two-thirds, was adjourned to the 10th of January, 1838, and again, from the same cause, to the 20th of February. On the latter day, before the holding of the meeting, the plaintiff and Mr. Clayton called on the defendant at his

Marginal note: Expenses incurred by the employment of an attorney by the landowners of a parish, to conduct the proceedings towards a commutation of the tithes of the parish, under the stat. 6 & 7 Will. 4, c. 71, are not "expenses of or incident to making the apportionment," within the 75th section of that act: and the attorney may therefore recover the amount of his bill for such services, in an action against the landowners who were parties to employing him.

(a) This case was decided in Hilary Term 1842, (Jan. 18), but is inserted here as having relation to the same subject as the preceding case.

residence, and he gave Mr. Clayton a power of attorney, which the plaintiff prepared (in the form subjoined to the 16th section of the 6 & 7 Will. 4, c. 71), to act for him at the meeting. At this meeting, an agreement for the commutation of the tithes of the township of Moston was concluded with Mr. Clayton, which was subsequently executed by a sufficient number of the landowners, as required by the act of Parliament, and confirmed by the Tithe Commissioners. On the 13th of March, another meeting, by adjournment from that of the 20th of February, was held, at which the defendant was present and acted as chairman; and the agreement confirmed by the commissioners was laid before the meeting by the plaintiff, who again acted as secretary, and took the minutes of the proceedings, which were signed by the defendant as chairman. The plaintiff, on that occasion, was also consulted by the defendant, and gave his advice, upon a question which was under discussion as to the mode of apportioning the rent-charge on some osier beds within the township. At this meeting a valuer was appointed under the 32nd section of the act. Several subsequent meetings took place, by adjournment and notice, (the plaintiff preparing the notices, some of which were signed by the defendant); at some of those meetings the defendant was present and in the chair: the apportionment and award were duly made and confirmed, the plaintiff conducting all the proceedings on the part of the landowners, and in the year 1839 the commutation was finally carried into effect. The plaintiff subsequently made out his bill, amounting in the whole to £162, for the business done from the period of his original employment by Mr. Clayton; and at his request, the valuer employed under the act apportioned it, together with his own bill, among the different landowners within the township, according to their interests in the lands subject to tithe: and the proportion thus assessed against the defendant was 41*l.* 13*s.* The plaintiff delivered a copy of the bill to the defendant, who kept it in order to examine the items, and on a subsequent application by the plaintiff, made objections to some of the items, and particularly specified a journey by the plaintiff to Chester to have an interview with the assistant tithe commissioner for the district, and another charge of a similar nature. He also objected to paying anything in respect of the two or three first meetings, at which he was not present.

Upon this evidence, it was insisted for the defendant, that the plaintiff clearly could not recover in respect of his services performed before the *agreement* was finally carried into effect at the meeting of the 13th of March, 1838, inasmuch as they were performed by him as the attorney and for the benefit of the tithe-owner; and that as to his subsequent services, his proper remedy was to have proceeded for the recovery of his charges under the 75th and 76th sections of the statute; which, indeed, he had admitted to be the proper mode of proceeding, by having his bill apportioned accordingly by the valuer. For the plaintiff it was answered, first, that the payment of a legal adviser to the landowners could not be considered as expenses " incident to making the apportionment," within the meaning of the 75th section; and secondly, that even if they were, his common-law remedy by action could not be taken away except by an express enactment. The Lord Chief Baron entertained considerable doubt on the subject, and at his suggestion it was agreed that a nonsuit should be entered, with liberty to the plaintiff to move to enter a verdict, for such sum as the Master should find to be due to him, if the Court should be of opinion that the defendant was liable, and according to the principle upon which the Court should decide as to the commencement and the extent of his liability.

In Michaelmas Term, *Evans* obtained a rule accordingly, against which

Jervis and *E. V. Williams* now shewed cause.—In the first place, it is clear that up to the time when the *agreement* was completed by the confirmation of the commissioners, the plaintiff was employed by Mr. Clayton, and could have no claim against the landowners. The power of attorney given by the defendant to Mr. Clayton on the 20th of February, was only to represent him in the making of the agreement. Neither did his acting as chairman at the meeting of the 13th of March, when the agreement was still in fieri, subject him to any liability to the plaintiff.

Secondly, as to the other part of the claim, the plaintiff's only remedy was by proceeding under the 75th and 76th sections of the act. The 75th section enacts, that " all the expenses of or incident to making any apportionment (except the salary or allowance to any commissioner or assistant commissioner, and except any expense which the commissioners or assistant commissioner may be authorized and may have ordered to be otherwise paid) shall be borne and paid by the owners of lands included in the apportionment, in rateable proportion to the sum charged on the said lands in lieu of tithes by such apportionment." And by section 76, " if any difference shall arise touching the said expenses, or the share thereof to be paid by any person, it shall be lawful for the commissioners or some assistant commissioner to certify under his or their hand the amount to be paid by such person; and in case any person shall neglect or refuse to pay his share so certified to be payable by him, and upon the production of such certificate before any two justices of the peace for the county," &c., the justices are required to issue a warrant of distress for the amount. These charges may reasonably be considered as " expenses incident to the making of an apportionment," being fairly and almost necessarily incurred by the landowners in order thereto. They employ the attorney to take care that the instrument of apportionment is properly and *Exch. of Pleas,* formally drawn up, so as to protect the interests of all 1842. parties. The 77th section affords a key to the construc- HINCHLIFFE tion of the 75th. That section enables the owner of an ARMITSTEAD. estate in land or tithes, less than an immediate estate in fee-simple or fee-tail, or in settlement, with consent of the commissioners, to charge, in the manner therein mentioned, so much of the "expenses of commutation" as is to be defrayed by him, upon the lands whereof the tithes are commuted, or upon the rent-charge to be received by him in lieu of the tithes, for twenty years subsequently. Would not a landowner be entitled under this clause to throw the charge of such expenses as these on the remainder-man? [*Alderson*, B.—The words of that clause, "expenses of commutation," are much more general than the words "expenses incident to making any apportionment."] The expenses referred to appear to be the same.

If, then, these are expenses falling within the 75th clause, the remedy given by the 76th ought to be pursued, and the party cannot proceed by action. The statute is not cumulative in this respect. The 75th section enacts, "that *all* the expenses of or incident to making any apportionment, with the exceptions therein mentioned, shall be borne and paid by the land-owners, in rateable proportion to their rent-charge." Then the 76th provides, that if any difference shall arise touching *the said expenses*, &c., it shall be determined by the commissioners or assistant commissioner, and payment enforced, in the manner therein stated. The obvious intention was, that, in order to prevent jobbing and fraud, all disputes as to the expenses of the proceedings should be summarily disposed of by the commissioners.

Evans and *Welsby*, in support of the rule, having intimated that they were willing to forego that part of the plaintiff's claim which was antecedent to the completion of the agreement with the rector, were not called upon to argue the other part of the case.

Lord ABINGER, C. B.—The Court are of opinion, that the plaintiff is entitled to recover against the defendant for that portion of his charges which was incurred after the meeting at which the defendant took the chair, and the tithe-owner's interest in the proceedings ceased. I should be sorry to hold that the words " expenses of or incident to making any apportionment" would justify the charging of an attorney's bill in every case, although I do not say that the services of an attorney may not be useful for many purposes. I think those words must reasonably be interpreted to mean incidental expenses arising in the cause of the survey and valuation themselves. The land-owners might choose to employ an attorney to receive tenders from different valuers, and that may be a benefi-cial course for their own protection; but surely his charges could not be considered as expenses incidental to the ap-portionment. Then, secondly, is the proper remedy by action? If these were not expenses incidental to the appor-tionment, it was not a proper course to apportion them among the landowners. The defendant, however, is bene-fited by that proceeding. But even if this were otherwise, it does not follow that the plaintiff's common-law remedy upon his contract is taken away. Where an act of Par-liament gives a new right, and a particular remedy for the enforcement of it, the party must pursue that remedy, and no other can be resorted to : but that is not the case here. The rule will therefore be absolute, to enter a verdict for the plaintiff for such sum as the Master shall find to be due to him; the bill to be taxed from the period when the agreement between the tithe-owner and the landowners was complete ; the amount, when so taxed, to be appor-tioned on the principle of the plaintiff's particulars, and the defendant to be liable for his proportion only.

ALDERSON, B.—I agree that it is very difficult indeed to say that the expenses of employing an attorney can be considered as expenses incident to making the apportionment.

GURNEY, B., concurred.

Rule absolute accordingly.

WILD and Others *v.* HOLT and Another.

THIS was an action of trespass for breaking and entering the plaintiffs' close, and getting and taking away their coal. Pleas, not guilty, and not possessed. The cause came on for trial at the last Spring Assizes at Liverpool, before *Rolfe*, B., when it was referred, by order of Nisi Prius, to a gentleman at the bar. The terms of the order were,— " that the verdict should be entered for the plaintiff for the damages in the declaration, subject to be reduced or vacated, or instead thereof, a verdict for the defendant *or a nonsuit* entered, according to the award thereinafter mentioned; and that this cause, and also all matters in difference between the parties, should be referred to the award, order, arbitrament, final end, and determination of" &c. &c. The arbitrator heard the evidence, and made his award, whereby, after reciting the submission as above, he awarded and directed "that the verdict entered for the plaintiffs should be vacated, and instead thereof a nonsuit should be entered." It did not appear that there was any matter in difference between the parties except the cause. *Cresswell* having obtained a rule to shew cause why the award should not be set aside, on the ground that it was not final,

R. V. Richards and *Tomlinson* now shewed cause.—

A cause and all matters in difference between the parties (there being no matters in difference except in the cause) were referred by order of Nisi Prius to the award, order, arbitrament, final end, and determination of A. B.; the order providing, that the verdict should be entered for the plaintiff for the damages in the declaration, subject to be reduced or vacated, or instead thereof a verdict for the defendant *or a nonsuit* entered, according to his award. The arbitrator, by his award, directed that the verdict entered for the plaintiff should be vacated, and a nonsuit entered:—*Held,* (*Parke,* B., dissentiente), that the award was bad, as not finally determining the matters in difference in the cause.

It does not appear, by the affidavit in support of this rule, that there was any matter in difference between the parties except in the cause: if there was, it lay on the plaintiffs to shew it: *Ingram* v. *Milnes* (a). It is therefore to be taken as being a mere reference of the cause: and in that cause there is express power given to the arbitrator, by the submission, to enter a nonsuit. He has, therefore, only given effect to the express agreement of the parties. [*Parke,* B.—The objection taken is, that entering a nonsuit is not final, and that he ought to have gone on to adjudicate on the matter in difference in the cause. The question turns entirely on the construction of the submission. Lord *Abinger,* C. B.—Either it is an adjustment of the cause or it is not. If the parties meant that a nonsuit should be considered as an adjustment of the cause, the award is final: if not, then they agreed that there should be no adjustment of it, and the arbitrator has disposed of the cause in the manner they agreed upon.] The Court then called on

Cresswell and *Cowling,* in support of the rule.—It is clear that the object of the reference was to enable the parties to get rid altogether of litigation on the matter in dispute in the cause. [Lord *Abinger,* C. B.—Why then give the arbitrator power to enter a nonsuit?] That might be a convenient mode of disposing of *the record*, but the arbitrator ought also to have disposed of the cause, that is, of the matters in difference in the cause, according to the justice of the case. Under this submission he had two things to do: first, finally to dispose of the cause and all matters in difference therein; and secondly, so to modify the record as to inform the officer of the Court how to enter up the judgment and tax the costs. He has performed the latter part of his duty only, and has in no way

(a) 8 East, 445.

expressed his "final end and determination" on the me-

rits of the cause. He ought to have decided either that
the plaintiffs were right or that they were wrong, whereas
all that he says is, that he is not satisfied with the plaintiffs' evidence. He has not given the parties that protection against future litigation which they were entitled to have by his award; if another action were brought
against the defendants, this judgment of nonsuit would be
no protection to them. [*Parke,* B.—No doubt they would
be liable to a fresh action; but the question is, whether
they have not so stipulated.] Surely the reasonable construction of the submission is, that the parties intended
that all litigation between them on the matters in difference in the action should cease. [*Parke,* B.—The matter
in difference in the action is the question which is raised
by the pleadings in the action; and that is decided by a
nonsuit.] How can it be said that the parties intended
that the arbitrator should dispose of the matters in difference in a manner which does *not* dispose of them? It
would have been perfectly correct to have said,—" I find
that the plaintiff has no cause of action, and therefore I
direct that a nonsuit shall be entered." The power to enter a nonsuit precedes the express reference of the matters
in difference, which also tends to shew that that was merely
considered as a mode of disposing of the record. It is not
that the arbitrator is to dispose of the matters in difference *by* entering a nonsuit; but that the verdict shall be
entered for the plaintiff, subject to be vacated and a nonsuit entered instead, *and* that the cause and all matters in
difference shall be referred to the award, final end, and
determination of the arbitrator. [*Parke,* B.—What are the
matters in difference but the issues in the cause? The arbitrator does dispose of them by the nonsuit.] It is submitted
that the true construction of the submission is, not that he
is empowered to make an end of the controversy between
the parties by entering a nonsuit, but that he may thereby,

if he think it expedient, dispose of the record. That is a power given diverso intuitu from, and only supplementary to, the power of deciding on the merits of the cause. Its origin appears to be this, that an arbitrator has no jurisdiction over the mode of entering a verdict, unless he has an express authority for the purpose; when that authority is given, nice questions may frequently occur as to the manner in which particular issues should be determined, and in order to enable him to evade those difficulties, a practice has arisen of allowing him to order a nonsuit to be entered.

Lord ABINGER, C. B.—Upon consideration, I am of opinion that this rule ought to be made absolute. I think that when parties refer all matters in difference in a cause, and the submission contains a power to the arbitrator to enter a nonsuit if he thinks fit, that does not abrogate his authority or his duty to decide all the matters in difference in the cause. A nonsuit does not decide the matters in difference between the parties; a verdict does. The power, therefore, of entering a nonsuit must have been given for some other purpose; probably, as has been suggested, because it was expedient not to perplex the arbitrator with the entry of the verdict on the several issues. But he must decide the matters in difference existing in the cause, which a nonsuit does not; because the plaintiffs may bring a fresh action for the same trespass against the same parties. He does not therefore decide the matter in difference, but only says he will not decide it. I think that the parties here did intend that he should finally decide all the matters in difference in the cause, and that he has not done so: I cannot think, because a power is given him to enter a nonsuit, that that makes it the less his duty to pronounce a final determination upon the matter litigated between the parties.

PARKE, B.—I am sorry to be obliged to differ from my

Lord in this case; but it appears to me, upon the true
construction of this submission, to be tolerably clear that
this award is sufficient. I cannot understand the difference between *the cause*, and the *matters in difference in*
the cause:—they depend altogether upon the issues raised
in the cause. Here the arbitrator is to decide on the matters in difference in the cause; but the parties have expressly given him power to dispose of the cause by entering a nonsuit: therefore, by the express contract of the
parties, that is a good and valid end and determination of
the cause, and therefore of the matters in difference in
the cause. The arbitrator has therefore made such a final
end and determination as the parties have agreed to, of
the matters in difference between the parties in the cause;
and it is admitted that there are none out of it. Mr. *Cowling's* argument proceeds upon the fallacy, that the matters in difference in the cause mean something beyond the
questions arising upon the issues on the record. There is no
ground whatever for the argument, that the entry of a
verdict or a nonsuit is merely the act of the officer of the
Court: it is that determination of the cause which the
parties themselves have stipulated for. I think, therefore,
that this award is perfectly good.

GURNEY, B.—I think this award is not good. The object of the parties doubtless was, finally to settle all the
matters in difference between them. The arbitrator is
empowered to dispose of the record by entering a nonsuit; but he ought to have gone on and said that the
plaintiffs had no cause of action.

ROLFE, B.—I agree in thinking that this is a bad
award. There could be no doubt upon the point, were it
not for the power given to the arbitrator to enter a nonsuit. Then the question is, how does that power alter the
case? I quite agree with my Brother *Parke*, that *the
cause*, and the *matters in difference in* the cause, mean the

Exch. of Pleas,
1841.

WILD
v.
HOLT.

same thing.   But here the cause and all matters in differ-ence are referred to "the award, order, arbitrament, *final end*, and determination" of the arbitrator: then a power is superadded, that, amongst other things, he may direct a nonsuit.   Now, this must mean one of three things: either, first, that he should terminate the cause and all matters in difference by a nonsuit, by the agreement of the parties; or secondly, that he should terminate this cause thereby, leaving it open to the plaintiffs to bring a new action; or lastly—and which I conceive to have been really his duty,—that, determining the matters in differ-ence, he might also dispose of the record, as the most convenient way of doing so in the particular case, by en-tering a nonsuit.   But he must also perform his duty by finally determining all the matters in difference between the parties.   I think, therefore, that the award is bad, and that this rule must be made absolute.

                                        Rule absolute.

Nov. 22.

Two clergymen being possessed of livings, a-greed to ex-change the one for the other, with the con-sent of their respective pa-trons, and the livings were accordingly re-signed into the hands of the bishop, and each party re-spectively was inducted into the other of them.   There was no specific agreement en-tered into upon

DOWNES *v.* CRAIG.

THIS was a special action on the case on the custom of England, brought by the plaintiff, as successor to the de-fendant in the Rectory of Fetcham, in the county of Sur-rey, to recover from the latter the sum of 99*l.* 10*s.* 6*d.* for dilapidations.   The declaration was in the ordinary form, commencing with the usual inducement, stating the cus-tom of England for rectors to repair their respective rec-tories, and deliver up the same so repaired to their suc-cessors, and that if they do not, then that they are bound to satisfy so much as should be necessary to be expended or paid for the necessary repairing thereof.   It then stated, that on the 4th of April, 1839, the defendant was rector of Fetcham, and as such seised in fee of the chancel of the

the subject of dilapidations, but it was found that neither party at the time contemplated any claim for dilapidations :—*Held*, in an action by one of the incumbents against the other, as his successor for dilapidations, that the plaintiff was entitled to recover.

church, and of a house, lands, and premises, and that he re-

signed the rectory to the bishop of the diocese, who accepted
the resignation thereof: That the plaintiff was afterwards
presented, instituted, and inducted into the said rectory,
and became and still continues seised in right thereof, of the
said chancel, house, lands, and premises, and was the next
successor to the defendant: That at the time of the resignation of the defendant the chancel, house, lands, and
premises were out of repair, and that the defendant had
not satisfied or paid the amount of those repairs.

The defendant pleaded, 1st, not guilty; and 2ndly, that
whilst he the defendant was rector of Fetcham, the plaintiff
was vicar of Leamington Priors, in the county of Warwick,
and that the plaintiff and the defendant thereupon, with the
assent of their respective patrons and diocesans, agreed to
exchange their respective livings in their then state and condition, and that the exchange was afterwards, in pursuance
of the agreement aforesaid, carried into effect, and the
plaintiff thus, and not otherwise, became successor to the
defendant as in the declaration mentioned. The plaintiff
joined issue on the 1st plea, and to the 2nd plea replied
that it was not agreed modo et formâ; whereupon issue
was joined.

The cause came on to be tried before Lord *Denman*, C. J.,
at the Surrey Spring Assizes, 1841, when a verdict for the
plaintiff was taken by consent, damages £92, besides costs
of suit, subject to the opinion of this Court on the following case.

Previous to the month of March, 1839, the plaintiff was
vicar of Leamington Priors, in the county of Warwick, and
the defendant was rector of Fetcham, in the county of
Surrey. Being so possessed of the respective incumben-
cies, the plaintiff and defendant agreed to exchange them.
This exchange was made with the consent of their respective patrons and diocesans. On the 14th of April, 1839,
the plaintiff resigned the vicarage of Leamington Priors
into the hands of the bishop of the diocese, and on the

17th of May, in the same year, the defendant was inducted into it.   On the 4th of April, 1839, the defendant resigned the rectory of Fetcham, into which the plaintiff was inducted on the 24th of June.   There was no specific agreement entered into upon the subject of dilapidations, but from the conduct of the parties at the time of and for several months after the exchange was agreed and acted upon, it is plain that neither party then contemplated any claim for dilapidations, and it was not till a dispute arose on another subject, that the plaintiff, at the latter end of October, 1839, first mentioned his claim for dilapidations. In the following January he had them surveyed, and the amount was then formally demanded.

On the 12th of August, 1839, there was a statement of accounts between the plaintiff and defendant, signed by them both, in which there was no mention of any claim for dilapidations.

The questions for the opinion of the Court are :—1st. Whether under the above circumstances there is sufficient evidence that the exchange was intended by the plaintiff and the defendant to be on the footing that each should take the living of the other in its then state and condition. 2ndly. Whether the law of England, with respect to the dilapidations claimed by the successor to a spiritual preferment from his predecessor, applies, under the above circumstances, to the case of an exchange of preferments.

The points marked for argument on the part of the defendant were as follow:—That the custom of England with respect to the liability of an incumbent to his successor for dilapidations, does not apply to the case of an exchange of livings : because a rector is a tenant for life, and the custom only differs from the ordinary law relating to the liability of tenants for life for waste, by allowing an action of waste to be brought by one party against another without there having been any privity of estate between them, and also against the executor of the tort feasor, notwithstanding the principle of " actio personalis moritur cum personâ:" consequently, the successor being in by Exch. of Pleas, 1841. his own contract, no action lies; at all events, the injury, if any, being the result of and springing from a contract, DOWNES v. CRAIG. and caused by the plaintiff's own act, an action of tort cannot lie: that the parties are not in merely by presentation and institution, but by contract, since if one had died before the induction of the other, or vice versâ, the institution and induction of the one would have been void. The defendant will also contend that a contract to exchange the livings in their then state and condition, is found in point of fact by the case: that the statement and signature of the accounts between the parties without reference to any claims for dilapidations, four months after the exchange, and two before any such claim, is conclusive evidence upon the subject: that therefore, according to the legal effect of an ordinary contract of exchange, and by the express terms of the present one, the defendant is entitled to have a verdict entered for him.

Thesiger, for the plaintiff.—The case finds that there was no specific agreement entered into upon the subject of dilapidations, and therefore merely raises the general question, whether, upon an exchange of livings, either party can maintain an action for dilapidations. [*Parke*, B.—The plea avers, that there was an agreement to exchange their respective livings in their then state and condition, and then it is found that there was no specific agreement entered into upon the subject of dilapidations, but from the conduct of the parties at the time of and for some months after the exchange was agreed and acted upon, it is plain that neither party then contemplated any claim for dilapidations. That might be because they did not know the extent of the dilapidations, and they might conceive that the amount in each was equal. The exchange of livings is only the case of each incumbent surrendering to his patron the living he holds.]

The only difference is, that there is a condition that if one of the parties should die before induction, the other party returns to his living on the former presentment. That is the only difference between this and a formal resignation; and in Gibson's Codex (a) it is said, that " no other collateral condition may be annexed to a resignation, in order to exchange, than what is expressed in the foregoing writ in these cases, and founded thereupon."—He was then stopped by the Court, who called upon

Fortescue, contrà.—It is assumed on the other side, that the parties are in the same situation as if they were in as successors the one to the other, in the ordinary way, by institution and induction; but that is not so; neither is the succeeding party the *successor* to any greater extent than a party is successor to another in an estate which he purchases from him. Succession, in the case of a corporate body, is analogous to descent in case of a natural body; there is no such succession here. These parties are in by contract. The law on this subject is correctly stated in Watson's Clergyman's Law, p. 28, where it is said: " Two persons, by an instrument in writing, do agree to exchange their benefices, which are both spiritual, and in order thereunto resign them into the hands of the ordinary. Such exchange being executed the resignations are good, but though the one is instituted and inducted into the other's benefice, yet if the exchange be not executed in both parts, the clerk on whose part the exchange was not executed may have his benefice again." This shews that the parties are not in *merely* by resignation on the one side, and presentation, institution, and induction on the other; for if so, on one being presented, instituted, and inducted, the estate and right of action would vest in him immediately; but it is not so in the case of an exchange, for so long as it is not executed on both sides the

(a) Page 821.

whole proceeding may be rendered void, and each may in

such case resume his old estate. The parties, therefore,
are not in by institution and induction : if they were, their
right of action would vest immediately, but it does not ;—
"for in this case of exchange the law doth annex this
condition to a resignation, if it be fully executed. But a
collateral condition may not be annexed thereunto." An
argument on the other side is built on this latter expression, which was read from Gibson's Codex, but it does not
affect the case at all. Lord *Coke* (a) compares the effect
of an agreement, in a case of this sort, to a deed to lead
the uses of a fine, and says, that to a fine no collateral
condition can be annexed; but who can doubt that it may
be contained in a deed to lead the uses of such fine?
The passage in Watson proceeds as follows : "But a
collateral condition may not be annexed thereunto, no
more than an ordinary may admit upon condition, or a
judgment be confessed upon condition, which are judicial
acts. And so if two, upon such an agreement, resign as
aforesaid, and the patrons, according to their agreement,
present cross de novo, (as they must do if the exchange
be executed), and the one is admitted, instituted, and
inducted into the other's benefice; and the other is likewise instituted into his, but the first dieth before he is
inducted into his benefice, although after a mandate
made by the bishop for his induction, (although the induction of the first was absolute), yet, because it was
directed by the precedent agreement, which ought to be
executed on both parts in the lifetime of the parties,
(which in this case it was not for want of induction), the
exchange is void. Fitzh. Abr., Exchange, 10, *Lord Crom-
well's case*, 2 Co. 74. b. The like law if before the completing of the exchange by mutual presentment, institution, and induction, the reason of the exchange fail; *Colt*

(a) See 2 Rep. 74 b.

and *Glover* v. *The Bishop of Lichfield and Coventry*, Hob. 150; for respect must be had to the resignation and protestation of both incumbents. And therefore either incumbent may return to his old benefice, in pristino statu, upon his former presentments." There is a case precisely to the same effect in Burn's Ecclesiastical Law, vol. 2, p. 242, where it is said: "Thus, where one is both instituted and inducted, and the other is only instituted and dies, or refuses to finish, in this case, though they have proceeded so far, yet the resignation and all that followeth upon it shall be void, and both (if both are living) may return to their former benefices upon the foot of former possession; or if one dies before he is inducted, and after the induction of the other, this induction and all that went before shall be void, because the exchange was not fully executed during the lives of the parties." For this Gibson's Codex, 821, is cited as an authority; and it is added from Degge's Parson's Counsellor, "and this is agreeable to the reason of the common law, for at the common law, if a man exchange lands, and the lands he receives in exchange be evicted, he may repair to his own lands and re-enter upon them." There is more analogy between estates ecclesiastical and estates at common law than may at first be supposed.

This is an action of tort, which is founded upon the estate of the parties. It is not annexed to the person in any way; and if the legal seisin in fee is not in the parties, the action cannot be maintained: *Wright* v. *Smythies*(a), *Browne* v. *Ramsden*(b). Those cases shew that the right of action is annexed to the estate. Then what estate has the parson in his glebe? In Co. Lit. 341. a. it is said,—"In whom the fee simple of the glebe is, is a question in our books. Some hold that it is in the patron; but that cannot be for two reasons. First, for that in the beginning the land was given to the parson and his successors, and the patron is no successor. Secondly, the

(a) 10 East, 409.   (b) 2 Moore, 612.

words of the writ of juris utrum be, 'si sit libera eleemo-
sina ecclesiæ de D.', and not of the patron. Some others
do hold that the fee-simple is in the patron and ordinary; but this cannot be for the causes above said: and
therefore, of necessity, the fee-simple is in abeyance, as
Littleton saith. And this was provided by the provi-
dence and wisdom of the law; for that the parson and
vicar have curam animarum, and were bound to cele-
brate divine service, and administer the sacraments; and
therefore no act of the predecessor should make a discontinuance to take away the entry of the successor, and to
drive him to a real action, whereby he should be destitute
of maintenance in the meantime. Upon consideration of
all our books I observe this diversity, that a parson or
vicar, for the benefit of the church and of his successor, is
in some cases esteemed in law to have a fee-simple qualified; but to do anything to the prejudice of his successor
in many cases, the law adjudgeth him to have in effect
but an estate for life." And he adds,—" Causæ ecclesiæ publicis causis æquiparantur; and summa ratio
est quæ pro religione facit. And Ecclesia fungitur vice
minoris; meliorem facere potest conditionem suam, deteri-
orem nequaquam. As a parson, vicar, archdeacon, pre-
bend, chantery priest, and the like, may have an action of
waste, and in the writ it shall be said, ad exhæredationem
ecclesiæ, &c. ipsius B. or præbendæ ipsius A." From this
circumstance, of the action of waste lying, it seems clear
that the action is annexed to the estate.

Hence it would seem that the parson for some purposes
has the fee, though for other purposes the law considers
him as having only a life estate. Then what estate has he
for the purpose of exchanging his benefice? If a fee, then
the whole fee would pass by the contract of exchange, and
any claim for dilapidations by either is out of the question :
if a life estate merely, the analogies which hold at common
law with respect to estates would apply here, and the plaintiff is in the situation of a remainder man who has pur-

chased from the particular tenant his life estate, and it is not for him to complain that he has not so good a bargain as he expected. It is, however, for certain purposes only that he has merely a life estate; for the purpose of an exchange he has an estate in fee. He has power by law to exchange with the consent of the patron and ordinary; for that purpose he has the fee, and by the contract he passes the whole fee, and not merely the estate of the person in remainder after him. If so, no right of action can pass to the present plaintiff. And if it were a life estate, the same argument would prevail to nearly the same extent. Where a party takes an estate by contract, he cannot resort to an action of tort at common law, for the doing that to which he was a party. It was suggested by the Lord Chief Baron, whether a party who contracted for his own benefit, and agreed to waive the claim for dilapidations, would not be chargeable with simony. It may be questionable whether he would. There may be cases in which it would be for the benefit of the church that a fresh incumbent should be made liable for the dilapidations; and there is the protection of the consent of the patron and ordinary being necessary to the exchange. It is clearly for the benefit of the church that parties should be allowed thus to exchange. The diocesan will take care of the interests of the church, and the patron will also take care that no injustice is done to that which cannot, perhaps, be said to be his own inheritance, but is pretty nearly so. The inconvenience would seem to be the other way. If an agreement upon the subject be simoniacal, how is the question to be settled between the parties? It can only be by two cross actions in every case of an exchange. It is a strong point in the defendant's favour, that no such action as this has ever been heard of, which tends to shew that such an action would not lie, as exchanges like this are of every-day occurrence.

Lord ABINGER, C. B.—It might be a very considerable question, whether, if a contract for the exchange of livings were made in writing, with an express declaration that

neither party should sue the other fort he dilapidations,—
if one party said, If you will admit me to your living, I will
admit you to mine, and I will make no claims for dilapidations,—it would not amount to a simoniacal contract, and
so would be void.   At present I do not see that it makes
any difference whether it be a contract with a party to resign in favour of another, or whether it be a contract for
an exchange, which may possibly fail in the completion.
But it is unnecessary in this case to pronounce a judgment
on that point, for here the exchange was made and completed.   Then the only question is, whether an agreement
simply to exchange, has necessarily and fairly engrafted
upon it the condition that neither party shall be liable to
the other for dilapidations.   I see nothing to shew that,
and I do not see any consequence, derived from the admitted contract to exchange, and the exchange actually
completed, operating against the right of the party entering to claim for dilapidations.   The facts found in this
case preclude the necessity of the Court considering the
effect of a positive agreement to that effect; there is no
such agreement here; the parties have the same right as
they would have in case of a presentation to a living, when
it is clear that the plaintiff would have a right to claim for
dilapidations against his predecessor.   I think, therefore,
that the judgment must be in his favour.

PARKE, B.—I entirely agree in opinion with the Lord
Chief Baron. The first question is, whether there is in
this case any agreement between the parties, that if the
living were exchanged, each should omit to sue the other,
and in effect give up to the other any claim for dilapidations. The case finds that there was no specific agreement, and it would be very wrong to infer from the facts
stated in the case, that there was such an agreement; and
even if there were, I cannot help concurring in the
doubt which has been expressed by my Lord, whether it

would be valid and binding. It appears to me to savour of simony.

The next question is, whether by law the claim for dilapidations does not apply to a successor by exchange, as well as to another. The law upon that subject is expressed in the written declaration of what was the common course in the olden times. In the case of *Wise* v. *Metcalfe* (a), that declaration will be found to be the foundation of the judgment of the Court, and it is extended to all rectors. It states in effect (b), that " all prebends, rectors, vicars, &c., shall be required to repair and support their parsonages, and so on, and to deliver them to their successor repaired and supported; and if they do not, they shall pay such a sum to their successors as shall be necessary for the reparation or necessary re-edification of the house or building." That statement of the law applies to all successors of persons ceasing to possess the living. If they have permitted dilapidations, they are to pay to their successors so much as shall be necessary to put the rectory into a proper state of repair. Such being the law, there is no doubt the plaintiff was the successor of the defendant. It is said that it could not be known till the exchange was completed whether he would be his successor; there can be no doubt that it was a defeasible right to the living, until the other incumbent was inducted; but I do not think there can be any doubt, that when induction took place on his taking possession, he became the successor, and his predecessor became liable for the dilapidations. The circumstance of the right being defeasible I do not think constitutes a defence; but it is unnecessary to decide that question here, because the other incumbent was inducted also. The case therefore appears to me to be clear on both points. It is found that there was no agreement between the parties that the one should give up the right to

(a) 10 B. & Cr. 299; 5 Man. & Ry. 235, 965.

(b) See 1 Lutw. 116; Degge's Parson's Counsellor, p. 138, pl. 94.

dilapidation as against the other, and there is no exemption to the operation of the general law applying to a case of mutual resignation with a view to an exchange of livings.

GURNEY, B.—It is found that there was no agreement here, and therefore the common law must prevail.

ROLFE, B.—I am of the same opinion. Suppose, instead of an exchange, it had been an acceptance by the other party of the living, there is no doubt the common-law right would have attached; and I see no ground for making the slightest difference. This is an acceptance of a living under a special contract,—a case in which the law allows a contract, that in consideration of one resigning his living, the other shall resign also. I do not enter into the argument as to what would be the law in the intermediate period between the first and the second presentation. I think the same principle would still apply, but there is a great analogy between this and the exchange of land—the exchange may become wholly void by the death of one of the parties before the transaction is completed. Upon the whole, I entirely concur in the opinion which has been expressed, and particularly in the doubt intimated by my Lord, whether an agreement to waive the claim for dilapidations would have been a valid agreement.

Judgment for the plaintiff.

Exch. of Pleas,
1841.

Nov. 24.

STANILAND *v.* HOPKINS.

By an act of
Parliament cre-
ating a Court
of Requests for
the borough of
Boston, it was
enacted, that
the mayor, re-
corder, deputy
recorder, alder-
men, and com-
mon councilmen
for the time be-
ing of the bo-
rough, the jus-
tices of the
peace for a cer-
tain district,
together with
other persons
therein men-
tioned, should
be the commis-
sioners thereof;
and that in case
of a vacancy in
the situation of
clerk of the
court, &c., the
mayor and al-
dermen of the

THIS was an action for money had and received by the
defendant to the use of the plaintiff, and on an account
stated between them. The defendant pleaded the general issue, non assumpsit, and a verdict was found for the
plaintiff, with £167 damages, subject to the following
case, with liberty for either party to turn it into a special
verdict.

By an act of the 47 Geo. 3, c. 1, s. 2, intituled "An
Act for the more speedy recovery of Small Debts in the
borough and parish of Boston, and the hundreds of Skirbeck and Kirton, except the parishes of Gosberton and
Surfleet, in the county of Lincoln," after reciting that the
borough of Boston is an ancient corporation, as well by
prescription as charter, and also that it would greatly
tend to the encouragement of trade in the said borough
and in the said parishes and places, if certain local acts
of Parliament were repealed, and more extensive powers

borough, for the time being, or the major part of them, should appoint a successor, and that
until such appointment should be made, the commissioners or any three or more of them should
nominate officers to do the business of the Court. At a meeting of the town council of B., specially summoned for the purpose of electing a clerk, the plaintiff, who was a member of the
council, was elected by the council, and before the end of the election he tendered to the
mayor his resignation of the office of town councillor, together with the sum of £50 as a fine
on resignation, under 5 & 6 Will. 4, c. 76, s. 51. No bye-law had been made to enforce a fine
on resignation, and therefore the mayor returned the £50, in the presence of the council, after
the election. The plaintiff's seat in the council was afterwards filled by the election of another
person, and at a quarterly meeting of the town council, held on the 7th of May, 1840, of which
no notice had been given, the plaintiff was again elected by the town council:—*Held*, first,
that neither the 73rd section of 5 & 6 Will. 4, c. 76, nor the 8th section of 6 & 7 Will. 4, c. 105,
was applicable to this case.

Secondly, that the case was within the 72nd section of 5 & 6 Will. 4, c. 76; the true construction of which was, that the body corporate, under that act, should be trustees or commissioners for executing, by the town council, the *powers and provisions* of all acts of Parliament, of
which *powers and provisions* the old body corporate, or any of the members thereof, in their
corporate capacity, were sole commissioners or trustees before the election of the town council:
and as the mayor and aldermen were, by the local act, sole trustees or commissioners for the
purpose of appointing the clerk, that their powers devolved upon the town council, and that
the plaintiff was duly elected at the first meeting: that, under all the circumstances of the case,
the plaintiff's resignation of the office of town councillor was sufficient: but that if it was not,
his election to the office of clerk had the effect of vacating his office of town councillor.

vested in commissioners, to hear and determine plaints con-

cerning debts not exceeding £5, arising within the said borough and parish of Boston, and the said hundreds of Skirbeck and Kirton, except the parishes of Gosberton and
Surfleet, it was enacted, "That the mayor, recorder, deputy recorder, aldermen, and common councilmen of the
said borough of Boston for the time being, the several justices of the peace for the parts of Holland in the said
county for the time being, residing in and acting for the
said parts, the several ministers of the parish churches
within the said hundreds of Kirton and Skirbeck, for the
time being, and the several other persons therein named,
should be and they were thereby appointed commissioners,
and they and their successors were thereby constituted a
court of justice, by the name of the Court of Requests for the
borough and parish of Boston, and the hundreds of Skirbeck and Kirton, except &c., in the county of Lincoln; and
the said commissioners were thereby empowered and required to meet and assemble, and to hold the said Court
on Monday in every week, in the Guildhall of the said
borough, or in some other convenient place within the said
borough, to be appointed by the major part of the said
commissioners for that purpose assembled; that the first
meeting of the said commissioners should be holden on the
third Monday next after the passing of the said act, and the
commissioners present should elect a chairman for that
meeting, and so at each succeeding meeting; and the said
commissioners, or the major part of them who should be
present at such meetings, not being less than three, (except as thereinafter mentioned), were thereby authorized
and empowered to hear and determine all such actions and
causes as were thereinafter mentioned, and to give such
judgments, and to make such orders and decrees therein,
and to award execution thereupon, with the costs, against
the body or bodies, or against the goods of all and every
other the person and persons against whom they should

give any such judgments, or make any order or decree as should to them seem just in law or equity; and in case of any equality of votes in any action, cause, or question before the said commissioners, the said chairman, so elected, should have the casting vote; and if it should happen that no chairman should have been previously elected at that meeting, then and in every such case the commissioner present, who should stand first in the list of names of the said commissioners, should have the decisive or casting vote. And it was thereby further enacted, that when and as often as it should happen that the office of clerk, or serjeant, or crier, or any other officer or officers, should become vacant, either through misbehaviour, death, or resignation, suspension, dismission, removal, or incapacity, then and in every such case it should and might be lawful for the mayor and aldermen of the said borough of Boston for the time being, or the major part of them, and they were thereby required to nominate and appoint another fit and proper person to be clerk, or serjeant, or crier, or other officer or officers of and in the said Court of Requests during his and their good behaviour, and until such nomination and appointments should be made as aforesaid, it should and might be lawful for the said commissioners of the said Court of Requests, or any three or more of them, assembled as aforesaid, to appoint such officers respectively to do the business of the said Court until such nomination and appointment should from time to time be made as aforesaid; and all persons so appointed by the said commissioners, or any three of them, should be and be deemed to be (during such time as they should respectively act) officers under the said act, to all intents and purposes whatsoever, and entitled to all the advantages and emoluments specified in the said act, and should be subject to be removed from their offices in like manner as the officers from time to time to be appointed by the mayor and aldermen of the said borough of Boston as aforesaid, or the major part of them, for the time being,

were subject to be removed."

By the 10th section of the act, the commissioners had power to remove the clerk for misbehaviour, and, subject to the control of the mayor and aldermen, to appoint a deputy during his removal. A copy of the above-mentioned act accompanied and was to form part of this case.

The council of the said borough, at the time of the several elections of the plaintiff and defendant respectively, as hereinafter mentioned, had not appointed any of their body, under the 73rd section of the 5 & 6 Will. 4, c. 76, to execute the powers, duties, and functions reposed in the mayor and aldermen by the above statute, or to act as commissioners under the above statute. On the 23rd of November, 1839, Mr. Francis Thirkill, the clerk of the said Court, died, and the office thereby became vacant. On the 2nd of December, 1839, at a meeting of the town council, specially summoned for the purpose of electing a clerk to the said Court, the defendant was first elected by the mayor and aldermen only, after which an election took place before the town council, at which both the plaintiff and the defendant were candidates. They were both members of the town council, and out of courtesy they each voted for the other at the election of the town council. Immediately after the plaintiff had voted for the defendant, and before the election was completed, he tendered his resignation to the mayor, in a letter, with £50. The mayor afterwards returned the £50. The plaintiff was elected by the council, eleven members of the council voting for the plaintiff, and ten for the defendant. There was no bye-law to enforce a fine on resignation; and therefore the mayor returned the £50 in the presence of the council after the election. Afterwards, on the 12th of December, the plaintiff's seat at the council was filled by an election of Mr. Wedd by the burgesses of the same ward. At a quarterly meeting of the town council, on the 7th of May, 1840, the plaintiff was re-elected by the council. No previous notice had been given of the intention to elect a clerk of the Court of Requests at that meeting. The defendant has always, since his election by the mayor and aldermen, acted as clerk of the said court, and has received fees to the amount of £167.

The question for the opinion of the Court was, whether the plaintiff had been duly elected clerk of the said court; if so, the verdict for the plaintiff was to stand; otherwise a verdict was to be entered for the defendant.

The case was argued early in this Term (Nov. 10), by

Hill, for the plaintiff.—The main question in this case is, in whom the right of election is vested. The Boston Court of Requests Act enacts, " that the mayor, recorder, deputy recorder, aldermen, and common councilmen of the Borough of Boston, with the justices of Holland, the ministers of certain parishes, and several other persons named in the act, shall be commissioners of the court;" and it also enacts, " that in case of a vacancy in the office of clerk, or serjeant, or crier, &c., of such court, it should be lawful for the mayor and aldermen of the said borough of Boston for the time being, or the major part of them, and they are thereby required to nominate and appoint another fit and proper person for that purpose." That power, which was formerly vested in the mayor and aldermen, the plaintiff contends, is now vested, by the Municipal Corporation Act, in the town council, and they having appointed him to the office in question, his appointment is valid. The case falls within the 72nd section of 5 & 6 Will. 4, c. 76, which enacts, " that the body corporate named in the said schedules (A) and (B) in conjunction with any borough, shall be trustees for executing, by the council of such borough, the powers and provisions of all acts of Parliament made before the passing of this act, (other than acts made for securing charitable uses and trusts), and of all trusts (other than charitable uses and trusts) of which the said body corporate, or any of the members thereof in their corporate capacity, was or were sole trustees before the time of the first election of councillors in such borough under this act." The effect of that section is to vest in the town council the execution of all the powers and provisions of all acts of Parliament made before the passing of the Municipal Act, of which powers and provisions the old corporations were the sole trustees and (by the interpretation clause, section 142) commissioners. The 73rd section enacts, " that in every borough in which the body corporate &c. was or were before the passing of this act trustees, jointly with other trustees, for the execution of any act of Parliament, or of any trust, or in which the body corporate &c. by any statute, charter, bye-law, or custom, was or were before the passing of this act lawfully appointed to or exercised any powers, duties, or functions whatsoever, not otherwise herein provided for, the council of such borough shall appoint a like number of councillors to be joint trustees as there were theretofore members or nominees of such corporate body." That section, therefore, provides for two other classes of cases: one where the old corporations were *joint* trustees with other parties; the other where they exercised powers and functions not otherwise provided for by the Municipal Corporation Act. The appointment of the clerk of the court under the local Act was vested solely in the mayor and aldermen, who were trustees of the *powers and provisions* of the local Act, and therefore it now vests in the town council under the 72nd section. The argument on the other side is, that the town council have no right to appoint the clerk; according to their construction of the 72nd section, the town council have only a right to interfere in cases where the old corporations were the trustees of *entire* acts of Parliament, and not merely of *some* of the powers and provi-

sions contained therein; and that as the mayor and aldermen of the old corporation were the commissioners, not
of the *whole* act of Parliament, but only of that part relating to the election of the clerk and officers of the Court,
the case falls within the 73rd section: and it will be contended that it was the duty of the town council to appoint
a certain number of their own body, in whom the right of
electing the clerk should vest. That construction, however, is at variance both with the grammatical interpretation of the section, and the object and purposes of the act.
Whatever was the intention of the last clause of the 73rd
section, it clearly refers to other duties and cases than
those mentioned in the 72nd section.

Secondly, the plaintiff was twice elected: first, on the
2nd of December, 1839, by the town council, at a meeting specially convened for that purpose, pursuant to the
69th section of 5 & 6 Will. 4, c. 76; and secondly, on the
7th of May, 1840, at a quarterly meeting of the town
council, of which, however, no notice was given. But no
notice was necessary, for the election of clerk fell within
the description of *general business,* which, by the 69th
section, might be transacted at a quarterly meeting without notice, or might be transacted at a quarterly meeting
by the town council under 6 & 7 Will. 4, c. 105, s. 8, which
provides that the town council may do at a quarterly meeting "every thing provided under any local act of Parliament to be done exclusively by any particular or limited
number, class, or description of the members of any
body corporate named in the schedules (A) and (B) annexed to the said act." The quarterly meeting, therefore, had jurisdiction and exercised it properly, and no
notice of those meetings was necessary, as they are fixed
by the act.

But, thirdly, it will be said that the plaintiff, being a
member of the town council at the time the election
began, was ineligible, because the town council as com-

missioners had power to remove officers of the Court of Requests, and he had thereby a control over his own removal. But the answer to that is, that at common law the functions of clerk and town councillor are not incompatible; and that the town council have joint and not exclusive powers of removing officers, the power of removal being in the commissioners generally, under the provisions of the local act. [*Parke*, B.—The town council are to elect commissioners to fulfil the duties of joint commissioners with the justices. If the plaintiff continues a member of the town council, there is a difficulty in saying that he is eligible as clerk, because he would have the right of voting for the commissioners, who have the power of appointment as to himself.] If the offices are incompatible, his office of town councillor would be vacated. In *Rex* v. *Tizzard* (a), where, in the borough of Weymouth, the appointment of the town clerk was in the mayor, aldermen, and bailiffs, to hold the office during their pleasure, with a salary which they had power to alter in amount or withdraw altogether; and one of the town clerk's duties was to attend all corporate meetings of the mayor, aldermen, &c., and draw up minutes of their proceedings under their inspection: it was held that the offices of alderman and town clerk were incompatible, because he would fill the situation of master and servant, and that an alderman by accepting the latter vacated the former office. That principle was recognised in *Rex* v. *Jones* (b), and also in *Rex* v. *Patteson* (c), where the offices of common councilman and town clerk were held not to be incompatible, because the common council were not the masters of the town clerk, and had no power of removing him or of fixing his salary. Again, the plaintiff, before the end of the election, tendered his re-

(a) 9 B. & Cr. 418.　　　　(b) 1 B. & Ad. 681.
　　　　(c) 4 B. & Ad. 9.

signation of the office of town councillor, which the council, being by the 6th section of the Municipal Act 5 & 6 Will. 4 invested with all the powers of the old corporation, were competent to accept. Besides, the 28th section of the 5 & 6 Will. 4, c. 76, is applicable to this case. That section enacts, "that no person shall be qualified to be elected, or to be a councillor or alderman" of any such borough, "during such time as he shall hold any office or place of profit other than that of mayor, in the gift or disposal of the council of such borough." This is a place of profit in the gift of the council, and might be given by them to the plaintiff. There is nothing in the act to prevent the town council from conferring such a place upon one of their own body. The effect of this section is, to disqualify the holder of a place of profit from being elected a town councillor, and as soon as he is elected to such an office he would cease to be a member of the town council.

The Solicitor-General, contrà.—The appointment of the clerk of the Court of Requests is not in the town council of this borough. The power to elect a clerk was, by the local Act, in a portion only of the corporation. This case does not fall within the 72nd section, as that was intended to apply to cases where the whole corporation were the sole trustees of "acts of Parliament" or of "trusts." Here the mayor and aldermen were not the sole trustees of the local act of Parliament, for the other commissioners were associated with them in its execution. The case comes within the 73rd section, which applies to cases where the old corporation were trustees *jointly* with other persons, or where a limited number of them were by any *statute,* bye-law, or custom, "appointed to or exercised any powers, duties, or functions whatsoever, not otherwise herein provided for." The use of the word *statute* shews that the powers there alluded to are not those of a corporate nature only. The town council ought to have appointed an equal number of their own body with those of Exch. of Pleas, the old corporation, who before had the power to elect the clerk of the Court of Requests. It may well be conceived that the legislature intended that the ten or twelve persons, who constituted the body of mayor and aldermen, were proper persons to make the appointment, and not that a meeting of the whole town council should proceed to a general election of the clerk. It is clear that the right to nominate the clerk is not in the town council, but in a limited number to be appointed by them.

But it is said that this case may fall within the 6 & 7 Will. 4, c. 105, s. 8, which enacts, " that every thing provided, under any local act of Parliament, to be done *exclusively* by any particular or limited number, class, or description of the members of any body corporate named in the schedules (A) and (B) annexed to the said act for regulating corporations, the continuance of which is not inconsistent with the provisions of the said act, and also every thing provided in any such local acts to be done by the justices, or by some particular class or description of members of such body corporate, being justices, at some court of general or quarter sessions assembled, and *which does not relate to the business of a Court of criminal or civil judicature,* shall and may be done by the council at some quarterly meeting of the council, or by some committee of the council, or any three or more of such committee to be appointed at a quarterly meeting of the council." It is said that this is something done *exclusively* under a local act of parliament by a limited number of the body corporate, "which does not relate to the business of a Court of civil or criminal judicature." But that is not so; for, first, the appointment of a clerk was not a thing to be done under the local act *exclusively* by the mayor and aldermen; for the commissioners generally, or any three of them, had the power to nominate a clerk until the mayor and aldermen have made the appointment;

secondly, that section is not in the plaintiff's favour, because the words ": which does not relate to the business of a Court of criminal or civil judicature," override the whole of the clause, and then the true construction of the clause is, that the town council shall execute no functions which relate to the criminal or civil business of a court of justice; the object being to prevent the town council from interfering with the administration of justice. [*Parke*, B. —The legislature seem to have thought, that by transferring all the business of a Court of criminal and civil judicature to the recorder, and all the other business done by justices at quarter sessions, not relating to criminal or civil judicature, to the council, they had disposed of the whole business.] The words "relating to a Court of criminal or civil judicature," it is submitted, extend to the whole of the section, and then the appointment of a clerk of the Court of Requests is a matter which relates "to the business of a court of civil judicature," and therefore does not belong to the town council. In *Palmer* v. *Powell* (a), it was held that the fees of the assessor and clerk of the Court of Requests did relate to the business of a Court of civil judicature, and therefore that the town council had no authority to reduce them. The words "business of a court" cannot be confined to its mere judicial business. The clerk transacts the whole ministerial business of the court. The object of the legislature was to prevent this large body of persons from interfering with anything relating to the business of a court or the appointment of its officers. Suppose, under the local act, the mayor had been a judge of the court, could it be contended that the town council would be the judges, and have power by vote at their quarterly meetings to sentence criminals to transportation? There would be no end to the absurdities that would follow if this is held to apply to the mem-

(a) 6 M. & W. 627.

bers of the corporate body. [*Rolfe*, B.—By the 118th section of the 5 & 6 Will. 4, c. 76, the town council have the power in certain cases of appointing the necessary officer, other than the recorder, for the trial of civil actions. That seems to shew that the object of the legislature was not to exclude the town council from the appointment.] It perhaps might be more correct to argue on behalf of the defendant, that, as this power is before vested in other persons, the 8th section does not apply to this case at all, but to those cases only which are omitted in the 73rd and other sections of the 5 & 6 Will. 4, c. 76. If this case is within the Municipal Act at all, it is within the 73rd section and not within the 72nd.

Then with respect to the objection that the plaintiff at the time of the election was a member of the town council. The offices of town councillor and clerk of the court are incompatible; for the plaintiff, in his capacity of town councillor, would, under the provisions of the local act, have a voice if a question as to his own removal should arise, and might thereby keep himself in office. In *Rex* v. *Patteson*, it is laid down that the acceptance of an incompatible office does not operate as an avoidance of a former office, where the party cannot divest himself of that office by his own act. These offices being incompatible, the plaintiff was therefore ineligible. He could not resign his office into the hands of the burgesses, who have the election of the town councillors, for they had no power to meet for the purpose of accepting his resignation, and the council had no power to accept his resignation, nor could he resign his office at all under the circumstances of the case. By the 51st section of 5 & 6 Will. 4, c. 76, it is provided that a councillor when elected shall accept the office, or in lieu thereof shall pay such fine, not exceeding £50, as the council by a bye-law shall declare. In this case no bye-law had been made fixing the sum to be paid on resignation; it could not therefore be paid, and no resignation could take place. Then the second election is void, because there was no notice of the meeting of the town council; for the appointment of a clerk of the Court of Requests is not such "general business" of the corporation as by the 69th section may be transacted without notice. But it is contended that the plaintiff's office of town councillor was vacated and made void by his acceptance of an office of profit in the gift of the town council; but if the office of town councillor could not be got rid of directly by resignation, neither could it by indirect means: and the plaintiff was therefore ineligible.

Hill replied.

Cur. adv. vult.

The judgment of the Court was now delivered by

Lord ABINGER, C. B.—The plaintiff in this case claims to be the clerk of the court for the recovery of small debts for the Borough of Boston, and certain hundreds of the county of Lincoln. His title to that office depends upon two questions:—first, whether the town council of Boston had the power of appointing that officer; and secondly, whether he was ineligible by reason of having been at the time of the election a member of the town council. By the local Act, 47 Geo. 3, establishing the small debts court above mentioned, the mayor, recorder, deputy recorder, aldermen, and common councilmen of Boston, and several other persons therein named, were made commissioners of the court. On the vacancy of the office of clerk of the court, the mayor and aldermen of Boston had power to nominate his successor, whenever such nomination should be made, and the commissioners at large were to appoint an officer to act in the meantime; and the clerk was liable to be removed for misbehaviour by the commissioners, acting in open court, and they might appoint a deputy during

his absence, subject to the control of the mayor and aldermen only. A vacancy having occurred in the office of clerk,
the town council proceeded to an election without having
at any previous time named an equal or any number
of persons to act as commissioners, and the first and most
important question in the case is, whether they were legally empowered to elect. This appears to us to depend
upon the construction of the 72nd clause of the Municipal
Act, which provides,—"that the body corporate named in
the said schedules (A.) and (B.), in conjunction with any
borough, shall be trustees for executing, by the council of
such borough, the powers and provisions of all acts of Parliament made before the passing of this act (other than
acts made for securing charitable uses and trusts), and of
all trusts (other than charitable uses and trusts) of which
the said body corporate, or any of the members thereof in
their corporate capacity, was or were sole trustees before
the time of the first election of councillors in such borough
under this act." Now we think that the 72nd clause may
reasonably be construed so as to bring the present case
within its provisions; and if so, the 73rd clause, which has
been the subject of much argument, and the object of
which (the latter part of it) is very obscure, is put out of
the question, because the only thing very certain in that
clause is, that it does not apply to any case before provided
for by that act. If, therefore, the particular case has been
before provided for, we ought not to search into the 73rd
clause for a different provision, nor for doubts to be thrown
on the fair interpretation of the preceding clause. If then,
for the purpose of construing the 72nd clause, we call in aid
the interpretation clause, sect. 142, by which it is provided
that the word "trustees" shall be taken to mean not only
trustees, but "commissioners or directors, or the person
charged with the execution of a trust or public duty," we may
read the clause thus:—"The body corporate of each borough
shall be trustees and commissioners for executing, or shall be

charged with the duty of executing, by the council of such borough, the powers and provisions of all acts of Parliament now made, and of all trusts, of which powers and provisions, or trusts, the body corporate, or any of the members thereof in their corporate capacity, was or were sole commissioners or trustees respectively, or were solely charged with the duty of executing them, before the time of the first election of councillors in such borough." And this, we think, is the true mode of construing the clause. It is however contended, that, by the grammatical construction of the 72nd section, the relative "which" applies to the next antecedent, namely, "acts of Parliament," and not to "powers and provisions," and that the section, therefore, must be read as applying only to those cases in which the body corporate, or a part of it, are sole commissioners in an act of Parliament, or solely charged with the duty of executing all the powers of it; but, besides the objection to this construction, that there is probably no act of Parliament in which a corporate body, or a part of it, is solely charged with all the duties prescribed by it, the relative may, without any impropriety, refer to "all powers and provisions," and not to the words "all acts of Parliament;" and the more so, as full operation is thereby given to this section, which, in the more limited construction, would be hardly applicable to any case whatever. It is true that, in strict grammatical construction, the relative ought to apply to the last antecedent; but there are numerous examples in the best writers to shew, that the context may often require a deviation from this rule, and that the relative may be connected with nouns which go before the last antecedent, and either take from it or give to it some qualification. Suppose, for example, this phrase —"If there be any powers or provisions of an act of Parliament, of which the corporation are sole commissioners for executing,"—is it not obvious here that the relative "which" refers to the "powers and provisions," and not to the " act of Parliament?" So in the 72nd clause, the *Exch. of Pleas,* 1841.

words " sole trustees," when properly interpreted, mean, with reference to the powers and provisions of acts of Parliament, sole commissioners for executing them. If, then, the clause in question may properly be read in this way, which we think it may, there can be no doubt that the town council were entitled to elect the clerk, provided the mayor and aldermen were before, by the local act, sole commissioners for that purpose, or solely charged with the duty of appointing the clerk; and we are all of opinion that they were, because, although the other commissioners were authorized to appoint ad interim, the mayor and aldermen alone could appoint absolutely. Upon the true construction of the 72nd section, the right of nomination and election was in the town council, and if they duly elected the plaintiff at the first meeting of the 2nd December, 1839, his title to the office is good, and it is unnecessary to consider whether it could have been maintained by the subsequent election on the 7th May, 1840, which took place by virtue of the 8th section of 6 & 7 Will. 4, c. 105, for this section is admitted to give an additional power to the town council, and not to repeal or alter the powers given before: and we all think that he was duly elected at the first meeting.

The next objection to the election was, that when the meeting commenced, the plaintiff was a member of the town council, and was therefore ineligible to the office of clerk of the Court of Requests, that office being incompatible with the office of town councillor, and that disability not having been removed when the election took place. But if the offices were incompatible, as we think they were, by reason of the control over the clerk given by the 10th section of the local act to the mayor and aldermen, and consequently, for the reasons before given, transferred to the town council as their substitute, the question still remains, whether the effect of such incompatibility was to render a town councillor ineligible, or whether the election and acceptance of the office of clerk absolutely vacated the office of town councillor. It has been argued, on the one hand, that the plaintiff could not resign his office of town councillor, because no bye-law had been made to impose a fine for the non-acceptance of the office, and by the 8th section of the 6 & 7 Will. 4, c. 105, the power of resignation there given is only conditional on the party paying such fine as shall have been imposed on him for non-acceptance of the office. On the other hand, it was said that a power of resignation to those who were competent to accept it, is by the common law incident to every corporate office; that the 8th section of 6 & 7 Will. 4, c. 105, was intended to extend that power to cases where the acceptance might be refused; that the town council were the only body now competent to accept the resignation, and that the law has been settled, that the appointment to an office incompatible with one held before by the same person, makes ipso facto the first office vacant, provided the person appointing was competent to have received the resignation of the first office. It was said, moreover, that the 5 & 6 Will. 4, c. 76, did not make it imperative on the town council to make any bye-law to impose a fine for the non-acceptance of office, and that it never could be intended that the majority of that body should have the power, by refusing to make such bye-law, to control the right of resignation intended by the last statute to be given to officers, whether the town council chose to accept the resignation or not; and then, having made no bye-law to impose a fine for non-acceptance, the party elected might either refuse to accept the office, or, having accepted it, might resign without paying any fine.

Again, it was insisted on the part of the defendant, that as, by the 28th section of the Municipal Corporation Act, no one could be elected or be a town councillor, during the time that he should hold an office of profit in the gift of the town council, it must be inferred that the town councillor was incapable of being elected to such office, and if so, that the present election was void. To which it was answered, that the effect of this clause was not to make a town councillor ineligible, but merely to vacate his office on his acceptance of an office of profit in the gift of the town council; not to make the election void, but to make him cease to be a town councillor by the very act of accepting the other office. The Court is well aware of the difficulty of putting a construction on this act of Parliament which is free from doubt and perplexity, arising from an endeavour to frame, by one act of Parliament, one universal charter for all municipal corporations, and to combine with that object all the principles of corporation law that are to be found in a long series of judicial decisions. If we are wrong in the conclusions we have formed in this case, it is some consolation to us to know that it will be open to the defendant to obtain the decisions of the other Judges, by turning the case into a special verdict. We are bound to express the best opinion we can form, on both views taken of this latter branch of the question; and that opinion is in favour of the plaintiff, that his resignation, under all the circumstances, was sufficient; but that if it was not, his election to the office now in question had the effect of vacating his office of town councillor; and therefore our judgment must be for the plaintiff.

Exch. of Pleas,
1841.
STANILAND
v.
HOPKINS.

Judgment for the plaintiff (a).

(a) See *Regina* v. *Hopkins*, 1 Ad. & E., N. S. 161.

Exch. of Pleas,
1841.

Nov. 22.

PURSSORD *v.* PEEK.

Assumpsit on a bill of exchange drawn by one S. B. upon and accepted by the defendant, for £25, payable three months after date.
Plea, that after the bill became due, and before the commencement of the suit, to wit &c., the said S. B. paid to the plaintiff divers monies, to the amount of £17, and did for the plaintiff work and labour to the value of £8, in full satisfaction and discharge of the sum of money in the bill specified, and of all damages sustained by the non-payment thereof, which were then accepted and received by the plaintiff in such full satisfaction and discharge: and further, that he the defendant accepted the bill at the request and for the accommodation of the said S. B., and not otherwise, and that there never was any considera-

ASSUMPSIT.—The declaration stated, that one S. Barley, on the 28th February, 1839, made his bill of exchange in writing, and directed the same to the defendant, and thereby required the defendant to pay to his the said S. Barley's order the sum of £25, three months after the date thereof, which period had elapsed before the commencement of this suit, and the defendant then accepted the said bill, and the said S. Barley then indorsed the same to the plaintiff, of all which the defendant then had due notice, and then promised, &c.

Plea, that after the said bill had become due and payable, and before the commencement of this suit, to wit, on the 29th of September, 1840, the said S. Barley, in the said first count of the declaration mentioned, paid to the plaintiff divers monies to a large amount, to wit, to the amount of £17, and did for the plaintiff work, and provided materials for the same, of a large price and value, to wit, of the price and value of £8, in full satisfaction and discharge of the said sum of money in the said bill specified, and of all damages sustained by the plaintiff by reason of the non-payment thereof, which payment, and which work and materials, were then accepted and received by the plaintiff of and from the said S. Barley, in such full satisfaction and discharge as aforesaid: and the defendant further says, that he accepted the said bill at the request, and for the accommodation of the said S. Barley, and not otherwise, and that there never was any consideration or value for the payment by the defendant of the said bill, or any part thereof, and that the plaintiff, at the time of the commencement of this suit, held, and

tion or value for the payment by the defendant of the said bill, or any part thereof, and that the plaintiff, at the time of the commencement of the suit, held and now holds the said bill without any consideration or value whatever:—*Held,* that the plea was bad for duplicity.

now holds the said bill without any consideration or value whatever. Verification.

Special demurrer, assigning for causes, that the said plea is double and multifarious, and contains two distinct answers or grounds of defence, either of which would, if the same were true, and could not be answered or avoided, constitute a bar to the said action, as regards the said first count; in this, to wit, that it is not only alleged in the said plea that the said S. Barley paid the plaintiff the said monies, and did the said work, and provided the said materials, in the said plea mentioned, in full satisfaction and discharge of the said sum of money in the said bill specified, and of all damages sustained by the plaintiff by reason of the non-payment thereof, and which payment, and which work and materials, were accepted and received by the plaintiff in such full satisfaction and discharge as aforesaid, such facts, if true, being a defence and answer to the said first count; but it is also averred and alleged in the said plea to the said first count, that the defendant accepted the said bill at the request and for the accommodation of the said S. Barley, and that there never was any consideration or value for the payment thereof by the said defendant, and that the plaintiff held and now holds the said bill without any consideration or value whatsoever, which latter circumstance, if true, would also afford a defence as regards the said bill. And also for that the said plea to the said first count is repugnant, and contains material allegations at variance and inconsistent with each other, in this, to wit, that although in the first part of the said plea it is alleged that the said S. Barley paid and satisfied the said bill as therein mentioned, and thereby admitted that the plaintiff was a holder for value, nevertheless in the subsequent part of the said first plea, the defendant avers and alleges that the plaintiff held and holds the said bill without any value whatsoever: and also for that the first part of the said plea to the said first count is a plea in satisfaction and discharge of the said bill in that count mentioned, and the latter part of the said plea is a plea by way of excuse for the non-payment of the same bill, which is against the rules of good pleading, and the plaintiff cannot take any certain or safe issue on the said plea.

Joinder in demurrer.

Hugh Hill, in support of the demurrer, was stopped by the Court, who called on

Warren to support the plea.—The declaration imports that the acceptance was an acceptance for value, and the bill is negotiable ad infinitum until it is paid or satisfied by the acceptor. To constitute a complete defence, it was necessary to shew, not only that Barley had satisfied the plaintiff, the indorsee, the amount of the bill, but also that the defendant accepted it for Barley's accommodation and without value. In *Callow* v. *Lawrence* (a), where the drawer of a bill payable to his own order, and indorsed by him to one Taylor, and by Taylor to Barnett, upon the bill being dishonoured, paid the amount to Barnett, who struck out his own and Taylor's indorsement, and returned it to the drawer, and the drawer afterwards passed it to the plaintiff; it was held that the plaintiff might recover against the acceptor. The bill is negotiable until it is paid by the acceptor. In *Hubbard* v. *Jackson* (b), where a bill payable to the order of the drawer was dishonoured by the acceptor, and paid by the drawer when due; it was held that the drawer might indorse it over a year and a half afterwards, and that his indorsee might recover against the acceptor. So here, until the plea shewed, not only that the drawer had paid and satisfied the plaintiff the amount of the bill, but that the defendant had accepted it for the drawer's accommodation, it was not a complete

(a) 3 M. & Selw. 95.   (b) 4 Bing. 390; 1 Mo. & P. 11.

defence. [Lord *Abinger*, C. B.—Is it not a complete defence to the action by the present plaintiff, that Barley had satisfied the bill in his hands?] The defendant contends that it is not. It would not appear from the first part of the plea that the defendant was an accommodation acceptor; and then the plaintiff might sue as trustee, until the bill was paid by the acceptor. The substance of the plea is, that the defendant accepted the bill for the accommodation of Barley, and that he satisfied the plaintiff its amount. If the plea had merely shewn satisfaction by the drawer, the plaintiff might have replied that he was suing as his trustee.

Hugh Hill, contrà.—The statement of the acceptance not being for value is not set forth as inducement to the other matter alleged. Those matters constitute two distinct answers. The first is accord and satisfaction, which is of itself a good answer. In *Sard* v. *Rhodes* (a), a plea, to an action on a bill of exchange for £43 by an indorsee against the acceptor, that after the bill became due, the drawer gave the plaintiff his promissory note for £44 in full satisfaction, and that the plaintiff accepted it in satisfaction, was held to be a good answer to the action. [Lord *Abinger*, C. B.—The plea in that case states, in the first instance, that the bill had been accepted for the accommodation of the drawer.] That is so, but it is so stated merely by way of inducement introductory to the satisfaction by the drawer, and there is no allegation as to whether the plaintiff was a holder for value. In *Shearm* v. *Burnard* (b), to an action by the indorsee against the maker of a promissory note, the latter pleaded, that before the making of the note in the declaration mentioned, he made another note for the accommodation of the indorser, who indorsed it to the plaintiff; that when it became due, he the defendant made the note in the declaration mentioned, and

Exch. of Pleas,
1841.

PURSSORD
v.
PEEK.

(a) 1 M. & W. 153.   (b) 2 Per. & D. 565; 10 Ad. & Ell. 593.

gave it to the indorser to take up such prior note; he then averred payment by the indorser to the plaintiff of the note in the declaration mentioned, and acceptance by the plaintiff: and it was held, that the only material part of the plea was payment of the note declared on, and that all the averments as to the prior note were surplusage. And *Littledale*, J., there says:—"If the whole averment as to the first bill be struck out, the plea would afford an answer to the action." [*Parke*, B.—The question is, whether the plaintiff, who has been paid the amount of the bill, could be the person to put the bill in suit without more. In *Callow* v. *Lawrence*, the drawer, after paying the bill, passed it to the plaintiff, who sued the acceptor upon it, and was held entitled to recover. This case goes a step further.] The very case of *Callow* v. *Lawrence* shews that this plea is double, since it first answers the original title which the plaintiff acquired by the indorsement to him from Barley, and then professes to answer a second title, which it is assumed the plaintiff may have as trustee for Barley, after Barley had satisfied the amount as alleged in the plea: so that viewing the plea in this light, it is clearly double, since it contains two answers, each being applicable to a distinct title to the amount of the bill. If the plea had merely alleged the satisfaction by Barley, and the plaintiff had relied on his supposed title as trustee, the plaintiff should in such case specially reply such title, and then the allegations contained in the latter part of the plea might have been rejoined. It is however submitted, that the latter part of the plea must be treated as a distinct and separate answer to the plaintiff's title by the indorsement to him, and that he could not acquire a title as trustee for the drawer, when his own claim as indorsee was satisfied. In *Bacon* v. *Searles* (a), it was held that the

(a) 1 H. Bl. 88.

indorsee of a bill of exchange, having received part of the

contents from the drawer, could not recover more than the residue from the acceptor; and that where the drawer pays the whole, the acceptor is entirely discharged. There Lord *Loughborough* says, " When a bill of exchange is drawn, the drawer orders the acceptor to pay so much of his money to a third person; but if he anticipates the acceptor, and pays the money himself, he thereby releases the acceptor from his undertaking: so that if the acceptor were to pay the bill after notice given him that the drawer had already paid it, an action would lie for the drawer against the acceptor to recover back the money so paid." *Gould,* J., says, " The doctrine contended for would go the length of proving, that the holder of a bill having received the whole money from the drawer, might recover it again from the acceptor." And *Wilson,* J., says, " The drawer having paid part and the acceptor the residue, the contract was at an end, the acceptor being the agent of the drawer." And he adds,—"the plaintiff has received all the money, and yet desires to be a trustee for the drawer, and receive again from the acceptor that which the drawer has paid." There the doctrine is repudiated, that after receiving payment of the amount, the holder can be trustee for the drawer. [Lord *Abinger,* C. B.—If that be the principle of that case, it may be a question whether, if it were now considered, it would not be overruled (a). Might not the plaintiff take issue on either one or the other of the allegations in the plea?] If he took issue on one, the other would be an answer. [*Parke,* B.—Suppose he denied the accord and satisfaction, would the other be an answer?] It is submitted that it would. The allegation is so extensive in its character, that it would let in proof not merely that there never had been any consideration, but also that the

(a) See *Johnson* v. *Kennion,* 2 Wils. 262: *Reid* v. *Furnival,* 1 C. & M. 538.

consideration had wholly failed. It is true, the last alle-gation in the plea, if it stood alone as an answer to the declaration, would be bad on special demurrer; but if found by the jury for the defendant, it would clearly be good after verdict. It is not necessary, in order to esta-blish duplicity in a plea, to shew that each part of the plea is well pleaded: it is sufficient if each of the alleged answers would be good after verdict. This is laid down in Com. Dig. Pleader (E. 2), citing 1 Sid. 176, and was recognised by the Court of Common Pleas in *Stephens* v. *Under-wood* (a). In that case, to an action against the acceptor of a bill of exchange, the defendant pleaded, that he made the acceptance by force and duress of imprison-ment, and that he never had any value for accepting or paying the bill; and it was held that the plea was bad for duplicity, though one of the grounds of defence was badly pleaded. It is therefore submitted that, at all events, the plea is bad as containing two distinct answers to the de-claration; but, further, that the position that the plaintiff may claim as trustee for the drawer is not tenable. Upon this last mentioned point it may be also noticed, that *Bacon* v. *Searles* is recognised in Bayley on Bills (b), which book on the same point cites *Pearson* v. *Dunlop* (c), as establishing that where the drawer of a bill has paid part of the amount to the holder, the holder cannot recover anything more from the acceptor than the balance remain-ing due.

Lord ABINGER, C. B.—I am disposed to come back to the opinion I originally entertained, that the plea is double. The language used at the conclusion of the plea, that the plaintiff held the bill without value, renders it double, and although that may be badly pleaded as an answer to the action, yet the plea is nevertheless demurrable on that

(a) 4 Bing. N. C. 655; 6 Scott,   (b) P. 276, 4th Ed.
402.   (c) Cowp. 571.

ground. However, upon payment of costs, and an affidavit of merits, the defendant may amend.

PARKE, B.—If the allegation had been that the plaintiff had never held for value, the plea would clearly have been double,—and it is not the less so that the latter part is badly pleaded.

Leave was then granted to amend on producing an affidavit of merits, and on payment of costs within a week. The defendant, however, did not amend within that time, and there was

　　　　　　　　Judgment for the plaintiff.

————◆————

FENTON v. THE TRENT AND MERSEY NAVIGATION COMPANY.

Nov. 24.

CASE.—The declaration stated, that before the committing of the grievances by the defendants as thereinafter

By a local act, 1 Will. 4, c. 55, the Trent and Mersey Navigation Company were empowered to take lands for the purposes of the navigation, and by section 118 and other sections, provision was made for ascertaining, by a sheriff's jury, the sum to be paid for the land, and for any damage occasioned by the company in carrying the provisions of the act into effect. And in order to protect the company from injury to arise from working any mines near two tunnels by which the canal passed under a certain hill, the act provided, by section 170, that no mine owner should work any mine in or under any land within forty yards of the tunnels, without leave of the company; and by section 171, that if the company, instead of insisting on their full right of having forty yards left unworked, should require less than thirty yards to be so left, then the mine owner might insist on the necessity of leaving, for his security, any greater quantity unworked not exceeding thirty yards, and the question so in dispute as to the quantity necessary to be left for the security of the mine owners was to be tried, settled, and determined, *by an issue at law.* And by section 172 it was provided, that whenever any mine became workable in ordinary course, within forty yards of the tunnels, the mine owner should give notice to the company, and thereupon the company should pay to the mine owner for so much of the mine within the forty yards as they should require to be left unworked for security of their works; or (as the case might be) for so much of the mines as, under the provisions of section 171, it might be ascertained to be necessary to leave unworked, for security of the mines. Provided, that no mines should in any case be worked under the tunnels; but whenever any such last-mentioned mines should become workable, satisfaction should be made by the company for the same, "*such satisfaction to be settled by an issue at law.*"

By the 178th section, the course to be taken in trying any feigned issue was pointed out, and it enacted, that after trial and verdict in such issue, the Court was to give judgment for the sum of money to be awarded by the jury:—Held, that by the express terms of the 172nd section, the owner of a mine which had become workable within the space of forty yards of the tunnels mentioned in the act, was entitled to be paid for the value of the forty yards of mine left unworked for the security of the navigation, the whole having been by the company required to be so left unworked; but that the only remedy open to him to enforce his right was by a feigned issue, and consequently that he was not entitled to proceed by an action on the case.

Exch. of Pleas, mentioned, by a certain act of Parliament passed in the
1841. first year of the reign of his late Majesty King William the
FENTON Fourth, intituled " An Act to consolidate and extend the
v. powers and provisions of the several Acts relating to the
TRENT AND Navigation from the Trent to the Mersey," amongst other
MERSEY
NAVIGATION powers and provisions therein contained, relating to certain
Co. mines and minerals in the said act mentioned, power was
given to the said company to require the owners and
workers of any mine or mines, mineral or minerals, in or
under any lands within the distance of forty yards from
certain tunnels through Harecastle Hill, or either of them,
in the said act mentioned, to leave the said last mentioned
mines and minerals unworked and ungotten, and the owners and workers of the said mines and minerals, and all
other persons whosoever, were by the said act prohibited
from working or getting any of the said mines and minerals so required by the said company to be left unworked
and ungotten as aforesaid. And it was by the said act
(amongst other things) further enacted, that when and as
often as any mines or minerals lying under the said tunnels through Harecastle Hill, or either of them, or in or
under any lands within the space or distance of forty yards
from the same respectively, should become workable in the
due and regular course of working and getting the same,
notice thereof in writing should be given by the owner or
worker of such mines or minerals to the said company
thereby established, and thereupon the said company
should pay to the owners or workers of such mines or minerals respectively, in proportion to their respective interests therein, for all or so much of the said mines or minerals so becoming workable, and contained in or under the
lands within the said space or distance of forty yards, as
should be required by the said company to be left ungotten or unworked, for the security or preservation of the
said tunnels and works, or any of them (as the case might
be), for so much of the said mines or minerals so becoming

workable as should be ascertained and determined in pursuance of the provision thereinbefore contained, to be necessary to be left unworked or ungotten for the security and preservation of the said mines: And whereas also, after the passing of the said act of Parliament, and before the giving of the notice by the plaintiff as hereinafter mentioned, and before the committing of the grievances by the defendants as hereinafter mentioned, and from thence hitherto, the defendants have been and still are the owners of certain tunnels over and near adjoining to certain mines and minerals, and strata of coal and ironstone hereinafter more particularly mentioned and described, of the said plaintiff, made, cut and driven through a certain hill called Harecastle Hill, situate, lying, and being in the township or hamlet of Ravenscroft, otherwise Ranscliffe, in the parish of Woolstanton, in the county of Stafford: And whereas also, after the passing of the said act of Parliament, and before the giving of the notice by the plaintiff as hereinafter mentioned, and before the committing of the said grievances by the defendants as hereinafter mentioned, and from thence hitherto, the plaintiff hath been and still is the owner of certain mines and minerals hereinafter more particularly mentioned and described, lying in and under certain lands in the township or hamlet of Ravenscroft &c., lately in the occupation of Robert Williamson Esq., within the space or distance of forty yards from the said tunnels through Harecastle Hill in the said act mentioned, and which said last-mentioned mines and minerals, and each and every of them, had, before the giving of the said notice by the plaintiff, and before the committing of the said grievances hereinafter mentioned, become and were workable in the due and regular course of working and getting the same: And whereas also, after the said last-mentioned mines and minerals, and each and every of them, had so become and were workable as last aforesaid, and before the committing

Exch. of Pleas,
1841.

FENTON
v.
TRENT AND
MERSEY
NAVIGATION
Co.

Exch. of Pleas,
1841.

FENTON
v.
TRENT AND
MERSEY
NAVIGATION
Co.

of the said grievances as hereinafter mentioned, to wit, on the 25th May, 1840, the plaintiff, as the owner of the said last-mentioned mines and minerals and each and every of them, did, in pursuance of the provision in that behalf in the said act contained, give notice in writing to the said company to the effect following (that is to say), that certain mines or strata of ironstone lying in or under certain lands in the township or hamlet of Ravenscroft, then or lately in the occupation of one Robert Williamson, Esq., within the space or distance of forty yards from the tunnels through Harecastle Hill in the said act mentioned, and which mines and strata of ironstone lie respectively between the two mines of coals respectively called Spend-croft coal and Ten-feet coal, and between the two mines of coals respectively called Ten-feet coal and Great-row coal, and between the two mines of coal respectively called Great-row coal and Little-row coal, had respectively become and were workable in the due and regular course of working and getting the said last-mentioned mines or strata of iron-stone respectively; and also that the said several mines of coal respectively called or known by the name of Ten-feet coal, Great-row coal, and Little-row coal, lying in and under certain lands in the township or liberty of Ravens-croft aforesaid, then or lately in the occupation of the said Robert Williamson, within the space or distance of forty yards respectively from the said tunnels respectively, had become and were workable in the due and regular course of working and getting the said mines of coals respectively; and the plaintiff did by the said notice require the said company to make satisfaction for and pay to the plain-tiff, as the owner of the said last-mentioned mines or minerals respectively, for his interest in all such parts of the said last-mentioned mines or minerals lying in or un-der the aforesaid lands, within the space of forty yards from the same tunnels respectively, as should be required by the said company to be left ungotten or unworked for the security or preservation of their said tunnels and works,

or any of them: and in case the said company should
consent that any part of the said last-mentioned mines
and minerals lying in or under any of the said lands,
within the said space of forty yards, should be worked
or gotten, then the plaintiff did by the said notice require the said company forthwith to declare and give
such consent in writing under their common seal, in manner mentioned in the said act, and by such consent to
specify and set forth how much and what part or parts
of the said last-mentioned mines and minerals, lying in
or under any of the said lands within the space or distance aforesaid, they required to be left ungotten or unworked, for the security or preservation of their said tunnels and works, or any of them: and the plaintiff did,
by the said notice, further require the same company
to make satisfaction and payment to the plaintiff, as the
owner of the said last-mentioned mines respectively, for
his interest in all the said last-mentioned mines and minerals lying in or under the said lands, within the space
or distance aforesaid, or as the case might be, for all such
parts, if not the whole, of the said last-mentioned mines
and minerals, as should be required by the said company
to be left ungotten or unworked as aforesaid; and for
that purpose the said plaintiff did by the said notice
further require the said company to ascertain and determine how much of the said last-mentioned mines and minerals were required by the said company to be left ungotten or unworked as aforesaid, and to proceed forthwith to a valuation or valuations of the said last-mentioned mines and minerals, or of such parts thereof as
should be required by the said company to be left ungotten or unworked as aforesaid, and of the plaintiff's
interest therein; and the plaintiff did then, by the said
notice in writing, further give notice to the said company,
that he the plaintiff was ready and willing to concur,
and the plaintiff did then offer to concur with the said

Exch. of Pleas,
1841.

FENTON
v.
TRENT AND
MERSEY
NAVIGATION
Co.

Exch. of Pleas,
1841.

FENTON
v.
TRENT AND
MERSEY
NAVIGATION
Co.

company in all proper and reasonable steps for or towards such valuation or valuations: And the plaintiff in
fact saith, that although afterwards, and after the giving
of the said notice in writing, and before the committing of the said grievances, to wit, on the 14th of July,
1840, the said company did require the plaintiff to leave
unworked and ungotten, for the security and preservation of the tunnels and works in and through Harecastle Hill aforesaid, the whole of the mines, minerals,
and strata of coal and ironstone, respecting which such
notice was given by the plaintiff to the said company
as aforesaid; and although the plaintiff did, in pursuance of such requirement by the said company, leave
unworked and ungotten, for the security and preservation
of the said tunnels and works in and through Harecastle
Hill aforesaid, the whole and every part of the said last-
mentioned mines, minerals, and strata of coal and ironstone, so required by the said company to be left unworked
and ungotten as aforesaid; and although the whole and
every part of the said last-mentioned mines, minerals,
strata of coal and ironstone have been, from the time
when the plaintiff was so required by the said company
as aforesaid, hitherto left unworked and ungotten, and
still are unworked and ungotten, of which the said company have always had notice: And although it thereupon became and was the duty of the said company to
pay to the plaintiff, as the owner of such last-mentioned mines and minerals, and strata of coal and ironstone,
for his the plaintiff's interest therein, the price and
value of all the said mines and minerals, strata of coal
and ironstone, so required as aforesaid by the said company to be left ungotten and unworked, for the security
and preservation of the said tunnels and works in and
through Harecastle Hill aforesaid: Nevertheless the plaintiff in fact saith, that the said company have not, although
often requested so to do, as yet paid to the plaintiff, as

Exch. of Pleas,
1841.

FENTON
v.
TRENT AND
MERSEY
NAVIGATION
Co.

the owner of such last-mentioned mines and minerals, strata of coal and ironstone, for his interest therein, the price and value of such last-mentioned mines and minerals, strata of coal and ironstone, or any of them or any part thereof, although a reasonable time for making such payment had long elapsed before the commencement of this suit, but have hitherto altogether neglected and refused and still do neglect and refuse so to do: By means of which said several premises the plaintiff hath been and is greatly injured, and hindered and prevented from working and getting his said mines and minerals, as he otherwise might and would have done, and the plaintiff hath also, by means of the said premises, altogether lost and been deprived of the price and value of the same, &c.

To this declaration the defendants pleaded, fourthly and lastly, that the plaintiff commenced his said action against the defendants in the Court of our Lady the Queen, before the Barons of her Exchequer at Westminster, in the county of Middlesex, after the making of the said act of Parliament in the said declaration mentioned, and that the said mines and minerals in the said declaration alleged to have become workable in the due and regular course of working and getting the same, were, at the said times in the said declaration in that behalf mentioned, and still are, lying under the said tunnels in the said declaration also mentioned, or one of them, or in or under the lands within the space or distance of forty yards from the same tunnels respectively: yet the plaintiff hath not delivered or tendered to the defendants any declaration in any action upon a feigned issue commenced in any of her Majesty's Courts of Record at Westminster, in which the said plaintiff is plaintiff and the said company are defendants, in respect of the said mines and minerals, or any of them, or in respect of payment or satisfaction for the same.—Verification.

The plaintiff demurred specially, assigning the following

Exch. of Pleas,
1841.

FENTON
v.
TRENT AND
MERSEY
NAVIGATION
Co.

causes :—that the plea does not sufficiently traverse or confess and avoid the causes of action in the declaration mentioned; that the plaintiff, by his declaration, seeks to recover damages against the defendants for a breach of duty as therein alleged, in respect only of the mines and minerals and strata of coal and ironstone belonging to the plaintiff, and lying respectively in and under the lands within the space or distance of forty yards from the said tunnels in the said declaration mentioned, whereas the defendants have, in and by their last plea, attempted to raise a defence in respect of other mines and minerals than those embraced by the plaintiff's declaration, viz. in respect of mines and minerals lying under the tunnels in the declaration mentioned, or one of them; and also for that the defendants, in and by their said plea, have attempted to raise a defence on the omission by the plaintiff to deliver or tender to the defendants any declaration in any action upon a feigned issue,· but the defendants do not, in their said plea, aver that the said mines and minerals in the declaration mentioned lie under the said tunnels through Harecastle Hill, or either of them, or in or under the lands within the space between the same tunnels, nor does the said plea contain any averment to shew that the provisions of the said act of Parliament, in the declaration mentioned relating to feigned issues, are applicable to the mines and minerals in the said declaration mentioned, or any of them; and for that the said plea is pleaded to the whole of the declaration, and ought to contain averments to shew that the whole of the mines and minerals in the declaration mentioned are subject to the provisions of the said act of Parliament relating to the feigned issues; and also for that, in and by the said act of Parliament in the declaration above mentioned, the method of trial by feigned issues is expressly confined and limited to such mines and minerals, and strata of coal and ironstone, as shall respectively lie under the said tunnels through Harecastle-hill, or either of them, or in or under the lands within the space between the same tunnels, whereas the claim of the plaintiff is only in respect of the mines and minerals, and strata of coal and ironstone, lying in or under the space or distance of forty yards from the external side of the said tunnels, or either of them, the whole of which said last-mentioned mines and minerals have been required by the defendants to be left ungotten and unworked by the plaintiff as aforesaid, and does not include any demand in respect of the mines and minerals lying under the said tunnels, or in or under the space between the same.

Exch. of Pleas,
1841.

FENTON
v.
TRENT AND
MERSEY
NAVIGATION
Co.

Joinder in demurrer.

The case was argued on a former day in this term (Nov. 10) by *Cresswell* for the plaintiff, and by *R. V. Richards* for the defendant; but as the question turns altogether on the construction of a local act of Parliament, and the arguments and different clauses are fully stated in the judgment, it has been thought unnecessary to detail them here.

The judgment of the Court was now delivered by

ROLFE, B.—The question in this case is, whether the plaintiff can recover, in an action on the case, the value of the mines which he has left ungotten for the convenience of the defendants, pursuant to the provisions of the 1st Will. 4, c. 55, the local act under which they are now incorporated, or whether he is not bound to assert his right by means of a feigned issue. The act is certainly somewhat obscure; but upon an attentive consideration of the different sections bearing on this case, we have come to the conclusion that the defendants are right in saying that the only remedy open to the plaintiff is that of a feigned issue.

Exch. of Pleas,
1841.

FENTON
v.
TRENT AND
MERSEY
NAVIGATION
Co.

The company is empowered, in the ordinary way, to take lands for the purposes of the navigation; and by the 118th and several subsequent sections, provision is made for ascertaining, by a sheriff's jury, the sum to be paid by the company, as well for the land taken as for any damage occasioned by the company in carrying the provisions of the act into effect. But this is not all. The navigation, it seems, traverses a mining district, and in that district passes through two tunnels under Harecastle-hill. In order to protect the company from injury to arise from working any mines too near to those tunnels, the act contains the following provisions.—First, by section 170, it provides that no mine-owner shall work any mine in or under any lands within forty yards of the tunnels without leave of the company. Secondly, section 171, for the security of the mine-owner, enacts, that if the company, instead of insisting on their full right of having forty yards left unworked, should require less than thirty yards to be so left, then the mine-owner may insist on the necessity of leaving for his security any greater quantity unworked, not exceeding thirty yards, and the question so in dispute as to the quantity necessary to be left for the security of the mine-owner is to be tried, settled, and determined by an issue at law.

Then follows the 172nd section, on which the question mainly turns. It is thereby provided, that whenever any mine becomes workable in ordinary course within forty yards of the tunnels, the mine-owner shall give notice to the company, and thereupon the company shall pay to the mine-owner for so much of the mine within the forty yards as they shall require to be left unworked for security of their works, or (as the case may be) for so much of the mines as, under the provisions of section 171, it may be ascertained to be necessary to leave unworked for security of the mines: provided that no mines shall in any case be worked under the tunnels, but whenever any such last-

mentioned mines shall become workable, satisfaction shall
be made by the company for the same, such satisfaction to
be settled by an issue.   The five following sections provide for working the mines within the forty yards not required by the company to be left unworked, and for com-
pensating the mine-owners for injuries to their mines
arising from the works of the navigation, and also for
working the mines in and under the lands adjoining the
rest of the line of the navigation, exclusive of the two
tunnels.   Section 178 then points out the course to be
taken for trying any feigned issue to be tried under the
provisions of the act, after the trial and verdict in which
the Court is to give judgment for the sum of money
awarded by the jury.

There is no doubt but that, by the express terms of the
172nd section, the plaintiff is entitled to be paid for the
value of the forty yards of mine left unworked for the
security of the navigation, and the only question is by
what proceeding is he to enforce his right.   Now it is to
be observed, that the clauses 170 to 180, both inclusive, all
relate to this question of working the mines in the immediate neighbourhood of the navigation, and providing compensation to the mine-owners for the mine of which they
are deprived by the company; and these clauses must therefore all be construed together, and with reference to one
another, as all forming parts of one general system of enactment.   It is admitted that the question of the amount to
be paid for the mine actually *under* the tunnels, is, by the
express terms of the 172nd section, to be settled by an issue.   So again, by the positive words of the 177th section,
the amount of mine to be left unworked at any part of the
line of navigation, other than within forty yards of the
tunnels, and *also the sum to be paid by way of compensation
for what is so left unworked,* is to be settled by an issue.   It
seems, therefore, impossible to believe that the legislature
could have meant to adopt so strange a course, as to pro-

Exch. of Pleas,
1841.

FENTON
v.
TRENT AND
MERSEY
NAVIGATION
Co.

Exch. of Pleas,
1841.

FENTON
v.
TRENT AND
MERSEY
NAVIGATION
Co.

vide a specific mode of ascertaining the compensation to be paid for mine left unworked *under* the whole line of the canal, and *adjoining* the whole line except for the space of forty yards from the two tunnels, and have left the quantum of compensation for those forty yards to be settled by an ordinary action on the case. No reason can be assigned why the value of the mine within the forty yards should be settled by a course of proceeding different from that by which the value of any other mine left unworked was to be determined; and we feel bound, if it be possible, to put such a construction on the 172nd section as shall prevent a consequence, which, it is quite obvious, the legislature could never have contemplated. Now we think this may be done without offering any material violence to the language of the 172nd section.

That section may be considered as divided into three branches, by every one of which the company is certainly made liable to pay money to the mine-owner, by way of satisfaction for mines of which he is deprived. 1st. The company shall pay the mine-owner for the mine within the forty yards, where forty yards are taken. 2nd. The company, in like manner, shall pay him for the mine, not exceeding thirty yards, left unworked for his security. 3rd. As to the mine actually under the tunnel, no person shall ever be at liberty to work it, but when workable, satisfaction shall be made for it by the company to the mine-owner. Then follow these words, " *such satisfaction to be ascertained, fixed, and determined by an issue at law.*"

Now it may be conceded that the more obvious construction of this clause would refer the words "such satisfaction," &c., only to the satisfaction immediately preceding, namely, the satisfaction to be paid at all events for the mines left unworked under the tunnels. There is, however, nothing grammatically incorrect in referring the words "such satisfaction" to every species of satisfaction mentioned in the clause; namely, to the payment to

be made for mine within the forty yards, for mine within *Exch. of Pleas,*
1841.

FENTON
v.
TRENT AND
MERSEY
NAVIGATION
Co.
the thirty yards, and for mine actually under the tunnels;
and in furtherance of what we cannot but suppose, from
the whole tenor of these eleven clauses, must have been
intended by the legislature, and to avoid the strange incongruity of having one mode of deciding questions as to
the value of mine within forty yards of the tunnels, and
another as to the value of mines along the rest of the line
of the canal, and under the tunnels themselves, we feel
bound to adopt the latter construction of the words "such
satisfaction," and to hold them applicable to every case for
which satisfaction is made payable under the 172nd section.

The necessity of such a construction may be made more
obvious, by considering that, unless it be adopted, there
must, when the mine-owner has got within forty yards of
the tunnels, and is there stopped by the company, be two
proceedings going on at the same time, in order to ascertain the compensation to which he is entitled; for it is
obvious that when the mine-owner has got up to within
forty yards of the tunnels, the mine under the tunnels
must have become " *workable,*" within the meaning of that
word as used in the proviso of the 172nd section, inasmuch
as the company, by preventing the mine-owner from working within the forty yards, will effectually prevent the mines
under the tunnels from ever being workable, unless they
are to be deemed so when the mine-owner has reached the
confines of the forty yards. The forty yards, therefore,
having become workable, and the mines under the tunnels
having become workable at the same time, the plaintiff
must contend that the legislature intended to impose on
him the necessity of instituting two proceedings, one to
recover by action compensation for the mine adjoining the
tunnels for a space of forty yards, and another to recover
by an issue compensation for the mine actually under the
tunnels.

Exch. of Pleas,
1841.

FENTON
v.
TRENT AND
MERSEY
NAVIGATION
Co.

Exactly the same anomaly would occur, whenever a mine-owner in the progress of his works approaches within forty yards of the tunnels, and at the same time within such a distance of the adjoining parts of the line of the canal, as, either by agreement of the parties, or by the result of an issue to be tried under the 177th section, is ascertained to be the distance within which the mines cannot further be worked with safety to the canal. In such a case, the value of the mine to be left unworked for the security of such part of the canal as does not pass through the tunnels, is, by the express provision of the 177th section, to be tried in an issue; and it is therefore impossible to suppose, that the value of that part which is left for the security of the tunnels, could have been intended to be tried by a different tribunal. The legislature seems to have considered the tunnels to be more exposed to danger from the mines than the rest of the line of the canal. This afforded a very good reason for not leaving it to a jury to say how much mine should be left for the protection of the tunnels, but to have fixed conclusively beforehand a depth of forty yards, as being necessary in case the company should choose to insist on having it; but we can see no imaginable reason why the value of this part of the mine should have been intended to be ascertained by a different proceeding from that which is clearly applicable to the rest.

Our view of the case is, perhaps, somewhat confirmed by considering that the 178th section seems to assume that in every case where an issue is to be tried, a sum of money will have to be awarded by the jury. Now that section expressly refers, amongst other issues, to issues to be tried under section 171, for ascertaining how much mine it may be necessary to leave for the security of the mine-owner; but it is clear that on such an issue, if nothing were to be ascertained but the quantity to be left unworked, no sum of money would be awarded at all; and it would seem, therefore, as if the legislature assumed that on the trial of such an issue the jury would be bound under the other provisions of the act to assess the value of what was left, and there certainly are no provisions applicable to such a case, unless they can (as we think they may) be found in the 172nd section.

On all these grounds, we think that the case is within the 172nd section and consequently there must be judgment for the defendant.

Exch. of Pleas, 1841.

FENTON
v.
TRENT AND
MERSEY
NAVIGATION
Co.

Judgment for the defendant.

————

•MENDELL *v.* TYRRELL.

Nov. 24.

COWLING had obtained a rule, calling upon the defendant to shew cause why he should not pay to the plaintiff two sums of £90 and 47*l.* 15*s.* 2*d.*, pursuant to an award, rule of Court, and the Master's allocatur. It appeared from the affidavit on which the rule was obtained, that the cause had been referred to arbitration, and that the arbitrator, by his award, ordered the defendant to pay to the plaintiff the sum of £90, with costs, which were subsequently taxed at 47*l.* 15*s.* 2*d.* The plaintiff afterwards filed an affidavit of debt in the Court of Bankruptcy, under the provisions of the stat. 1 & 2 Vict. c. 110, s. 8 (*a*). The defend-

An arbitrator having by his award ordered the defendant to pay to the plaintiff a sum of money, the plaintiff filed an affidavit of debt in the Court of Bankruptcy, under stat. 1 & 2 Vict. c. 110, and the defendant gave a bond, with sureties, conditioned for payment of the money, but

omitting the alternative in the statute, of rendering himself to custody:—*Held*, that the plaintiff's having adopted this proceeding did not preclude him from applying for an attachment for non-performance of the award and rule of Court thereon.

(*a*) Which enacts, "that if any single creditor, or any two or more creditors being partners, whose debt shall amount to £100 or upwards, or any two creditors whose debt shall amount to £150 or up- wards, or any three or more creditors whose debts shall amount to £200 or upwards, of any trader within the meaning of the laws now in force respecting bankrupts, shall file an affidavit or affidavits in her

ant entered into a bond with two sureties, conditioned "to pay such sums as should be recovered in any action or actions which had been brought or should thereafter be brought for the recovery of the said debts, together with such costs as should be given in the same," but omitting the alternative mentioned in the act, viz., "that he render himself to the custody of the gaoler of the Court," &c. No further proceedings were taken in the Court of Bankruptcy, but the present rule was obtained.

Pashley shewed cause.—The plaintiff has elected as his remedy to enforce the award under the act, and not to proceed by attachment, and therefore the Court will not now interfere, especially as the plaintiff has by that proceeding obtained full security for the payment of his debt. The object and practice of the Courts has been to discourage a multiplicity of proceedings for the same subject of

Majesty's Court of Bankruptcy, that such debt or debts is or are justly due to him or them respectively, and that such debtor, as he or they verily believe, is such trader as aforesaid, and shall cause him to be served personally with a copy of such affidavit or affidavits, and with a notice in writing requiring immediate payment of such debt or debts; and if such trader shall not within twenty-one days after personal service of such affidavit or affidavits and notice, pay such debt or debts, or secure or compound for the same to the satisfaction of such creditor or creditors, or enter into a bond in such sum and with such two sufficient sureties as a commissioner of the Court of Bankruptcy shall approve of, to pay such sum or sums as shall be recovered in any action or actions which shall have been brought or shall thereafter be brought for the recovery of the same, together with such costs as shall be given in the same, or to render himself to the custody of the gaoler of the Court in which such action shall have been or may be brought, according to the practice of such Court, or within such time and in such manner as the said Court, or any judge thereof, shall direct, after judgment shall have been recovered in such action, every such trader shall be deemed to have committed an act of bankruptcy on the 22nd day after service of such affidavit or affidavits and notice, provided a fiat in bankruptcy shall issue against such trader within two calendar months from the filing of such affidavit or affidavits, but not otherwise.

claim. If a party bring an action on an award, he is precluded from moving for an attachment for not performing it: *Stock* v. *De Smith* (a). It was there argued that it was as reasonable to grant an attachment whilst an action was pending on the award, as to permit the several remedies which are allowed upon mortgages, such as a bill for foreclosure, an action upon the bond, and an ejectment to get the possession; but Lord *Hardwicke*, C. J., said, "I am satisfied you ought not to have an attachment while an action is pending; and this not like the several remedies allowed on mortgages, for they are for different purposes; as the ejectment to gain the possession of the land, the action on the bond to recover the money, and the bill for foreclosing the equity of redemption; they are all remedies which the party is entitled to by course of law, and needs not the leave of the court: now in this case there are two remedies, one by action, to which you are entitled by course of law, but the other depends upon the discretion of the Court: and both are for the very same purpose, viz., for the money awarded: for the Court will not deliver the party from an attachment till he has paid the money." So, in *Badley* v. *Loveday* (b), the Court refused to grant an attachment for non-performance of an award pending an action brought on the award, or to allow the plaintiff to waive the action in order to apply for the attachment; the Court saying he had made his election. And in the *Earl of Lonsdale* v. *Whinnay* (c), the defendant having been taken under an attachment for non-performance of an award, went to prison, refusing to pay the money; the plaintiff afterwards commenced an action on the award; and on motion that the plaintiff might be compelled to discontinue, or that the defendant might be discharged out of custody, the Court ordered him to be discharged,

(a) Ca. Temp. Hardw. 106. (b) 1 Bos. & Pull. 81.
(c) 1 C. M. & R. 591.

on giving a bond to the plaintiff, with sureties to the Master's satisfaction, conditioned to the same effect as in a recognisance of bail. *Paull* v. *Paull* (a) is to the same effect. There an attachment was resisted on the ground of the pendency of an action on the award, and it appearing that the party was in contempt before the action was commenced, the Court granted the attachment on the plaintiff's undertaking to discontinue the action and pay the costs. Here the giving of the bond is equivalent to the commencement of the action. The plaintiff has obtained ample security for his debt and costs by the bond. [Lord *Abinger*, C. B.—The bond is not a bond within the statute.] The plaintiff ought to shew some reason for abandoning his primary proceeding.

Cowling, in support of the rule.—The authorities cited are not applicable to the present case, for no action has been commenced on the award, but all that appears is that the plaintiff has obtained a security for his debt.

Lord ABINGER, C. B.—I am of opinion that this rule ought to be made absolute. If any action has been commenced on the award, the defendant should have shewn that fact; as he has not done so, it must be taken that no action has been commenced, and that circumstance distinguishes the present case from those cited. If an action had been commenced, the Court would not, by making this rule absolute, allow a double remedy. But in the present case, the plaintiff's sole object seems to have been to render the defendant a bankrupt, and that object has been defeated by the defendant's providing sureties for the payment of the debt. The rule will be absolute, on the plaintiff's undertaking not to bring any action on the award.

PARKE, B.—A rule of Court, under the recent statute,

(a) 2 C. & M. 235.

calling upon the defendant to pay the sum awarded, is *Exch. of Pleas*,
analogous to an attachment under the old law; therefore, 1841.
if the plaintiff had actually commenced an action on the MENDELL
award, the authorities cited would have been in point. But *v.*
it is not so here. Besides, the bond is not conditioned ac- TYRRELL.
cording to the statute, for the payment of the debt, or the
render of the defendant; the latter part seems by mistake
to have been omitted.

Rule absolute.

HAMMOND *v.* NAIRN, Clerk. *Nov. 25.*

PLATT had obtained a rule, calling upon the defendant The costs of an
to shew cause why it should not be referred to the Master interpleader
rule obtained
to tax the plaintiff's costs of and incident to the writ of by a sheriff or
other similar
fieri facias de bonis ecclesiasticis issued in this cause, and officer, cannot
be considered
why the Bishop of Norwich should not levy the same, to- as "expenses of
gether with the sum of £4 omitted by mistake, and inter- the execution,"
which may be
est on the judgment from the 27th of November, 1838. It levied under the
appeared from the affidavits, that a writ of fi. fa. de bonis stat. 43 Geo. 3,
c. 46, s. 5.
ecclesiasticis, directed to the Bishop of Norwich, had been
issued against the defendant; but that, by a clerical error,
the sum indorsed thereon was less by £4 than it ought to
have been. The execution issued under the stat. 1 & 2
Vict. c. 110, s. 18, but before the promulgation of the
forms of writs framed by the Judges under that statute;
and no interest on the judgment was indorsed on the writ,
from want of knowledge of the form in which it should be
claimed. A sequestration was granted by the bishop, but,
the defendant having become insolvent, the provisional
assignee of the Insolvent Debtors' Court claimed the rents,
tithes, &c., by virtue of a prior execution. In Hilary Term,
1840, the bishop obtained an interpleader rule, calling
upon the plaintiff and the provisional assignee to appear
and state their claims; which rule was discharged without
costs, the Court holding that it was not a case in which the

bishop could have relief under the Interpleader Act. A second sequestration at the suit of another creditor had since issued against the defendant.—Against the present rule

Archbold now shewed cause for the defendant.—The main object of this application is to obtain, as incident to the execution, the costs which this Court, on the discussion of the interpleader rule, refused to allow to the plaintiff. But it cannot possibly be said that those costs fall within the meaning of " fees and expenses of the execution," within the stat. 43 Geo. 3, c. 46, s. 5. The defendant had not even notice of the interpleader rule. [*Parke,* B.— Those are not costs incident to the execution, but costs occasioned by the sheriff's asking for the interpleader rule.] And even if it were otherwise, the rule ought to be upon the bishop, who is bound to levy the expenses of the execution, not on the defendant.

Secondly, it is too late now to recover the interest: it ought to have been claimed on the back of the writ: and other parties are now interested in the fund, under the intervening sequestration. [*Parke,* B.—Then it must not, at all events, be levied until that sequestration is satisfied.]

With respect to the £4, the affidavits do not shew with certainty of what it consisted, or how it was omitted out of the indorsement, and the Court will not re-open the proceedings on that account, after this lapse of time.

Platt, in support of the rule, urged that at all events the plaintiff ought to be allowed to levy for the interest, and that on the part of the defendant, who alone came to shew cause against this rule (which had been served also on the bishop), it was no answer to the rule to say that other parties were interested, or ought to have been served; that was a matter in which he had no interest.

PER CURIAM.—It is quite clear that the plaintiff is not entitled to recover the costs of the interpleader rule as expenses of the execution, which mean only such expenses as the sheriff, &c., is put to in keeping possession of the goods, selling, &c. As to the £4 omitted from the indorsement, it is not shewn how the amount was £4 less, or how it was a clerical error. As to those two matters, the rule must be discharged with costs. With respect to the interest, the rule may be enlarged on payment of costs by the plaintiff, in order to serve it upon the other execution creditor.

Exch. of Pleas,
1841.

HAMMOND
v.
NAIRN.

Rule accordingly.

RYAN *v.* SMITH.

Nov. 25.

ON shewing cause against a rule nisi for an attachment against the defendant for disobedience to a rule of Court, *Cresswell,* for the defendant, proposed to read an affidavit of the defendant, sworn on the 10th of November, and filed in Court, which was made in support of a former rule obtained by the defendant for rescinding an order of *Rolfe,* B., ordering the defendant to deliver up certain documents and vouchers. That rule was granted on certain terms, which the defendant declined to accept, and therefore did not draw up the rule; but the plaintiff's attorney was informed that the affidavit was filed, and took an office copy of it. The order of *Rolfe,* B., was afterwards made a rule of Court, which rule the defendant was now charged with having disobeyed; and the affidavit in support of the present application referred to the defendant's affidavit of the 10th November.

A party shewing cause against a rule has a right to read an affidavit of his filed in Court, which was made in support of a former application for a rule involving the same question, and of which the other side took an office copy.

Crowder, for the plaintiff, objected to the affidavit being used, inasmuch as it was sworn upon a mere ex-parte application, and could contain no answer to the present rule.

The Court held that the affidavit might be read.

Exch. of Pleas,
1841.

Nov. 25.

Costs of attend-
ances to serve
the writ of
summons.

TAPPING *v.* GREENWAY.

SMIRKE, on behalf of the plaintiff's attorney, obtained a rule calling upon the defendant and his attorney to shew cause why the Master should not review his taxation of the costs of service of the writ of summons, and why the defendant's attorney should not pay the costs of this application. It appeared that the plaintiff sued out the writ of summons indorsed to levy the debt and 1*l.* 17*s.* for costs, and on Friday, the 5th of November, sent a person to serve it at the defendant's dwelling-house. He was there informed that the defendant would not be at home until the following day at eight o'clock, at which hour he called again; but not finding the defendant within, he made a further appointment for the Monday following, on which day he again called, and saw the defendant's mother, who said her son was out of town, and would be back on Wednesday. He then, however, left a copy of the writ of summons, and did not call again. The 1*l.* 17*s.* indorsed for costs included the costs of three attendances. The defendant, within four days afterwards, called at the office of the plaintiff's attorney, and paid the debt and costs. The Master first allowed the plaintiff the costs of two attendances, but subsequently, in pursuance of an order of *Alderson,* B., the taxation was reviewed, and the costs of one attendance only was allowed; the result of which was, that more than one sixth was struck off the amount of costs claimed.

Miller shewed cause, and contended that, under the circumstances, the party ought not to have left the copy of the writ on the Monday, but to have waited until the Wednesday; and that the Court, being apprised of the circumstances, would not have granted any distringas, in which case one attendance only would be allowed.

Smirke, contrà, insisted that the attorney was clearly entitled to the costs of *two* attendances; and

Exch. of Pleas, 1841.

TAPPING
v.
GREENWAY.

PER CURIAM.—The call on the Monday was unnecessary; the party might have left the process on the Saturday; but still the plaintiff is entitled to the costs of two attendances. As this, however, is an appeal against the order of a Judge, the rule will be absolute on the terms of the attorney on each side paying his own costs.

Rule absolute accordingly.

WILLIAMSON *v.* HARRISON.

Nov. 25.

MARTIN had obtained a rule, calling upon the plaintiff to shew cause why the rule of Court, or the attachment issued thereon against the sheriff of Yorkshire, should not be set aside on payment of costs. It appeared that a writ of testatum fi. fa. having issued, directed to the sheriff of Yorkshire, he was directed, by a Judge's order obtained in vacation (28th October), to return the same. The time for the return expired on the 6th of November, but the writ was not returned until the 10th of November, and on the afternoon of that day the Judge's order was made a rule of Court, and a rule for an attachment was obtained.

The rule of M. T., 3 Will. 4, r. 13, applies only to the case of writs issued *and returnable* in vacation; in the case of a fi. fa. issued in vacation, but returnable, under a Judge's order obtained in vacation, on a day in term, the plaintiff must still pursue the old practice, and cannot bring the sheriff into contempt after the writ has been actually returned, although after the day on which it was returnable.

W. H. Watson shewed cause.—It will be said that the proceeding in the present case was irregular, and that the plaintiff ought to have obtained a side bar rule, according to the old practice before the Uniformity of Process Act, 2 Will. 4, c. 39, and the rule of Court founded thereon, M. T., 3 Will. 4, r. 13. That depends upon the interpretation to be put upon that rule, which prescribes that, " in case a Judge shall have made an order, in vacation, for the return of any writ issued by the authority of the said act, or any writ of ca. sa., fi. fa., or elegit, on any day in the vacation, and such order shall have been duly served, but obedience shall not have been paid thereto, and the same shall have been made a rule of Court in the term then next following, it shall not be necessary to serve such rule of Court, or to make any fresh demand of performance thereon, but an attachment shall issue forthwith for the disobedience of such order, whether the thing required by such order shall or shall not have been done in the mean time." It is submitted that that rule applies to the present case, the order having been made in vacation.

PARKE, B.—The rule of Court does not apply to this case. It was introduced to obviate the evil that existed under the old practice, when rules to return writs in vacation never need be complied with at all, if the sheriff could obtain time until the first day of term. In that case, if subsequent compliance could purge the contempt, he might inconvenience parties by neglecting to return a writ until the first day of term, and yet escape an attachment. But the rule does not apply to the case of writs ordered to be returned in term. According to the old practice, if the order were complied with before a rule was obtained for an attachment, that was sufficient; and the rule of M. T., 8 Will. 4, applies only where the order is both made and returnable in vacation.

The other Barons concurred.

Rule absolute.

Exch. of Pleas,
1841.

REGINA v. RYLE.

Nov. 25.

ON the 8th of July, 1841, a commission was issued upon a suggestion that the defendant was indebted to the Crown for monies deposited in his hands by Lieutenant-Colonel Egerton, for the service of the Cheshire yeomanry cavalry. The commission was in the usual form, empowering the commissioners " to inquire as well on the oaths of good and lawful men of the county of Middlesex, by whom the truth may be the better known, as by the testimony on oath of any other credible person or persons, whether the said John Ryle is now indebted to us in any and what sum of money on the account aforesaid; and therefore we command you, that at such day and place as you shall for that purpose appoint, you diligently attend in and about the premises with effect, and duly take an inquest thereof on the oaths of such good and lawful men, and have the same before the Barons, &c. And we hereby command our sheriff of Middlesex, that he cause to come before you, at such day and place as you shall appoint, twelve good and lawful men of his bailiwick, by whom the truth may the better be known, and we empower you to summon before you such person or persons as you shall think proper, and carefully examine them in the premises on their corporal oaths, &c." An inquisition was accordingly taken; and the only evidence brought before the jury, on the execution of the commission, was an affidavit of Henry Hill, Esq., captain and adjutant of the Cheshire yeomanry cavalry, " that John Ryle, of &c., is justly and truly indebted to our Sovereign Lady the Queen in the sum of 2,492*l.* 7*s.* 7*d.*, being so much of her Majesty's monies deposited in his hands by Lieutenant-Colonel Wilbraham Egerton, for the service of the said regiment, and unaccounted for by the said John Ryle, and that he verily believes that the said John Ryle

In the case of an immediate extent, on an inquisition to find debts, the jury may find the fact of a debt being due to the Crown, on the sole evidence of an affidavit that the debt is due.

has stopped payment, and is in embarrassed and insolvent circumstances, and that unless some method more speedy than the ordinary course of proceeding at law be forthwith had against the said John Ryle for the recovery of the debt so due and owing to her Majesty as aforesaid, the same is in danger of being lost." The jury found that the defendant was indebted to the Crown in the sum mentioned in the affidavit, and thereupon a Judge's fiat was obtained for a writ of *immediate* extent to issue, which was issued accordingly.

Cowling had obtained a rule, calling upon the *Attorney-General* to shew cause why the inquisition, and all the subsequent proceedings taken thereunder, should not be set aside for irregularity.

The affidavit of Mr. Hobbs, who for twenty years has acted as a commissioner upon commissions to find debts due to the Crown, stated, in answer to the application, that whenever it had been found inconvenient or impossible to obtain, in time to make the proceedings available, the attendance of witnesses to give vivâ voce evidence, the jury had found the debt upon affidavit only; and that he believed this has been the invariable practice from the most ancient period up to the present time.

The *Solicitor General* and *Waddington* shewed cause.— It will be contended on the part of the defendant, that as the evidence used before the jury was an affidavit only, and no witness was examined vivâ voce, the proceeding was irregular and contrary to practice; for that, as the jury were empanelled under the commission to inquire whether or not a debt was due to the Crown, no evidence could be legal but that which was given by witnesses vivâ voce upon oath; and the case of *Rex* v. *Hornblower* (a) will be relied upon. That, however, was the case of an extent

(a) 11 Price, 29.

in aid, and no such decision has been come to in the case of an extent in chief. But even in the case of an extent in aid, according to the practice of this Court, and the established course of proceeding with respect to Crown debts, the course pursued on this occasion was the proper one. It appears not only upon the affidavit filed in this case, but is admitted in the case of *Rex* v. *Hornblower*, to have been of very long usage. The object of finding the debt under the commission is merely to have the debt entered of record. The Crown can have no writ against the body or the goods of the debtor, without first applying to a judge upon an affidavit of debt, that the party is insolvent, and the debt is in danger. In order to issue an extent, it is necessary that the debt should be entered of record; but the inquiry under the commission is purely an ex-parte proceeding, and the party has no notice to attend, nor can he, nor has he ever been known to attend the inquiry; nor, if any witness were examined vivâ voce, could he cross-examine him. The debt is not conclusively found by the inquiry before the jury under the commission, but the party is at liberty to traverse the debt in the proceedings which subsequently take place. If it could be shewn that any grievance resulted from the practice, or that any advantage would be obtained by the party in having the witness examined vivâ voce, it might be a reason against the continuance of the practice, and for an alteration of it by the legislature; but that cannot be suggested. When the extent is issued, and the inquisition is held by the sheriff and a jury, the party may attend and traverse the debt;—he is not bound by the preliminary proceeding. [*Parke*, B.—In *Rex* v. *Hornblower*, the Court placed some reliance upon the language of the commission.] There is nothing whatever in the form of the commission to render it necessary to examine the witnesses vivâ .voce. All that is required is, that the jury are to be satisfied by testimony on oath. The commissioners are to inquire " on the oaths of good and lawful men, and by the testimony on oath of other credible persons." This affidavit is evidence upon oath; it is not necessary that it should be stated vivâ voce before a jury. Mr. West, in his book on Extents, admits the practice, although he says that no length of time can legalize it. He says (a), "No notice is given to the defendant of the execution of this commission; and the usual, if not universal practice is, to adduce no evidence of the debt before the jury, except the affidavit which is prepared for the purpose of obtaining the immediate extent. On this affidavit, and this affidavit alone, usually, if not universally, the jury find the debt." The affidavit of Mr. Hobbs confirms this statement, and shews that notwithstanding the decision of *Rex* v. *Hornblower*, this has continued to be the universal practice to the present time. [*Parke*, B.—Certainly, that decision has never been acted upon.] It has never been acted upon, because the impression was that it was an erroneous decision, come to without properly investigating the grounds upon which this mode of proceeding was adopted. This proceeding is founded on the statute of 33 Hen. 8, c. 39, which regulates the proceedings to recover debts due to the Crown. The 55th sect. enacts, "that all and every suit and suits, which hereafter shall be had, made, or taken of, for, or upon any debt or duties which heretofore hath grown or been due, or that hereafter shall grow or be due, to the king, in the several offices and courts of his exchequer, Duchy of Lancaster, augmentations of the revenues of his crown, surveyors-general of his manors, lands, and tenements, master of the wards and liveries, and court of the first fruits and tenths, or in any of them, or by reason or authority of any of them, shall be severally sued in such one of the said courts and offices, in which court and office, or by reason of the which court and office, the same

(a) Page 22.

debt or duty did first grow or become to be due, or hereafter shall grow or become due, or in the which office and
court the recognisance, obligation, or speciality is or shall
be or remain. And every such several suit and suits shall
be made in every of the said several offices and courts,
under the several seals of the said several courts, by capias, extendi facias, subpœna, attachments, and procla-
mations of allegiance, if need shall require, or any of
them, or *otherwise as unto the said several courts shall be
thought by their discretions expedient for the speedy recovery of the king's debts.*" Now *this* has been thought a proper and expedient mode of commencing the suit, and it is
the only mode in which the debt could be recovered, viz. by
making the mode of commencing the suit a secret and ex-
parte proceeding. The distinction between the inquisition
to find debts and the inquisition taken before the sheriff
was not adverted to in *Rex* v. *Hornblower*, and the arguments
there used apply very well to the latter inquisition taken before the sheriff, by which the party is to be concluded, but
are perfectly inapplicable to the former, which is a matter of
form, necessarily ex-parte, and of which the party has not
and cannot have notice, because giving notice to the debtor
would at once destroy the whole effect of the proceeding,
and render it useless and unavailing. This preliminary
proceeding comes to nothing, unless it turns out that the
Crown is entitled, on the debt being traversed by the
debtor upon the inquisition before the sheriff. One or two
of the judges, in *Rex* v. *Hornblower*, seemed to think that
there is an express rule of the English law which cannot
be dispensed with, requiring that where a jury is summoned, the witnesses should be summoned and produced
before them: but there is no such rule, and there are
many cases, even of issues joined at common law, and
where courts of equity direct issues to be tried, in which
the personal appearance of the witnesses is dispensed with,
and their depositions are received in evidence. And those

are cases of a contest between litigating parties: but here, if the witnesses were produced, the party has no right to appear or cross-examine them. There are very few cases on this subject to be found in the books; the first is in the reign of Chas. II., *The Attorney-General* v. *Sparrow* (a); but in that case it does not appear upon what evidence the debt was found. In *Rex* v. *Knight* (b) it does appear that it was upon affidavit; and the affidavit having been objected to, the objection was overruled.

Cresswell and *Cowling,* in support of the rule.—This affidavit was not proper evidence to be laid before the jury. From the form of the commission itself, it may be inferred that it was not intended that such evidence should be received. It empowers the commissioners to inquire " as well on the oaths of good and lawful men of the county of Middlesex, by whom the truth may be the better known, as by the testimony of any other credible person or persons." If the meaning of that be that they are to summon a jury, and that the jury are to decide for the commissioners, then the jury surely ought to have before them the credible person or persons. The commissioners have no power to summon and examine them in private, and lay before the jury the result of that examination. If it be contended that the commissioners have power to inquire not only through a jury, but by any other means, then they need not lay the affidavit before the jury at all, provided they, the commissioners, are satisfied. But if they are to inquire through the medium of the inquest, then they are to summon before the jury persons who are to be there examined on their corporal oaths, and *the jury* are to ascertain whether the evidence of those persons is satisfactory. The effect of the inquest is to give the Crown a judgment against the body, lands, and goods of the debtor: the debt

(a) Hardr. 227.   (b) Bunbury, 318.

becomes a debt of record; and the Crown is entitled, under the extent and the statute of Hen. 8, to take the body, lands, and goods of the debtor.

It is said this commission is as old as the statute 10 Edw. 1; but if that statute be looked into, it will be apparent that the commission mentioned therein is not the same, but a different one, which had not the effect of giving the Crown a power of proceeding against the body, lands, and goods; and if the commission were taken under that statute, the Crown would be bound to let the party come in and be heard: for the 8th sect. enacts as follows: —" That certain persons assigned thereunto on our behalf shall be sent into every shire, which shall have full power to inquire of such manner of debts; and also to call afore them solemnly, as well the sheriffs, as their heirs and assigns, and the tenants of their lands, in case they be dead that have received the debts; and also, if need be, to proceed to the taking of such manner of inquests, whether the parties (against whom the foresaid tallies were shewed) do come or not; so that the sheriff do return a reasonable summons made to them therefore; and so the truth being inquired and discussed in presence of the parties, (if they will be there), the inquisitors shall make rolls of them that shall be convicted afore them, so that the foresaid debts being confessed and inrolled, the tallies of the same shall be forthwith broken." That is an entirely different proceeding from the present. The party is charged with his debt; the sheriff is to give him a summons; if he chooses to appear he shall be heard; if not, they proceed without him, and then the debt is to be inrolled. The practice pointed out by this statute has been neglected, and these inquisitions are now held privately; and the cursus scaccarii has been to abstain from giving that summons, and the Crown has fallen into the habit of fixing the person with the debt without giving him an opportunity of appearing. And accordingly we find in the stat.

1 Hen. 8, c. 8, s. 8, that it is enacted, "that every escheator and commissioner shall sit in convenient and open
places, according to the statutes heretofore made, and that
the said escheators and commissioners shall suffer every
person to give evidence openly in their presence to such
inquest as shall be taken before any of them, upon pain of
£40." It may be presumed that that statute was passed
in consequence of the directions in the statute of Edw. 1
not having been pursued. It has been argued on the other
side, that it is in the power of this Court to say how the
king shall recover his debts, and that this is *their* construction of the stat. 33 Hen. 8, c. 39, s. 55; but that is
not so. The Court may devise some other writ instead of
a capias or extendi facias, or subpœna or attachment, and
they might perhaps devise a new writ or writs, or direct
a particular sort of information to be filed; but they cannot say what amount of evidence shall be sufficient to bind
the rights of the subject, and render the body, lands, and
goods of the debtor liable to execution; if that were so, it
would go the length of saying that the Court might admit
hearsay evidence of the debt to be received, or that there
need not be any evidence upon oath at all. The cases
which have been alluded to, in which depositions are admitted instead of vivâ voce testimony, all shew that the
common-law principle is, that no man shall be bound by
evidence which he has not had an opportunity of testing by
cross-examination; because the depositions are only admitted where such an opportunity has been given. And the
stat. 1 Hen. 8, c. 8, s. 3, confirms that view; for the sheriffs, commissioners, and escheators are there directed to
hold their commissions openly. There is, therefore, nothing
in favour of the Crown but this practice. But it is said it
would be idle to have witnesses present, because the party
is not summoned, and could not know where the inquisition is to be held, and therefore vivâ voce testimony would
be useless: but the same observation would have applied

to the inquisition held under the extent before the sheriff,

where no notice was formerly given; and it was argued
that the party had no right to be there and be heard,
until the decision in *Rex* v. *Bickley* (a), when this Court
held that the subject had a right to come in and be heard.
It was there contended, as here, that as the Crown was
not bound to give any notice, it would be quite impossible
to hold that the party had a right to be there and be
heard. The Court took time to consider, and Lord Chief
Baron *Thompson*, in giving his judgment, says,—" It is not,
I believe, very usual in point of practice to have these inquisitions, which are stated to be ex-parte proceedings, much
attended to; but there is no reason why the parties may
not attend them, and why they ought not to be allowed to
propound all such questions to the witnesses as may be
deemed necessary to prove the property in others than the
defendant. And the case of *The King* v. *Bulley and Blo-
mart* (b), which was much relied on, is of great weight;
indeed it is directly in point; but it is one which I never
heard of, (so little has it ever been acted upon), till it was
cited upon this occasion. There the Court held, that a
witness should be examined to prove the property; it does
not appear that there was any refusal to cross-examine the
witnesses; but here there is the additional circumstance,
that the cross-examination was refused. It was laid down
that the writ of extent was a right in the king, not at
common law, but given by the statute of Henry the Eighth,
and the learned person who stated that said, that he himself had attended inquisitions on elegits and outlawries.
Undoubtedly this is a very strong authority, and it seems
to have with it all the reason of the thing; for, as it was
stated in the argument, had this case been then entered
into, the expense and trouble of traversing the inquisition
would have been avoided. And it seems to be no answer

(a) 3 Price, 454.   (b) Bunb. 233.

that you may plead the claim; for meanwhile irreparable injury may be done, when, if the evidence had been suffered to proceed, and had the questions proposed been allowed to be received, it would have shewn the truth of the matter. It seems to us, therefore, that this is an irregular proceeding, and the inquisition must, for that reason, be quashed." Again, in *Rex* v. *Hornblower* this matter was fully considered, and it was expressly decided by the Court in that case, notwithstanding what was said of the previous practice, that that practice was wrong; and the inquisition was set aside. And when not a single trace can be found in the books of any dissatisfaction expressed by the Court with that decision, it seems extraordinary that the practice of the officers should have been in defiance of it. There is nothing in the statutes of Edw. 1 or Hen. 8, nor in the power thereby given to this Court to deal with suits for the recovery of Crown debts, which can authorize the Court to depart from the rules of evidence establish for the decision of rights in this kingdom, or can establish one species of evidence for the Crown and another for the subject. It is a mere mockery to call a jury together to find upon their oaths whether a debt exists or not, upon the mere production of an affidavit; for they could not inquire whether the affidavit was true or false, nor as to the means of knowledge of the deponent, but must be bound by his mere statement that a certain debt existed. The Crown relies upon its being the practice; but that practice is not prescriptive. It cannot be older than the reign of Henry the Eighth at the utmost, and all that has been shewn in its favour is stated by persons now living. There is no case to shew that it has ever been brought under the attention of the Court and confirmed; on the contrary, the moment the attention of the Court was called to it, it was disallowed.—They referred also to *Rex* v. *Cooke*, cited in West on Extents, 22, and relied upon *Rex* v. *Hornblower.*

The *Solicitor-General* in reply.—The stat. of 10 Edw. 1, which has been referred to, is not the stat. under which this proceeding takes place, and has nothing to do with this question. That was an act passed on account of some temporary frauds upon the Crown; it was not an act making any permanent regulations, but directing certain commissioners to proceed into different counties to inquire concerning the King's debts, and where they had not been paid, to break the tallies. The other statute also, of the 1 Hen. 8, c. 8, has no application to the present question. It directs certain escheators and commissioners to sit in open and public places, to hold inquisitions upon the deaths of the King's tenants in capite, and to inquire into the escheats and forfeitures due to the Crown. It was passed in consequence of the exactions of Empson and Dudley in the latter part of the reign of Hen. 7, and the mode in which they had conducted the inquisitions, and it was enacted that the escheators and commissioners should sit and examine witnesses openly. The Crown do not set this up as a prescriptive right, but as the invariable usage of the Court, under the 55th section of the 33 Hen. 8, c. 39, by which, it is submitted, the Court may make such orders for the speedy recovery of the King's debts as to it shall seem fit. It is apprehended that the Court, under that statute, might have made a rule of Court regulating the practice, as was suggested in argument in *Rex* v. *Hornblower.* It is not conceded that the writ of extent is no older than the stat. of Hen. 8; it is considerably older; and there is in Price's Exchequer Practice a form of a writ of extent in the time of Edw. 1. [Lord *Abinger,* C. B.—The stat. of Hen. 8 refers to it as one of the writs existing for the recovery of the Crown debts. *Parke,* B.—That is a matter which it is not necessary to enter into. It does not follow that there may not have been commissioners to find debts by the ordinary process; but the question is as to the validity of the practice of receiving this species of evidence upon the execution of the commission to find debts.] The question is, what has been the usage as far as it can be traced? If we can find no time in which this species of evidence has not been received, the question then arises, whether it is so illegal that it must necessarily be put an end to. It is a strong argument against its illegality, that it has existed so long. But why is not an affidavit legal evidence before a jury for this purpose? It is said it is hearsay evidence; but it is not so; it is a statement upon oath made by a party respecting the debt, not vivâ voce, but sworn before a competent authority. That is not hearsay evidence, the witness being examined upon oath. But then it is said you must take the first species of evidence, and not secondary; but this is not secondary: it is a positive statement upon oath that such a person is indebted to the Crown, the deponent stating the facts which constitute the debt. That is not secondary evidence. It is true, that in every cause where there are contested questions, and where the matter is to be laid before a jury, the practice has been universal to examine witnesses vivâ voce. But this is a process simply to put the Crown's debt on record, or put the Crown in a situation to sue for it. If the Crown do not proceed by sci. fa., and the Court think that the writ of extent ought to issue, then the entering the debt on record is in no way binding on the party, who may traverse the debt. There is, therefore, nothing illegal in this practice, and no ground for interfering with it.

Lord ABINGER, C. B.—I am of opinion that this rule ought to be discharged. The objection taken on the part of the defendant is founded upon the proceeding on the inquest, under a commission of this Court, to find whether a debt was due from him to the Crown; and it is stated, that in order to support the existence of that debt, no other evidence was adduced before the jury than an affidavit of debt, and that that was illegal evidence. Now I am at a loss to know upon what authority, either of statute or of common law, it is to be said that in an ex-parte proceeding of this kind, an affidavit is illegal evidence. We have not had brought before us any authority or case to shew that upon inquisitions of various natures that were issued before, evidence of affidavits, or even, in many instances, hearsay evidence, was excluded. The notion of legal evidence on trials before juries, in our law, is the effect of long practice and usage, the decision of Judges, and the practice at Nisi Prius, which has grown into a system, and which forms a part, and a very important part, of the law of the land. But where is the analogy that binds us to apply that practice to ex-parte proceedings on inquests for particular purposes, which are mere matter of form? There is no case that decides that, on inquests to be taken under provisions of this nature, there shall be none but vivâ voce evidence, or none but that which, in common-law trials before juries, may be considered as legal evidence.

I do not apprehend, therefore, that the application is well founded, when it assumes that this affidavit was not legal evidence, and that it was not competent for the jury to found their verdict upon it. I think that it was. When we find that the practice for so many ages has been consistent with the present form, that alone is sufficient evidence, I think, to shew that, till the practice is altered by special authority, we ought not to interpose to alter it.

Such being the case, let us see what is the object of this inquiry. The debts due to the Crown are to be recovered by certain forms of process, but there has been an understanding which is in some measure technical, though I admit the force of it from long usage, and nothing else, that there can be no debt of the Crown upon which process can issue, except it be a debt on record. Upon what is that rule founded? Upon nothing but usage. One does not see any principle why the Crown should not be able to

Exch. of Pleas,
1841.

REGINA
v.
RYLE.

proceed for the recovery of a debt in the same way as a subject, but a usage has grown up which we do not disturb, that the debts of the Crown must be found by record— must be on the records of the Court, before the process can issue from this Court to enforce them. Formerly that process called upon the party to appear, and to contest his debt in the suit. The statute of the 33 Hen. 8 was passed for the purpose of giving the Crown a more rapid procedure, and for the very purpose of securing the debt before the party should have time to abscond or make away with his goods. The process by scire facias would give him that opportunity. The legislature, therefore, in the time of Henry the 8th, passed this act for the purpose of authorising the Court of Exchequer, or any other Court in which the King's debt is entered on record, to issue an immediate process for execution, a capias, extendi facias, or a subpœna. But that statute has provided a remedy for all possible inconvenience that might result; for it enacts, by the 79th section, "that if any person or persons of whom any such debt or duty is or at any time hereafter shall be demanded or required, allege, plead, declare, or shew, in any of the said Courts, good, perfect, and sufficient cause and matter in law, reason, or good conscience, in bar or discharge of the said debt or duty, or why such person or persons ought not to be charged or chargeable to or with the same, and the same causes or matters so alleged, pleaded, declared, or shewed, be sufficiently proved in such one of the said Courts as he or they shall be impleaded, sued, vexed, or troubled for the same, then the said Courts, and every of them, shall have full power and authority to accept, adjudge, and allow the same proof, and wholly and clearly to acquit and discharge all and every person and persons that shall be so impleaded, sued, vexed, or troubled for the same." That clause allows the party to plead to the extent, or to apply by summary motion, which is very often done, to the Court, for the pur-

Exch. of Pleas, 1841.

REGINA
v.
RYLE.

pose of shewing good grounds to discharge him from that process, and the Court often act upon it; and hence, as as well in law as in equity and good conscience, the Court has an equitable jurisdiction, in all cases of process of this sort, to enter upon the whole merits of the case, and to discharge the party, if, upon equity and good conscience, he ought to be discharged. Therefore no detriment arises to the subject. This is a mere form to put the debt upon record, in order to authorise the issuing of the process.

That being the case, I see no inconvenience, I see no prejudice, I see no injustice whatever arising to the individual, from the form being pursued according to the ancient practice.

But we are told that the case of *Rex* v. *Hornblower* is an authority the other way. If I could consider that case as an unequivocal authority the other way,—though it has never been acted upon,—it would undoubtedly deserve very grave consideration; but I think I cannot take it as any authority at all. In the first place, the case was discussed by counsel only on behalf of the private prosecutor, the interest of the Crown not being supported by the Crown. In the next place, when I look at the reasoning of the counsel and the judgment of the learned Judges, I do not find any satisfactory grounds assigned for the decision; far from it, because in that case, looking at the particular circumstances, nobody could doubt that the evidence before the inquest was perfectly legal, and would be competent evidence to prove a debt before a Judge and jury impanelled to try it; it was an affidavit of *the debtor* that he owed the Crown the debt, which would be evidence before any jury at any time. The Lord Chief Baron says, "It is impossible that we can interfere in the manner proposed on the part of the defendant; we are called upon by this motion merely to determine whether the objections which have been made to this extent are well founded, in other words, to say whether the extent has been well issued or not. I am clearly of opinion that it has been improperly issued, because the fiat upon which it was obtained was founded on an inquisition improperly taken, and therefore it must be set aside." He gives, therefore, no reasons at all, but in as far as he incorporates the reasons of the advocate, they are evidently inconsistent with reason or with justice. Then I do not find that Mr. Baron *Graham* gives any reason; he only says that he is of opinion that the inquisition is not properly found. Mr. Baron *Wood* gives no reason. He says, "There ought to be an affidavit made, to be produced before the Judge, and an inquisition must be taken before a jury." Whether he means an affidavit to justify the issue of the extent, I do not know, but he does not give any answer to the question about the commission; he enters in no degree into the reasoning about it. The judgment of Mr. Baron *Garrow* is given at greater length, and I observe, that though he coincides with the rest of the Court, he gives reasons which I cannot conceive were properly reported. He says this:—"The nature of the process requires that it should be strictly correct in all its stages. The seizure of a defendant's person and effects is, in most instances, the first intimation that he has of it; the party, who may be in fact a very responsible person, cannot hear, generally speaking, except from information or by accident, that on the taking of the inquisition against him no witness was examined before the jury, and that the only evidence given of any debt being due from him was an affidavit of this description; that is stated to have been the course pursued on the present occasion; and although it has been objected that the affidavit of the facts is founded on information and belief, yet, in the present case, I think that is quite sufficient, because the party has in such cases seldom any better means of knowledge." Therefore he seems to have thought the affidavit was sufficient, but he does not enter into the reasoning in support of it at all. There is nothing stated about the

Exch. of Pleas, 1841.

REGINA
v.
RYLE.

practice—nothing stated about the statute, and the jurisdiction it gives to the Court of Exchequer; all that is entirely left out of view, which has been so fully discussed to-day: and I do not find, except to one learned individual, that this authority of *Rex* v. *Hornblower* has ever given any satisfaction. That individual is Mr. West, who has written upon extents.

It appears to me that it is our duty to support the uniform and constant practice of the Court, when we do not find it inconsistent with any positive law. In this case it appears to me not to be inconsistent with any law whatever. I think the evidence was not illegal under the circumstances. I think it was such evidence as the jury might take, and find the debt upon. The party is not prejudiced by not being summoned to attend before them, because the appeal is open to him afterwards when the process is issued, and the very object of the statute of Hen. 8 was to enable the Court to issue a more immediate process, leaving it open to the party to plead before execution as he might have done previously. I am of opinion, therefore, that this rule ought to be discharged.

PARKE, B.—I agree with my Lord Chief Baron that this rule ought to be discharged. Two points have been discussed yesterday and to-day, upon which I think it unnecessary to give an opinion: one is, whether this extent is grounded upon the common law, or upon the statute of Hen. 8. It appears to me to be entirely immaterial to discuss any question of that kind. Another is, whether the inquisition that is taken in order to find the debt, is such a public proceeding that the debtor and all the world have a right to be present. It is unnecessary to give any opinion upon that; it may be, that it is so by common law only, but that the right is restrained by the operation of the statute of Hen. 8, to which reference has been made.

The simple question for us to decide is, whether an inquisition taken upon a commission to find debts, (which we may presume to have existed before the time of Hen. 8), is properly executed by receiving evidence of a person not called before the jury, which evidence would be inadmissible in any trial between party and party. Now, as my Lord Chief Baron has very properly observed, the rules of evidence, as applicable to trials between party and party and criminal trials, have been the result of practice established, not by the law of the land, but the Judges seeing that the species of evidence given in cases between party and party, and between prosecutor and the accused, was much more lax than in the present day, have prescribed certain rules which have been adhered to; but the question is, whether the practice has laid down any such rule with regard to inquests of this description, which are not final in their nature, but are only preliminary, and may be traversed by any person whose rights are affected thereby. That appears to be a question to be determined by practice and usage, and the authority of decided cases. Now, in this case there is no doubt that the practice and usage have prevailed for a century back. I have always understood that such was the regular established usage in all cases of proceeding upon extents, and we can only learn what the practice has been in ancient times from the practice of modern times: and I apprehend that it would be difficult to produce any authority to shew that, in a proceeding which was not finally binding upon the rights of parties, juries have been tied down to hear only such evidence as would be received in cases binding between party and party.

That being so, according to established usage, I apprehend this affidavit would be admissible in evidence. Then is there any authority which could preclude us from acting upon the acknowledged practice? The only case is that of *Rex* v. *Hornblower.* That authority, for the reasons given by my Lord Chief Baron, I do not think ought to bind us. The principal reason is, that that was an extent in

aid, and we all know that extents in aid were very much
abused, and were a very great grievance to the subject,
and that the Courts had begun to lend a ready ear to objections taken to them. Again, the Crown was not heard
upon that occasion to enforce its rights to recover Crown
debts. Therefore I do not feel that we are bound to
yield to the authority of that case, so much as I should
have done if the matter had been fully discussed, and
with somebody present to represent the interests of the
Crown.

I had some doubts in the course of the argument, whether the form of the commission might not have precluded the taking of the evidence by affidavit. Had the
commission been in the form in which it has occasionally
been, that the commissioners were to inquire " by all
other means in their power," there would be no doubt of
the admissibility of the evidence. But I have come to
the conclusion, that the particular form makes no difference. By the terms of the commission, the jury are
empowered to satisfy themselves upon all such evidence as
would lead them to find the truth of the debt upon their
oaths,—such evidence as would satisfy them that the debt
existed in point of fact, and I think that they are not confined to that species of evidence which is specifically pointed
out in the commission, the examination of witnesses upon
oath. Those words are introduced into the commission in
order to enable the commissioners to summon witnesses and
to administer an oath to them; but it does not appear to
me that they are, by the terms of the commission, confined
to evidence upon oath only. For these reasons, I am of
opinion that the rule ought to be discharged.

GURNEY, B.—I concur in opinion with my Lord Chief
Baron and my Brother *Parke,* for the reasons they have
given.

The case of *Rex* v. *Hornblower* cannot be considered

as any authority, when we find that the evidence which was there considered as inadmissible clearly was admissible, as being the statement of the party himself made against himself, and that that decisive proof of its admissibility was never brought before the Court. It appears that the Court were not assisted by counsel for the Crown in that case; if they had been, it is scarcely possible that the case should have been so imperfectly argued.

ROLFE, B.—I am of the same opinion. Suppose the practice, instead of that which has been proved, had been, that upon the Crown making an affidavit, the debt should be entered on record; if that had been the practice uniformly pursued, nobody could have said it was a proceeding so unjust as on the face of it to carry its own refutation, and to be necessarily illegal. Now the practice has been, not that the debt is entered on record upon affidavit alone, but upon the finding of the jury; the jury upon that affidavit finding that the debt is due. That is somewhat more protection than the party would have had if an affidavit only had been required.

That there is no injustice in this case appears further from this, that under the statute of Henry 8, the party interested in contesting the debt has a full right to do so; and I cannot but assume from the language of that statute of Henry 8, in the 79th section, that when it speaks of debts, it contemplated debts which the party had had no previous opportunity of contesting; for I can see no reason for giving a party an opportunity of contesting the proceeding upon execution, if he had had an opportunity of contesting it before. Mr. *Cresswell's* argument went not so much upon the injustice of proceeding upon the affidavit, as upon that of proceeding without calling the party in in the first instance, and allowing him to contest the debt; and it seems to me that the legislature contemplated the debts being debts in respect to which there

was no such opportunity, otherwise they would not have
allowed the party to contest them upon the subsequent
proceeding.

For these reasons, I concur with my Lord and my
learned Brothers, that this rule must be discharged.

Lord ABINGER, C. B.—I wish to add, that the foundation
of the former jurisdiction of this Court in quo minus, is the
assumption that the party suing is a debtor to the Crown;
but it was nothing but the practice of the Court that permitted the declaration of the plaintiff that he was a debtor
to the Crown to be received as sufficient evidence of that
fact, to give him the process to call his debtor into Court.
It might have been urged with equal propriety as in this
case, that it was very hard to allow a provision of that sort to
entitle a party to issue a capias, and take a man in arrest;
and yet the long-established practice of the Court gave the
jurisdiction.   In like manner in the King's Bench, with
respect to the custody of the marshal.   The ancient established practice of the Court is not to be objected to in
modern times, merely because it is not founded upon
exact statute.

                                        Rule discharged.

Nov. 25.

Where a rule
nisi for judg-
ment, as in case
of a nonsuit, is
discharged on a
peremptory un-
dertaking,
either party
may draw up
the rule con-
taining the un-
dertaking, and
if the defendant
does so he must
serve the plain-
tiff with it, to
enable him to
try according to
the undertak-
ing; and where
the plaintiff
gave a peremp-
tory undertak-
ing to try at the
sittings after
term, and on
default a rule
absolute was
obtained for
judgment, as in
case of a non-
suit; the Court
set aside that
rule and all
proceedings
thereon for ir-
regularity, the
defendant not
having served
the plaintiff
with the rule
containing the
undertaking
until the first
day of the
sittings.

SAWYER *v.* THOMPSON and Another (*a*).

IN this case judgment as in case of a nonsuit had been moved for in Trinity Term, and the rule discharged on an undertaking to try at the sittings after that term. The plaintiff did not draw up the rule for the undertaking, or proceed to trial; but the defendant drew it up, and served it on the first day of the sittings. In this term, the defend-ant obtained the ordinary rule absolute for judgment as in case of a nonsuit, on the usual affidavit that the plain-tiff had not proceeded to trial pursuant to his undertak-ing. *Willes* had obtained a rule to set aside the latter rule and all proceedings thereon, on the ground that the defendant had not drawn up the rule in time to enable the plaintiff to go to trial, and must therefore be consi-dered as having abandoned it.

Humfrey and *James* now shewed cause, and contended that it was the plaintiff's rule, and that he could not take advantage of his own laches in not drawing it up.

Willes, in support of the rule, referred to *Gingell* v. *Bean* (*b*), where the defendant having, in Hilary Term, ob-tained a rule nisi for judgment as in case of a nonsuit, which was discharged on a peremptory undertaking to try at the sittings after term; but the rule containing the undertaking not having been drawn up until after the time to which it related had expired, a rule absolute in the first instance for judgment as in case of a nonsuit, obtained in Easter Term, and all proceedings thereon, were set aside for irregularity.

(*a*) This case was decided by *Alderson*, B., sitting alone on the last day of the term.

(*b*) 1 Man. & G. 50; 1 Scott, N. R. 153.

ALDERSON, B.—That case is in point, and it is consist- Each. of Pleas, 1841.
ent with common sense, that if the defendant means to
act upon the undertaking he should give the plaintiff notice in time that he does so.

SAWYER v. THOMPSON.

Rule absolute.

VACATION SITTINGS AFTER MICHAEL-
MAS TERM.

NORTH v. INGAMELLS.

Nov. 26.

TRESPASS.—The declaration alleged, that the defendant, with force and arms, &c., broke and entered " a certain close of the plaintiff, situate and being in the parish
of Hickney in the county of Lincoln, abutting on the south
upon lands now in the occupation of the defendant, and in
other part upon lands now in the occupation of John
Smith," and there with spades, &c., dug up, turned up,
and subverted the soil, &c.

In trespass qu. cl. fr., a description of a close by two abuttals only is a sufficient compliance with the rule of H. T. 4 Will. 4, trespass, 1.

Special demurrer, assigning for cause that the said close
in which, &c., is not sufficiently described in the declaration by name or abuttals, or other description.

Wallinger, in support of the demurrer.—The declaration
does not comply with the rule of Court. Hil. Term, 4 Will.
4, tit. " Trespass" 1, which requires that " in actions of
trespass quare clausum fregit, the close or place in which,
&c., must be designated in the designation, by name or
abuttals, or other description; in failure whereof the defendant may demur specially." This close is described by
two abuttals only, which is not a compliance with the rule.

Willmore, in support of the declaration.—The plaintiff is
not bound to set out the abuttals all round the close.

Here two abuttals have been given, by which the rule has been sufficiently complied with. [*Parke*, B.—The rule means all the abuttals, and you have set out only two.] It is submitted that that is sufficient. The plaintiff has used the ordinary mode of description which was in use before the rule of Court. In *Walford* v. *Anthony* (a), two abuttals only were given, and although the case turned on an objection to the abuttals, no objection was taken on that ground. If the plaintiff in the present case attempted to set out all the abuttals, he would probably be nonsuited at the trial for want of proof of the abuttals, as the title to the other adjoining closes is disputed. If the close was not sufficiently described, so as to know which was the close intended, the defendant might have applied to a Judge at Chambers to compel the plaintiff to give a better description of the abuttals, and ought not to have demurred. The rule requires a designation by name or abuttals; and any name would be a compliance with its terms, though it afforded no information to the defendant. In *Cocker* v. *Crompton* (b), where the plaintiff named his close the Foldyard, and the defendant pleaded liberum tenementum generally, without giving any further description of the close, it was held that the plaintiff was not driven to a new assignment, but was entitled to recover upon proving a trespass done in a close in his possession bearing the name given in the declaration, although the defendant had a close called the Foldyard in the same parish. So here, two abuttals would be a compliance with the terms of the rule, and they have been given.—He cited also *Lethbridge* v. *Winter* (c).

Wallinger, in reply.—The object of the rule was to avoid ambiguity, and to prevent the plea of liberum tenementum, and the consequent necessity of a new assignment. It is

(a) 8 Bing. 75; 1 M. & Scott, 126.

(b) 1 B. & Cr. 489; 2 D. & R. 719.

(c) 2 Bing. 49; 9 Moore, 95.

admitted that one abuttal would not be a compliance with the rule, and it has never yet been decided that two abuttals are sufficient. The circumstance of the other boundaries of the close not being known, is no excuse for not complying with the rule. The demurrer is expressly given by the rule, if there is a failure of compliance with it.

PARKE, B.—I think the description is sufficient to satisfy the rule of Court. The rule was introduced to prevent the plea of liberum tenementum, and the necessity of a new assignment; and it directs the close to be set out by name, abuttals, or other description. It was settled in *Cocker* v. *Crompton*, that if there be a description of the close in the declaration, liberum tenementum is not a common bar, because the defendant must be taken to know what close is meant; and the question is whether the close so described is or is not the close of the defendant. I therefore think it is sufficient to give such a description that the party may know what close is intended. If this description should be insufficient, the defendant may apply on affidavit to a Judge at chambers, stating that he does not know in respect of what close the plaintiff complains. If indeed it had been decided, that to a plea of liberum tenementum a replication setting out two abuttals only had been bad, I should have been disposed to think that the same rule would have applied to the declaration; but there is no such decision. The practice of pleaders has been not to insert too many abuttals in the declaration, in order to avoid being nonsuited at the trial. I think the plaintiff is within the terms of the rule, and that he may be considered to have done enough in the first instance, to prevent the defendant from having recourse to the plea of liberum tenementum. The description is in accordance with the old practice, under which it was sufficient to shew two abuttals. The defendant may withdraw his demurrer on payment of costs.

ALDERSON, B.—The object of the rule in requiring the close to be described by name, abuttals, or other description, was to prevent the ambiguity that would arise if the name of the parish alone were given. The plaintiff must give a sufficient description to shew that he is suing for a trespass to a particular close, and that is done when a plaintiff gives two abuttals or the name. It is clear that no rule could be made in this case so as to exclude all possible ambiguity. If the defendant can shew that there is a real ambiguity, and that he cannot see distinctly what close is indicated by the plaintiff's declaration, he may apply to a Judge for a better description.

GURNEY, B., and ROLFE, B., concurred.

Judgment for the plaintiff.

———◆———

Nov. 26.

FLETCHER, Public Officer, *v.* CROSBIE, BARLOW, and Others.

A declaration described the plaintiff as "one of the present public officers of certain persons united in co-partnership *for the purpose of carrying on the trade and business of banking in England, according to the stat. 7 Geo. 4, c. 46:*—*Held* bad on *special demurrer*, for not stating that the copartnership was carrying on the trade and business of bankers, or had carried on such trade.

ASSUMPSIT for money lent, money paid, interest, work and labour, and on an account stated. The declaration commenced as follows:—" John Fletcher, the plaintiff in this suit, one of the present public officers of certain persons united in co-partnership, for the purpose of carrying on the trade and business of bankers in England, according to the statute made and passed in the 7th year of the reign of his late Majesty King George the 4th, entitled ' An Act for the better regulating Co-partnerships of certain Bankers in England,' &c., which said John Fletcher had been duly nominated and appointed, and now is one of the public officers of the said co-partnership, according to the form and effect of the said act of Parliament, complains," &c.

Special demurrer, assigning for causes, that it nowhere appears by the declaration, that the said co-partnership ever in fact carried on business under the provisions of the said act, or that the said supposed debt accrued from the defendant Barlow to the said co-partnership whilst carrying on business under the provisions of the said act, or that the said defendant was indebted to the said co-partnership, as a co-partnership carrying on business under the provisions of the said act, at the time of the commencement of the said suit.

Joinder in demurrer.

Tomlinson, in support of the demurrer.—As the right of action arises under a statute, 9 Geo. 4, c. 46, and did not exist at common law, the plaintiff is bound to bring himself within the provisions of the statute. The statute confines the right to sue to parties to a co-partnership which has actually carried on business, and as it does not appear that the parties here ever carried on business as bankers, the plaintiff has not brought himself within it. The 9th section of the 7 Geo. 4, c. 46, enacts,—" that all actions and suits, and also all petitions to found any commission of bankruptcy, against any person or persons who may be indebted to any such co-partnership, *carrying on business* under the provisions of this act," &c. &c., shall be commenced in the name of any one of the public officers for the time being, of such co-partnership. Similar language is used in the act for extending it, 1 & 2 Vict. c. 96, s. 1, by which it is enacted,—" that any person now being, or having been, or who may hereafter be or have been, a member of any co-partnership now carrying on or which may hereafter carry on the business of banking under the provisions of the said recited acts, shall, &c." So that the right of a banking co-partnership to sue in the name of their public officer, is confined to cases where they are *actually* carrying on business, and not merely to cases where they intend doing so. The carrying on business is conditional to the right to sue. Here the allegation in the

Exch. of Pleas, 1841.

FLETCHER
v.
CROSBIE.

declaration is, that they are united in co-partnership *for the purpose* of carrying on the trade and business of bankers. It is consistent with that allegation, that the co-partnership has never carried on business at all, but only contemplates doing so. By the rule of Hil. T. 4 Will. 4, pl. 21, the character in which a party sues or is sued " shall not in any case be considered as in issue, unless specially denied." In the present case there is no averment which is capable of being traversed. *Spiller* v. *Johnson* (a) will perhaps be relied on by the other side, but there this objection was not pointed out as a cause of demurrer.

Crompton, contrà.—The form here used is the same as that in *Spiller* v. *Johnson* and *Christie* v. *Peart* (b), and is the form now given in the books of pleading. In *Spiller* v. *Johnson, Alderson,* B., says, " In actions by the assignees of a bankrupt, it is not necessary to state in the declaration that they were elected by the creditors." It cannot be necessary, to entitle co-partnerships to sue by their public officer, that they should actually be carrying on business at the time of the action; otherwise the consequence would be, that if they ceased to carry on business they could neither sue nor be sued; whereas the fourth section of the act provides that *before* they begin to issue bills or notes, &c., the names of two or more persons shall be given as public officers, in whose name the co-partnership shall sue and be sued: *Edwards* v. *Buchanan* (c). [*Parke,* B.—The act provides that certain acts shall be done before they "shall begin to issue any bills or notes, or borrow, owe, or take up any money on their bills or notes;" but it does not follow that they cannot borrow money or act as bankers in other respects.] According to the argument on the other side, no indictment could be maintained for stealing the property of the co-partnership,

(a) 6 M. & W. 570.   (b) 7 M. & W. 491.   (c) 3 B. & Adol. 788.

as it might be a good defence to say that they were not carrying on business. *Exch. of Pleas,* 1841.

FLETCHER
v.
CROSBIE.

Tomlinson, in reply.—The objection is, that it does not appear that they ever carried on business. If the members of this co-partnership once carried on business, and were winding up their affairs, they might still be considered as carrying on business within the meaning of the act. It is analogous to the case of a partnership, where after the dissolution the partners still remain liable. The privilege is confined to persons carrying on business, or who have carried on business.

PARKE, B.—The declaration is bad on special demurrer. It ought to have stated that the co-partnership were *carrying on* business, and it would be sufficient proof of that allegation, if it were traversed, that they had once begun to carry it on. The plaintiff may amend by inserting the word " and," so that the sentence will run thus, " for the purpose of *and* carrying on the trade and business &c."

Leave to amend accordingly, otherwise

Judgment for the defendant.

Exch. of Pleas,
1841.

Dec. 2.

HUNTING *v.* SHELDRAKE and Others.

Where the obligor of a bond, having devised his land, died before the passing of the stat. 1 Will. 4, c. 47: —*Held,* that the specialty creditor could not maintain an action against the devisee alone, there being no heir, under 3 W. & M., c. 14, s. 3.

DEBT on bond.—The declaration stated, that William Clarke, of whom the said defendants are devisees (*there being no heirs* of the said William Clarke), theretofore and in the lifetime of him the said William Clarke, to wit, on the 27th of June, 1821, by his certain writing obligatory, sealed, &c. (profert), acknowledged himself to be held and firmly bound unto the plaintiff in the sum of £100, to be paid to the plaintiff, and for the true payment whereof the said William Clarke did, by the said writing obligatory, bind himself and his heirs to the plaintiff: and the plaintiff avers that the said William Clarke departed this life after the making and passing of a certain act of Parliament passed in the first year of the reign of his late Majesty King William 4th (*a*), intituled "An Act for consolidating and amending the Laws for facilitating the Payment out of Debts of real Estates," to wit, on the 17th of July 1831 ; and the plaintiff further saith, that the said William Clarke died without having or leaving any heir or heirs ; nevertheless the said William Clarke in his lifetime, and the defendants, so being his devisees as aforesaid (there being no heir of the said William Clarke), have not nor hath any or either of them paid the said sum of £100 above-mentioned, or any part thereof, but to pay the same have wholly neglected and refused, and the said defendants still refuse to pay the same, or any part thereof.

(*a*) 1 Will. 4, c. 47; by the 4th section of which it is enacted, that if in any case there shall not be any heirs-at-law, against whom, jointly with the devisee or devisees, a remedy is hereby given, in every such case every creditor to whom by this act relief is so given, shall and may have and maintain his, her, and their action and actions of debt or covenant, as the case may be, against such devisee or devisees solely; and such devisee or devisees shall be liable for false plea as aforesaid.

Plea, that the said William Clarke departed this life before the making and passing of the said act of Parliament in the declaration mentioned, to wit, on &c., without this, that the said William Clarke departed this life after the making and passing of the same act, modo et formâ.

Special demurrer, assigning for cause, that the defendants have, by their said plea, taken an immaterial issue.

Joinder in demurrer.

The following was the point marked for argument on the part of the plaintiff:—The plaintiff will rely upon the cause of demurrer specially assigned, viz. that the defendants have by their plea taken an immaterial traverse; and will insist that it is immaterial, on the ground that the action was maintainable against the devisee alone (there being no heir) under the 3 W. & M. c. 14.

The case was argued on a former day (Nov. 26) by

Manning, Serjt., in support of the demurrer.—By the 3 W. & M. c. 14, s. 2, it is enacted,—" that all wills and testaments, limitations, dispositions, or appointments of or concerning any manors, messuages, lands, tenements, or hereditaments, or of any rent, profit, term, or charge out of the same, whereof any person or persons, at the time of his, her, or their decease, shall be seised in fee-simple in possession, reversion, or remainder, to have power to dispose of the same by his, her, or their last wills or testaments, to be made after the 25th day of March, 1692, shall be deemed and taken (only as against such creditor or creditors as aforesaid, his, her, and their heirs, successors, executors, administrators, or assigns, and every of them) to be fraudulent, and clearly, absolutely, and utterly void, frustrate, and of none effect, any pretence, colour, feigned or presumed consideration, or any other matter or thing to the contrary notwithstanding." And the 3rd section enacts,—" And for the means that such creditors may be enabled to recover their said debts, be it further enacted, that in the case before mentioned, every such creditor shall and may have and maintain his, her, and their action and actions of debt upon his, her, and their said bonds and specialties, against the heir and heirs-at-law of such obligor or obligors, and such devisee and devisees jointly, by virtue of this act; and such devisee or devisees shall be liable and chargeable for a false plea by him or them pleaded, in the same manner as any heir should have been for any false plea by him pleaded, or for not confessing the lands or tenements to him descended." The latter section merely means, that where there is an heir he must be joined, otherwise the defendant may plead the non-joinder in abatement but where there is no heir, the devisee may be sued alone. If the section has not that construction, it will have the effect of narrowing very considerably the operation of the enactments in the second section. The statute was passed to prevent creditors from being defrauded of their debts, and it ought therefore to be liberally construed, as was said by Lord *Hardwicke* in *Kinaston* v. *Clark* (a). At common law lands were not devisable, and all specialty creditors might recover their debts against the heir. The stat. 32 Hen. 8, c. 1, enabled persons to devise all lands held in socage, and two-thirds of lands held by knight-service, or in the nature of socage, of other lords than the King. And the stat. 12 Car. 2, c. 24, s. 1, by abolishing tenure by knight-service, had the effect of rendering all lands devisable; by which means persons were enabled, by devising their lands, to defraud their creditors. It was to remedy this evil that the stat. 3 W. & M., c. 14, was passed. In *Gawler* v. *Wade* (b), where a bill in equity was filed against the devisee alone, there being an heir in existence, it was held that the heir ought to be joined; and Lord *Cowper*, C., there says,—" It is the act of Parliament makes this assets in the devisee's hands, and that requiring

(a) 2 Atk. 205.   (b) 1 P. Wms. 100.

the heir to be made a defendant, you must follow the re- *Exch. of Pleas,*
medy therein prescribed; and this bill in equity is an action at law; *otherwise, if there were no heir;* and perhaps it
might be otherwise too, if the bill had charged that the
plaintiff had made inquiry, and could find or discover no
heir." That passage was misunderstood by *Lawrence*, J.,
in *Wilson* v. *Knubley* (a); for there is no ground for sur-
mising that Lord *Cowper* thought, that if there had been
no heir, it would have been a reason for the creditors going
into equity. The effect of the decision in truth is, that
both at law and in equity the devisee may be sued alone,
when there is no heir.

F. *Robinson*, contrà.—The issue is not immaterial, for
the allegation that the obligor died before the passing of
the stat. 1 Will. 4, c. 47, is a good traverse. The stat.
3 W. & M., c. 14, was intended to give a remedy to specialty creditors in those cases only where there was an
heir and also a devisee, and there is no reason to assume
that the legislature intended to give a remedy where there
was no heir. In *Wilson* v. *Knubley*, where the plaintiff
declared in covenant against the defendant as devisee of
the lands, "there being no heir" of the testator, Lord
Ellenborough says—"Supposing, therefore, that we could
go to the extent of saying that an averment of there being
no heir is equivalent to joining the heir, where there is
one, in the action—supposing we could get over that difficulty, how could we, construing a comparatively recent
act of Parliament, where a particular remedy is given, by
action of debt, on bonds and specialties, where no remedy
was before, extend it to actions of covenant?" That case
was recognized by the Court in giving judgment in *Farley*
v. *Briant* (b). The only authority cited on the other side

(a) 7 East, 133. (b) 3 Ad. & Ell. 839; 5 Nev. & M. 42.

is an obiter dictum of an equity Judge in *Gawler* v. *Wade,* and which was not necessary to the decision of the case. [*Alderson,* B.—In those days the equity Judges knew and were in the habit of practising the common law.] Even admitting Lord *Cowper* to be as good an authority in law as in equity, it was not necessary for him to determine this point, because he decided against the creditor. It has been held that, under certain circumstances, the heir is liable to make contribution to the devisee; which is in favour of the defendant: *Chaplin* v. *Chaplin* (*a*), *Galton* v. *Hancock* (*b*). The legislature may have intended to give a remedy to a certain extent only, and may never have contemplated this case: if so, it is casus omissus, and the Court cannot supply it. In *Jones* v. *Smart* (*c*), *Buller,* J., says—" A casus omissus can in no case be supplied by a Court of law, for that would be to make laws." The same rule is laid down by *Vaughan,* C. J., in *Bole* v. *Horton* (*d*). *Doe* dem. *Howson* v. *Waterton* (*e*), and *Bradley* v. *Clark* (*f*), are authorities to the same effect. In the latter case *Buller,* J., says, " In early times the legislature used (and I believe it was a wise course to take) to pass laws in general and in few terms; they were left to the Courts of law to be construed, so as to reach all the cases within the mischief to be remedied. But in modern times great care has been taken to mention the particular cases in the contemplation of the legislature, and the Courts are not permitted to take the same liberty in construing them as they did in expounding the ancient statutes." This statute gave a new remedy, and must be construed strictly. It may be admitted that if before the stat. 3 W. & M. there had been a remedy against the devisee of land, the words of the act might admit of the construction contended for by the plaintiff; but

(*a*) 3 P. Wms. 365.
(*b*) 2 Atk. 430.
(*c*) 1 T. R. 52.

(*d*) Vaugh. 373.
(*e*) 3 B. & Ald. 149.
(*f*) 5 T. R. 197.

it is otherwise when a statute, as in this case, gives a remedy unknown to the common law. In *Townsend's case* (a) it is said, "And so is the diversity where a statute makes an ordinance by affirmative words touching a thing which was before the common law, and which was not before at the common law." In *Wethen* v. *Baldwin* (b), *Windham*, J., says, "When an act of Parliament is introductory of a new law in affirmative words, it has the force of negative words." And in *Pool* v. *Neel* (c), *Glyn*, C. J., says, "It is to be observed that acts which give new remedies shall not have a liberal construction." The devisee is not, therefore, solely liable where there is no heir.

Manning, Serjt., in reply.—It is admitted on the other side, that if any remedy had existed at common law against the devisee, the plaintiff's construction would be correct: but that makes no difference. The object of the statute was to make lands devised by will subject to specialty debts, and that if a devise was in fact made, the devisee should be liable. Its effect was to place the devisee in the situation of the heir, and to make him liable to specialty debts. The case is precisely within the words of the act, which apply to all devises which contain no provision for the payment of debts; the object being to provide for the payment of all persons who were creditors of the testator; the remedy against him being co-extensive with the assets. The obligation to pay debts necessarily arose from the power to devise.

Cur. adv. vult.

The judgment of the Court was now delivered by

ROLFE, B.—The question in this case was, whether before the passing of the stat. 11 Geo. 4 and 1 Will. 4, c. 47, by

Exch. of Pleas, 1841.

HUNTING
v.
SHELDRAKE.

(a) Plowd. 113.   (b) 1 Sid. 56.   (c) 2 Sid. 63.

which the laws for facilitating the payment of debts out of real estate were consolidated and amended, the creditor of a deceased devisor, being creditor by a bond in which the heirs were bound, could maintain an action of debt against the devisees alone, stating in his declaration that the devisor had died and left no heir.

The question turns entirely on the construction of the 3 W. & M., c. 14, commonly called the Statute of Fraudulent Devises. That statute in its preamble recites, that it is not just that by the practice of any debtors their creditors should be defrauded of their just debts, but that nevertheless it has often happened that persons having, by bonds or other specialties, bound themselves and their heirs, have died seised in fee of lands, and have by their wills, in fraud of their creditors, devised their lands in such manner as that their creditors lost their debts. And then in the second section, for remedying of this evil, it enacts that all wills of lands, whereof any person shall die seised in fee-simple, shall be deemed (only as against such creditors as aforesaid) to be fraudulent and void, and of none effect. The third section then proceeds to enact, that in case of such devises the creditor shall and may maintain his action of debt against the heir and devisee jointly. No provision is made in the act for the case of a devisor dying without an heir; but on the part of the plaintiff it was argued, that such a case being manifestly within the mischief intended to be remedied, the Court would construe the third section so as to give an effectual remedy. The legislature, by the second section, makes void, as against creditors, all wills whatever, without regard to the fact of the devisor having or not having an heir; and it was strongly pressed on us in argument, that the subsequent provision in the third section, as to suing the heir and devisees jointly, must be taken only as pointing out the course of proceeding in those cases (by far the most common) where there is an heir, and not as narrowing the enactment in the previous section, whereby *Exch. of Pleas,* all wills of land whatever are made void against specialty 1841. creditors.

At the commencement of the argument of this case, we were very much inclined to adopt this view of the subject; but on a more attentive consideration of the statute, we have come to a contrary conclusion, and are all clearly of opinion that no remedy whatever is given, or was intended to be given by the statute, in the case of a debtor by specialty dying without an heir.

The evil recited in the preamble of the statute is the devising of lands *to the defrauding of creditors*, and the remedy applied is the making void of all such devises as against the creditor.

Before the statute, if the obligor in a bond, wherein the heirs were bound, died intestate, his land descended on the heir, and the heir (to the extent of the land descended) was liable to the creditor. If the obligor devised away his land, so that nothing descended, the right of the creditor was defeated. The heir was not liable, because by the act of the debtor in devising away his land the heir was enabled to plead riens per discent. The devisee was not liable, for the bond or other specialty in no way affected him. To remedy this evil the legislature interposed, by putting the creditor in all cases in the same situation *as if no will had been made;* it declared all wills void as against him. Such is the express enactment of the 2nd section. But if the statute had stopped there, the creditor might have had considerable difficulty in knowing how to proceed. His obvious course would seem to have been to proceed against the heir, for, the will being declared void as against creditors, he might have contended that the lands had descended on the heir. On the other hand, the will not being void against the heir, the heir might have truly pleaded riens per discent. To obviate this incongruity, the 3rd section gives a remedy of a special nature, by enabling the creditor to sue the heir and devisee jointly, in analogy probably to the case of an obligor dying and leaving two distinct classes of heirs, viz. one ex-parte paternâ and the other ex-parte maternâ, or leaving some lands held in free and common socage, and other lands held in gavelkind, where the heirs will be divisible.

These clauses thus give a complete and effectual remedy to the creditor, in all cases in which the debtor *might* have left the lands to descend to his heir, so as to become liable to the demand of the creditor, but has, in order to avoid payment or from any other motive, devised them away.

How is it then in a case where the debtor devising away his lands has left no heir? We think that case is left altogether untouched by the statute. In such a case the will could not by possibility work any injustice to the creditor; for, if there had been no will, he could have had no right against the land. The will makes no difference; the heir, it is true, was bound by the bond or other specialty; but, if there is no heir, the lord claiming by escheat certainly is not liable to the creditor. He, in the language of the law, comes in not in the *per* but in the *post*, and is an entire stranger to the obligations of the tenant whose land has escheated.

For these reasons, we think that the statute does not at all apply to the wills of persons dying without heirs; and in confirmation of this view of the case it may be observed, that the only relief given is to make void all wills as against creditors, a species of relief obviously inapplicable to a case where, supposing the will out of the way, the creditor has no right against the land which forms the subject of the devise.

In putting this construction on the statute, we are not acting against any decided case. Indeed, the only authority at all relied on by the plaintiff is the dictum of Lord *Cowper* in *Gawler* v. *Wade* (a). We agree with the obser-

(a) 1 P. Wms. 100.

vation, that what was there said, though referable only to the course of proceeding in equity, is equally applicable to an action at law. For in enforcing the payment of debts against devisees, under the statute of Fraudulent Devises, courts of equity were merely enforcing legal rights, and must of course strictly follow the law. But with all respect for the high authority of the distinguished judge to whom the dictum is attributed, we cannot think it of sufficient weight to countervail what appears to us to be the plain and obvious construction of the statute, a construction, we may add, by which we fully carry out all the purposes declared in the preamble, and give effect to every part of the enactments. Our construction, it is true, does not in all cases make the land assets in the hands of a devisee, which it has been the object of more recent acts to do. But it carries into effect all which the statute itself states as its object; and whether the omission of the case of a party dying without an heir was the result of accident, or, as we believe it was, of design, in neither case do we feel justified in doing violence to the positive words of the legislature, merely in order to effect something not stated on the face of the statute as one of its objects.

On these grounds we think there must be judgment for the defendant.

Judgment for the defendant.

Exch. of Pleas,
1841.

Dec. 2.

WALKER *v.* J. S. SHERWIN, Esq., and G. WRAGGE.

By a local act, for raising the sum of £21,000 to pay the amount of damages recovered of the hundred of B. for the partial destruction of Nottingham Castle by rioters, the justices of the peace for the county of N. were empowered to borrow the required sum by mortgage, or a sale of annuities

THIS was an action of trespass for breaking and entering the dwelling-house of the plaintiff, situate in the parish of Radford in the county of Nottingham, and there taking his goods and chattels, until the plaintiff, in order to redeem the same, was obliged to pay the defendants 181*l.* 5*s.* 9½*d.* The defendants pleaded not guilty, and issue having been joined thereon, the cause came on to be tried at the last Summer Assizes for the county of Nottingham, when a verdict was found for the plaintiff for 181*l.* 5*s.* 9½*d.* damages, and 10*s.* costs, subject to the opinion of the Court upon the following case :—

The plaintiff, at the time of the committing of the al-

secured on the proportion of the county rate chargeable on the inhabitants of the hundred of B. And by sect. 5, the justices were required to charge the proportion of the county rate to be raised upon the inhabitants of the hundred (except as thereinafter mentioned) not only with the interest of the money borrowed, but also with the payment of such further sum as should insure the payment of the sum borrowed within seven years, or with the payment of such annuities for the like period, as should be agreed to be paid or granted in respect of any part of the money so borrowed ; and such sums should be assessed and recovered on the hundred in such manner as county rates are directed to be assessed and recovered ; and should be paid and applied under the direction of the justices in discharge of the interest, and so many of the principal sums secured, or of such annuities, as such money would extend to discharge in each year, until the whole of the money should be paid. The 8th sect. provided a method for each parish to exempt itself from the operation of the act, by paying its proportionate quota in the first instance, and for that purpose directed the justices, after ascertaining the amount of the sum to be borrowed, to specify and declare the sum to be paid or contributed by each parish as the proportionate quota or share of the whole sum so ascertained ; and also to appoint a day on or before which the churchwardens or overseers of the poor of any such parish, desirous of paying the full amount of its proportionate quota, might pay the same to the person appointed as receiver under the act; and upon payment thereof, such parish should be discharged from all future payments relating to the integral sum whereof such quota should have been so paid, and from the interest thereof, and also from any share of the expenses, &c. And the 9th sect. enabled the churchwardens and overseers in every such parish, to raise the sum required as the quota of such parish, by loan on the security of their parochial rates, to be repaid within seven years.

In pursuance of the 8th sect. the justices fixed the quota of each parish in the hundred. Four availed themselves of the option of paying their quota. The parish of R., and thirty more, did not; and the justices raised the required sum, after allowing for these payments, by granting annuities of £3,600 per annum for seven years.

Held, that the effect of the 8th and 9th sections was to exempt from the operation of the 5th section those parishes only who paid their ascertained quota; that the annuities granted by the justices to pay the remainder were to be secured upon the portion of the county rate raised upon the hundred of B., with the exception of those parishes which had paid; and that the county rate, with those exceptions, was liable in the aggregate to the incumbrance, which was to be raised, in addition to the ordinary county rate, by order of the justices, in the same way in all respects as the other county rate is levied.

leged trespasses, was one of the overseers of the poor
of the parish of Radford, in the hundred of Broxtowe,
in the county of Nottingham. The defendant Wragge
then was and still is the high constable for the south division of the said hundred (within which division the parish
of Radford is situated), and committed the trespasses as
alleged in the declaration, and kept the goods seized until
the plaintiff paid him the said sum of 181*l.* 5*s.* 9½*d.* to redeem the same. The entry and seizure were made by the
defendant Wragge under and by virtue of the warrant
(hereinafter mentioned) of the other defendant Sherwin,
one of her Majesty's Justices of the Peace for the county
of Nottingham. The proper notices were duly served upon
the defendants, and a copy of the warrant duly demanded,
as required by law.

In the autumn of 1831, various persons riotously and tu-
multuously assembled in different places within the hundred
of Broxtowe in the county of Nottingham, and then feloni-
ously demolished and destroyed Nottingham Castle, and
divers other houses, mills, and other buildings, and the furniture and goods therein. Shortly afterwards several persons commenced and prosecuted actions at law, and proceeded to final judgment therein against the said inhabitants
of the hundred of Broxtowe, for damage and injury respectively sustained by them in consequence of such felonious
destruction of property, and recovered large sums of money
as compensation for such damages and for costs of suit, and
those sums of money were wholly or in part levied upon
and paid by the inhabitants of the said hundred. And the
Duke of Newcastle, as owner of Nottingham Castle, situate within the said hundred, also commenced and prosecuted an action at law against the said inhabitants for the
damage and injury sustained by him in consequence of the
demolition of the said castle and property therein, and obtained a verdict for £21,000, together with costs of suit,
and the inhabitants of the said hundred expended a con-

siderable sum in their defence of the said action, whereupon it became manifest that the said sum of £21,000 so recovered by the said Duke, with costs of suit, and the expenses incurred by the inhabitants of the said hundred, could not be immediately raised and forthwith levied upon the said inhabitants without occasioning very serious distress and inconvenience; it therefore became expedient that power should be granted for borrowing money to satisfy and discharge such damages, costs, and expenses, and accordingly, in March, 1833, an act of Parliament was obtained, intituled " An Act for raising Money to pay Compensation for Damages committed within the Hundred of Broxtowe in the County of Nottingham, during the late Riots and Tumults therein," which is declared to be a public Act, and is to form part of this case, and to be referred to by either party if necessary. By the said Act, sect. 1, it is enacted,—" That the justices of the peace acting in and for the county of Nottingham, assembled in General Quarter Sessions, or at any adjournment or adjournments thereof, should, and they were thereby required, authorized, and empowered to ascertain the amount of the damages and costs of suit recovered by the said Duke of Newcastle against the inhabitants of the said hundred of Broxtowe, and the costs, charges, and expenses incurred by them, or in their behalf, and duly allowed to them, in consequence of the said suit, and after having ascertained the same, to borrow and take up on mortgage of the portion of the rate or assessment for the county of Nottingham, charged upon the inhabitants of the said hundred, according to the laws then in force for assessing county rates (except as thereinafter mentioned), by instrument in the form contained in the schedule to the said act annexed, marked A. or to the like effect, any sum or sums of money not exceeding the amount so ascertained as aforesaid, either by way of loan at interest, or by sale of annuities for the term of seven years, as to the said justices should appear necessary

and expedient for the purposes aforesaid, and to secure
every such sum of money so borrowed upon the credit of
such proportion of rate; and that it should be lawful for
the justices so assembled, and they were thereby authorised, to treat and agree with any person or persons for the
loan of any such sums of money, and by their order to
confirm every such agreement; and every such agreement,
signed by the chairman and any two or more justices present at the time of making such order, should be and the
same was thereby declared to be effectual for securing
every such sum of money so advanced, with interest
thereon to the person or persons advancing the same, on
such terms as in and by such agreement should be stipulated."

By sect. 2, it was further enacted, "That it should be
lawful for the said justices from time to time, or at any
one time, to borrow from the Exchequer Bill Loan Commissioners the whole or any part of the money thereby
authorised to be borrowed and raised, either in one sum
or in separate sums, and either by way of loan or sale of
annuities for the term of seven years, upon the credit of
the rates authorized to be made, raised, and assessed as
hereinbefore mentioned, without requiring personal security, and that it should be lawful for the said justices of
the peace to mortgage or assign the said rates to the said
commissioners or their secretary for the time being, in
such manner and form as they the said commissioners
should direct and appoint, as security for the payment of
the principal and interest of any sum or sums so to be advanced, until the principal money advanced by the said
commissioners in Exchequer bills or otherwise, and all
interest thereon and arrears of annuity due or owing to
them, should be fully paid and satisfied." And by sect. 3,
it was enacted, "That it should be lawful for the respective persons entitled to any of the securities to be given
by virtue of that act, and their respective executors,

assigns, &c., at any time by writing under their hands and seals, to transfer such securities to any person or persons by indorsement on the back of such security, or any writing to be annexed thereto in the form mentioned in the schedule to the said act annexed."

By section 5, it was enacted, "That it should be lawful for the said justices of the peace, and they were thereby authorized and required, from time to time to charge the proportion of the county-rate to be raised upon the inhabitants of the said hundred of Broxtowe, (except as thereinafter mentioned), not only with the interest by half-yearly payments of the money so borrowed by way of lease, but also with the payment of such further sum as should insure the payment of the whole of the sum so borrowed within seven years from the time of borrowing the same, in equal yearly payments, and with the payment of such annuities for the like period, as should be agreed to be paid or granted for and in respect of any part of the money so borrowed, together with the expenses incident to the obtaining and passing the said act and of executing the same; and such sums should be assessed and recovered on the said hundred, (except as thereinafter mentioned), in such manner as county rates are directed to be assessed and recovered under the laws in force for that purpose, and should be paid and applied under the direction of the said justices of the peace, in discharge of the interest of so many of the principal sums on the said securities, or of such annuities as such money would extend to discharge in each year, until the whole of the money for which such securities should be made, and the interest thereof, should be fully paid and discharged. And the said justices of the peace should and they were thereby required to fix one or more day or days in each year in which such payment should be made, and should make orders for assessment in due time, so as to provide for the regular payment thereof, and which justices should also and they were thereby required

to appoint a proper person to receive all and every the
rates charged upon the said hundred, for the purposes of
the said act, and to apply the same in conformity to the
provisions of the said act, and to the orders of the said
justices in that respect." By sect. 8, it was further enacted, " That the said justices of the peace should, and they
were thereby required, immediately after ascertaining the
amount of the sums authorized to be borrowed under the
provisions of the said act, at such general quarter sessions
or at any adjournment thereof as aforesaid, to specify and
declare, by public advertisement in one or more of the
newspapers printed or circulated in the said county of
Nottingham, or by notice signed by the clerk of the peace
and delivered to the churchwardens and overseers of the
poor, or the person or persons authorized to collect the
county rates of such parish, township, or place within the
said hundred, the sum to be paid or contributed by each
parish, township, or place, as the proportionate quota or
share of the whole sum of money so ascertained as aforesaid, and which the inhabitants of the said hundred would
have been liable to pay in case this act had not been
passed; and also to appoint a day on or before which
the churchwardens or overseers of the poor of any of such
parish, township, or place, desirous of paying the full
amount of such proportionate quota or share, might pay
the same to the person appointed as receiver under the
said act, and upon payment thereof accordingly, such
parish, township, or place should be discharged from all
future payments relating to the integral sum whereof
such quota or share should have been so paid, and from
the interest thereof, and also from any share of the expenses of obtaining the said act, or relating to the execution thereof."

And by sect. 9, it was further enacted, "That if the inhabitants of any parish, township, or place within the said

hundred, should be desirous of borrowing the money to be
required for the purposes of the said act, upon the securities
of their respective parochial rates or assessments, it should
be lawful for the churchwardens and overseers of the poor
in every such parish, township, or place, or, if there were no
churchwardens, then for the overseers of the poor for any
such parish, township, or place, (with the consent of the
inhabitants thereof in vestry assembled), to raise the sum or
sums of money required as the quota or share of such parish, township, or place, for the purposes of the said act, by
loan to be repaid within seven years from the time of borrowing the same, in equal half-yearly payments, or by the
sale of annuities for the like term of seven years. And
the churchwardens and overseers of the poor should, and
they were thereby authorized, by instrument in the form
contained in the schedule annexed to the said act marked
C., or to the like effect, to secure the money to be so
borrowed upon the credit of the respective parochial rates
or assessment on any such parish, township, or place, with
the repayment of the principal sum which should have
been so borrowed, and the interest thereof, or with the
payment of the annuity thereby granted, (as the case might
be), and such securities should be registered with the clerk
of the peace for the said county, (for each of which a fee
of 2s. 6d. should be paid). And it should be lawful for
each and every person who should be entitled to the money thereby secured, and such person was thereby empowered, by indorsing his or her name on the back of such
security, to transfer the same, and his or her right to the
principal money and interest thereby secured, unto any
other person or persons : and every such assignee might,
in like manner, transfer the same again, and so toties
quoties, and the person to whom such security or any assignment thereof should be made, and his executors, administrators, and assigns, should be creditors upon the
said rate in an equal degree one with another, and

should not have any preference with respect to the priority of any money so advanced; provided nevertheless, that such parish, township, or place should not, by reason of exercising the powers aforesaid, be exempt from the payment of their proportionate quota or share of the expenses of obtaining the said act, or relating to the execution thereof."

At the general quarter sessions of the peace held at Nottingham, on Saturday the 18th day of May, 1833, pursuant to public notice, the justices acting in and for the same county then and there assembled, in exercise and execution of the several powers and provisions of the said act, ascertained and fixed the amount of damages and costs of suit, recovered by the said Duke of Newcastle against the inhabitants of the said hundred of Broxtowe, and the costs, charges, and expenses incurred by them or on their behalf, and duly allowed to them, in consequence of the said suit, at the sum of 28,830*l*. 3*s*., and immediately after ascertaining the amount of the said damages and costs, the said justices duly apportioned the same amongst all the parishes, townships, and places within the said hundred, according to the then existing county rate, as specified in the under-written table, being the "Table of Rates charged on the Hundred of Broxtowe, for the Payment of the above-mentioned Damages and Costs." [The table was here set out, containing the names of thirty-five parishes, and amongst others Radford—a statement of the "annual value for county rates" of each parish—the amount of the rate—and the quota of each person.]

The hundred of Broxtowe comprises the thirty-five parishes or townships mentioned in the foregoing table, and the sum to be paid or contributed by each parish, township, or place, as the proportionate quota or share of the sum so ascertained as aforesaid, varied in amount, as appears by the above table, the lowest being 48*l*. 11*s*. 11*d*.

and the highest being 2988*l.* 6*s.*; all the sums being calculated and apportioned according to the amount which the said thirty-five parishes were respectively at that time assessed to the county rate.

The said justices, after having so ascertained the amount of the said damages and costs, and made their apportionment of the several proportionate quotas or shares thereof, as hereinbefore mentioned, specified and declared the same by their sessions' order, and by public notice in the manner prescribed by the said act; and they directed the clerk of the peace to issue notices to be signed by him, and to be delivered to the overseers of the poor of all the parishes, townships, or places within the said hundred, specifying and declaring (as set forth in the foregoing table) the sum to be paid or contributed by each parish, township, or place, as the proportionate quota or share of the whole sum of money so ascertained as aforesaid.

The said justices at the said adjourned sessions appointed Friday, the 31st day of May then instant, as the day on or before which the overseers of the poor of any of the said thirty-five parishes, desirous of paying the full amount of their several specified and declared proportionate quotas or shares, might pay the same to the receiver appointed under the said act, for the purpose of being exempted from the expenses and operation thereof. And the said justices then appointed Mr. Godfrey (the clerk of the peace for the county of Nottingham) the receiver under the said act,

Pursuant to the order of the said justices at the said adjourned sessions, as hereinbefore mentioned, the clerk of the peace issued and delivered to the overseers of the poor of the parish of Radford a notice signed by him, specifying and declaring that the sum to be paid or contributed by that parish, as their proportionate quota or share of the whole damages and costs so ascertained as aforesaid, amounted to the sum of 1,092*l.* 0*s.* 1*d.*

Four of the parishes mentioned in the foregoing

table (the aggregate of their respective proportionate quotas or shares, so declared as aforesaid, amounting to 1,575*l.* 17*s.* 10*d.*) did, on or before the said 31st day of May then instant, pay to the said receiver their respective proportionate quotas or shares so specified and declared as aforesaid, but the remaining thirty-one parishes or townships, including the parish of Radford, did not pay theirs, hence leaving a sum of £22,254 to be provided, and which, in furtherance of the provisions of the said act, was borrowed from the Exchequer Bill Loan Commissioners by the said justices, and was by them applied for the purposes of the said act. And in consideration thereof, the said justices in open court mortgaged, charged, and assigned all and every the rates authorized to be made, raised, and assessed upon all the parishes within the said hundred of Broxtowe, under the description of county rates, (except in respect of the four parishes before mentioned as having paid their respective proportionate quotas or shares), to secure to the said commissioners an annuity or sum of £3,600, to be paid and payable for the space of seven years, by half-yearly payments of £1,800 each, on the 10th of February and 10th of August in each year, the first of such half-yearly payments to be made on the 10th of February, 1834, and the last of such half-yearly payments to be made on the 10th of August, 1840.

Thenceforth the said parishes in the hundred of Broxtowe (exclusive of the said four parishes which had paid their quotas) were charged half-yearly, not only with the payment of their proportion of the ordinary and usual county rate assessed upon the rest of the county, but also with their proportion of the last half-yearly instalment payable in respect of the said annuity, which had been made payable to the Exchequer Bill Loan Commissioners, for and in consideration of the integral sum borrowed to discharge the amount left unpaid by the thirty-one parishes, in respect of the proportionate quotas of shares so declared and specified as aforesaid.

This was done by the justices making, at the Epiphany and Midsummer Sessions in each year, two orders for the collection of rates, one being a common order upon the county generally, for a certain number of rates for the ordinary and usual county purposes; the other order being a special order upon the several parishes in the said hundred of Broxtowe (the said four parishes excepted), to pay to the high constable a certain number of rates expressly for the purpose of raising the half-yearly instalments of the said annuity payable in respect of the money borrowed under the provisions and for the purposes of the said act.

From the adjourned Sessions, held in May 1833, up to the Epiphany Sessions 1837 inclusive, seven of the above-mentioned special orders were made, each requiring the high constable to deliver his warrant to the overseers of the poor of the several parishes within the said hundred of Broxtowe (except the said four parishes) forthwith, to levy, collect, and pay to the said high constable seventeen farthing rates, to be by him paid to the receiver appointed under the directions of the said act, and by virtue of such half-yearly special orders the high constable did issue and deliver his warrant to the overseers of the poor of the parish of Radford, requiring them to raise, levy, and pay to him, out of the money collected or to be collected for the relief of the poor of the said parish, the sum of 88*l.* 14*s.* 4½*d.* No other half-yearly sum than the said sum of 88*l.* 14*s.* 4½*d.* was demanded during the said period from May 1833, to the Epiphany Sessions in 1837, as the half-yearly sum payable by that parish towards the instalment of the said annuity, nor was any other sum during that period due or payable.

The said sum of 88*l.* 14*s.* 4½*d.* bears the same proportion to the whole amount of the half-yearly instalment of the said annuity, as the said sum of 1,092*l*. 0*s*. 1*d*. bore to the integral or aggregate sum so required and borrowed under the said act as aforesaid.

At the Easter Sessions, 1837, the justices made a new assessment or county rate on all the rateable property in the whole county, for the ordinary and usual county purposes, and by which new assessment the parish of Radford then was and now is rated and assessed to the county rate at £13,310 instead of £5,010, the amount at which it had been assessed to the county rate since 1833.

The table of rates or apportionment made by the justices in May 1833, and by them then charged upon the hundred of Broxtowe, for the payment of the said damages and costs, has never been altered by the justices, nor have they ever made any alteration in the apportionment of the several quotas in that table specified and declared as the sums to be paid or contributed by the several parishes in the said hundred of Broxtowe, as their proportion respectively of the ascertained damages and costs.

At the Midsummer Sessions, 1837, the justices again made two orders as theretofore—one a common order upon the county generally, for a certain number of farthing rates for the ordinary and usual county purposes; the other a special order upon the several parishes in the said hundred of Broxtowe (the said four parishes excepted), for payment of thirteen farthing rates to the high constable.

Those orders were made for the purpose of raising the half-yearly instalments of the said annuity, payable in respect of the money borrowed under the provisions and for the purposes of the said act; and by virtue of that special order the high constable issued and delivered his warrant, dated the 29th day of June, 1837, directed to the churchwardens and overseers of the poor of the parish of Radford, requiring them to raise and levy out of the money collected for the relief of the poor of that parish the sum

of 180*l*. 4*s*. 9½*d*., and the parish of Radford paid that sum
to the high constable under protest, denying the liability
of the parish to pay, and the legality of the increased
demand.

After the Midsummer Sessions, 1837, and at each subsequent Epiphany and Midsummer Sessions, the justices
made two orders as theretofore for collecting of rates—one
a common order on the county generally for a certain
number of farthing rates for the ordinary and usual purposes; the other a special order upon the several parishes
in the hundred of Broxtowe (the said four parishes excepted) for thirteen farthing rates.

Those special orders were made for the purpose of raising the half-yearly instalments of the said annuity; and
the high constable, by virtue of such special orders, issued
and delivered to the overseers of the poor of the parish of
Radford his warrant, requiring them to raise, levy, and
pay to him, out of the poor-rate of that parish, the sum of
180*l*. 4*s*. 9½*d*., and pursuant to such warrant the parish
paid him under protest four several sums of 180*l*. 4*s*. 9½*d*.
each.

At the Midsummer Sessions, 1839, the justices of the
peace again made two orders as theretofore—one a common order upon the county generally, for a certain number
of farthing rates for ordinary and usual county purposes;
the other a special order upon the several parishes in the
said hundred of Broxtowe (the said four parishes excepted)
for payment of thirteen farthing rates to the high constable.

That special order was made for the purpose of raising
the half-yearly instalments of the said annuity, payable in
respect of the money borrowed under the provisions and
for the purposes of the said act.

Under the last-mentioned special order, the high constable again issued and delivered his warrant, dated the
6th day of July, 1839, directed to the overseers of the

poor of the parish of Radford, requiring them to raise, levy, and pay to him, out of the poor-rates of that parish, 180*l.* 4*s.* 9½*d.*, to be applied for the purposes of the Broxtowe Compensation Act: but the parish of Radford having then already paid several sums, amounting altogether to a sum exceeding in amount their said declared and specified proportionate quota or share of the said ascertained damages and costs; and their share of the expenses incurred in reference to the said act, refused to pay that demand; and after a due and proper summons and appearance, the defendant Sherwin directed his warrant, dated 4th September, 1839 (which, if any thing was then due from the said parish of Radford in respect of the said annuity, it is admitted was a good and valid warrant), and made in proper form under his hand and seal, to the defendant Wragge (as such high constable as aforesaid), to distrain the goods and chattels of the overseers of the poor of the parish of Radford for the sum of 180*l.* 4*s.* 9½*d.*, together with the costs of making such distress. And the defendant Wragge thereupon made his entry and seizure in due form of law upon the plaintiff's goods and chattels.

The proportionate quota or share to be paid by the parish of Radford in respect of the said ascertained damages and costs, was specified and declared by the justices at the adjourned sessions in May, 1833, to be the sum of 1,092*l.* 0*s.* 1*d.*

The proportionate share of the parish of Radford, of the costs of obtaining the said Act, was the sum of 20*l.* 10*s.* 3*d.*

The parish of Radford, prior to the time when the defendant Wragge made the said entry and seizure, had paid to the receiver, in pursuance of the several before-mentioned special orders, several sums, amounting altogether to 1,868*l.* 1*s.* 8*d.*, being £276 over and above the said original apportionment.

The Court is empowered and authorized to draw inferences from the facts stated, in the same manner as a jury

Exch. of Pleas, 1842.

WALKER
v.
SHERWIN.

might or could draw inferences from the same facts, if proved.

The questions for the opinion of the Court are—1st, Whether, when the parish of Radford had paid (or there had been levied) the full amount of the said proportionate quota apportioned on them as aforesaid, and all the said costs, charges, and expenses of obtaining the act as abovementioned, the parish was liable, under the circumstances stated, to pay any further sum, and what.

2nd, Whether the assessments and rates made after Easter, 1837, were properly made and levied according to the new assessment or county rate then first made, or whether they ought not to have been levied according to the assessment or county rate, as it was when the proportionate quotas were ascertained in 1833.

3rd, Supposing that the parish of Radford was liable to pay a larger sum than their said proportionate quota, costs, charges, expenses, and expenses of obtaining the act, whether the further sums after Easter, 1837, ought to have been raised and levied according to the new county rate or assessment then first made, or according to the assessment or county rate, as it was when the proportionate quotas were ascertained in 1833.

The case was argued in Michaelmas Term, by *Whitehurst* for the plaintiff, and by *N. R. Clarke* for the defendants; but as it entirely turned on the construction of the local act, it has been thought unnecessary to detail the arguments at length.

The Court took time to consider, and now the judgment of the Court was delivered by

PARKE, B.—This is an action of trespass, brought by the plaintiff as overseer of the parish of Radford, against the defendants, one a magistrate of Nottinghamshire, the other the high constable of the hundred of Broxtowe, for entering the plaintiff's house and seizing his goods, and com-

pelling the plaintiff to pay £180 and upwards. The question is, whether the defendants were justified in what they
did by the provisions of the local act, which passed in the
year 1835, for raising the sum of £21,000, in order to pay
the Duke of Newcastle the amount of his damages recovered of the hundred of Broxtowe for the partial destruction of Nottingham Castle by rioters.

Upon a full consideration of the different clauses of this
act, the impression which was at first entertained as to its
meaning is removed, and we are all now of opinion that the
defendants pursued the proper course, and were justified in
what they did, and the reasons which have induced us to
come to that conclusion may be very shortly stated.

The act, in the first place, empowers the justices to
borrow the required sum by mortgage of, or a sale of annuities secured on, the proportions of the county rate
charged upon the inhabitants of the hundred of Broxtowe
(with the exceptions after mentioned); and the 5th section
empowers and requires the justices from time to time to
charge the proportion of the county rate to be raised upon
the inhabitants of the said hundred of Broxtowe (except as
thereinafter mentioned), not only with the interest by
half-yearly payments of the money so borrowed by way of
loan, but also with the payments of such further sum as
shall insure the payment of the whole of the sum so borrowed, within seven years from the time of borrowing the
same, in equal yearly payments, or with the payment of
such annuities for the like period as shall be agreed to be
paid or granted for and in respect of any part of the money so borrowed, together with the expenses incident to
the obtaining and passing the act, and of executing the
same; and such sums shall be assessed and recovered on
the said hundred (except as thereinafter mentioned) in such
manner as county rates are directed to be assessed and recovered under the laws in force for that purpose, and shall
be paid and applied, under the direction of the said justices

of the peace, in discharge of the interest, and of so many of the principal sums on the said securities, or of such annuities, as such money will extend to discharge in each year, until the whole of the money for which such securities shall be made, and the interest thereof, shall be fully paid and discharged.

This is the *only* section which directs the mode of levying the sum charged on the hundred; and that mode is simply by adding the sum to the proportion of the county rate to be raised on that hundred.

The 8th section provides a method for each parish to exempt itself from the operation of the act, by paying its proportionate quota in the first instance, and for that purpose directs that the justices shall, after ascertaining the amount of the sums authorized to be borrowed under the provisions of the act, specify and declare by public advertisement, or by notice signed by the clerk of the peace, and delivered to the churchwardens or overseers of the poor, or the person or persons authorized to collect the county rates of each parish, township, or place within the said hundred, the sum to be paid or contributed by each parish, township, or place, as the proportionate quota or share of the whole sum of money so ascertained as aforesaid, and which the inhabitants of the said hundred would have been liable to pay in case the act had not been passed, and also to appoint a day on or before which the churchwardens or overseers of the poor of any such parish, township, or place desirous of paying the full amount of such proportionate quota, or share, may pay the same to the person appointed as receiver under the act, and upon payment thereof accordingly, such parish, township, or place, shall be discharged from all future payments relating to the integral sum whereof such quota or share shall have been so paid, and from the interest thereof, and also from any share of the expenses of obtaining the act, or relating to the execution thereof.

The 9th section enables the churchwardens and overseers *Exch. of Pleas,* of the poor in every such parish, township, or place, to raise 1841. the sum or sums of money required as the quota or share WALKER of such parish, &c., for the purposes of the act, by loan on *v.* the security of their parochial rates, to be repaid within SHERWIN. seven years. In pursuance of the 8th sect., the justices fixed the quota of each of the thirty-five parishes in the hundred. Four availed themselves of the option of paying their quota. The parish of Radford, and thirty more, did not; and the justices raised the required sum, after allowing for these payments, by granting annuities of £3,600 per annum for seven years. The question then is, how that annual sum is to be raised.

We think that the effect of the 8th and 9th sects. is only to exempt those parishes who pay their ascertained quotas pursuant to those sections from the operation of the fifth clause; all the other parishes, who do not pay, are liable to it, and remain a part of the hundred for the purpose of being charged under that clause with the residue, not satisfied by the quotas so paid. The annuities, therefore, granted by the justices to pay the remainder, are to be secured upon the portion of the county rate raised upon the hundred of Broxtowe, with the exception of those parishes which have paid. The county rate on the hundred, with those exceptions, is liable in the aggregate to the incumbrance, which is to be raised in addition to the ordinary county rate by order of the justices, in like manner in all respects as the other county rate is to be levied. There is no power in the act to make the orders on each parish separately in the ascertained proportions, and no authority to the high constable to make any distinction between the levying of this or the general county rate. This is the course which the magistrates have pursued, and, we think, rightly pursued. That the parish of Radford has eventually had more to pay than it would have paid, if it had availed itself of the option given by the

8th or 9th sect., is a matter of accident. It might have had less, if it had happened that the wealth of the parish had been found on the new valuation in 1837 to have decreased in proportion to the rest of the hundred.

Judgment for the defendants.

———————

Dec. 3.

A partner has no implied authority by law to bind his co-partners by his acceptance of a bill of exchange, except by an acceptance in the true style of the partnership.
   Therefore, where a firm consisted of J. B. & C. H., the partnership name being "J. B." only, and C. H. accepted a bill in the name of "J. B. & Co.," it was held that J. B. was not bound thereby.

KIRK *v.* JOHN BLURTON and CHARLES HABERSHON.

ASSUMPSIT.—The declaration stated, that the defendants, *by and under the name, style, and firm of John Blurton & Co.*, on the 12th March, 1841, made their bill of exchange in writing, and directed the same to Messrs. Smith, Payne, & Smith, and thereby required them to pay to the order of the defendants £50, two months after date, which period had then elapsed; and the defendants then indorsed the said bill to William Unwin, who indorsed it to Andrew Duncan, who indorsed it to the plaintiff. Breach, in non-payment by Messrs. Smith, Payne, & Smith, of which the defendant had due notice.

The defendant Habershon allowed judgment to go by default. The defendant Blurton pleaded four pleas; 1st, that he did not make the bill; 2ndly, that he did not indorse it; 3rdly, that Blurton and Habershon were partners as printers, and that Habershon made and indorsed the bill in fraud of his partner, for purposes not connected with the partnership, and that the bill was indorsed by him to Unwin, by Unwin to Duncan, and by Duncan to the plaintiff, with notice of the fraud; 4thly, that the bill was so made in fraud of Blurton, and that the same was indorsed respectively by the indorsers thereof, without value or consideration. On these pleas issues were taken and joined.

At the trial before Lord *Denman*, C. J., at the last Summer Assizes for the county of York, the bill was produced in evidence, and was as follows:—

"Sheffield, March 12th, 1841.
"Two months after date pay to our order £50, for value received. John Blurton & Co.
"At Messrs. Smith, Payne, & Smith's,
Bankers, London."

Indorsed—"John Blurton & Co., Wm. Unwin, Andrew Duncan."

The bill was drawn and indorsed by the defendant Habershon.

It appeared that the defendants carried on business as printers at Sheffield, under the name of "John Blurton," that being the name over the door. A witness was called, who stated that the firm had been in the habit of drawing bills, and that he had seen them, but he could not take upon himself to say whether they were in the name of "John Blurton," or of "John Blurton & Co."

Cresswell, for the defendant Blurton, objected, that Habershon had no authority from Blurton to draw bills, except that which the law implied, namely, to do so in the partnership name, which was "John Blurton" only; and therefore that this bill being drawn in the name of "John Blurton & Co.," the defendant Blurton was not liable. The learned Judge, however, was of opinion that there was primâ facie evidence of authority in either partner to draw bills in the name of "John Blurton & Co.," and overruled the objection. The case then proceeded upon the question of fraud; but the jury were of opinion that no fraud was shewn, and they thereupon found a verdict for the plaintiff, leave being reserved to the defendant Blurton to move to enter a verdict for him on the first and second issues.

Creswell, in Michaelmas Term, obtained a rule accordingly, against which

Dundas and *Pashley* now shewed cause.—The persons composing the firm are Blurton and Habershon, and the bill is drawn in the name of "Blurton & Co.," which is sufficient to charge both. Habershon was a partner, as was proved, in the habit of drawing bills, and he had, therefore, authority to draw in the name of himself and his partner under the name of "Blurton & Co." In *Faith* v. *Richmond* (a), it was held that, where a partner accustomed to issue notes on behalf of the firm indorses a particular note in a name differing from that of the partnership, and not previously used by the firm, which note is objected to on that account, in an action brought upon it by the indorsee, the proper question for the jury is, whether the name used, though inaccurate, substantially described the firm, or whether it so far varied that the indorser must be taken to have issued the note on his own account, and not in the exercise of his general authority as partner. Here the name used did substantially describe the firm. *Williamson* v. *Johnson* (b) is in point. There the declaration stated that a bill of exchange was indorsed by certain persons trading under the firm of H. & F., by procuration of J. D., and it was held that this allegation was supported by evidence of J. D.'s handwriting, and that he, being the managing partner in a firm which carried on all its business of buying and selling under the designation of H. & F., was in the habit of indorsing bills in that manner, although there was no such person as F. in the firm, and no direct proof that the other members of it were privy to those transactions. And *Holroyd,* J., there intimates his opinion, that evidence of J. D.'s handwriting *alone,* as between third persons, would have been sufficient without proof of

(a) 11 Ad. & Ell. 33; 3 P. & D. 187.   (b) 1 B. & Cr. 146.

any usage on his part to indorse bills in the manner stated.

[*Alderson*, B.—The learned Judge says, *as between third persons;* here you seek to bind the party himself.] In *Mason* v. *Rumsey* (a), the bill was drawn upon " Messrs. Rumsey & Co.," and T. Rumsey, jun., wrote on it—" Accepted, T. Rumsey, sen." Lord *Ellenborough* ruled at Nisi Prius that both the partners were bound by this acceptance, and that ruling was confirmed by the Court on motion for a new trial. So, in *Lord Galway* v. *Matthew* (b) the principle was distinctly laid down, that the signature of a bill by one of several partners (presuming his authority) bound the whole firm. *Drake* v. *Elwyn* (c) is precisely in point. There the defendant Elwyn and P. & S. Wittaker were sued as partners, makers of a note. Elwyn signed the note " Elwyn & Co." A partnership was proved, but not that the defendants traded under the name of Elwyn & Co. The Supreme Court held, that as such a signature imported a co-partnership, and a co-partnership did exist at the time between Elwyn and the other defendants, it was to be *presumed* that such was the name of the firm, and it was sufficient to cast upon the defendants the burden of proving what was the name of the firm, if a different name existed. In Story on Agency, 100, n., the general principle is stated, that " each partner is held out to the public as the general agent of the partnership; and consequently his acts will bind it, notwithstanding he may have violated his private instructions, or the express terms of the secret articles of partnership."—They also cited *Siffkin* v. *Walker* (d), and *Dickinson* v. *Valpy* (e).

Cresswell, contrà.—None of the cases cited on the other side touches the principle upon which this rule was obtained. It is obvious that no man can be bound by the

(a) 1 Camp. 384.	(d) 2 Camp. 308.
(b) 10 East, 264.	(e) 10 B. & Cr. 128; 5 Man. &
(c) 1 Cain. American Rep. 184.	R. 126.

acceptance or indorsement of a bill of exchange, unless it were written by himself or some other authorized by him. If an agent accept a bill for his principal, he must pursue his authority correctly. In the case of a partnership, which is only a form of principal and agent, each partner has an implied authority to bind the partnership firm by his signature to a bill, if it be necessary or incident to the dealings of the partnership to accept bills. But there is no implied authority to any partner so to bind the firm by his acceptance of a bill, except *in the true style of the partnership*. Then is there anything in the cases cited to shew that "John Blurton" and "John Blurton & Co." here mean the same thing? The former was the true style of the partnership, and in that alone had Habershon authority to sign, so as to bind his partner. *Faith v. Richmond*, if properly examined, will be found to be an authority in favour of the defendant. [He was then stopped by the Court.]

ALDERSON, B.—The Court do not entertain any doubt as to the principle of law applicable to this case. One partner can bind his co-partners only to the extent of the authority which is given to the partners generally, to enable them to carry on the partnership business together. The true principle is that which has been stated by Mr. *Cresswell*, that, in the case of a partnership, the authority which each partner has is an authority given by law to do such things as are necessary for carrying on the partnership. If bills are necessary, then they have a power to accept bills, and so to bind each other. If there is an express contract amongst themselves different from that which the law implies, that express contract must prevail. What authority is there in a case like the present? An authority to bind the firm *in the name of the partnership*, and in that only. In those cases where the question has been left to the jury, it has been whether substantially there was any difference between the signature and the name of the partnership. For instance, if the signature were *Coal* & Co., and the true designation of the partnership were *Cole* & Co., it would no doubt be for the jury to say whether it was in substance the same. Upon the whole, I am of opinion that Habershon had no authority to bind Blurton, except in the partnership name, which, upon the evidence, appears to have been "John Blurton" only; and therefore the verdict on the first and second issues must be entered for the defendant.

GURNEY, B.—I quite agree, and I do not see that there is any hardship on the plaintiff: he should have inquired before he took the bill.

ROLFE, B.—The question would probably never have arisen, if the difference between the two names had not happened to be a little less here than in some other cases. I think it would not be right to enter into the extent of the difference: it is better to adhere to the rule, that the partnership name shall in these cases be used. The law seems to be perfectly reasonable; it implies no authority to bind the partnership in any other name than that held out to the world as the name of the firm. The signature, therefore, of "John Blurton & Co." did not operate to bind the defendant Blurton.

ALDERSON, B., added, that in coming to this conclusion, the Court did not mean at all to cast any doubt on the authority of the American case cited from Caines's Reports.

Rule absolute.

END OF MICHAELMAS TERM.

Exch. of Pleas,
1841.

KIRK
v.
BLURTON.

REPORTS OF CASES

ARGUED AND DETERMINED

IN

The Courts of Exchequer,

AND

Exchequer Chamber.

HILARY TERM, 5 VICTORIÆ.

Exch. of Pleas,
1842.

Jan. 12.

COOZE *v.* NEUMEGEN.

Where the date of the writ of summons, and the recital of the writ itself, were omitted in the issue, but the writ of trial was correct in these particulars, and the defendant, at the trial, protested against the irregularity, and refused to take any part in the proceedings; a rule afterwards obtained to set aside the issue and all subsequent proceedings was discharged with costs, on the ground that the defendant ought to have returned the issue when delivered, or applied before the trial to set it aside.

THIS was a rule calling on the plaintiff to shew cause why the issue, writ of trial, verdict, and all subsequent proceedings, should not be set aside for irregularity, with costs. It appeared that the issue was delivered on the 5th of November last, and commenced as follows:—" London, to wit: W. J. Cooze, the plaintiff in this suit, by F. T. S. his attorney, complains of L. Neumegen, the defendant in this suit, who has been summoned to answer the plaintiff in an action of debt; for that whereas the defendant heretofore," &c. No part of the issue made any mention of the date of the writ of summons, nor was there any recital that the defendant had been summoned "by virtue of a writ of summons," as required by the forms given in the rules of Hilary Term, 4 Will. 4, Nos. 1 and 4.

The cause came on for trial before the Secondary of London, on the 16th of November, when the defendant's attorney attended, but protested against the proceedings on the ground of this irregularity, and took no part in the trial. The writ of trial was perfectly correct in the recital and date of the writ of summons. A verdict having been found for the plaintiff, the present rule was obtained on the 17th of November; against which

Lush shewed cause.—The defendant ought, on discovering the error in the issue, to have returned it within four days; and it was too late to make the objection, after the cause was tried.—He was then stopped by the Court, who called upon

Petersdorff to support the rule.—The objection is, that the writ of trial varies from the issue, and that it introduces matters which are not to be found in the issue. The case of *Lycett* v. *Tenant* (a) is precisely in point. There the date of the writ of summons, not being inserted in the issue delivered to the defendant, was inserted by the plaintiff in the writ of trial, and this was held to be an irregularity for which the writ of trial might be set aside, notwithstanding the defendant had appeared under protest at the trial. In *Worthington* v. *Wigley* (b), the omission to transcribe into the issue delivered the dates of the pleadings, was held to constitute a variance, of which the defendant was entitled to avail himself after trial and the roll being made up, although the dates appeared on the roll. There *Tindal*, C. J., says—" The omission to state the true date would clearly be such an irregularity, that, if it occurred in the record itself, it might be complained of at any time. . . . . . The objection is one certainly of a very captious nature; but still one that the party had an undoubted right to insist upon."

(a) 4 Bing. N. C. 168; 5 Scott, 479. (b) 3 Scott, 555; 5 Dowl. P. C. 209.

Lord ABINGER, C. B.—I think this rule ought to be discharged. If the writ of trial had strictly followed the issue, the defendant would no doubt have applied to set it aside, on the ground it was not in accordance with the form prescribed by the rule of Court. The defendant must have known of the defect in the issue when it was delivered, and he ought then to have applied to set it aside; but instead of objecting to it, he allows the plaintiff to go on, and makes the proceedings a vehicle for incurring costs, which may have to be paid by his own client.

ALDERSON, B.—I think the decision of this Court in *Farwig* v. *Cockerton* (a) was right. If a defendant wishes to take advantage of an irregularity in the proceedings, he should not appear at all at the trial, but should allow the plaintiff to go on at his peril. Here a considerable time elapsed between the delivery of the issue and the trial, and no application was made to set the former aside. This case must be governed by the rule, which prescribes that no advantage shall be taken of an irregularity after the party has taken a fresh step.

GURNEY, B., concurred.

The Court were disposed to discharge the rule without costs, on the ground that the plaintiff had acted on the authority of a decided case; but *Lush* having referred the Court to the more recent decision in *Currey* v. *Bowker* (b), they said the rule must be discharged with costs.

Rule discharged, with costs.

(a) 3 M. & W. 169.   (b) 9 Dowl. P. C. 523.

Exch. of Pleas,
1842.

Jan. 12.

DUNN v. WARLTERS.

ASSUMPSIT. The declaration stated an agreement by
the plaintiff to build a house for the defendant, and that
the defendant should supply him with timber, slates, and
all other materials for the completion of the house; and
alleged as a breach the non-supply of timber only.

The defendant pleaded, first, non assumpsit; secondly, that
he did supply the plaintiff with timber; thirdly, payment
of part of the sum claimed, on which issues were joined.
At the trial the cause was referred to an arbitrator, with
power "to settle the cause and all matters in difference
between the parties," and to determine what should be
done by the parties respecting the matters in dispute.
The arbitrator made his award in these terms:—" I, the
said arbitrator, having heard and weighed the evidence
produced by both parties *touching the matters in difference,*
do make and publish this my award in writing *of and concerning the premises,* in manner following; that is to say,
I award and adjudge that a verdict shall be entered for
the plaintiff upon so much of the first issue joined between the parties in the said cause, as relates to the agreement alleged in the first count of the declaration, and for
the defendant upon the residue of that issue; and that
a verdict shall be entered for the defendant upon the second issue, namely, that he did supply the necessary timber according to the terms of the said agreement; and
for the plaintiff upon the third issue."

A rule nisi had been obtained for setting aside the
award, on two grounds;—first, that the arbitrator " had
not awarded on a matter in difference submitted to him;"
secondly, that the award was not final. It was stated in the
affidavits in support of the rule, that evidence was given

*In a rule nisi
for setting aside
an award, an
objection "that
the arbitrator
has not awarded
on a matter in
difference sub-
mitted to him"
is sufficiently
specific.*

*A declaration
on an agree-
ment to supply
timber and
slates to the
plaintiff for the
building of a
house, alleged
as a breach the
non-supply of
timber only.
The defendant
pleaded—1st,
non assumpsit;
2nd, that he did
supply timber;
3rd, part pay-
ment. The
cause and all
matters in dif-
ference were re-
ferred, and the
arbitrator, by
his award, after
reciting that he
had heard the
evidence pro-
duced "touch-
ing the matters
in difference,"
stated that he
made his award
" of and con-
cerning the pre-
mises," and
then proceeded
to find specially
on each of the
issues in the
action:—Held,
that the award
was sufficient,
although it ap-
peared that*

there was a matter in difference submitted to the arbitrator as to the non-supply of *slates.*

before the arbitrator of the plaintiff's having been prevented from completing his contract by the neglect of
the defendant to supply him with sufficient *slates*. An
affidavit was thereupon made by the arbitrator, in which he
stated that he had taken into his consideration the alleged
breach of agreement as to the slates.

W. J. Alexander shewed cause against the rule.—In the
first place, the rule nisi does not disclose, with certainty
sufficient to satisfy the rule of Court on this subject, the
matter in difference which it is alleged has not been adjudicated on by the arbitrator.   Statements of objections in
the rule nisi ought to be more specific than this : *Boodle*
v. *Davies* (a).   In that case, and also in *Gray* v. *Leaf* (b),
it was held not to be sufficient to state in the rule, " that
the arbitrator had exceeded his authority."   This is a general statement of a similar kind.   [*Alderson*, B.—The
object of the rule is, that the parties may not wander
about in search of the defect relied upon by their oppo-
nents.   In *Boodle* v. *Davies*, the statement was very vague
indeed, because there is a multitude of ways in which
an arbitrator may exceed his authority; but here the affidavits direct the attention immediately to that matter in
difference which it is alleged by the rule has not been
awarded upon.]

Secondly, the award is sufficient.   The objection to it
is that the arbitrator has not adjudicated in specific terms
with respect to the complaint as to the slates.   They are
not included in the breach laid in the declaration, but
they were in fact, as the arbitrator himself states, taken
into consideration by him.   And the award recites that
the arbitrator had heard and weighed the evidence " touching the matters in difference," and professes to be made
" of and concerning the premises. "   *Gray* v. *Gwen-*

(a) 3 Ad. & Ell. 208 ; 4 Nev. & M. 788.　　　(b) 8 Dowl. P. C. 654.

nap (a) is in point. There a verdict was found for the

plaintiff in an action of tort, subject to a reference of all matters in difference. The defendant claimed before the arbitrator a sum of money due to him on the balance of an account, which was admitted by the plaintiff to be due. The award, after stating that it was made *of and concerning the premises,* merely directed a verdict to be entered for the plaintiff with damages. It was objected that this was an adjudication only on the subject-matter of the action, but the Court held the award sufficient. *Platt* v. *Hall* (b), *Brown* and *Croydon Canal Company* (c), and *Allenby* v. *Proudlock* (d), are also authorities in support of this award. The Court will not encourage technical objections of this kind to awards, the object of which is to put an end to litigation.

Erle and *Gray*, contrà.—This award is no determination of all the matters in difference between the parties; it contains nothing but a finding on the three issues raised on the record in the action. A specific award on certain matters therein mentioned cannot be taken to extend also to other matters not mentioned: *Doe* d. *Madkins* v. *Horner* (e), *Gyde* v. *Boucher* (f). Suppose there were a reference of a claim on a bill of exchange, a trespass, and a demand for the price of goods, and the arbitrator decided on the first only; could it by any possibility be intended that he had determined the other matters also? And the Court will not listen to the statement of the arbitrator himself, after he has made his award, for that would be to allow him to supply a fact necessary to give it validity, after his authority has expired. The rule is clear, that if, on a reference of several matters of difference, the arbitrator omit to decide one of them, that vitiates the whole

(a) 1 B. & Ald. 106.
(b) 2 M. & W. 391.
(c) 9 Ad. & Ell. 522; 1 P. D. 391.
(d) 4 Ad. & Ell. 326.
(e) 8 Ad. & Ell. 235; 3 N. P. 344.
(f) 5 Dowl. P. C. 127.

award: *Randall* v. *Randall (a)*, *Mitchell* v. *Staveley (b)*, *Birks* v. *Trippet (c)*.

Lord ABINGER, C. B.—If this matter had been res integra, I should certainly have been disposed to think that this award was void; but we are bound by the authorities which have been referred to, and cannot set it aside. Our judgment, however, will not be final, since the matter may be reviewed in an action brought on the alleged breach of contract respecting the slates. But for those authorities, I should certainly have thought, that as the award must be in writing, its silence as to any matter in difference brought before the arbitrator prevented it from being a sufficient exercise of the authority vested in him by the submission. There would be much weight in the argument, that the words " of and concerning the premises" shewed that the matter in question had been disposed of, if that matter had been previously mentioned in specific terms; but that has not been done. The authorities, however, especially the case of *Gray* v. *Gwennap*, are too strong to be got over, and therefore the rule for setting aside the award must be discharged.

ALDERSON, B.—I think this case must be governed by the decision in the case of *Gray* v. *Gwennap*. There can be no doubt that an arbitrator is bound to decide upon all the matters in difference; but the question is, whether he is bound to decide them in express terms. In *Hayllar* v. *Ellis (d)*, where there were counter-claims, an award that the plaintiff had no cause of action was held to be sufficiently certain.

GURNEY, B., concurred.

Rule discharged.

(a) 7 East, 81.   (c) 1 Saund. 28 c.
(b) 16 East, 58.   (d) 6 Bing. 225; 3 M. & P. 553.

Exch. of Pleas,
1842.

Jan. 13.

GABRIEL and Another *v.* EVILL.

ASSUMPSIT for goods sold and delivered, and on an account stated. Plea, non assumpsit. At the trial before Lord *Abinger*, C. B., at the London sittings after Michaelmas Term, it appeared that the defendant was sought to be charged as a partner with B. & S. Vanderplank, to whom the goods in question had been actually delivered, and who carried on business in partnership as woollendrapers, in the city. The defendant, a clothier, who had supplied them with goods, and to whom they were considerably indebted, in May 1839, proposed to become a partner with them; and the terms of the intended partnership were settled in a written memorandum, which, however, was never signed by either of the parties. The defendant was to bring in £1,000 in money and £1,000 in cloths, and to be entitled to one-third of the profits, and was to be a dormant partner, without any power of interference as to the management of the concern; the name of the firm was to be changed to that of B. & S. Vanderplank & Co., and the partnership was to date from the 1st April, 1839; but under the circumstances, the defendant reserved to himself the option of determining, at any period within twelve months after that day, whether he would become a partner. The name of the firm was altered accordingly, and a new banking account was opened in the name of B. & S. Vanderplank & Co.; and evidence was given from which it might be inferred, that the defendant had made the advance of £1,000 in money and £1,000 in goods to the firm; but, within the twelve months, the defendant declared his determination not to enter into the partnership. The firm of B. & S. Vanderplank & Co. was dissolved in August, 1840, and no account of profits was rendered to the defendant, nor did he ever claim any profits. The

In May, 1839, A., a creditor of the firm of B. & S., proposed to become a partner with them, the terms of the intended partnership being, that A. should bring in £1,000 in money and £1,000 in goods, and should be entitled to one third of the profits, and be a dormant partner; the name of the firm was to be changed to B. S. & Co., and the partnership was to date from the 1st April, 1839, but A. reserved to himself the option of determining, at any period within twelve months from that day, whether he would become a partner. The name of the firm was altered accordingly, and a new banking account was opened in the name of B. S. & Co.; and A. advanced the £2,000 to the firm; but within the twelve months he declared his determination not to enter into the partnership:—*Held,* that A. was not liable

for goods supplied to the firm after May, 1839, for that he never became a complete partner.

Lord Chief Baron was of opinion, upon this evidence, that the defendant was not liable, and accordingly directed a nonsuit.

Erle now moved for a new trial, and contended that, as against third persons, the circumstances proved at the trial constituted the liability of a partner. The option was in the defendant, and the facts shewed that it was exercised; at all events, there was evidence to go to the jury that it was. Whenever a concern is carried on with the joint assent of several persons, and any one of them has a right to file a bill for an account of the profits, that is a partnership ab initio. [Lord *Abinger*, C. B.—The whole agreement here is, that if the defendant shall agree to become a partner with the others from a given day, they shall divide the profits from that day.] It is against the policy of the law that a party shall be allowed to reserve a right to divide the profits of a concern, with such an option in the mean time. Is he, after watching the progress of business for years, to have a right to take away a share of the profits ab initio, if it be a profitable business, or to take the funds as a creditor if it be not? [*Rolfe*, B.—It is a fallacy to say the defendant becomes a partner from the beginning of the twelve months; he becomes a partner from the time when he declares himself such, with a right retrospectively to an account of the profits. *Alderson*, B.—And here he declares within the time limited that he will not be a partner.] If he retains the option, the law casts on him the liability of a partner. He had always the power of giving himself the right to an account of the profits: but that is an option which the law will not allow to subsist.—He cited *Howell* v. *Brodie* (a).

Lord ABINGER, C. B.—The defendant clearly was not a partner until he had exercised the option given him of

(a) 6 Bing. N. C. 44; 8 Scott, 372.

declaring himself such. He never had a right to an account of the profits of the concern.

ALDERSON, B., and ROLFE, B., concurred.

Rule refused.

———

LOVELL *v.* ELIZABETH WALKER, sued as ELIZABETH WINSTANLEY.

DEBT by the payee against the acceptor of a bill of exchange, with counts for goods sold and delivered, work and labour and materials, and upon an account stated. To the first two counts the defendant pleaded her coverture in abatement, and to the residue of the declaration, that she was never indebted. The former plea not being accompanied by any affidavit of verification, the plaintiff signed judgment as for want of a plea.

Ogle now moved for a rule to shew cause why that judgment should not be set aside for irregularity, upon affidavits which stated, that the action was brought (independently of the bill of exchange) to recover the amount of a dress-maker's bill; that the defendant had intermarried after the acceptance of the bill of exchange, but that a considerable portion of the other claim had accrued since her marriage.—The first question is, whether the plea of coverture is to be considered a dilatory plea within the stat. of 4 Anne, c. 16, s. 11, and therefore requiring an affidavit of verification. It has been decided that it is not a plea falling within the provisions of the stat. 3 & 4 Will. 4, c. 42, s. 8: *Jones* v. *Smith* (a). Neither is it, as to the causes of action which accrued before the marriage, a dilatory plea within the statute of Anne. As to them, the defendant's defence is, that she is entirely discharged by her marriage, all her property having passed to her hus-

A plea in abatement to an action of debt, of the defendant's coverture, is a dilatory plea requiring an affidavit of verification under the stat. 4 Anne, c. 16, s. 11: and if there be no such affidavit, the plaintiff is entitled to sign judgment as for want of a plea, although part of the cause of action accrued after the coverture.

(a) 3 M. & W. 526.

Exch. of Pleas,
1842.

LOVELL
v.
WALKER.

band, and he being the only party against whom execution can issue. [Lord *Abinger*, C. B.—I have always understood that a dilatory plea is one that does not deny the plaintiff's right of action, but says that it is not brought in the proper form against the proper party. *Alderson*, B.— This plea only means—I am not liable for this debt during my husband's lifetime.] . The defendant says, that by the marriage all her liability is transferred to her husband. It is like a plea of the defendant's bankruptcy. [*Alderson*, B. —That shews that the defendant never can be liable.]

Secondly, the plea of coverture, at all events, covered all that part of the clause which accrued after the marriage, and as to that it was not necessary, before the new rules, to verify it by affidavit. [*Alderson*, B.—When the plaintiff comes to assess his damages on the writ of inquiry, he will only take out execution for the amount of the goods supplied before the coverture. If he takes out execution for the whole, the defendant may apply to set it aside as to the residue.] He has taken his judgment for the whole, and therefore for too much. [Lord *Abinger*, C. B.—How could the plaintiff split the plea? The defendant pleads her coverture as to all to which it can apply, and the plea of never indebted as to the rest.]

PER CURIAM,   Rule refused.

———◆———

Jan. 14.   CARPENTER and Another *v.* SMITH.

The "public use
and exercise" of
an invention,
which pre-
vents it from
being consi-
dered a novelty,
is a use *in pub-*
CASE for the infringement of a patent for certain improvements " in locks and other securities applicable to doors and other purposes." Pleas, first, not guilty; secondly, that the plaintiffs were not the true and first in-

lic, so as to come to the knowledge of others than the inventor, as contradistinguished from the use of it by himself in private; and does not mean a use *by the public generally.*

Therefore, where an improved lock, for which the plaintiff had a patent, had previously been used by an individual on a gate adjoining a public road, for several years; and several dozens of a similar lock had been made at Birmingham from a pattern received from America, and sent abroad; it was held that this constituted such a public use and exercise of the invention as to avoid the patent.

ventors of the said improvements; thirdly, that the said
improvements were not a new invention as to the public
use and exercise thereof; on which issues were joined.

At the trial before Lord *Abinger*, C. B., at the Middlesex sittings after Michaelmas Term, the main question
between the parties was, whether the plaintiffs' invention,
the principle of which was a combination of the bolt and
latch of the lock within one hasp, was or was not a novelty. A witness called by the defendant proved, that in
the year 1816 he received from a house in the United
States a pattern of a lock similar in principle to the plaintiffs', and that he procured several dozens to be made at
Birmingham according to the pattern, and sent them to
America. The defendant also produced a lock similar to
that of the plaintiffs, which he proved to have been used
for sixteen years on a gate adjoining a public road, belonging to a clergyman of the name of Davies, residing near
Birmingham. For the plaintiffs it was contended, that
inasmuch as there was no proof that the locks in question
had been brought into public general use in this country,
the plaintiffs' might nevertheless be considered a new invention. The Lord Chief Baron, in summing up, stated
that an invention could not be considered new, which had
been in *public use* before; that the word *public* was not
equivalent to *general*, but was distinguished from *secret*
use: and he expressed his opinion that the circumstance
of a lock, similar in principle to the plaintiff's, being on
Mr. Davies's gate for so long a period, and the manufacture of several dozens by an English artist for money,
without secrecy, amounted to a public use of those locks.
The jury having found a verdict for the defendant,

Kelly now moved for a new trial, on the ground of misdirection.—The rule of law on this subject is not so narrow
as it was stated to be by the learned Judge. The mere
manufacture or use of an invention by an individual who

may himself have discovered it, even in such a manner that a particular portion of the public in his particular locality may have access to it, but without its being sold or brought into the market, does not constitute such a "public use or exercise" of that invention as to prevent another person, who does not *copy* it, from afterwards obtaining a patent for the same principle: *Morgan* v. *Seaward* (a). [*Alderson*, B.—How then do you get over the case of the invention for which a patent was avoided, because it had been previously published in a book (b)?—the principle being, that it could be appropriated by any body, because it had already been given to every body.] All that is required by the statute 21 Jac. 1, c. 8, s. 6, is, that the grant shall be made "to the first and true inventors of such manufactures, which others at the time of the making of the grant did not use." The statute intended to prevent loss to the inventor of a useful instrument, who brings it into public use and exercise, by reason of the making of a former similar invention *not* brought into practice, or the use whereof may be said to have ceased. [Lord *Abinger*, C. B.—By how many of the public would you allow it to be known, and what are the public? How vague a rule you would establish for each case! Would you say that the use by a particular club would be a use by the public? or suppose the inventor of a machine gives away a hundred among his friends, and they use it?] In *Lewis* v. *Marling* (c), a model and a specification of a machine similar to that for which the patent was granted, had been brought over from America and shewn to several persons: but it was held, that as no machine had been manufactured and brought into use, and as the patentee had not seen that model or specification, he might still be considered the inventor. So, in *Jones* v. *Pearce* (d), where it was proved for the defendant that a Mr. Strutt had

(a) 2 M. & W. 544.   (c) 10 B. & Cr. 22.
(b) Dr. Brewster's Kaleidoscope.   (d) Godson on Patents, 46.

constructed wheels similar in principle to that of the plaintiffs, *Patteson*, J., in summing up to the jury, said, that if it appeared that the wheel "was used openly in public, so that every body might see it, and the plaintiffs had continued to use the same thing up to the time of taking out the patent, undoubtedly that would be a ground to say that the plaintiffs' invention was not new." [*Alderson*, B.— That is the very same principle of law as was laid down by my Lord in the present case : the only restriction I should put upon it would be, that it need not appear that the machine was used up to the time of taking out the patent.] People would not become acquainted with the principle of this invention by passing along the road past the gate by thousands; and yet thereby a person bonâ fide discovering it for himself, and bringing it into public use in another part of England, is to be precluded from taking out a patent. Such a construction of the law is surely too large.

ALDERSON, B.—I think there ought to be no rule in this case. I have not the least doubt that that is the right construction of the law which my Lord has put upon it. "Public use" means a use *in public*, so as to come to the knowledge of others than the inventor, as contradistinguished from the use of it by himself in his chamber. How, then, can it be contended that the lock which has been used in public by Mr. Davies for so many years, is a new invention? If the plaintiffs' doctrine is correct, it would follow that if Mr. Davies were to change his lock to another gate, he would be liable to an action for an infringement of the plaintiffs' patent. The case of *Lewis* v. *Marling* went to the very extreme point of the law.

GURNEY, B., concurred.

Lord ABINGER, C. B.—I agree in thinking that there

x 2

Exch. of Pleas, 1842.

CARPENTER v. SMITH.

is no ground for disturbing the verdict. I was counsel in the cases of *Lewis* v. *Marling* and *Jones* v. *Pearce,* and I recollect that those cases proceeded on the ground of the former machines being in truth mere experiments, which altogether failed. The "public use and exercise" of an invention means a use and exercise *in public,* not *by the public.* There are some expressions in former cases which were referred to on the trial, which rather leant towards Mr. *Kelly's* argument, and I therefore thought it fit to lay down the rule of law in the broad terms I did. I have always entertained the same opinion on the subject.

Rule refused.

Jan. 14.

Where a material fact alleged in pleading is not traversed by the subsequent pleading, it is not therefore admitted *as a fact,* so as to dispense with proof of it before the jury.

To a declaration in assumpsit by indorsee against maker of a promissory note, the defendant pleaded, that the note was indorsed and delivered to the plaintiff by his indorser, in violation of good faith, and in

ASSUMPSIT by indorsee against maker of a promissory note, indorsed and delivered by the defendant to F. & Co., who indorsed it to G. V. & Co., who indorsed it to the plaintiff.

Plea, that the said several indorsements in the declaration mentioned were indorsements in blank; and that after the indorsement of the said note by the defendant to F. & Co., and before the delivery thereof to the plaintiff, the note was in the hands of G. V., who, at the time of making the order of Nisi Prius hereinafter mentioned, was the lawful owner thereof; that whilst the note was so in the hands of G. V., it was by an order of Nisi Prius, by consent of the said G. V., ordered that the said note and the claim of the said G. V. thereon should be referred to

fraud and contempt of an order for referring the claim of that indorser to arbitration; and that the plaintiff took the note with full knowledge of the premises. The plaintiff replied that he had not, when he took the note, any knowledge of the premises in the plea mentioned. Issue thereon:—*Held,* that upon these pleadings the defendant was bound to begin at the trial, and to prove the plaintiff's knowledge of the fraud; and that the plaintiff was not bound in the first instance to prove consideration given for the indorsement to him.

arbitration: that the note was delivered by G. V. to the plaintiff after the making of the said order, and before any award was made in the premises, and in violation of good faith, and in fraud and contempt of the said order; and that the plaintiff took the said note with full knowledge of the premises. Verification.

Replication, that the plaintiff had not, at the time when he so took the said note, any knowledge of the premises in the plea mentioned, upon which issue was joined.

Notice was given to the plaintiff to prove the consideration for the indorsement to him.

At the trial before Lord *Abinger*, C. B., at the Middlesex sittings after Michaelmas Term, it was contended on the part of the defendant, on the authority of *Bingham* v. *Stanley* (a), that inasmuch as the replication admitted a fraudulent delivery of the note to the plaintiff by G. V., the plaintiff was bound to begin, and in the first instance to prove consideration. The Lord Chief Baron, however, was of opinion, that even though the fraud of G. V. was admitted by the replication, still, as the note was not therefore absolutely void as against the plaintiff, but only capable of being made so by proof of his knowledge of the fraud, that fact was to be proved affirmatively by the defendant. The defendant accordingly began, and failing to prove the plaintiff's knowledge of the fraud, the plaintiff had a verdict for the amount of the note and interest.

Crowder now moved for a new trial, on the ground of misdirection.—The learned Judge ought to have called upon the plaintiff to prove consideration for the note. The replication, by omitting to traverse the material allegation of fraud contained in the plea, must, according to the rules of pleading, be taken to have admitted it: and where fraud in the transmission of the instrument to the

(a) 1 G. & D. 237.

holder is proved or admitted, he is bound to shew that he was not cognizant of that fraud, and that he gave value. The cases of *Bingham* v. *Stanley*, and of *Edmunds* v. *Groves* (a), in this Court, are at variance as to the effect of admissions on the record. In the latter case, *Alderson*, B., laid it down that "an admission on the record is merely a waiver of requiring proof of those parts of the record which are not denied, the party being content to rest his claim on the other facts in dispute; but if any inferences are to be drawn by the jury, they must have the facts, from which such inferences are to be drawn, proved like any other facts." On the other hand, Lord *Denman*, C. J., in delivering the judgment of the Court in *Bingham* v. *Stanley*, says, in reference to the case of *Edmunds* v. *Groves*, " Upon full consideration, we cannot agree with the doctrine thus stated. We think that an admission made in the course of pleading, whether in express terms or by omitting to traverse what has been before alleged, must be taken as an admission for all the purposes of the cause, whether the facts relate to the parties or to third persons, provided the allegation so made be material. We find no authority to the contrary; and indeed, in former times, before the new rules, such admissions, in the absence of a protest, estopped the party, even in another cause, from disputing the fact so admitted." [*Alderson*, B.—If the allegation of knowledge of the fraud was a necessary allegation in the plea, was it not for the defendant to prove it?] The admission made by the plaintiff on the pleadings, that the transfer of the note to the plaintiff arose out of a fraud, cast upon the plaintiff's title such an impeachment as to shift the onus of proof, and threw it upon him to shew, not only that he had no knowledge of the fraud, but that he gave value for the note. There can be no real distinction between the effect of the admis-

(a) 2 M. & W. 642. See also   661; *Bennion* v. *Davison*, 3 M. &
Nicolls v. *Bastard*, 2 C., M. & R.   W. 182.

sion of a fact by the party on the record, and the proof of it by the mouths of witnesses. The defendant in this case, therefore, stood in just the same position as if he had called witnesses, and had tainted the instrument with fraud. [Lord *Abinger*, C. B.—The mere circumstance of the plaintiff being the holder of the note, primâ facie imports that he is the holder for value. If this case had been tried on non assumpsit, before the new rules, would not the defendant have been bound to prove fraud in connexion with the note, and a knowledge of that fraud in the plaintiff?] The course of proceeding before the new rules would have been this:—the plaintiff would first have put in the note, and there rested his primâ facie case: the defendant must then have given evidence to shew that the transfer of the note was tainted with fraud; and having done that, the plaintiff would have been compelled to shew that he gave value for the note, and that he had no knowledge of the fraud. And here the situation of the plaintiff was this, that he was the holder of a note admitted by himself to have been fraudulently negotiated: he, therefore, was equally bound to shew that he had given value, and that he had no knowledge of the fraud. [*Alderson*, B.—Assuming, for the sake of the argument, that the circumstances of fraud alleged in the plea are admitted as facts by the replication, how do they afford primâ facie evidence of the plaintiff's *knowledge* of that fraud? Where a plea, as in this case, states facts amounting to fraud, and alleges that the plaintiff had knowledge of them, the issue, according to your argument, is on the plaintiff: then suppose he proves *consideration*, which way ought the verdict to be? His having given consideration proves nothing conclusively as to his want of knowledge of the fraud.] The plaintiff is bound, under such circumstances, to go further, and to prove also that he took the instrument under such circumstances as shew him not to have been cognizant of the fraud. Issue is constantly taken on the

Exch. of Pleas,
1842.

SMITH
v.
MARTIN.

double averment, that consideration was given, and that the plaintiff had no knowledge of the alleged fraud. The rule on this subject is laid down in *Mills* v. *Barber* (a). That was an action by indorsee against acceptor of a bill of exchange: plea, that the bill was an accommodation bill, and that no consideration passed between any of the parties to it: replication, that the drawer indorsed it to the plaintiff for consideration, on which issue was joined: and it was held that the plaintiff was not bound, in the first instance, to prove that he gave value for the indorsement to him, but that it lay on the defendant first to impeach his title, by shewing fraud or duress, or that the bill had been lost or stolen. Here the plaintiff's title *is* impeached on the ground of fraud, his primâ facie title arising from the possession of the note being rebutted by his own admission on the record, that it is a note tainted with fraud, whereby he stands in the same position as if that fact had been proved against him by witnesses.

Lord ABINGER, C. B.—I think no rule ought to be granted in this case. If we entertained any doubt on the point, we should think it a fit case for further discussion; but the arguments which have been used have not shaken the opinion we had formed at the commencement of the case.

ALDERSON, B.—I must say it seems to me to be unjust and unreasonable to prevent a party, by the rules of pleading, from denying a particular fact, and yet to call upon the jury to treat that fact as proved. If that be the law, then a double replication is of the very essence of justice. Personally, I should desire to have the matter fully discussed; but as the opinion of this Court is at variance with that which has been expressed by the Court of Queen's Bench, the difference can be settled only in a

(a) 1 M. & W. 425.

Court of error. I have considered the decision of the Court of Queen's Bench with every possible respect; but I must say it is not satisfactory to my mind, and appears to me to present many difficulties.

Exch. of Pleas,
1842.

SMITH
v.
MARTIN.

GURNEY, B.—I agree in thinking that there ought to be no rule in this case. I think it is too much, upon these pleadings, to throw upon the plaintiff the burthen of proving that he had no knowledge of the fraud. The defendant has averred affirmatively that the plaintiff had knowledge of the fraud, and the defendant ought to prove the fact.

Rule refused (a).

(a) See *Lewis* v. *Parker*, 4 Ad. & Ell. 838; 6 Nev. & M. 294.

———◆———

SERLE v. NORTON.

Jan. 14.

ASSUMPSIT on a banker's cheque, dated March 19, 1841, made by the defendant, delivered by him to J. Wright, and by Wright to the plaintiff. There were also counts for money paid, and on an account stated. The defendant pleaded to the first count, that he did not make the note, and also pleas denying due presentment and notice of non-payment; and to the other counts, non assumpsit. At the trial before Lord *Abinger*, C. B., at the London sittings after Michaelmas Term, it was proved by the defendant that the plaintiff received the cheque from Wright (to whom he gave value for it) some days before the date which it bore. It was contended for the plaintiff, that he might still recover on the count for money paid, and that the cheque, though post-dated, was evidence to support that count. The learned Judge thought otherwise, and directed a verdict for the defendant, giving the plain-

A post-dated cheque is altogether void, and cannot be received in evidence for any purpose. Therefore, the plaintiff cannot, in an action on such an instrument, resort to the count for money paid, because he cannot prove it without producing the cheque.

tiff leave to move to enter a verdict for him on the second count for the amount of the cheque.

S. Temple now moved accordingly.—The money paid by the plaintiff to Wright on the transfer of the cheque was money paid to the use of the defendant, and the cheque might be used as evidence of it. In Bayley on Bills, 358, (5th edit.), it is laid down that " a bill is primâ facie evidence of money lent by the payee to the drawer, and a note of money lent by the payee to the maker, and each, consequently, of money had and received by the drawer or maker to the use of the holder, and of money paid by the holder to the use of the drawer or maker." The case of *Dimsdale* v. *Lanchester* (a) shews, that an action for money had and received may be maintained by the indorsee of a promissory note against the maker. The party originally giving the cheque acknowledges himself to have money in his hands to the use of the party to whom he gives it, and so also of the person to whom that party gives it for value. [Lord *Abinger*, C. B.—That is to make an action on an implied contract assignable.] The maker calls upon each bearer to pay the amount to the party from whom he receives it, and undertakes that either his banker or he will pay it to the holder. *Eales* v. *Dicker* (b) may appear to be an authority against the plaintiff; but it is distinguishable, because there the party sought to be charged on the count for money paid, was not the drawer or maker, but the *acceptor* of a bill. The acceptor admits a debt due to the *drawer*, and therefore the indorsement by him is the assignment of a chose in action; but the drawer may be said to require all the subsequent parties to pay the amount to his use. [Lord *Abinger*, C. B.—How does the present question arise? The cheque, being post-dated, was void, and therefore not receivable in evidence.] It may be

(a) 4 Esp. 201, n.   (b) Moo. & M. 324.

looked at to shew the terms on which the money was advanced by the plaintiff to Wright. [*Alderson*, B.—Wright
could not have enforced payment of the cheque against the
defendant. Then how can the payment to him on a cheque
on which the defendant is not liable be payment to the use
of the defendant?] According to *Sutton* v. *Toomer* (a), a
promissory note which was given as a security for a deposit, and afterwards altered, may be given in evidence to
shew the terms on which the deposit was made; yet there
the note could not be enforced as a security. [Lord *Abinger*, C. B.—There the note was originally a good note, and
it still remained a note for its original purpose; the objection was, that the banker had made another note without
a new stamp.] The ground of decision was, that although
the plaintiff could not recover by force of the instrument
itself, he might recover on the count for money lent, and
give the note in evidence for that purpose.

Lord ABINGER, C. B.—I think there is no ground for a
rule. The case cited rests on a different principle. Suppose the case of a bond, which was originally good, but
was afterwards destroyed or altered; the party could not
declare upon it, because he had made it void as a security
by his consent; but it would still be evidence to shew the
nature of the transaction. Here the cheque could not be
read at all; it was altogether void.

ALDERSON, B.—This was a paper altogether inadmissible
as evidence.

GURNEY, B., concurred.

Rule refused.

(a) 7 B. & Cr. 416; 1 M. & R. 125.

Exch. of Pleas,
1842.

Jan. 14.

Where goods
are sold for
ready money,
and payment is
made accord-
ingly, no *debt*
arises, and such
payment is
therefore prove-
able under the
general issue.

BUSSEY *v.* BARNETT.

DEBT for goods sold and delivered, and on an account stated. The particulars of demand claimed the sum of 3*l.*5*s.*6*d.*, being the balance of an account for goods sold and delivered by the plaintiff to the defendant. Pleas, except as to the sum of 4*s.* 6*d.*, parcel &c., nunquam indebitatus; as to that sum, a tender, which was denied by the replication. At the trial before the under-sheriff of Middlesex, it appeared that the action was brought to recover an alleged balance of a disputed account for goods bought by the defendant, for ready money, at the plaintiff's shop. The defendant produced evidence to prove that, within ten minutes after the delivery of the goods at his house, he paid for them in full, with the exception of the 4*s.* 6*d.* as to which the tender was pleaded. It was objected for the plaintiff, that it was not competent to the defendant to give evidence of this payment, there being no plea of payment on the record: but the under-sheriff thought that, under the circumstances, no debt ever arose between the parties, and therefore the evidence was admissible under the plea of nunquam indebitatus, and he accordingly received it: and the tender being also proved to the satisfaction of the jury, the defendant had a verdict on both issues.

C. Jones now moved for a new trial, on the ground of misdirection, and contended that the defence was inadmissible without a plea of payment. [*Alderson,* B.—The plea of nunquam indebitatus means, that there never was a sale of goods to the defendant *on credit.* This was a mere exchange of goods for money, and no debt ever arose. Lord *Abinger,* C. B.—There was no contract whereby the defendant became indebted to the plaintiff.] In *Goodchild*

v. *Pledge* (a), where to a count in debt for £20 for goods sold and delivered, the defendant pleaded, that before the commencement of the suit, and when the said sum of £20 became due and payable, to wit, on &c., the defendant paid the plaintiff the said sum of £20, according to the defendant's said contract and liability; this plea was held bad on demurrer for concluding to the country, and not with a verification; and *Parke*, B., there says, "The moment the goods are delivered, is there not a cause of action, throwing the proof of its discharge on the defendant?" And he adds—"The new general issue, that the defendant never was indebted, that is, at no instant of time, was framed for the express purpose of making all these defences pleadable by way of discharge." [*Alderson*, B.— What the learned Judge there means is, that the moment goods are delivered *on credit*, a contract arises whereby the defendant becomes indebted. No doubt that was a proper case for a plea of payment.] This was a defence in the nature of confession and avoidance.

Lord ABINGER, C. B.—In this case the goods were not delivered upon a contract out of which a debt arose: there was no promise to pay, but immediate payment.

ALDERSON, B.—Where there is a contract for the sale and delivery of goods for ready money, and ready money is paid, there is no debt.

GURNEY, B., concurred.

Rule refused.

(a) 1 M. & W. 363.

Exch. of Pleas,
1842.

Jan. 17.

GREENSHIELDS *v.* CRAWFORD.

In an action by
indorsee against
acceptor of a
bill of ex-
change, it ap-
peared that the
bill was direct-
ed to " Charles
Banner Craw-
ford, East India
House," and
accepted " C. B.
Crawford." It
was proved that
this signature
was the hand-
writing of a
gentleman of
that name, for-
merly a clerk
in the East
India House,
who had left it
five years ago :
—*Held,* that
this was suffici-
ent evidence of
the identity of
the defendant
with the person
whose hand-
writing was
proved.

ASSUMPSIT by indorsee against acceptor of a bill of
exchange. Plea, denying the acceptance, and issue thereon. At the trial before *Rolfe,* B., at the Middlesex sittings
in this Term, the bill, when produced, appeared to be directed to " Charles Banner Crawford, East India House."
A witness called for the plaintiff stated, that the handwriting of the acceptance, " C. B. Crawford," was that of
a gentleman of that name, who was formerly a clerk in the
East India House, but had left it five years ago; but he
did not know whether that Mr. Crawford was the defendant in this action. It was contended for the defendant,
that there was no sufficient evidence of the identity of the
person whose handwriting on the note was proved, with
the defendant. The learned Judge overruled the objection, and the plaintiff had a verdict.

Corrie now moved for a new trial, and re-urged the objection taken at Nisi Prius; citing *Parkins* v. *Hawkshaw* (a),
and *Whitelocke* v. *Musgrove* (b).

Lord ABINGER, C. B.—I am of opinion that the evidence was quite sufficient. Here the bill is drawn upon
Charles Banner Crawford, and addressed to him at the India House. The evidence is, that there is a person of the
name of Charles Banner Crawford; that he once belonged to
the India House; and that the acceptance is in his handwriting. That is surely sufficient evidence of identity,
especially as no affidavit is produced to shew that he is not
really the defendant in the action. The case of *Whitelocke*
v. *Musgrove* was quite different in its circumstances. There
the learned Judge at the trial was inclined to think, that
mere evidence of the handwriting of the attesting witness,
and that he had gone to America, was not sufficient proof

(a) 2 Stark. 239.   (b) 1 C. & M. 511.

of the signature to the note, which was that of a marks- *Exch. of Pleas,*
man; but he left it to the jury to determine whether they 1842.
were satisfied with the evidence, and they found a verdict GREENSHIELDS
for the defendant. The jury were the proper judges, and *v.* CRAWFORD.
they thought the evidence was not sufficient. The Court
thought their verdict ought not to be set aside, because
they could not see that they had come to a wrong conclusion; and I quite agree in that decision.

ALDERSON, B.—I think there was abundant evidence of
identity in this case. It is quite a different question whether, if you allow the handwriting of an attesting witness
to be proof, it is sufficient to shew the identity of the attesting witness, and it is thence to be inferred that he saw
the party execute the instrument, whether by name or
otherwise. I agree that in such case there should be some
additional evidence, beyond the mere identity of the attesting witness.

Rule refused (a).

(a) See *Simpson* v. *Dismore*, ante, 47; *Jones* v. *Jones*, ante, 75.

PISTOR v. CATER. *Jan.* 17.

COVENANT.—The declaration stated, that by articles By agreement
of agreement, dated 20th October, 1824, made between the dated 20th
October, 1824,
plaintiff of the first part, John Evans and A. J. Mackenzie, reciting a
former agree-
ment in 1819,
for the grant of a lease of copyhold premises to A. B. for twenty-one years, from the 25th of
March, 1820, and that A. B. had requested, and the plaintiff had agreed, that the defendant
should be accepted as tenant, and a lease should be granted to him instead of to A. B., on the
same terms; and that the plaintiff was desirous to let the premises to the defendant so soon as a
good license for that purpose should be granted to him by the lord of the manor, but not before:
the plaintiff, in consideration of the covenants and agreements thereinafter contained on the part
of the defendant, covenanted that he would, so soon as a good license for that purpose should
have been procured by him from the lord, at the defendant's expense, lease the premises to the
defendant for all the residue then unexpired of the term of twenty-one years from the 25th of
March, 1820, &c.: and the defendant thereby covenanted, from thenceforth yearly during the remainder to come of the said term, to pay the plaintiff the rent, and also that he would *from time to
time during the term to be granted as aforesaid,* keep the premises in repair, &c. &c. The agreement
contained also a covenant by the plaintiff for quiet enjoyment during the remainder of the term,
on payment of the rent and performance of the covenants. The defendant entered upon the
premises, and occupied them until the expiration of twenty-one years from the 25th of March,
1820:—*Held,* that he was liable on the covenant for repair, although no lease had ever been
made to him pursuant to the agreement, nor any license obtained from the lord for that purpose.

the then churchwardens of the parish of St. Mary Walthamstow, and James Turner and James Vickery, the then overseers of the poor of the said parish, of the second part, Elizabeth Price, widow and administratrix of William Price, deceased, of the third part, Charles Rowland and Janet his wife, and Mary Maclaurin, (executors of Duncan Maclaurin, deceased), of the fourth part, and the defendant of the fifth part (profert); after reciting an agreement, dated 29th November, 1819, whereby the then churchwardens and overseers of the poor of the said parish agreed to make and execute a lease to the said William Price of the hereditaments therein mentioned, for the term of twenty-one years, to commence from the 25th of March, 1820, at the yearly rent of 47*l.* 5*s.*, and reciting that the said William Price afterwards contracted and agreed with the said Duncan Maclaurin that the said lease should be made to him in lieu of the said William Price; that the said C. Rowland and Janet his wife, and Mary Maclaurin, had applied to the said churchwardens and overseers, parties thereto, and requested that the defendant should be accepted tenant of the same premises, and that a lease thereof should be granted to him instead of the lease so contracted to be granted to the said William Price, on such terms and conditions as were mentioned and contained on the part of the said William Price in the said first-mentioned agreement; and that the plaintiff, with the consent of the said churchwardens and overseers, had agreed to accept the defendant as tenant, and to comply with the request of the said C. Rowland, &c.; and that the hereditaments in the said articles of agreement mentioned were of copyhold or customary tenure, and held of the lord of the manor of Walthamstow, Torrey, and High Hall, in the county of Essex, and no license had then been granted by the lord of the said manor to the plaintiff to demise the said hereditaments to the defendant; and that the plaintiff was willing and desirous to let and demise the hereditaments in the said articles of agreement mentioned to the defendant, his executors and administrators, when and so soon as a good and sufficient license for that purpose should be granted to him by the lord of the said manor, *but not before:* he the plaintiff, *in consideration of the covenants and agreements thereinafter contained* on the part of the defendant, his executors, &c., did for himself, his heirs and assigns, covenant, promise, and agree with the defendant, his executors and administrators, in manner following (that is to say); that he the plaintiff, his heirs or assigns, should and would, when and so soon as a good and sufficient license for that purpose should have been procured by the plaintiff, his executors or administrators, from the lord of the manor aforesaid, at the proper costs and charges of the defendant, his executors, &c., demise and lease all that piece or parcel of land, and all that messuage or dwelling-house and premises, in the said articles particularly mentioned, unto the defendant, his executors, &c., for all the residue and remainder then to come and unexpired of the term of twenty-one years, to be computed from the 25th of March, 1820, at and under the yearly rent of 47*l.* 5*s.*, by two equal half-yearly payments, &c. And the defendant, for the considerations aforesaid, did thereby, for himself, his heirs, executors, and assigns, covenant, promise, and agree with the plaintiff, his heirs and assigns, that he the defendant, his executors, &c., should and would from thenceforth yearly and every year during the residue and remainder then to come *of the said term*, well and truly pay or cause to be paid to the plaintiff, his heirs and assigns, the said rent of 47*l.* 5*s.*, at the days and times and in the proportions aforesaid. [Then followed covenants by the defendant, from time to time *during the term thereby agreed to be granted*, to pay all taxes charged on the premises: from time to time *during the term to be granted as aforesaid*, to repair the premises, and to paint the outside once in each three years during the term; and a covenant by the plaintiff for quiet enjoyment by the defendant during the remainder of the term, on

payment of the rent and performance of the covenants.]
And lastly, it was by the said articles agreed and declared
by and between the said parties thereto, that such lease,
when granted in pursuance of such license so to be obtained
as aforesaid, should contain covenants, provisoes, and
agreements similar to and founded upon the several covenants, provisoes, and agreements, therein contained, and
none other. The declaration then averred, that after the
making of the said articles of agreement, to wit, on &c.,
the defendant, under and by virtue of the said articles,
entered into and upon the said premises mentioned therein, and became and was possessed thereof, and continued possessed thereof, under and by virtue of the said
articles of agreement, from thence until the 25th day of
March, 1841, *when the said term mentioned in the said
articles of agreement expired by effluxion of time;* and assigned breaches of covenant in not keeping the premises
in repair, and not painting, pursuant to the agreement.

Special demurrer, assigning for causes, first, that the
declaration does not shew that the premises mentioned in
the articles of agreement declared upon were at any time
demised and leased by the plaintiff to the defendant for
the term of years mentioned in the said articles, in pursuance of the plaintiff's covenant therein contained; and
secondly, that it appears by the declaration, that the premises agreed to be demised to the defendant were copyhold premises, and that, in order to enable the plaintiff to
demise the same, it was necessary that he should procure
the license of the lord of the manor for that purpose, but
it is nowhere alleged or shewn in the declaration, that the
plaintiff did ever apply for or obtain, or use any endeavour
to obtain such license from the lord of the said manor, or
that any license was ever granted to the plaintiff by the
lord of the said manor, to enable him to demise the premises to the defendant. Joinder in demurrer.

Fish, in support of the demurrer.—The declaration discloses no legal liability on the part of the defendant to re- pair the premises. The covenants are only to pay rent, to repair, &c., during the term thereby agreed to be granted, i. e., during the remainder of the term of twenty-one years of which a lease is thereafter to be made by the plaintiff to the defendant. The defendant's liability, therefore, did not attach until the remainder of that term had been granted to him by a valid lease. The articles of agreement themselves did not and could not constitute an actual demise, it being necessary first to obtain a license from the lord. The parties have made the grant of that license a condition precedent to the granting of the term, during which alone the defendant's liability under the covenants is to subsist. [Lord *Abinger*, C. B.—The declaration shews that the defendant has in fact entered on the premises, and held them during the whole remainder of the twenty-one years. Suppose he had been turned out by the lord, and had sued the plaintiff on his covenant for quiet enjoyment, what defence would he have had? The defendant has had the whole benefit of the lease without the license, and yet, at the end of the twenty-one years, says he is not liable on the covenants.] It is clear no term actually vested in the defendant: but the covenant is only to repair *during the term*. Until a license was obtained, and a valid grant of the term made to him, he was not bound by this covenant. It would be unreasonable to suppose that he should, since he might have been turned out by the lord the day after he had put the premises into complete repair. [Lord *Abinger*, C. B.— On the other hand, he might be content to rest upon the covenant for quiet enjoyment, without the license being obtained.] If there be any hardship on the plaintiff, he has brought it upon himself by not procuring the license and tendering the lease. In *Doe* d. *Coore* v. *Clare* (a), it was held that an instrument on an agreement stamp,

Exch. of Pleas,
1842.

PISTOR
v.
CATER.

(a) 2 T. R. 739.

Y 2

reciting that A., in case he should be entitled to certain copyhold premises on B.'s death, would immediately demise them to C., and declaring that he did thereby agree to demise and let the same, with a subsequent covenant to procure a license to let from the lord, operated only as an agreement for a lease, and not as an actual demise. That case shews that the license of the lord is a condition precedent essential to a valid lease. The same appears from the case of *Doe* d. *Nunn* v. *Lufkin* (a). If the license had been refused by the lord, the defendant could not have enforced a specific performance of the agreement; why then should the plaintiff be at liberty to take advantage of it in the absence of such license, and of the lease to be founded thereon?

Cleasby, contrà, was stopped by the Court.

Lord ABINGER, C. B.—It is clear that by these articles of agreement, the parties intended to covenant with each other, independently of the lease to be afterwards granted. If this had been an ejectment by the landlord, after six months' notice to quit, the cases cited might have applied; but then an action might have been brought by the defendant against the plaintiff, on his covenant for quiet enjoyment, for turning him out of possession. This is a contract which is to bind both parties even if no lease be granted, and in addition, the defendant was to have a lease, if the license should be obtained. No lease having been made, but the defendant having occupied for the whole of the term agreed upon, and having had the full benefit which he could have enjoyed under the lease, he cannot now say that the covenants are not binding, because the lease was not granted.

ALDERSON, B., and GURNEY, B., concurred.

Judgment for the plaintiff.

(a) 4 East, 221.

Exch. of Pleas,
1842.

STERICKER and Another *v.* BARKER.

Jan. 19.

Assumpsit by indorsee against drawer of a bill of exchange. The declaration alleged, that the defendant, on the 5th May, 1841, made his bill of exchange in writing, and directed the same to one George Baxter, and thereby required the said George Baxter to pay to the order of the defendant 103*l.* 7*s.* 6*d.*, two months after the date thereof, which period had elapsed before the commencement of this suit; and the defendant then indorsed the said bill to the plaintiffs; and that the said George Baxter did not pay the said bill, although the same was presented to him on the day when it became due, whereof the defendant then had notice.

Plea, that the defendant had not notice of dishonour of the said bill of exchange on the day when the same became due, modo et formâ.

Special demurrer, assigning for cause, that the defendant was not entitled to notice of the dishonour of the bill on the day when it became due, and that the pretended traverse in the plea raised an issue wholly immaterial. Joinder in demurrer.

The points marked for argument by the defendant were, that the declaration was insufficient; first, because it stated that the defendant had notice on the day of the dishonour of the bill; secondly, because it contained no averment of any promise by the defendant.

Ball appeared to support the demurrer, but the Court called on

Wordsworth, contrà.—The plea undoubtedly cannot be sustained. But the declaration is bad on general demurrer, for want of an allegation of a promise to pay. That is

In an action by the indorsee against the drawer of a bill of exchange, the omission of a promise by the drawer to pay is at most merely matter of form, which can only be taken advantage of on special demurrer.

And *semble,* the allegation of a promise is in such case altogether unnecessary.

a defect not of form merely, but of substance; *Henry* v. *Burbidge* (a). That was an action by the indorsee against the drawer of a bill of exchange, and no promise to pay was alleged. *Tindal*, C. J., says—" In this action, which is against the drawer, the bill does not constitute a debt, but raises a promise by implication of law, to pay in case of the acceptor failing to do so. That promise, I am of opinion, ought to be alleged in the declaration." The cases of *Hayter* v. *Moat* (b), and *Harding* v. *Hibel* (c), are authorities to shew that a promise to pay is necessary in an indebitatus count, and that such promise is matter of substance, and not of form merely. Where the action is against the *acceptor*, indeed, no promise to pay need be alleged, because his liability is not implied and conditional, like that of the drawer, but express and absolute on the face of the contract. *Griffith* v. *Roxbrough* (d) will probably be cited on the other side. There, undoubtedly, this Court appeared to think that no promise to pay need now be alleged in a count on a bill or note, and held that at all events the omission of it could only be taken advantage of on special demurrer: but the cases of *Hayter* v. *Moat* and *Harding* v. *Hibel* were not referred to.

Ball, in reply.—The objection to the declaration is, at all events, matter of form only, and not of substance. The count pursues the form given in the rule of Trin. T., 1 Will. 4. The promise to pay is not now traversable, and therefore none need be alleged. Besides, this is an action against the drawer by his indorsee, on a bill payable to the order of the drawer, and there is therefore a privity of contract between the parties.

Lord ABINGER, C. B.—It is clear that the defendant

(a) 3 Bing. N. C. 501; 4 Scott, 296.   (c) 4 Tyrw. 314.
(b) 2 M. & W. 56.   (d) 2 M. & W. 734.

could not have traversed the promise to pay, and therefore I think the plaintiffs were not bound to allege it. If that view of the case had been presented to the Court of Common Pleas in the case of *Henry* v. *Burbidge*, I cannot but think that they would have formed a different conclusion. The judgment must be for the plaintiffs.

Exch. of Pleas,
1842.

STERICKER
v.
BARKER.

ALDERSON, B.—It is sufficient to say, as I said in the case of *Griffith* v. *Roxbrough*, that the promise to pay, in this case, not being traversable by the defendant, the omission of it is, at all events, mere matter of form, which cannot be taken advantage of except on special demurrer.

GURNEY, B., concurred.

Judgment for the plaintiffs.

———————

VESEY v. MANTELL.

Jan. 19.

DEBT on bond. The declaration stated, that the defendant, by his writing obligatory, bearing date the 2nd September, 1840, acknowledged himself to be held and firmly bound to the plaintiff in the penal sum of £100, subject to a condition therein contained, whereby, after reciting that one Mary Ann Torwood had exhibited her bill of complaint in the High Court of Chancery against Isabella Rooks, Charles Brutton (and several other parties therein named), and the now defendant, as defendants; the condition of the said writing obligatory was declared to be such, that if the now defendant, his heirs, &c., should well and truly pay or cause to be paid all such costs as the said Court should think fit to award to *all* the said defendants

The condition of a bond, after reciting that one A. B. had filed a bill in Chancery against several persons (naming them) and the now defendant, as defendants, was, that the now defendant should pay all such costs as the Court of Chancery should award to *all* the said defendants:—
Held, that the construction of this condition

was, that the defendant should pay the costs awarded to all or any of the defendants except himself.

in the said cause, then the said writing obligatory should be void, &c. Averment, that the said Court awarded to the said Isabella Rooks and Charles Brutton, the defendants in the said cause, the sum of 45*l.* 18*s.* 11*d.*, for their costs, &c. Breach, non-payment of that sum by the defendant.

General demurrer, and joinder.—The ground of demurrer stated in the margin was, that by the condition the payment was to be of costs awarded by the Court to *all* the defendants in the said suit ; whereas the declaration shewed an award of costs to some of the defendants only, and not to all.

Erle, in support of the demurrer.—The declaration does not shew any breach of the condition of this bond. The condition was, that the defendant should be liable to payment of the costs only in case of their being awarded to *all* the defendants. He has not made himself responsible for costs which may become payable to a single defendant. In *Kipling* v. *Turner* (a), where the condition of the bond, after reciting that three parties had filed their bill in equity against two defendants (naming them), was, that the obligor should pay such costs as the Court of Chancery should award *to the defendants,* the majority of the Court were certainly of opinion that the death of one defendant, before any award of costs, could not be pleaded in discharge of the bond ; but *Abbott,* C. J., dissented, and said,—" I doubt whether we can properly introduce the words ' or either of them ' into the condition of this bond, in order to satisfy the intention of the parties." A long series of cases, from that of *Lord Arlington* v. *Merricke* (b), down to that of *The University of Cambridge* v. *Baldwin* (c), has fully established the principle, that the strictest construction is to be applied to the obligation of sureties. In

(a) 5 B. & Ald. 261.

(b) 2 Saund. 403 ; and see

the cases collected in the notes.

(c) 5 M. & W. 580.

suits in equity, a plaintiff is sometimes directed to pay costs to one defendant, and to receive them from another; and it is not at all necessarily implied in this condition, that the defendant should pay the costs which may be awarded to one defendant only.

Montague Smith, contrà.—The word " all " must, in order to effectuate the plain intention of the parties, be construed distributively, as in *Kipling* v. *Turner.* [*Alderson*, B.— The construction for which Mr. *Erle* contends would lead to this absurdity, that the defendant is to pay the costs that may be awarded to himself.]—He was then stopped by the Court.

Erle was heard in reply.

Lord ABINGER, C. B.—It is clear that the word " all " cannot mean that the defendant is to pay the costs that may be awarded to all the defendants *jointly*, for then the absurdity would follow, to which my brother *Alderson* has referred, that he would have to pay them to himself. The construction of the condition must therefore be, that the defendant shall pay the costs that may be awarded to all or any of the defendants in the suit except himself. The judgment must be for the plaintiff.

ALDERSON, B.—I am clearly of the same opinion. The word " all " must be taken distributively; it cannot have been meant to be used in the joint sense, otherwise it would import that the defendant was bound to pay such costs as should be awarded to himself and others.

GURNEY, B., concurred.

Judgment for the plaintiff.

Exch. of Pleas.
1842.

Jan. 19.   SPAETH *v.* HARE, Knt., and Others.

Declaration in
assumpsit
stated, that the
defendants
bought of the
plaintiff a
quantity of lin-
seed, to be
worked by the
buyers in 14
days from the
ship's arrival in
the river, the
price to be paid
in ready money,
less 2½ per
cent. discount,
or by the de-
fendants' ac-
ceptance at two
months. Aver-
ment, that the
linseed arrived
and was ready
for delivery;
that the 14 days
had elapsed;
and although
the plaintiff ten-
dered it to the
defendants for
their accept-
ance, and
would have re-
ceived their
acceptance at
two months for
the price, and
although the
defendants
were requested
to pay in ready
money, or to
give their ac-
ceptance, and
refused to do
the latter, and
discharged
the plaintiff
from tendering

ASSUMPSIT.—The declaration stated, that whereas the defendants, on &c., bought of the plaintiff a certain quantity of linseed, on board a certain ship, to be worked by the buyers in fourteen days from the ship's arrival at the river Thames, and the seed being ready for delivery, and the amount to be paid either in ready money, less 2½ per cent. discount, or by the defendants' acceptance at two months. Averments, that the linseed arrived in the river Thames, and was ready for delivery, and that fourteen days from its being so ready had elapsed; and although the plaintiff would have delivered the said linseed, and then tendered and offered the same to the defendants for their acceptance, and would also have drawn upon the defendants, and have received their acceptance at two months, for the price of the same, of which the defendants had notice, and were then requested to pay for the said linseed in ready money, or to give their said acceptance; and although the defendants then wholly neglected and refused so to give such acceptance as aforesaid, and then discharged and exonerated the plaintiff from drawing upon them, or tendering for their acceptance any bill of exchange, yet that the defendants did not nor would accept the said linseed, nor work the same, nor pay the price thereof in ready money to the plaintiff.

Third plea, that the defendants were not requested by the plaintiff to pay for the said linseed in ready money, or to give their said acceptance, modo et formâ. Fourth plea, that the defendants did not refuse to give such ac-

a bill for their acceptance, yet they did not accept or work the linseed, or pay for it in ready money.—Pleas, first, that the defendants were not requested to pay for the linseed in ready money, or to give their acceptance: 2nd, that they did not refuse to give their acceptance, or discharge the plaintiff from tendering a bill for their acceptance:—*Held*, that both pleas were bad, as traversing averments which were immaterial to the maintenance of the action.

ceptance, or discharge or exonerate the plaintiff from
drawing upon them, or tendering to them for their acceptance any bill of exchange, modo et formâ.

Special demurrer to the third plea, assigning for causes,
that the defendants have therein attempted to take issue
on an averment in the declaration, not material to the
plaintiff's claim to damages, and not constituting a condition precedent to the plaintiff's right to sue: and that the
plea furnishes no answer to the plaintiff's claim to damages
in respect of the defendants not having accepted the said
goods, and not having worked them. There was also a
demurrer to the fourth plea, assigning in substance the
same causes. Joinders in demurrer.

Barstow, in support of the demurrers.—These pleas pro-
fess to answer the whole count, but they give no answer
whatever to that part of the breach which complains of the
non-acceptance of the linseed, and the not working it out
of the ship within the fourteen days. All that the third
plea says is, that the defendants were not requested to pay
in ready money or to give their acceptance. That is quite
immaterial to the maintenance of this action. The same
objection applies to the fourth plea. A clear cause of action, therefore, remains upon the declaration unanswered.

Swann, contrà.—The pleas are good, for they traverse a
material averment, which was essential to the maintenance
of the action. Upon the true construction of this contract,
the tender of the bill by the plaintiff for acceptance, and
the acceptance of the goods by the defendants, were mutual
conditions: and the defendants were not bound to accept
the goods until the plaintiff tendered them a bill for acceptance, that being the special mode of payment agreed upon.
The plaintiff was to do the first act, namely, to draw the bill.
If this averment had not been introduced into the declaration, it would be consistent with it that the defendants
refused to receive the goods, because the plaintiff would

not draw the bill. The defendants had the option of paying
by bill at two months if they thought fit, and their contract was to accept the goods only provided the plaintiff
would receive payment in that mode. The law on this
subject is thus stated in the note to *Peeters* v. *Opie* (a):—
" Where two concurrent acts are to be done, the party who
sues the other for non-performance must aver that he has
performed, or was ready to perform, his part of the contract." The averments traversed by the pleas were therefore material and traversable, and the issues are well
taken upon them.

Lord ABINGER, C. B.—The plaintiff has averred in his
declaration all that he was bound to do in order to maintain
the action. The contract was, that the defendants should
buy of the plaintiff a quantity of linseed, to be worked by
them within fourteen days after it arrived in the river and
was ready for delivery, and to be paid for in ready money,
minus a certain discount, or by their acceptance at two
months. The declaration states the arrival of the linseed,
and that it was ready for delivery, and avers that it was
duly tendered to the defendants for their acceptance, and
that they were requested to pay for it in ready money, or
to give their acceptance, which they refused to give, and
discharged the plaintiff from drawing upon them: and it
is then averred as a breach, that the defendants did not
accept or work the linseed, or pay for it in ready money.
To this the defendants plead, that they were not requested
to pay in ready money, or to give their acceptance, and in
another plea, that they did not refuse to give their acceptance, or discharge the plaintiff from drawing upon them or
tendering a bill for their acceptance. That is no answer to
the breach of contract alleged in the declaration; it leaves
it in doubt whether they had or had not refused to accept
the goods. Why should the plaintiff request them to pay

(a) 2 Saund. 352, b.

either in bills or cash, until they had accepted the goods? They might have said that they were willing to pay by a bill, but that the plaintiff required cash, and that would have been a good defence; but the issues raised by these pleas are altogether immaterial. Our judgment must therefore be for the plaintiff.

ALDERSON, B.—I am of the same opinion. The facts stated in these pleas are wholly immaterial to the maintenance of the action, on the state of facts set forth in the declaration. The agreement of the defendants is, that they will accept the goods, and pay for them in one of two modes. As soon, therefore, as the plaintiff tendered the goods, and the defendants refused to receive them, the contract was broken, and the right of action accrued.

GURNEY, B., concurred.

Judgment for the plaintiff.

HORNE *v.* RAMSDALE.

Jan. 19.

ASSUMPSIT. The declaration stated, that by a certain agreement made between the plaintiff, as clerk to the commissioners for building a certain bridge, to wit, at Staines, in the county of Middlesex, of the first part, one W. Taylor of the second part, and G. Simpson and the defendant of the third part, it was agreed, that whereas the commissioners were empowered to erect a certain toll-gate, and the said W. Taylor had been and was declared the renter of the tolls to be received at the said gate, and had proposed the said G. Simpson and the defendant as his sure-

To a declaration stating that T. was the lessee of certain tolls, and that S. and the defendants agreed to join with T. in a bond conditioned for payment of the rent under the lease; and alleging as a breach that the defendant refused to join T. in the bond: the defendant

pleaded, first, that at the time of tendering the bond to him, S. had not executed the same, nor was he present ready to execute it jointly with the defendant: 2nd, that S. died before the commencement of the suit, and that before his death the bond was not tendered to the defendant for execution, nor was he requested to execute it:—*Held*, that the pleas were bad.

ties; and whereas the said W. Taylor had agreed to execute a counterpart of the lease which the commissioners should execute to him of the said tolls; and the said G. Simpson and the defendant undertook, on their parts, for the punctual payment of the rent according to the terms of that agreement, and to join with the said W. Taylor in a bond in the penal sum of 1000*l.*, for the due performance of the covenants and payment of the rent in the said lease contained and reserved, &c. The declaration then averred, that the commissioners did execute a lease to Taylor, pursuant to the agreement; and that although Taylor and Simpson did afterwards, to wit, on &c., execute a certain bond in the penal sum of 1000*l.*, for the due payment of the rent reserved by the said lease; and although the defendant was afterwards, to wit, on &c., requested by the commissioners to join in the said bond, and to execute the same, and although the said bond, after the same was executed by the said W. Taylor, was tendered to the defendant to be executed by him; yet the defendant did not nor would join with the said W. Taylor in the said bond, whereby the commissioners were unable to recover from the defendant the sum of 800*l.* then due from the said W. Taylor to the said commissioners for the rent of the said tolls, &c.

Pleas:—First, that at the time of tendering and offering the said bond to the defendant to be executed by him, as in the declaration mentioned, the said G. Simpson had not executed the same, nor was he present on that occasion, ready to execute the same jointly with the defendant; secondly, that the said G. Simpson departed this life before the commencement of this suit, and that before the decease of the said G. Simpson, the said bond was not tendered or offered to the defendant for his execution, nor was he, before the decease of the said G. Simpson, requested to execute the same.

To these pleas the plaintiff demurred specially; assigning for causes of demurrer, that the facts of Simpson's not

having executed the bond before it was tendered to the defendant for his execution, and of his having died before it was so tendered, were no answer to the action. Joinder in demurrer.

Cleasby, in support of the demurrer.—These pleas furnish no answer to the action. The first appears to suppose it to have been material that the sureties should both execute the bond at the same time and place. But there is no agreement on the part of one surety, that the other shall also execute; otherwise it would only be for two of the obligors to refuse to meet for the purpose of executing it, and the lessor would be left without any mode of obtaining security. The second plea merely amounts to this, that Simpson had not executed the bond when it was tendered to the defendant for execution. If that be a defence, each surety has but to refuse to execute, and the plaintiff is without remedy. There is no condition that either of them shall not join the principal in the bond, unless the other has first executed, or is ready to join in the execution. They cannot be compelled to meet for the purpose. —The Court then called upon

Erle, contrà.—It is part of the stipulation between the parties that there shall be *two* sureties: but the commissioners have executed the lease with one surety only, and, having lain by until the other is dead, and the principal has become insolvent, now call upon the former for payment of the whole sum due. This amounts to such laches on their part as discharges the defendant from his obligation; since he may reasonably allege, that one motive for his becoming a surety was that his co-surety would exercise some control over the principal: his situation has therefore been altered to his prejudice, by the neglect of the commissioners to obtain the signature of both sureties pursuant to the agreement. In *Bellairs* v. *Ebsworth* (a), the defendant gave a bond to the plaintiffs for the due accounting of the principal, who afterwards, with the plaintiffs' knowledge, took a partner : it was held that the defendant was thereby discharged from liability. In *Dance* v. *Girdler* (b), where the defendant gave a bond to the plaintiffs, payable to them and their successors, as governors of a society, conditioned for the faithful accounting with them and the successors, governors, &c., of a collector ; and the society was afterwards incorporated by letters patent ; it was held, that the defendant was not liable for the default of the collector subsequently to such incorporation. [*Alderson*, B.—Here the parties agree to join with Taylor in the bond ; the only material thing, therefore, was that Taylor should execute it.] Suppose, when the parties met, one refused to execute ; might not the other take advantage of his refusal ? If, before the bond was tendered to the defendant for execution, Simpson had been released, the defendant would surely have been discharged. But further, the declaration is defective : the agreement ought to have been made with the commissioners ; and unless it were so made, there was no consideration for the defendant's promise, inasmuch as it does not appear that the plaintiff had any authority to make the agreement on their behalf. The whole of the consideration is the lease of the tolls to Taylor by the commissioners.

Lord ABINGER, C. B.—I am clearly of opinion that the plaintiff is entitled to the judgment of the Court. The agreement must receive the same interpretation as it would have borne at the time when it was signed. It is a contract by each of the intended sureties to join in the bond with Taylor, the principal ; i. e. to execute the bond in the character of surety. It is not a contract that they shall

(a) 3 Campb. 53.   (b) 1 N. R. 34.

execute it in the presence of each other, or that if one die, the other shall be at liberty to refuse to execute it. As to the other point, I think the declaration is quite sufficient.

ALDERSON, B.—I am of the same opinion. What the defendant undertook was, to join with Taylor in the bond. The only condition precedent was the execution of the bond by Taylor. He has executed it, but the defendant refuses to do so. I think he has no right so to refuse; it is no part of the agreement that he shall join with the other surety in the execution.

GURNEY, B., concurred.

Judgment for the plaintiff.

Exch. of Pleas, 1842.

HORNE *v.* RAMSDALE.

ENGLAND and Another, Executors, *v.* WATSON, Executor.

Jan. 19.

DEBT on bond by the plaintiffs, as executors of the surviving executor of the will of W. Pinning, the survivor of Samuel Bean, against the defendant as executor of John Watson. The declaration stated, that John Watson in his lifetime, by his writing obligatory &c., acknowledged himself to be held and firmly bound to the said W. Pinning and S. Bean in the sum of £3000; and averred as a breach the non-payment thereof by John Watson in his lifetime, or by the defendant as executor since his decease.

The plea set out the bond and condition on oyer. The condition, after reciting, that by a marriage intended to be solemnized between the said John Watson and Elizabeth Robinson, he the said John Watson would receive with his said intended wife the sum of £2000 and upwards, stated, that the bond was to be void, if, after the marriage, the said John Watson should die in the lifetime of his said intended wife, and his heirs, executors, &c., should, within six months after his decease, pay to the said W. Pinning

Payment of money into Court, under the 4 & 5 Ann. c. 16, s. 13, in discharge of principal and interest on a bond, and costs, cannot be *pleaded* to an action on the bond.

and S. Bean the sum of £1500, in trust for his said intended wife; but if she should die in his lifetime, the bond was to be void in case he should make payment to the person or persons to whom she should, by any will or other testamentary writing, give or bequeath all or any part of the said sum of £1500. The plea then alleged payment into Court of the sum of £315, principal money and interest due upon the bond, together with the further sum of £11 for costs; and averred that those sums were the full amount due for principal, interest, and costs. Verification.

General demurrer and joinder.

The points marked for argument on the part of the plaintiffs were :—1st, that payment of money into Court, under the stat. 4 & 5 Anne, c. 16, in discharge of all principal and interest due upon a bond, and of costs incurred in any suit at law or in equity, could not be pleaded : 2ndly, that the provisions of the 4 & 5 Anne, c. 16, s. 3, did not apply to the case of a bond conditioned, like the present, for the payment of uncertain amounts, contingent on uncertain events : 3rdly, that under the stat. 8 & 9 Will. 3, c. 11, the plaintiffs were entitled to have judgment for the whole penalty on the bond, to stand as a security for future breaches.

The defendant's points were :—1st, that the bond in question was a bond with a condition of defeasance, to make void the same upon payment of a less sum at a day certain, within the 4 Anne, c. 16, ss. 12 & 13 : 2ndly, that by that statute, payment into Court of the sum actually due upon such a bond at any time, with costs, might be pleaded, and, if no more were actually due, was a complete answer to the action upon it : 3rdly, that the plea stated a traversable fact, viz. that no more than £315 was due upon the bond, and that a good issue might be taken thereon.

Crompton, in support of the demurrer.—This plea is

altogether unwarranted by precedent. It is an attempt to
extend the provisions of the stat. 4 & 5 Anne, c. 16, ss. 12
& 13, to the case of a bond debt payable on a contingency.
Such a construction is altogether opposed to the established
sense of the statute. The 12th section enacts, that where
an action of debt is brought "upon any bond which hath
a condition of defeasance to make void the same upon
payment of a lesser sum at a day or place certain," if the
obligor has, before action brought, paid the principal and
interest due by the defeasance, although not strictly according to the condition, such payment may be pleaded to
the action, and shall be an effectual bar. The 13th section
enacts, "that if at any time, pending an action upon any
such bond with a penalty, the defendant shall bring into
the Court where the action shall be depending, all the
principal money and interest due on such bond, and also
all such costs as have been expended in any suit or suits
at law or in equity upon such bond, the said money so
brought in shall be deemed and taken to be in full satisfaction and discharge of the said bond; and the Court
shall and may give judgment to discharge every such defendant of and from the same accordingly." The clear
meaning of that section is, not that the amount of the debt
is to be found and settled by a jury, but that it is to be
ascertained by the officer of the Court.—He was then
stopped by the Court, who called on

W. H. Watson, contrà.—The defendant is entitled to
plead the payment into Court in this case. Before the
stat. 3 & 4 Will. 4, c. 42, s. 21, and the rules of Court
founded thereon, of Hilary Term, 4 Will. 4, and Trinity
Term, 1 Vict., the general rule was, that money could be
paid into Court only in actions of debt or assumpsit, where
the plaintiff demanded a sum certain, or one capable of
being ascertained by mere computation. There were also
several particular statutes, under which it would be paid

z 2

Exch. of Pleas,
1842.

ENGLAND
v.
WATSON.

in, *e. g.*, the Carriers' Act, 1 Will. 4, c. 68. But, until the recent statute and the new rules, it could in no case be *pleaded.* Now the rule of Trinity Term, 1 Vict., is in the most general terms: it directs, that when money is paid into Court, it shall be pleaded in all cases. Secondly, this bond is within the 4 & 5 Anne, c. 16, s. 12; for, being payable six months after Watson's decease, it is a bond payable "at a day certain." A bond payable on a contingency, when the contingency has happened, is within the statute. In *Murray* v. *Earl of Stair* (*a*), which was the case of a post obit bond, payable six months after the decease of the then Earl of Stair, *Abbott*, C. J., thought it was within the statute. In *Ex parte Winchester* (*b*), Lord *Hardwicke* thought it was not a case falling within the statute; but there the contingency had not happened, because the principal money had not become due. [*Alderson*, B.—This is not like the case of a bill of exchange, which shews on the face of it how much is due; it is the case of money payable at a certain time after a man's death: is the Master to determine the fact or the time of the death? There may in such a case be matters in controversy, which the party has a right to have brought before a jury. The case is different where the contingency has already happened, and nothing more is required than mere computation; here it has to be ascertained whether the contingency has in fact happened or not.] The test is, whether it is a case in which it is necessary to assign breaches under the stat. 8 & 9 Will. 3, c. 11, s. 8; if it be not, the case is governed by the statute of Anne. In *Cardozo* v. *Hardy* (*c*), where the bond was payable at a day named, or within a month after the death of the obligee, which should first happen, it was held to be a case in which it was not necessary to assign breaches.—He cited also *Smith* v. *Bond* (*d*). [Lord *Abinger*, C. B.—Should not the plea

(*a*) 2 B. & Cr. 82.   (*c*) 2 Moore, 220.
(*b*) 1 Atk. 118.   (*d*) 10 Bing. 125 ; 3 M. & Scott, 528.

have stated the time when the money became due?] That
would be a question to be determined by the jury.

Crompton, in reply.—The new rules have no application
whatever to this case. They are applicable to those cases
in which, previously, money could have been paid into
Court: but the Court did not, under the former practice,
allow money to be paid into Court in an action of debt on
bond. The rule is correctly stated in Selwyn's Nisi Prius,
tit. Debt, Vol. 1, p. 542, (8th edit.):—" In debt upon
bond, the Court will not permit money to be paid into
Court, but will refer it to the Master to compute what is
due for principal and interest." Under the stat. 4 & 5
Anne, c. 16, the application is made to the equitable jurisdiction of the Court, and *the Court* exercises a discretion
upon it; it is in no respect the province of the jury, nor
can money be paid into Court in such a case, so as to affect
the pleadings.

Lord ABINGER, C. B.—I am of opinion that the plaintiffs are entitled to the judgment of the Court. Under
the statute of Anne, a defendant, in certain cases of debt
upon bond, may pay into Court the principal money and
interest, with costs of suit, the whole to be computed by
the Master, and the Court may thereupon stay the proceedings in the action. But it does not at all follow that
the defendant can plead such payment; indeed, it must
often happen that the proceedings will be stayed before he
will be required to plead. The new rules have no application to such a case as this; all that they do is to direct
that payment of money into Court must be pleaded, which
applies to those cases where the payment is made without
leave of the Court.

ALDERSON, B.—I am of the same opinion. The payment of money into Court under the new rules has nothing

whatever to do with the present case. There the defendant fixes the amount himself, and pays it in at his peril: but under the statute of Anne, the Court is to ascertain, through its officer, the amount due for principal and interest, and costs upon the bond, and to discharge the defendant from the debt. In this case, the defendant claims himself to determine the amount due from him for principal, interest, and costs, and wants the jury to decide whether he is right or wrong: but the statute declares that that is a question for the Court.

GURNEY, B., concurred.

> Judgment for the plaintiffs.

———————•———————

TYLER *v.* BLAND.

ASSUMPSIT for work and labour, money paid, and on an account stated.

Plea, as to the sum of 4*l.* 16*s.*, parcel &c., that after the making of the promises by the defendant in the declaration mentioned, and before the commencement of the suit, to wit, on the 28th of June, 1841, the defendant was ready and willing to pay, and tendered to the plaintiff the sum of 4*l.* 16*s.*, and that, after the making of the promises as to that sum, he hath always been and still is ready to pay the said sum of 4*l.* 16*s.* to the plaintiff, and now brings the same into Court, &c.

plaintiff, and now brings the same into Court, &c.—Replication, that before the making of the tender in the plea mentioned, and before and at the time of the demand and refusal hereinafter mentioned, a larger sum than 4*l.* 16*s.*, to wit, 7*l.* 12*s.*, that sum including the 4*l.* 16*s.*, was due from the defendant to the plaintiff on account of divers of the causes of action in the declaration; and that before the making of the said tender, to wit, on &c., the plaintiff demanded of the defendant payment of the said sum of 7*l.* 12*s.*, which so included the said sum of 4*l.* 16*s.*; yet the defendant did not pay the said sum of 7*l.* 12*s.*, or any part thereof, but refused to pay the same and every part thereof, and that no set-off or other just cause then existed for the non-payment:—*Held,* on special demurrer, that the replication was good.

Replication, that before the making of the said tender
in the said plea alleged, and before and at the time of the
demand and refusal hereinafter mentioned, a larger sum
than 4*l.* 16*s.*, to wit, the sum of 7*l.* 12*s.*, the said last-mentioned sum including the said sum of 4*l.* 16*s.*, was due from
the defendant to the plaintiff on account of divers of the
said causes of action in the declaration mentioned; and
that before the making of the said tender in the said plea
alleged, to wit, on the 25th of June, 1841, the plaintiff
demanded of the defendant payment of the said sum of
7*l.* 12*s.*, which so then included the said sum of 4*l.* 16*s.*,
yet the defendant did not pay to the plaintiff the said sum
of 7*l.* 12*s.* or any part thereof, but then wholly neglected
and refused to pay the said sum of 7*l.* 12*s.* and every part
thereof; and that no set-off or other just cause then existed
for non-payment by the defendant of the said sum of 7*l.*
12*s.* or any part thereof.—Verification.

Special demurrer, and joinder in demurrer.

Ogle, in support of the demurrer.—This was a good tender
of the 4*l.* 16*s.* The plaintiff seeks to recover on several
causes of action, and the defendant in such case has a right
to plead a tender to one of them. Suppose the defendant
were charged as obligor on two bonds, one for 300*l.* and
the other for 200*l.*, might he not plead a tender as to one
of them, denying his liability on the other? In Bac. Abr.,
Tender, 449, it is laid down that " if A. be indebted to B.
in divers distinct sums of money, he may make a tender
of any one of the sums." *Cotton* v. *Godwin* (a) will be relied
on for the plaintiff, but that case is distinguishable, because
there there was but a single cause of action. Here the
defendant was always ready to pay, so far as regards this
sum of 4*l.* 16*s.* The plea is good as to that amount, and
the replication contains no answer to it.

(a) 7 M. & W. 147.

Martin, contrà.—The replication is good. The cause of
action disclosed by the declaration is one which the plaintiff might enforce at once, without any demand of payment.
Then the plea of tender means this: that the debtor,
though he was bound to pay without demand, may tender
the sum due; and if he can also make out that he was
always ready to pay it, the law excuses him from any damages subsequent to such tender. He must shew affirmatively, that from the time of the accruing of the debt he
was *always* ready to pay; and therefore it is that a demand and refusal previously to the tender prevents him
from ever availing himself of the tender, because he has once
made a default. Now this replication shews that there was
a time when the defendant was not ready to pay the 4*l.* 16*s.*,
viz., when he refused payment "of the said sum of 7*l.* 12*s.*
(which included the 4*l.* 16*s.*), and every part thereof."
[*Alderson,* B.—If the words "and every part thereof" are
a material part of the averment, you are right.] The defendant might have rejoined a tender of the 4*l.* 16*s.* [*Alderson,* B.—The question is, whether this replication does
state a demand and refusal of the 4*l.* 16*s.* Suppose the
one party demands 7*l.* 12*s.*, and the other says, I do not
owe you more than 4*l.* 16*s.*, and no more passes; is that a
refusal of payment of the 4*l.* 16*s.*?] Yes, because it is the
duty of the debtor to pay the sum justly due, and there is
no obligation on the creditor to demand it; and it makes no
difference whether it be demanded as part of a larger sum
or not. A tender, at the time of the demand, of the 4*l.* 16*s.*,
would indeed have been an answer to this replication; but
on these pleadings it appears to be a *previous* demand of
the 7*l.* 12*s.*, and a refusal of all and every part of that sum.
[Lord *Abinger,* C. B.—Are we bound to assume that the
tender stated in the plea, and admitted by the replication, was made at a different time from the demand? It
might have been immediately after, and part of the same
transaction. A *previous* demand means a demand made on

a substantially different occasion.] It is admitted by this *Exch. of Pleas,* demurrer, that a larger sum than 4*l.* 16*s.*, and including 1842. that sum, was due; that the plaintiff demanded it, and the TYLER defendant refused to pay the same and every part thereof; *v.* and all that appears further is, that on a subsequent occa- BLAND. sion, the defendant tendered the 4*l.* 16*s.* only; but his previous default had incapacitated him from setting up that defence. *Cotton* v. *Godwin* is precisely in point.

Ogle, in reply.—The whole appears on the pleadings to have been one and the same transaction. [Lord *Abinger*, C. B.—To make out your defence, you ought to shew that then and there you tendered the whole sum demanded, or that no more was due than 4*l.* 16*s.*, and that you then tendered that.] How could the defendant rejoin, but by repeating the tender, as alleged in the plea? The replication ought to have shewn that a larger sum was due than the amount tendered, on the same cause of action. In *Cotton* v. *Godwin*, the replication was applied to the specific cause of action as to which the tender was made; but that is not so here. [*Alderson*, B.—Why could not you rejoin that when the plaintiff demanded the 7*l.* 12*s.*, you tendered the 4*l.* 16*s.*? you ought to amend by so rejoining.]

Lord ABINGER, C. B.—Where the replication to a plea of tender re-enforces the demand, and sets it up again, the rejoinder must either deny or confess and avoid that demand, otherwise it must be taken that the whole sum is due. Therefore, although the original plea of tender does not admit the whole sum to be due, it is admitted on this demurrer. The defendant should have rejoined by re-alleging a tender, at the time of the plaintiff's demand of 7*l.* 12*s.*, of the smaller sum of 4*l.* 16*s.*, and denying that more was due.

ALDERSON, B.—All the facts stated in the replication are admitted by the demurrer, and facts may be supposed which make them all true; as a demand of the whole, afterwards payment of part, and then a tender of the residue.

GURNEY, B. concurred.

Leave to amend on payment of costs; otherwise judgment for the plaintiff.

Jan. 21.

A Judge made an order for the arrest of the defendant for £422. The capias was indorsed for 422*l.* 13*s.* 4*d.*, (the real amount of the debt). The Court refused to discharge the defendant out of custody, and directed the writ to be amended on payment by the plaintiff of the costs of the application for the defendant's discharge.

PLOCK and Another *v.* PACHECO.

R. V. RICHARDS moved for a rule to shew cause why the defendant in this cause should not be discharged out of custody, and why the plaintiffs should not pay the costs of this application. It appeared from his affidavit, that the defendant, having gone on board a vessel at Southampton bound for the West Indies, was arrested at Falmouth on a capias issued in pursuance of a Judge's order under 1 & 2 Vict. c. 110, s. 8. The learned Judge, before making the order, inquired the amount of the debt, and being informed that it was 422*l.* 13*s.* 4*d.*, he indorsed on the order the sum of £422. The defendant was arrested for the sum of 422*l.* 13*s.* 4*d.*, for which amount the capias was indorsed.

Richards contended that the arrest was bad, having been made for a larger amount than that ordered by the Judge. The statute empowered an arrest only "for such sum as such Judge should think fit, not exceeding the amount of the debt or damages," and enabled the plaintiff to sue out thereon a writ of capias, in the form contained in the schedule annexed to the act; according to which form, the writ was to be indorsed for the amount of bail ordered by the Judge. He cited *Hodgkinson* v. *Hodgkinson* (a), where the defendant was discharged out of cus-

(a) 1 Ad. & Ell. 533; 3 Nev. & Man. 564.

tody, on the ground that in the copy of the capias the direction appeared to be to the sheriff of "Middesex."

Cleasby shewed cause against the rule in the first instance; and also applied for a cross rule to shew cause why the writ of capias should not be amended, by substituting thereon the sum of £422 instead of 422*l*. 13*s*. 4*d*. He urged that the Courts had always acted on the principle of allowing amendments in writs, where the justice of the case requires them, and where no injury is done to any party. In *Laroche* v. *Wasbrough* (*a*), which was an application to amend a writ, Lord *Kenyon* said, "The justice of the case requires that we should permit the plaintiff to amend. If the defendant had indeed suffered by the excess in the execution, that might have varied the case; but here he has not sustained any damage by it." So here, the defendant can have sustained no damage whatever by being held to bail for the odd shillings and pence beyond the sum directed by the Judge. The Court is expressly empowered, by the 6th section of the act, upon the application of a party by rule or order for his discharge from arrest, to make absolute or discharge such rule or order, or " to make such other order therein as to such Judge or Court shall seem fit."

Richards, in reply.—In *Trotter* v. *Bass* (*b*), the Court held that they had no jurisdiction to amend a writ of summons. Such an amendment was indeed allowed in *Lakin* v. *Watson* (*c*), but that was in order to save the Statute of Limitations; and *Parke*, B., in his judgment, appears to confine such amendments to cases of that nature. [*Alderson*, B.—The stat. 1 & 2 Vict. c. 110 had not then passed; and therefore the exception could not have been extended

(*a*) 2 T. R. 737.   (*b*) 1 Bing. N. C. 516; 1 Scott, 403.
(*c*) 2 C. & M. 685.

to a case like the present.] *Partridge* v. *Wallbank*(a) is an authority to the same effect.

Lord ABINGER, C. B.—In this case, as no oppression appears to have been exercised towards the defendant, and as we are empowered, by the 6th section of the act, to make such order in the matter as we shall think fit, under all the circumstances, we think the defendant should pay into Court the sum of £422, and £20 in lieu of bail, with liberty to take out those sums on putting in and perfecting special bail : Mr. *Cleasby's* rule for amending the writ will be made absolute, and Mr. *Richards's* rule discharged, the plaintiffs paying the costs of this application.

ALDERSON, B.—I agree in opinion that this writ ought to be amended, and think that, in so doing, we are not departing from any principle laid down by this Court in former cases. We have allowed writs to be amended, where justice appeared to require it, and the situation of the parties has not been changed by the amendment, as in the case of the Statute of Limitations. Here the Judge thought the plaintiffs were in danger of losing their debt by the defendant's quitting England in case he were at large; and it seems to me that that circumstance brings the case within the same principle that governed the Courts in regard to the Statute of Limitations. Here, too, we have something by which the writ can be amended. The rules will therefore be disposed of in the manner which has been stated by my Lord Chief Baron; and the plaintiffs will be quite sufficiently punished for their mistake by paying the costs of these applications.

GURNEY, B., concurred.

Rule accordingly.

(a) 1 M. & W. 316.

Exch. of Pleas,
1842.

BALL and Others *v.* GORDON and Others.

Jan. 24.

ASSUMPSIT by indorsees against acceptors of a bill of exchange. The declaration stated, that " whereas certain persons using the name, style, and firm of M'Leod & Co., on the 14th day of July, 1841, made their bill of exchange in writing, and thereby required the defendants to pay, four months after the date thereof, to them the said M'Leod & Co., or order, 132*l.* 0*s.* 7*d.* value received, which period has now elapsed; and the defendants accepted the said bill, and the said M'Leod & Co. then indorsed the same to W. J. Strickland, who then indorsed the same to the plaintiffs," &c.

Special demurrer, assigning for causes, that the alleged drawers of the bill were not sufficiently described, as they ought to have been described by their christian or names of baptism, and surnames, or by the initial or contraction of their christian or first names, in addition to their surnames; that the description is vague and uncertain: and that even if " M'Leod & Co." is a sufficient description, yet it is not alleged that the supposed drawers in fact drew the bill in that name, or by means of such description. Joinder in demurrer.

Declaration by indorsee against acceptor of a bill of exchange stated it to be drawn by " certain persons using the name, style, and firm of M. & Co.," and that " the said M. & Co." indorsed it. Semble, that this was not a sufficient description, as it did not shew that M. & Co. drew or indorsed the bill in that name.

Bovill, in support of the demurrer.—The description of the drawers of the bill in this declaration is not sufficient. The rule of the common law, is that the christian and surnames of all persons mentioned in the pleadings should be accurately set out; Stephen on Pleading, 329 (4th edit.), citing Com. Dig., Abatement (E. 20), (F. 19); *Buckley* v. *Thomas* (a), and *Rowe* v. *Roach* (b). The authority of this rule is recognized also in *Gamly* v. *Bechinor* (c). And the stat. 3 & 4 Will. 4, c. 42, s. 12, has no application to this

(a) Plowd. 128 a.   (b) 1 M. & Selw. 304.   (c) 2 Lev. 197.

case, because it applies only to parties who are described in written documents by the initial letter or contraction of the christian or first name, which is not the case here. In *Reg.* v. *West* (a), where goods the property of the Hull and Selby Railway Company were described in a coroner's inquisition as the property of "The Proprietors of the Hull and Selby Railway," it was held that the inquisition was therefore bad. [*Alderson*, B.—It is consistent with this declaration, that although the parties used the name of M'Leod & Co., they made the bill in their own proper names.] Then, with respect to the indorsement, it is not even said that the said persons using the name, style, and firm of M'Leod & Co. indorsed, but merely "the said M'Leod & Co." If the plaintiffs do not know the names, there should be an averment to that effect.

R. V. Richards, contrà.—The declaration is sufficient. It is in the form constantly used in such a case. In the form given by the rule of Trinity Term, 1 Will. 4, all that is stated is, that ".one E. F. made his bill of exchange in writing," &c.; it is not said that he made it *in the name of* E. F. [Lord *Abinger*, C. B.—The difficulty is this, that it is possible the persons using the name of M'Leod & Co. may have drawn bills and used a different name or names; so that the defendants may plead to it, supposing it to be drawn in the name of M'Leod & Co., whereas you may prove a bill drawn in another name.] It is certain to a common intent, and must mean that the drawers used that name in the instrument declared on. In *Bass* v. *Clive* (b), the declaration was on a bill drawn "by certain persons trading under the name, style, and firm of E. N. & Co.," payable to their own order; and it was held, as against the acceptor, who had accepted the bill so drawn, that it was no variance if it were proved that the firm consisted of one

(a) 1 G. & D. 481.   (b) 4 M. & Selw. 13.

person only. [*Alderson*, B.—Would it be sufficient to say that "a certain person made his bill of exchange," &c.?] It is submitted that it would.

THE COURT(a) intimated their opinion that the allegation was not sufficient, and gave *Richards* leave to amend on payment of costs; otherwise

Exch. of Pleas,
1842.

BALL
v.
GORDON.

Judgment for the defendants(b).

(a) Lord *Abinger*, C. B., *Alderson*, B., and *Gurney*, B.
(b) See the next case.

TIGAR and Another *v.* GORDON and Others (c).

ASSUMPSIT by indorsees against acceptors of a bill of exchange. The declaration stated, "that whereas certain persons, by and under the name, style, and firm of James Gale & Son, on the 18th day of October, 1841, made their bill of exchange in writing, and directed the same to the defendants, and thereby required them to pay to the order of the said persons so using the said name, style, and firm of James Gale & Son, 66*l.* 7*s.* 11*d.*, for value received, four months after the date thereof, which period had elapsed before the commencement of this suit; and the defendants then accepted the said bill, and the said persons, by and under the said name, style, and firm of James Gale & Son, then indorsed the said bill to the plaintiffs," &c.

Special demurrer, assigning for causes, that the drawers and indorsers of the bill are not sufficiently or properly designated or described. Joinder in demurrer.

Bovill, in support of the demurrer, relied on *Ball* v. *Gordon* (d), and, in addition to the authorities there cited, referred to *Rex* v. *Harrison* (e). The only distinction between the case of *Ball* v. *Gordon* and the present is, that here it is stated that certain persons, *by and under* the name, &c., drew

Declaration by indorsee against acceptor of a bill of exchange, stated it to be drawn by "certain persons, by and under the name, style, and firm of G. & Son," and that " the said persons, by and under the said name, style, and firm of G. & Son," indorsed it:—*Held*, on special demurrer, that this was a sufficient description of the drawers and indorsers.

(c) Decided at the sittings after Trinity Term, 1842 (June 22).
(d) Ante, 345.
(e) 8 T. R. 508.

the bill. But that is not enough to satisfy the rule of law, that the names of all persons mentioned in the pleadings should be correctly stated. It may be said that the acceptor is estopped to deny that the bill was well drawn in the name of James Gale & Co.; but at all events there is no such estoppel as to the indorsement: the act of acceptance is not even primâ facie evidence of the indorsement being correct. And even as to the drawing, it is not a conclusive admission, but only affords primâ facie evidence that the bill is properly drawn. It is but a rule of evidence, and does not apply to the statement on the pleadings.

R. V. Richards, contrà.—This is the usual and invariable form of declaration which has long been adopted in declaring on a bill or note made by a firm. The *drawing* is admitted by the acceptance; and the declaration states the bill to be indorsed by "the said persons" who are so admitted to have drawn it. If this declaration be not sufficient, the difficulties in the way of mercantile transactions will be insurmountable. Suppose the case of a foreign bill in parts, one of which comes over to this country and is accepted, and then another arrives covered with indorsements by foreign firms, how is the party suing to set them all out by christian and surname? Then it is said he must aver that he does not know them:—does that mean that he must shew he has no knowledge of them, or no means of knowledge? If the latter, must he send out a commission to India or China to ascertain the names, before he can declare upon the bill? It will be wholly impossible for the negotiation of bills of exchange to be carried on, if the holder is obliged to state all the names of all the persons composing the different firms that appear on the face of them. [*Parke,* B.—You may have an issue on that most complicated of all questions—partnership—raised upon every indorsement.] The declaration here is distinguishable from that in *Ball* v. *Gordon,* because it

states not only that Gale & Co., under that name, drew **Bach. of Pleas,**
the bill (which is admitted by the acceptance), but also **1842.**
that the same persons by the same name indorsed it. **TIGAR**
[*Parke,* B.—And that you are bound to prove; therefore **v.**
if there be such a rule as is contended for by the defend- **GORDON.**
ants, it is impossible for the plaintiff to succeed, unless
either he strikes out all such names, and so loses the security of them, or is able to prove the Christian and surname
of them all, though they may be foreign firms from the
most remote parts.] *Rex* v. *Harrison* and *Regina* v. *West*
were cases of coroner's inquisitions, which are not at all
applicable to the case of a bill of exchange.—He again
referred to *Bass* v. *Clive* (a).

Bovill, in reply.—It is true this form of declaration has
been ordinarily used, but that cannot repeal the rule of
law. In *Wright* v. *Welbie* (b), it was held that an averment, in a declaration on a policy of insurance, that certain persons named, and also "certain persons trading
under the firm of E., F., & Co.," were interested in the
property, was sufficient after verdict; but the Court ·
strongly intimated their opinion that it would have been
bad on special demurrer. This general form may not
have been before objected to, from an apprehension that
there would be relief given by amendment, and then that
the defendant might have stricter terms imposed on him
in the subsequent stages of the cause. All the alleged
inconvenience is avoided by stating the names to be unknown. [*Parke,* B.—And then there might be an issue
whether they were known or unknown. What matter the
names, if the bill were made by the firm?] The defendants rely upon the strict rule of pleading.

PARKE, B.—I think this demurrer ought to be overruled.
As to the case of *Ball* v. *Gordon,* it certainly appears that
in that case there was a strong intimation of the opinion

(a) 4 M. & Selw. 13.   (b) 1 Chit. Rep. 49.

of the Court that the declaration was insufficient, and an amendment in consequence; but it is sufficient to say that it is distinguishable upon the ground stated by Mr. *Richards :* here it does appear that the bill was drawn in the name of the firm. According to all the precedents, that is sufficient. That is the form in the precedent given by Mr. Justice *Bayley* (a); and from my own experience I can say that for a long series of years such has been the established practice. I should not be disposed to depart from that practice without strong reason; and there is none. at all here: on the contrary, the inconvenience of holding this form defective would be immense; it would be almost impossible to go on in the negotiation of foreign bills, if it were necessary that they should be traced with precision through so many names. It is said the inconvenience may be avoided by saying that the names are unknown to the plaintiff; but then there would be an issue on that question, whether they were known or unknown. The case of a declaration upon a policy of insurance is different in two respects: in the first place, the interest is never stated to be in *firms*, but in *individuals;* and in the next place, the parties in whom the interest is are in fact the plaintiffs, and therefore the declaration ought to state their names. The case of a bill of exchange is widely different, and the established form of declaration is such as has been adopted in the present case. It states that the bill was drawn by certain persons using the name, style, and firm of James Gale & Co.—that it was drawn in that name —and that it was indorsed by the same persons in that name. I think, therefore, that it is sufficient, and that our judgment should be for the plaintiff.

GURNEY, B., and ROLFE, B., concurred.

Judgment for the plaintiff.

(a) Bayley on Bills, (5th edit.) 375.

Exch. of Pleas,
1842.

Jan. 12.

GIBBS *v.* PIKE.

CASE.—The declaration stated, that, after the passing of a certain act of Parliament made and passed in the second year of the reign of her Majesty Queen Victoria, intituled " An Act for abolishing arrest on mesne process in civil actions, except in certain cases, and for extending the remedies of creditors against the property of debtors, and for amending the laws for the relief of insolvent debtors in England," and before the committing of the grievances, &c., a certain suit was and still is depending in the High Court of Chancery, before the Master of the Rolls, in which said suit Elizabeth Wells, and one Fanny Wells Freeman, Richard Freeman, Robert J. Freeman, and James W. Freeman, infants, by the said Elizabeth Wells, their next friend, were plaintiffs, and John Gibbs, and one Richard Freeman, and Fanny Freeman, were defendants : And whereas also, before and at the time of the committing of the grievances, the plaintiff was and still is seised in his demesne as of fee of and in divers lands, tenements, and hereditaments, with the appurtenances, situate, lying, and being in the county of Kent : And the plaintiff further saith, that after the making of the said act of Parliament, and before the committing of the grievances, &c., and while the said suit was so depending, by a certain order of the Right Hon. Henry Lord Langdale, in the said suit, bearing date &c., after reciting that counsel for the plaintiffs had that day moved the Court, that the defendant, John Gibbs, or the said defendants, John Gibbs and Richard Freeman, might be ordered, on or before the 26th day of June then next, to transfer into

Where, in a suit in equity, an order was made that one G. should pay into the name of the Accountant-General, in trust in the cause, a certain sum admitted by his answer to have been the amount of the sale of a trust fund; and the solicitor for the plaintiff in the suit registered it under 1 & 2 Vict. c. 110, s. 19, and G. was in consequence prevented from disposing of his lands :—*Held,* that the registering of the order was not of itself a wrongful act, and that no action could be maintained for it without proof of malice.

Semble, that such an order is within the equity of the stat. 1 & 2 Vict. c. 110, s. 19.

Where evidence is rejected by a judge at *Nisi Prius,* the counsel proposing it ought to make a formal tender of it to the judge, and request him to take a note of it, or he will not be allowed to raise before the Court any questions arising out of such evidence, if the judge's note does not shew the point to have been raised at the trial.

the name of the accountant-general of the said Court, in
trust in the said cause, the sum of 1637*l.* 8*s.* 6*d.*, £3 per
cent. Consolidated Bank Annuities, being the amount of
the fund admitted by the answer of the same defendants
in the said suit to have been invested in their names,
upon the trusts of the indenture or marriage-settlement
of the 8th day of December, 1819, in the pleadings mentioned, and to have been sold out by them on the 17th
day of January, 1829; or that the said defendant John
Gibbs, (meaning thereby the said plaintiff), and Richard
Freeman, might be ordered, on or before the 26th day of
June next, to pay into the name of the said accountant-
general, in trust in the said cause, the sum of 1404*l.* 2*s.*,
admitted by the answer of the said defendants, the said
John Gibbs and Richard Freeman, to have been the
amount of the proceeds of the sale of the said trust fund
of 1637*l.* 8*s.* 6*d.*, £3 per cent. Consolidated Bank Annuities, received by the said defendant, John Gibbs; and
that such sum of 1404*l.* 2*s.*, when so paid in, might be invested by the said accountant-general in £3 per cent.
Consolidated Bank Annuities, in trust in the said cause,
&c.: upon hearing the said defendant's, John Gibbs'
(meaning the said plaintiff) answer read, and what was
alleged by the counsel on both sides, the said Right Hon.
Henry Lord Langdale did order, that the said defendant
John Gibbs, (meaning thereby the said plaintiff), should,
within a month from that time, pay into the bank, with
the privity of the accountant-general of that Court, to the
credit of the said cause, the sum of 1404*l.* 2*s.*, admitted by
the answer of the said defendants, the said John Gibbs
and Richard Freeman, to have been the amount of the
proceeds of the sale of the trust-fund of 1637*l.* 8*s.* 6*d.*, £3
per cent. Consolidated Bank Annuities, received by the
said defendant, the said John Gibbs; and it was ordered,
that such sum of 1404*l.* 2*s.*, when so paid into the bank,
should be laid out in the purchase of bank £3 per cent.

annuities, in the name and with the privity of the said
accountant-general, in trust in the said cause; and he was
to declare the trust thereof accordingly, subject to the
further order of the said Court: and for the purposes
aforesaid, the said accountant-general was to draw on the
bank according to the form prescribed by the act of Parliament, and the general rules and orders of the said
Court in that case made and provided. And the said
John Gibbs in fact saith, that after the making of the said
order of the said Right Hon. Henry Lord Langdale, they
the said Charles Andrews Pike and Elizabeth Wells, well
knowing the premises, and well knowing, as the fact was
and is, that the said order was not a decree or order of a
court of equity, whereby any sum of money, or any costs,
charges, or expenses, were payable to any person within
the said act of Parliament, or the intent or meaning thereof, but contriving and intending to oppress, harass, and
aggrieve the said John Gibbs, and to prevent him from
disposing of any part of the said lands, tenements, and
hereditaments, with the appurtenances, of him the said
John Gibbs, and to deprive him thereby of the means of
paying the said sum of 1404*l*. 2*s*., in the said order specified, and satisfying the said order, and to injure and prejudice him in his credit and circumstances, to wit, on, &c.,
wrongfully, maliciously, oppressively, and unlawfully, and
under colour and pretence of the said last-mentioned act
of Parliament, left and caused and procured to be left
with the senior Master of the Court of Common Pleas, at
Westminster, a certain memorandum or minute in writing, containing the name and the usual or last-known
place of abode, and the title, trade, or profession of the
said John Gibbs (the said plaintiff), whose estate was intended to be affected thereby, and the Court, and the title
of the cause in which such order was obtained and made,
and the date of such order, and the amount of the monies
thereby ordered to be paid; and which same particulars

contained in the said memorandum or minute, so left and caused and procured to be left by the said Charles Andrews Pike and Elizabeth Wells, as aforesaid, were, by such leaving as aforesaid, and by and through the wrongful, malicious, and unlawful procurement of the said Charles Andrews Pike and Elizabeth Wells, forthwith entered in a book by the said senior Master of the Court of Common Pleas, according to the provisions of the said act of Parliament, as and for a memorandum or minute in writing of a decree or order of a Court of Equity, whereby a sum of money, or certain costs, charges, and expenses, were payable to a person within the said act, whereby, after such entry by the said senior Master of the Court of Common Pleas as aforesaid had been made as aforesaid, it then and there appeared, from and on the face of such entry in the said book as aforesaid, that the said order so made by the Right Hon. Henry Lord Langdale, so being the said Master of the Rolls as aforesaid, was an order within the intent and meaning of the said act of Parliament; that is to say, an order of a Court of Equity, whereby the said sum of 1404l. 2s. was payable to the said Elizabeth Wells, &c., and had the effect of a judgment in a superior court of common law, affecting the said lands, tenements, and hereditaments of the said John Gibbs; and that the said Elizabeth Wells, and that the said Fanny Wells Freeman, Richard Freeman, Robert John Freeman, and James William Freeman, were thereby to be deemed judgment creditors within the meaning of the said act; by means of which said several premises, and by reason of the said order, from such entry so made as aforesaid, appearing and purporting to have the effect of a judgment against the said John Gibbs, and so affecting the said lands, tenements, and hereditaments of the said John Gibbs as aforesaid, by such wrongful, malicious, and unlawful procurement of the said Charles Andrews Pike and the said Elizabeth Wells as aforesaid, he the said John Gibbs has

been hindered and prevented from selling and disposing
of certain lands, tenements, and hereditaments of him the
said John Gibbs, which he otherwise might and would
have sold and disposed of for divers large prices and sums
of money, for the purpose of paying the said sum of
1404*l.* 2*s.* in the said order mentioned.

The defendant pleaded not guilty.

At the trial before Lord *Abinger*, C. B., at the London
Sittings after last Trinity Term, it appeared that the plaintiff, who was the trustee of a settlement executed in 1828,
on the marriage of a person of the name of Freeman with
the mother of the defendant, E. Wells, had, with the con-
nivance of those parties, who were only the *cestui que*
trusts for life, sold out the trust fund, consisting of a sum
of £1404 2s., he paying them a higher rate of interest,
and giving his bond for the security of the principal.
After the death of Freeman, the defendant E. Wells, who
had a reversionary interest in the fund, with the assistance
of the defendant Pike, who acted as her attorney, filed a
bill in Chancery against Gibbs to compel a re-investment
of the trust-money; and an order for that purpose, bearing the date and in the terms mentioned in the declaration, was made by the Master of the Rolls. In order to
raise money to comply with this order, Gibbs, in the
month of October, 1840, put up for sale certain freehold
land of which he was seised, and purchasers offered themselves for different lots; but they having discovered that
the above order had been previously registered under 1 & 2
Vict. c. 110, s. 19, as an order directing a sum of money
to be paid by Gibbs, and as such having the force of a
judgment at common law, declined to complete the purchases. An application was subsequently made to the
Master of the Rolls to get rid of the registered order, who
refused to interfere, saying that he had no jurisdiction
over the officers of the Court of Common Pleas. On this
evidence, the Lord Chief Baron told the jury, that without

giving an opinion as to whether the above order was an order for the payment of money within the meaning of 1 & 2 Vict. c. 110, s. 19, and as such entitled to be registered, it appeared to him, that, in registering it, the defendant Pike had done no more than his duty; that there did not appear any evidence of his having been actuated by a malicious motive in so doing, or that any injury had resulted to the plaintiff from it; but that, if the jury could see either, they would find a verdict for the plaintiff. The jury having found for the defendants,

Platt obtained a rule nisi for a new trial, on the grounds, first, that the learned Judge had misdirected the jury in leaving the question of malice or no malice for their consideration, as the law always inferred malice on proof of a wrongful act; and secondly, that he had improperly rejected certain evidence which tended to establish malice, namely, the subsequent sequestration of the plaintiff's property, and suing out a writ of rebellion, by force of which the plaintiff had been taken and committed to the Fleet under circumstances of aggravation. When, however, the Lord Chief Baron's note was read, it was silent as to the fact of this evidence having been tendered.—Against this rule

Hayes shewed cause.—The defendant, in registering this order, did nothing more than his duty as solicitor in the suit. If there were any doubt whether the order was an order within the 1 & 2 Vict. c. 110, he was bound to register it; and if he had not done so, he might have been liable for negligence. There is nothing to shew that he was actuated by malice, and malice cannot be inferred. The plaintiff will probably rely on what is laid down by Lord C. B. *Comyn* (a), that "where a man sustains a temporal loss

(a) Com. Dig., Action on the Case, (A).

or damage by the wrong of another, he may have an action on the case;" that is admitted, but the act here is not wrongful in itself, and the same principle applies as that which governs the cases of actions for criminal prosecutions. The declaration here avers not only malice, but a scienter, which was not proved. In *Scheibel* v. *Fairbain* (*a*), the plaintiff sued out a capias ad respondendum against the defendant, and before the latter was arrested, he paid the debt; but it was held that no action would lie against the plaintiff for neglecting to countermand the writ, unless malice was averred and proved. So, in *Page* v. *Wiple* (*b*) it was held, that no action will lie for not preventing, but permitting and suffering the plaintiff to be arrested after payment of debt and costs owing to the defendant, upon a writ sued out before such payment: Lord *Ellenborough*, C. J., saying that he thought the case not distinguishable from *Scheibel* v. *Fairbain*. In the recent case of *Saxon* v. *Castle* (*c*), the plaintiff gave the defendant a warrant of attorney to enter up judgment, if certain costs should be unpaid within four days after the Master should have taxed the same; the defendant procured a taxation ex parte, and by an incorrect representation to the Master, obtained from him an allocatur for more costs than he was entitled to; by order of a judge, on summons, a new taxation was directed, pending which the defendant arrested the plaintiff. The declaration alleged only that the defendant had " wrongfully and injuriously" delivered the writ to the sheriff, and the Court being of opinion that it was necessary that malice should be averred, arrested the judgment. So, in *Gibson* v. *Chaters* (*d*), it was held that, in an action for maliciously holding to bail, it was not sufficient to prove that the writ was sued out after payment of the debt, if the circumstances afford no inference of malice; but in such case evidence of

Exch. of Pleas,
1842.

GIBBS
v.
PIKE.

(*a*) 1 Bos. & P. 388.
(*b*) 3 East, 314.

(*c*) 6 Adol. & Ell. 652.
(*d*) 2 Bos. & P. 129.

actual malice must be given. In *Mitchell* v. *Jenkins* (a), it was held, that in an action for a malicious arrest, malice is a question of fact for the jury, who are at liberty, but not *bound*, to infer it from the want of probable cause; and that the jury ought to be directed to find whether there was malice or not. [*Alderson*, B.—The rule on this subject is correctly laid down in the note to *Hodgson* v. *Scarlett* (b), which I can vouch was furnished by the late Mr. Justice *Holroyd*.] In *Porter* v. *Weston* (c), the defendant having told a bail that his principal was likely to abscond, procured from him directions to take his affidavit of justification off the file. The directions having been given too late, the defendant obtained by means of them an order of a judge for the render of the principal; and it was held that an action did not lie against him for this proceeding at the suit of the principal, without alleging and proving express malice. All the authorities shew that an averment of a want of probable cause is necessary, and that the action cannot be maintained without proving it.

Platt, in support of the rule.—It is not contended on the other side, that the order was one which fell within the act of Parliament, and which the defendant had a right to register; and that being so, the act itself was wrongful, and it was not necessary that actual malice should be proved. Where a man sustains an injury and a loss by the act of another, an action on the case may be maintained. Com. Dig., Action on the Case, (A). In the cases cited, it does not appear that the plaintiff sustained any injury by the mere act of indictment or arrest; but here both a damnum and an injuria are alleged in the declaration. Every man must be taken to know the law, and then the scienter must be taken to be proved.

(a) 5 B. & Adol. 588.   (b) 1 B. & Ald. 232.
(c) 5 Bing. N. C. 715 ; 8 Scott, 25.

[*Alderson* B.—The scienter means actual knowledge.] The defendant committed an injuria by registering the plaintiff's property when he had no right to do it. [*Alderson*, B.—What is the injuria? The registering of an order that is not binding can do no harm: the defendant has merely done a nugatory act.] By so doing, he has prevented the plaintiff from realizing the amount which he might have obtained for his property. In *Beaurain* v. *Scott* (a), it was held that an action on the case may be maintained against a judge of the Ecclesiastical Court, who excommunicates a party for refusing to obey an order which the Court has not authority to make, or when the party has not been served with a citation or monition, nor had due notice of the order. But further, if malice was requisite, there was evidence of malice tendered, which ought to have been left to the jury.

Lord ABINGER, C. B.—No doubt the plaintiff in this case has suffered great prejudice; but he has done so in common with all others who are unfortunately placed in the same predicament with himself; and I cannot see that, in registering this order, the defendant Pike did more than it was proper for him to do as an attorney acting for the benefit of his client in a suit in equity. If he were guilty of a mistake in unnecessarily registering this order, I do not see how it could operate to the injury of the plaintiff, for the register refers to the order, which would speak for itself, and which any one is at liberty to inspect; and therefore, even assuming the argument to be well founded, that this was an order not proper to be registered, no one could make a mistake, or be misled by that circumstance, since, unless supported by the order, the registry is a nullity as to any effect it might have on the property of any person, and therefore cannot work any in-

(a) 3 Camp. 387.

jury. On the other hand, if it is a matter of doubt whether or not a particular order of this kind ought to effect the benefit conferred by the late act, of binding the estate of the party, this would be a proper case to register it; for here we have a trustee who admits, by his answer in Chancery, that the trust-funds were remaining in his hands, and the attorney had good reason to think that his real estate would be subject to the order of the Court: but even supposing him to be wrong in this view, still, if there was a reasonable doubt on the subject, there was a probable cause for his registering the order. So that, take it either way, the conduct of the defendant protects him from the charge of having acted maliciously and wrongfully, and with intent to injure the plaintiff. If the order and the registry are a nullity, there is no harm done; if they are not so, they would be good and valid, and so no wrong be done. But then it is said, that the Master of the Rolls doubted, and I confess I entertain doubts myself, whether this is an order within the words of the 1 & 2 Vict. c. 110, ss. 18, 19; and on the first .blush of the matter, I was inclined to say it was not; but I think it comes within the equity of the statute, and was one which might fairly be registered, with the view of raising the question. That appears to dispose altogether of the case. But Mr. *Platt* says, that he tendered evidence of malice; still, unless it would go far enough to shew that the defendant knew he was doing wrong, it could not make out the plaintiff's case. But I cannot agree to the principle of taking the statements of counsel on such a point as that. What record can you properly appeal to for what took place at the trial, except the judge's notes? It is always in the power of counsel, who is dissatisfied at the rejection of a piece of evidence, to tender a bill of exceptions; or he may first ask the judge to make a note of the tender, and if the request is denied, then tender his bill of exceptions. But in the course of a trial, many points of evidence are suggested, *Exch. of Pleas*, on which the judge gives a hasty opinion; and if counsel 1842. do not press the point, or ask the judge to make a note of it, what is the Court in banc to do, when the question of GIBBS the admissibility of the evidence is brought before them? *v.* PIKE. If they depart from the judge's note as the record of what took place at the trial, what a wide field of discussion would be opened! They would have to take, in the first instance, whatever the objecting counsel might suggest, whose representation of the facts would, in all probability, be denied by the counsel on the other side, and the Court would be plunged into a sea of difficulty. Is it not better to take the judge's note as authority? and when a particular fact is not found there, counsel ought not afterwards to raise a question upon it. I should never feel offended at a bill of exceptions being tendered; and in the present case, I should have taken a note of the point, if pressed to do so; but as I have no note of its being tendered, I cannot admit its rejection as the ground for a new trial.

ALDERSON, B.—I quite agree with my Lord Chief Baron on the main point in this case, and also as to the necessity of counsel distinctly making a formal tender to the Judge at Nisi Prius of evidence which he has declared inadmissible. Such a course puts the fact beyond all dispute at a subsequent period, and saves all the difficulties which might arise from a contest between the opposite counsel as to what took place at the trial. Upon the general question, however, it appears to me that this rule ought to be discharged. In order to sustain this action, the plaintiff is bound to shew an injury done to him; and the question is, whether the mere act of registering this order in the Common Pleas office does per se constitute one. It is an order by which the Court of Chancery orders the plaintiff to pay a sum of 1404*l.* 2*s.* into Court to the credit of a cause; and the

question is, is that an order of the Lord Chancellor or
Master of the Rolls, whereby a sum of money is made
payable to any person, within the meaning of 1 & 2 Vict.
c. 110, s. 18? Now, whether it be such an order or not,
is a proposition on which I do not mean at present to give
any definite opinion; but it is certainly within the equitable meaning of the clause, because it is intended to take
effect against the property of the party, and not to be defeated because he chooses to remain in prison and refuses
to pay; in such case it was the general object of the act
to render his property liable. Now, although that section
confers on an order of this nature the effect of a judgment
at common law, it still renders it necessary to be registered,
in order to bind the land of the party against whom it is
obtained. Here, then, that party is in possession of the
land, and the party by whom the order was obtained regis-
ters it. If that order will bind the land, he has only done
what he ought to do; and if it will not, it becomes of
course inoperative and harmless. How then is his registering the order an injurious or wrongful act to any one?
It is clear it is not. It causes no damage—it is no injurious act; and therefore, in order to enable the plaintiff to
maintain this action, it is incumbent on him to shew that
this act, in its nature not wrongful, has become so in consequence of its having been done through a bad motive.
For this purpose, and in order to render the act wrongful
and injurious, he is bound to add to the fact of registering
the order the absence of reasonable and probable cause,
and a malicious motive for doing so. If those motives are
relied on and averred, they should be proved. I do not
think we ought to take into our consideration the evidence
referred to by Mr. *Platt;* but suppose it were admitted,
how would it prove the want of reasonable and probable
cause, or that this was not a proper order to be registered?
On the contrary, the jury, had the point been left to them,
would probably have found that the defendant Pike, when

he did the act, did so fairly, under the belief that he was only doing what was right.

GURNEY, B., concurred.

Rule discharged.

LLOYD and Another *v.* BLACKBURN.

COVENANT on an indenture of apprenticeship against the father of the apprentice, assigning breaches by the apprentice.

The defendant, being under terms of pleading issuably, after setting out the indenture on oyer, pleaded, that at the time of making the said indenture, the plaintiffs carried on the business of engineers, as copartners; that the apprenticeship and covenant were made with them as such copartners, and not otherwise; and that before any breach of duty by the defendant, the plaintiff dissolved partnership.

Peacock having obtained a rule, calling upon the defendant to shew cause why this plea should not be set aside, on the ground of its not being an issuable plea—

Byles now shewed cause.—The plea is an issuable one. The apprentice has covenanted to serve the two partners, and when the partnership is dissolved, there necessarily is an end of the apprenticeship, as the apprentice cannot serve them both. There is an implied condition that the partnership shall continue. If it were not so, the greatest inconvenience might result. Suppose, after the dissolution, one of the partners were to reside in Yorkshire, and the other in London, which of them is the apprentice to serve and be with? In case a master dies, there is clearly

Jan. 12.

Where, to an action of covenant on an indenture of apprenticeship against the father, for breaches by the apprentice, the defendant, being under terms of pleading issuably, pleaded that the plaintiffs carried on the business of engineers as copartners, that the covenants were made with them as such copartners; and that before any breach of duty, they dissolved partnership:— *Held*, that the plea was an issuable one, and ought not to be set aside.

a dissolution of the contract; there is, however, no such condition expressed; but there is an implied condition. This at least shews that the plea is an issuable one, and it ought not, therefore, to be set aside.

Peacock, contrà.—There is a covenant in the deed to teach the apprentice the trade and business; but there is no allegation in the plea, that anything has occurred to put it out of the plaintiff's power to teach the apprentice. It simply amounts to this, that there has been a dissolution. The deed contains no stipulation limiting the apprenticeship to the duration of the partnership, and the dissolution cannot put an end to the contract of apprenticeship.

Lord ABINGER, C. B.—I am of opinion that this plea ought not to be set aside as not being an issuable one, as it raises a fit question for discussion. I do not express any opinion upon the question itself. It may be possible that where, on a dissolution of partnership, one partner agrees to resign the apprentice to the other, the apprenticeship may still subsist. On that, however, I give no opinion. It is sufficient to say the plea ought not to be set aside.

ALDERSON, B., and GURNEY, B., concurred.

Rule discharged.

Exch. of Pleas,
1842.

Jan. 15.

NICHOLSON and Others *v.* HOOD.

ASSUMPSIT.—The declaration stated, that on the 6th
April, 1838, in consideration that the plaintiffs, at the request of the defendant, would from time to time supply
goods to one Charles Nash on credit, the defendant promised and guaranteed to the plaintiffs the payment of the
price of any goods the plaintiffs should at any time supply
to the said C. Nash, to the extent of £30; and the plaintiffs aver, that they, confiding in the said promise of the
defendant, did afterwards, to wit, on the day and year
aforesaid, and on divers other days and times, &c., supply
the said C. Nash with, and sell and deliver to him, goods, the
prices whereof amounted to a large sum, to wit, 51*l.* 15*s.*,
on certain credit then agreed on between the plaintiffs and
the said C. Nash; and although the said credit, and the
time for the payment of the said prices of the said goods,
had elapsed before the commencement of this suit, and
although the said C. Nash hath paid and satisfied the
plaintiffs the sum of £25, parcel of the said sum of 51*l.* 15*s.*,
yet the said C. Nash hath not (although he was afterwards,
to wit, on the 7th December, 1840, requested by the plaintiffs so to do) as yet paid to them the residue of the said
sum of 51*l.* 15*s.*, such residue amounting to 26*l.* 15*s.*, or
any part thereof, &c., but hath hitherto neglected and
refused so to do, of which the defendant had notice, &c.

Pleas: first, non assumpsit; secondly, that the plaintiff
did not supply the said C. Nash with, or sell and deliver
to him, the said goods; thirdly, that the goods in the declaration mentioned to have been supplied to the said C.
Nash, and sold and delivered to him by the plaintiffs as
therein mentioned, were commodities for the removal of
which a permit was, at the time of the removal thereof as
hereafter mentioned, by law required; and which said
commodities were before then, to wit, on the days and

*Where G.,
the licensed
keeper of a
public house,
sold the lease
of it to N., who
entered into the
occupation of it,
the license still
remaining in
the name of G.;
and a quantity
of spirits, which
required a per-
mit for its re-
moval under 2
Will. 4, c. 16,
was supplied by
a distiller on the
order of N., and
delivered on
the premises in
question:—
Held, that a
permit made
out in the name
of G. was a
valid permit
under the
statute.*

times in the said declaration in that behalf mentioned, supplied, and sold and delivered by the plaintiffs to the said C. Nash, and removed from and out of certain stock of the plaintiffs, and by them delivered to the said C. Nash, without a permit accompanying them, or any or either of them, or any part thereof, contrary to the form of the statute in such case made and provided, &c. Verification.

Replication to the last plea, that a permit, at the time of the removal of the said goods, did accompany them according to the statute, &c.; on which issue was joined.

At the trial before Lord *Abinger*, C. B., at the Middlesex Sittings after last Trinity Term, it appeared that a person of the name of Gilmore, being in the occupation of a public-house, sold the lease of it to one Charles Nash, for whom a guarantee had been given, and who entered into the occupation of the premises, but the license was continued in the name of Gilmore, until a new one could be procured in the name of Nash. The goods in question, being a quantity of spirits which required a permit for their removal, were supplied to Nash at this public-house, but the permit was made out in the name of Gilmore. One of the officers of excise, on being examined, said that the permit was in the proper form, and if it had been made out to Nash instead of Gilmore, he should have seized the goods. On this evidence, the defendant's counsel objected that the permit was not in accordance with the provisions of the act 2 Will. 4, c. 16, for consolidating and amending the laws regulating the granting and issuing of permits (*a*); but the learned Judge overruled the objec-

---

(*a*) The following are the sections of the stat. 2 Will. 4, c. 16, which were referred to in the argument:—

Sect. 5 enacts, " That no permit shall be granted by any officer of excise, until a request note, or requisition in writing, shall have been delivered by or in behalf of the person requiring such permit; and every permit which shall be granted without a request note or

tion, and left the case to the jury, who found for the plain-

tiffs for the amount claimed; leave having been reserved

requisition being delivered in manner required by this act, shall be actually void, and shall not protect any goods, wares, or merchandize mentioned in such permit."

The 6th sect. enacts, " That every request note for any permit shall contain the date thereof, and the name of the place from which and the place to which the commodities therein mentioned are to be carried, and the mode of conveyance by which such commodities are to be removed, and shall likewise contain the real name and surname, and place of abode, of the person or persons sending such commodities, and of the person to whom they are to be sent, and, in case of a company or copartnership, the name of the firm, company, or copartnership, together with such other particulars as the commissioners of excise shall from time to time direct or appoint, or as shall be required by any act or acts relating to the commodities in respect of which the permit shall be required; and every such request note shall be signed by the person requiring the permit, or by his or her known clerk or servant; and no permit shall be granted on any request note which shall not be so signed, and contain the several particulars aforesaid."

The 7th sect. enacts, " That every permit to be granted for the removal of any commodities, shall be made out in conformity with the request note; and every such permit shall be in such form, and shall

be marked, stamped, and printed with such stamps, marks, figures, and devices, and shall contain such particulars, as the commissioners of excise shall direct."

The 8th sect. enacts, " That every officer of excise, empowered to grant permits, shall express and limit in every permit granted by him, as well the time during which such permit shall be in force for removing the commodities for which the permit shall be obtained from and out of the stock of the person taking out such permit, as also the time within which the same commodities shall be delivered and actually received into the stock of the person or persons to whom the same shall be so permitted to be sent; and every permit which shall not be actually used, as directed by this act, within the time expressed and limited in such permit, shall, within the said time, be returned and redelivered by the person who shall have obtained the same to the proper officer of excise; and if any permit shall not be so returned as aforesaid, and, upon taking an account by any officer or officers of excise, of the stock remaining in the hands or custody of the person or persons from or out of whose stock the commodities mentioned in such permit were thereby authorized to be removed, there shall not appear a sufficient decrease to answer the removal of the commodities mentioned in such permit, then the person or persons from or out of whose stock the commodities

to the defendant to move to enter a verdict. A rule was obtained accordingly in Michaelmas Term, against which

mentioned in such permit were thereby authorized to be removed, shall forfeit and lose the like quantity of commodities so permitted to be removed and not removed according to such permission, and the same may be seized by any officer of excise ; and in case any commodities specified in any permit shall be removed from the stock of the person taking out such permit, and the same shall not, within the time expressed and limited in such permit, be actually delivered and received into the stock of the person or persons to whom the same are mentioned in such permit to be sent, then and in every such case, all such commodities so removed as aforesaid shall be deemed to be goods removed or removing without permit, and shall be forfeited and seized accordingly."

By sect. 11, all goods removed without a permit are to be forfeited, and the person removing them is to forfeit £200.

By sect. 12 it is enacted, " That in any action or suit at law or in equity on any bond, bill, note, or other security, contract, agreement, promise, or undertaking, where the whole or any part of the consideration thereof shall be for the value or price of any commodities, for the removal of which a permit is or shall be required, and for and with which a proper permit shall not have been given, the defendant in such action or suit may plead and give in evidence that such commodities were delivered without a

permit accompanying them ; and if the jury shall find that such goods were delivered without a true and lawful permit having been obtained for the removal thereof, they shall find a verdict for the defendant ; and if such commodities shall have been sold for ready money, or if the person selling the same shall otherwise have been paid or satisfied for the value or price thereof, it shall be lawful for the person who shall have paid or satisfied such value or price, within twelve calendar months after payment or satisfaction made, to recover back from the seller of such commodities the amount of the value or price of such commodities, to be sued for and recovered by action of debt, or on the case in any of his Majesty's courts of record."

And by sect. 19, " Whenever, on the trial of any information, suit, action, or other proceeding at law, it may be necessary to prove the issuing of any permit, or the contents thereof, the counterpart of such permit, together with the request note, may in all cases be admitted as evidence and proof that such permit was granted and issued, and of the contents thereof, according to the purport of such counterpart and request note, without producing or requiring the production of the original permit ; and it shall not be necessary to prove any order of the commissioners of excise, appointing or directing the form of any such permit, or of any counterpart thereof respectively."

Otter and *Hugh Hill* now shewed cause. The permit

granted for the removal of these goods was sufficient in point of law. It is to be presumed that the provisions of the act have been complied with, rather than the contrary ; and therefore the onus of shewing the insufficiency of the permit lay upon the defendant. Now it is not pretended that the permit is at variance with the request note, or that the commodities are improperly described ; but the objection is, that that part of the 6th section has not been complied with, which requires "that every request note shall contain the real name and surname and place of abode of the person sending such commodities, and of the person to whom they are to be sent :" that the real name of the party to whom these goods were to be sent was incorrectly given, inasmuch as Nash, and not Gilmore, was the real purchaser of the goods. But the evidence of the excise officer shewed that the permit was correct in point of form, and that if it had been in the name of Nash, he should have seized the goods. The 6th section is merely a direction to the officers of excise as to what they shall put into the permit; and it does not say that the permit shall be void if those provisions are not complied with. It cannot be that a person selling spirits is bound to find out the real name of the person to whom the goods are to be sent. In *Rex* v. *The Commissioners of Excise* (a), *Ashhurst*, J., said that these statutes ought to receive a liberal construction. The 7th section, as to the form of the permit, is altogether directory; and it does not say that an informal permit shall be void, or inflict a penalty for it, in which last case it might be constructively void: *Bartlett* v. *Vinor* (b). There is no form of a permit given in this statute, nor does it require that it shall contain all that is stated in the request note. It may be assumed that the request note stated what it ought to do.

(a) 2 T. R. 381.   (b) Carthew, 251.

C C 2

This is a case of great importance, for if this permit be held to be insufficient, every man who sells any quantity of spirits will be bound to find out the real name of the purchasers before he sends them out.

Petersdorff, contrà.—The words of the 8th section clearly shew that this permit is invalid; for they provide " that every officer of excise empowered to grant permits, shall express and limit in every permit granted by him, as well the time during which such permit shall be in force for removing the commodities for which the permit shall be obtained, *from or out of the stock of the person taking out such permit*, as also the time within which *the same commodities shall be delivered and actually received into the stock of the person to whom the same shall be permitted to be sent, &c.*" That shews that the permit is to be made out, not in the name of the person to whom they are nominally sent, but in the name of the person of whose stock they are to form a part. And adverting to the whole tenor of the act, the legislature shews a clear intention that no person's name shall be inserted except the name of the person to whom the goods are really sent, and of whose stock they are to form part. If the question were left to the jury to say to whom were these goods sent, they could never be said to have been sent to Gilmore, who was a mere stranger, having no interest whatever in them. If this permit were to be held sufficient, it would open a wide door to frauds upon the revenue, and defeat the intention of the legislature, which was to prevent the frauds resulting from permits being taken out in the name of fictitious or nominal parties.

Lord ABINGER, C. B.—This is a case in which I have felt considerable doubt, but upon the whole we think the rule ought to be discharged. The only question is, whether the regulations required by the commissioners of excise, relative to the matters to be inserted in every permit, have been duly complied with. The commissioners see the person to whom the goods are sold, and, as they have no power to send them except to the premises of that party, we must presume they had directions to send them to Gilmore, and make out the permit in his name. That they accordingly do; and we have it in evidence, that if this permit had been made out in any other way, the commissioners would have deemed it an illegal one. There is no evidence to shew that this permit was contradictory to the request note; nor is there any fraud on the revenue in this mode of proceeding, inasmuch as the whole is under the control and supervision of the commissioners of excise, to whose discretion it was manifestly the intention of the legislature to commit it.

ALDERSON, B.—There is this difficulty pressing on the defendant in this case, that the onus lies upon him to shew that this permit is bad. The 7th section of the statute requires every permit to be made out in such form as the commissioners of excise shall direct; and the 19th provides, that a counterpart of such permit shall be evidence, without requiring the production of the original. Now, we must take it for granted that the evidence of the officer of excise, in this case, is equivalent to the production of the counterpart, otherwise there would be no evidence of the contents of this permit at all; and if we take his evidence on the subject, it is to the effect that he considered the permit a regular one. Now, there are no directions given in the statute as to the mere form of the permit; and the section I have already referred to says, that the counterpart is to be admissible in evidence in all cases where it shall be necessary to prove the issuing of any permit, or the contents thereof; thus, as it should seem, rendering the counterpart or evidence of the excise officer, evidence not only of the fact of such permit having been issued, but also of its contents. In short, the effect

Exch. of Pleas, 1842.

NICHOLSON v. HOOD.

of the 19th sect. is to substitute parol evidence for that which would otherwise be the strict legal evidence, namely, the permit itself; and, if this parol evidence is receivable, does it not go to the length of shewing that a legal permit was issued in compliance with the requisition of the 7th section?

GURNEY, B.—These goods are forwarded to the premises of Gilmore, accompanied by a permit in his name. What possible objection can there be to Nash going to the excise officer to request liquors to be sent to Gilmore, with a permit accordingly?

Rule discharged.

———•———

DOE d. HUGHES v. JONES.

Jan. 20.

Where the sheriff sells a term taken in execution under a *fi. fa.*, to the execution creditor, but executes no assignment in writing of the term, the estate remains in the debtor, and the execution creditor has no defence to an ejectment at his suit.

AT the trial of this ejectment, before *Wightman,* J., at the last assizes at Lancaster, it appeared that one Wright, the owner of the premises in question, had in the year 1827 leased them to the lessor of the plaintiff for fourteen years, at a rent payable half-yearly, and that the plaintiff had occupied and paid rent up to the year 1839, when a fieri facias was put in at the suit of the defendant, under which the lessor of the plaintiff's goods, and the lease of the premises, were taken in execution, and sold by the sheriff. The defendant became the purchaser of the lease, which was accordingly handed over to him, and he entered and paid rent to the owner; but no assignment in writing of the lease had been made by the sheriff to the defendant. Under these circumstances, the learned Judge was of opinion that there was no defence at law to this ejectment, and under his direction a verdict passed for the plaintiff.

Dundas, in Michaelmas Term last, obtained a rule to shew cause why there should not be a new trial, on the ground of misdirection.

W. H. Watson (*Cresswell* was with him) shewed cause.— This is a case clearly within the Statute of Frauds, and the interest remains in the lessor of the plaintiff. The 3rd section of that statute enacts, " that no leases, estates, or interests, either of freehold or terms of years, or any uncertain interest, not being copyhold or customary interest, of, in, to, or out of any messuages, manors, lands, tenements, or hereditaments, shall at any time be assigned, granted, or surrendered, unless it be by deed or note in writing, signed by the party so assigning, granting, or surrendering the same, or their agents thereunto lawfully authorized by writing, or by act and operation of law." Now here there is no assignment in writing, and the question is, was there one by act and operation of law? Clearly not; for the sheriff had no interest in the lease; he had merely a power to dispose of it, which he could only execute by an instrument in writing. The effect of a seizure under a fieri facias is to give the sheriff only a special property in the goods; the general property of the owner is not divested: *Morland* v. *Pellatt* (a). In the case of a leasehold interest, the sheriff has no right whatever to enter into possession of the premises, but has only a power to sell and assign the lease. There are a variety of cases as to the manner in which the sheriff should execute the writ. One of them is *Palmer's case* (b). In *Rex* v. *Deane* (c), it was held that if a sheriff, on a fieri facias, sell a lease or term of a house, he cannot and must not put the person out of possession, and the vendee in; but the vendee must bring his ejectment. That is a strong authority, because it

(a) 8 B. & C. 722 ; 2 Man. & R. 411.   (b) 4 Co. 74 ; Cro. Eliz. 584.
(c) 2 Show. 85.

shews that when he has assigned the lease, he merely confers the title, not the possession. It has never been said
that the sheriff, by selling the lease, interfered with the
possession. There are some dicta which would seem to the
contrary in *Taylor* v. *Cole* (a), but the point has never yet
been decided. Under a fi. fa. the sheriff merely takes the
parchment containing the lease, with a power to dispose of
it. The sheriff has done nothing here but made a mere
seizure of the lease. If the Court were to hold that the
seizure of the lease amounted to an assignment by operation of law, the sheriff would become liable to the covenants. It has been held that a provisional assignee is not
an assignee of such a nature as so to become liable. The
lessor of the plaintiff has still the legal interest in him, and
is therefore entitled to recover. The sheriff has a collateral power; but it is only a power which he may still
exercise, and assign the lease back to the plaintiff.

Dundas and *Crompton*, in support of the rule. There was
in this case an assignment by act and operation of law. This
is the very case to which the Statute of Frauds has reference.
Before the statute, chattels real as well as personal passed
by parol. In cases of bankruptcy the property passes by
operation of law, and this is in principle the very same
case as that of bankruptcy. Although it is usual for the
sheriff, under such circumstances, to execute a deed of
assignment, it is not in strictness necessary; for the assignment is complete by operation of law the moment the purchaser accepts the lease. It is remarkable, that it is no
where said that the sheriff must execute an assignment.
In *Doe* d. *Mitchinson* v. *Carter* (b), it was held that the
sale of a lease, under an execution against the lessee, did
not operate as a forfeiture of the lease under the covenant
not to assign. In *Higgins* v. *M‘Adam* (c), the Court said,

(a) 3 T. R. 292.   (b) 8 T. R. 57.   (c) 3 You. & J. 13.

"The rule is, that when execution is executed the property is changed, and execution is said to be executed when a sale has taken place." That was a case of execution against the goods, but there is no distinction in that respect. In *Giles* v. *Grover* (a), *Alderson*, B., adopts that rule, and lays it down thus: "It is not until after the sale that the right of the execution creditor is consummate." After being put into possession under the sale, could the Crown take the term under an extent? *Swain* v. *Morland* (b) shews that they could not, and that as soon as the execution was executed the Crown had no right. In this case, when the defendant was put into possession by the bill of sale, the title was consummated. In *Doe d. Stevens* v. *Donston* (c), the sheriff under a fieri facias seized the lease of premises, and sold the term before the writ was returnable, but did not execute the assignment to the vendee till a subsequent period; and it was held that the assignment was valid. The sheriff may therefore still proceed to assign the lease. [*Alderson*, B.—In the case of an assignment by operation of law, there is a designation of the party to whom the property shall go; but here there is nothing of that kind; the sheriff may assign, as long as he has the power, to any one he likes.] They also referred to *Stratford* v. *Twynam* (d), and *Taylor* v. *Cole*.

Lord ABINGER, C. B.—I am of opinion that this rule ought to be discharged. The Court was induced to grant a rule in this case, chiefly on the ground that, assuming the defendant not to be in possession of these premises by act and operation of law, it might still be a question whether the plaintiff, from whom they had been taken by operation of law, could recover them back. But, on hear-

(a) 9 Bing. 159; S. C., 2 M. & Scott, 197; M'Clel. & Y. 232; 12 Price, 2.

(b) 1 Brod. & B. 370.
(c) 1 B. & Ald. 230.
(d) Jacob, 418.

ing the argument of the plaintiff's counsel to-day, we think this rule must be discharged. Here something is to be done by the sheriff before the title of the execution debtor is divested out of him, or that of the purchaser is completed; namely, an assignment of the lease. Now, if a sheriff is bound to execute such an instrument, ought he not to do it in compliance with the established rules of law? In order to give a title to the property, he must find a specific person to assign it to, and give that person an assignment in writing, according to the express words of the Statute of Frauds. If there be any circumstance of hardship in this case, the defendant must seek his remedy in a court of equity.

ALDERSON, B.—I am of the same opinion. It seems to me that this is an imperfect assignment, and that the property in these leasehold premises must be considered as still remaining in the party in whom it was originally vested, unless it is shewn to be transferred in a legal manner to some one else. How was it then in the present case? First of all, has it been transferred to the *defendant* by operation of law? The answer to that is, that every assignment by operation of law contains a designation of the person to whom the property is assigned; which is not the case here, for it is clear that something is to be done by the sheriff before any title can vest in the purchaser; and this it is which distinguishes the present case from what I said in *Giles* v. *Grover*, which has been referred to; for my observation there was, that the transfer of the property was consummated by the act of sale. In an execution against the goods it is so. Then comes the next question—is the property in the sheriff? No; for he has nothing more than a power to transfer it; and then comes the further question, has he legitimately exercised that power? It appears that he has made a parol assignment to the defendant. Now a parol assignment by a sheriff is open to all the evils of a parol assignment of property by any one else; parties would be setting up claims to property under pretence of such assignments; and the object of the statute, which was to prevent such practices, and the numerous perjuries and frauds resulting therefrom, would be entirely defeated. And not only the Statute of Frauds, but the object of all the registry acts, would be equally defeated; because a parol sale by the sheriff would of course not be registered like a regular assignment. In the present case, therefore, however unfortunate it may be that the execution debtor must be allowed to recover this property back from the execution creditor, it is out of our power to prevent it; for this case comes before us in the shape of an action of ejectment, when nothing is in issue but the *legal* title and right to the possession of the land. If the defendant has any remedy, it is in a court of equity.

GURNEY, B., concurred.

Rule discharged.

Exch. of Pleas,
1842.

DOE
d.
HUGHES
v.
JONES.

THE ATTORNEY-GENERAL *v.* LOCKWOOD.

The keeper of a beer-shop, licensed under 1 Will. 4, c. 64, & 4 & 5 Will. 4, c. 84, is liable to the penalties imposed by 56 Geo. 3, c. 58, s. 2, for having in his possession any of the prohibited articles therein specified, or any other article or preparation to be used as a substitute for malt or hops.

In order to render such a person liable to those penalties, for having in his possession any of the articles *enumerated* in the 56 Geo. 3, c. 58, s. 2, it is unnecessary to aver or prove, either that the party had them in his possession to be used as a substitute for malt or hops, or that he had them in his possession with any criminal intention. But where the information is for his possession any article *not designated by name* in that section, it is necessary to shew that it was intended to be used as a substitute for malt and hops in the making of beer.

THIS was an information against the defendant under 56 Geo. 3, c. 58, s. 2, for that he, being a retailer of beer, after the 5th July, 1817, and before the exhibiting of the information, to wit, on &c., at &c., received and took into and had in his custody and possession, a large quantity, to wit, 500 pounds weight of liquorice, contrary to the form of the statute in that case made and provided, whereby, and by force of the statute &c., the said William Lockwood, so being such retailer of beer as aforesaid, and so offending as aforesaid, hath, for his aforesaid offence, forfeited and lost the sum of £200. There was a second count, for receiving into his custody and possession an article or preparation as a substitute for malt and hops, he being a retailer of beer; a third for having in his custody and possession liquorice, he being a *dealer* in beer; and a fourth, for having in his possession a certain preparation as a substitute for malt and hops, he being a *dealer* in beer.

The defendant pleaded not guilty.

At the trial before Lord *Abinger*, C. B., at the Middlesex Sittings after last Easter Term, it appeared that in the month of February, 1840, the defendant was licensed to sell beer by retail, under 1 Will. 4, c. 64, and 4 & 5 Will. 4, c. 84. The license was to sell beer, ale, and porter, by retail, in the dwelling-house of the said William Lockwood, and in the premises thereunto belonging, but not to be drunk or consumed in the house or premises. On the 29th of February, 1840, the officers of excise found upon the defendant's premises 28 lbs. of liquorice in a sack of roasted malt. It was contended that the possession of the liquorice under the circumstances was an offence against the act

56 Geo. 3, c. 58, s. 2. The facts above stated were admitted at the trial, and a verdict was taken for the Crown on the first count of the information, for one penalty of £200, subject to the opinion of the Court, the Crown to be at liberty to enter the verdict on any count of the information that might be applicable to the facts proved. In Trinity Term, 1841, *Kelly* obtained a rule to enter a verdict for the defendant, upon the ground that the defendant, being licensed under the beer acts, was not liable to the penalties under the 56 Geo. 3, c. 58, s. 2; or to arrest the judgment, on the ground that the count applicable to liquorice contained no allegation that it was for or as a substitute for malt or hops.

The *Solicitor-General, Jervis,* and *Wilde,* shewed cause. —It will be contended on the other side, first, that as this was the case of a person selling beer, not under a magistrate's license, but under and by virtue of the stat. 11 Geo. 4 & 1 Will. 4, c. 64, continued by 4 & 5 Will. 4, c. 84, the provisions of the 56 Geo. 3, c. 58, do not apply; and secondly, that the information is defective, in not stating that the defendant had the liquorice in his possession as a substitute for malt and hops. As to the first objection,—the words of the stat. 56 Geo. 3, c. 58, s. 2, are, " That from and after the 5th day of July, 1817, no brewer or brewers of, or dealer or dealers in, or retailer or retailers of, beer, shall receive or take into, or have in his, her, or their custody or possession, or make, or use, or mix with, or put into any worts or beer, any liquor, extract, calx, or other material or preparation, for the purpose of darkening the colour of worts or beer, or any liquor, extract, calx, or other material or preparation, such as has been heretofore or as shall hereafter be made use of for or in the darkening of the colour of worts or beer, other than brown malt, ground or unground, as commonly used in brewing, or shall receive or take into, or have in his, her, or their custody or posses-

Exch. of Pleas,
1842.

ATT.-GEN.
v.
LOCKWOOD.

sion, or use, or mix with, or put into any worts or beer, any molasses, honey, liquorice, vitriol, quassia, coculus Indiæ, grains of Paradise, quinea pepper, or opium, or any extract or preparation of molasses, honey, or liquorice, &c. &c., *or any article or preparation whatsoever for or as a substitute for malt or hops;* and if any such brewer or brewers of, or dealer or dealers in, or retailer or retailers of beer, shall receive or take into, or have in his, her, or their custody or possession, or make or use in brewing, or mix with or put into any worts or beer, any liquor, extract, calx, or other material, or preparation, for the purpose of darkening the colour of worts or beer, or any liquor, extract, calx, or other material or preparation, such as has been heretofore or as shall hereafter be made use of for or in the darkening of the colour of worts or beer, other than brown malt, ground or unground, as commonly used in brewing, or shall receive, or take into, or have in his, her, or their custody or possession, or shall use, or mix with, or put into any worts or beer, any molasses, honey, liquorice, &c., or any extract or preparation of molasses, honey, liquorice, &c., or any article or preparation whatsoever, for or as a substitute for malt or hops; all such liquor, extract, calx, molasses, &c. &c., article and preparation as aforesaid, and also the said worts and beer respectively, shall be forfeited, together with the casks, vessels, or other packages containing the same, and shall and may be seized by any officer or officers of excise; and such brewer or brewers of, dealer or dealers in, or retailer or retailers of beer, so offending as aforesaid, shall for each and every such offence forfeit and lose the sum of £200." It will be said that the stat. 11 Geo. 4 & 1 Will. 4, c. 64, has made an alteration in the law, and that the stat. 56 Geo. 3, c. 58, does not apply to a person who sells beer by retail under that act. But the state of the law is this. Persons who retailed beer were required originally, as alehouse-keepers, by the stat. 5 & 6 Edw. 6, c. 25, to take out a magistrate's

license. The stat. 11 Geo. 4 & 1 Will. 4, c. 64, has done
no more than allow persons to sell beer by retail, without having that particular sort of license; it has not
introduced any new traffic of any kind; a person sells
beer by retail, and keeps an alehouse, now as he did
before; but the legislature enables him to do so without
a magistrate's license. That act does not at all affect the
question, whether he is to be considered a seller of beer by
retail; all that can be said is, that such person is not a
seller of beer who is required to take out a magistrate's
license. The object of the legislature was, that retailers
of beer should not have it in their power to adulterate the
beer they sold to the public, and it can make no difference
whether the retailer of beer has a magistrate's license or
not.

The stat. 11 Geo. 4 & 1 Will. 4, c. 64, recites, that it is
expedient for the better supplying the public with beer in
England, to give greater facilities for the sale thereof than
are at present afforded by licenses to keepers of inns, alehouses, and victualling-houses; and it enacts, that it shall
be lawful for any person who shall obtain a license for
that purpose under the provisions of this act, to sell beer,
ale, and porter by retail in any part of England in any
house or premises specified in such license. It enables
them to do so without having a license under the former
statutes, having taken out one under that statute; but the
act itself shews that such a person is a retailer of beer;
and it then goes on to state the mode in which the license
is to be obtained. The 13th section enacts, that if any
person so licensed as aforesaid shall knowingly sell any
beer, ale, or porter made otherwise than from malt and
hops, or shall mix or cause to be mixed any drugs or other
pernicious ingredients with any beer sold in his house or
premises, or shall fraudulently dilute or in any way adulterate any such beer, such offender shall for the first
offence forfeit any sum not less than £10, nor more than

£20, as the justices before whom such offender shall be convicted shall adjudge. The 14th section regulates the time for keeping open the houses, and imposes a penalty for a breach of that regulation; and the 15th points out the mode in which the penalties may be recovered. It is clear that those penalties are imposed on breaches of the act by the keepers of beerhouses under that statute, but there is nothing preventing the general regulations applying to those persons who retail beer, whether under that act or under former acts of parliament. The imposition of a new penalty could not abrogate the former penalty for a different species of offence. There are a great number of acts of parliament pointing out the distinction between a seller of beer by retail, and a retailer of beer. Such are the statutes 12 Car. 2, c. 23, & 25 Geo. 3, c. 73. There is a recital in the latter act which shews what the distinction is; and it enacts, that every common brewer who shall sell beer or ale, or worts, in any less quantity at any one time than in a whole cask containing four gallons and a half, shall be deemed to sell beer or ale by retail. This is the case of a person selling beer by retail, not to be consumed upon the premises, under an excise license obtained under the Beer Act. There is a definition of an alehouse-keeper in Burn's Justice, title "Alehouses." "Every inn is not an alehouse, nor every alehouse an inn; but if an inn uses common selling of ale, it is then also an alehouse; and if an alehouse lodges and entertains travellers, it is also an inn." So, if a party sells beer by retail, he comes under the common designation in the acts of parliament, of a retailer of beer, or a keeper of a beer or alehouse, and is within the statute 56 Geo. 3. It never could be the intention of the legislature, when they allowed this greater facility for the opening of beerhouses, to remove from the keepers of them all those restrictions which applied to persons who kept beerhouses or alehouses under the license of the magistrates. The statute 1 Will. 4, c. 64, was passed in the same session as the 1 Will. 4, c. 51; *Exch. of Pleas,* and it appears by the statement in the latter act, that it was supposed by the framers of it that the act, c. 64, would pass first. That act (c. 51) was passed for the same purpose, of giving facilities for the sale of beer, and taking away the license of the magistrates, and giving other means of licensing. It repealed various acts of Parliament with relation to the duties and restrictions imposed on the keepers of alehouses, but expressly kept alive the provisions of the statute 56 Geo. 3; it is enacted by section 3, "that all brewers of beer or ale for sale, and all and every person who shall be licensed under any act as a brewer, dealer in or retailer of beer, shall continue subject to the provisions, enactments, and regulations in the said last-mentioned act contained; and the said provisions, enactments, and regulations, shall continue to be respectively executed and put in force by the commissioners and officers of excise in Great Britain, as fully and effectually as if this act had not been passed." Then the 22nd section shews that the framers of this act supposed the other act would have passed first, for it begins by reciting, "And whereas an act was passed in this present session of Parliament, intituled 'An act to permit the general sale of beer and cider by retail in England.'" These two acts shew distinctly that the legislature intended to keep alive, and in operation upon retailers of beer, the provisions of the statutes 56 Geo. 3. In *The Mayor &c. of Leicester* v. *Burgess* (a), it was held that the statute 11 Geo. 4 & 1 Will. 4, c. 64, for permitting the general sale of beer by retail in England, did not supersede the custom of a borough, that no person should carry on the trade of an alehouse-keeper therein who is not a burgess.

The second question is, whether it was necessary for the

1842.

ATT.-GEN.
v.
LOCKWOOD.

(a) 5 B. & Adol. 246.

information to state that this prohibited article was intended to be used as a substitute for malt and hops. The words of the act are, "that no brewer or brewers, &c., shall have, receive, or take into, or have in his, her, or their custody or possession, or shall use, or mix with, or put into any worts or beer, any molasses, honey, liquorice, &c., respectively;"—then come these words—"or any article or preparation whatsoever, for or as a substitute for malt or hops." Parties may have articles of the kind here mentioned as a substitute for malt or hops, or they may have them innocently in their possession; but the legislature has said, that any person carrying on this trade shall be liable to a penalty if he has any of the articles *enumerated* in his possession; and the officers of the revenue are bound to enforce it. In the previous act of the 51 Geo. 3, c. 87, s. 16, the words are—" no maker or makers of any such liquor as aforesaid, nor any brewer or brewers of beer, shall receive or take into his, her, or their custody or possession any molasses, honey, &c., respectively;" and there is nothing said as to a substitute for malt and hops. Unless persons carrying on this trade were altogether restricted from having these articles in their possession, it would be necessary to give evidence of the purpose for which the party had the article in his possession, which it would be very difficult to prove, unless you could shew the actual use. The act, therefore, says that the possession shall not be permitted. [Lord *Abinger*, C. B.—No person can put this law in force except the Attorney-General, and he would not do so absurd a thing as to put it in force where there was not a suspicion that the article was kept for improper purposes. The act of 51 Geo. 3, c. 87, does not contain the words, " or any article or preparation whatsoever, for or as a substitute for malt or hops," which this act has, in addition to those enumerated.] Precisely so; this act was intended to be more stringent; for it is recited in the preamble that the former provisions were not found sufficiently effectual. In *The Attorney-General* v. *King* (a), where a party had the article in his possession innocently, in his trade as a distiller, but he also carried on the trade of a brewer, it was held that he was liable to the penalties imposed by 51 Geo. 3, c. 87, for receiving and taking into his possession articles prohibited by that statute. An argument may also be drawn from the 3rd section of the 56 Geo. 3, c. 58, applicable to druggists and persons selling articles to brewers, as in that case it is not necessary that the article should be used as a substitute for malt and hops, but the penalty applies merely for selling or delivering to any licensed brewer or dealer or retailer of beer, knowing them to be so, any liquor, &c. The stat. 56 Geo. 3, c. 58, enumerated various articles, which were supposed more likely to be fraudulently used, but the legislature thought the enumeration might be defective, and therefore added the words "any other article or preparation for or as a substitute for malt or hops," lest there should be anything else which the ingenuity of the brewer might suggest as a substitute. It will also abundantly appear, from the first part of this section, that the intention of the legislature was to impose a penalty on any dealer or trader who had in his possession any of the articles ordinarily used for the purpose of darkening or colouring beer. The words are, that he shall not "have in his possession, or make or use or put into any worts or beer, any liquor, calx, or other materials or preparation used for the purpose of darkening the colour of worts or beer." It might with equal justice be contended, that in order to bring a trader within that part of the clause, it was necessary he should have the material in his possession for the purpose of darkening beer; but the words which follow shew that such was not the intention of the legislature; but that, if he

(a) 5 Price, 195.

D D 2

had in his possession articles ordinarily used for that purpose, he should be liable. The words are, " or any liquor, extract, calx, or other material or preparation, such as has been heretofore or as shall hereafter be made use of, for or in the darkening the colour of worts or beer." It is clear from that, that if the trader had in his possession any articles ordinarily used for that purpose, or which might be so used, he would be within that clause, though he did not intend so to use them. The argument on the other side must go to this extent, that it is legal to put the various enumerated articles into beer, provided they are not used as a substitute for malt and hops. Upon such a construction, the long enumeration of these articles is perfectly useless.

Kelly and *Bramwell*, contrà.—This act, imposing as it does a severe penalty, must be construed strictly. At the time the stat. 56 Geo. 3, c. 58, passed, there were several classes of persons carrying on the business, who are pointed out by the act. These were, first, the brewers, the actual manufacturers of the beer; dealing to a very considerable extent; secondly, dealers in beer, which does not include merely retailers of beer, but persons who sell beer in quantities of not less than four gallons and a half at a time; and thirdly, the keepers of hotels, taverns, and public-houses, and licensed victuallers. Those were classes of persons well known to the law, and of a very different description from that which came within the operation of the recent beer acts, and who hold licenses under those acts. Such were the three classes of persons existing at the time the stat. 56 Geo. 3 passed, and on whom its large penalties were imposed. That state of the law continued as long as those classes alone existed, and indeed still continues as affects them. Then the 1 Will. 4, c. 64, the beer-act, passed, and an entirely new and different class of persons was brought into existence, of an inferior description—inferior in the extent of their deal-

ings and property, and their means of paying penalties;
persons who keep beershops of a lower class, and take
out these licenses to sell beer by retail. That act contains distinct enactments, rendering them liable, not to
heavy penalties of £200, which they were thought not able
to pay, but to penalties which, according to their means,
would guarantee the observance of the law : penalties very
much smaller in amount, for offences of much more serious
evil. The stat. 56 Geo. 3, c. 58, was intended to apply to
the classes of brewers and dealers in and retailers of beer
who then existed. The words "brewer of or dealer in beer,"
are not to be taken in their extended, but in a restricted
sense. The statute says, "every person who shall sell
any beer or ale in quantities not less than four gallons
and a half, or two dozen reputed quart bottles, to be drunk
or consumed elsewhere than on the premises where sold,
shall be deemed a dealer in beer." The words "retailer
or retailers of beer," in the 3rd section, were intended
to apply to licensed victuallers, who were a class of
persons then in existence, and to them only. The
keepers of beershops are a new class of traders, carrying
on business in an entirely different way, under different
licenses, to whom these penalties are not applicable, although the words may be capable of reaching them. The
legislature, at the time the beer-act passed, were not un-
mindful of the protection necessary for the excise; and the
act provides, that the keepers of beershops shall only trade
under certain licenses, which contain a great number of
minute and express conditions and regulations, and they
are liable to penalties for any breach of those regulations;
and the legislature have thereby provided for every case in
which it was considered at all probable they would violate
the law. The 13th sect. of the 1 Will. 4, c. 64, provides,
that every seller of beer, ale, and porter by retail, having a
license under the provisions of this act, who shall permit

any person or persons to be guilty of drunkenness or disorderly conduct in the house or premises mentioned in such license, shall for every such offence forfeit the respective sums following; and every person who shall in any way transgress or neglect, or shall be a party in transgressing or neglecting, the conditions and provisions specified in such license, or shall allow such conditions or provisions to be in any way transgressed or neglected in the house or premises so licensed, shall be deemed guilty of disorderly conduct; and every person so licensed, who shall permit any such disorderly conduct, shall for the first offence forfeit any such sum, not less than 40s. nor more than £5, as the justices before whom such retailer shall be convicted of such offence shall adjudge; and for the second such offence, any sum not less than £5, nor more than £10; and for the third such offence, any sum not less than £20, nor more than £50; and it shall be lawful for the justices before whom any such third offence shall take place, to adjudge, if they shall so think fit, that such offender shall be disqualified from selling beer by retail for the space of two years next ensuing such conviction. The persons to whom such licenses are granted, and who comprise the whole class of beershop-keepers, whether they sell beer alone in their shops, or have a chandler's-shop and sell beer also, or in whatever other way, all have a license in this form:—It recites that a bond has been entered into by the beerhouse-keeper and a surety, the conditions of which are, that the former does not sell any beer, ale, or porter, made otherwise than from malt and hops, nor mix, or cause to be mixed, any drugs or other pernicious ingredients in beer, ale, or porter; nor fraudulently dilute, deteriorate, or adulterate any beer, ale, or porter; nor sell any beer, ale, or porter, knowing the same to have been fraudulently diluted, deteriorated, or adulterated; nor use in selling any beer, ale, or porter, any measures which are not of the legal standard; nor wilfully

o̓r knowingly permit any drunkenness, or any violent or
quarrelsome or other disorderly conduct in his house or
premises, &c. &c.: and that the license shall cease and determine, and shall become void, in case any of the conditions or regulations contained therein shall be transgressed. [Lord *Abinger*, C. B.—What was the form of
license under the former act? The *Solicitor-General.*—
It was exactly the same, which is important.] By the
18th section, not only the license may be forfeited, but
specific penalties may be imposed for adulterating, di-
luting, or mixing beer. Can it be supposed that the legislature intended to apply this penalty of £10 or £20 only
for actually adulterating beer in however injurious a manner, and that a penalty of £200 is to be imposed on the
party for merely having an article calculated for that
purpose in his possession? When the legislature have
said that persons keeping beershops shall be liable to a
penalty of £10 or £20, they cannot have intended to continue in operation a penalty of ten times the largest of
those amounts for merely having the articles in their possession. The intention of the legislature appears to be
still further illustrated by the provision on which the second objection has been taken. This penalty is imposed
under the act upon any person, whatever the trade he
carries on, who shall have any of these numerous articles
in his possession—molasses, honey, liquorice, &c., &c.,
which it must be observed are articles invariably and necessarily in the possession of that class of chandlers'-
shop keepers, as part of their stock-in-trade; but at the
time of the passing of the statute 56 Geo. 3, it was hardly
to be contemplated that the person who had a brewery,
and brewed beer, would keep a grocer's shop, or that the
wholesale dealer in beer, or the licensed tavern-keeper·
or hotel-keeper, should do so. [Lord *Abinger*, C. B.—It
may be a question whether a shopkeeper taking out a
license to sell beer must not relinquish dealing in such

articles.] The Court, in construing the act, and considering how far it imposes a large penalty on an individual, will look to the common practice in trading under these licenses. It is not an impossible case, that, under the former act, a person might be a brewer, a wholesale dealer, and a publican in one part of the town, and in another part of the town carry on a grocer's or chandler's shop; but it would be so peculiar a case that it could hardly be supposed to have been in the contemplation of the legislature. But more than one-half the persons who carry on trade in these beer-houses, do so also in chandlers' or grocers' shops. It could not be the intention of the legislature to apply so severe a provision to this new class of persons; their liability is limited to the penalties recoverable under the 13th sect. of the act of Parliament constituting them, and they are not liable to the penalties directed by the 56 Geo. 3, c. 58.

But assuming the Court to be of opinion that the defendant was a retailer of beer within the 56 Geo. 3, c. 58, and subject to its penalty, the further question remains, whether that penalty is not repealed, in point of law, by the imposition of a smaller one, for one at least of the offences included in the 56 Geo. 3, by the 1 Will. 4, c. 64, s. 13. In *Henderson* v. *Sherborn* (a), it was held that a parish officer who supplies goods for his own profit to an individual pauper is not liable to the penalty imposed by the 55 Geo. 3, c. 137, s. 6; and there is a quære (added to the marginal note) whether that clause is not impliedly repealed by the 4 & 5 Will. 4, c. 76, s. 77. There Lord *Abinger*, C. B., says, "The principle adopted by Lord *Tenterden* (b), that a penal law ought to be construed strictly, is not only a sound one, but the only one consistent with our free institutions. The interpre-

---

(a) 2 M. & W. 236.

(b) In *Proctor* v. *Mainwaring*, 3 B. & Ald. 145.

tation of statutes has always in modern times been highly *Exch. of Pleas,* 1842. favourable to the personal liberty of the subject, and I hope will always remain so. But I think there is another ground for not disturbing this nonsuit. If the 77th sect. of the new Poor Law Act embraces this case, I do not agree that it does not amount to a repeal of the former enactment. If a crime be created by statute, with a given penalty, and be afterwards repeated in another statute with a lesser penalty attached to it, I cannot say that the party ought to be held liable to both. There may, no doubt, be two remedies for the same act, but they must be of a different nature. The new act, then, would be in effect a repeal of the former penalty." The effect of that judgment is, that where there is a penalty imposed by an act of Parliament upon an offence created in that act, and subsequently a fresh penalty is imposed by another act, that repeals the former penalty. *Rex* v. *The Trustees of Northleach and Witney Roads* (a), and *Barrett* v. *The Stockton Railway Company* (b), are authorities in favour of the same principle. [Lord *Abinger*, C. B.—My judgment was founded on the principle, that where the same offence is re-enacted with a different punishment, it repeals the former law. If the conditions of the license contained all the things mentioned in the old act of Parliament, and there had been a clause forbidding the same things by a different punishment, I should agree it had repealed the former act.] The stat. 56 Geo. 3, imposes a penalty of £200 for having in possession certain articles, and using and mixing those articles; the penalty for using and mixing those articles is reduced to £10 by stat. 1 Will. 4, c. 64; and as a person cannot use an article without first having it in his possession, the legislature cannot have intended to continue the penalty of £200. That would be quite incon-

ATT.-GEN.
v.
LOCKWOOD.

(a) 5 B. & Ad. 978.
(b) 2 Man. & G. 15; 1 Hud. & Br. (Irish), 304.

sistent. This argument rests on the assumption that the defendant was a retailer of beer within the act 56 Geo. 3; but he is not a retailer absolutely, he is merely a retailer sub modo, namely, of beer to be drunk off the premises, and on that ground also he is not within the act.

The other question is, whether the words at the conclusion of the sentence, "or any article for or as a substitute for malt or hops," are to be read "or any other article;" or whether these words, "for or as a substitute for malt or hops," govern the whole of the antecedent part of the sentence, and render it necessary to aver, in an information for the penalty, that the article was found in the possession of the party, *and* that it was intended to be used "for or as a substitute for malt or hops." Now, independently of the rule that these statutes must be construed strictly, there is reason for holding that these latter words govern the whole of the antecedent provisions. There are two purposes to which these articles can be applied, of an unlawful nature, which it was intended to prevent. One is the colouring of beer, the other is the using them as a substitute for malt or hops. Each article enumerated in the second section of the 56 Geo. 3, c. 58, is of a description which brewers might have used for the purpose of colouring, or as a substitute for malt and hops, but no other. The enacting words are, " That no brewer or distiller, or retailer of beer, shall have in his custody or possession, or make or use, or mix with or put into any worts or beer, any liquor, extract, calx, or other material or preparation, for the purpose of darkening the colour of worts or beer, or any liquor, extract, calx, or other material or preparation, such as has been heretofore or as shall be hereafter made use of for or in the darkening of the colour of worts or beer, other than brown malt, ground or unground, as commonly used in brewing:"—so far the legislature has provided against the colouring of beer, or there being in the possession of the party any article by which that can be done. Then follows *Exch. of Pleas,* 1842. another provision, to prevent persons from having in their possession any article to be used as a substitute for malt and hops:—" or shall receive or take into, or have in his custody or possession, or use or mix with, or put in any worts or beer, any molasses, &c.," enumerating a dozen different articles, " or any article or preparation whatsoever for or as a substitute for malt or hops." The meaning is, that no person shall have in his possession any article for the colouring of beer—whether he uses it or not is immaterial,—or any article to be used as a substitute for malt or hops. The purpose to which the articles are capable of being applied forms a part of the sentence, and a part of the description of the article itself. Those words, being put at the end, govern the sentence, and it must be not the mere absolute fact of having such articles in his possession, but the having them "for or as a substitute for malt and hops," that renders the act unlawful. In the first part of the clause, the party is prohibited from having any of those articles in his possession which would have the effect of darkening the colour of beer, without saying, as in a subsequent part of it, for the purpose of so doing. The legislature, if they had intended to prohibit the one absolutely and positively like the other, would have put both together in the same branch of the enactment. The words "for or as a substitute for malt and hops," therefore, override the former words, and render it necessary to aver an intention so to use the article.

The *Solicitor-General*, in reply, was directed to confine himself to the argument as to the clause in the 56 Geo. 3, c. 58, being repealed by the 13th section of the Beer Act, quoad this matter.—The argument is, that the provision in the latter act is virtually a provision against the same offence as the one mentioned in the 56 Geo. 3, c. 58, and imposes a minor penalty, and therefore is a repeal of the former statute, according to the decision of this Court in *Henderson* v. *Sherborn.* But the principle of that decision, which it is not intended to controvert, is not applicable. The answer is, that the offences in the 1 Will. 4, c. 64, and the 56 Geo. 3, c. 58, are not the same offences, and their provisions are not directed to the same object. Under the stat. 56 Geo. 3, the main object was to protect the revenue. With that view, all prosecutions for the breach of it were to be in the hands of the Attorney-General. The object was to raise the revenue upon malt and hops, and the excisable articles, the provisions of the 1 Will. 4, relating to the penalties for breach of the license, are provisions relating to the management of the house, as a species of public regulation; and in that act there is no offence created for merely having in possession pernicious articles, which may be a fraud on the revenue; the offence is the doing an act upon the premises, and selling beer so adulterated. Its object is to prevent the sale by beerhousekeepers of those articles which are pernicious to the public; the prohibition is confined to the offence of *selling.* [*Gurney,* B. : " Or mixing."] "Mixing, or causing to be mixed with any beer *sold on the premises."* That is a part of the police regulation, to prevent parties from selling those deleterious articles. The question is, whether these provisions of these several acts are incongruous and inconsistent, so that one of them must necessarily be a repeal of the other. Now in order to determine that, the object and intent of both acts must be looked at. The provisions of the latter act cannot operate as a repeal, because the stat. 1 Will. 4, c. 51, which is part of this measure, distinctly states that the stat. 56 Geo. 3, c. 58, shall continue in full force. The objects of the two statutes are altogether distinct : one is to protect the revenue ; the other a matter of regulation, to provide not only against the house being a disorderly one, but also against articles being sold to the Exch. of Pleas,
1842.
Att.-Gen.
v.
Lockwood. public which may be prejudicial to their health; and therefore both provisions may well stand together, and one is not a repeal of or incongruous with the other. [He was then stopped by the Court.]

Lord ABINGER, C. B.—There are two objections made to this proceeding. The first is, that the defendant is not a licensed dealer within the meaning of the 56 Geo. 3, c. 58. I cannot accede to that proposition. It appears to me that that act applies to every dealer, and I am not prepared to say (though I will not say to the contrary) that it might not apply to a dealer without any license at all; but if it were made applicable to existing licensed dealers, and an act of Parliament were afterwards passed, making it unnecessary for parties to have a license, but without repealing this clause, I should say that it would still apply to all those who dealt in beer, though they had not licenses at all. I do not see any difficulty in that construction. Then if so, the passing of another act, to create another set of dealers with another set of licenses, would make them retailers of beer, and bring them within the former act; and I cannot enter into a speculation of what might have been in the contemplation of the legislature, because they have not stated what they contemplated. Mr. *Kelly's* argument was, that they must have contemplated dealers of a smaller class,—I do not know that; at all events I cannot be sure that they did. The act of Parliament practically has had, I believe, a very pernicious effect—an effect not at all contemplated—but we cannot construe the act by that result.

The next question was, whether this act of Parliament is to be so construed, as that the offence which is prohibited thereby, and which is the subject of the penalty, namely, having possession of any of those ingredients, is not contemplated unless the party has them in his possession for the particular purpose named in the act. Now I think a mere reference to the act of Parliament itself, and to the words of it, is sufficient to shew that that is not the proper construction of it. Where a person mixes liquor for that specific purpose, the act of Parliament has a distinct provision against it; but it likewise prohibits the possession by retail dealers of certain specified articles; and the former act of Parliament, of which this clause is an enlargement, did not contain the words "any other article;" but this act of Parliament, in order to extend the provisions of the former, thought it right to prohibit the possession, not only of any of the specified articles, but also of any other articles which the legislature might not contemplate at the time, which might be used for the same purpose as those contemplated might possibly be used for; the prohibition is upon the party having in his possession any article not specified, used for the purpose of or as a substitute for malt or hops. It seems to me that the construction is very plain and distinct, and therefore I think the judgment cannot be arrested.

Mr. *Bramwell*, in a very ingenious argument, which struck me forcibly, put this case,—that it appeared from the license under the last act, that one of the penalties which was enacted in the 56 Geo. 3, was introduced into the act of the 1 Will. 4; namely, the penalty upon mixing any drugs or other pernicious ingredients with beer; and he contended, that if the party mixed any drugs or pernicious ingredients in beer, it might be said that that was equally an offence within the 56 Geo. 3, and subject to the larger penalty. The argument is undoubtedly very plausible, and it certainly made an impression upon my mind; for to suppose that the legislature imposed a penalty of £200 upon a party for having an article in his possession, and that it imposed a penalty of £10 for

mixing that article with beer sold, would certainly be supposing the legislature not to act very reasonably, if that
were contemplated. But there are two answers to that
objection. The first is, that such certainly is not the
offence for which this information is filed; it is a distinct
offence. It is clear that the offence for which this information is filed, is not made the subject of any lesser penalty,
and it is only by inference and ingenious argument that
it can be made so. We cannot suppose the intention
of the legislature against the express words; and supposing the fact to be, that they have selected one of those
particular offences,—that is, the mixing,—and fixed that
at a lower penalty, and thereby so far have repealed the
first act, it would not interfere with the other class of
offences not repealed in the same manner. But I think
the *Solicitor-General* has given the true answer; namely,
that these clauses were passed with a distinct view; that
this condition in the license is one which is introduced,
with a class of others of the same nature, intended to preserve good order in the house, and to prevent the persons
who are therein from being immediately imposed upon by
the sale of adulterated beer. It appears that in the former
license, before this act was passed, there was a clause in
the conditions that might, by interpretation, have been
construed as referring to one of those offences specified in
the 56 Geo. 3; clearly the argument, therefore, applies to
that, because the act of the 56 Geo. 3 was passed after the
form of that license was known. I think, therefore, that
the infraction of the conditions of *this* license, to which the
penalty of £10 is annexed in the terms of the statute,
must be construed to refer, not to the same class of
offences as are specified in the 56 Geo. 3, but to offences
against the good order of the house, in conducting the
business, and immediate imposition upon persons in that
house, who are drinking beer; that it relates to the sale of

beer in the house, and the maintenance of good order there. I think, therefore, we cannot construe that, by inference, as a repeal of the penalty for keeping and having in possession the prohibited article. The judgment therefore ought not, in my opinion, to be arrested upon that ground.

ALDERSON, B.—I am entirely of the same opinion. The rule of law, I take it, upon the construction of all statutes, and therefore applicable to the construction of this, is, whether they be penal or remedial, to construe them according to the plain, literal, and grammatical meaning of the words in which they are expressed, unless that construction leads to a plain and clear contradiction of the apparent purpose of the act, or to some palpable and evident absurdity. Now, that being the rule upon which we are to construe statutes, let us apply that rule to the statute before us. We find that all dealers in or retailers of beer have certain regulations imposed upon them. Now I agree that, looking at the law as it stood before, and as it is to be found here, inasmuch as we find the words " dealer in beer " and " retailer of beer," you are to construe the words " dealer in beer " as designating a wholesale dealer in beer, because the legislature has subsequently used the words " retailers of beer " to distinguish them from the other. Therefore, the act of Parliament applies to two classes,—to wholesale dealers, that is, to persons who sell at one time more than four gallons and a half; and to retailers, that is, persons who sell less than four gallons and a half at one time. Those are the sets of persons upon whom the act of Parliament imposes certain regulations; and, among others, they are prohibited from having in their possession certain articles, which are enumerated in the act of Parliament. In the first place, then, does the present defendant fulfil any one of those conditions? It is clear that he is a retailer of beer, for he is a person who sells beer in quantities less than four gallons and a half; and in order to make it lawful for him to be such a retailer of beer, which is the definition given in the very act of Parliament, he must take out a license under the statute of 1 Will. 4, c. 64; and he takes out a license accordingly to retail beer. It is palpable, then, that he is a retailer of beer within the 56 Geo. 3, c. 58.

Then Mr. *Kelly's* argument is, that the statute is to be confined in construction to those persons, and those persons alone, who were retailers of beer at the time the act of Parliament passed. But the act of Parliament does not say so; and the plain grammatical and literal meaning of the act is, to construe those words in a general sense, as applicable to all retailers of beer—both to those who were in existence at the time that act passed, and to those who, by any lawful means, hereafter should become retailers of beer. Nay, it seems to me that an absurdity would follow from not using the words in the general sense; for, as has been well pointed out in the argument of the counsel for the Crown, if we were to introduce the construction suggested by Mr. *Kelly,* we should decide that any change in the license, or in the condition of the license required by law, would put an end to all the provisions of the 56 Geo. 3— an absurdity so great, that the counsel on the part of the defendant disclaims it; but it seems to me necessarily to follow, unless we adopt the rule that the expressions " retailer of beer," and " dealer in beer," must be considered as applying to those who might exist at the time the act passed, and to those who might subsequently exist. Therefore it appears to me, that, in the first place, the counsel for the defendant have to make out that the literal construction of the words, and the grammatical construction, which is general, is to be restrained by reason of

some absurdity which would follow from their being construed generally; but it seems to me that the absurdity
would be in the construction pointed out by them. These
words must, therefore, be taken in their large and general
sense. That disposes of the first question.

The second question is as to the articles enumerated;
and it turns upon this, whether we are to apply the last
words of the sentence, " for or as a substitute for malt or
hops," to all the articles specially enumerated, or to confine them to the latter words, " any article or preparation
whatsoever." Now, let us look and see what would be the
plain and grammatical construction of the words. If Mr.
Kelly's argument is correct, we ought to have the words
" or any *other* article or preparation whatsoever for or as
a substitute for malt or hops;" if those had been the words
used, it might have been said, that inasmuch as the articles and the preparations mentioned were to be any other
of the like kind with those which had been enumerated
before, and as those last words were clearly restrained by
the words " for or as a substitute for malt or hops," the
same restriction might also very fairly, in construction,
have been applied to the former words. But the words are
not so; the words are " or any article," not " any other
article." Therefore, according to the plain and grammatical meaning of them, the latter words control the words
" any article or preparation whatsoever," and those alone.
If we look at the former part of the section, we see how
the legislature express it when they mean to bind up the
general words. We find that they speak of " any liquor,
extract, calx, or *other* material or preparation for the
purpose of darkening the colour of worts or beer," that
is, liquor for the purpose of darkening the colour of worts
or beer, extract for the purpose of darkening the colour of
worts or beer, calx for the purpose of darkening the colour
of worts or beer, or any other article for the purpose of

darkening the colour of worts or beer; but when they come to this part of the section, they leave out the word "other," and say, "any article or preparation for or as a substitute for malt or hops." It seems to me, therefore, that the plain grammatical meaning of the clause confines these latter words to the words "any article or preparation," and excludes them from the other words of the clause.

Let us try this matter in the way I have suggested before. Does any absurdity follow from our so construing the act? On the contrary, may it not have been a very reasonable intention on the part of the legislature to say thus?—There are certain things which it is very important should not be in the hands of persons of this description at all; but inasmuch as we cannot know whether, at some future time, ingenious persons may not discover articles that may fall within the same category, we will add "other articles;" but as that will be too general, we will restrain those words by saying, "any other articles for or as a substitute for malt or hops;" when we do use the general words, we will add to them the purpose to which those other articles are to be applied. It seems to me no more than reasonable, when using general words, to restrain them by subsequent words introduced into the clause, and when using particular words, not to restrain them, in order to impose an absolute and intelligible prohibition.

Very stringent provisions are sometimes enacted by the legislature for purposes of general public good, involving great restrictions upon particular classes of men. We all know very well that, in the West Riding of York and Lancashire, persons are not allowed to be in possession of weft of a particular description without proving that they have come honestly by it, which is contrary to the general law. If a man is in possession of a certain quantity of weft, he is presumed to have embezzled it,

Exch. of Pleas, 1842.

ATT.-GEN. *v.* LOCKWOOD.

unless he can prove that he came honestly by it; which is a breach of the general principle of law, that every man is presumed innocent till he is found guilty; but that act has been passed in order to prevent that which I presume was a frequent crime, the embezzlement of the property of employers by their workmen.

Then the last question is, has this enactment been repealed? If this had been an information for using and mixing articles of this description with beer, there might have been some possible ground for contending that the penalty of the 56 Geo. 3, c. 58, had been repealed or altered by the 13th section of the Beer Act; I say possibly, but even as to that, it seems to me that the argument of the *Solicitor-General* is entitled to great weight. I think that it is not even in that case repealed; but when we come to look at this part of the section, there is not a single syllable in the subsequent act which touches that; and all the argument amounts to is, that if the legislature had thought about it, it is not probable that they would have altered the penalty for mixing, which could not be done without the party's having the article in his possession, and have left the penalty of £200 for having it in his possession. But the act of Parliament is to be construed according to its plain meaning. The legislature have not said so; possibly they never thought about it, and this is an ingenious construction of the clause very contrary to their intention. Why should we, when such is not clearly the intention of the legislature, attempt to arrive at the intention by any reasoning? It seems to me, therefore, that there is no ground for saying that this penalty has been altered by the subsequent act of Parliament; and, applying the rule of construction which I first laid down, I think the Crown is entitled to judgment.

GURNEY, B.—I am of the same opinion. There would

be no ground whatever for the application, provided this case stood upon the 56 Geo. 3, c. 58, alone, and the 1 Will. 4 had not passed, because the defendant is clearly a retailer of beer, and he has done that which the 56 Geo. 3 prohibits; but it is contended that the act of 1 Will. 4 has introduced a new species of retailer of beer, subject to smaller penalties. I think my Lord Chief Baron has given the answer to that, that it matters not what description of retailer of beer he is; every retailer of beer is the same, whether under one act of Parliament or the other; he is a retailer of beer, and subject to every provision of the acts of Parliament which apply to retailers.

Then it is contended that under the 1 Will. 4, c. 64, other penalties are inflicted for the same offences; but the obvious answer is, that this is not an offence created by the 1 Will. 4; that the offence upon which this information is founded is not that for which any penalty is inflicted by that statute. And still further, that by another act of Parliament, which passed within a week, and which must be taken to be part of the same provision, the enactments of the 56 Geo. 3 were kept alive.

I think, therefore, upon the whole case, without going further into it, that this rule ought to be discharged.

Rule discharged.

Exch. of Pleas,
1842.

Jan. 24.

FRESHFIELD and Others *v.* REED and Others, Executors.

A power to demise premises with the consent of A. B., in writing, *duly attested,* is not well executed by a demise which professes to be made with the consent of A. B., " testified by his being a party to those presents ;" the meaning is, that the written consent shall be signed in the presence of a witness.

COVENANT for rent arrear, by the assignees of the reversion against the executors of the assignee of the lessee. The declaration stated, that one Thomas Watson being seised in fee of the premises thereinafter mentioned, heretofore, to wit, on the 8th day of March, 1777, by a certain indenture made between himself of the first part, Elizabeth Susanna Watson of the second part, and certain trustees of the third part, it was declared, that it should be lawful for the said Thomas Watson in his lifetime, and for the said trustees after his death, with the consent and approbation of the said Elizabeth Susanna Watson, while living, in writing, *duly attested,* to make demises of the premises in the manner therein mentioned. The declaration then averred, that by an indenture of demise, made on &c., the said trustees, by and with the consent and approbation of the said Elizabeth Susanna Watson, " testified by her being a party to the said indenture, did demise," &c. the premises in question. On demurrer to one of the pleas,

Ogle, who appeared in support of the plea, objected that the declaration was bad, the terms of the power not having been complied with, inasmuch as it was not alleged that the lease was made with the consent of E. S. Watson " in writing, duly attested." The averment that she was a party to the deed was not equivalent to an allegation that she gave her consent in writing, and that that was duly attested; nay, it was not even alleged that she executed the deed.

Addison, contrà, urged, that the power did not require that the consent should be attested *by witnesses,* but that any attestation by writing was sufficient; that the word " attested " had the same meaning as " testified ;" and that the parties to the lease might be considered as so many witnesses to her consent.

But PER CURIAM.—The term " attest " manifestly implies that a witness shall be present, to testify that the party who is to execute the deed has done the act required by the power; the object of which was, that some person should verify that the deed was signed voluntarily.

Leave to the plaintiffs to amend on payment of costs; otherwise

Judgment for the defendants.

BUTCHER *v.* G. D. STEUART.   *Jan.* 24.

ASSUMPSIT.—The declaration, after stating that the plaintiff had recovered in an action against one Robert Steuart the sum of £3000 and upwards, and had sued out a writ of capias ad satisfaciendum, under which the said R. Steuart had been taken in execution, alleged, that in consideration that the plaintiff would procure the release of the said R. Steuart from custody under the said writ, the defendant promised to pay the plaintiff the sum of that the plaintiff would procure the release of R. S. from custody, the defendant promised to pay him £500. Averment, that the plaintiff did procure the release of R. S. from custody. Breach, in nonpayment of the £500.

Declaration in assumpsit, stating that the plaintiff had recovered in an action against R. S. the sum of £3000, and had sued out a ca. sa. under which R. S. had been taken in execution, alleged, that in consideration

The defendant pleaded as follows:—1st. That R. S. was a member of the House of Commons, and entitled to privilege of Parliament, and freedom from arrest; that his release from custody was only on the ground of his being so privileged; that he afterwards ceased to be a member of the House, and became and still is liable to be taken in execution at the suit of the plaintiff; that the promise of the defendant was a promise to answer for the debt of another, and that there was no memorandum in writing thereof.

2nd. That R. S., at the time of his becoming indebted to the plaintiff, was a member of the Commons House of Parliament, and that whilst he continued such member, the plaintiff recovered judgment and issued a ca. sa., under which he was taken into custody; that R. S. was as such member entitled to his discharge from arrest, and that during the continuance of his privilege, a judge ordered his discharge out of custody, and he was discharged accordingly; and that, save as aforesaid, there never was any consideration for the defendant's promise:—*Held,* on special demurrer, that the first plea was bad for duplicity, and the second, as being an argumentative traverse of the allegation in the declaration, that the plaintiff had procured the release of R. S. from custody.

£500. The declaration then averred, that the plaintiff
did procure the release of the said R. Steuart, but that the
defendant had not paid the plaintiff the said sum of £500,
or any part thereof.

Fifth plea.—That the said R. Steuart, before and at the
time of making the said promise of the defendant, and
from thence until and at and after the discharge of the
said R. Steuart from custody as aforesaid, was a member of
the House of Commons, and entitled to his privilege of
Parliament, and freedom from arrest and imprisonment
on civil process; and that the procurement of the release
of the said R. Steuart, and his release from custody, were
only on the ground of his being so privileged; that afterwards, and before the commencement of this suit, the said
R. Steuart ceased to be a member of the said House; and
that before the commencement of this suit, he the said
R. Steuart became and was, and still is, liable to be taken
in execution at the suit of the plaintiff: That the said
promise of the defendant in the declaration mentioned,
was and is a promise to answer for the debt and default of
another, and that there was no memorandum or note in
writing of the said promise.—Verification.

Sixth plea.—That the said R. Steuart, at the time of his
becoming indebted to the plaintiff as in the declaration
mentioned, was a member of the Commons House of Parliament, and that whilst he continued such member, the
plaintiff recovered judgment for the said debt, and issued
a writ of capias ad satisfaciendum thereon against him,
under which the said R. Steuart was taken into custody:
That, from the time of contracting the said debt until the
time of the discharge of the said R. Steuart from custody,
he was, as such member, entitled to his discharge from
such arrest and imprisonment; that whilst the said R.
Steuart was so in custody as aforesaid, and during the continuance of the said privilege, the said R. Steuart being
privileged from arrest as aforesaid, it was ordered by the

Hon. Mr. Justice *Patteson* that the said R. Steuart should be discharged out of custody, and he was discharged accordingly; and that, save as aforesaid, there never was any consideration for the making of the said promise of the defendant in the declaration mentioned.—Verification.

To these pleas the plaintiff demurred specially; and assigned for causes, as to the fifth plea, First, that the same was double, and contained two distinct grounds of defence, namely, that the said R. Steuart was entitled to privilege of Parliament and freedom from arrest, that the procurement of his discharge was on that ground only, and that he was liable to be again taken in execution; and also, that the defendant's promise was to answer for the debt and default of another, and that there was no note or memorandum thereof in writing : Secondly, that the plea was an argumentative denial of the plaintiff's procurement of the release of the said R. Steuart, and amounted to non assumpsit. The causes of demurrer to the sixth plea were, that the plea amounted to an argumentative denial of the procurement of the release of R. Steuart, and did not shew with certainty that the plaintiff had not, by his personal labour, procured the discharge of the said R. Steuart, and that the plea amounted to non assumpsit.—Joinder in demurrer.

Byles, in support of the demurrer.—These pleas are bad. With respect to the fifth plea, if the first part of it means that R. Steuart was discharged by reason of his privilege of Parliament, and therefore that the original debt still subsists, that of itself is an answer to the declaration, and the plea is double, because it goes on to set up a second defence also, namely, that the promise is void, because it is not in writing pursuant to the Statute of Frauds. First, the defendant says that there was no consideration for the promise, because the plaintiff has done no more than by law he was bound to do; secondly, he says that the case is within the Statute of Frauds. If the first be an answer to the action, so is the second. But in truth, the first part of the plea affords no answer whatever. The allegation in the declaration is, that in consideration that the plaintiff would *procure* the release of R. Steuart from custody, the defendant promised to pay the £500. That could only be by some application to the Court or a Judge: and there is nothing in the plea to shew that the plaintiff has not incurred expense and trouble in procuring that discharge, or that the defendant has not received a benefit by his interposition. *Procuring,* ex vi termini, imports the doing of something whereby the discharge was facilitated or accelerated; and the plea does not deny that the plaintiff did that. Again, if the party were discharged by his own procurement, the debt continues; but if the plaintiff procured it, then, he being discharged by the act of the plaintiff, and not solely by the act of law, the remedy for the debt is extinguished, and there is a good consideration for the defendant's promise. But supposing the plaintiff has *not* lost his remedy against R. Steuart, then the Statute of Frauds is an answer to the action, and the plea is bad for duplicity.

Secondly, the plea is bad in form, as amounting to an argumentative traverse of the allegation of procurement by the plaintiff, and perhaps also as amounting to the general issue. Under a direct traverse of that allegation, the defendant might have given in evidence that R. S. was entitled to privilege of Parliament, and that he was discharged on that ground alone. Whatever be the sense attributable to the contract between these parties, the plaintiff has averred performance of it: if the defendant says that another sense is to be attributed to it, he ought to have traversed it as alleged.—The sixth plea is bad for the same reason.

Gurney, contrà.—The fifth plea is not bad on the

ground of duplicity. Although each part of it may be in *Exch. of Pleas,* itself a defence, if they constitute parts of another entire 1842. defence, the pleading is not therefore bad. Here the BUTCHER several allegations are constituent parts of one defence. *v.* The answer given by the first part of the plea is not STEUART. merely the discharge of R. Steuart on the ground of privilege, but that he continues liable to be taken in execution. That is stated to shew that the promise of the defendant was not an original one, but was a promise to pay the debt of a third party, and therefore within the Statute of Frauds. It is a necessary inducement to the latter part of the plea, which constitutes the real answer on which the defendant relies. [Lord *Abinger*, C. B.—You say the plea shews that in fact this was the debt of a third person, because the original debtor, having been discharged on the ground of privilege, continues liable to be taken in execution. But is it not to be inferred from the declaration, that his discharge was to be so procured as that the original debt should be destroyed?] It is submitted that there is no such necessary inference, and that the plaintiff would not be bound so to prove at the trial. It would be sufficient for him to shew any procurement; and such, indeed, is the argument on the other side. [Lord *Abinger*, C. B.—Then supposing the construction of the agreement to be that the debt is *not* extinguished, but that the plaintiff may retake his debtor, is not the defendant's promise nudum pactum?] Perhaps so; but the defendant desires to have also the defence to the contract, upon the other construction of it, that even if there was a promise which otherwise would have been binding, he is not liable, because it is void by the Statute of Frauds.

As to the sixth plea, the objection is, that it is an argumentative traverse of the alleged procurement. [*Alderson*, B.—What is it but a circuitous denial of the procurement, concluding with a verification? Lord *Abinger*, C. B.—

Neither does it allege who took out the summons before the judge; it may be that the plaintiff did.]

Byles, in reply.—It is assumed on the other side, that if there be two defences, one of which is pleaded as *inducement* to the other, the plea is not double; but that is not so. Nor is the plea the less double because one of the defences is informally pleaded: *Purssord* v. *Peek* (a). But the substantial objection to this plea is, that it does not shew any absence of consideration. It may be that after his discharge R. Steuart went abroad, or that another privilege supervened: if so, the plaintiff would be much prejudiced. He has parted with his present right of arrest; and the contingency of not retaking the debtor is a sufficient detriment to constitute a good consideration.

Lord ABINGER, C. B.—I think this plea is bad. I entained some doubt at first as to the sufficiency of the consideration, supposing the intention of the agreement to be that the plaintiff should reserve his right of re-arresting the party. But the consideration may be equally good notwithstanding, by the detriment arising to the plaintiff by the suspension of his remedy. If the original debt was not extinguished by the discharge, the plea is double, as containing two entire defences; if it was, the rest of the plea amounts to nothing. As to the sixth plea, that only amounts to a circuitous denial of the discharge by the procurement of the plaintiff.

ALDERSON, B., and GURNEY, B., concurred.

Judgment for the plaintiff.

(a) Antè, 196.

Exch. of Pleas,
1842.

WALKER *v.* ROSTRON.

Jan. 21.

ASSUMPSIT for money had and received, and on an account stated. Plea, non assumpsit. At the trial before Lord *Abinger*, C. B., at the London sittings after Trinity Term, 1841, the following facts appeared:—

This was an action brought by the plaintiff, a manufacturer at Nottingham, to recover from the defendant, who was a partner in a mercantile house, carrying on business at Manchester under the firm of Rostron, Dutton, & Co., and at Rio de Janeiro and Bahia under the firm of Rostron, Hall, & Co., the sum of £1080, with interest, claimed to be due under the following circumstances. The plaintiff had sold goods to one Bull, receiving his acceptances for the price, and transmitted them to the defendant as Bull's agent; and the defendant consigned them to his partners at Rio de Janeiro and Bahia. While the acceptances were outstanding, the plaintiff having doubts as to Bull's solvency, and wishing for further security, it was agreed between the plaintiff, his agent Mr. Moylan, Bull, and a Mr. M'Kinwell, one of the defendant's partners, authorized by the defendant for that purpose, that Bull should write to the defendant the following letter; which was written by him accordingly, and delivered to the defendant:—

Mr. Richard Rostron, 24th October, 1839.

Sir,—Mr. Richard G. Walker, of Nottingham, holding my acceptances for £1100 (say eleven hundred pounds) or thereabouts, for goods consigned by him, on my account, to your firms at Rio de Janeiro and Bahia, I hereby au-

The plaintiff sold goods to B., taking his acceptances for the price, and sent them to the defendant as B.'s agent, who consigned them to his Partners abroad for sale. While the acceptances were running, the plaintiff, doubting B.'s solvency, required further security; whereupon it was agreed between the plaintiff, B., and the defendant, that B. should write and deliver to the defendant a letter authorizing him, out of any remittances he might receive against the net proceeds of the above consignments, to pay the acceptances as they became due, if not honoured by him, B., previously to the receipt of such net proceeds. The letter was accordingly delivered to the defendant, and

he assented to the terms of it. Before the bills were due, B. became bankrupt, and the defendant, having received the net proceeds of the goods, refused to pay any part thereof to the plaintiff, but handed them over to B.'s assignees:—Held, that the plaintiff was entitled to recover the amount of the acceptances from the defendant in an action for money had and received; this being an appropriation irrevocable except by the consent of all parties, for which the existing debt, although not then payable, was a good consideration.

Held, also, that the letter did not require a stamp, either as an inland bill or as an agreement

thorize and direct you, from and out of the remittances that you may receive against net proceeds of any consignments made by me to either of your above firms, subsequent to the 1st of May last, to pay such acceptances upon and as they become due, or afterwards, if previously to the receipt of such net proceeds of such consignments the said bills are not honoured by me.

Yours respectfully,

Signed in the presence of us   ANTHONY BULL.

J. H. M'KINWELL.

W. MOYLAN.

Bull afterwards directed the defendant to pay his own debt out of the residue of the proceeds. One of the acceptances became due on the 17th August 1839, but was renewed by Bull. The next would have been due on the 15th December following. On the 2nd December, however, Bull committed an act of bankruptcy, on which a fiat issued on the 2nd January 1840. The plaintiff took up the bill which fell due on the 15th December. The defendant, having received the proceeds of the consignments in question, and having paid out of them his own demand on Bull, handed over to Bull's assignees, under an indemnity from them, the remainder of the proceeds.

Upon the letter of the 24th October being tendered in evidence by the plaintiff, it was objected that it ought to have borne a stamp, either as an inland bill, within the stat. 55 Geo. 3, c. 184, sched. pt. 1, title ' Inland Bill,' or as an agreement. It was also contended for the defendant, that the order itself, being conditional and contingent in its terms, did not amount to an appropriation, or to an equitable assignment, of any part of the proceeds of the goods; and the cases of *Carvalho* v. *Burn* (a), and *Hutchinson* v. *Heyworth* (b), were cited. The Lord Chief Baron

(a) 4 B. & Ad. 382; 1 Nev. &   Ell. 883; 4 Nev. & M. 889.
M. 700; *S. C.* in error, 1 Ad. &   (b) 9 Ad. & Ell. 375; 1 P. & D. 266

reserved both points, and a verdict was found for the
plaintiff for the amount claimed, the defendant having
leave to move to enter a nonsuit.—In Michaelmas Term,

Thesiger moved accordingly.—He admitted that *Hutchinson* v. *Heyworth* was an authority that the order did not
require an inland bill stamp, but contended that it ought
to have had an agreement stamp; for that unless it
amounted to an agreement whereby the funds of Bull in
the hands of the defendant were bound, the plaintiff could
have no right of action.

PER CURIAM.—This is a mere order, and not a memorandum in which both parties have reduced to writing the
binding terms of their agreement, and which, whether
signed or not, requires a stamp. It is more like a pro-
posal, or a valuation of work done, which, though it be
afterwards assented to by the other party, may be read in
evidence without a stamp. It is in truth a parol agreement so far as respects the defendant. On this point
therefore there will be no rule.

On the other point reserved a rule was granted, against
which

Erle and *Gray* shewed cause in the same term (November 16). It will be contended for the defendant, that,
inasmuch as Bull's acceptances were not due at the time
when the order of the 24th of October was given, there
was no consideration for the giving of it, and therefore the
order was revocable by Bull, and was consequently revoked
by his bankruptcy. No question of *consideration* is raised
in the cases on this subject, an order of this kind being held
to be irrevocable, where the party to whom it is directed
has accepted it, and pledged himself to act upon it. It is
not like the case of an agreement under which a party is
to do more than he was before liable to do, and for which

there must be a consideration: here the acting upon the order could be only carrying into effect that which by a subsisting agreement, by means of the bills, Bull had already contracted to do. If it had been an authority to pay before the bills became due, the case might be different; but, in truth, it is no more than the reiteration of his previous promise on the bills. [Lord *Abinger*, C. B.—That is what they say on the other side; that it is no more than he had before agreed to do, and therefore he might revoke it; and, the bankruptcy having revoked it, it is at an end.] But the defendant has accepted it, and given a pledge to be bound by it. The question arises as to the consideration between the plaintiff and Bull; and that, it is contended, is sufficient, because by the order Bull contracts to do no more than he was already liable to. Where there is a subsisting debt, although not yet payable, the creditor may take a further security, without any other consideration than the existing debt; *Crosby* v. *Crouch* (a). The assent of the party to whom the order is directed is the material fact; after such assent, *he* cannot say that it was without consideration. *Robertson* v. *Fauntleroy* (b) and *Hodgson* v. *Anderson* (c) are authorities for the plaintiff. [*Rolfe*, B.—Those were cases of a debt then due and payable.] The implied undertaking, to pay out of the proceeds, would be a consideration subsisting at the time of the agreement, though not to be performed till afterwards, and would prevent the order from being revocable. [*Parke*, B.—You would contend, that if I owed a debt, to be paid on the 1st January next, and gave an order on my banker to pay it, and on my creditor's going to him he promised to do so, that order would not be afterwards countermandable.] Yes, if the debtor intends that it shall thenceforth be a security to the creditor, as was the case here. Suppose, in consequence of this

(a) 2 Campb. 166; *S. C.* 11 East, 256.
(b) 8 Moore, 10.   (c) 3 B. & Cr. 842; 5 D. & R. 735.

order, the plaintiff had made further advances to Bull, could he afterwards turn round and say that it was revocable for want of consideration? Here the plaintiff did afterwards take up the bill which fell due on the 15th of December; it is sufficient, however, if his position *might* have been altered to his prejudice in consequence of the order. *Gibson* v. *Minet* (a) may be cited on the other side. That was the case of an order given by the plaintiff upon his banker to a third person, directing the banker " to hold over from his private account £400 to the disposal of " the third person. The banker accepted the order, by writing on the debit side of the plaintiff's account that this money was to be held at the disposal of that person; but it was not paid over to him, or appropriated to his credit. There the order was held to be revocable, but that was upon the finding of the jury that it was executory, and had not been acted upon; Lord *Gifford* laying it down, that if it was an absolute order, and accepted as such by the banker, the plaintiff had no right to revoke it. So, in *Williams* v. *Everett* (b), where a party residing abroad remitted a sum of money to the defendants, his bankers, with directions to pay it to the plaintiff, but they *refused* to do so, it was held, on the ground of such non-assent on their part, that they were not liable to the plaintiff in an action for money had and received: but there also the general principle is distinctly stated, that, after an engagement by the remittee, whereby he has appropriated the remittance to the use of the person who is the object of it, he cannot retract his consent, but is bound to hold it for his use. The same principle is recognised in *Hutchinson* v. *Heyworth*. But further, this may be considered as an authority coupled with an interest, and therefore not revocable. *Gaussen* v. *Morton* (c). It may

Exch. of Pleas, 1842.

WALKER
v.
ROSTRON.

(a) 2 Bing. 7; 9 Moore, 31. (b) 14 East, 582.
(c) 10 B. & C. 731.

be said there is no interest because there is no consideration, and therefore that in truth it is the same question in other words. But this is an authority to do an act in which the party, in whose favour it is given, has an interest. It is not like a case where, if the authority be executed, he will not be benefited, and if it remain unexecuted, he is not prejudiced: here it is obvious an interest was intended to pass. Or it may be regarded as an equitable assignment of the specific fund to which it relates—the proceeds of consignments already made—a fund capable of being assigned, and the assignment of which was enforceable in equity, and which is therefore irrevocable. *Crowfoot* v. *Gurney* (a); *Carvalho* v. *Burn* (b). The case last cited was a case of an appropriation of funds to secure the payment of bills not yet due, so that it entirely resembles the present.

Thesiger and *Crompton*, in support of the rule.—The transaction in question amounted merely to an order capable of being revoked by Bull, and therefore revoked in fact by his bankruptcy. In order to render it such an appropriation, or equitable assignment, of the fund, as cannot be revoked, it must appear that there is a binding consideration of some kind between the party giving the order and the party in whose favour it is given; and that is an ingredient in all the cases cited on the other side. Here it is admitted that there was no fresh credit given to Bull, and no fresh duty imposed on him. In *Hutchinson* v. *Heyworth*, the case was put upon the ground that there was a consideration by the forbearance of the bankers towards the party who made the order, and the guarantee given by them to the defendants. In *Hodgson* v. *Anderson*, the order was held to be irrevocable on the ground that the defendant, from whom the debt was due, had pledged himself to pay it to the appointees, and that the plaintiff had

(a) 9 Bing. 372; 2 M. & Scott, 473.   (b) 7 Simons, 109.

received forbearance from the banking company, his credi- *Exch. of Pleas,* tors. So, in *Crowfoot* v. *Gurney*, it was held that there <u>1842.</u> was an equitable assignment, the consideration of which WALKER was the forbearance of the appointee to sue the appointor. ROSTRON. A debt can be well assigned only where there is a binding agreement amongst all the three parties to the transaction, for good consideration, the extinguishment of the original debt being deemed a good consideration. *Wharton* v. *Walker* (a); *Fairlie* v. *Denton* (b). But the mere precedent liability to the debt is only sufficient to ground a promise which is coextensive with, and would arise in law out of, that liability; it is not sufficient to raise any new obligation: *Hopkins* v. *Logan* (c). The only case which resembles this in the circumstance of the bills not being at maturity at the time of the order, is that of *Bailey* v. *Culverwell* (d). The authority of that case has been questioned: there, however, there was a complete transfer *of the goods* by the order, and on that ground the case is distinguishable from the present. Here both parties, after the giving of the order, remained in *statu quo;* no fresh forbearance or credit was given to Bull, nor was any detriment sustained by the plaintiff. But further, there was no appropriation of any *specific part* of the proceeds of the goods to the payment of the acceptances; and that brings the case within the authority of *Burn* v. *Carvalho*, where Lord *Lyndhurst*, C. B., says (e)—" Here is no immediate assignment of any certain or specified amount of property, but at most only an agreement to assign on a contingency, and goods of an uncertain quantity." So here there is no specified amount of property whereon the order is to operate, and there is also a contingency, for the proceeds are not to be paid to the plaintiff, in case Bull should honour his acceptances. It is

(a) 4 B. & Cr. 163; 6 D. & R. 288.
(b) 8 B. & Cr. 395; 2 Man. & R. 353.
(c) 5 M. & W. 241.
(d) 8 B. & Cr. 448; 2 Man. & R.
(e) 1 Ad. & Ell. 894.

said that the assent of the party ordered to pay the money is sufficient to make the transaction binding; but that is not so. Where there is an actual transfer of the goods, so that trover would lie, the case is different; but a gift not perfected by delivery of possession may be revoked, notwithstanding an assent. A *consideration* is also necessary. In *Bradbury* v. *Anderton* (a), where creditors of a trader who had committed a secret act of bankruptcy, procured a person to whom they were indebted to purchase goods of the trader, with whose assent that person credited them in account for the price, it was held that if the appropriation of the money to them was merely in consequence of the direction of the trader, it was revocable, and was revoked by his bankruptcy. The Court there treat it as entirely a question of *contract*. There must be something *in the contract* to make such an order irrevocable—*primâ facie* it is revocable, although it has been assented to by the party on whom it is made. *Gibson* v. *Minet.*

Then it is said that this is an authority coupled with an interest, which therefore could not be revoked. But to make that rule of law applicable, it is necessary that the interest should be in the party to whom the authority is given; as in *Gaussen* v. *Morton*, where it was held that a debtor could not revoke an authority given by him to his creditor to sell his, the debtor's, lands, and pay his own debt out of the proceeds. In the present case, the defendant had no authority to pay his own debt out of this fund, by virtue of the direction given by Bull with the plaintiff's assent; his authority to pay himself was derived out of another instrument.

Neither is this an *equitable assignment*, which a Court of Equity would enforce by compelling an actual assignment. If it be a mere equitable right of lien, that gives the plaintiff no title to recover at law. But further, a binding bar-

(a) 1 C., M. & R. 486.

gain is equally necessary to its operating as an equitable assignment.   [*Parke*, B.—Is not an equitable assignment of a chose in action the same in equity as the assignment of a chattel at law? Then this is the case of a plaintiff suing the party, who has agreed to become his agent for the amount of that equitable lien.]   But to arrive at that conclusion, we have to come round to the agreement of the parties, for which there must be a consideration.— They cited also *Lepard* v. *Vernon*(a).

Exch. of Pleas,
1842.

WALKER
v.
ROSTRON.

Cur. adv. vult.

The judgment of the Court was now delivered by

Lord ABINGER, C. B.—In this case the question arose upon the effect of a written arrangement entered into by the defendant, Mr. Rostron, that he would deliver over to the plaintiff the proceeds of certain consignments that were to come to his hands, the goods being in the possession of two foreign houses, in which he was a partner. This was to be done in order to satisfy certain bills of exchange, accepted by a person of the name of Bull, payable in favour of the plaintiff for goods sold by him, and which Bull had consigned to the defendant's house abroad. The bills of exchange, at the time the alleged appropriation was made, were not due. The circumstances were these: —The defendant, Rostron, was a merchant residing in Manchester, and the plaintiff being the holder of these bills of exchange, and having some doubt of the solvency of Bull, there was an understanding that he was to have some further security. The defendant was aware of this, and directed his partner to go with the plaintiff to Bull, in order to arrange with him the sort of collateral security that the plaintiff was to have for the payment of the bills. The plaintiff went accompanied by his agent, and several

(a) 2 Ves. & B. 51.

suggestions having been made at the meeting by the agent, and not approved of, the gentleman who represented the defendant suggested an expedient which appeared to satisfy all parties; it was arranged that Bull should write the letter on which the action was brought. He accordingly wrote that letter, the particular terms of which it is unnecessary to state,—the result was, that the defendant engaged, on Bull's direction, to pay such proceeds as should come to his hands from the goods consigned, as were necessary to satisfy the bills of exchange, in case they were not paid at maturity. The paper was accordingly handed to him, having been approved of by both parties, and he and his agent undertook to comply with its terms. The remainder of the proceeds was to be applied by the defendant in satisfaction of a debt of his own. Bull eventually, and before the bills became due, became a bankrupt. The defendant, having received the proceeds of the goods from his house abroad, paid out of them what was due to himself from Bull, and then, taking an indemnity from the assignees, paid them the sums that the plaintiff contended ought to have been paid to him. Upon this, the plaintiff brought the present action; and on the trial, I directed the jury that the plaintiff was entitled to the verdict. An objection was taken on the part of the defendant, and was argued before us in the last term, which resolves itself into two points: first, whether there was any good consideration given to Bull, in the letter in question, for his appropriating the proceeds in the manner therein mentioned. Upon consideration, the Court are of opinion that there was a good consideration; for the existence of a debt, although it be not due instanter, is a good consideration; and so it is to take lawful and proper means to provide for payment, even though they be conditional. If we were to hold otherwise, you might deny the consideration for a collateral security for any debt which might not be due at the moment, although it is a very common thing to require and obtain such security. It *Exch. of Pleas,* cannot be doubted that if a man held a bill of exchange, 1842. of which another was the acceptor, and both were to go WALKER together to a banker, who had money of the acceptor's *v.* deposited with him, and it were agreed amongst them that ROSTRON. the banker should hold that money until the bill of exchange should be satisfied, and if not satisfied, that he should pay the bill out of that money, that would constitute a good consideration, and it could not be altered afterwards, except by the consent of all parties. The next objection was, that the letter itself did not bind the defendant; that it was only directory as to what should be done with the proceeds; and that Bull himself, before his bankruptcy, might have altered the appropriation then made. That turns on this question, whether the defendant had accepted it, and bound himself so to appropriate the proceeds. I think there can be no doubt, upon the whole, that the real transaction, and the real object and arrangement of the parties, was this—to apply the proceeds in the hands of the defendant as far as it could be done, the goods being abroad, but the proceeds being destined to come to him; and that he should undertake so to apply them. If that be the case, how could the bankrupt have made any such alteration? He could not alter the direction of the consignments; they were already in the defendant's hands, or in those of his partners abroad, and the proceeds were to come to the defendant. The question is, whether he could authorize the defendant to disregard the arrangement so made, and to pay the proceeds to anybody else. If he could, of course his assignees had the same power. But we are of opinion that neither he nor his assignees could do so. This is a case of a party engaging himself to appropriate the proceeds of the goods according to certain directions of the owner, and appears to us to fall within that class of cases where, when an order has been given to a person who holds goods

Exch. of Pleas,
1842.

WALKER
v.
ROSTRON.

to appropriate them in a particular manner, and he has engaged to do so, none of the parties are at liberty, without the consent of all, to alter that arrangement. We are therefore of opinion, that the acceptance of that arrangement made on the part of the bankrupt was binding on the defendant. The verdict was therefore right, and this rule must be discharged.

Rule discharged.

Jan. 22.

WATKINS *v.* BENSUSAN.

To an action by the indorsee against the acceptor of a bill of exchange, the defendant pleaded, first, that before and at the time of the indorsing of the bill by the drawer, he, the drawer, was indebted to the defendant in a sum of money exceeding the amount of the bill: and that after the bill became due, in order to deprive the defendant of his right of set-off in respect of the debt, he fraudulently indorsed the bill, to enable the plaintiff to sue the defendant on the bill, and without any consideration for the indorsement. The defendant pleaded, secondly, that the drawer, before he indorsed the bill, petitioned for relief under the Insolvent Debtors' Act, whereby the right and title to the bill vested in his assignees :—*Held,* that both were issuable pleas.

ASSUMPSIT by the indorsee against the acceptor of a bill of exchange, in which the declaration alleged, that Thomas Trueman, the drawer, had indorsed the bill to one Bincks, who indorsed to one B. Binckley, who indorsed to the plaintiff. To this declaration the defendant, who was under terms of pleading issuably, pleaded, first, that before and at the time of indorsing the said bill of exchange by the said Thomas Trueman, as in the declaration mentioned, the said Thomas Trueman was and still is indebted to the defendant in the sum of £100 for work and labour, money lent, and on an account stated, payable on request, to an amount exceeding the amount of the said bill of exchange, and of all damages thence resulting:—the plea then went on to allege, that the said Thomas Trueman, whilst the said money was due and unpaid, and after the bill of exchange in the declaration became due, in order to deprive the defendant of his right of set-off in respect of the aforesaid debts, did, in fraud of the defendant, and in collusion with the said Bincks, Binckley, and the plaintiff, indorse the said bill to the said B. Bincks, who indorsed the same to Binckley, who indorsed it to the plaintiff, which said indorsements were the indorsements in the declaration mentioned, in order to enable the plaintiff to sue the defendant on the said bill, without any consideration for the said indorsements, or any of them, and that the plaintiff sued in this action as agent of the said Thomas Trueman, according to such fraud and collusion, and that the money due to the defendant from Trueman still remained unpaid. The defendant also pleaded, that before the commencement of the suit, and the indorsing of the bill, as in the declaration mentioned, the said Thomas Trueman was a prisoner for debt, and whilst holder of the bill, and before the same was indorsed over, applied to the Insolvent Debtors' Court by petition for relief, whereby the right to the said bill vested in his assignees. The plaintiff treated these two pleas as being non-issuable pleas, and signed interlocutory judgment.

Butt, having obtained a rule to set aside this judgment,

Pearson now shewed cause.—These pleas are not issuable. The first plea attempts to affect the plaintiff with the equities between the drawer and acceptor, with which he has nothing to do. In *Burrough* v. *Moss* (a), it was held that although the indorsee of an overdue promissory note is liable, in an action against the maker, to all the equities arising out of the note transaction itself, yet he is not liable to a set-off in respect of a debt due from the indorser to the maker of the note, arising out of collateral matters. That case was confirmed by *Stein* v. *Yglesias* (b), where, in an action by the indorsee against the acceptor of a bill of exchange, the defendant pleaded, that before the indorsement the indorser was indebted to the defendants in a sum of money exceeding the amount of the bill; and it was held

Exch. of Pleas,
1842.

WATKINS
v.
BENSUSAN.

(a) 10 B. & C. 558.   (b) 1 C., M. & R. 565; 3 Dowl. P. C. 252.

rrough v. *Moss*. ... nis is a bad plea, ... effect that the ... and has no right ... so for the pur- ... ght of set-off. ... in effect the ... plaintiffs. ... *Sanger* v. ...

Exch. of Pleas,
1842.

SPENCER *v.* BAROUGH.

Jan. 22.

ASSUMPSIT against the defendant as the maker of a promissory note. Plea, that the defendant did not make the note.—No notice had been given, pursuant to the rule of Hilary Term, 4 Will. 4, s. 20, to admit the signature; the reason for which omission was, that the defendant's attorney having been applied to to admit it, he refused to do so, saying that the bill was a forgery. The cause having been tried, and a verdict found for the plaintiff, the Master, on taxation, refused to allow the costs of proving the signature.

S. Temple now moved to review the taxation. — The rule was never intended to apply to cases where the validity of the document was put in issue on the record, and where there had been a positive refusal by the defendant to admit the signature on the ground that the instrument was a forgery. Under the stat. 22 & 23 Car. 2, c. 136, a judge's certificate to entitle the plaintiff to costs was held unnecessary where a battery was admitted on the record.

ALDERSON, B.—The rule is imperative, and applies to all cases, whether the document proposed to be given in evidence is put in issue on the record or not. In either case the plaintiff is obliged to give the defendant notice, in order to give him an opportunity of admitting it. It is every day's practice. If we were once to accede to applications of this nature, it would be urged as an excuse in every case for non-compliance with the rule by the attorney of the opposite party, that the application to admit would not be complied with.

A party who proposes to adduce in evidence a document at the trial, is bound in every case, in order to entitle himself to the costs of proving it, to give a notice to admit, under R. 20 of H. T. 4 Will. 4, to afford the other party an opportunity of admitting it, notwithstanding the document is put in issue on the pleadings, and although, on application to the attorney on the other side, he had refused to make the admission on the ground that the document was a forgery.

Lord ABINGER, C. B., and GURNEY, B., concurred.

Rule refused (a).

(a) See *Rutter* v. *Chapman*, 8 M. & W. 388.

Jan. 27.

Doe d. WALKER v. ROE.

It is not too late to move for judgment against the casual ejector, in the term following that in which the tenants have had notice to appear; whether the cause be a town or country cause.

IN this case *Hayes* moved for judgment against the casual ejector. It appeared that the venue was laid in Middlesex, and the notice was to appear in last term.—The officers of the Court object that the motion in the present term is too late, and have refused to draw up the rule. Upon this point the decisions are at variance. In *Doe* d. *Greaves* v. *Roe* (a), *Coleridge*, J., held that the practice of allowing judgment to be signed against the casual ejector in the following term, where the term in which the appearance is required has elapsed before service has been effected, applies only to country causes: whilst in *Doe* d. *Wilson* v. *Roe* (b), the Court of Common Pleas, under similar circumstances, granted a rule nisi, to be served on the tenant. This latter case was a decision of the full Court, the former being that of a single judge only. In *Doe* d. *Greaves* v. *Roe*, the cases of *Doe* v. *Roe* (c) and *Doe* v. *Roe* (d) were cited, in which the rule laid down by the Court was, that if only one term was allowed to elapse after the service the Court would grant the rule; but it does not appear from the report whether those were town or country causes.

PARKE, B.—There is certainly a discrepancy between the practice of the Common Pleas and the Queen's Bench on this point; but there does not appear to be any satisfac-

(a) 4 Dowl. P. C. 88.   (c) 1 Dowl. P. C. 495.
(b) 4 Dowl. P. C. 124.   (d) 2 Dowl. P. C. 196.

tory reason why parties, in cases of this nature, should be put to the trouble of bringing a fresh ejectment; in addition to which, the case in the Common Pleas was a decision of the full Court. You may therefore take your rule to shew cause, to be served on the tenant in possession.

ALDERSON, B.—In addition to what has been said, we must remember that the present mode of proceeding is the cheapest, and we ought therefore to abide by it.

Rule accordingly.

MORGAN *v.* SMITH.

THIS cause was referred to arbitration by order of Nisi Prius, " the costs of the cause to abide the event, and the costs of the reference and award to be in the discretion of the arbitrator, who shall ascertain the same." The arbitrator by his award directed that the costs of the reference and award should be paid by the defendant; but he omitted to ascertain the amount of the costs, and they were subsequently taxed by the Master.

E. V. Williams had obtained a rule to shew cause why the award should not be set aside on the above ground, contending that the arbitrator alone had authority to determine the amount of those costs.

W. M. James shewed cause.—The terms of the submission were not intended to oust the Court of its jurisdiction to tax the costs by its proper officer. This being an order of Nisi Prius made a rule of Court, the costs must be ascertained by the Master. In *Fox* v. *Smith* (a), which was debt on an administration bond, the defendant pleaded

By the terms of an order of reference at Nisi Prius, the costs of the cause were to abide the event, " the costs of the reference and award to be in the arbitrator, who shall ascertain the same:"—Held, that the arbitrator was bound to ascertain and determine the costs of the reference and award.

(a) 2 Wils. 267.

no award, and the plaintiff replied setting out the award, by which it was ordered that the defendant should pay the plaintiff a certain sum, " and all such costs, charges, and expenses, as the plaintiff had been put to in a certain cause depending between the parties;" it was objected on the part of the defendant, that no certain costs, charges, and expenses, were set down and averred : but the Chief Justice said, " A benign construction of awards hath taken place in modern times, though formerly courts of justice looked nicely and critically into them; we will intend that by costs, charges, and expenses, are meant such costs, &c., as Courts will take notice of by their officer; it might be said that all costs between the attorney and client are meant thereby, but we will take the words of the arbitrators to mean the same as if they had been the words of the Court." In *Beale* v. *Beale* (a), an award to pay the charges in a certain suit was held good, " for they are certain enough when the attorney hath made a bill of charges." In *Hanson* v. *Liversedge* (b), the award was that " the defendant should pay to the plaintiff twelve guineas, and all such monies as he had expended circa prosecutionem placiti prædicti; it was objected that it was not sufficient to award payment of the charges in such a suit, it being altogether uncertain what the sum would be; but the Court held that the award was good; "for it may be easily reduced to a certainty when it is made appear what was laid out in that suit." The same language was used in a recent case, *Cargey* v. *Aitcheson* (c), where *Bayley*, J., says, " The sum to be paid might be ascertained either by fixing it in the award, or referring it to an officer, whose duty it is to say what shall be the whole sum paid for costs." These authorities shew that the arbitrator does ascertain the costs, when he leaves their amount to be determined by the officer of the Court. [*Alderson*, B.—The Master is

---

(a) Cro. Car. 383.　　　(b) 2 Ventr. 242.　　　(c) 2 B. & Cr. 174.

to ascertain the costs of the cause, but the arbitrator is to *Exch. of Pleas,* ascertain the costs of the reference. *Parke*, B.—The 1842. parties might have thought that the arbitrator would form MORGAN a better judgment of their amount than the Master.] It *v.* is conceded, that if the arbitrator direct a party to pay SMITH. only a portion of the costs, he should name the amount; but where he directs a party to pay the whole, it is enough to order costs to be paid, which will afterwards be taxed by the Master. At all events, the award is not bad in toto, but only as to so much as respects the costs.

E. V. Williams, in support of the rule, was stopped by the Court.

Lord ABINGER, C. B.—It is perfectly clear, in my opinion, that by the terms of this submission the arbitrator is to ascertain the costs. When the words of a document are clear, it is of no avail to argue that the party meant the arbitrator to do what he has done, and to quote authorities. Words must be construed according to their plain grammatical meaning. I am of opinion that these costs ought to have been ascertained by the arbitrator; but if the party is willing to waive them, I think we ought not to disturb the remainder of the award. The award will then be set aside so far as regards the costs of the reference, but will stand as to the rest.

PARKE, B., and ALDERSON, B., concurred.

James consented to waive the costs, and a rule was granted to reduce the judgment by the amount of the costs of the reference.

suggestions having been made at the meeting by the agent, and not approved of, the gentleman who represented the defendant suggested an expedient which appeared to satisfy all parties; it was arranged that Bull should write the letter on which the action was brought. He accordingly wrote that letter, the particular terms of which it is unnecessary to state,—the result was, that the defendant engaged, on Bull's direction, to pay such proceeds as should come to his hands from the goods consigned, as were necessary to satisfy the bills of exchange, in case they were not paid at maturity. The paper was accordingly handed to him, having been approved of by both parties, and he and his agent undertook to comply with its terms. The remainder of the proceeds was to be applied by the defendant in satisfaction of a debt of his own. Bull eventually, and before the bills became due, became a bankrupt. The defendant, having received the proceeds of the goods from his house abroad, paid out of them what was due to himself from Bull, and then, taking an indemnity from the assignees, paid them the sums that the plaintiff contended ought to have been paid to him. Upon this, the plaintiff brought the present action; and on the trial, I directed the jury that the plaintiff was entitled to the verdict. An objection was taken on the part of the defendant, and was argued before us in the last term, which resolves itself into two points: first, whether there was any good consideration given to Bull, in the letter in question, for his appropriating the proceeds in the manner therein mentioned. Upon consideration, the Court are of opinion that there was a good consideration; for the existence of a debt, although it be not due instanter, is a good consideration; and so it is to take lawful and proper means to provide for payment, even though they be conditional. If we were to hold otherwise, you might deny the consideration for a collateral security for any debt which might not be due at the moment, although it is a very common thing to require and obtain such security. It cannot be doubted that if a man held a bill of exchange, of which another was the acceptor, and both were to go together to a banker, who had money of the acceptor's deposited with him, and it were agreed amongst them that the banker should hold that money until the bill of exchange should be satisfied, and if not satisfied, that he should pay the bill out of that money, that would constitute a good consideration, and it could not be altered afterwards, except by the consent of all parties. The next objection was, that the letter itself did not bind the defendant; that it was only directory as to what should be done with the proceeds; and that Bull himself, before his bankruptcy, might have altered the appropriation then made. That turns on this question, whether the defendant had accepted it, and bound himself so to appropriate the proceeds. I think there can be no doubt, upon the whole, that the real transaction, and the real object and arrangement of the parties, was this—to apply the proceeds in the hands of the defendant as far as it could be done, the goods being abroad, but the proceeds being destined to come to him; and that he should undertake so to apply them. If that be the case, how could the bankrupt have made any such alteration? He could not alter the direction of the consignments; they were already in the defendant's hands, or in those of his partners abroad, and the proceeds were to come to the defendant. The question is, whether he could authorize the defendant to disregard the arrangement so made, and to pay the proceeds to anybody else. If he could, of course his assignees had the same power. But we are of opinion that neither he nor his assignees could do so. This is a case of a party engaging himself to appropriate the proceeds of the goods according to certain directions of the owner, and appears to us to fall within that class of cases where, when an order has been given to a person who holds goods

" that no tenant or lessee shall recover in any action for
any such unlawful act or irregularity as aforesaid, if tender
of amends hath been made by the party or parties distraining, his, her, or their agent or agents, before such
action brought." This case is not within that section,
as there is no tender before, but the money is paid into
Court after, action brought. Then the 31st sect. enacts,
" that in all actions of trespass or upon the case, to be
brought against any person entitled to rents or services of
any kind, his bailiff or receiver, or other person, relating to
any entry, by virtue of this act or otherwise, upon the
premises chargeable with such rents or services, or to any
distress or seizure, sale or disposal of any goods or chattels
thereupon, it shall be lawful for the defendant in such actions to plead the general issue, and give the special matter
in evidence, any law or usage to the contrary notwithstanding: and in case the plaintiff in such action shall
become nonsuit, discontinue his action, or have judgment
against him, the defendant shall recover double costs."
That applies to cases where the plaintiff had no good cause
of action at the time of the action being brought; but
here the defendant, by paying money into Court, admits
that the plaintiff had a good cause of action. It is clear
the statute was only intended to apply to cases where the
defendant has judgment upon the whole cause of action;
but here he has only judgment on the issue that the plaintiff has not sustained damage to a greater extent than the
sum paid into Court.

R. V. Richards, in support of the rule.—Under the old
law, before the new rules, a defendant, by paying money
into Court, when tendered before action, admitted a cause of
action, as much as he does now since the new rules. After
the money is paid into court, the action goes on for the
excess, and is nothing less than a new cause of action; and
the defendant, obtaining judgment, is entitled to double

costs. Suppose the plaintiff fails for want of proving the introductory averments in the declaration, the defendant would be entitled to judgment, and to his double costs. The payment of money into Court cannot affect his right to them. In all cases where the defendant obtains judgment, he is entitled to double costs under the statute.

Lord ABINGER, C. B.—In order to have the benefit of the 11 Geo. 2, c. 19, it appears to me that the defendant ought to shew that he tendered sufficient amends before action brought, or that the plaintiff had no cause of action, which has not been done in the present case.

PARKE, B.—The sole question is, whether the rule of Court, which says, that in the event of the issue being found for the defendant, he shall be entitled to judgment and his costs of suit, means, that the defendant shall have judgment for costs under the statute, or whether it means simply, that as the payment into Court is a proceeding in the suit, the defendant is to have only his ordinary costs. My impression is, that it means the ordinary costs of suit.

ALDERSON, B.—Under the law as it stood after the passing of the 11 Geo. 2, c. 19, the defendant in this case would not have been entitled to double costs, but on the contrary, would have had to pay the plaintiff's costs. Then the 3 & 4 Will. 4 is passed, and a rule is made in pursuance of it, which says, that if the plaintiff go on after money is paid into Court, to recover further damages, and fails, he shall pay the defendant's costs; that means, ordinary costs of suit.

Rule discharged.

Exch. of Pleas,
1842.

HANDCOCK
v.
FOULKES.

Exch. of Pleas,
1842.

Jan. 26.

NEWTON *v.* SCOTT.

A landlord dis-
trained the
goods of A. on
his tenant's
premises, for
rent; the ten-
ant afterwards
became bank-
rupt, and ob-
tained his cer-
tificate:—*Held*,
that the certifi-
cate did not
operate as a re-
lease of the
rent, and there-
fore that the
landlord had a
right, in reple-
vin at the suit
of A., to avow
for a return of
the goods.

REPLEVIN.—The defendant made cognizance as bailiff of T. Berry, and justified the taking for a quarter's rent due from one J. Warren as tenant to Berry of the dwelling-house in which, &c. Plea in bar, setting forth that Warren had become bankrupt, and obtained his certificate; and alleging, that the said arrears of rent became due to the said T. Berry before Warren became a bankrupt. Re-plication, that the defendant took the said goods before the said certificate in the said plea mentioned was signed and allowed, to wit, on &c.

Special demurrer, assigning the following amongst other causes:—That the said rent was due before the bankruptcy, and was a debt provable under the fiat, and one from which Warren was absolutely discharged by his certificate: that neither the said T. Berry, nor the de-fendant as his bailiff, ought to have judgment to recover the said arrears of rent; the effect of the return of the goods, and of the judgment, being to compel Warren to pay a debt from which he had been discharged, and which he had been deprived of the means of paying, by the ap-pointment of assignees under the fiat, and the vesting of his estate and effects in them.—Joinder in demurrer.

The following point was stated for argument on the part of the defendant:—That it was no plea, in an action of replevin, that the tenant, having become a bankrupt, had, since the distress, obtained a certificate of conformity under the Bankrupt Acts; and that the rent accrued due before the bankruptcy, and the legal lien upon the goods under the distress was not discharged by such cer-tificate.

R. V. Richards, in support of the demurrer.—The ques-tion in this case is, whether the discharge of Warren, the

tenant, under his bankruptcy, does not also operate to discharge the liability of the plaintiff, whose goods have been
distrained on Warren's premises for arrears of rent which
became due before the bankruptcy. The effect of the
bankruptcy was, that the rent was no longer due from
Warren, and therefore the landlord could not distrain for
it. [*Parke*, B.—The rent was due until the certificate,
which was not until after the distress.] It is *the bankruptcy* which constitutes the discharge; the certificate is
no more than the evidence of conformity under the bankruptcy, and when obtained, is evidence by relation to the
bankruptcy. [*Parke*, B.—But in the mean time the distress was lawful. The landlord distrains, having at the
time a clear right to do so; then the plaintiff wrongfully
replevies the goods : could he thereby prevent the landlord
from proceeding to a sale of the goods so distrained?]
The defendant might perhaps have *justified* the taking, but
he could not avow for a return of the goods. The remedy
by distress is only a process whereby the lord compels the
performance of personal services or the payment of rent;
and the only effect of a replevin, and of a judgment pro
retorno habendo, is that the lord holds the goods irreple-
viable, until the tenant performs the service or renders
the rent : and here the tenant was discharged of the rent
by the bankruptcy. [*Parke*, B.—The tenant is personally
discharged by the certificate, but the debt is not released
thereby : and all collateral securities remain in force notwithstanding the bankruptcy.] That which exonerates
the tenant from payment of the rent must exonerate him
also from that which is merely a process for obtaining it.
At common law, the lord has no power to use or sell goods
distrained for rent, and if he does so he is a trespasser ab
initio. They are in no way convertible into the amount of
rent. The proper course in such a case is to justify, and
shew that the distress was lawful at the time, although by
matter subsequent the defendant is prevented from having

a return: *Camplin* v. *Baker* (a). [*Parke*, B.—Your argument would have great weight if the certificate were a release of the debt; but it is not. The certificate does not extinguish the landlord's remedies against collateral parties.] It is not necessary to shew that it operates as a release of the debt; if the principal be discharged from the debt, the landlord surely cannot indirectly make a third party liable for it. An avowry is in effect a declaration in debt for the rent; and here it is clear debt would not lie for the rent. The distress does not amount to a *security*—there is no lien; it is merely a process for compelling payment of the rent by the tenant. Then, when his person and property have been discharged by the certificate, can the landlord take the goods of a third party, to hold them till payment of that debt which the law has said he is not bound to pay?—He cited *Bradyll* v. *Ball* (b). [*Parke*, B.—Nothing turned upon the effect of the certificate in that case: it merely decides that the landlord has no lien on the goods distrained; and he could not have a return, because the assignees of the tenant had sold the goods; but he would not lose his rent, because he would have a right to proceed against the sureties on the replevin bond.]

Martin, contrà, was stopped by the Court.

Lord ABINGER, C. B.—This case turns altogether on the question, whether the certificate obtained by a bankrupt tenant amounts to a *release* of the rent. If it had that effect, there would be great weight in Mr. *Richards's* argument, that the landlord, the certificate having released the rent, has lost his collateral remedy against the goods. But a certificate does not amount to a release, although in certain cases it may prevent the creditor from proceeding against

(a) Lutw. 1139.   (b) 1 Bro. Ch. C. 427.

the goods of the bankrupt. Here the landlord was entitled

to his distress, and the goods were wrongfully replevied :
the question is, whether he is entitled to have a return.
The general rule is, that where the distress is lawful, and
the landlord is entitled to a return, an avowry may be
made ; and that is the case here, for the landlord is entitled
to have the goods returned, the rent not being released.
It is not like the case of *Bradyll* v. *Ball :* there the landlord could not have a return, because the property in the
goods had passed to the assignees, and he had no lien upon
them.

PARKE, B.—I entirely agree. The sole question is,
whether the certificate amounts to a release of the debt.
If it had that effect, the plea, although no answer to a
justification of the distress, would be a good answer to an
avowry for a return. But the only effect of the certificate
is to discharge the person and goods of the bankrupt ; it
is no release of collateral remedies. Let us then consider
what is the nature of the landlord's remedy by distress.
It gives him no *lien*, because the goods are in the custody
of the law ; therefore the case of *Bradyll* v. *Ball* was
rightly decided ; but he has a right to enforce the payment
of the rent through the medium of the goods distrained ;
and, as the rent is not released by the certificate, he still
retains the right to work out the payment of it by means
of those goods. The plea in bar is therefore bad, and our
judgment must be for the defendant.

ALDERSON, B., concurred.

Judgment for the defendant.

CHRISTY *v.* TANCRED & THOMPSON.

Where pre-
mises are let
for a certain
term to A. and
B., and A.
holds over after
the expiration
of the term,
with B.'s as-
sent, both are
liable in an ac-
tion for use and
occupation, for
so long as A.
continues ac-
tually to occu-
py, but no
longer.

Quære, whe-
ther both are so
liable where A.
holds over with-
out B.'s con-
sent.

A judgment
obtained by A.
in an action of
use and occu-
pation, against
B. and C., is
no evidence to
charge B. in a
subsequent ac-
tion brought by
A. against him
alone, for the
use and occu-
pation of the
same premises
for a subse-
quent period.

THIS was an action of assumpsit, commenced on the
21st of December, 1840, to recover the sum of 498*l.* 13*s.* 8*d.*
The declaration contained an indebitatus count for use
and occupation, a count for money paid by the plaintiff
for the use of the defendants, and for money found to be
due on account stated. The defendants severally pleaded
non assumpsit, upon which issue was joined. The cause
came on to be tried before Lord *Abinger,* C. B., at the
sittings for London after Hilary Term, 1841, when a
verdict was found for the plaintiff, damages 498*l.* 13*s.* 8*d.*,
subject to the opinion of the Court upon the following
case, with liberty for either party to turn it into a special
verdict.

By articles of agreement, bearing date the 12th July,
A. D. 1838, and purporting to be made between the
plaintiff of the one part, and Sir James Douglas Hamilton
Hay, Bart., Sir John Ross, Knt., Alexander Finlay, Au-
gustus Warren Payne, the above-named defendants Charles
Tancred and Charles Thompson, and Thomas Tisdall,
Calder Campbell, Cay Lewis, and Christian Hesse, of the
other part, which said articles of agreement were signed
by all the parties thereto except the said Augustus Warren
Payne and Thomas Tisdall, who did not sign the same,
the plaintiff agreed to let unto the said Sir J. D. H. Hay,
Sir J. Ross, A. Finlay, A. W. Payne, the defendants
Charles Tancred and Charles Thompson, and T. Tisdall,
C. Campbell, C. Lewis, and C. Hesse, and the said parties
agreed to take from the plaintiff, the premises in question,
for the term of one year, to be computed from the 24th
June then last, at the rent of £420; such rent to be
payable quarterly, on the 29th September, the 25th of
December, the 25th of March, and the 24th of June, then
next ensuing, the first of such payments to be made on the

29th of September then next ensuing. At the time of the

making of the above agreement, the defendants, and all the other parties to the agreement, except the plaintiff, were provisional directors of a joint-stock banking company called "The London and Dublin Trades Banking Company." It appeared in evidence that the defendant Tancred, on the 17th of April, 1838, applied for and obtained from the secretary of the company a certificate in the following form :—

"LONDON AND DUBLIN TRADES BANK.
"*London, April 17th,* 1838.

"This is to certify, that Charles Tancred, Esq., will be entitled to five shares of £10 each in the London and Dublin Trades Bank, (upon which £1 per share has been paid), on his signing the deed of settlement, and conforming to the regulations of the company.

"J. T. SCOTT,
"THOMAS TISDALL, } Provisional Directors.
"FREDERICK EDGELL, Secretary."

The defendant Tancred paid £5 deposit on obtaining the said certificate. The defendant Thompson also, in like manner, applied for and obtained a similar certificate, and paid a deposit thereon. But neither of the defendants ever signed the deed of settlement, nor was the same signed by any one.

Shortly after the date of the above agreement, viz. on the 19th of July, 1838, the defendants and the said Sir J. D. H. Hay, Sir J. Ross, A. Finlay, C. Campbell, C. Lewis, and C. Hesse, were let into possession of the said premises by the plaintiff under the above agreement, and occupied the same for the purposes of the said banking company.

The defendant Tancred ceased to be a director in January, A. D. 1839. After the defendant Tancred retired, some new directors were appointed.

The premises were not delivered up to the plaintiff on the 24th of June, 1839, but continued to be occupied up to the 7th of November, 1839, by the said banking company, of which the defendant Charles Thompson continued up to that time a director. The rent was paid under the above agreement up to the 25th March, 1839.

The plaintiff, on the 21st November, 1839, commenced an action of assumpsit against the above-named defendants, and A. Finlay, C. Campbell, C. Lewis, C. Hesse, and Sir J. D. H. Hay. The plaintiff's particulars stated, that the action was brought to recover the sum of £210, due for half-a-year's rent, from the 25th March, 1839, to the 29th of September in the same year, of certain premises occupied by the defendants, and 5*l.* 11*s.* 4*d.* for insurance premiums. The plaintiff recovered a general verdict, and judgment was entered up thereon for £110, in addition to the sum of 110*l.* 11*s.* 4*d.*, paid into Court by the defendant Tancred. The judgment in such action was to be referred to, if necessary, and to be considered part of the case, subject to any objection as to its admissibility in evidence.

Public notice was given, on the 7th of November, A.D. 1839, that the said banking company had stopped payment. On the 7th of December, 1839, Frederick Edgell, who had been secretary to the banking company, tendered to the plaintiff, unconditionally, the key of the premises in question. The plaintiff referred the said F. Edgell to Mr. Murray, his solicitor, and the attorney in the previous action. Mr. Edgell subsequently, on the 9th of December, wrote to Mr. Murray, who, upon the representation of the said F. Edgell that he came from a committee of shareholders of the said banking company, refused to accept the key of the premises, until the said F. Edgell should procure an authority for giving up the same from the defendants and the other parties who, by the articles of agreement, had originally taken the said premises from

the plaintiff. Mr. Edgell then tendered the key unconditionally to the said Mr. Murray, who then refused to
receive it. The defendant Thompson was a member of
the said committee of shareholders, and he was one of the
persons who authorized the tender of the key, but his name
was not mentioned to Mr. Murray. On the 24th December, 1839, the said F. Edgell packed up the key in a
parcel, and addressed it to the plaintiff, and sent it to the
plaintiff's house by a porter, who left it there on the same
day.

The question for the opinion of the Court is, whether
the plaintiff is entitled to recover for the use and occupation of the premises from the 29th of September, 1839, to
the 30th of November, 1840, or any and what portion of that
period. If the Court should be of opinion that the plaintiff
was entitled to recover for the whole or any portion of that
period, a verdict was to be entered for him, with damages,
to be calculated at the rate of 427*l*. 8*s*. 6*d*. a year, for such
period as the Court might think him entitled to recover,
and costs, 40*s*. But if the Court should be of opinion
that the plaintiff was not entitled to recover from the defendants for any part of the said period, then a nonsuit
was to be entered.

R. V. Richards, for the plaintiff.—The defendants are
not charged in the character of *tenants*, but for the use and
occupation of the premises : and that they did so occupy,
the judgment in the former action against them and other
co-defendants (*a*) is conclusive evidence. In the course of
the argument in that case, *Parke*, B., says—" Suppose there
had been no negotiation between the parties, and some of
the defendants had continued to occupy, they would all
have remained liable. It is their duty, at the end of the
term, to give up the tenancy ; if by themselves, or by sub-

(*a*) *Christy* v. *Tancred*, 7 M. & W. 127.

tenants, or joint-tenants, they remain in, they are liable as holding over." In the present case, therefore, the question will mainly resolve itself into one of fact, when the possession was given up to the plaintiff. [*Parke*, B.—Is the judgment in the former action evidence in this? the parties are constituted differently.] There were more defendants in that action than in this, including these two defendants, who therefore are liable to the effect of that judgment. In *Blakemore* v. *Glamorganshire Canal Co.* (a), it was held that a verdict recovered for the same cause of action by one of the then plaintiffs, Blakemore, against the same defendants, was evidence for both the plaintiffs in that action. [*Parke*, B.—If the parties in the former action and in this had been the same, a judgment obtained against the former would be evidence against the latter : but there is no authority that a judgment against A. & B. jointly is evidence in an action against A. alone, because it may have proceeded on the admission of B., which might or might not be evidence against A. according to circumstances. In *Blakemore* v. *The Glamorganshire Canal Co.*, the other plaintiff claimed under Mr. Blakemore.] It is submitted that it is evidence to shew that these two defendants and others paid rent for the premises up to a certain time.

The main point however is, when the possession was given up. The onus of shewing that is upon the tenant. As to the rent from the 29th September to the 7th Dec. 1839, there can be no question. Then the tender of the key on that day, not being shewn to have been made on behalf of these defendants, did not amount to a surrender. The plaintiff had nothing to do with the "committee of shareholders." [*Parke*, B.—The case does not state in terms that the committee were the persons who carried on the business of the bank on the premises.] Neither

(a) 2 C., M. & R. 133.

did the subsequent sending of the key to the plaintiff's
house, without proof of its having reached him, constitute a delivery of possession. *Harland* v. *Bromley* (a) is in
point.

Kelly, contrà.—The defendants must be jointly liable or
neither. This is not an action *on a demise,* or on an agreement for a continuing tenancy, but for use and occupation.
Now, one of these defendants, Tancred, has never actually
or constructively occupied during the period comprised in
the particulars. It was the *Company* who actually occupied, of which it does not appear that he had ever become
a member. [*Parke,* B.—The case finds that he entered on
the premises, and occupied them for the purposes of the
Banking Company.] He never became a complete partner, and before the 24th June, 1839, his connexion with
the Company ceased altogether. Now, to charge a party
in an action for use and occupation, one of three things
must be proved : either, 1st, that he was actually a tenant
under a demise, not under seal; or, 2nd, that he actually
occupied; or, 3rd, that there has been an occupation by
some other parties standing in such a relation to him that
their occupation is his, and he is personally liable for it.
The present case must be brought into the last class, if
into any. But in order to do that, it must appear that the
occupation was by some person who could reasonably be
said to occupy at the instance and request of the defendant. The decision in the former case of *Christy* v. *Tancred* might perhaps be questioned in point of law; but it is
distinguishable from the present. [*Parke,* B.—The question whether Tancred continued a partner is one which
should have been found by the jury. There is ample
evidence that he acted as a partner, although the terms of
the original contract were not complied with.] If it was

(a) 1 Stark. Rep. 455.

necessary to shew him to have been a partner in fact, the plaintiff should have had that fact found by the jury, and introduced into the case. If it be a question of law, then it is contended that he was not a partner, because the case only states him to have been a provisional director, which he ceased to be before the occupation began for which this action is brought.

But it is said, that where there is a lease to two or more persons for a term certain, it is the duty of each and all of them to deliver up the possession at the end of the term, and that if one of them hold over, even without the concurrence or against the will of the others, all remain liable. But it is submitted that such is not the law. It may be conceded, that where parties refuse to give up possession at the end of the term, they would be liable in a special action on the case for damages in not delivering up possession: and it is reasonable that such should be the remedy. It may not be in their physical power to deliver up the possession: for instance, an under-tenant may refuse to go out. [*Parke*, B.—Your argument is, that though there may be an action against all on their covenant, the landlord can only treat those who remain in as trespassers or as tenants.] Yes: he recovers against *all* the damages proportionable to his real injury, viz. the value of the land while he is so kept out of possession : but the damages ought to be limited to that, and the parties ought not to be made tenants against their will. [Lord *Abinger*, C. B.—The rest of the company came in with the consent of Tancred, and have had the enjoyment of the premises taken by him; must they not be taken to be his tenants?] But not only has he ceased to be a partner, but his term has ceased. As to the period between the end of June and the 7th December, the question is, whether the possession of the Banking Company was in law the possession of the defendant Tancred. Upon that point the former case of *Christy* v. *Tancred* is certainly a direct

authority; but the Court is called upon to review that
decision. *Harding* v. *Crethorne* (a) is distinguishable, because there the holding over was by an under-tenant of
the original lessee.   But this is not the case of an *under-*
tenancy.   The Company did not come in *under* Tancred:
they were let into possession by the plaintiff himself.   The
case of a co-tenant is very different from that of an under-
tenant: the party has no control over his co-tenant, who
may continue to occupy against his will.   And in the case
of a term which expires of itself by effluxion of time, it is
not necessary for him, as against the co-tenant, to give
notice to quit, or to give notice that the other party
occupies without his consent. [Lord *Abinger*, C. B.—
Are not *both* bound to give up possession? if they do not,
what becomes of the premises?]   The relation of tenancy
cannot continue, because it is at an end by the expiration
of the lease; but the landlord has a right to treat the continuing party as a trespasser; or, by virtue of a new contract with him, as a tenant; but he has no right to treat
as a tenant the party who has ceased to occupy, and he
does not remain liable merely because he cannot give up
the premises.   In *Hirst* v. *Horn* (b), which was an action
for double rent against two co-tenants for holding over,
one only having actually occupied, *Alderson*, B., says—" I
do not, as at present advised, entirely accede to the doctrine
that one tenant is necessarily bound by the wilful holding
over of his co-tenant."   *Nation* v. *Tozer* (c) was an action
for use and occupation against two persons who were executors of a deceased tenant for years, but one of whom only
had entered and taken possession ; and it was held that
the action could not be maintained. *Parke*, B., there says—
" Such enjoyment is not by law the possession and enjoyment by both, and it does not render both chargeable to
the lessor, to pay a compensation to him for it, as joint occu-

Exch. of Pleas,
1842.

CHRISTY
v.
TANCRED.

(a) 1 Esp. 57.   (b) 6 M. & W. 393.   (c) 1 C., M. & R. 172.

piers in their own right. But in order to support this action for use and occupation, it is necessary that the land should have been occupied by the defendant, *his agents or under-tenants,* during the term for which the compensation is claimed for use and occupation." Now it cannot be said that the implied relation of co-tenants is that one shall be the agent of another to this extent. [*Parke,* B. —Your argument would be more forcible in an action of trespass, but I do not say that it has not made considerable impression on my mind. This question, however, arises only in case the defendant Tancred did not continue a partner in the banking business; and although the case is defective on that point, there is ample evidence for a jury that he did so continue.]

Lord ABINGER, C. B.—I am of opinion that, upon the facts stated in this case, the plaintiff is entitled to our judgment for the amount of that portion of the rent which accrued due between the 29th of September and the 7th of December, 1839. With respect to the question intended to be raised by Mr. *Kelly,* I entirely agree with the doctrine laid down by Lord *Kenyon,* that the landlord is entitled to treat a lessee, who has not given up the possession at the end of the term, as still occupying by the party who has come in through his instrumentality : and I think we cannot escape from the conclusion, that here the defendant Thompson continued in by the assent of Tancred. It is true the latter had ceased to be a director, but there is nothing to shew that he was not a partner, and that he did not, as such, assent to the premises being still occupied by the Company, for the benefit of all who held shares. It cannot be assumed, until the contrary appears, that he meant to give up the possession, and that the other parties were holding over against his will. Where two persons become parties to a lease, the landlord is entitled to hold both of them to all the obligations of the lease, and where one refuses to give up possession, he may hold both liable. It is said the landlord may bring an ejectment; but he is not bound to do so. The case of two tenants is a stronger one than that of a tenant and an under-tenant; both in effect hold over till both deliver up possession; the landlord is therefore entitled to his remedy against both. On the whole, I think it sufficiently appears that the other parties held over with the consent of Tancred: he gave no notice of his dissent: therefore he continued liable as long as the others did, that is, as long as they actually occupied.

PARKE, B.—I also think that the plaintiff is entitled to recover a compensation for the use and occupation of the premises during the period of actual occupation by the banking company; viz., from the 29th of September to the 7th of December, 1839. If this had been the case where, a lease being granted to two persons, one of the tenants had remained in occupation of the premises after its expiration and the other had not, that would have raised the same question as was decided in the former case of *Christy* v. *Tancred,* and I should have thought that we must be bound by that decision, although I own that Mr. *Kelly's* able argument has made me doubt whether it was a correct one, and whether there is not a distinction between the case of a co-tenant and that of an under-tenant. If, however, that decision be wrong, it should be questioned in a Court of Error. But in the present case, the facts stated remove the difficulty. The case discloses ample evidence of the defendant Tancred's having continued a partner in this banking company, by agreeing to go on upon other terms than were originally contemplated on the formation of the company; and if he continued a partner, then, if his co-partners occupied, it is the same as if he himself carried on the business of the bank there. But he is liable only during the period of their actual occupation;

and when the key was unconditionally tendered to the plaintiff, there being no actual occupation afterwards, I think the liability under the original contract ceased, and therefore that the defendants are not liable after the 7th of December.

ALDERSON, B.—I am of the same opinion. I consider the Court precluded from questioning the former decision in *Christy* v. *Tancred* on the present occasion. When the question arises, I should wish for time to consider whether, in the case of a lease granted to two parties, one of whom is desirous of giving up possession, and notifies his desire to the other, who nevertheless holds over, the party who is out of possession can be made liable to an action for use and occupation. If the holding over by one is with the consent of the other, then the case falls within that of *Harding* v. *Crethorne;* but if such an inference were not warranted by the facts of the case, I should be disposed to consider the question before I came to that conclusion. But the circumstances which appear in this case render it unnecessary to do so, because from them the consent of the defendant Tancred to the occupation by the other parties may be presumed.

Judgment for the plaintiff.

———◆———

REGINA *v.* The SHERIFF of MONTGOMERYSHIRE, in a cause of ROGERS *v.* ASTLEY.

A plaintiff does not waive his right of exception to bail put in under the stat. 1 & 2 Vict. c. 110, s. 4, by delivering a declaration in chief, and consenting to further time to plead.

IN this case the defendant was arrested on the 11th December, 1841; on the 18th bail was put in conditionally, and filed; on the 28th the plaintiff delivered a declaration with a demand of plea; on the 4th January the defendant

took out a summons for ten days' time to plead, to which
the plaintiff consented; and on the 6th January the plaintiff excepted to the bail.

Exch. of Pleas,
1842.

REGINA
v.
SHERIFF OF
MONTGOMERY-
SHIRE.

Jervis now moved for a rule, calling upon the plaintiff
to shew cause why the attachment issued against the
sheriff of Montgomeryshire, for not bringing in the body,
should not be set aside.—The question turns on the construction to be put upon the 4th section of the stat. 1 & 2
Vict. c. 110, which enacts, that "such defendant, when so
arrested, shall remain in custody until he shall have given
a bail-bond to the sheriff, or shall have made deposit of the
sum indorsed on such writ of capias, together with £10
for costs, according to the present practice of the superior
Courts; and all subsequent proceedings, as to the putting
in and perfecting special bail, or of making deposit and
payment of money into Court instead of putting in or perfecting special bail, shall be according to the like practice
of the said superior Courts, or as near thereto as the
circumstances of the case will admit." Under the old
practice, the plaintiff, by delivering a declaration in chief,
and consenting to time to plead, would have waived his
right to except to the bail; and the practice is not altered
by the recent statute. [*Parke*, B.—The capias has now
nothing to do with the steps in the cause; it is merely a
proceeding in aid. The meaning of the statute is, that the
times for excepting, &c., shall be the same as before.
Alderson, B.—Under the old practice, taking a step in
chief was a waiver, because it admitted that the defendant
was in Court.]

PER CURIAM,

Rule refused (*a*).

(*a*) See *Betts* v. *Smyth*, 1 G. & D. 284.

Exch. of Pleas,
1842.

HOYLE *v.* COUPE.

Jan. 27.

In an action by
the lord of a
manor against a
copyholder, for
taking stones,
where the de-
fendant justifies
under an
alleged custom
of the manor,
entitling the
copyholders
to take the
stones to be
used on premi-
ses within the
manor, any
other copy-
holder is a
competent wit-
ness for the
defendant since
the stat. 3 & 4
Will, 4, c. 42,
ss. 26, 27.

TROVER for stones. Pleas, first, not guilty; secondly, a denial of the plaintiff's property in the stones; on which issues were joined. At the trial before *Wightman*, J., at the last assizes at Lancaster, it appeared that the plaintiff claimed the stones in question as lessee under the lord of the manor of Accrington, in that county, of certain stone and slate mines; and the defendant, who was the occupier of a copyhold farm within the manor, justified under an alleged custom of the manor for all the copyholders to get stone within the manor, and use it upon other premises within the manor, not being copyhold. Another of the copyholders, being called for the defendant to prove the custom, was objected to, on the ground that he was interested in the event of the suit, and therefore could not be rendered competent by the operation of the stat. 8 & 4 Will. 4, c. 42, s. 26: and the learned judge being of that opinion, rejected the witness, and the plaintiff recovered a verdict.

In Michaelmas Term, *Wortley* obtained a rule nisi for a new trial, on the ground that the evidence was improperly rejected. In the present term (Jan. 21),

Cresswell, W. H. Watson, and *Cardwell* shewed cause.— There can be no doubt that this was a custom which, if established, was highly beneficial to all the copyholders within the manor, and therefore to the witness : he, therefore, had a direct interest in establishing it. The exercise of the right, under the verdict obtained by his evidence for this defendant, would be evidence for himself. He comes to sustain a user, which will necessarily raise the value of his own copyhold. He has thus an interest, which nothing could remove but his ceasing to be a copyholder. *Bailiffs* of *Godmanchester* v. *Phillips* (a). It appears clear, there- Exch. *of Pleas,* fore, that before the stat. 3 & 4 Will. 4, c. 42, this witness would have been incompetent; and giving that statute the largest construction, it meant only to remove the disability of the witness, in cases where by the indorsement of his name on the record under the 27th section, the parties can be made equally secure as if no such record existed. If he has any the least interest ultra, the objection on the score of that interest is not removed by the statute. It has indeed been said in some cases, that the statute meant to remove the objection to the competency of the witness in all cases where a release would be necessary; but that construction can hardly be maintained; and besides, here the witness could not release his right to the other copyholders. The question therefore is, whether the sole objection to the witness was his liability to have the record used against him, or his privilege to use it for himself. Now if the verdict were found against the defendant, he could no longer exercise the right; if for him, he would go on exercising it; and such his exercise of it would be evidence of the right for all the copyholders. The witness is interested, not merely in the record, but in the fact of the existence of the custom; and the establishment of the custom would be followed by an exercise of the right, which would be necessarily for the benefit of the witness. And the verdict itself, though it could not be used for him by reason of the statute, would be evidence for another copyholder, and the recovery by that other would be evidence for the witness. He has therefore an interest ultra the verdict, and is not rendered competent by the statute. [They cited *Pickles* v. *Hollings* (b), *Stewart* v. *Barnes* (c), *Steers* v. *Carwardine* (d), *Wedgewood* v. *Hartley* (e), *Parker* v. *Mitchell* (g).]

(a) 4 Ad. & Ell. 550; 6 Nev. & M. 211.

(b) 1 M. & Rob. 468.

(c) Id. 472.

(d) 8 C. & P. 570.

(e) 10 Ad. & Ell. 619; 4 P. & D. 84.

(g) 11 Ad. & Ell. 789; 3 P. & D. 655.

Wortley and *Cowling*, contrà.—It may be admitted that
the true construction of the stat. 3 & 4 Will. 4, c. 42, s.
26, is, that it removes the incompetency only where the
objection is that the verdict might be used for or against
the witness. The object was not to prevent the necessity
of a release, but, as appears from the recital in the preamble, to prevent the frequent rejection of witnesses on
the ground of interest. In cases where a release could
operate, the grievance would be far less great. And the
question is, whether *in the event of this suit,* this witness
had a *direct* interest, as distinguished from a *contingent*
interest, or an interest derived from the verdict being evidence. The interest which is capable of excluding a witness ought to be a direct and immediate one, not, as in the
present case, a remote, indefinite, and contingent benefit.
[They referred on this point to *Rex* v. *Bray* (a), *Walton* v.
Shelley (b), *Bent* v. *Baker* (c), *Rex* v. *Prosser* (d), *Doe* d.
Teynham v. *Tyler* (e), *Clark* v. *Lucas* (f).] Here the *right*
is left as it was before; the verdict decides nothing but
the damages in trover : the only difference is, that if any
future action be brought against another party, and the
same question again arises, this verdict will be evidence.
The consequence may be that the witness's land may be
made more valuable; but that is not such a direct interest
in the suit as will exclude him; his estate remains the
same; and the lord might contest the right with him
again the next day, and shew this verdict to have proceeded on erroneous grounds. He is indeed interested in
the general question; but he has no interest whatever
which the law can take notice of, directly consequent on
the result of this suit. It may be that other copyholders
would in consequence of a verdict for this defendant exercise acts of ownership, and therefore that the witness may
be benefited, because the custom would thereby be strength-

(a) Cas. temp. Hardw. 360.   (d) 4 T. R. 17.
(b) 1 T. R. 296.   (e) 6 Bing. 390; 4 M. & P. 29.
(c) 3 T. R. 27.   (f) Ry. & Moo. 32.

ened; but that is an interest far more remote than in several of the cases which have been cited. A creditor, however large, called for an insolvent plaintiff in an action of
debt, is not therefore incompetent; yet there is a far
greater possibility of gain there than here. But there is
another class of cases which shew at least the impression
of the profession that the objection to the competency of
commoners was their interest by the use of the verdict:
see *Walton* v. *Shelley, Anscomb* v. *Shore* (a), Bull. N. P.
288, *Reed* v. *Jackson* (b), *Lord Falmouth* v. *George* (c).
The stat. 3 & 4 Will. 4, c. 42, s. 26, is to be liberally construed: *Pickles* v. *Hollings, Russell* v. *Blake* (d), *Poole* v.
Palmer (e). [They referred also to *Bowman* v. *Willis* (f),
Creevey v. *Bowman* (g), *Yeomans* v. *Legh* (h), and *Steers* v.
Carwardine.]

Cur. adv. vult.

The judgment of the Court was now delivered by

Lord ABINGER, C. B.—There was a case of *Hoyle* v.
Coupe, which was argued a few days ago. It was an action
by the lord of the manor against a copyholder within the
manor, for getting stone to be used by his tenant; and the
defendant justified upon a title or custom for all copyholders within the manor to get stone, not only to be used
upon his own premises, but upon other premises; and in
order to sustain that right, he called as a witness another
copyholder, who appeared to be in the same situation, and
he was rejected. On the discussion before us, it was argued that the witness ought to be rejected, because he did
not come within the provisions of the late statute; that he
was not rendered competent by the indorsement of his name
upon the record, to prevent the judgment and verdict

(a) 1 Taunt. 261.
(b) 1 East, 355.
(c) 5 Bing. 286; 2 M. & P. 457.
(d) 2 Scott N. R. 574; 2 Man.
& G. 374.

(e) Ante, p. 71.
(f) 3 Bing. N. C. 671; 4 Scott,
387.
(g) 1 M. & Rob. 496.
(h) 2 M. & W. 419.

being evidence against him afterwards. It was thought by the learned judge who tried the cause, that this was not a case within the statute, for that this was an interest inde‑pendent of the verdict and judgment, inasmuch as the party came to increase the value of his own premises by proving a general custom. We think, upon consideration, that the learned judge was mistaken, and that the statute could have no operation at all, unless it were applied to cases of this sort. There has been no previous example of any ob‑jection to a witness of this description, except upon the ground that the verdict and judgment were evidence in his favour, there being a verdict or judgment in support of the custom; and none of the cases (and they are numerous) have ever adverted to any other. It is true in one sense, that such a witness may have an interest in support of the custom, but yet the particular verdict could not immedi‑ately and directly affect it; it could only affect it incident‑ally, as it were, by a circuitous process, as supporting the evidence in other cases at the suit of other landlords against other copyholders. But it was said the verdict might be evidence for another copyholder, although it could not be given in evidence by this person; and that, if it could be given in evidence for another copyholder, it would tend to support the custom, though it could not be given in evidence by the particular witness; and then that the second verdict might be given in evidence for him; so that circuitously it might operate in a way to his advantage; but still it would not increase the value of his estate, or give him any interest in the result of the suit, except by a contingency or remote probability, which is not within the contemplation of the principle which excludes a witness from being competent. We are of opinion, there‑fore, that the learned judge was mistaken in thinking the statute did not apply to this case, and that the rule ought to be made absolute.

Rule absolute.

Exch. of Pleas, 1842.

DOE d. ELLIS v. OWENS.

Jan. 28.

THIS ejectment was commenced in Michaelmas Term, 1839. On the 6th March, 1840, notice of trial was given for the ensuing spring assizes for Carnarvonshire; and on the same day, a copy of an order of *Alderson*, B., admitting the plaintiff to sue in formâ pauperis, was served on the defendant. The order contained no provision as to the costs previously incurred: The cause was tried at the Spring assizes, 1841, when a verdict was found for the defendant. A rule was afterwards obtained for a new trial, which was discharged on the 1st June 1841: on the 9th June judgment was signed. On the 14th January (before any taxation of costs had taken place), *Jervis* obtained a rule calling on the plaintiff to shew cause why the order of *Alderson*, B., should not be set aside, as having been improperly issued after the commencement of the action: citing *Casey* v. *Tomlin* (a) and *Brunt* v. *Wardle* (b).

Townsend now shewed cause.—This application, after judgment, is too late; the cause is then at an end. In *Jenkins* v. *Hyde* (c), it was held that a plaintiff could not be dispaupered after judgment as in case of a nonsuit. [*Parke*, B.—The signing of judgment and taxation of costs are one act.] Secondly, the order was regular. There had certainly been some cases in this Court which threw a doubt on the question whether a plaintiff could be admitted to sue in formâ pauperis after the commencement of the action; but in *Casey* v. *Tomlin*, the Court expressly reserved its decision upon the point; and in *Brunt* v. *Wardle*, where all the cases are collected, it was expressly held that the Court had jurisdiction at common law to admit a pauper to sue at any period of the cause. *Langley*

A plaintiff may be admitted to sue in formâ pauperis after the commencement of the suit.

(a) 7 M. & W. 189. (b) 4 Scott. N. R. 188.
(c) 6 M. & Selw. 228.

v. *Blackerby* (a), and *Brittain* v. *Greenville* (b), there cited, are express authorities to the same effect: and such was the invariable practice until the case of *Foss* v. *Racine* (c). The stats. 11 Hen. 7, c. 12, & 28 Hen. 8, c. 15, were merely enabling statutes, and did not affect the power of the judges at common law to relieve a poor suitor from certain costs.

Jervis, contrà.—First, the defendant is not too late in his application. It would not have been proper to make it while the rule for a new trial was pending: and the plaintiff has taken no step on the faith of the order which the defendant could have prevented by an earlier application. There is no judgment *pronounced* until the costs are taxed; and there was no necessity for the defendant to come to the Court until the time when the order would operate upon the costs.

Secondly, this rule may be made absolute consistently with the decision in *Brunt* v. *Wardle*. This order is in contravention of a rule of this Court, of the year 1717, stated in Com. Dig., *Formâ Pauperis*, (A), that "if admitted after the commencement of the suit, the pauper is to give security to pay the costs before admittance:" it ought therefore to have contained such a provision. But further, the true construction of the statutes is this: the stat. 11 Hen. 7, c. 12, enacts, "That every poor person or persons, which have or hereafter shall have cause of action or actions against any person or persons within this realm, shall have, by the discretion of the Chancellor of this realm for the time being, writ or writs original, or writs of subpœna, according to the nature of their cause, therefore nothing paying'; and after the said writ or writs be returned, &c., the justices shall assign to the same poor person or persons counsel learned &c., and shall appoint attorney and

(a) Andr. 306.   (b) 2 Stra. 1121.
(c) 4 M. & W. 610.

attornies for the same poor person'or persons, &c. &c." That
statute, therefore, contemplates something to be done by
the Court after the commencement of the suit. But the
stat. 23 Hen. 8, c. 15, s. 1, is express, that all poor persons, plaintiffs, " which *at the commencement of* their suits
or actions, shall be admitted to have their process of cha-
rity, &c.," " shall not be compelled to pay any costs by virtue and force of this statute," which imposed costs generally
on plaintiffs in case of a verdict for the defendant or a nonsuit.   Therefore, where they are admitted before the commencement of the suit, they are to pay no costs on a verdict
for the defendant or a nonsuit ; but it is quite consistent
with that, that although admitted subsequently, they
may, under the stat. of Hen. 7, have their own counsel,
attorney, &c., gratuitously. The present defendant, therefore, is at all events entitled to the costs antecedent to the
order of the learned judge.

Exch. of Pleas,
1842.

Dos
d.
ELLIS
v.
OWENS.

PER CURIAM.—If that be the correct construction of
the statutes, you do not want to dispauper the plaintiff ;
but you should proceed to taxation, and then the question
may be raised.   Your argument shews the order to be
right, because it admits that it has some effect.

Rule discharged, with costs.

Exch. of Pleas,
1842.

PARRATT *v.* GODDARD and Another, Executrix and Executor of H. Goddard.

Jan. 28.

To a declaration in debt against executors, containing a count for non-payment of money due on a covenant of the testator, with counts for money paid and on an account stated, the defendants, being under terms of pleading issuably, pleaded, 1. that "the writing in *the declaration* mentioned" was not the deed of the testator; 2. that "the said writing in the declaration mentioned" was executed for an immoral consideration:— Held, that these were not issuable pleas, being in form pleaded to the whole declaration, whereas they applied to the first count only.

DEBT. The declaration contained a count for non-payment of money due on a covenant of the testator, together with counts for money paid to the use of the defendants, and on an account stated. The defendants, being under terms of pleading issuably, pleaded, first, " that the said writing *in the declaration* mentioned is not the deed of the said H. Goddard;" concluding to the country; secondly, " that the said writing in the declaration mentioned was sealed and delivered by the said H. Goddard," &c., [stating an immoral consideration for the deed.] The plaintiff having signed judgment as for want of a plea, on the ground that the pleas, although applicable to the first count of the declaration only, were in form pleaded to the whole declaration, and therefore were not issuable pleas, a rule nisi was obtained for setting that judgment aside: against which

Badeley now shewed cause.—These pleas, being without the proper formal commencement, must be taken to be pleaded to the whole action, and are therefore not issuable pleas. They would be bad on special demurrer: *Putney* v. *Swann* (a). Where a defendant, being under terms of pleading issuably, pleaded nunquam indebitatus to a declaration containing counts on bills of exchange, as well as for goods sold and delivered, it was held that the plaintiff might treat the plea as a nullity and sign judgment; *Sewell* v. *Dale* (b).

Thomas, contrà.—The plaintiff ought not to have signed judgment; his proper course was to have demurred. A plaintiff who has consented to a rule to plead several matters, cannot apply to set aside any of the pleas on the

(a) 2 M. & W. 72.   (b) 8 Dowl. P. C. 309.

ground that they are no answer to the action: *Howen* v. *Carr* (a). In *Wood* v. *Farr* (b), where, in debt for £150, the defendant pleaded to the whole action, that he had paid the plaintiff £50, judgment signed by the plaintiff by nil dicit for £100, was held irregular. [*Parke*, B.—The question here turns on the ground of the defendants being under terms to plead issuably.]

Exch. of Pleas,
1842.

PARRATT
v.
GODDARD.

PER CURIAM.—These pleas apply substantially to the first count, but being in form pleaded to the whole declaration, would be bad on special demurrer. But the present question is, whether they are issuable pleas; and we think they are not—they are not pleas on which the plaintiff could join issue, and go to trial upon the merits. If the defendant had in terms pleaded to the first count only, the plaintiff might have signed judgment on the other issues. The judgment may be set aside on payment of costs.

Rule absolute on payment of costs.

(a) 5 Dowl. P. C. 305.   (b) 5 Bing. N. C. 247; 7 Scott, 270.

RICHARDS, Public Officer, &c., *v.* DISPRAILE.

A RULE had been obtained, calling upon the plaintiff to shew cause why an order of *Gurney*, B., for issuing a capias against the defendant, should not be rescinded, and why the defendant should not be discharged out of the custody of the Warden of the Fleet Prison. The objection was, that there was a variance between the affidavit on which the capias was obtained, and the title of the cause in the writ: the former describing the plaintiff as " John Richards, one of the public officers of the Western District Banking Company for Devon and Cornwall," whereas in the writ the words " for Devon and Cornwall " were omitted.

Jan. 28.
The affidavit in support of a capias described the plaintiff as " J. R. one of the public officers of the Western District Banking Company *for Dev'n and Cornwall:*" in the writ these last words were omitted: The court discharged without costs a rule for discharging

the defendant out of custody on the ground of the variance, upon the plaintiff's filing a fresh affidavit, omitting those words in the title.

Exch. of Pleas,
1837.

RICHARDS
v.
DISPRAILE.

Erle shewed cause.—This variance is wholly immaterial. The plaintiff was not obliged to describe himself, in the title of the cause in the writ, as one of the public officers; he need not do so at any earlier stage of the proceedings than the declaration. It is not like the case of an assignee, where a statutable right is given to him in that capacity. Here he has, in the affidavit, given his correct title, only he has added the locality for which he acts. That does not vitiate the affidavit.

PER CURIAM.—It is not alleged that the defendant has been improperly arrested. The rule will, therefore, be discharged without costs, on the defendant's filing a fresh affidavit, omitting the words " for Devon and Cornwall " in the title.

Rule discharged accordingly.

———————

Jan. 28.

FYSON, Administratrix of CROFT, Deceased, *v.* CHAMBERS.

TROVER for goods, brought by the plaintiff as administratrix of John Croft.—Pleas, first, not guilty; secondly, a denial of the plaintiff's possession as administratrix: on which issues were joined. At the trial before Lord *Abinger*, C. B., at the London Sittings after Trinity Term, the following facts appeared in evidence.

The intestate, John Croft, died on the 21st of January, 1839, possessed of certain household furniture and effects, the subject of the present action. No administration having been taken out by the next of kin, the plaintiff, who was a creditor of the intestate, applied for and ob-

A certificate under the Bankrupt Act is evidence, as against the bankrupt, of a valid bankruptcy, without proof of the petitioning creditor's debt, &c.

A party who has taken possession of the goods of an intestate after his death, cannot set up as a defence to an action of trover by the administra-

tor, that the intestate had been first insolvent and then bankrupt, and had not paid 15s. in the pound under the fiat, and that therefore the property in the goods vested absolutely in the assignees; the goods having being acquired by the intestate after the bankruptcy, and he having been allowed by the assignees to retain possession of them.

tained letters of administration, dated 10th October, 1840. In January 1841, the plaintiff discovered that the defendant, who was an auctioneer, had sold the goods by direction of the next of kin, who had made himself executor de son tort. For the defendant it was proved, that in 1828 the intestate took the benefit of the Insolvent Debtors Act, and it was proposed also to shew that he had subsequently become a bankrupt, for which purpose the depositions and the certificate were put in, but no specific evidence was given of a petitioning creditor's debt, or of the other previous requisites to a valid bankruptcy; and on the face of the depositions there was some ambiguity in the statement as to the date of the petitioning creditor's debt. It was proved also, that the intestate did not pay 15*s.* in the pound under the alleged commission, and that he acquired the goods in question subsequently to the date of the certificate, so that the property in them vested absolutely in the assignees under the Bankrupt Act, 6 Geo. 4, c. 16, s. 127. No evidence was given to shew the application of the proceeds of the sale. It was contended for the plaintiff, first, that the depositions and certificate were no sufficient proof of the issuing of a fiat, or of the existence of a petitioning creditor's debt; and secondly, that the defendant could not, in this action, set up the title of the assignees against the plaintiff's claim as administrator. The Lord Chief Baron reserved the points, and a verdict passed for the plaintiff for the value of the goods, with leave to the defendant to move to enter a verdict for him on the second issue.

In Michaelmas Term, *Erle* obtained a rule nisi accordingly, against which, in the same term (Nov. 23),

Kelly and *Butt* shewed cause.—First, the defendant was bound, in order to establish the proposed defence, to prove a valid commission of bankruptcy issued against the intestate, and he did not 'prove it by merely shewing the existence of a certificate. The petitioning creditor's debt, the trading, &c., ought to have been proved by specific evidence. It is impossible for the alleged bankrupt to defeat such a primâ facie case, if it be one, by shewing that he has *not* committed an act of bankruptcy. Proof by the statement in the depositions, that a petitioning creditor's debt was due at the date of the commission, is no proof of its having been due at the time of the act of bankruptcy: *Clarke* v. *Askew* (a). *Haviland* v. *Cook* (b) will be cited for the defendant, but the authority of that case has been shaken by subsequent decisions. It is only in favour of the bankrupt, when pleading his bankruptcy, that the certificate is made evidence by sect. 126 of the Bankrupt Act. In *Pitt* v. *Chappelow* (c), it was held that a defendant who pleads the bankruptcy of the drawer of a bill of exchange as an answer to an action against him by an indorsee, is bound to set forth fully all the requisites to establish a valid bankruptcy. [*Parke*, B.—The allowance of the certificate is not conclusive against the bankrupt; but surely it is good primâ facie evidence that all the previous steps have been regular, and that evidence is not disproved by a mere ambiguous statement in the depositions.]

Secondly, the plaintiff, representing the intestate, might well maintain this action against the defendant, who stands in the situation of a mere wrong-doer, and claims no title under the assignees. It has been held that an uncertificated bankrupt may sue in trover a wrong-doer who takes his goods; and that, so long as the assignees permit him to deal with subsequently acquired property as his own, the wrong-doer cannot set up against him the jus tertii: *Webb* v. *Fox* (d); *Drayton* v. *Dale* (e). The bankrupt may

(a) 1 Stark. Rep. 458, n.   (d) 7 T. R. 391.
(b) 5 T. R. 655.   (e) 2 B. & Cr. 293; 3 D. & R.
(c) 8 M. & W. 616.   534.

sue as the trustee of the assignees: *Cumming* v. *Roebuck* (a). And the 127th sect. of the Bankrupt Act has the same operation as to after-acquired property, in the case of a second commission under which 15s. in the pound has not been paid. The other side will rely on *Young* v. *Rishworth* (b), in which it was held to be a good defence to an action of assumpsit for money had and received, that the plaintiff had been twice a bankrupt, and had not paid 15s. in the pound under the second commission; but there the defence was specially pleaded. [*Parke*, B.—What special plea of that kind could you draw which would not amount to an argumentative denial of the plaintiff's being possessed?] The plea in *Young* v. *Rishworth* was held good on special demurrer. [*Parke*, B.—The demurrer was not on the ground that it amounted to not possessed.] The rule as to the interpretation of the plea of not possessed is laid down in the case of *Purnell* v. *Young* (c), where it is said, " The plea denying the close to be the plaintiff's is a denial of possession, if the defendant be a wrong-doer; if otherwise, of the right to the possession." If, therefore, the bankrupt has a possessory title, which is good against a wrong-doer, a party who comes to justify under the right of the assignees should plead specially, giving the plaintiff colour: *Morant* v. *Sign* (d). [*Parke*, B.—The question is not whether you might not have given colour, and pleaded specially, but whether the plea of not possessed is not sufficient. It means this :—Although I, the defendant, have converted the goods, you, the plaintiff, have no lawful title to them as against me]. Then the answer is, that the bankrupt has a lawful title as against all but the assignees. [Lord *Abinger*, C. B.—I cannot see that the effect of sect. 127, at most, is more than to place a certificated bankrupt under a second commission upon which he has not paid

(a) Holt's N. P. C. 172.
(b) 8 Ad. & Ell. 470; 3 Nev. & P. 588.
(c) 3 M. & W. 288.
(d) 2 M. & W. 95.

15*s.* in the pound, in the same situation as an uncertificated bankrupt under the 5 Geo. 2, c. 30, s. 9.] There cannot be any valid distinction between the rights of the assignees in the one case and in the other. In *Carter* v. *Johnson* (a), it was held that a defendant in trespass, under a plea that the goods were not the plaintiff's, could not set up property in a stranger under whom he did not justify, in answer to the plaintiff's possession. *Carnaby* v. *Welby* (b) is also an authority that the issue on not possessed in trespass is simply as to the plaintiff's actual possession, and that no question can be raised under it whether the possession was fraudulent.

Erle and *Barstow*, contrà.—In the first place, the defendant was at liberty, on this record, to set up the present defence. In trover, the plea that the goods are not the plaintiff's puts in issue the right of the plaintiff to the possession, as against the defendant, at the time of the alleged conversion: *Isaac* v. *Belcher* (c); *Owen* v. *Knight* (d). *Butler* v. *Hobson* (e) is a clear authority for the defendant on this point. [*Parke*, B.—Surely there can be no doubt on this part of the case—that this plea raises the whole question between the parties.] The actual possession is enough, no doubt, in trespass; but it is different in trover. This is an issue who is entitled to the property. [*Parke*, B. —It is not a case of simple possession, but of possession coupled with a kind of bailment: the intestate is in possession by consent of the assignees.]

Then the plea discloses a complete defence to the action. *Young* v. *Rishworth* is an express authority, that after-acquired property of a bankrupt, who has not paid 15*s.* in the pound under a second commission, vests absolutely in

(a) 2 M. & Rob. 263.
(b) 8 Ad. & Ell. 872; 1 P. & D. 98.
(c) 5 M. & W. 139.

(d) 4 Bing. N. C. 54; 5 Scott, 307.
(e) 4 Bing. N. C. 290; 5 Scott, 798.

the assignees, and that the bankrupt therefore can maintain no action upon a contract in respect of it. It is said it must be taken that the goods were in the lawful possession of the intestate by the consent of the assignees. That was a question of fact. But, if he held the possession as their agent, either his agency determined by his death, or the defendant is in under the same agency. [*Parke*, B.— The first question is, whether the intestate could sue ; and the second, whether, if he could, the title relates back so that his administrator can sue. It may be that there is thé same relation back in cases where the intestate had a special property in the goods, as where he had the absolute property. This was a question much considered in *Elliott* v. *Kemp* (a), where it was held, that there was not such relation back as to chattels in which the intestate had no personal interest, but was merely the administrator of another. The question is, has the bankrupt such a title as is *descendible,* so to speak, or has the party title who is in by the authority of the assignees? Lord *Abinger*, C. B.— Your argument is, that though a possessory title is good against a mere wrong-doer, that has no application where the party suing has no possession, and where the party under whose title he comes in had no possession at the time of the wrong done, being then dead ; and therefore that it is a mere issue on *title.*] Yes. And it is submitted that there is a material difference between the case of an uncertificated bankrupt, and of a bankrupt who has not paid 15s. in the pound under a second commission. The words of sect. 127 are stronger than those of the 5 Geo. 2, c. 30, s. 9. The latter merely made the after-acquired property " liable to the creditors ;" the former vests it in the assignees. And in *Ex parte Robinson, in re Freer* (b), the Vice-Chancellor of England held, that under that clause it vests in them absolutely, and ab initio. The bankrupt

(a) 7 M. & W. 306.   (b) Mont. & M'Arth. 44.

himself, therefore, could not have sued; but much less his administrator. For what purpose could *he* sue? The goods when recovered must be assets; yet it 'is clear the assignees could claim them, and that the plaintiff could not distribute them. This supposed license or permission of the assignees, therefore, if it exist at all, was personal to the bankrupt, and does not survive to his representative.

Lord ABINGER, C. B.—It appears to me to be sufficiently clear, upon all the authorities, that this action might have been maintained by the bankrupt himself in his lifetime, on the principle that a possession by the consent of the true owner is a lawful possession against a third party: but my doubt is, whether the same principle applies to the administrator, unless the wrong were done in the lifetime of the intestate. On that point we will take some time to consider.

PARKE, B.—That appears to me to be the only point on which consideration is required. It is clear that the applying for and obtaining a certificate of conformity is evidence against the party of the validity of the bankruptcy; not conclusive indeed, but evidence; and it is clearly not disproved by the depositions put in, which seem, indeed, to have been admitted per incuriam, for I do not see how they were admissible at all. Then as to the next point, I do not see any difference between the position of a bankrupt after a second commission, who has not paid 15*s.* in the pound, and that of an uncertificated bankrupt: both have a kind of special property of the same description. In *Ex parte Robinson,* the attention of the Vice-Chancellor does not appear to have been called to the analogy between their two characters. In both cases, the bankrupt has a kind of special property against all but the assignees, and may maintain trover against a wrong-doer.

It is different from the case of a mere naked possession :

the question whether *that* will entitle a party to maintain trover, even against a wrong-doer, is one upon which I entertain considerable doubt, and which has yet to be determined. The question then here is, whether the right of the bankrupt to this after-acquired property stops with his life, or passes to his administrator. The case of *Young* v. *Rishworth* decides nothing as to the difference between after-acquired property in the case of a bankrupt under a second commission, not having paid 15*s.* in the pound, and in that of an uncertificated bankrupt. The plea there did not state that it was after-acquired property, but only that the plaintiff had become bankrupt a second time, and had not paid 15*s.* in the pound; and all that the Court decided was, that the plea was primâ facie an answer to the declaration, and that the facts ought to have been replied.

Cur. adv. vult.

The judgment of the Court was now delivered by

Lord ABINGER, C. B.—There was a case of *Fyson* v. *Chambers* discussed last term, in which Mr. *Erle* moved for a rule to show cause why the verdict should not be set aside, and a verdict entered for the defendant, or a non-suit had. The case was this:—The plaintiff was the administrator of a person of the name of Croft, but he did not take out letters of administration for many months after Croft's death. It appeared that after Croft's death, there were two persons who were connected with him, one of whom had possession of his goods, which remained in his house undisposed of until the period when the defendant, who was an auctioneer, disposed of them. Some time after that the plaintiff, who was a creditor of Croft, took out administration to his effects, and then brought this action against the defendant for the conversion by

the sale of the goods. At the trial it appeared to me
that the plaintiff, having taken out administration so
long after the event had happened, was rather acting
sharply towards the defendant in bringing this action, and
I was disposed, if possible, to have defeated his object;
but however, I did not think myself entitled upon the
evidence to say that the goods were not the administrator's.
Then Mr. *Erle* raised another objection, which he endeavoured to support by evidence; viz. that Croft had been
twice a bankrupt, and had not paid 15*s.* in the pound
under the second commission, and therefore that the
goods vested in and still remained the absolute property
of the assignees. The Court was very desirous, if possible,
of giving effect to one or the other of the objections to this
verdict for the plaintiff; but, upon consideration, we apprehend we cannot do so. With regard to the first objection, it was proved that the plaintiff took out administration
many months after the deceased died, not until after the act
of conversion had taken place; and if the conversion of
these goods had actually taken place by the relatives of
the deceased before the defendant had interfered, so as to
pass the property, the subject of that conversion, to somebody else, I for one should be unwilling to say that the
administrator could have retained the property and sued
for such conversion. But, on considering this case, it appears that the first act of conversion done, after the death
of the deceased, was the very sale of the goods, in which
the supposed executor and the defendant were actually
concerned together, and that all parties were therefore
liable in an action of trover. Now it is very true, if an
action had been brought in trover by the administrator
against the executor de son tort, the cases have decided
that an executor de son tort may recoup himself in
damages for all money he has paid bonâ fide on account of
the testator; and so might the defendant in this case, if
he had given any evidence that the executor de son tort

had paid the debts of the testator out of the proceeds of *Exch. of Pleas,*
1842. the sale. No such evidence was given, and it therefore remains a conversion without any thing to excuse it, or to FYSON
v.
CHAMBERS. diminish the amount to be recovered. And as to the second point, it appears to us, on consideration of all the facts, that this case falls within a class of cases in which it has been decided, that where the assignees have permitted the bankrupt to remain for a considerable time in possession of property acquired after his bankruptcy, although they may interfere and take it away, it is not competent to third parties to set up a claim which the assignees themselves do not think fit to insist upon. We therefore think that there was a good title in the bankrupt against all the world but the assignees. Now the defendant in this case is not the assignee, and has no right to set up a title of third persons to cover his own default: we think, therefore, that the verdict should stand for the plaintiff, and that the rule must be discharged.

Rule discharged.

THE EARL OF FALMOUTH v. ROBERTS. Jan. 29.

ASSUMPSIT.—The declaration stated that the defendant had become and then was tenant to the plaintiff of a certain messuage, farm, and lands, except as in a certain wards signed an agreement containing certain stipulations as to the mode of tillage. In an action by the landlord for breaches of these stipulations, the agreement, on being produced, contained an erasure in the term of years mentioned in the habendum, which was altered from seven to fourteen:—*Held*, that in this action the agreement might be received in evidence without any explanation of the erasure, the term of years being immaterial to the parol contract between the parties, to hold from year to year, subject only to the terms of the agreement as to the cultivation of the land.

The agreement was attested by the landlord's steward, who, after having been apprehended for embezzlement, had absconded, and could not be found after search at his house, and at the inns he was in the habit of frequenting:—*Held*, that evidence of his handwriting was properly received.

Where, A. B. the elder being summoned on a special jury, A. B. the younger, of the same place, by mistake answered to the name, was sworn, and sat as a special juror on the trial of a cause ; the Court, in its discretion, refused a new trial, after verdict for the plaintiff, it appearing that the defendant's attorney's clerk was aware of the mistake at the time of the trial, and made no objection, and the attorney himself not negativing his knowledge of the mistake.

The defendant became tenant to the plaintiff of a farm from year to year, by parol, but after-

agreement theretofore made between the plaintiff and the defendant is excepted, subject to the defendant's keeping, as such tenant, certain terms and agreements, that is to say &c. The declaration then set out the terms of an agreement relating to the mode of farming the land, by laying thereon a certain quantity of manure, not converting meadow land into tillage, &c. &c., and assigned various breaches in respect thereof. At the trial before *Rolfe*, B., at the last Cornwall Assizes, it appeared that the farm was originally let by parol by the plaintiff's steward to the defendant, as tenant from year to year; and that afterwards the defendant signed an agreement containing certain terms and stipulations as to the mode of tillage. The attesting witness to this agreement was the steward; who, being afterwards apprehended under a warrant for embezzling the plaintiff's rents, had been liberated on a promise to attend at a certain time and place to investigate his accounts, but, instead of doing so, absconded. Inquiries had been made for him at his house, and at the inns he had been in the habit of frequenting, but without success. The learned Judge, under these circumstances, admitted evidence of his handwriting.

The agreement, on being produced, appeared to contain an erasure and interlineation as to the term of years mentioned in the habendum, which appeared to be altered from seven to fourteen; whereupon it was objected for the defendant, on the authority of *Knight* v. *Clements* (a), that, without some explanation given by the plaintiff of the time at which the erasure was made, the agreement could not be read in evidence. The learned Judge, however, admitted it, and the plaintiff had a verdict, damages £20.

In Michaelmas Term last (Nov. 6), *Crowder* moved (b) for a rule to shew cause why a new trial should not be had, on the ground of misdirection.—First, there was not

(a) 8 Ad. & Ell. 215; 3 Nev. & P. 375.
(b) Before Lord *Abinger*, C. B., *Parke*, B., *Gurney*, B. and *Rolfe*. B.

sufficient proof of search for the attesting witness to let in the evidence of his handwriting. No application was shewn to have been made to any member of his family. [The learned Judge read his notes of the evidence as to this point, and the Court held that it was clearly sufficient.] Secondly, the agreement having been altered in a material part, and there being no proof when that alteration was made, it óught not to have been admitted. The onus was upon the plaintiff to shew that the alteration was made before the execution of the instrument, or with the consent of the parties. *Henman* v. *Dickinson* (a), *Johnson* v. *Duke of Marlborough* (b), *Knight* v. *Clements.* [*Parke*, B.—The general rule undoubtedly is, that where there appears to be an alteration in the document, it lies upon the party producing it to explain it. But, in truth, the holding here is under a parol agreement, only incorporating so much of the written instrument as is applicable to a yearly holding. In that point of view, the duration of the term therein mentioned, whether seven or fourteen years, is immaterial; it is altogether dehors the agreement, and quite independent of the contract which the parties have entered into, to farm the land according to the stipulations of that agreement. The alteration of the instrument could not make the defendant hold according to the custom of the country, instead of according to the terms of their agreement. Suppose the paper were destroyed, the parol agreement would still remain. The rule of law applies where the obligation is by reason of the instrument; here the obligation is by reason of the parol contract of the parties, quite independent of the subscription of that paper, and arising from the occupation of the land upon all the terms of that instrument which are applicable to a tenancy from year to year; as to which, an alteration in the term of years is wholly immaterial. *Rolfe*, B.—This declaration

(a) 5 Bing. 183; 2 M. & P. 289.   (b) 2 Stark. Rep. 313.

is framed on an assumption that the contract operated to create a tenancy from year to year, on the terms of that agreement as to the cultivation of the land.]

Thirdly, there was a mis-trial.—On this point the learned counsel produced affidavits, from which it appeared that one William Rogers, the younger, of Sideford, in the parish of St. Germains, was sworn as a special juror, and sat as such on the trial of this cause, not being duly qualified to sit either as a special or a common juror, though without any fraudulent intention, or collusion with either the plaintiff or the defendant; that William Rogers, the elder, of the same place, was the party named in the precept, and had been duly summoned in pursuance thereof; that the clerk of the defendant's attorney was present at the trial, and was personally acquainted with both the elder and the younger Rogers.—Neither the attorney nor his clerk negatived their knowledge of the mistake at the time of the trial.—A rule having been granted on this point only.

Erle and *Montague Smith* now shewed cause, and urged that this was a matter entirely for the discretion of the Court; *Hill* v. *Yates* (a); and as there was no pretence for saying that any injustice had been done in the present case, the Court in their discretion would not grant a new trial, it appearing that the defendant's attorney's clerk must have known of the mistake at the time, and yet made no objection, and neither he nor his employer denying such their knowledge. In *Dovey* v. *Hobson* (b) the objection was taken before trial. *Rex* v. *Tremearne* (c) was the case of an indictment for perjury, and there the juror was not only disqualified but under age.

Crowder and *Bere*, in support of the rule, admitted that it

(a) 12 East, 229.   (b) 2 Marsh. 154; 6 Taunt. 460.
(c) 5 B. & Cr. 254.

was a matter for the discretion of the Court, but submitted that as the party who sat as the juror was altogether unqualified, and it did not appear that the attorney or his clerk knew of the mistake before the jury were sworn, it was fit that the verdict should be set aside.

Exch. of Pleas,
1842.

EARL OF
FALMOUTH
v.
ROBERTS.

PARKE, B.—*Rex* v. *Hunt* (a), and the other cases which have been cited, shew that it is altogether discretionary with the Court whether under such circumstances they will grant a new trial. Now, here the affidavit of the defendant's attorney's clerk shews his knowledge of the parties at the trial, and no affidavit is made by the attorney himself that he was ignorant of the mistake at all. I think, therefore, that we shall exercise our discretion properly in discharging this rule.

The other Barons concurring,

Rule discharged.

(a) 4 B. & Ald. 430.

BILTON *v.* CLAPPERTON.

IN this case, the defendant, who had been conditionally discharged under the Insolvent Debtors Act, 1 & 2 Vict. c. 110, s. 84, was arrested under a writ of capias, issued in pursuance of the 85th section of the same act, which provides, that in all cases where it shall have been adjudged by the Insolvent Debtors Court, that any prisoner shall be discharged conditionally, " such prisoner shall be subject and liable to be detained in prison, and to be arrested and

Jan. 31.

Where a defendant has been conditionally discharged under the Insolvent Debtors Act, 1 & 2 Vict. c. 110, s. 84, and is again arrested under a writ of capias, issued pursuant to the 85th sect. of the same

Act, it is not necessary that a judge's order should have been taken out for the defendant's arrest under the 3rd section of the Act.

Where an affidavit of debt described the plaintiff as " W. B. the younger," but in the capias he was called " W. B." only, his father bearing the same name and residing in the same town as himself:—Held, that the writ was bad, but the Court allowed the plaintiff to amend it on payment of costs, on the ground that the plaintiff might suffer a detriment if the defendant were discharged out of custody, and it not being a mere question of costs.

charged in custody, at the suit of any one or more of his or her creditors with respect to whom it shall have been so adjudged, at any time before such period shall have arrived, in the same manner as he would have been subject thereto if this act had not passed." The capias, which was issued out of this Court, and tested in the name of the Lord Chief Baron, was indorsed as follows:—" Issued under the authority of 1 & 2 Vict. c. 110, s. 84, by virtue of an adjudication of the Court for the relief of Insolvent Debtors." The order of the Insolvent Debtors Court was grounded on an affidavit intitled in the Court of Exchequer, disclosing a debt exceeding £20 due to the plaintiff, and in the form of an old affidavit to hold to bail.

W. H. Watson, on a former day in this term (Jan. 20), moved to set aside the capias and all subsequent proceedings as irregular, on the ground that there ought to have been a judge's order for holding the defendant to bail, under the 3rd section of the statute; and if so, that the affidavit ought to have shewn a sufficient cause of action, and sufficient facts to give a judge jurisdiction under that section.

Lord ABINGER, C. B.—If a judge's order were necessary for this arrest, there might be some ground for objecting to the form of this affidavit; but the plaintiff is entitled to make this arrest in the same manner as if the statute had never been passed; and consequently, all the provisions in the 3rd section are irrelevant to the present question. There is therefore no ground for granting a rule on that point.

ALDERSON, B.—The effect of the 85th section of this statute is to render every party discharged by the Insolvent Debtors Court, in the manner this defendant has been, as liable to be arrested by force of a writ of capias, as if the other provisions in the act for the abolition of arrest upon

mesne process had never been passed. Now, previous to
the statute, a party might have been arrested on such a
writ, provided a proper affidavit were made, sufficiently disclosing a debt, to the amount of £20 or more, due from him
to the plaintiff. So, since the statute in the present case,
the arrest is lawful, provided a sufficient affidavit of debt is
produced, and unless you can shew, by affidavit, something
to taint the arrest with illegality.

Rule refused on that point.

Watson then moved for and obtained a rule to shew
cause why the writ should not be set aside, and why the
bail-bond should not be delivered up to be cancelled on
the ground of variance, the plaintiff having been described
in the affidavit of debt as " Walter Bilton the younger,"
whereas in the writ of capias he was described as " Walter
Bilton " only. It appeared that the plaintiff resided at
Hull, where his father, whose name was " Walter Bilton,"
also resided, but the father was not a creditor of the defendant.

Martin now shewed cause.—There is no necessity for
stating that the " Walter Bilton " who is sued was Bilton
the younger. It is a mere question of identity, and it appears
from the affidavits that Bilton the elder was not a creditor
of the defendant, and that Bilton the younger was the
party who made the affidavit of debt and sued out the writ
against the defendant. There may be a trifling variance
between the affidavit to hold to bail and the writ, but the
Court will not set the proceedings aside on that ground, and
there is no authority for saying that a party is bound to
describe himself as " the younger, " or " the elder ". Perjury might well be assigned on this affidavit, if it were un-

true. It is a mere question whether the party making the affidavit of debt, and the party suing out the writ, are the same. In ——— v. *Rennolls* (*a*), it was held that a variance between the affidavit to hold to bail and the writ, in the letters of the defendant's name, as *Rennoll* instead of *Rennolls*, did not vitiate the affidavit. It is sufficient to shew that the action is brought by Walter Bilton, the same person who made the affidavit of debt. At all events, if the writ be wrong, the Court will amend it.

Watson, contrà.—The variance is a material one, and the defendant is entitled to be discharged. In Com. Dig. (E 22), it is said, " So if the plaintiff sues by his christian or surname with an addition, and in other actions the addition is omitted, it shall be pleaded in abatement : as, if he sues by the name of Henry Norman, of B., and, in other writs against the same defendant in another county, is named Henry Norman only, the other writs shall abate where the addition is omitted; though it was objected that perhaps there was another of the same name in the county where the first action was brought, and not in the county where the other actions are brought." In *Grindall* v. *Smith* (*b*), where the plaintiff had described himself as Charles Edmund in the affidavit to hold to bail, and was called Charles only in the writ and declaration, it was held that the defendant ought to have applied to set aside the writ. Secondly, the Court will not amend the writ unless it be shewn that if it be not allowed the defendant would be able to avail himself of the Statute of Limitations, which has not been done here.

ALDERSON, B. (*c*).—It appears by the affidavit, that there

(*a*) 1 Chit. Rep. 659, n.
(*b*) 1 M. & P. 24.
(*c*) This case was heard before *Alderson*, B., sitting alone, on the last day of term, but before delivering this judgment he consulted the rest of the Court.

are two persons named Walter Bilton, in the town of Hull. *Exch. of Pleas,*
Now, when no addition is made to the name, does it not
imply that the party intended was Walter Bilton the elder?
The Masters all say that the proper way to sue out the
writ was in the name of Walter Bilton the younger. The
plaintiff has, therefore, a good affidavit of debt, but not a
good writ. I have, however, conferred with the rest of the
Court, and they think that the writ in this case ought to
be amended, on payment by the plaintiff of the costs of
this application. The principle acted upon by the Courts
appears to be this, that an amendment will not be allowed,
where the sole object is to save costs; but where the refusal to amend would deprive a party of his remedy, as
where the Statute of Limitations would apply if an amendment were not made, or the plaintiff would suffer any material detriment (*a*) if the defendant were discharged out
of custody, there the Courts will allow the writ to be
amended. The present case falls within that principle, for it
involves something more than a mere question of costs.
The object of arresting this party is, to carry into effect
the punishment inflicted under the Insolvent Act, to which
the defendant ought to submit. I think, therefore, that the
writ must be amended, and that the plaintiff must pay the
costs of this application.

Exch. of Pleas,
1842.

BILTON
v.
CLAPPERTON.

Rule discharged accordingly.

(*a*) Referring to *Plock* v. *Pacheco*, ante, p. 342.

TAYLOR *v.* WHITWORTH.

Jan. 31.

An affidavit of service of a rule nisi stated that the deponents served " the above-named defendant with a true copy of the rule, by delivering and leaving with one H., at the defendant's residence, situate &c., a true copy of the said rule, and at the same time shewing the original thereof, and that the said H. promised to deliver the said copy to the defendant:"— *Held* to be insufficient, as it did not shew a service on any person connected with the defendant's residence.

THIS was a rule to compute principal and interest on a bill of exchange, and the question was as to the sufficiency of the service of the rule nisi. *R. Denman*, in moving to make the rule absolute, produced an affidavit which stated that the deponent, on Saturday, the 29th January, did serve the above-named defendant with a true copy of the rule hereto annexed, by delivering and leaving with one Hitchcock, at the said defendant's residence, situate in Ravenhurst Street, Birmingham, a true copy of the said rule, and at the same time shewing the original thereof, and that the said Hitchcock promised to deliver the said copy to the defendant.

ALDERSON, B. (*a*)—The affidavit is insufficient. It does not appear who Hitchcock is; he may be the deponent's own clerk whom he took with him to the defendant's dwelling-house. It should appear that there was a service upon a servant of the defendant's, or some other person who is connected with his residence.

Rule refused.

(*a*) Sitting alone on the last day of term.

———◆———

BURGH *v.* SCHOFIELD.

Jan. 31.

Where an application for an interpleader rule is made to a judge at Chambers, pursuant to the stat. 1 & 2 Vict. c. 45, s. 2, a judge at chambers only, and not the court, has authority as to the costs of the proceedings.

THIS was a rule calling upon the claimants on a sheriff's interpleader rule to pay the plaintiff's costs of appearance, they having abandoned their claim. The application of the sheriff was made by summons to a judge at chambers pursuant to the stat. 1 & 2 Vict. c. 45, s. 2, who heard the summons, and on the 15th December made an order for an issue, which was subsequently abandoned.

Hayes shewed cause, and contended that the Court had no power under such circumstances to make any order as to the costs, but that the application must be made to the learned judge before whom the previous proceedings had taken place. The stat. 1 & 2 Vict. c. 45, s. 2, enacts, "that it shall be lawful for any judge of the supreme courts to exercise such powers or authorities for the relief and protection of the sheriff or other officer, as may, by virtue of the Act 1 & 2 Will. 4, c. 58, s. 6, be exercised by the said several Courts respectively, and to make such order therein as shall appear to be just;" "and the costs of such proceedings shall be in the discretion *of such judge.*" The statute, therefore, delegates the whole authority of the Court to the individual judge; and the discretion as to the costs may much more fitly be exercised by the judge who has heard all the circumstances of the case. Such a construction is in accordance both with the express words of the Act, and also with all convenience and justice.

Martin, contrà.—According to the rule laid down by the Courts as to the construction of the 1st section of the Interpleader Act, 1 Will. 4, c. 58, the plaintiff had a right to make this application to the Court. According to the interpretation put by the other side upon the Act 1 & 2 Vict. c. 45, nobody has any jurisdiction in this respect but the individual judge who made the order. But it never could have been the intention of the legislature to oust the general jurisdiction of the Court over matters occurring in the Court, whether at Chambers, or elsewhere; that could not be done without express words. Under the 1 Will. 4, c. 58, s. 1, it has been held, that though a judge had originated the proceedings, the Court has jurisdiction as to the costs; yet there "the Court, or any judge thereof," are respectively spoken of throughout the section. The latter act was passed for the express purpose of putting the sixth section on the same footing in all respects as the

Exch. of Pleas,
1842.

BURGH
v.
SCHOFIELD.

first: and there are no words sufficient to deprive the Court of its power to regulate its own proceedings, whether at Chambers or in banc.

Lord ABINGER, C. B.—There is some perplexity in this matter, but upon the whole, it appears to me that by this act of Parliament the discretion is vested in the judge. The case was not provided for by the first act, and the second was no doubt passed to remedy that defect: but the express words of that act give the discretion as to the costs of the proceedings to the judge, and it is sought to be taken away only by a construction founded on the supposed intention of the legislature. There appears to be no inconvenience, however, in construing the act literally, except, indeed, in the event of the judge dying, or being removed to another Court. In the 1st section of the 1 & 2 Will. 4, c. 58, the words are alternative, " the Court, or any judge thereof." Most probably the Court, even if it possessed jurisdiction, would refer the matter back to the judge who had entertained it at Chambers, except in a very plain case. We think, however, that the case is not within the words of this act, and we are not disposed to enlarge them by construction. The rule will therefore be discharged.

PARKE, B.—I also think that this case should be referred back to the judge; and I am strongly inclined to think (although perhaps such a construction is contrary to the intention of the legislature), that the act means that the Court shall have power over the costs where the order was made by the Court, and a judge where the proceedings were before a judge. I should hardly be disposed to restrict the authority to *the individual* judge who made the order. The words may be construed either way, and I should be disposed to put the more enlarged construction upon them, any other leading to much inconvenience. But I think that the case must be worked out by a judge, where the proceedings originated before a judge.

ALDERSON, B., and GURNEY, B., concurred.

Rule discharged.

DAVENPORT *v.* COLTMAN.

THIS was a case sent by his Honour the Vice-Chancellor of England, for the opinion of this Court.

George Coltman, at the time of making his will, and at his death, was seised in fee-simple of the house in Stanley-place, Chester, in his will mentioned, and also of a certain tenement in the county of Lincoln, and a certain other tenement in the county of Hertford. The said George Coltman being so seised, and being also possessed of certain sums of money in the £3 per cent. and £4 per cent. Bank Annuities, and of an interest in the leasehold houses at Liverpool, in the will mentioned, and of the other personal estates therein also mentioned, made his last will and testament, dated the 26th March, 1828, and duly executed and attested so as to pass real estates, in the words following :—" To my son, Thomas Coltman, I bequeath my gold watch, chain, and seals, my carriages, harness, and horses, and cows, market cart, and harness for the same, also whatever is considered as belonging to me at my new residence in Hagnaby Priory. To my daughter, Mary Newbold, I bequeath the sum of £250

A testator, being possessed of estates in the counties of L. and H., bequeathed certain legacies and annuities to his two sons and two daughters. The will then proceeded thus: " That my wife, M. C., may be left in as comfortable a situation as possible, I bequeath to her, for her natural life, the possession of my house in Stanley-place, Chester, together with the use of the plate, linen, &c., and all the joint property in houses in Liverpool, and likewise of interest of money as often as due, arising from the £3 and £4 per

cents., and to have and to hold the same during her natural life, save and except the clauses in favour of my daughters, as already mentioned; at her decease, it is my will and pleasure that M. N., and C. C., (his daughters), shall divide equally between them, *as residuary legatees, whatever I may die possessed of,* except what is already mentioned in favour of others." The will, after giving the executors the power of selling certain leasehold houses in Liverpool, concluded thus :—" But the house in Chester must not be sold as long as my wife lives :"—*Held,* that the residuary legatees took the estates in L. and H. for an estate in fee-simple, commencing at the death of the wife, and that they took the Stanley-place house in fee-simple in remainder, expectant on the death of the wife. *Held,* also, that the wife did not take any interest for life by implication, in the estates in L. and H.

per annum, and, in case of her death, and without issue, the same sum to her husband for his natural life, and afterwards to be equally divided between my son George Coltman and daughter Charlotte Coltman. To my daughter Charlotte Coltman, I bequeath the sum of £250 per annum, and in case she should continue unmarried, or die without issue, the same shall be taken possession of by her brother, George Coltman. To my son, George Coltman, I bequeath the sum of £3000, which he is not to receive till after the death of his mother, and likewise, at her decease, all the plate which I may die possessed of; but, at my decease, he is to have immediately the whole of my library at his own disposal. That my wife Mary Coltman may be left in as comfortable a situation as possible, I bequeath to her, for her natural life, the possession of my house in Stanley-place, Chester, together with the use of the plate, china, linen, and household furniture, and all the joint property in houses in Liverpool, and likewise of interest of money, as often as due, arising from the £3 and £4 per cents., and to have and to hold the same during her natural life, save and except the clauses in favour of my daughters, as already mentioned. At her decease, it is my will and pleasure, that Mary Newbold and Charlotte Coltman shall divide equally between them, as *residuary legatees, whatever I may die possessed of*, except what is already mentioned in favour of others."

The testator then, after giving two small legacies, appointed his wife, John Eden, Esq., and his son Thomas Coltman, his executrix and executors. " As for the houses in Liverpool, they may dispose of any one or the whole of them, whenever the same may be thought advisable for the benefit of the parties concerned; but the house in Chester must not be sold, so long as my wife lives." The houses in Liverpool were leasehold.

The testator died in 1828, without having revoked or altered his said will, leaving his wife, the said Mary Coltman, and also the four children named in his said will,

that is to say, Thomas Coltman, who was his eldest son
and heir-at-law, George Coltman, Mary Newbold, and
Charlotte Coltman, (who has since become the wife of John
Davenport the younger), his only next of kin him surviving.

The questions for the opinion of the Court were, first,
what estate (if any) did Mary Coltman, the wife of the testator, take in the tenements in the counties of Lincoln
and Hertford under the will? Secondly, what estate (if
any) did Mary Newbold and Charlotte Davenport, the
daughters of the testator, or either and which of them,
take in the said tenements in the counties of Lincoln and
Hertford, under the will? And, thirdly, what estate (if
any) did Mary Newbold and Charlotte Davenport, or either
and which of them, take in the said house and tenement in
Stanley-place, Chester, under the same will?

The case was argued in Michaelmas Term (Nov. 15), by

Erle, for the residuary legatees.—The two daughters, by
the residuary clause, took remainders in fee in the house in
Stanley-place, Chester, and also estates in fee in the property in Lincolnshire and Hertfordshire, expectant on the
death of the testator's widow. It will be said that the
words "residuary legatees" apply to chattel interests only,
and it is admitted that they generally do so, and that the
word "possessed" has been held to apply rather to chattel
interests only. But in this case the context shews that the
words are intended to be applied to lands also. The testator clearly shews that he was not acquainted with legal
and technical language. Having given legacies to his two
sons, and annuities to his daughters, and having created a
freehold estate to his wife for life in the house in Stanley-
place, he makes his daughters residuary legatees of *whatever he may die possessed of*, except what is already men-

tioned in favour of others. The intention was not to prevent any property, except what had been previously excluded, from passing under the residuary clause. The
exception to prevent property before devised from falling
into the residue plainly shews an ignorance of technical
language. The last clause in the will—"as for my houses
in Liverpool," (which were leasehold), "the executors may
dispose of any one or the whole of them, whenever the
same may be thought advisable for the benefit of the
parties concerned, but the house in Chester must not be
sold so long as my wife lives," plainly indicates that the
testator was not acquainted with the distinction between
chattel interests and freehold estates, for there is an express exclusion of the house in Chester from the powers of
the executors. In *Wilce* v. *Wilce*(a), the testator commenced his will as follows:—"As touching such worldly
property wherewith it hath pleased God to bless me, I
give, devise, and dispose of the same in manner following:"
and after various bequests and devises concluded:—"all
the rest of my worldly goods, bonds, notes, book-debts,
and ready money, and every thing else I die possessed of,
I give to my son George;" and it was held that George
took a fee in lands of the testator not specifically devised
by the will. *Tindal*, C. J., there says, after commenting
on the will, "by *everything else* must be understood everything else not before disposed of." In *Pitman* v. *Stevens*(b) the devise was —"I give and bequeath all that I
shall die possessed of, real and personal, of what nature
and kind soever," without saying to whom, but adding,
"I appoint P. my residuary legatee and executor," which
was followed by a bequest of certain annuities and legacies, &c.; and it was held to shew the testator's intention
to make P. the residuary legatee of his real estate in fee.
So in *Noel* v. *Hoy*(c), the nomination of the testator's

(a) 7 Bing. 664; 5 M. & P. 682.   (b) 15 East, 505.   (c) 5 Madd. 38.

wife as executrix, and a bequest of "all the property of

whatever description or sort that I may die possessed of," was held sufficient to pass a copyhold estate; and Sir *John Leach,* V. C., said, " A testator is not to be confined to the technical sense of the words which he uses." In *Hopewell* v. *Ackland* (a), a devise with the words " whatsoever else I have in the world," was held to pass an estate in fee. In *Huxtep* v. *Brooman* (b), a devise of " all I am worth" was held sufficient to pass a real estate. In *Brady* v. *Cubitt* (c), *Hope* v. *Taylor* (d), *Hardacre* v. *Nash* (e), and *Pitman* v. *Stevens,* the words " legacy" and " legatee," it was decided, might be applied to lands, if the context of the will shewed it to be the testator's intention so to use them. Devises appointing persons " executors of his houses" have been held to pass lands in fee: *Doe* d. *Hickman* v. *Haslewood* (f); *Doe* d. *Pratt* v. *Pratt* (g). So the words " executors of all my lands for ever:" *Doe* d. *Gillard* v. *Gillard* (h). So, a power to a devisee of lands and goods, to " give what she thought proper of her said effects," it was held, enabled the devisee to devise the real estate: *Doe* d. *Chillcott* v. *White* (i). So in *Doe* d. *Andrew* v. *Lainchbury* (k), the words " property and effects" were also held to pass real estate. *Camfield* v. *Gilbert* (l) may be relied upon by the other side, but the principle is in favour of the residuary legatees. There one, seised in fee of real estate, by her will first made a disposition of her real estates to two persons for life, reserving a rent-charge out of the same, payable first to her uncle for life, and then to her *heir* at law *for life;* which, " together with the repairs during the term, should be considered as *his*

(a) 1 Com. Rep. 164.

(b) 1 Bro. Cha. Ca. 437.

(c) 1 Doug. 31, 40.

(d) 1 Burr. 268.

(e) 5 T. R. 716.

(f) 6 Ad. & Ell. 167; 1 Nev. & P. 352.

(g) 6 Ad. & Ell. 180; 1 Nev. & P. 366.

(h) 5 B. & Ald. 785.

(i) 1 East, 33.

(k) 11 East, 290.

(l) 3 East, 516.

rent for the said farm;" and afterwards she proceeded to make a disposition of her personal property, and then bequeathed and *devised* " all the rest, residue, and remainder of her *effects,* wheresoever and whatsoever, and of what nature, kind, or quality *soever,* (except her wearing apparel and plate), to certain nephews and nieces, to be equally divided between them by her *executors;*" and it was held, that the reversion in fee in the real estate did not pass by the residuary clause, but descended to the heir at law. But there the exception in the residuary clause clearly shewed that the word " effects" was intended to apply to personalty. Here the exception in the residuary clause is of freehold interests, which shews that it was intended to apply to the other freehold interests. In *Doe* d. *Tofield* v. *Tofield* (a), it was held that *real* property might pass under the description of *"personal estates"* in a will, where it was manifest from the whole of the instrument that such was the devisor's intention. Here the testator has used words large enough to include *real* as well as *personal* estate, and must therefore be taken to have intended to include the former; and if the words are large enough to include the house in Stanley-place, they will also include the lands in the counties of Lincoln and Hertford.

Mylne, for the widow.—The words used in the will are large enough to comprehend whatever the testator might die possessed of, both real and personal, and the effect of it was to give the widow an estate for life by implication in the Lincolnshire and Hertfordshire property. In *Saumarez* v. *Saumarez* (b), Lord *Cottenham,* C., says, " In considering gifts of residue, whether of real or personal estate, it is not necessary to ascertain whether the testator had any particular property in contemplation at the moment.

(a) 11 East, 246.   (b) 4 Mylne & Cr. 339.

Indeed, such gifts may be introduced to guard against the testator having overlooked some property or interest in the gifts particularly described. If he meant to give the residue of his property, be it what it may, it is immaterial whether he did or did not know what would be included in it; and if so, it cannot make any difference that such ignorance is manifested upon the face of the will, unless the expressions manifesting it are sufficient to prove that the testator did not intend to use the words of gift in their ordinary, extended, and technical sense." The words of this will are large enough to pass both the real and personal estate; and if so, they are large enough to pass an estate for life to the widow. Two of the persons mentioned in the residuary clause are persons who are next of kin to the testator. In *Roe* d. *Bendale* v. *Summerset* (a), where a testator, being possessed of a term for ninety-nine years, if he or his daughter Betty, or John Bendale, should so long live, devised the premises as follows: "Item, I give to my daughter Mary, after the decease of my daughter Betty, my house, &c., during the life of John Bendale;" it was held that Betty took an estate for life by implication. In *Blackwell* v. *Bull* (b), where a testator directed his business to be carried on by his wife and son for the mutual benefit of the family, and devised his property in trust that at his wife's decease the whole of it, as well freehold as personal, should be equally divided among his children; it was held that the testator, in the words " my family," intended to comprise his wife; and as to the testator's property devised after his wife's decease to his children, it was held upon the whole will, and what appeared to be the evident intention of the testator, that the wife took a life interest by implication, as well in the real as in the personal estate.

(a) 5 Burr. 2608.　　　　(b) 1 Keen, 176.

Cresswell, for the heir-at-law.—In construing this will the Court will no doubt look at the intention of the testator; but the rule is, that in giving effect to that intention, technical words must be allowed to have a technical meaning, unless clearly used by the testator in a different sense. The words "legacy" and "legatee" generally apply to personal property, and it is incumbent on the residuary legatees to shew that the testator intended by these words to pass his real estate. In *Wilce* v. *Wilce* the testator began his will by a recital manifesting a clear intention of not dying intestate as to any portion of his property. In *Noel* v. *Hoy*, the words used were of a very comprehensive description. In *Roe* d. *Helling* v. *Yeud* (a), the words, "all the remainder of my property, whatsoever and wheresoever, to be divided equally," &c., were held not sufficient to pass the real estate, because they were controlled by the latter part of the will. *Mansfield*, C. J., says, "There is no introductory clause in this will, indicating an intention of the testator to dispose of his whole property; nor is there any one provision throughout the will, which has the least relation to real estate." So, in this will, there is no mention of real property except what relates to the house in Stanley-place. *Doe* d. *Bunny* v. *Rout* (b) is to the same effect. *Hardacre* v. *Nash* comes nearer the present case, but there the testator clearly shewed, that by the word "legacies" he intended to denote real estate. Here, no words of inheritance are used in describing the real property. The testator could not have intended his daughters to take a fee-simple in the lands, when it is plain he did not mean them to have an absolute interest in the annuities and legacies. He may, perhaps, have intended that they should take all that the wife took for her life. The word *legatees* in this instance ought to receive its ordinary

(a) 2 N. R. 214.   (b) 7 Taunt. 79.

import, because there is nothing here to indicate clearly that he contemplated anything different from it. Then follows the curious provision as to the houses in Liverpool. " As for the houses in Liverpool, they may dispose of any one, or the whole of them, whenever the same may be thought advisable for the benefit of the parties concerned ; but the house in Chester must not be sold so long as my wife lives." He seems to have thought that the executors had the power of selling the houses ; if he did, he did not contemplate that he had given the remainder in fee in the house in Chester to his daughters. The words would be well satisfied by holding that they were meant to include that which he had before specifically bequeathed to his wife. Then the only other question is, what becomes of the life estates in the property in Lincolnshire and Hertfordshire The widow took no estate for life by implication in that property. In *Roe* d. *Bendale* v. *Summerset*, the parties would have taken nothing but for the devise. Here the heir-at-law would be entitled.

Erle, in reply. — The residuary legatees do not rely merely upon the word *legacy* being construed to refer to real estate, but upon the words " whatever I may die possessed of." Those words have not a technical meaning, but apply equally well to a freehold estate as to a chattel interest, and they are to be construed in their ordinary sense, and are sufficient to convey the fee. In *Doe* d. *Wall* v. *Langlands* (a), a testator, possessed of real and personal estate, after several pecuniary legacies, " gave and bequeathed all and every the residue of his *property*, goods, and chattels, to be divided equally between A. and B., share and share alike, after all his debts paid." The personalty was not quite sufficient to pay all the debts and legacies ; but it was held, that the word *property*, though

(a) 14 East, 370.

thus followed by *goods and chattels*, was sufficient of itself to pass the realty. There Lord *Ellenborough*, C. J., in delivering the judgment of the Court, said, " We think this case distinguishable from *Roe* d. *Helling* v. *Yeud*, where the bequest was to five persons, whom the testator made his executors, and where the enumeration at the end of his will was very particular, and was considered by the Court as incapable of meaning anything but an enumeration of what the testator supposed to be included in his bequest. The clause in that case specified goods, stock, bills, bonds, book-debts, securities, and funded property : and if it were so incapable of being understood otherwise than as enumerating what he meant to include in his expression of *property*, (and which that Court appears to have thought), the conclusion was necessary, that personal property only could pass. The words in this case do not seem to us as requiring any such limited construction of the word *property* before used ; and, therefore, we think the two messuages passed to the devisees." [He cited also *Denn* d. *Gaskin* v. *Gaskin* (a).]

Cur. adv. vult.

The judgment of the Court was now delivered by

ROLFE, B.—This was a case sent by his Honour the Vice-Chancellor of England for the opinion of this Court, as to the construction of the will of George Coltman.

The will, which was duly executed and attested for passing real estates, bears date the 26th of March, 1828, and is in the following words :—[The learned Baron here read the will.]

The testator, at the date of his will, was, and until his decease (which happened a few months afterwards) continued, seised in fee of a freehold house in Stanley-place, Chester, being the house mentioned in the will, and of two

(a) Cowp. 657.

real estates, situate the one in the county of Lincoln and the other in the county of Hertford; and the questions on which our opinion is desired are, 1st, whether the widow took any and what interest in the Lincolnshire and Hertfordshire estates; and, 2ndly, whether the daughters took any, and, if any, what interest in those estates, and in the Stanley-place house, or either of them.

The case turns on the construction to be given to the words in the will following the gift to his wife, viz., "at her decease it is my will and pleasure that Mary Newbold and Charlotte Coltman shall divide equally between them, as residuary legatees, whatever I may die possessed of, except what is already mentioned in favour of others."

On the part of the daughters it is contended, that under this clause they take the fee-simple of all the real estates, subject only to the widow's life interest in the Stanley-place house.

The heir-at-law, on the other hand, contends, that the clause in question does not extend to real estate at all, but is confined to the leasehold houses in Liverpool, and the other personal estate.

Although, in cases like the present, it is always difficult to arrive at conclusions entirely satisfactory, yet, on a full consideration of this will, we think it clear, beyond any fair judicial doubt, that under the words "*whatever I may die possessed of*," the testator intended to include his real estate, as well that in the counties of Herts and Lincoln, as the house in Chester.

The testator was evidently making his own will without legal assistance to guide him in the use of his expressions; and though the words in question are not those which a conveyancer would have employed to include real estate of which a party may die seised, yet they cannot be said to be insufficient to embrace property of that description, if they were meant to do so.

In *Huxtep* v. *Brooman* (a), a gift of "*all I am worth*" was held by Lord *Thurlow* to include real estate, and the authority of that case has never been questioned; on the contrary, in *Doe* v. *Rout* (b), *Gibbs*, C. J., expressly says that Lord *Thurlow* decided rightly. In *Doe* d. *Morgan* v. *Morgan* (c), Mr. Justice *Bayley* assumes it as quite clear, that the words "*all I have, and all I am worth*," would clearly include real estate. Now, surely it would be very difficult for a person not conversant with legal language to understand that the expression, *whatever I may die possessed of*, should not be at least as comprehensive as the words *all I am worth*, or *all I have*. It rarely happens, in fact, that a party making a will does not intend to include every thing over which he has a disposing power; and it is in a great measure from this consideration that the Courts have been led to give a comprehensive meaning to general expressions used by a testator in disposing of his estate. Whether it might at first have been wiser to require, before the heir should be disinherited, expressions of a less equivocal or more technical nature, it is no part of our business to discuss; the principle of a more liberal construction having been adopted, we think it would be very unsafe to admit of refined distinctions between such expressions as *all I am worth, all I have*, and *all I am possessed of*, which, according to the common usage of mankind, would, as we think, certainly be considered as having precisely the same import.

It is not, however, absolutely necessary for us to say what might have been the effect of the words in question if they had stood alone, for we think that there are other parts of this will strongly indicative of an intention to include real estate in the general residuary gift. In the first place, the testator had clearly real estate in his mind, since

(a) 1 Bro. Cha. Ca. 437.   (c) 6 B. & C. 518; 9 D. & R.
(b) 7 Taunt. 82.   633.

he expressly gives a life interest to his wife in the Stanley- *Exoh. of Pleas,*
1842.

DAVENPORT
v.
COLTMAN. place house; and this has always been considered as a circumstance favouring the presumption that general words were intended to include real as well as personal property. But that presumption is, in this case, very much strengthened by the concluding paragraph of the will, in which the testator directs that the Stanley-place house should not be sold till after his wife's death. That paragraph can hardly be read as a power to sell, but rather as a restriction imposed on a power of sale, which the testator assumes to have been already given expressly or impliedly by the previous provisions in the will. There is no charge of debts, —no purpose whatever for which a sale could possibly be necessary or expedient, except that of more conveniently *dividing the house,* as part *of what he died possessed of,* between his daughters.

We think it impossible not to see that the testator considered that the proceeds to arise from the sale of the Stanley-place house (if it should be sold) were to go in the same manner as the proceeds of the sale of the leasehold houses, and this could only be because the former, as well as the latter, were supposed by him to be included under the words, " whatever I may die possessed of."

The Stanley-place house was (if it should be deemed expedient) to be sold *by the executors,* but not till after the wife's death, and then whenever it might be thought advisable for the benefit *of the parties concerned.* It is surely impossible that the testator would have authorized his executors to make sale of a house after it should have become the absolute property of the heir, or that he would have described *the heir* as *the parties concerned.*

These considerations appear to us to lead irresistibly to the inference that the testator considered the Stanley-place house as part of what he had given under the description of *all I may die possessed of.* And that being so, we think the other real estates are also necessa-

rily included; for if the words in question, "*all I may die
possessed of,*" extend to real estate at all, there is nothing
to point their meaning to one part of his real estate alone,
and to exclude the rest. The argument on which we have
relied, as arising out of the direction concerning the sale,
is founded indeed on a matter not applicable to the Hertfordshire and Lincolnshire property; but what we deduce
from the argument is, that the testator considered himself
to have used the words, "*all I may die possessed of,*" in a
sense which must include the Stanley-place house, and
which can only include it by also including the whole of
the real estate.

We further think, that the estate which the daughters
take cannot be less than an estate in fee-simple, for the
testator looked to the probable expediency of a sale and
division of the proceeds, as the most convenient method of
dividing what he had given, and this is evidently inconsistent with the notion of the daughters taking only a partial interest for their lives, or for any other term.

On the part of the heir-at-law, it was pressed on us in
argument that, on the authority of several decided cases,
we ought to restrict the meaning of the word "possessed"
to objects of the same nature as those previously disposed
of, more especially looking at the direction that the subject-
matter of the gift should be divided between his daughters
as residuary legatees—an expression, it was contended,
strongly indicative of an intention to dispose of personal
estate only. But in answer to this argument it must be
remembered, that the previous gifts had not been confined
exclusively to personal estate; and after all, the rule of
construction, which in the cases referred to would confine
the general words to personal estate, is a rule which must
always give way where there exist, as we think there do in
this case, other circumstances plainly and strongly show-
ing that the words were meant to have their fullest
import.

The words *residuary legatees* are certainly not quite technical, when applied to devisees of real estate. But the testator was evidently unacquainted with the ordinary language of conveyancers, and he might have thought that as a sale would probably take place, and so his daughters would take the money-value of the property and not the property itself, therefore the words *residuary legatees* would be the most appropriate; at all events, the use of these words does not appear to us to raise a doubt sufficiently strong to outweigh the other circumstances to which we have adverted.

It seems, however, to us to be clear, that the daughters took nothing till after the wife's death, and we shall therefore certify our opinion that they took the Stanley-place house in fee-simple in remainder expectant on the death of the wife; and that they took the other real estates for an estate in fee-simple, commencing at her death.

With regard to the claim of the wife, we think it altogether unfounded. The circumstance that a devise is not to take effect until after the death of a third person is not sufficient to give to such third person an estate by implication, unless there be something to shew that the land could not have been intended to go to the heir in the meantime—as where the devisee is himself the heir. Nothing of the sort occurs here. The testator might have meant the Hertfordshire and Lincolnshire estates to go to the heir during the widow's life; at all events there is nothing to shew the contrary, and it is pretty plain, from the express gift of the Stanley-place house to the wife for her life, that no other part of the real estate was intended for her. On these grounds we shall certify our opinion that she took no interest whatever in the Herts and Lincolnshire property.

———

The following certificate was afterwards sent:—

"We have heard this case argued, and have considered it, and are of opinion,

"First, that Mary Coltman, the wife of the testator, took no estate in the tenements in the counties of Lincoln and Herts;

"Secondly, that Mary Newbold and Charlotte Davenport took an estate as tenants in common in fee-simple in the tenements in Lincoln and Herts, under the said will, commencing at the death of the said testator's widow;

"Thirdly, that the said Mary Newbold and Charlotte Davenport took an estate as tenants in fee-simple in the Stanley-place house, in remainder expectant on the life estate of the widow.

"ABINGER.

"J. PARKE.

"J. GURNEY.

"R. M. ROLFE."

———◆———

Jan. 31.

JENNINGS and Wife *v.* BROWN and Others, Executors.

The reputed father of an illegitimate child promised to pay the mother an annuity if she would maintain the child, and keep secret their connexion:—
Held, that the maintenance of the child was a sufficient consideration to sustain assumpsit.

ASSUMPSIT.—The declaration stated, that before the making of the promise of the said A. B. B. (the defendants' testator), to wit, on the 1st January, 1833, the plaintiff Mary, being then sole and unmarried, and having theretofore always conducted herself with chastity and decorum, was seduced by the said A. B. B., who then debauched and carnally knew the said plaintiff Mary, so being sole and unmarried as aforesaid, and by means of which said seduction and carnal knowledge the said plaintiff Mary then became pregnant, and afterwards, and in the lifetime of the said A. B. B., and before the making of the said promise, to wit, on the 3rd November, 1833, was delivered of a bastard child, to wit, a daughter, which said child had been and was begotten by the said A. B. B., and is still living; and whereas also afterwards, and in the lifetime of the said A. B. B., and before the making of the said promise as aforesaid, the said plaintiff Mary, so being then sole and unmarried as aforesaid, and having wholly

relinquished and given up all cohabitation and immoral
intercourse with the said A. B. B., had, at his request,
undertaken, and then had the care and nurture of the said
child; and thereupon afterwards, and in the lifetime of
the said A. B. B., to wit, on the day and year last aforesaid, in consideration of the premises, and that the said
plaintiff Mary would continue to take charge of the said
child, and would thenceforth conduct herself correctly and
virtuously, and would also keep secret the said fact that
the said A. B. B. had so seduced and debauched the said
plaintiff Mary, and was the father of the said bastard
child, he the said A. B. B. then promised the said plaintiff Mary, then being sole and unmarried as aforesaid,
that he the said A. B. B., his executors or administrators, should or would punctually pay or cause to be paid
to the said plaintiff Mary, an allowance of £60 a-year
during her natural life, by four quarterly payments in
every year, to wit, on &c. in each year; and the said
plaintiffs aver, that the said plaintiff Mary hath always,
from the time of the making of the said promise of the
said A. B. B. as aforesaid, continued to take charge of
the said bastard child, and that the said plaintiff Mary
hath also, from the time of the making of the said promise
hitherto conducted herself correctly and virtuously, and
did not at any time after the making of the said promise,
and during the lifetime of the said A. B. B., cohabit or
have any immoral intercourse with the said A. B. B., and
hath also always hitherto kept secret the said fact that the
said A. B. B. did so seduce and debauch the said plaintiff
Mary, and was the father of the said bastard child as aforesaid; of all which several premises respectively the said
defendants, executors as aforesaid, have continually had
notice; and the plaintiffs in fact say, that afterwards,
and after the death of the said A. B. B., and after the
said intermarriage of the plaintiffs, and before the commencement of this suit, to wit, on the 12th November,

1841, a large sum of money, to wit, the sum of £180 of the said yearly allowance of £60, for twelve quarters of a year, which then, and as well after the said death of the said A. B. B. as after the said intermarriage of the plaintiffs had elapsed, became due and payable to the plaintiffs under and by virtue of the said promise of the said A. B. B. in that behalf; nevertheless the defendants, executors as aforesaid, not regarding the said promise of the said A. B. B., have not at any time paid to the plaintiffs the said sum of £180, or any part thereof, (although often requested so to do), but have hitherto wholly neglected and refused so to do, and the same is still wholly due and unpaid, contrary to the said promise of the said A. B. B. in that behalf made as aforesaid.

The defendants pleaded non assumpserunt, and other pleas;—traversing the seduction; that the child was begotten by the testator; alleging that the plaintiff Mary had not, at the time of making the promise, relinquished cohabitation with the plaintiff; nor had she undertaken nor had the care or nurture of the child; nor had she continued to take charge of the child, nor kept secret the fact that the testator did seduce the plaintiff Mary, and was the father of the child. But all these pleas, on which issues were taken, were negatived by the finding of the jury.

The cause was tried before *Rolfe*, B., at the London sittings in this Term. It appeared that the action was brought to recover twelve quarterly payments of an annuity of £60 a year, under the following circumstances. The testator, in the year 1833, became acquainted with the plaintiff Mary, a servant in his establishment, and the result was the birth of a child in the month of November in that year, which, by a letter to her father, he acknowledged himself to be the father of, and said that she and her child were amply provided for. It appeared that he paid her an annuity of £60 a year, and refrained from further criminal intercourse with her. Shortly after, the plaintiff Mary entertained intentions of getting married, and applied to the testator for the purpose of getting the annuity previously settled upon her. In reply to which the testator wrote her the following letter :—

" MARY,   Dec. 31st, 1834.

" I received your letter of yesterday, and feel a little annoyed at the distrust you entertain for my not providing for your child while I live, and after my decease. You seem to have got some would-be cunning adviser, which, if you do not mind, will cause you to lose a friend, instead of making one. Your father, by writing an imprudent letter, was very near doing you harm. When I spoke of an annuity, I did not consider that, from your youth and good health, the office would require (to allow the sum of £60 a year) a large deposit of some thousands, and which, were you to die the day after, would be entirely thrown away, besides its being a sum I am neither willing nor able to lay down."

And after stating other matters, and that her marrying would not alter his intentions, he adds :—

" Thus, then, as long as your future conduct is correct, and the situation you have been placed in remains a secret, my allowance to you of £60 a year will be paid with punctuality; but I must remind you, were it to become known, the allowance of a magistrate would be 4s. 6d. or 5s. per week, which is £13 per annum. Under these circumstances, I should recommend you to consider me your friend, and place that confidence in me which you never had reason to doubt. Should you marry, for your mutual happiness, I would never see you but in the presence of your husband."

Shortly after this the plaintiffs were married, and a letter of congratulation, dated January 31, 1835, was written to her by the testator, which contained, amongst others, the following passage :—" The allowance I told you I would make for the maintenance of Emma shall always be punctually paid quarterly."

The annuity was accordingly paid up to the testator's death, in March 1839; but his executors not feeling themselves justified in paying the annuity without the sanction of a court of law, refused to pay it, and the present action was brought. It was proved that the child was now living with the plaintiffs. The above facts having been proved, and the letters read in evidence, the counsel for the defendants objected that there was nothing in the correspondence which made out the consideration as expressed in the declaration. The learned Judge, however, overruled the objection, and the jury found a verdict for the plaintiffs, with £80 damages, leave being reserved to the defendants to move to enter a nonsuit.

Humfrey now moved to enter a nonsuit accordingly. The letters written by the testator, and produced in evidence, do not shew a sufficient consideration to support the action. This is not the case of an instrument under seal, but a mere assumpsit, which is invalid for want of a consideration, and cannot be enforced either at law or in equity. *Binnington* v. *Wallis* (a) is in point. There the declaration stated that the plaintiff had cohabited with the defendant as his mistress; that it was agreed that no further immoral connexion should take place between them, and that the defendant should allow her an annuity so long as she should continue of good and virtuous life and demeanour; that afterwards, in consideration of the premises, and that the plaintiff would give up the annuity, the defendant promised to pay as much as the annuity was reasonably worth. The Court, on general demurrer, held the declaration bad. The only difference between that case

(a) 4 B. & Ald. 650.

and this is, that here it is stated that the testator seduced her, but that makes no difference. [*Parke*, B.—No, that makes no difference; but here the woman has supported the child, and that is a good consideration. It is a matter of bargain, that she is to take care of the child, and to exonerate the father.] In *Binnington* v. *Wallis* there was abundant proof of consideration, for the plaintiff had given up the annuity. [*Parke*, B.—No, that was not part of the consideration; it was a mere moral consideration, which is nothing.] The Courts have never yet gone to the extent of holding such an agreement valid.

Exch. of Pleas,
1842.

JENNINGS
v.
BROWN.

PER CURIAM.—The father might have had the child affiliated on him, and the consideration must be understood to be for ordinary provision. We think that a sufficient consideration.

Rule refused.

RODWELL *v.* PHILLIPS.

Jan. 31.

THIS was an action of assumpsit, brought against the defendant for not permitting the plaintiff to gather certain fruit and vegetables, which had been sold by the defendant to the plaintiff, and which the declaration alleged were growing and being on a close of the defendant's (*a*). Plea, non assumpsit. At the trial before Lord *Abinger*, C. B., at the London sittings after Easter Term, 1841, it appeared that the plaintiff and defendant had entered into the following written (unstamped) agreement, for the sale to the plaintiff of a quantity of fruit and vegetables, growing in the defendant's garden:—

An agreement for the sale of growing fruit is an agreement for the sale of an interest in land, and if of the value of £20 requires a stamp.

"Memorandum of agreement this 14th day of July,

(*a*) See the declaration more fully set forth in the judgment, *post*, p. 504.

1840. Thomas Phillips agrees to sell to Mr. Rodwell all the crops of fruit and vegetables of the upper portion of the garden, from the large pear trees, for the sum of £30; and Lionel Rodwell agrees to buy the same at the aforesaid price, and has paid £1 deposit. Witness our hands.

"THOMAS PHILLIPS.

LIONEL RODWELL."

It was objected for the defendant, that this was the sale of an interest in land, within the meaning of the Stamp Act, 55 Geo. 3, c. 184, sched. Part I., title "Conveyance," and therefore required a stamp; and the Lord Chief Baron, being of that opinion, directed a nonsuit.

In Trinity Term following, *Shee*, Serjt., obtained a rule nisi for a new trial, on the ground of misdirection, against which, in Michaelmas Term (Nov. 23),

E. James shewed cause.—This is a sale of an interest in land, and the agreement, therefore, was not admissible without a stamp. The cases on this subject are all collected and reviewed in *Jones* v. *Flint* (a); and throughout the judgment in that case, the same distinction is taken, as in *Evans* v. *Roberts* (b), between a contract for the sale of fructus industriales, and of things which are the natural product of the earth, as is fruit. Growing fruit goes to the heir-at-law, and is not seizable by the sheriff. The purchase of a growing crop of grass, to be mown and made into hay by the vendee, is an interest in land: *Crosby* v. *Wadsworth* (c); *Carrington* v. *Roots* (d). Here the plaintiff's declaration itself sets up an interest in the land, entitling him to enter and take away the fruit and vegetables. The property vested by the contract itself, and the plaintiff might, if he chose, have entered and gathered them unripe.

(a) 10 Ad. & Ell. 753; 2 P. & D. 594.   (c) 6 East, 602.

(b) 5 B. & C. 829; 8 D. & R. 611.   (d) 2 M. & W. 248.

Shee, Serjt., contrà.—This is a sale of goods, wares, and merchandises, and is therefore within the exemption in the Stamp Act. It is a mistake to say these are not fructus industriales: they may be strawberries and asparagus,— can it be said that those are the natural products of the soil? All fruits and vegetables, in truth, are brought to maturity and perfection in this country by cultivation and manurance. [Lord *Abinger*, C. B.—The difference appears to be between annual productions, raised by the labour of man, and the annual productions of nature, not referable to the industry of man, except at the period when they were first planted.] *Crosby* v. *Wadsworth* is distinguishable on the grounds stated by *Bayley*, J., in *Evans* v. *Roberts*, that there the grass was the natural produce of the land, and also was to be mown by the buyer. *Waddington* v. *Bristow* (a), in which the sale of growing hops was held to be the sale of an interest in land, is of questionable authority. [*Parke*, B.—Hops are fructus industriales. That case would now probably be decided differently. The distinction is pointed out in *Sainsbury* v. *Matthews* (b).] In that case, as also in *Warwick* v. *Bruce* (c), and *Evans* v. *Roberts*, a sale of potatoes growing on the land, even though they were to be dug up by the buyer, was held to be a sale of goods and chattels. *Smith* v. *Surman* (d), *Parker* v. *Staniland* (e), and *Jones* v. *Flint*, are also authorities for the plaintiff. Here he buys only the fruit which the trees may produce; he could not take any part of the tree itself. It is unnecessary for the purpose of the contract to give him an interest in the land; it is sufficient that he have an easement to go upon it, for the purpose of gathering the fruit; and that is implied in the contract of sale: Bac. Abr. Grant, (I.) 89; 1 Saund. 323, n.

Exch. of Pleas, 1842.

RODWELL
v.
PHILLIPS.

Cur. adv. vult.

(a) 2 Bos. & P. 452.
(b) 4 M. & W. 343.
(c) 2 M. & Selw. 205.

(d) 9 B. & Cr. 561; 4 Man. & R. 455.
(e) 11 East, 362.

The judgment of the Court was now delivered by

Lord ABINGER, C. B.—This was the case of an action
upon a contract, setting forth that the plaintiff had bought
of the defendant a quantity of fruit and vegetables, then
growing and being in a certain close of the defendant's, at
a certain rate agreed upon between them, the price of £30,
and in consideration thereof, and that the plaintiff, at the
request of the defendant, had then promised the defendant
that he would accept and receive the said fruit and vegetables, and pay the defendant for the same at the rate or
price aforesaid, the defendant then promised the plaintiff
that he would permit and suffer the plaintiff, and the servants and agents of the plaintiff in that behalf, to enter
into the said close, and with all necessary and convenient
tools, utensils, and implements, to gather and take the
said fruit and vegetables, as and when the same should be
fit for being gathered and taken, and to allow him to have
proper access to the said fruit and vegetables for the purpose aforesaid: And although the said fruit and vegetables
afterwards, to wit, on the day and year aforesaid, became
fit to be gathered and taken, and the plaintiff, with his
servants and agents in that behalf, was then ready and
willing to gather and take the same, and to pay for the
same after the rate aforesaid, whereof the defendant then
had notice; and although the defendant did then permit
and suffer the plaintiff to gather and take a very small
part, to wit, fifty bushels of the said fruit and vegetables,
yet the defendant, not regarding his said promise, did not
nor would permit or suffer the plaintiff, or his servants or
agents in that behalf, to gather or take the residue of the
said fruit, or any part of such residue, although often requested so to do. And then the declaration goes on to
allege, that after the making of the said contract with the
defendant, and confiding in his promise, the plaintiff
entered into and made certain agreements with divers

other persons, for the sale to them of parcels of the said

fruit, which, by the defendant's refusal to permit his servants to take the residue, he was unable to perform, and
that he lost money by the contract.

When the contract was produced at the trial, it appeared
that it was not so extensive in its provisions as set forth in
the declaration. It was answered, that though the contract did not in terms express it, yet it implied all that
was alleged in the declaration. Then the objection was
taken, that it was not a contract for the sale of goods,
wares, and merchandizes, but of an interest in land, and
therefore required a stamp; and I was of that opinion.
There is a great variety of cases, in which a distinction is
made between the sale of growing crops and the sale of an
interest in land; and it must be admitted, taking the cases
altogether, that no general rule is laid down in any one of
them that is not contradicted by some other. It is sufficient, however, for us to say, that we think this case ought
not to be governed by any of those in which it is decided
that a sale of growing crops is a sale of goods and chattels.
Growing fruit would not pass to an executor, but to the
heir; it could not be taken by a tenant for life, or levied
in execution under a writ of fi. fa. by the sheriff; therefore
it is distinct from all those cases where the interest would
pass, not to the heir at law, but to some other person.
Undoubtedly there is a case (a) in which it appears that a
contract to sell timber growing was held not to convey any
interest in the land, but that was where the parties contracted to sell the timber at so much per foot, and from the
nature of that contract it must be taken to have been the
same as if the parties had contracted for the sale of timber
already felled. In this case, there seems to be no doubt
that this was a sale of that species of interest in the produce of the lands which has not been excepted by the

(a) *Smith* v. *Surman,* 9 B. & Cr. 561.

Stamp Act, and that it is not a sale of goods and merchandize; and the contract is of a sufficient value to require a stamp. The nonsuit, therefore, must stand, and the rule must be discharged.

Rule discharged.

———◆———

Jan. 31.

WHITEHEAD and Others, Assignees of BENBOW, a Bankrupt, *v.* WALKER.

The holder of a bill of exchange, on *non-acceptance,* and protest and notice thereon, has an immediate right of action against the drawer, and does not acquire a fresh right of action on the *non-payment* of the bill when due. The Statute of Limitations, therefore, runs against him from the former and *not* from the latter period.

To an action of assumpsit by the fourth indorsee of a foreign bill of exchange against the first indorser, alleging *for* breach non-payment by the drawee, the defendant pleaded, that before the bill became due, and after the indorsement to the third indorsee, and before the indorsement to the plaintiff, the bill was refused acceptance, and was protested; that the third indorsee and the plaintiff, at the time of the indorsement to the latter, had notice of the non-acceptance and protest; and that the defendant had not due notice of the non-acceptance or of the protest:—*Held,* on special demurrer, that a replication de injuriâ to this plea was good.

ASSUMPSIT by the indorsee against the indorser of a foreign bill of exchange. The declaration stated, that heretofore, to wit, on the 8th of August, 1834, and before the bankruptcy of Benbow, in parts beyond the seas, certain persons made their bill of exchange in writing, directed to Messrs. Grayhurst and Company, and thereby requested them to pay to the defendant, ninety days after sight, 721*l.* 0*s.* 3*d.*, value received: that the defendant indorsed the said bill to W. Swainson, who indorsed it to Willis & Co., who indorsed it to Benbow; and that the said Grayhurst & Co. had sight of the said bill, but *had not paid* the same.

Seventh plea.—That before the said bill became due, or had been presented for payment, and after the indorsement of the same to Willis & Co., and before the indorsement to Benbow, the said bill was presented to Grayhurst & Co. *for their acceptance;* that Grayhurst & Co. refused to accept the same; that thereupon the bill was protested for non-acceptance; and that Benbow, as well as Willis & Co., at the time of the indorsement to Benbow, had notice that the said bill had been so presented, and had been so refused, and protested for non-acceptance. Verification.

Eighth plea.—That before the said bill became due, or was presented for payment, and after the indorsement to Willis & Co., and before the indorsement to Benbow, the bill was presented to Grayhurst & Co. for their acceptance, but that they refused to accept the same, and the bill was thereupon protested for non-acceptance; and that the defendant had not due notice of the non-acceptance of the bill, or of its having been so protested; and that Benbow, as well as Willis & Co., at the time of the said indorsement to Benbow, had notice that the bill had been so presented for acceptance, and refused and protested for non-acceptance. Verification.

Ninth Plea.—That before the said bill had become due, or had been presented for payment, and after the indorsement thereof to Willis & Co., and before the indorsement to Benbow, the bill was presented to Grayhurst & Co. for their acceptance, and was refused acceptance; that the bill was thereupon, and before the indorsement to Benbow, duly protested for non-acceptance, whereof the defendant afterwards, and before the indorsement to Benbow, had notice, whereby an action then accrued to Willis & Co. to recover the amount of the bill from the defendant; that Benbow, as well as Willis & Co., at the time of the indorsement to Benbow, had notice that the bill had been so presented for and refused acceptance, and protested for non-acceptance; and that the cause of action in this plea mentioned did not accrue to Willis & Co. at any time within six years, and before the commencement of this suit. Verification.

To the seventh plea there was a general demurrer; the ground of demurrer stated was, that it was no answer to an action for non-payment of a bill of exchange to shew that it was dishonoured when presented for acceptance, and that the party taking it, and suing on it, had notice of such dishonour.—Joinder in demurrer.

To the eighth plea, the plaintiff replied de injuriâ.

To the ninth plea he demurred specially: the causes assigned were, that the cause of action was for *non-payment* of the bill, whereas the plea answered a cause of action for *non-acceptance;* that there is an implied promise on the part of the drawer and indorsers of a bill of exchange, that it shall be paid as well as accepted; that it was the duty of the drawer and indorsers, on notice of the non-acceptance, to enable the drawer to pay the bill, from the neglect to do which a fresh promise arose; that it was no answer to an action for such breach, to shew that there had been a previous breach of such promise; that the plaintiffs might waive the first breach, and bring an action on the second breach; that the remedy for the first breach having expired, was no answer to an action on the second breach; that the Statute of Limitations ran from the time when the cause of action mentioned in the declaration accrued, and not before; and that the plea was double.—Joinder in demurrer.

There was also a special demurrer to the replication, assigning for causes, that the traverse de injuriâ was inadmissible, because the eighth plea relied on matter of discharge by laches, and shewed a release to the defendant by operation of law, and did not consist of matter of excuse. —Joinder in demurrer.

The case was argued at the sittings after last Michaelmas Term (Nov. 26 and 27) by

Crompton, for the plaintiffs.—The pleas demurred to afford no answer to this action. The contract of the drawer of a bill of exchange is, that the drawee not only shall *accept* the bill, but shall *pay* it at maturity; and therefore a cause of action accrues to the holder on its non-payment when due. No doubt the drawer may be *Exch. of Pleas,*
1842. sued upon the breach of his contract by the non-acceptance by the drawee; *Mitford* v. *Mayor* (*a*); but no case can be cited to shew that he *must* be so sued, and that the holder may not take advantage of the subsequent breach by non-payment. *Dunn* v. *O'Keefe* (*b*) is an authority to shew, that a drawer who has had no notice of the non-acceptance may yet be sued by an indorsee for value who had no knowledge of the dishonour. But the argument for the defendant must be, that a right of action having once vested by the non-acceptance, the Statute of Limitations runs from that period, even against an innocent indorsee. The rule of law which compels a party who takes a qualified acceptance to give notice of that fact to the drawer, (*Sebag* v. *Abitbol* (*c*); Bayley on Bills, 253, 5th edit.), clearly implies that he is to have a right of action against the drawer on *non-payment* of the bill; for such notice can only be required for the purpose of preserving a right to sue on the non-payment. [*Parke,* B.—The reason of the notice in that case is, that, inasmuch as the acceptance is not in the form which had been stipulated for by the drawer, he is entitled to be informed of that fact; and the notice may constitute some evidence of his having assented to the acceptance in a qualified form. *Alderson,* B.—Why is notice given of non-acceptance? because the contract is then broken; then if so, can it be broken again?] The breach of contract by non-acceptance may be waived, and the drawer may be sued on the non-payment. Marius, in his "Advice concerning Bills of Exchange," p. 19, (4th edit.), says, "If a bill so made payable [after sight] be omitted to be presently upon refusal protested for non-acceptance, all that time which shall run out between the private presenting of the bill and protesting thereof is lost time, and is not to be ac-

WHITEHEAD
v.
WALKER.

(*a*) 1 Dougl. 55.   (*b*) 5 M. & Selw. 282; *S. C.* in error, 6 Taunt. 305.
(*c*) 4 M. & Selw. 466.

counted as part of the number of days mentioned in the bill of exchange, except the party on whom the bill was drawn do, of his own free will, acknowledge to have seen the bill from the first day it was privately presented to him." And after saying that if a bill is refused acceptance, it shall be protested for non-acceptance, and thereupon the drawer and indorser must give security for payment, with damages and costs, if it be not paid by him to whom directed, at the time limited in the bill; he adds, (p. 28), " But if a protest be returned for want of payment, and if you have had security already given you on the protest for non-acceptance, or for want of better security, then, upon receipt of your protest for non-payment, you may only acquaint the drawer (or party that took up the money) therewith, and tarry out the same proportion of time at which the bill was made payable, to be accounted from the time it fell due, before you demand your principal money, with the re-exchange and charges, of the party that drew the bill, or his surety; who, according to the law of merchants, are bound, jointly and severally, to repay the same upon the protest for non-payment." These passages are adopted as law into Comyns' Digest, tit. " Merchant," (F. 8), (F. 9), and shew clearly that the holder has a right to retain a bill after acceptance has been refused, and to sue the drawer on non-payment at maturity. So also, where a bill has been accepted suprà protest, for the honour of the drawer, and has been presented for payment to the drawee, and to the acceptor for honour, the drawer may be sued for the non-payment: *Hoare* v. *Cazenove* (a); *Williams* v. *Germaine* (b). There are precedents in 1 Wentw. 302, and 2 Chitty on Pleading, 100, of declarations by the first indorsee against the first indorser, after protest for non-acceptance, and also for non-payment. See also another precedent, similar in

(a) 16 East, 391.   (b) 7 B. & Cr. 468 ; 1 Man. & R. 394.

principle, in 1 Wentw. 315. And in *Auriol* v. *Thomas* (a), Exch. of Pleas, the interest was calculated from the notice of *non-payment*.

Secondly, the replication de injuriâ is good. The substance of the 8th plea is, that the drawer was discharged by the neglect of a prior indorser to give him notice of the non-acceptance or protest. That, as against the plaintiff, a subsequent party to the bill, is mere matter of *excuse* for the non-performance of the defendant's contract by non-payment. The case is expressly within the authority of *Humphreys* v. *O'Connell* (b), where de injuriâ was held a good replication to a plea by the acceptor that the bill was accepted for a gaming debt, and that the plaintiff, before the indorsement to him, had notice of that fact.

Bovill, contrà.—The general rule on this subject, as laid down in all the text-books of authority, is, that although the holder of a bill of exchange is not bound to present it for acceptance, yet if he thinks fit to do so, and acceptance is refused, he is bound to give notice of that fact to all the parties to the bill to whom he desires to resort for payment: Molloy, de Jure Maritimo, b. 2, c. 10; Chitty on Bills, 272, (9th ed.); Bayley on Bills, 252, (5th ed.). And after presentment for acceptance and refusal, a right of action vests immediately, and the holder need not again present the bill for acceptance; *Hickling* v. *Hardey* (c); or if he does so, and acceptance is again refused, he is not bound, if payment be also afterwards refused, to protest it for non-payment; *De la Torre* v. *Barclay* (d). For by the refusal of acceptance he acquires a complete cause of action against the drawer and the indorsers: *Starke* v. *Cheeseman* (e); *Mitford* v. *Mayor.* It is at that period, accordingly, that the liabilities of all the parties to the bill are to be determined; and all who take the bill subse-

Exch. of Pleas,
1842.

WHITEHEAD
v.
WALKER.

(a) 2 T. R. 52.   (d) 1 Stark. Rep. 7.
(b) 7 M. & W. 370.   (e) 1 Ld. Raym. 538; 1 Salk.
(c) 7 Taunt. 312; 1 Moore, 61. 128; Carth. 509.

Exch. of Pleas,
1842.

WHITEHEAD
v.
WALKER.

quently to the non-acceptance and protest, take it with all its infirmities; *Crossley* v. *Ham* (a); unless, indeed, in the case of a subsequent holder for value who takes it without notice of the dishonour: here, however, it is admitted by the demurrer that the bankrupt had notice of the non-acceptance and protest before the indorsement to him, and he therefore stands in the same situation as the previous indorsees. It follows from these principles of law, that another new cause of action cannot afterwards arise on the *non-payment* of the bill; if it could, then a recovery in an action brought on the non-acceptance would be no bar to a subsequent action against the same party on the non-payment. The drawing of a bill of exchange is the creation of a debt; it is evidence of an existing debt from the drawer to the payee: *Starke* v. *Cheeseman; Macarty* v. *Barrow* (b); *Bishop* v. *Young* (c); *Workman* v. *Leake* (d): and the contract of the drawer is, that another person, the drawee, shall take upon himself payment of such his debt, according to the terms of the bill; and the moment the drawee commits an unqualified breach of that engagement, the debt becomes payable immediately, and the right of action against the drawer is vested. The plaintiffs must contend for the existence of two concurrent causes of action against the same party arising out of the same contract, which is altogether repugnant to legal principles.

Secondly, the replication de injuriâ is bad. The eighth plea amounts to a discharge of the defendant's promise, and not merely to an excuse for the non-performance of it. It shews, in truth, that no implied promise to pay on the part of the drawer ever arose. And the rule is, that wherever the plea amounts to a denial or avoidance of the contract declared on, the replication de injuriâ is inapplicable:

(a) 13 East, 498.
(b) 2 Stra. 949; *S. C.* cited 3 Wils. 16.
(c) 2 Bos. & P. 83.
(d) Cowp. 22.

Parker v. *Riley* (a); *Howden* v. *Clifton* (b); *Schild* v. *Kil-*
pin (c).

Crompton, in reply.—The argument on the other side is, that because a right of action vests on the non-acceptance, therefore the second breach, by non-payment, never comes into operation; but that is assuming the whole question in dispute. And the passage already quoted from Marius shews clearly, that after protest for non-acceptance recourse may be had to the drawer on default in payment. The position, that the mere drawing of a bill of exchange creates a present debt from the drawer, is questioned by Lord *Ellenborough*, in *Storey* v. *Barnes* (d). Secondly, the replication de injuriâ is clearly good. [On this point he was stopped by the Court, who expressed a clear opinion, that, as between the parties to this record, the plea amounted merely to matter of excuse, and therefore that the replication was good.]

Cur. adv. vult.

The judgment of the Court was now pronounced by

PARKE, B.—The question raised by the pleadings in this case is, whether, if the indorsee of a foreign bill of exchange has presented it for acceptance, and (acceptance having been refused) has duly presented it and given notice to the drawer, (for the defendant, the indorser, is in the same situation), and so has acquired a right of action against him by reason of the non-acceptance, a new right of action afterwards accrues to him on the subsequent presentment of the bill for payment, and non-payment according to its tenor. The plaintiffs, indeed, are not the indorsees who presented the bill, but they are averred to have taken the bill with notice of the fact of presentment and dis-

(a) 3 M. & W. 230.
(b) 1 G. & D. 22.
(c) 8 M. & W. 673.
(d) 7 East, 440.

honour, and therefore stand in the same situation, and are not to be considered as having a title as innocent indorsees; *Dunn* v. *O'Keefe* (a). The practical importance of the point in the present case arises from the delay of the holder in bringing his action. The non-acceptance and the protest thereon occurred in September 1834. The bill, according to its tenor, would not be payable till the subsequent month of December, and this action was commenced in November 1840; so that if a right of action accrued in December 1834, the Statute of Limitations cannot be successfully pleaded; whereas, if there was no right of action accruing subsequently to the protest for non-acceptance in September 1834, the statute is a bar.

On the part of the plaintiff it was contended, that although he undoubtedly might have brought an action in the month of September 1834, founded on the non-acceptance, yet it was optional with him to do so or not; that he might, if he thought fit, waive that action, and proceed merely on the ground of the subsequent non-payment in December 1834. For the drawer of a bill, it was contended, enters into a double engagement with the payee, and through him with the successive holders of the bill, namely, *first*, that the drawee shall accept the bill when regularly presented to him for acceptance; and *secondly*, that he shall pay the bill when regularly presented to him for payment. And if this be a correct representation of the engagement entered into by the drawer, the conclusion seems unavoidable, that whatever right of action the holder might have acquired by the non-acceptance, he certainly is not precluded from suing in respect of the default of payment. But we are of opinion that the contract entered into by the drawer is not such as is contended for by the plaintiff, and that he in fact enters into one contract only; namely, in the case of a bill made

(a) 5 M. & Selw. 282.

payable after sight, that the drawee shall, on the bill being *Exch. of Pleas,* 1842. presented to him in a reasonable time from the date, accept the same, and having so accepted it, shall pay it WHITEHEAD when duly presented for payment according to its tenor; WALKER. and in the case of a bill payable after date, that the drawee shall accept it if it is presented to him before the time of payment, and having so accepted it, shall pay it when it is in due course presented for payment; or if it is not presented for acceptance at all, then that he shall pay it when duly presented for payment.

The counsel for the plaintiff, in support of his view of the law, relied mainly on some passages which he cited from the work of Marius on Bills of Exchange, some of which are adopted in Comyns' Digest, tit. "Merchant," (F. 8) & (F. 9). But with respect to those passages, we must remark that the work of Marius, though undoubtedly one of authority in its way, is scarcely to be looked at as a legal treatise on the subject of bills of exchange. It is, as its title imports, a work giving good practical advice from a practical man to persons receiving and negotiating bills of exchange. The author was a public notary, who lived in the middle of the seventeenth century, when questions of mercantile law were much less perfectly understood than they are now. In some of his notions he was clearly mistaken; as for instance, he considers the holder of a bill of exchange to be in all cases bound to present it for acceptance; and it seems very doubtful whether he supposed the effect of non-acceptance to be anything more than that of rendering it incumbent on the drawer to find better security for the satisfaction of the holder. It is not, however, absolutely necessary to decide that Marius is wrong, for he no where lays down the proposition now insisted on, namely, that after a protest for non-acceptance, a second right of action accrues to the holder on the non-payment. He speaks, indeed, of the holder retaining the bill after non-acceptance, and applying for payment, and suing on default of payment; and this, as a matter of prudence, may probably be the wisest course which a party can pursue.   In spite of the non-acceptance, the drawer still may pay the bill when at maturity, and the holder having by protest and notice on non-acceptance put 'himself in a condition to sue the drawer, may very reasonably, as a matter of prudence, retain the bill, and endeavour to obtain payment when the bill is at maturity, and not involve himself in litigation until there has been a failure of payment as well as of acceptance.   It by no means, however, follows, because this is spoken of as being, what probably it still is, the usual course, that any second right of action arises on the second default.   For let us consider what is the nature of the right which the holder acquires on the default of the drawee to accept.   It is clear (whatever might formerly have been considered on the subject), that by the non-acceptance, followed by the protest and notice, the holder acquires an immediate right of action against the drawer—a right of action, be it observed, not in respect of any special damage from the non-acceptance, but a right of action *on the bill,* i. e. a right of action to recover the full amount of the bill.   The effect of the refusal to accept is (according to the language of the Court of King's Bench in *Macarty* v. *Barrow,* as quoted by C. J. *Wilmot,* in 3 Wils. 16), that the drawee says to the holder, " I will not pay your bill; you must go back to the drawer, and he must pay you."   The holder thus acquires by the non-acceptance the most complete right of action against the drawer which the nature of the case admits, and no subsequent act or omission of the drawee can give him a more extensive right against the drawer than he has already acquired.   But further, on failure of acceptance, the holder is bound to give immediate notice to the drawer, and if he omits to do so, he forfeits all right of action against him, not only in respect of the default of acceptance, but also in respect of the subsequent non-payment.

Now it is very difficult to reconcile this doctrine with the notion that a new right of action arises from the non-payment; for if that were so, it could hardly be that such new right of action could be destroyed by the previous neglect to give notice of a matter unconnected with that out of which the second right of action is supposed to arise. The argument of the plaintiffs must be, that a second right of action on the bill arises from the default of payment in those cases only in which the holder has duly given notice of the non-acceptance, i. e., in those cases only in which the holder, by the hypothesis, must have already acquired a right of action precisely similar to and co-extensive with that which is thus supposed to vest in him by the default of payment. This seems to us to be a proposition so much fraught with inconsistency, and so entirely destitute of principle and authority, that we cannot hold it to be law. It may be added, that if the law were as is contended for the plaintiffs, this inconvenience would follow, that the holder of a bill might at the same time be prosecuting two actions on the same bill against the same party, for the recovery of precisely the same sum.

On these grounds we are of opinion that there must be judgment for the defendant on the demurrers to his 7th and 9th pleas. With regard to the 8th plea, we think the replication de injuriâ is good, and judgment on that plea will therefore be for the plaintiffs.

Exch. of Pleas, 1842.

WHITEHEAD
v.
WALKER.

Judgment accordingly.

Exch. of Pleas,
1842.

Jan. 31.

WHITEHEAD and Others, Assignees of Richard Benbow, a Bankrupt, *v.* ANDERSON and Others.

A notice of stoppage in transitu, to be effectual, must be given either to the person who has the immediate custody of the goods, or to the principal whose servant has the custody, at such a time, and under such circumstances, as that he may by the exercise of reasonable

TROVER for timber, alleging the possession by the plaintiffs as assignees, and a conversion by the defendants after the bankruptcy.

Pleas, first, not guilty; secondly, a denial of the plaintiffs' possession of the goods. All points as to any right of stoppage in transitu were to be raised upon the first and second pleas.

At the trial, at the Liverpool Spring Assizes, 1841, a verdict was found by consent for the plaintiffs, damages £2000, subject to a special case for the opinion of this Court, to be stated and settled by a barrister; wherein it

diligence communicate it to his servant in time to prevent the delivery to the consignee. Therefore, where timber was sent from Quebec, to be delivered at Port Fleetwood in Lancashire, a notice of stoppage given to the shipowner at Montrose, while the goods were on their voyage, whereupon he sent a letter to await the arrival of the captain at Fleetwood, directing him to deliver the cargo to the agents of the vendor—was held not to be a sufficient notice of stoppage in transitu.

The vessel arrived in port on the 8th of August, on which day, before the captain had received his owner's letter, the agent of the assignees of the vendee (who had become bankrupt) went on board, and told the captain he had come to take possession of the cargo. He went into the cabin, into which the ends of timber projected, and saw and touched the timber. When the agent first stated that he came to take possession, the captain made no reply, but subsequently, at the same interview, told him that he would deliver him the cargo when he was satisfied about his freight. They then went on shore together. Shortly afterwards the agent of the vendor came on board, and served a notice of stoppage in transitu upon the mate, who had charge of the cargo; and a few days afterwards received possession of the cargo from the captain:—*Held*, that, under these circumstances, there was no *actual* possession taken of the goods by the assignees; and that, as there was no contract by the captain to hold the goods as their agent, the circumstances did not amount to a *constructive* possession of the goods by them.

Quære, whether the act of marking, or taking samples, or the like, without any removal of any part of the goods from the possession of the carrier, even though done with the intention of taking possession, will amount to a *constructive* possession, unless accompanied by circumstances denoting that the carrier was intended to keep, and assented to keep, possession of the goods as the agent of the vendee.

Before the consignor knew of the bankruptcy of the consignee, he had sent three letters to the manager of a bank in Liverpool, inclosing bills drawn by himself upon certain parties, and he referred therein to the defendants as persons who would settle any irregularity that might occur respecting the acceptances. These letters were communicated to the defendants, and assented to by them. Another letter to the same party inclosed a bill drawn upon the consignee for the price of the timber in question:—*Held*, that the letters were admissible in evidence, and were some evidence to shew an authority in the defendants to stop the cargo in transitu.

The consignor, *before* the stoppage in transitu, wrote a letter to the defendants, in which he assumed that they had stopped the cargo, and gave directions as to the sale of it. This letter did not reach the defendants until *after* the stoppage. Quære, whether it gave authority to them to stop the cargo at the time of the stoppage, or amounted to a valid ratification of that act.

was agreed that, if the opinion of the Court should be in favour of the defendants, then the verdict so found for the plaintiffs should be set aside, and a verdict entered for the defendants; but if the opinion of the Court should be in favour of the plaintiffs, then that the damages should be subject to reduction according to the finding of the barrister.

Richard Benbow, before his bankruptcy, was a timber merchant at Liverpool, and on the 12th of March, 1840, contracted with Charles Birnie, owner of the ship Monarch, that the ship should proceed to Quebec, and there load a full cargo of timber, and should proceed therewith to Wyrewater, otherwise called Port Fleetwood, in the county of Lancaster, and deliver the same, on being paid freight for the timber at a certain rate. It was also agreed that the ship should be consigned to Thomas Benbow, of Wyrewater, the brother of Richard Benbow.

On the 1st of April, 1840, R. Benbow contracted with George Burns Symes, a merchant at Quebec, then at Liverpool, for a cargo of timber for the Monarch, to be shipped at Quebec, and to be paid for by the purchaser's acceptance of the seller's draft at ninety days; and on the 25th of June, the Monarch sailed with the cargo. On the 1st of July, 1840, Symes wrote a letter to John Chaffers, the manager of the Royal Bank in Liverpool, with which bank Symes had an account, inclosing in the letter a bill of exchange, drawn by him on R. Benbow, for 533*l.* 8*s.* 6*d.*, the price of the Monarch's cargo.

On the 27th of June, 1840, a fiat of bankruptcy issued against Benbow, founded on an act of bankruptcy committed on the 26th of June, 1840, and he was duly declared a bankrupt, and the plaintiffs were, on the 8th of July, 1840, appointed his assignees.

On the 9th of July, Mr. Birnie, the owner of the Monarch, having heard some rumours affecting the credit of R. Benbow, wrote from Montrose a letter to the captain of the Monarch, stating the rumours, and requesting the captain to intimate to Thomas Benbow, that before the delivery of the cargo, he, T. Benbow, must produce approved security. The plaintiffs directed T. Benbow to take charge of the cargo of the Monarch for the assignees, on her arrival at Wyrewater. The bill drawn by Symes on Benbow for the price of the cargo was not accepted, and has not been paid.

The defendants, who are merchants at Liverpool, are correspondents of Symes, and on the 18th of July, 1840, dispatched Richard Grindley, one of their clerks, to Wyrewater, with instructions to go on board the Monarch on her arrival there, to serve the notice of stoppage in transitu on the master. The defendants also wrote a letter from Liverpool, on the 18th of July, to Birnie, in consequence of the receipt of which, Birnie, on the 20th of July, wrote a letter to the captain, apprising him of the failure of Benbow, and appointing Grindley, or Mr. Lewtas, of Garstang, near Wyrewater to take charge of the cargo.

The Monarch arrived at Wyrewater between seven and eight o'clock on Saturday evening, the 8th of August, 1840. As she was entering the harbour, T. Benbow saw her, and having hailed the captain and ascertained her name, took a boat to go on board. The vessel let go her anchor, and he got on board about eight o'clock P. M., as the crew were furling the sails. The Monarch was then at the usual anchoring and discharging ground, opposite to the Custom-house, and then came to anchor with a single anchor, at the spot where her cargo was subsequently discharged; but in such a tide-way as there is at Wyrewater, it was necessary that the vessel should be moored with a second anchor, in order to discharge in safety, and the second anchor was not in fact got out until four o'clock next morning, the 9th of August, until which time the pilot remained on board in charge of the vessel. Thomas Benbow so went on board the Monarch for the purpose of taking possession of the cargo, and told the captain that

the ship was consigned to him by the charter-party, and
that he had come to take possession of the cargo. He
told the captain that he, Benbow, had got the bill of
lading; but he did not produce it. The captain invited
Thomas Benbow into the cabin. The bulkheads of the
cabin had been removed, as is usual in timber vessels, and
the ends of the timber, part of the cargo, projected into
the cabin, and Thomas Benbow saw and touched them.
When Thomas Benbow first stated that he came to take
possession, the captain made no reply; but he subsequently, at the interview, told Thomas Benbow that he
would deliver him the cargo when he was satisfied about
the freight; and he did not, at this interview, consent to
deliver immediate possession, or to waive his lien on the
cargo for the freight. Thomas Benbow offered to advance
the captain any money he might want: the captain said
he would require money for various purposes, and that he
expected a letter from his owner; and he then accompanied
Thomas Benbow ashore. At this time the captain received his owner's letter of the 9th of July. T. Benbow,
at the same time, advanced him £40 on account of freight,
to be applied by the captain for the disbursements of the
ship. At this time T. Benbow had not informed the captain, nor had the captain any knowledge, of the bankruptcy
of R. Benbow; and this payment being only a partial
satisfaction on account of the freight, did not alter the
captain's intention to withhold his consent to deliver the
cargo until he was satisfied for the whole of the freight.

Grindley, the defendant's clerk, on the same 8th of
August, got on board the Monarch, about half-an-hour
after the captain had gone on shore with T. Benbow. He
there told the mate that the consignees had failed, and
that he had come to prevent the cargo falling into their
hands. He then delivered to the mate the notice, stating
that it was intended for the stoppage in transitu of the

cargo. Grindley then went on shore, and delivered to the captain the letter of the ship-owner of the 20th of July, whereupon the captain promised and consented to deliver the cargo to Grindley. The following day, the captain tendered to T. Benbow the £40 that he had received from him; but the latter declined to receive it. The cargo was afterwards entered at the Custom-house by Benbow, and the captain consented to deliver the cargo to him. This entry, however, was not acted on, and it was subsequently entered by Grindley, to whom the captain again promised to deliver it. Part of the timber was afterwards put over the ship's side, and delivered to Grindley, Benbow, who was present, making claim to and demanding possession of it. The rest of the cargo was also subsequently delivered to Grindley. The Monarch never moved from the place where she first came to single anchor, and where Benbow first got on board, until after the delivery of the cargo was completed.

It has been already stated, that the defendants were agents for Symes; but the extent of their authority as agents was disputed. Part of the evidence tendered to shew such a general authority from Symes as would warrant the defendants in stopping this cargo in transitu, consisted of letters written by Symes on the 27th of May, the 28th of May, and the 12th of June, 1840, to Mr. Chaffers, the manager of the Royal Bank of Liverpool, which letters had been received, communicated to the defendants, and had been assented to by them, before they interfered to stop in transitu, as stated in the present case. In these three letters, which inclosed bills drawn by Symes on the various parties, and which he directed Chaffers to forward for acceptance, he stated that if any irregularity or informality should occur respecting them, the defendants would assist in getting them in order. There was also a letter of the 1st of July, 1840, written by Symes to Chaffers, in which he inclosed a bill drawn by

him on the bankrupt, Richard Benbow, for the amount of *Exch. of Pleas,* 1842.
the cargo in question, and requested Chaffers to get it accepted. The admissibility of all these letters was objected   WHITEHEAD
to. If these letters, or any of them, are admissible, and   *v.*
are any evidence to shew such general authority, they, to-   ANDERSON.
gether with the other evidence given, suffice to prove such
general authority; and it must be assumed as a fact in the
case, that the defendants had authority from Symes to
stop this cargo in transitu, before they took any steps for
that purpose. If these letters are not any evidence to
prove such authority, then it must be assumed that the
defendants had no authority from Symes to stop this cargo
in transitu, when they interfered for that purpose, unless
such authority was conveyed by the letter next hereinafter
mentioned.

On the 24th of July, 1840, Symes wrote a letter to the
defendants, in which he assumes that they have taken possession of the cargo, and sold it on his account. This
letter was posted on the 24th of July, 1840, and received
by the defendants in Liverpool on the 15th of August,
1840. If this letter could give the defendants authority
from Symes to stop this cargo in transitu, at the time they
interfered for that purpose, it must be taken that they
then had such authority. If this effect cannot be legally
attributed to this letter, Symes by it ratified and confirmed
all that was done by the defendants to stop this cargo in
transitu, and take possession of it.

If the Court should be of opinion that the plaintiffs are
entitled to recover, the verdict is to be entered for them,
damages £460; but if the Court should be of opinion in
favour of the defendants, then the verdict found for the
plaintiffs is to be set aside, and a verdict entered for the
defendants.

The case was argued at the sittings after last Michaelmas
Term, (Nov. 27), by

Crompton, for the plaintiffs.—First, the notice given by the defendants to Birnie, the ship-owner, by the letter of the 18th of July, did not amount to a stoppage in transitu, not being directed to the party who had possession of the goods, and could act upon it. Could a notice given to an owner, residing in Canada or the East Indies, operate to stop in transitu goods on their way to England? To have that eeffct, it ought to be given to the captain, or at all events to the owner within such reasonable time and distance that he may communicate with the captain. [*Parke*, B.—Suppose it were a case of carriage by land; would a notice to Pickford's in London be sufficient, or must it be given to the carrier on the road?] A notice to them might be sufficient, if given in time for them to write and stop the goods. The test is, whether the party receiving the notice would be liable in trover as for a conversion by non-delivery of the goods pursuant to the notice. [*Parke*, B.—Then, in the case of a ship at sea, there must always be a sort of race, and the vendor must take the chance of the consignee's first reaching the port of discharge.] The notice ought surely to be given to the person who can act upon it at the time: otherwise parties may have assumed the possession, and acted as owners of the goods, and their rights may afterwards be devested by a communication coming from the owner abroad, of a notice of stoppage given to him. The rule of law used to be, that a stoppage in transitu could be effected only by the corporal touch of the goods, but that undoubtedly is now otherwise: *Litt* v. *Cowley* (a). But in that case trover would have lain against the carrier for not delivering the goods accordingly; but not so here, unless laches were shewn, or it appeared that the ship-owner could have acted on the notice in time. If the defendants had gone to him at Montrose, and there demanded the goods, his refusal to deliver them would clearly not have amounted to a conversion.

(a) 7 Taunt. 169.

Secondly, the goods came to the possession of the as- *Exch. of Pleas,*
signees on the 8th August, before any act of stoppage in 1842.
transitu. On that day their agent went on board, declar- WHITEHEAD
ing his intention to take possession, and had actual corporal *v.*
touch of the goods; and the captain agreed to hold the ANDERSON.
goods for them, and attorned to their title, for he promised to deliver them on payment of certain freight, which
was afterwards paid accordingly. He became thenceforward
ward the agent of the plaintiffs, to hold the goods for
them. In *Crawshay* v. *Eades* (a), which may be cited for the
defendants, the carrier had not delivered the property to
the consignee, nor agreed to hold it for him, but expressly
retained it by way of lien for his freight. There was in
that case nothing to amount to an attornment by the bailee
in possession of the goods. In *Hawes* v. *Watson* (b), it was
held, that an attornment by a warehouseman to the title of
the vendee, subject to the payment of warehouse rent and
charges, put an end to the right of stoppage. So in *Gosling*
v. *Birnie* (c), where a wharfinger had agreed to hold
timber on his wharf for the plaintiff, a vendee, he was held
liable in trover for the value, notwithstanding his claim for
wharfage. These cases shew that the continuance of the
carrier's lien does not prevent the determination of the
right of stoppage in transitu. *Allan* v. *Gripper* (d) and
Rowe v. *Pickford* (e) are authorities to the same effect. If
it were otherwise, the right of stoppage never would be
gone in cases where the goods are held by warehousemen
·or wharfingers as agents for the vendee, for in all such cases
there is an existing lien. Then, as to the mode of taking
possession, *Ellis* v. *Hunt* (f) is an authority to shew that it
was sufficient in this case. There possession taken by the
consignee's putting his mark upon the goods in the carrier's
warehouse was held sufficient. The present case is stronger;

(a) 1 B. & Cr. 181; 2 D. & R. 228.   (d) 2 C. & J. 218.
(b) 2 B. & Cr. 540; 4 D. & R. 22.   (e) 8 Taunt. 83.
(c) 7 Bing. 339; 5 M. & P. 160.   (f) 3 T. R. 464.

here the plaintiffs, by their agent, had actual touch of the goods, and had the 'carrier's assent to hold for them. More could not have been done; for the goods were to be delivered afloat. In *Jackson* v. *Nichol* (a), where the right of stoppage was held to be undetermined, there was a mere *demand* by the vendee, without any delivery; and the holder had refused to deliver the goods. Here they had come to their ultimate destination, and the captain had agreed to hold them for the benefit of the plaintiffs: and all that was afterwards done by Grindley on behalf of the vendors, could not affect the previous transaction of the 8th of August.

But, thirdly, the defendants had no sufficient authority to stop the goods in transitu. The letters prove no *prior* authority, and a subsequent ratification is not sufficient for such a purpose. [The learned counsel read the letters stated in the case.] The letter from Symes of the 24th July, although written before the stoppage, was not communicated to the defendants until after that event, and therefore cannot be considered as having authorized them to stop the cargo. [*Alderson*, B.—Can you say the letters are not *some evidence* towards proving a general authority? and if they are, the fact is found that the defendants had such authority.] It is submitted that they are not evidence at all. The other letters refer to other transactions, and have no relevancy to this issue. They amount at most to evidence of a special authority to interfere with respect to the bills mentioned in them. And with respect to that of the 24th July, it can only be regarded as a subsequent ratification of the defendant's act, which is not sufficient. In *Nicholls* v. *Le Feuvre* (b), the Court appeared to doubt whether a stoppage in transitu, made by an unauthorized party, could afterwards be ratified. See also *Siffkin* v. *Wray* (c). A subsequent ratification cannot be equivalent

(a) 5 Bing. N. C. 508; 7 Scott, 577.   (b) 2 Bing. N. C. 81.
(c) 6 East, 371.

to a previous authority, where the rights or estates of third *Exch. of Pleas,* parties are to be affected thereby. In this case, if it were *1842.* sufficient, the captain would be made a wrongdoer by re- WHITEHEAD lation, and the assignees would be left in an uncertainty *v.* ANDERSON. whether they had a right to the possession or not. On the same principle, a recognition of a notice to quit, given by an authorised person after it has begun to run, is ineffectual. *Right* v. *Cuthell* (a); *Doe* d. *Mann* v. *Walters* (b). The law is laid down in accordance with this distinction in Story on Agency, 208, 209; and Paley's Principal and Agent, 345, 346, (3rd Edit.)

Cresswell, for the defendants.—In the first place, the letters are amply sufficient to shew an authority given to the defendants to exercise the right of stoppage in transitu on behalf of the vendors. They are obviously the same for this purpose as if they had been addressed to the defendants themselves, having been communicated to and assented to by them. They are not merely *admissible,* but *the best* evidence for the purpose; and they clearly tend to shew a general authority to act on behalf of the vendors, in all cases with relation to unpaid bills which should render such interference necessary. And the finding in the case is express, that if the letters are admissible, and are *any* evidence to shew such general authority, they suffice, with the other evidence in the case, to prove it. But further, the letter of the 24th July, which was written before the stoppage, is no mere act of *ratification;* it professes to *confer* an authority, and takes effect from its date. It is in this respect like a power of attorney, which would become operative from the period of its execution and delivery, though it might not come into the agent's hands until after he had done the act authorized by it. But even if this be not so, it is good as a ratification of the acts

(a) 5 East, 491. (b) 10 B. & Cr. 626; 5 Man. & R. 357.

N N 2

of the defendants. This case differs essentially from those which have been cited, of unauthorized notices to quit afterwards ratified. There a party is called upon to give up a right, or his position is sought to be altered, by force of a document which, at the time, gives him no countervailing protection, for the tenant would remain liable to the rent, notwithstanding the receipt of the unauthorized notice. The same doctrine may perhaps apply as between the principal and *the carrier*, with relation to the stoppage of goods in transitu; and if this were an action by the vendees against the carrier for delivering the goods to the buyers notwithstanding this notice, it might not be sufficient; but the case is different as between these parties. In *Bailey* v. *Culverwell* (a), the general doctrine, that the ratification of an act done for the benefit of the party is equivalent to a previous authority, was distinctly recognised, and has never been disputed, except in the instances falling within the principle stated in *Right* v. *Cuthell*. The same law is broadly laid down in *Whitehead* v. *Taylor* (b).

Secondly, there was in fact a sufficient stoppage in transitu. According to *Litt* v. *Cowley*, the letter to Birnie of the 18th July, if not per se, yet coupled with his consequent letter to the captain, was a sufficient exercise of the right of stoppage. In *Litt* v. *Cowley*, the goods were delivered to Pickford & Co. at Manchester; before they arrived at London, notice of stoppage was served on Pickford & Co. in Manchester; and that was held sufficient. It is said the notice in this case was insufficient, because it did not come to the hands of the captain in time, and he did not act upon it: the same fact existed, and the same argument might have been used, in the case of *Litt* v. *Cowley*. Birnie, who is *the carrier*, assents to stop the goods, and communicates that intention to the master, who then has

(a) 8 B. & Cr. 448; 2 Man. & R. 564.
(b) 10 Ad. & Ell. 210; 2 P. & D. 367.

the goods in his possession, as his servant. That is a suf- Exch. of Pleas, 1842.
ficient act of stoppage.

Thirdly, there was no such previous delivery of the WHITEHEAD v. ANDERSON.
cargo as could defeat the right of stoppage in transitu on
the 8th August. The voyage was not ended at the time
when the agent of the assignees came on board, for the
ship was not so moored as to be ready for the delivery of
the cargo. And it clearly never was in the contemplation
of the parties that the ship should be the warehouse of the
purchaser for the deposit of the goods. There is no agreement on the part of the captain to give up the goods *on
board the ship,* but only that the assignees should receive
them afloat, at the usual place of mooring. The question
then comes to this, was there an *intention to deliver* the
cargo, or a delivery in fact? In *Crawshay* v. *Eades,* the
delivery on the wharf would primâ facie have appeared to
be a delivery to the purchaser; but the Court held that it
could not be so construed, because there the party could
not have intended to part with his lien. So, the purchaser's
act of marking the goods does not of itself import a delivery. [*Parke,* B.—No, the question is quo animo the act
is done. My notion has always been, that the question is
whether the consignee has *taken* possession, not whether
the captain has *intended* to *deliver* it.] Suppose he refuses to deliver, can the consignee take possession in invi-
tum? [*Parke,* B.—Yes, subject to his lien. In *Ellis* v.
Hunt and *Rowe* v. *Pickford,* there was no intention on the
part of the carrier to deliver, so as to devest his lien.] But
there was no intention to withhold the possession—no
adverse demand of lien. Those cases proceeded on the
ground of the place being treated as the warehouse of the
purchaser, and the contemplated end of the transitus. But
further, here there was no actual delivery or taking possession of the goods. There was no assent to their immediate delivery, nor is it said that the agent touched them
with intent thereby to take possession; his doing so might

be merely accidental. There was no such taking possession as would have imposed upon the assignees the duty of taking the cargo out of the vessel. The cases as to an *attornment* are of quite a different character, and amount to this only, that, as between the warehouseman and a second purchaser, the former is estopped by the entry and transfer in his books; such are *Hawes* v. *Watson* and *Gosling* v. *Birnie :* but in such cases the rights of the original vendor remain unaffected. A *symbolical* taking of possession cannot be made operative, and equivalent to actual possession, without the consent of both parties. Suppose the captain had received authority to stop in transitu, could this transaction have prevented it? It clearly amounts to no more than *evidence* of possession, which is rebutted by the other circumstance of the case. *Dixon* v. *Yates* (a) shews that the whole question, whether there has been a delivery or not, depends on the intention of the parties. Here the captain shews his intention, by refusing to deliver till the freight is paid; he merely promises to deliver in futuro, on being satisfied as to the freight, and enters into no engagement to hold for the vendees in the meantime.

Crompton, in reply.—First, no sufficient authority in the defendants is found for the Court to act upon it. [*Parke*, B. —Surely every evidence of a special is evidence of a general authority. *Alderson*, B.—The letters are not admissible, because not relevant, *otherwise* than as shewing a general authority; but surely they are some evidence of that.] The letter of the 24th July could give no authority, except from the time when it was received. [*Alderson*, B. —That question is material only in case the other letters are inadmissible; and the Court have little doubt that they are admissible.]

Secondly, the letter to Birnie, even coupled with his

(a) 5 B. & Adol. 313.

letter thereupon to the captain, was no sufficient stoppage *Exch. of Pleas,* in transitu. Birnie never communicated his assent *to the* 1842. *defendants.* No doubt, his letter to the captain would WHITEHEAD have been a sufficient authority to *him* to stop, if he had *v.* received it before the 8th of August. Those letters would ANDERSON. not have been sufficient evidence to make Birnie liable in trover, if the captain had delivered the goods to the assignees. In *Litt* v. *Cowley,* the facts established that the carriers had the immediate power of doing the act necessary to the stoppage.

Thirdly, there was a sufficient taking of possession by the assignees. It is argued that there was no *intention* on the part of the captain *to deliver;* but that was immaterial. What it is necessary to prove is, either that *actual possession* has been taken, or that the master has become the agent of the vendee, to hold for him; and in this case there was evidence of such agency. It is strictly a case of estoppel, by attornment of the master to the title of the assignees.

Cur. adv. vult.

The judgment of the Court was now delivered by

PARKE, B.—The question for our decision in this case is, whether the unpaid vendor of a cargo of timber legally stopped it in transitu before the transitus was at an end.

The material facts may be stated in a few words.— Benbow, a merchant in Liverpool, ordered a cargo of timber of Symes, a merchant at Quebec, which was dispatched from thence on board a ship belonging to Birnie, of Montrose, chartered by Benbow. The timber was deliverable at the port of Fleetwood, in Lancashire. The price was not paid; and, before the arrival of the vessel in England, Benbow became bankrupt; thereupon the defendants, who were the correspondents of the vendor, gave, on the 18th of July, to Birnie, the owner, at Montrose, a notice of stoppage in transitu, on behalf of the vendor; and Birnie, on the 20th, wrote to the captain, directing him to hold the cargo at the disposal of the defendants' agents, and sent the letter to await the arrival of the vessel at Fleetwood. On the 8th of August, the captain arrived there with the vessel and cargo; but, on that evening, and before the receipt of the letter by the captain from his employer, an agent of the assignees of Benbow went on board to take possession of the cargo, and had a communication with the captain on the subject, and did certain acts on board, which are stated in the special case. The captain went on shore with the agent of the assignees, and soon after, on the same evening, the defendants' agent went on board the vessel, and delivered a notice of stoppage in transitu to the mate, who was left in charge of the cargo. Afterwards, the defendants got the actual possession of the cargo, and the plaintiffs, the assignees of Benbow, bring this action to recover it.

Upon these facts, the first question is, whether the notice given by the defendants to Birnie, on the 18th July, was a sufficient stoppage in transitu; for if it was, the alleged taking possession of the cargo by the agent of the assignees of the purchaser was too late. We think it was not.

It being admitted by the plaintiffs that a notice to the carrier, on the part of the unpaid vendor, is generally a sufficient stoppage in transitu, two objections were taken to this notice; the one, that the defendants, the correspondents of the vendor, were not authorized by him to give it, (and the same objection applies to every other act of the defendants which is put forward as a stoppage in transitu): and the other objection is, that the notice to the ship-owner, who had not himself personally the custody of the goods, was, under the circumstances of this case, insufficient.

Whether the defendants had authority to make a stop-

page in transitu for the vendor, turns upon this point. *Exch. of Pleas,*
Certain letters were offered in evidence, written and sent 1842.
by Symes at a prior time from Quebec to a Mr. Chaffers, WHITEHEAD
the manager of a bank at Liverpool, all referring to the ANDERSON.
defendants as persons who were to act for Symes in case
any difficulty should arise, with respect to different bills
of exchange mentioned in those letters, or to any others,
(amongst which latter was a bill drawn by Symes in favour
of Chaffers, on account of the very cargo of timber in
question). All these letters had been communicated to
and assented to by the defendants, before they interfered; and the special case, in which the facts were found
by an arbitrator, states, that if those letters, or *any* of
them, were admissible to shew such a general authority
as would warrant a stoppage in transitu, they, together
with other evidence in the cause, were, in the judgment of
the arbitrator, sufficient to prove it; and it must be
assumed as a fact, that there was such an authority. We
have no difficulty in saying, that the appointment of the
defendants by Symes to act for him, with respect to *other*
dishonoured bills, and particularly the bill for the cargo
in question, is *some* evidence of a general authority to act
for him, or at least of an authority to take such steps as
they should think fit for the purpose of securing those
bills; and, by implication, an authority to stop the cargo,
for the price of which one of the bills was drawn. And if
it be *any* evidence, the mode of stating the special case
precludes any question (if there were any) as to its
weight.

There is no doubt, therefore, of the authority of the
defendants to make a stoppage in transitu.

The next question is, whether the notice to Birnie, the
ship-owner, living at Montrose, given on the 20th July, is
such a stoppage of the cargo then being on the high seas
on its passage to Fleetwood. We think it was not: but
to make a notice effective as a stoppage in transitu, it

must be given to the person who has the immediate custody of the goods; or if given to the principal, whose servant has the custody, it must be given, as it was in the
case of *Litt* v. *Cowley* (a), at such a time, and under such
circumstances, that the principal, by the exercise of reasonable diligence, may communicate it to his servant in
time to prevent the delivery to the consignee; and to hold
that a notice to a principal at a distance is sufficient to
revest the property in the unpaid vendor, and render the
principal liable in trover for a subsequent delivery by his
servants to the vendee, when it was impossible, from the
distance and want of means of communication, to prevent
that delivery, would be the height of injustice. The only
duty that can be imposed on the absent principal is, to
use reasonable diligence to prevent the delivery; and in
the present case such diligence was used.

The case, therefore, is resolved into this question, whether the circumstances which occurred on the evening of
the 8th August, when the agent of the assignees went on
board, amounted to a taking possession, so as to determine
the right to stop in transitu.

The law is clearly settled, that the unpaid vendor has a
right to retake the goods before they have arrived at the
destination originally contemplated by the purchaser, unless in the meantime they have come to the actual or constructive possession of the vendee. If the vendee take
them out of the possession of the carrier into his own
before their arrival, with or without the consent of the
carrier, there seems to be no doubt that the transit would
be at end: though, in the case of the absence of the carrier's consent, it may be a wrong to him, for which he
would have a right of action. This is a case of *actual*
possession, which certainly did not occur in the present
instance. A case of *constructive* possession is, where the

(a) 7 Taunt. 169.

carrier enters expressly, or by implication, into a new
agreement, distinct from the original contract for carriage,
to hold the goods for the consignee as his agent, not for
the purpose of expediting them to the place of original
destination, pursuant to that contract, but in a new character, for the purpose of custody on his account, and subject to some new or further order to be given to him.

It appears to us to be very doubtful, whether an act of
marking or taking samples, or the like, without any removal from the possession of the carrier, so as though
done with the intention to take possession, would amount
to a constructive possession, unless accompanied with such
circumstances as to denote that the carrier was intended
to keep, and assented to keep, the goods in the nature of
an agent for custody. In the case of *Foster* v. *Frampton* (a),
it is clear that there were such circumstances; whether in
that of *Ellis* v. *Hunt* (b) is doubtful; but it is unnecessary
to determine this point, as there is no finding in this case
even of any act done to the timber *with intent to take
possession*. It is said, indeed, that the agent of the assignees touched the timber, but whether by accident or
design is not stated. There being then no such act of
ownership, it seems to us that unless, by contract with the
captain, express or implied, the relation in which he stood
before, as a mere instrument of conveyance to an appointed
place of destination, was altered, and he became the agent
of the consignee for a new purpose, there was no constructive possession on the part of the vendee.

There is no proof of any such contract. A promise by
the captain to the agent of the assignees is stated, but it is
no more than a promise, without a new consideration, to
fulfil the original contract, and deliver in due course to the
consignee, on payment of freight, which leaves the captain
in the same situation as before; after the agreement he

Exch. of Pleas,
1842.

WHITEHEAD
v.
ANDERSON.

(a) 6 B. & C. 107; 9 D. & R. 108.   (b) 7 T. R. 46.

Exch. of Pleas, remained a mere agent for expediting the cargo to its
1842. original destination.

WHITEHEAD We therefore think that the transaction on the 8th
v. August did not amount to a constructive possession by the
ANDERSON. vendees, and therefore the defendants are entitled to our
judgment.

Judgment for the defendants.

———— ◆ ————

Jan. 31.   ELSLEY *v.* KIRBY.

The sheriff or *PEARSON* had obtained a rule to shew cause why a
other inferior
judge to whom suggestion should not be entered on the record, in order
a writ of trial is to give the defendants costs, under the Tower Hamlets
directed out of
a superior court Court of Requests Act, 23 Geo. 2, c. 30 (*a*). It appeared
has no authority
to certify, under
the Tower Hamlets Court of Requests Act, 23 Geo. 2, c. 30, s. 8, that there was a probable
and reasonable cause of action for 40s. or more.

A party who sues in a superior court a defendant residing within the jurisdiction of the
Tower Hamlets Court of Requests Act, for a debt being the balance of account on a demand
originally exceeding £5, but reduced below that amount by payments before action brought,
is not liable to costs, though he recover less than 40s.

(*a*) Sect. 7 whereof enacts,
"that if in any action of debt, or
action on the case upon an assumpsit, for recovery of any debt
to be sued or prosecuted against
any person or persons aforesaid,
in any of the King's Courts at
Westminster, or elsewhere out of
the said Court of Requests, it shall
appear to a judge of the Court
where such action shall be sued or
prosecuted, that the debt to be
recovered by the plaintiff in such
action doth not amount to the sum
of 40s., and the defendant in such
action shall duly prove by sufficient testimony, to be allowed by
the judge or judges of the said
Court where such action shall depend, that at the time of commencing such action such defendant was resident within the district
thereinbefore described, and was
liable to be warned or summoned
before the said Court of Requests
for such debt; then and in such
case the said judge or judges
shall not allow to the said plaintiff
any costs of suit, but shall award
that the said plaintiff shall pay so
much ordinary costs to the party
defendant as such defendant shall
justly prove, before the said judge
or judges, it hath truly cost him in
the defence of the said suit.

Sect. 8 provides, that where the
plaintiff shall, upon any action
brought in any of the King's

from the affidavits, that the action was by the indorsee against the drawer of a bill of exchange for 17*l.* 13*s.* 7*d.*, but by the particulars the plaintiff claimed only a balance of 8*l.* 15*s.*, principal and interest, giving credit for £11 paid in respect of the bill. The bill itself, when produced on the trial, which took place before the Secondary of London, under a writ of trial, bore an indorsement in the plaintiff's handwriting, acknowledging the receipt of £7. It was proved that the defendant resided within the district comprised in the Court of Requests Act, and was liable to be summoned to that Court. The Secondary left it to the jury to say whether this was a payment in addition to the £11; they thought it was, and gave a verdict for the plaintiff for 1*l.* 15*s.* only. The Secondary certified, under the statute 23 Geo. 2, c. 30, s. 8, that there was a probable and reasonable cause of action for £5.

C. Jones now shewed cause.—The certificate of the Secondary, by the express provision of the 8th section, prevents the operation of the disabling clause of the act of Parliament, and the plaintiff is therefore entitled to his costs. [*Parke*, B.—Is the certificate of the Secondary sufficient for that purpose? It has been held that the

---

Courts at Westminster, obtain a verdict for less than 40*s.*, if the judge or judges who shall try the said cause shall certify that there was a probable or reasonable cause of action for 40*s.* or more, in every such case the plaintiff shall not be liable to pay costs, but shall recover his costs of suit as if this act had not been made.

Sect. 21 enacts, that no action or suit for any debt not amounting to the sum of 40*s.*, and recoverable by virtue of this act, in the said Court of Requests, shall be brought against any person residing or inhabiting within the jurisdiction thereof, in any other court whatsoever.

By the 2 Will. 4, c. 65, the jurisdiction of the above court is extended to debts amounting to £5; and s. 10 provides, that nothing in the recited act (23 Geo. 2, c. 30), or in that act, shall enable the commissioners to decide on any debt, for any sum being the balance of an account on a demand originally exceeding £5.

sheriff, or other inferior judge, to whom a writ of trial is directed, cannot certify to deprive the plaintiff of costs under the stat. 43 Eliz. c. 6, s. 2 (*a*).] That statute requires the certificate of the *justices* before whom the action shall be tried, and it has been held that the sheriff is not a justice within the act; but here the act of Parliament speaks of "the judge or judges who shall try the said cause," and the Secondary is clearly within those words. But, further, the stat. 2 Will. 4, c. 65, s. 10, saves the jurisdiction of the superior courts in a case like this, where the demand originally exceeded £5, and has been reduced below that amount by payments. *Green* v. *Bolton* (*b*) is an express decision to that effect, upon the words of this very act. [*Parke*, B., referred to *Pope* v. *Banyard* (*c*).]

Pearson, contrà.—First, the Secondary had no power to certify. The words of the statute of Elizabeth are much more extensive than those of this act: viz., that "if upon any action personal, to be brought in any of her Majesty's courts of Westminster, it shall appear to the judges of the same Court, and be so signified and set down by the justices *before whom the same shall be tried*, &c. &c., in every such case the judges or justices, before whom any such action shall be pursued, shall not award for costs," &c. &c. In *Wardroper* v. *Richardson, Littledale*, J., says, "The words 'judges' and 'justices' cannot mean any but the judges and justices of the Courts at Westminster." The same construction must be put upon the words "judge or judges" in this statute: they clearly mean the same persons as are mentioned in section 7, where they are expressly designated as "the judge or judges *of the Court* where such action shall be sued." [*Parke*, B.—Those

---

(*a*) *Jones* v. *Barnes*, 2 M. & W. 313; *Wardroper* v. *Richardson*, 1 Ad. & Ell. 75 : 3 Nev. & M. 839.

(*b*) 4 Bing. N. C. 308; 5 Scott, 746.

(*c*) 3 M. & W. 424.

words certainly mean a judge or judges of the superior Court. The question therefore is, whether this is the balance of a debt or demand originally exceeding £5.] The stat. 2 Will. 4, c. 65, s. 10, ought not to be construed to take away any power given by the former statute; that act was meant to be enabling, not restrictive. But further, the 21st section of the 23 Geo. 2, c. 30, imposes an absolute prohibition on the suing in any other court for any debt not amounting (*i. e.* at the time of action brought) to 40*s.*, and recoverable in the Court of Requests; and the 2 Will. 4, c. 65, contains no repeal of that clause.

PARKE, B.—With respect to the first answer which has been given to this rule, that the Secondary, who tried the cause, has granted a certificate that the plaintiff had a reasonable and probable cause of action to a greater amount than £5, I am of opinion that that is not a certificate of a judge within the meaning of the act of Parliament. Then the other question is, whether this case is within the operation of the proviso in the 10th section of the stat. 2 Will. 4, c. 65. This is clearly a debt which could have been sued for in the Court of Requests, under the statute of 23 Geo. 2, c. 30, and the only question is, whether it is within the subsequent act. The proviso refers expressly to the former act, and, as it seems to me, controls the meaning of that act. It provides, that nothing in the recited act, or in that act, shall enable the commissioners to decide on any debt for any sum being the balance of an account on a demand originally exceeding £5. Therefore, although the plaintiff recovers less than 40*s.*, the effect of this clause is to prevent the commissioners from entertaining any jurisdiction over the balance of any debt originally exceeding £5. That brings the question to what is meant by " a demand originally exceeding £5." Now, in the case which has been cited, of *Green* v. *Bolton*, the Court of Common

Exch. of Pleas,
1842.

ELSLEY
v.
KIRBY.

Exch. of Pleas,
1842.

ELSLEY
v.
KIRBY.

Pleas held, that a debt which originally exceeded £5, but had been reduced below that amount by payments from time to time before action brought, was within this 10th section. This was a debt, therefore, which was properly sued for in the superior Court, and the rule must be discharged.

Lord ABINGER, C. B., GURNEY, B., and ROLFE, B., concurred.

Rule discharged.

————•————

Jan. 29.

JEWISON *v.* DYSON.

By charter of the 23 Edw. 3, the King granted to the Earl (afterwards Duke) of Lancaster, (inter alia,) that he might have the return of all writs of the King and his heirs, and summons of the Exchequer, and *the attachment as well of pleas of the Crown*

CASE.—The first count of the declaration stated, that the liberty and franchise of the honour of Pontefract, in the county of York, is an ancient liberty and franchise of our Sovereign Lady the Queen, in right of the Duchy of Lancaster, of great extent, to wit, of the extent of 100,000 acres, and including therein divers, to wit, 200 townships: And whereas our Sovereign Lady the Queen, in right of her said duchy, before and at the time of the making of the letters patent hereinafter mentioned, was, and continually from thence hitherto

[attachiamenta de placitis coronæ] as of other pleas whatsoever, in all his lands and fees, so that no sheriff or other bailiff or minister of the King, or his heirs, might enter those lands or fees to execute the same writs and summons, or to make attachment of pleas of the Crown, or other pleas aforesaid, or to do any other office there, unless in default of the same Earl and his bailiffs and ministers in his lands and fees aforesaid:—*Held*, that thereby the right to appoint coroners within the Duchy of Lancaster was granted, and that such right was an exclusive one: that, therefore, notwithstanding modern usage to the contrary, the county coroner had no authority to exercise the office within any of the possessions of the duchy, concurrently with the duchy coroners, nor unless in default of their performance of the office.

Upon a question whether the Crown, in right of the Duchy of Lancaster, had the exclusive right, under the above grant, of appointing a coroner within the honour of Pontefract, evidence of appointments of coroners, and of their acting, in other parts of the duchy, out of the honour of Pontefract, was held admissible.

By an order made in 1670, by the Chancellor and Council of the Duchy of Lancaster, after reciting that the Court was informed that the coroner within the honour of Pontefract, parcel of the duchy, had usually returned their inquests to the Crown Office, without taking notice therein that they arose within the liberties of the duchy, it was ordered that the coroners should thenceforward specify in their returns when and where the inquests were held:—*Held* admissible in evidence, although no proof was given of any thing done under it.

.hath been and still is lawfully entitled to appoint the coroner of and within the said liberty and franchise, and no other person whatsoever, at the time of the committing of the several grievances by the defendant hereinafter mentioned, had lawful right or authority to perform or execute any duty within the said liberty and franchise, or take any fees, profits, or emoluments, to the said office of coroner appertaining, for any such duty performed or executed within the said liberty and franchise, unless in default of our said Lady the Queen, or of the coroner appointed by her: And whereas our said Lady the Queen, heretofore, to wit, on the 1st day of December, 1837, by her said letters patent, sealed with her seal of the said Duchy of Lancaster, [profert], gave and granted to the plaintiff the office of coroner of and within the said liberty and franchise, together with all and singular the pre-eminence, fees, rewards, profits, and emoluments to the said office belonging, to have, hold, enjoy, occupy, and exercise the said office during her Majesty's pleasure: provided, that the plaintiff should not in any manner interfere with or execute his said office of coroner, by taking any inquests on the body or bodies of any person or persons who might die within the gaol of the said honour; and provided also, that the said letters should be enrolled within three months then next ensuing, &c.: as by the said letters patent, reference being thereunto had, will more fully appear. The count then averred the due enrolment of the letters patent, the acceptance thereof by the plaintiff, and that he had from thence hitherto been and still is the coroner of and within the said liberty and franchise, her Majesty's pleasure never having been in any way determined or revoked; whereby the plaintiff, at the time of the committing of the grievances by the defendant, was, and continually from thence hitherto hath been, and still is, the coroner of and within the said liberty and franchise as aforesaid, and lawfully possessed of the said office, and by reason thereof,

Exch. of Pleas,
1842.

JEWISON
v.
DYSON.

during all the time last aforesaid, of right had and hath had, and still of right ought to have, the exclusive right to take and hold inquests within the said liberty and franchise, upon the view of the bodies of persons lying dead, and who have come by their death within the same, and whereof inquisitions ought by law to be taken, save and except upon the body or bodies of any person or persons who might die within the gaol of the said honour, and to divers fees, profits, and emoluments to the said office of coroner belonging and appertaining, unless in default of our said Lady the Queen, or of him the plaintiff, whereof the defendant, during all the time aforesaid, had notice. It then alleged, that before and at the time of the committing of the grievance by the defendant hereinafter next mentioned, and after the making of the said letters patent, and the acceptance thereof by the plaintiff as aforesaid, and whilst he was such coroner as aforesaid, to wit, on the 8th July, 1839, one Edward Nicholls was suddenly slain and dead, and came to his death within the said liberty and franchise, and not within the said gaol, and his body was lying dead within the said liberty and franchise, and an inquisition ought by law to have been holden and taken upon the view thereof; and the plaintiff was then ready and willing to hold and take the same in pursuance of his said office, and in performance of his duty in that behalf, and neither our said Lady the Queen, nor the plaintiff, had made any default of any kind in their duty in that behalf, whereof the defendant then also had notice. Nevertheless the defendant, well knowing the premises, but contriving and intending to injure the plaintiff, and wrongfully to deprive him of the fees, profits, and emoluments which ought to, and otherwise would, have accrued to him in that behalf, and to intrude upon and disturb him in the possession and enjoyment of his said office, heretofore, to wit, on &c., without any lawful right or authority whatsoever, performed and exercised the office and duty of coroner within the *Exch. of Pleas,* said liberty and franchise, to wit, at the township of Heath, 1842. within the same, and then took and held within the same, JEWISON that is to say, at Heath aforesaid, an inquisition upon the DYSON. view of the body of the said Edward Nicholls, so lying dead within the same as aforesaid, and afterwards, to wit, on &c., received and took to his own use divers fees, profits, and emoluments for and in respect of the said inquisition so taken and held by him as aforesaid, and wrongfully and illegally defrauded the plaintiff thereof, and prevented him from receiving the same, and from exercising his said office of coroner of and within the said liberty and franchise, and intruded upon and disturbed him in the possession and enjoyment thereof.

There were three other counts in the declaration, in respect of inquisitions held by the defendant on the bodies of other persons, at other places within the honour.

To this declaration the defendant pleaded :

First, That our Lady the Queen did not grant to the plaintiff the office of coroner of and within the said liberty and franchise, modo et formâ.

Secondly, That our Lady the Queen, at the time of the said making the said letters patent in the declaration mentioned, was not lawfully entitled to appoint the coroner of and within the said liberty and franchise, so and in such manner that no other person whatsoever should have lawful right and authority to perform or execute the duty and office of coroner within the said liberty and franchise, and to take the fees, profits, and emoluments to the said office of coroner appertaining for any such duty performed or executed within the said liberty or franchise, unless in default of our said Lady the Queen, or of the coroner appointed by her, as in the declaration alleged.

Thirdly, That the defendant, at the several times when, &c., was one of the coroners for the county of York, duly elected and sworn in that behalf, and at the said several times when, &c. had, as such coroner, lawful right to perform and execute within the said liberty and franchise the office and duties of coroner, and to take the fees, profits, and emoluments to the said office and duty within the said supposed liberty and franchise appertaining, the said supposed liberty and franchise being at those times within and part of the said county of York; without this, that the coroner appointed by our said Lady the Queen had at the said times when, &c., exclusive right and authority to perform or execute the office and duty of coroner in the said liberty and franchise, &c. &c., modo et formâ.

Fourthly, That the defendant, at the time of the committing the said several supposed grievances, &c., was one of the coroners for the county of York, duly elected and sworn in that behalf, and at the said times when, &c., had, as such coroner, lawful and concurrent right with the plaintiff to perform and execute within the said liberty and franchise the office and duties of coroner, &c., the said supposed liberty and franchise being at the said several times when &c., within and part of the said county of York: without this, that no other person whatsoever, other than the coroner appointed by our said Lady the Queen, at the time &c., had lawful right or authority to perform or execute any duty within the said liberty or franchise, or take any fees &c. to the office of coroner appertaining &c., modo et formâ.—On all these pleas issues were joined.

The cause was tried before Lord *Denman*, C. J., at the last York assizes. For the plaintiff, there was first put in a charter of the date of 25th September, 23 Edw. 3, (A. D. 1349, whereby that king granted to Henry, then Earl, afterwards Duke, of Lancaster (on the surrender of a former charter granted to his father, in the 16 Edw. 3), inter alia, "that the same Earl may have the return of all writs of us and our heirs, and summons of the exchequer of us and our heirs, *and the attachment, as well of pleas of the crown as of other pleas whatsoever,* [attachiamenta tam

de placitis coronæ quam de aliis quibuscumque], in all his lands and fees, so that no sheriff or other bailiff or minister [vicecomes vel alius ballivus aut minister] of us or our heirs may enter those lands or fees to execute the same writs and summons, or to make attachment of pleas of the crown, or other pleas aforesaid, or to do any other office there [seu ad attachiamenta de placitis coronæ vel aliis prædictis, aut aliquod aliud officium ibidem faciendum], unless in default of the same Earl and his bailiffs and minis- ters in his lands and fees aforesaid." And it was con- tended that the necessary inference from these words was, that the power to appoint a coroner within the lands of the grantee passed thereby, inasmuch as the coroner was the only officer who by law could hold pleas of the crown, by virtue of the Stat. of Westminster the 1st, 3 Edw. 1. Several subsequent charters of the 38 Edw. 3, the 20 Ric. 2, 1 Hen. 4, 2 Hen. 5, and 1 Edw. 4, confirming the privi- leges and franchises granted by the original charter, were also put in and read. The inquisitio post mortem taken on the death of Henry first Duke of Lancaster, A. D. 1361, was also read, whereby it was found that he died seised (inter alia) of the castle, town, and honour of Pontefract, with the manor, lands, and tenements, &c., thereunto be- longing. Next were produced letters patent of the 1 Hen.5, A. D. 1413, whereby John Frankys was appointed *"feodary* of the honour of Pontefract, in the county of York, during the king's pleasure, to be answerable from time to time for what pertained to his said office, during his continuance therein, receiving for the discharge of the said office the fees and wages therefore due and accustomed." Similar subsequent appointments in the years 1425, 1461, 1485, 1501, 1526, and 1559, were also put in. The accounts of Wm. Gyrlington, the feodary appointed in 1526, were read, wherein he rendered to the crown an account (inter alia) of certain chattels of Robert Mawe, late of Gyrlington, in the honour of Pontefract, " a felon who fled, and was taken and seized by the aforesaid feodary." Letters patent of the 3rd Eliz. 1561 were next read, whereby John Malet was appointed to the office of " feodary and bailiff of the liberties and franchises of the honour of Pontefract, part of the duchy of Lancaster, in the county of York, and the offices of escheator, *coroner*, and clerk of the market of the duchy aforesaid, in the said honour of Pontefract, in the county aforesaid; to have, enjoy, occupy, and exercise the offices aforesaid, and either of them, to the aforesaid John Malet, by himself and by his sufficient deputy or deputies for whom he will answer, during pleasure, with the wages and fees to the same office anciently lawfully due, and of right accustomed," &c. &c.   Subsequent appointments in the same terms, of the dates of 1572, 1608, and 1613, were also given in evidence.   It then appeared, that by a marriage settlement made on Queen Henrietta Maria, the wife of Charles I., (11th July, 1629), inter alia, the castle of Pontefract, bailiwicks of East Pontefract, South Pontefract, West Pontefract, and North Pontefract, &c., with several wapentakes, &c., all described as " being within and parcel of the honour of Pontefract, and also all rents and farms, and fines for respite of homage, with their appurtenants, charged in the account of the feodary of the honour of Pontefract, as appeareth by the account of the feodary thereof, mentioned to be of the yearly value of 34*l.* 19*s.* 11¾*d.*," were conveyed to the Earl of Holland and others, as trustees for securing a jointure to her Majesty: and in the 17 Car. 1, (1642), and again in the 12 Car. 2, (1660), and the 13 Car. 2, (1661), there were letters patent, granting to certain persons appointed by the trustees, the office of feodary and coroner of the honour.   In the 24 Car. 2, (1672), the same possessions were, on the death of Queen Henrietta Maria, settled upon Catharine of Braganza, the queen of Charles II.   Previously, in the same year, a lease had been made by the former queen and her trustees for forty years, if the lessees should so long live, of " the bailiwicks of East, South, West, and North Pontefract," &c., " together with the office or offices of bailiff or bailiffs, and collector of the rents and profits within all and singular the said bailiwicks," &c., and also all that the liberty and franchise of the said honour, and the office of bailiff and collector of all fines, amerciaments, estreats, and forfeitures, in every the courts, &c., to be forfeited within the said honour and premises, to be levied and collected by the bailiffs thereof, and the execution and return of all and singular writs, precepts, process, and of all and singular the courts, justices, commissioners, and estreators of the King's Majesty, and the execution thereof within the said honour and premises, with all and singular their rights, members, and appurtenances."   And, in the 28 Car. 2, (1675), and again in 3 Ann. (1704), Queen Catharine and her trustees demised the reversion of the same premises, expectant on the determination of the existing lease, for a further term of forty years, determinable on the life of the lessee.   In 1706, Queen Anne, by letters patent, granted to Nathaniel Booth the office " of feodary and bailiff of the liberties and franchises of the honour of Pontefract, together with the return of writs of and in the same, and the office of escheator, coroner, and clerk of the market in the said honour, and also the office of bailiff and collector of the rents, farms, and revenues of East Pontefract, and the office of collector of the courts there, &c. &c., during pleasure."   Another grant to John Clay, in 1728, in the same terms; also subsequent leases, of the dates of 1749, 1756, and 1765, of the same premises as were comprised in the lease of 1762, were also read.   In 1766, Richard Towne, the lessee under the lease of 1675, by virtue of a license obtained from the Duchy Office, assigned his interest in the demised premises, *except* the office of coroner; and in 1786, the party in whom the interest under the assignment had then vested, took a new lease from the crown, including that office, for twenty years from the 13th March, 1796. In 1793 the office of coroner of the honour was again granted to Thomas Laing; in 1801 it was demised for thirty-one years to William Carratt; in 1815 that lease was surrendered to the Crown, and a new lease for thirty-one years from that date was granted to the same person; in 1819 Carratt obtained a license to assign the office to the plaintiff, and assigned it accordingly by deed dated 17th May, 1819; and in 1828, 1830, and 1837, there were successive grants of the office to the plaintiff by letters patent, by George IV., William IV., and her present Majesty.

It was then proposed, on the part of the plaintiff, to give in evidence grants by the Crown of liberties and offices within other parts of the Duchy of Lancaster, not parcel of the honour of Pontefract. This evidence was objected to by the defendant's counsel, but the learned Judge, after argument, admitted it. Accordingly, a grant was read of the 22 Ric. 2 (A. D. 1399, on the death of John of Gaunt, Duke of Lancaster), to Thomas Duke of Surrey, of the custody of the manor of Rodley and Minsterworth, in the county of Gloucester, with its appurtenants, " and also with waifs, strays, cognizance of pleas, return of writs, courts baron, forests, &c.. chattels of fugitives and felons, with all other liberties and franchises to the aforesaid manor appurtenant," &c.: and also another grant of the same date, to Edward Duke of Albemarle, of the custody of " the castle, lordship and honour of Pontefract, and of the castle and lordship of Bolingbrook," with like general words as above mentioned; " and also with all manner of offices of stewards, *coroners*, constables, surveyors, receivers, auditors, bailiffs, &c., and all other offices whatsoever, to the aforesaid castles, lordships, and honours, pertaining or appendant, together with all manner of issues, revenues, emoluments, and profits thence proceeding," &c.; to hold until the return of Henry of

Lancaster, Duke of Hereford, (afterwards Henry IV.), to this kingdom. Grants to different persons of the office of coroner in the possessions of the Duchy, in the counties of Norfolk, Suffolk, and Cambridge, and also of Essex, Herts, Middlesex, and London, in the reigns of Henry VII. and Henry VIII., were also read. These patents contained a recital as follows:—"Whereas we, in right of our Duchy of Lancaster and by authority of Parliament, among other liberties and privileges, have the authority of keeping and appointing our coroner or coroners within all honours, lordships, &c., within our same duchy and every parcel thereof." Grants of the dates of the 14th and 24th Eliz. of the offices of "feodary and bailiff of the liberties, and escheator, coroner, and clerk of the market of the Duchy of Lancaster, in the county of Lancaster," were then read; and also the accounts of the feodary for the years ending at Michaelmas in the 31st and 34th Eliz., wherein he accounted for deodands upon inquisitions taken on the bodies of persons accidentally killed, and for the value of the chattels of persons found on inquisitions taken to have died felo de se, and also charged his fee as coroner under the statute of Henry 7. A grant to Henry Agard, of the 9 Jac. 1, of the office of feodary, together with those of clerk of the market, coroner, and escheator, within the honour of Tutbury, in the counties of Stafford, Derby, &c., which was also put in, had the following recital:—" Whereas all and singular feodaries by patent of us and our progenitors, of any of the possessions of our Duchy of Lancaster, by force of the letters patent made them under the seal of the said duchy of the office of feodary of any of the same possessions, without any further or larger words, have notwithstanding time out of mind had, used, enjoyed, and exercised the offices of *coroner* and clerk of the market, and also the office of escheator, for seizing the escheats, casualties, and forfeitures within the same liberty or liberties whereof they were so feodaries by patent as is aforesaid, as

Exch. of Pleas, 1842.

JEWISON *v.* DYSON.

belonging to the said office of feodary, as by surrender of precedents and records, proving the common and continual usage thereof, may plainly and evidently appear," &c.

The next piece of evidence tendered was an order of the Chancellor and Council of the Duchy of Lancaster, dated June 17, 1670, which, after reciting that the Court was informed that the coroners within the honour of Pontefract, parcel of his Majesty's ancient possessions of the Duchy of Lancaster, in the county of York, have usually returned all their inquests into the Crown office, without taking notice therein that the same did arise within the liberties of the duchy, from whence the King's officers had taken occasion to issue out process for the seizure and recovery of the deodands, &c., ordered that the coroners should thenceforth specify in their returns when and where the inquests were held. This document was objected to on the part of the defendant, as being no more than a mere private direction by the officers of the duchy to their servants, and no proof being offered of anything done under it. The learned judge, however, received it. There was read also a charter of the 4th Hen. 7, granting to the mayor and burgesses of the borough of Pontefract, that they and their successors should have in the borough the exclusive power and jurisdiction of executing the office of coroner.

There was no proof of any inquisitions actually held within the honour of Pontefract by the duchy coroner, earlier than the year 1798; but two inquisitions taken before one of the coroners of the duchy, in the county of Middlesex, in the 12th & 14th Car. 2, were produced. It was stated not to have been the custom to return them at that period. An order, made at the West-Riding sessions, in May 1758, that the several coroners within the riding should bring in their accounts to the quarter sessions, was put in, and it appeared that from that period down to about 1789 there were entries in the books of the sessions of payments made to the coroners of the honour of Pontefract for their charges for inquisitions taken within the honour: the whole number so proved being about 70. In 1797 the then coroner of the honour obtained a mandamus to the justices of the West-Riding, commanding them to pay him the fees and charges of his office in respect of inquisitions taken within the honour, and it was shewn that payments were subsequently made to him and his successors, down to the present time. It appeared, that during most part of the same period, similar payments had been made also to the county coroners, in respect of inquests held within the honour of Pontefract. It was proved that the plaintiff had taken, between 1819 and 1838, 647 inquisitions; and his predecessor, Mr. Carratt, between 1798 and 1819, 147.

For the defendant, reliance was in the first instance placed on the statute 3 Edw. 1, providing that "through all shires sufficient men shall be chosen to be coroners," &c., as being anterior to the charter of 23 Edw. 3, and declaratory of the common-law right of election in the freeholders of the county. It was contended also, that inasmuch as the right of holding inquests within the honour had been exercised concurrently for a long period of time by the coroners of the county and of the honour, the words of the charter ought not to be construed as conferring an exclusive right within the honour; and if they did, that the grant must be presumed to have been subsequently determined by act of Parliament, release, or some other means. Inquisitions, and also appeals of murder, taken before the coroner of the county, in respect of deaths occurring within the honour of Pontefract, commencing in the reign of Edward 2, and proceeding through most of the subsequent reigns down to the year 1826, were then proved. One was in the 4th Elis., the year in which the grant of the office of coroner of the honour was made by the Crown to John Malet. The accounts of some of the coroners in early times were also put in, wherein they

charged themselves with the receipt of the goods of persons found in some of the inquests so held to have died
felo de se. A lease for twenty-one years in the 87th Eliz.
(A. D. 1595) was put in; it stated the demise as being
of "all profits and commodities happening and arising
within the office of feodarer of the honour of Pontefract,
that is to say, the profits of the goods and chattels of
felons, and felons of themselves, fugitives, outlaws, deodands, waifs, and estrays, being parcel of the possessions
and revenues of the queen and of her Duchy of Lancaster," &c. It was also proved by parol evidence, that
the coroners of the county in recent times had been in
the habit of holding inquests within the honour without
interruption. And it appeared that in the year 1797,
after the issuing of the mandamus against the justices,
an arrangement was made between the county coroner
and the honour coroner, which was sanctioned by the sessions, that they should hold inquests concurrently within
the honour, according as each should be nearest to the
place of the death; which arrangement was abided by
until the appointment of the plaintiff.

The learned Judge, in summing up the case to the jury,
after going through all the evidence, told them that the
only question for their consideration was, what was the
construction to be put upon the original grant contained
in the charter of the 23 Edw. 3 to Henry Earl of Lancaster; and expressed his opinion, that if they thought the
evidence shewed that it was a grant of such privileges as
could only be exercised by an officer entirely analogous to
a coroner at this time, then it was in terms an *exclusive*
grant of such office. His Lordship then left it to the jury
to say whether they were satisfied that the word "feodary,"
as used in the early documents, meant the word "coroner,"
as it had now come into common use and general understanding; and stated, that if they were of opinion that
there was a grant of the office of coroner by the charter of

Edward 3, they could not be asked to presume an act
of Parliament to set up the right of the county coroner,
nor could any other course of proceedings in point of law
vary the effect of the grant, or create a *concurrent* jurisdiction. The jury found a verdict for the plaintiff.

In Michaelmas Term (*Nov.* 9), *Wortley* moved for a rule
to shew cause why the verdict should not be set aside,
and a new trial had.—The learned Judge misdirected
the jury in several particulars: first, in not leaving to
them the usage, ancient and modern, for the coroner of
the county to act within the honour of Pontefract, as
evidence that there was *no* grant by the Crown of the
office of coroner of the honour; and also in stating, that if
there was such a grant by the charter of Edward 3, the
right of appointment thereby granted must in point of
law be *exclusive*. He ought to have laid before them the
whole evidence of usage, as affording strong ground for an
inference that the terms of the charter never were intended
to convey any such grant at all. It is laid down in *Jenkins* v. *Harvey* (a), that from uninterrupted modern usage a
jury *ought* to presume the immemorial existence of the
right in question. [*Parke*, B.—All the evidence of usage
by the county coroner was consistent with an exclusive
right in the Crown: it may all have taken place when he
was absent, or in default of appointment by the Duchy.]
But the case of the plaintiff was, that the appointment was
always regularly made by the name of *feodary*. It was
argued that the words "quod habeat attachiamenta de
placitis coronæ" inferred a power to appoint coroners, the
coroner being the only officer who could by law attach
pleas of the Crown: but the sheriffs and bailiffs of the
Crown had the same power. That appears from the
stat. 8 Edw. 1, c. 10, which, after directing that "through

Exch. of Pleas,
1842.

JEWISON
v.
DYSON.

(a) 2 C. M. & R. 894.

all shires sufficient men shall be chosen to be coroners, the most wise and discreet knights, which know, will, and may best attend upon such offices, and which lawfully shall attach and present pleas of the Crown ;" enacts also, " that sheriffs shall have counter-rolls with the coroner, as well of appeals as of inquests, of *attachments,* or of other things which to that office belong." It is not, therefore, a necessary inference from these words that there should be a coroner. Neither was the appointment of " feodary" at all identical with that of coroner. The feodary appears to have been an officer attached to the Court of Wards, and accompanying the escheator in the execution of his duties. It is true that it appeared from the appointments and accounts of these feodaries, that they took the goods of felons and fugitives, and felos de se ; but that is by no means conclusive as to the nature of their office. [*Parke,* B.—The description of the " feodary" in Spelman's Glossary is nothing like a coroner. It was an official appointment by the Master of the Court of Wards.] The verdict for the plaintiff doubtless proceeded much upon the assumption that the feodary was the coroner. [*Parke,* B.— It is quite clear that under this charter it is an exclusive appointment or nothing ; because there is an express prohibition for any other King's ministers to interfere.] There is one case in which it is actually provided that there shall be a concurrent jurisdiction between coroners, for the convenience of the public, namely, in the case of the coroners of the verge of the palace, by the stat. 28 Edw. 1, c. 5. Again, the Lord Chief Justice of the Court of Queen's Bench, and all the other Judges of that Court, are concurrent coroners wherever they go. There is, therefore, nothing illegal or repugnant in such a concurrent jurisdiction. The terms of the grant are very ambiguous, and therefore the evidence of usage ought to have been applied to interpret them, and to ascertain of what it was a grant, and how far an exclusive one. [*Parke,* B.—It seems to me to be clear,

that if it granted the right to appoint a coroner at all, it *Exch. of Pleas,* 1842.
granted an exclusive right.]

JEWISON
v.
DYSON.

Secondly, the learned Judge misdirected the jury also, in stating to them that they could not presume an act of Parliament, or any other means whereby such grant by the Crown, if it carried the coronership, could have been revoked or extinguished. [Lord *Abinger*, C. B.—Who ever heard of the presumption of an act of Parliament against the Crown? It has been said that a private act of Parliament might be presumed for the purpose of supporting private rights.] It is not necessary to presume an act of Parliament; there are many other processes by which this right may have been lost, *e. g.* by release, or by merger. In 9 Rep. 26, it is laid down, that "when the king grants any privileges, liberties, or franchises, in his own hands, as parcel of the powers of his Crown, as bona et catalla felonum, fugitivorum, utlagatorum, et bona et catalla waviata, extrahia, deodanda, urecium maris, &c., within such possessions, then if they come again to the King, they are merged in the Crown, and he has them again in jure coronæ." So, this right of the Duchy may have merged in the Crown. [Lord *Abinger*, C. B.—The stat. of the 1 Hen. 4, which provided for the separation of the Duchy of Lancaster from the Crown, would prevent that.] In *Bedle & Beard's case* (a), it was held that a grant might be presumed against the Crown. So, in *Mayor of Horner* v. *Hull* (b), and *Powell* v. *Milbanke* (c), it was held that a grant or charter from the Crown, which ought to be matter of record, might be presumed, though within the time of legal memory. The same doctrine is recognised in the recent case of *Regina* v. *The Chapter of Exeter* (d). In ancient times, the office of coroner was rather of a burthensome than a lucrative nature, and whether the Duchy appointed or not would not be matter of general

(a) 12 Rep. 5.
(b) Cowp. 102.
(c) Id. 103, n.
(d) 4 P. & D. 252.

interest, so that the right might be put an end to without its being known by what precise means.

Thirdly, the evidence relating to appointments made and acts done in other parts of the Duchy of Lancaster, not within the Honour of Pontefract, was not receivable in this case. It did not go to prove any general custom prevailing in several districts held under the same tenure. It was not shewn at what period, under what circumstances, or by what grants, any portion of those possessions had become parcel of the Duchy. [*Rolfe*, B.—There could not be any acquisition by the Duchy after Henry the Fourth came to the crown. *Parke*, B.—It is evidence of what the Duke of Lancaster has done by virtue of the original charter. If it appears that he has appointed coroners in many other places comprised in the original charter, that is strong evidence to shew that he has the right in the Honour of Pontefract. Contemporaneous usage is always evidence to explain a charter.] The case of *Rowe* v. *Brenton* (a), on the authority of which the Lord Chief Justice admitted the evidence, is different, because there confessedly all the tenants in the different manors set up the same right, and the only question was, what was the nature of that general right. The party against whom the evidence was adduced had either the same identical title, or none at all. [*Parke*, B.—So it is here; these places are all comprised in the same grant.]

Lastly, the order of the Duchy Court in 1670 was no evidence. It was no more than a mere private direction to the servants of the Duchy, not shewn to have been communicated to the inhabitants of the Honour, or in any way made public, nor was there any proof of anything done under it. The direction of a lord of the manor, many years ago, to his bailiff, to claim all the minerals throughout the manor, never acted upon, might as well be made evidence against a tenant of the manor. [Lord *Abinger*, C. B.—Is it not like the common case of proving

(a) 8 B. & Cr. 765; 3 Man. & R. 143.

ancient leases, without shewing anything done upon them? *Parke*, B.—The only question for us is as to the admissibility of the evidence; we have nothing to do with the weight of it. Lord *Abinger*, C. B.—This is not like a mere private declaration; it is an act done by a public body, acting under the appointment of the Crown. The Chancellor and Council of the Duchy issue an order, which they are competent to issue. It is not to affect the rights of private persons: it is a question between the Crown in one capacity and the Crown in another.]

He moved also on the ground that the verdict was contrary to the evidence.

The Court took time to consider whether they would grant a rule, and on a subsequent day a rule was granted only on the point relating to the construction of the charter of Edw. 3, and refused as to the other grounds on which it was moved. Against this rule cause was shewn in this term (Jan. 21 and 27) by

Cresswell, *T. F. Ellis* (Attorney General of the Duchy of Lancaster), *Martin*, and *Robinson*.—[Lord *Abinger*, C. B., intimated that the Court were satisfied, that if the charter of Edw. 3 gave the right to appoint a coroner, it gave the exclusive right: and that the only question to be argued was, whether the words were sufficient to give the right at all.] In the first place, the plaintiff, having obtained the verdict, on the question distinctly left to the jury, upon all the evidence of usage, whether the words of the charter were or were not sufficient to confer the right, is not now bound to establish that it *must* have passed thereby, but the defendant is bound to shew that it *could not*. Lord Coke, in his Commentary on the first statute of Quo Warranto, 2 Inst. 282, says, " Where any claimed before the justices in eyre any franchises by an ancient charter, though it had express words for the franchises claimed; or if the words were general, and a continual possession pleaded of the franchises claimed; or if the claim was by old and obscure words, and the party in pleading, expounding them to the Court, and averring continual possession according to that exposition; the entry was ever *inquiratur super possessionem et usum*, &c., which I have observed in divers records of those eyres, agreeable to that old rule, *optimus interpres rerum usus*." There is, however, little difficulty in shewing that, by a necessary implication, the terms of this charter did carry a grant of the office of coroner. It cannot be necessary that the instrument should in terms give to the grantee a power to appoint any particular officer by name. If it grant the power of exercising certain functions and discharging certain duties, which are properly to be discharged by an officer bearing a particular title, it necessarily gives the power to appoint such officer for that purpose. Thus, a person having the return of writs has, without any express authority for that purpose, the power to appoint bailiffs to execute the writs and make the returns: *Newland* v. *Cliffe* (a), *Atkyns* v. *Clare* (b). In the present charter, the clause respecting the return of writs and summonses does not expressly give the power to appoint officers, and yet in the non-intromittant clause it assumes them to exist, " unless in default of the same Earl and his bailiffs and ministers." The original words of the clause in question are—" Quod idem comes et hæredes sui prædicti in perpetuum habeant retorna omnium brevium nostrorum et hæredum nostrorum, et *attachiamenta tam de placitis coronæ* quam de aliis quibuscumque, in omnibus terris et feodis suis; ita quod nullus vicecomes vel *alius ballivus seu minister noster*, vel hæredum nostrorum, terras seu feoda illa ingrediatur, ad executiones eorundem brevium et summonitionum, seu ad attachiamenta de placitis coronæ vel aliis prædictis, aut

(a) 3 B. & Adol. 630.   (b) 1 Ventr. 399.

aliquod aliud officium ibidem faciendum, nisi in defectu ipsius comitis Lancastriæ, et hæredum suorum prædictorum, ac ballivorum et ministrorum suorum." Now, first, the words "ballivus seu minister noster" are sufficient to include the coroner. In Magna Charta, c. 17, (the chapter taking away power to hold pleas of the Crown), the coroner is enumerated together with other bailiffs of the king:— " Nullus vicecomes, constabularius, *coronatores*, vel *alii balivi nostri* teneant placita coronæ nostræ." The sheriff, the constable, and the coroner, are all alike designated as bailiffs of the Crown. But further, the power to make attachments of pleas of the Crown carried with it the power to perform—under what title is immaterial—the office and duties of a coroner. And the words "attachiamenta de placitis coronæ," and " attachiamenta placitorum," are equivalent in effect. In the book entitled " Placita de Quo Warranto," (printed under the authority of the Record Commissioners), p. 28, it appears that "the abbot of St. Albans was summoned to answer the King, (temp. Edw. 3), by what warrant he claimed (amongst other things) to have the return of all writs touching his liberty, and to make a coroner in his liberty;" and his answer was, that, as regarded the making of coroners within his liberty, he produced the charter of King Edward I., in which it was contained, "that whereas the abbot and convent of St. Albans laid claim to such a franchise of old, viz. that the steward of their liberty of St. Albans, and his clerk, should discharge the office of coroners within their liberty, and the justices in eyre, by reason of the insufficient execution of the said office, had taken that franchise into the King's hands, &c.; the King pardoned the said abbot and convent the trespass aforesaid, and granted to them that they, in their Court of St. Albans, without the King's writ, might be able, at the due and necessary times, to choose and create from among the better and more lawful of their freeholders coroners in

Exch. of Pleas, 1842.

JEWISON
v.
DYSON.

their liberty of St. Albans, *to make attachments of the pleas of the Crown* (attachiamenta placitorum coronæ) arising in all places within the same liberty," &c. This proceeding shews, in the first place, that the *name* of coroner was not necessary to the execution of the office, which was there exercised by the *steward* of the liberty; and, in the next place, that the making attachments of pleas of the Crown was the peculiar duty of the coroners. Again, at p. 121, it appears that the Prior of the church of St. Mary of Carlisle was summoned (temp. Edw. 1) to answer by what warrant he claimed, amongst other things, "that neither the sheriff, nor any other bailiff of the Lord the King, should enter his fees to make summonses and attachments, distress, or any other office to exercise, without the license and will of the same prior," &c.: and the prior comes and claims those liberties by charter of 53 Hen. 3, wherein was contained a grant to the Bishop of Carlisle, (afterwards confirmed to the prior and his successors), "that no sheriff, constable, or other bailiff of the lord the king might have entry or power in the aforesaid lands or men, but that the whole might pertain to the aforesaid bishop and his successors, and their bailiffs, except the attachments of pleas of the Crown, [attachiamenta de placitis coronæ], which when the coroners should come to make, they should so make them that the franchise of the aforesaid bishop or his successors should be in nought impaired." In another place (p. 176) appears a claim by the Abbot of Glastonbury, in the same reign (Edw. 1), under charter of Hen. 3, that no sheriff, constable, or other bailiff of the king might have entry or power in the lands of the abbey, except the attachments of pleas of the Crown [attachiamenta de placitis coronæ]: and the like claim is made in the same reign by the Bishop of Salisbury (p. 801), " præter attachiamenta placitorum coronæ." And in the concluding clause of the charter now in question, it is granted that the Earl of Lancaster, by himself, or by his bailiffs or ministers, may have and levy certain fines, amercements, forfeitures, &c., " sine occasione vel impedimento nostri vel hæredum nostrorum, justitiariorum, escaetorum, vicecomitum, *coronatorum, vel aliorum ballivorum seu ministrorum nostrorum quorumcumque.*" The Crown, therefore, was in no way whatsoever to interfere by its coroners or other officers, within the district over which the Earl was by the charter authorized to exercise the functions therein mentioned, for which purpose he must have the power to appoint the proper officers. Now, by the stat. of Westminster 1st, 3 Edw. 1, c. 10, it is provided that the *coroners* to be chosen as therein directed " lawfully shall *attach and present* pleas of the Crown." And the counter-roll thereby directed to be kept by the sheriff, is merely as a check to shew what the coroner has done : the sheriff is not thereby authorized to attach or present pleas of the Crown. An appeal of murder has been quashed, on the ground that it had been taken by the sheriff instead of by the coroner. Then from the stat. 4 Edw. 1, De Officio Coronatoris, which states with great particularity the duties of the coroner as they existed at the common law, it appears that almost every duty which was commenced by the coroner terminated in attachment. Those who are found guilty upon an inquest super visum corporis, are to be taken and delivered to the sheriff (not to be taken *by* the sheriff) and committed to gaol, " and such as be founden, and be not culpable, shall be *attached* until the coming of the justices." So, in the case of persons drowned or suddenly dead, "if they were not slain, then ought the coroner to attach the finders, and all others in company." So, in the case of treasure found, he is to inquire who were the finders, and who is suspected thereof, " and hereupon he may be attached for this suspicion, by four or six more pledges, if they may be found." " Further, if any be appealed of rape, he must be attached, if the appeal be fresh," &c. So in the case of wounds, "any

Exch. of Pleas, 1842.

JEWISON
v.
DYSON.

that be appealed of the force shall be attached also, and surely kept in ward, until the principal be attained or delivered." Deodands are to be valued, and delivered in to the towns where the death took place: and wreck of the sea, if any lay hands on it, is to be attached by sufficient pledges. So that throughout his office, the coroner is to take proceedings which terminate in attachment. The like description of the duties of the office at common law is given by Bracton, lib. 3, c. 5, fol. 121.

But further, the grant by the charter of 22nd Richard 2, to the Duke of Surrey, of the custody of a part of the possessions of the Duchy of Lancaster, and also the grant of the same date to the Duke of Albemarle, which comprises the Honour of Pontefract itself, in their enumeration of the officers of which they give the right of appointment, *expressly* include the coroner. That is a contemporaneous exposition of the previous grant of Edw. 3, operating against the Crown, and shewing the extent of the privileges and franchises which had been granted away by the Crown. The King thereby admits, that whenever the Duke of Hereford should come in, he would have a right to take those lands, and the privileges belonging to them, again from the Crown: and thus makes the concession against himself, that the power to appoint the coroner had been included in the charter of Edw. 3.

Nor has there been any usage which really conflicts with this construction. From the time of Queen Elizabeth downwards, it appeared that coroners have regularly been appointed by that name, in the Honour of Pontefract: and from a much earlier period an officer was shewn to have been appointed, who, under the name of feodary, was competent to discharge and did discharge the duties of the coroner. But the only question now being, whether the charter is capable of receiving the construction contended for on behalf of the Crown, the evidence of acts done under it need not be entered into, after the finding of the jury, which the Court has intimated its intention not to disturb, in case the grant itself be capable of such an interpretation (a). [*Wortley* here intimated that he intended also to dispute the verdict on the ground that, even supposing the words of the charter to be susceptible of the construction that it gave the right of appointing a coroner, yet the grant was invalid, for that the Crown could not confer such power by the ambiguous and general words used therein, but only by express words. The plaintiff's counsel objected that the rule had not been granted on this point; but the Court thought that it would be convenient to have it finally settled. *Wortley* then referred to 1 Roll. Abr. 491 as an authority shewing that a grant by the Crown to hold cognizance of pleas does not give the grantee power to appoint a judge.] Because, if the grant is for such a purpose, he must himself be the grantee of the judicial office, and cannot delegate the appointment to another. But if, as is conceded, the Crown has power to grant by *express words* the power to appoint a coroner, why not also by implication? The only argument that can be advanced against a grant in general terms is, that the Crown may have been deceived, and may not have known what it was granting; but that brings back the question to what is the reasonable construction of this grant, as explained by the contemporary documents, and whether the exercise of the functions of coroner was not plainly within its contemplation. If it be, it is as good to bind the Crown as if express words had been introduced. And how can this defendant, representing, not the Crown,

(a) At the conclusion of *Cresswell's* argument, the other counsel for the plaintiff were relieved from arguing the point as to the effect of the word "ballivus," and of the words "ad attachiamenta de placitis coronæ faciendum." See further, as to the former, Fleta, pp. 20, 22, and the Stat. of Exeter, 14 Edw. 1; and as to the latter, Bracton, 121, b; Fleta, lib. i. cc. 18, 25, (p. 20); 22 Assis. pl. 94, (22 Edw. 3); and the Placita de Quo Warranto, p. 333, (post, 556).

but the freeholders of Yorkshire, use against the Crown a principle of law established for the protection of the Crown? It was expressly decided in the *Case of the Duchy of Lancaster* (a), that all the rights which belonged to the Duchy of Lancaster are, since its annexation to the Crown, to be exercised with all the privileges and prerogatives belonging to the Crown. Suppose the charter, instead of being in these words, had run thus—that the grantee should have the privilege of discharging, by himself and his officers, the duties, amongst others, of coroner, though without giving expressly the power to appoint the coroner; can it be doubted that that would have been sufficient? Or suppose it had been that the grantee should have the power of executing and returning writs, of holding inquests, making deodands, attaching pleas of the Crown, and so forth, and that he should appoint all the necessary officers for those purposes; would not that give the power to appoint a coroner? And the terms actually used are fully equivalent to this, inasmuch as the grantee is to exercise such functions, and no sheriff or other minister of the Crown is to interfere unless in default of the grantee and his bailiffs and ministers. The implication is a necessary one, that the grantee is to have the power of appointing that officer who alone could discharge the duties and enjoy the privileges thus vested in the office. The charter of 1 Hen. 4 being a statutory charter, and confirmed by the parliamentary charters of 1 Edw. 4 and 1 Hen. 7, the only question which can properly arise is as to the effect of the grant, and none can be raised as to the power of the Crown to make it. If however that shall be insisted upon, there is the clearest authority on that point. The saving clause of the stat. 28 Edw. 3, which expressly reserves the right of all lords of franchises, coupled with the admitted doctrine that no right could be claimed but by charter from

---

(a) Plowd. 212, b.

Exch. of Pleas, 1842.

JEWISON
v.
DYSON.

the Crown, of itself shews that the Crown could grant the right to appoint a coroner. In Coke's Entries, p. 544, there is an information against Lord Paget, for claiming " habere ballivum suum dictæ villæ de Burton fore coronatorem domini regis infra manerium et hamlet prædictum, et quod nullus alius coronator dicti domini regis vel hæredum suorum comitatuum Stafford vel Derby se intromittat." Lord Paget in that case sets out the grant by which he claims the right of appointing a coroner, and the Attorney-General confesses the plea, and judgment is given allowing the liberties claimed. This point, therefore, being beyond doubt, it must be contended that it is necessary to name the officer in the charter, in order to pass the right of appointment. In the book already cited, the Placita de Quo Warranto, there are some entries strongly applicable to this part of the case. In p. 333, is an entry of an information in quo warranto against the Abbot of Battle, wherein he is summoned to answer (inter alia) why he claims " habere infangenthef et utfangenthef et habere coronatorem proprium in hundredo suo de Wy." The Abbot asserts his claim to these franchises by his plea as follows:—As to infangenthef and utfangenthef, he says that William the Conqueror " concessit ipsi ecclesiæ manerium quod dictum Wy, cum membris suis, et saka et soka, tol et them, et infangenthef et utfangenthef, et eâ ratione clamat habere furcas," &c. Then he sets up another charter of Henry 3, granting treasure trove, " et quod nec abbas nec monachi ad quoslibet comitatus vel shires vel hundreda venire cogantur, sed habeant per omnia maneria sua curiam, cum regiâ libertate et consuetudine." Then he goes on to claim the office of coroner, on the ground that his predecessors " virtute cartæ prædictæ regis Conquestoris, et concessionum et confirmationum aliorum regum super dictorum, habuerunt coronatorem suum proprium usque jam triginta annis elapsis, tempore domini regis Edwardi, patris domini regis:"—that by the negligence of one of

his predecessors the county coroners had intromitted into
the office, but that he had obtained the charter of the
Crown, and notwithstanding such non-user, he was entitled to exercise the right, and had accordingly appointed
his own coroner, as his predecessors had been used to do.
Then follows a writ to the justices in eyre, commanding
them, that if on inspection of the rolls of pleas of the
Crown, or otherwise, it should appear to them that any of
the Abbot's predecessors had appointed his own coroner by
virtue of the said charters, they should permit him to have
his coroner within his liberty without impediment: and
the record goes on to state, that on inspection of the rolls
an entry was found of the appointment of a coroner of the
liberty. It appears, therefore, that in this instance the
right to appoint a coroner was claimed under charters containing no special words whatever referring to the office,
and that the claim, being referred to the proper authorities,
was allowed, notwithstanding a period of thirty years' non-
user. It further appears in the same case, that thereupon
the Archbishop of Canterbury came in and alleged that he
was prejudiced thereby, for that if the Abbot had the right
of appointing a coroner within the hundred, it interfered
with his, the Archbishop's, right of having the return of
writs, and *attachments*, &c. within his manor of Broke, in
the same hundred. This record, therefore, throws light
also on the interpretation of the word " attachiamenta ;"
for in the grant to the Abbot there is no mention whatever
of attachments by name. In the same book, (p. 305),
there is another case, in which the Abbot of Ramsey is
summoned to answer " quo warranto clamat habere coronatores proprios, et amerciamenta quorumcumque tenen-
tium, et catalla felonum et fugitivorum," within his liberty
of Ramsey: and he pleads, that Henry 2 granted to the
Abbey of Ramsey " sokam, sak, tol et theam, infangenthef, forstall, et blodewite, et murdrum, et inventionem
thesauri, et omnes alias libertates coronæ suæ pertinen-

tes in terrâ suâ, &c., et omnia alia placita coronæ regis Exch. of Pleas,
pertinentia, sicut ipse melius et plenius habuit in regno 1842.
suo, &c.; et inde dicit, quod per prædictam cartam clamat JEWISON
habere thesaurum inventum, et retornum brevium, et reci- DYSON.
pere brevia originalia, et ea placitare per justiciarios suos
proprios, *et habere proprios coronatores,* et placita coronæ
infra libertatem placitare;" &c.   The Attorney-General,
in answer to the plea, objects that the charters ought to
be judged of and interpreted by the king and his council,
to what liberties they ought to be extended, inasmuch as
in them are contained *general and obscure words;* and he
demands that the Abbot be put to his election, whether he
claims them by prescription or grant, "cum non sit juri
consonum, quod quis possit se per duos baculos defendere."
This case also shews that it was usual to claim the grant
of the office under words not expressly referring to it.   In
the 2 Inst., 496, Lord *Coke,* commenting on these words
of the Statute of Quo Warranto — "Et illi qui habent
chartas regales, secundum chartas illas et earundem plenitudinem judicentur,"—says, "Here is an excellent rule
for construction of the king's letters patent, not only of
liberties but of lands, tenements, and other things which
he may lawfully grant; that they have no strict or narrow
interpretation, for the overthrowing of them, sed secundum earundem plenitudinem judicentur; that is, to have
a liberal and favourable construction, for the making
of them available in law usque ad plenitudinem, for the
honour of the king."   The first case in which the expression " general words" occurs with relation to grants by
the crown, is in 17 Vin. Abr. 180 (Prerogative (C. c.)),
where it is said, (citing from the Year Book, 8 H. 4, f. 2),
"the right of the king shall not pass by general words."
But, on looking at the case in the Year Book, it appears
that the question was, whether the goods of a prisoner,
who, standing mute, suffered the peine forte et dure, and
died under it, were felon's goods within the meaning of a

Exch. of Pleas,
1842.

JEWISON
v.
DYSON.

grant from the Crown, and not whether all felons' goods did not pass under such words. In the note in the same page of Vin. Abr. it is said, "what he can grant only by his prerogative can never pass by general words, and therefore choses in action will not pass without special words:" but the reason of that, as appears by the case to which reference is made, in 12 Rep. 2, is, not that what he possesses because he happens to be king shall not pass by general words, but that that which in the mouth of a subject would have passed shall be considered to pass, but it shall not comprehend anything else: that is, the words shall not be strained beyond their ordinary meaning. So, where it is said that the grant of cognizance of pleas does not give the right to hold an assize, the explanation of that is also to be found in the Year Book, 9 H. 6, 27 b; not that it is too general, and therefore the assize, being one species of plea, shall not pass; but that it is no plea at all—"assize non est placitum, sed querela." In *Evans* v. *Ascough* (a) there is this dictum of *Jones*, J.—"If the king grant an ecclesiam, the advowson passes; for the intent, and not the precise words, are to be observed in the grants of the Crown" (b). An authority may be referred to on the other side in 17 Vin. Abr. 142, where it is said, "If the king grants to another to hold pleas before his bailiffs, stewards, or justices, if he had no such officers before the grant, he cannot make them by it." That also is an extract from the Year Book, 7 H. 4, f. 5 b: and it is remarkable that Brooke, in his Abridgment, (Patents, pl. 9), puts precisely the opposite interpretation on the same passage: but assuming the construction in Vin. Abr. to be the right one, the meaning is, that if the grantee has no such officers, it is a grant de non existentibus, and therefore void; and he cannot claim by implication the

---

(a) Latch, 248.
(b) See also *Whistler's case*, 10 Rep. 65, where it was held that the advowson of a manor passed by general words.

right of making such offices. [Lord *Abinger*, C. B.—
There is another principle applicable to that case; that
the grant to a well-known existing officer of a judicial
power is good; but the Crown cannot grant the power of
delegating it to a third person.] Accordingly, in the same
note, citing from the 2 Hen. 7, fol. 18, it is laid down—" If
the king grants conusance of pleas to one N., and does
not say before whom it shall be held, the grant is void;
for the grantee cannot make a judge; but if he had
court before, then the grant is good." This passage occurs
in the Year Book only incidentally, in illustration of the
question, whether the king could by implication grant the
power to make a corporation, by granting that which could
be done only by a corporation. However, in the Lib. Ass.,
37 Edw. 3, fol. 217, there is a case where the bailiff of the
town of Beverley claimed to have cognizance of all manner
of pleas, under a charter whereby the king granted to the
provost of the town " curiam suam," and the franchise
was allowed; and it was held that the court might be held
by the provost's steward or bailiffs. Again, in 17 Vin.
Abr. 89, is this passage:—" The king cannot dispose of
his crown by testament, though it be under the great seal;
nor of the ports of the kingdom, nor of the jewels of the
crown, nor of power to pardon treason or felony within
this kingdom, nor of power to make judges, justices of the
peace, or sheriffs, nor of such which concern government in
a high degree : of these the king can neither make a grant
nor a testament. He may grant the lands which he has in
jure coronæ by his letters patent, or by his will under the
great seal." To which there is a note, which is cited from
the Y. B. 1 Hen. 7, fol. 16 :—" The king cannot grant a
power to any to make justices of oyer and terminer, but he
ought to constitute such justices himself; for it is a high
prerogative." But the case itself does not go so far; it is
as follows :—" Grant of the king made to the abbot of St.
Albans to make justices is not good, for it is a thing an-

nexed to the crown, and cannot be severed, as grant to make denizen or to pardon felons is not good ; contrary of steward in leet, or justice where conusance of plea is, for those are the stewards or justices of the king; but the grant above to the abbot to make justiciarios suos is not good, and such cannot allow clergy to a felon," &c. It would seem, therefore, that the difficulty rather was on the language of the charter, in giving the grantee power to make *his own* justices, and not *the king's*. But none of these authorities are applicable to the quasi judicial office of a coroner, but only to judges in the higher and proper sense of the word. In Com. Dig., Courts, (P. 2), it is said—" So the king may grant conusance of pleas, by which the grantee shall have conusance of all pleas commenced in other courts out of such precinct," &c. : then follows an extract from 1 Roll. 491 :—" So an ancient grant de curiâ regali, or omni regiâ potestate, is sufficient, if conusance upon it has been allowed." " So such ancient grant is sufficient, though no judge be named, where the bailiff of the grantee has always used conusance." In Com. Dig., Franchises, (A. 1), the author adopts the rule laid down by Lord *Coke* in the 2 Inst. 282 (a), as a true rule for the construction of franchises. And again, in Com. Dig., Grant (G.), where the whole law on the subject of the construction of grants by the crown is collected, under the article (G. 5)—(" Grant by the Crown in respect of certainty,") the rule laid down, taken from the 9 Rep. 47a, is—" So a grant of the king, which has sufficient certainty for shewing fully that the king was not deceived, will be good." And every instance there given, of uncertainty sufficient to avoid such a grant, has reference to matters which belong to the king by right of his prerogative, which cannot pass by mere general words ; as for instance, by the grant of a manor, which has come by forfeiture or otherwise into the

(a) Cited ante, p. 557.

hands of the crown, with all liberties, privileges, &c. there-

with formerly held, felons' goods would not pass, although
they had formerly been granted and held with the manor.
Now the right of appointing a coroner is not a matter which
the crown has in right of its prerogative; in the absence
of any grant from the crown, it would have remained in
the freeholders of the county, according to the stat. of 3
Edw. 1. By the grant of a manor, with general words, an
advowson has been held to pass: *Whistler's case* (a). So,
by the grant of a hundred, Lord *Hale* says (b) that there
passed "not only a liberty which had a court, and also
commonly a leet, which is called the leet of the hundred,
but there was also an implied power of making a bailiff."
So, by the grant of a forest, cum omnibus incidentibus,
appendiciis, et pertinentiis, it was held that the grantee
should have courts of attachment and *swanimote*, though
not a justice-seat; "because that was necessary to give any
validity to the forest as a forest:" Manwood's Forest
Laws, 36. So also here, if the coroner be the proper
officer to make attachments of pleas of the crown, the
right of appointing that officer as clearly passed.

[They argued also, that the words "ex speciali gratiâ,"
in the grant, indicated the liberality with which the king
intended to grant, and so favoured a liberality of construction; and cited as to this point Jenkins's Century, p. 255,
pl. 45, and p. 209, pl. 47; *Harris* v. *Wing* (c), and *The Case
of Mines* (d).]

Wortley, *W. H. Watson*, and *Hardy*, in support of the
rule (Jan. 27 and 28).—The question in this case is,
not whether this grant gave the Duke of Lancaster the
power to appoint an officer to attach pleas of the Crown,
but whether the terms of it, by a necessary implication, gave him the power to appoint *a coroner*, for all

(a) 10 Rep. 65.   (c) 3 Leon. 249.
(b) 1 Ventr. 403.   (d) Plowd. 330, b.

the purposes incident to that office, to the exclusion of the coroners who, by the statute of 3 Edw. 1, were ordained to be elected by the counties: there being no non obstante clause, which, if the crown had meant to set aside the operation of the statute, one would have expected to find in the charter. If, therefore, this grant is to take effect in derogation of the general rights of the Crown and of the public, it ought to be at least by a necessary and positive implication, which the Court cannot resist. But the terms of the charter may be satisfied without the supposition of the existence of a coroner at all. Now there are several cases in which a grant of this nature can have no legal effect whatever. If it professes to grant a part of the king's prerogative, it is invalid; so also, if it be uncertain, the grant is therefore invalid; for the law supposes that the king did not know the extent of the grant he was making, and it is said that "dolus latet in generalibus." Again, if it appear to have been made under a mistake of existing circumstances, or if it have a double intent—that is, if professing to do one thing it will have the effect of doing two,—the grant is void as against the crown.

First, as to the particular words used in this grant. The words "attachiamenta placitorum" appear to be the larger expression, and to include the phrase "attachiamenta de placitis;" but there is an observable difference between them: nor is there a single instance to be found of an admitted power to appoint a coroner, given by words like these. The most obvious meaning is, that it is a grant of the return of writs, of summonses, and of attachments of the Crown which partake of the nature of writs and summonses, namely, attachments on writs at the suit of the Crown. The words "attachiamenta placitorum coronæ" can only be construed "attachments of pleas of the crown;" but the words "attachiamenta de placitis coronæ" (it not being said "de *omnibus* placitis coronæ") mean rather attachments of and concerning—*arising out of*—pleas of the Crown. [Lord *Abinger*, C. B.—In these old charters both expressions seem to be very often used synonymously.] There appears to be no greater reason for supposing that these words should convey the right to make a coroner, than that the words " retorna brevium " should convey the right to make a sheriff.   Then as to the non-intromittant clause, that does not in terms exclude the county *coroner*, and the more express words at the end of the charter, which make mention of the coroner by name, rather imply that such is not its proper construction.   But this is in truth a common clause, introduced into all such ancient grants, even where a coroner has existed before; as in the case of the charter of the Cinque Ports : and the reasonable construction of it appears to be, to exclude any interference of the king's sheriffs, bailiffs, or other officers, who shall pretend to interfere with any thing which by the effect of the charter *has been already granted*.   If otherwise, it would go to exclude coroners of all sorts—even the Lord Chief Justice of the Queen's Bench, and the other judges of that Court.   The coroner was at that period an officer of much greater rank and consequence than at present; and it appears to have been his principal duty to accompany the sheriff, and to *record* the pleas of the Crown.   In Staunford's Pleas of the Crown, 48, it is said—" Coroner est un ancient officer deins cest realm, ordains d'estre un principal conservator ou gardein de la peas, a porter record des pleas del corona, et de son view, et de abjuratione, et de utlagariis, &c.; sel definition est done per Britton."   Fitzherbert gives a definition to the same effect (*a*); and, in the 2nd Inst., 31, Lord *Coke* gives also another from the Mirror:—" His name is derived a coronâ, so called because he is an officer of the Crown, and hath conusance of some pleas which are called ' placita coronæ.'   For his

*Exch. of Pleas,
1842.*

*JEWISON
v.
DYSON.*

(*a*) Fitz. N. B. 163.

antiquity see the Mirror, who (treating of articles established by the ancient kings, Alfred, &c.) saith, ' Auxi ordains fuer coronours in chescun county, et viscounts, a garder le peace quant les countis soy demisterent del gard, et bayliffes in lieu de centeners :' that is, coroners in every county, and sheriffs, were ordained to keep the peace when the earls dismissed themselves of the custody of the counties, and bailiffs in place of hundredors. For his dignity and authority, Britton saith, in the person of the king, 'Pur ceo que nous volons que coroners sont in chescun county principals gardeins de nostre peas, a porter record de pleas de nostre corone, et de lour views et abjurations, et de utlagariis, volons que ily sont eslieus solonque ceo que est contein in nous statutes de lour election.' " It appears, therefore, that from time immemorial they were high and important elective officers, even before the passing of the statute which ordained the mode of their election : and charters such as this cannot properly be construed without reference to the character and dignity of the office at the time when they were made.

With reference to this part of the case, it is important to consider the effect of the statute of 3 Edw. 1, c. 10; because the Crown could have no power to create an office of this kind in contravention of an act of Parliament. For instance, the stat. of 18 Edw. 1, having provided that fines should be levied before the justices of the common bench, and not elsewhere, it was held that the king could not, in the face of those negative words, erect a court for the purpose of levying fines. Com. Dig., Fine, (D). It is true that the words of the 3 Edw. 1, c. 10, are not negative, but their effect is the same; because it is said that the coroner shall in all counties be elected in the manner therein mentioned; whereas this charter is to be construed as saying that no coroner shall act within the Honour of Pontefract, comprehending a large portion of the county of York, who is so elected. [Lord *Abinger*, C. B.—The statute also says that it is not to affect local franchises.] But the question is, whether this franchise was created by the subsequent grant. In most of the grants which avowedly convey the right to appoint a coroner (e. g. in that already referred to, to the abbot of St. Albans (a)), the power is granted by express words, " eligere et facere coronatorem," which might not be in contravention of the statute, inasmuch as the only effect of such words would appear to be, to give to the grantee of the franchise power to issue his writ to the sheriff, or other proper officer, for the election of a coroner, therefore by no means divesting the commonalty of the ancient right which they had at common law, and under the statute, to elect their own coroners. [Lord *Abinger*, C. B.—Can it be supposed that the abbot of St. Albans was to issue a writ for that purpose to the sheriff? *Parke*, B.—There may be an election by one, as well as by many.] The words are certainly capable of that construction. But the argument remains, that the grant of the power to appoint a coroner, to the exclusion of the county coroner, is contrary to the statute, and, at all events, ought not to have such an effect in the absence of a non obstante clause : and no instance has been adduced, with the exception of that cited from the Placita de Quo Warranto, p. 333, of such a grant made by words of like generality with these. But in that case there occur the words " regiæ libertates ;" and it may be that the Abbey of Battle had rights in the nature of jura regalia by prescription before the Conquest, which would entitle them, without charter, to exercise the right of appointing a coroner, as in the case of a county palatine. The extraordinary extent of the privileges granted to that abbey by William the Conqueror appears from Camden's Britannia, Vol. I. p. 209.

It appears to be clear, on all the old authorities, that

(a) Ante, 559.

the coroner was not the only officer who made attachments of what are termed "pleas of the Crown." The Statute of Westminster, 3 Edw. 1, c. 9, says, "For as much as the peace of this realm hath been evil observed heretofore, for lack of quick and fresh suit making after felons in due manner, and mainly because of franchises where felons are received, it is provided that all generally be ready and apparelled at the commandment and summons of sheriffs, and at the cry of the county, to sue and arrest felons, when any need is: And if the *sheriffs, coroners, or other bailiffs,* within franchise or without, for reward or for prayer, or for fear, or for any manner of affinity, conceal, consent or procure to conceal, the felonies done in their bailiwicks, or otherwise will not *attach* nor arrest such felons there as they may, or otherwise neglect to do their office in any manner in favour of such misdoers, and be attainted thereof, they shall have one year's imprisonment," &c. &c. Then, when c. 10 of the same statute, speaking of the duties of the office of coroner, refers to appeals, inquests, attachments, and presentments, it would seem that the word "attachment" there means no more than an arrest in pursuance of the before-mentioned proceedings. That construction is confirmed by the provisions of the same Statute of Westminster 1, c. 15. The words of this charter would therefore be fully satisfied by holding that the "attachiamenta" therein mentioned mean criminal arrests, founded on previous proceedings taken before the sheriff or other similar officer. That the sheriff had the power of taking inquisitions, and of arresting and imprisoning persons found culpable thereon, clearly appears also from the Statute of Westminster 2, 13 Edw. 1, c. 13. So also, from the stats. 1 Edw. 3, c. 17, and 25 Edw. 3, c. 14, it is plain that attachments were made, and what are technically termed pleas of the Crown were held, by the one as well as by the other officer. And the saving clause of the stat. 28 Edw. 3, c. 6, which reserves " to the king and other lords which ought to make such coroners, *Exch. of Pleas,* their seigniories and franchises," may receive full effect by 1842. applying it to *immemorial* franchises of that nature; and JEWISON so, accordingly, it was claimed in the case of the Lord *v.* Paget, already cited from Coke's Entries, p. 544 (a), the party not being satisfied to rely only on the grant from the Crown which he pleaded, which, however, it may be observed, gave in *express words* the right to appoint a coroner. In the same collection, p. 530. b, there is the case of a quo warranto for exercising various franchises, not affecting the exercise of the office of coroner: and the plea claims under a grant by the Crown to Queen Cathe-rine of Arragon, the wife of Henry the Eighth, to have for her life "the return of all writs, as well of assize, of certifi-cates, and *attachments*, as of all other briefs and precepts of the king, his heirs and successors, and also summonses, extracts, and precepts of the Exchequer." Here, there-fore, a grant of attachments is not pretended to import the right to appoint a coroner. Again, at p. 537 is to be found a quo warranto against the inhabitants of Denbigh, for having a court before their bailiffs, and there precisely the same words occur as here :—" Nec non attachiamenta tam de placitis coronæ quam aliis in dictâ villâ :" yet no notion was entertained of claiming under these words the right of appointing a coroner. In truth, the only pleas of the Crown which the coroner was to *attach,* were those that appeared before him *upon his own view,* either super visum corporis, or when, in old times, he had the power of taking inquests upon other felonies. The other side have relied much upon the authority of Bracton, as shewing that the duties of the coroner generally terminated in an attachment of the person. But it is remarkable that Bracton nowhere says, in express words, that *the coroner* is to attach. His words are not "attachiat coronatorius," but "attachiendus," "let him be attached." Indeed, in

(a) Ante, p. 564.

ancient times, when the counties were first divided into tithings, it will be found that the decennaries were the parties responsible for the attaching of persons suspected of homicide or other felonies. In the preface to Horne's Mirror, the editor, speaking of the duties of the decennary, says—" This decennalis fidejussio, or decemvirale collegium, by our author is called the decennary, who were charged to bring forth the person of every offender to answer unto the law; whereof Mr. Bracton speaketh in these words—' De eo autem qui fugam fecerit (he speaketh of one after a felony committed) diligenter erit inquirendum si fuerit in franciplegio et decennâ, et tunc erit decenna in misericordiâ coram justiciariis, quia non habent ipsum malefactorem ad rectum.' And, according to that law, if a felon, after his flying or conviction, were possessed of goods, the town or decennary was answerable for the same: and if the same were embezzled or holden from them, the decennary might seize those goods, in whosesoever possession they were found, as appeareth by 3 Edw. 3, in Fitzherbert's Abridgement, title ' Coronæ,' 366." The passage thus cited from Fitzh. Abr. is as follows :—" Nota quod vicecomes et decennarii seisire possunt catalla fugitivorum in manus domini regis, et vicecomes catalla illa liberabit villatæ, ad respondendum domini regis in itinere; et si vicecomes nec decennarii seisierint, villa respondebit regi itinere." In another place (p. 186), Fitzherbert, in enumerating the duties of the coroner, does not say that he is to *attach* pleas of the Crown, but that he is to *keep* the record of his view, &c., (" doit porť son record de son view," &c.) So, in Horne's Mirror, 38, the author says—" To coroners anciently were enjoyned the *keeping* of the pleas of the Crown, which extend now but to felonies and adventures." The same view is borne out by a curious entry in the Parliamentary Petitions, in the case of the Abbot of Furness, (vol. 1, p. 436), from which it appears that the sheriff was in the habit of taking inquisitions super visum corporis. It is a petition from the Abbot of

Furness, complaining of a great mortality in the district,

and reciting that divers inquests had been held before the sheriffs and coroners of Lancashire, ("devaunt visconates et coronours fers a Lancastre.") Again, in Dalton, p. 157, in setting forth the duties of *sheriffs*, it is said—"Nota quod pro transgressione contra coronam regiam quæ tangit vitam et membrum, defendens seu delinquus *attachiatus erit* per corpus," &c. In Bracton, p. 137, there is a writ set out, directed to the sheriff, directing him that in case of the arrest of a party for felony, "super visum custodum placitorum coronæ nostræ, et super visum tuum et ballivorum tuorum et legalium hominum, apprecientur catalla ipsius capti," &c. &c. And Dalton, in the chapter on bailiffs of franchises, (p. 463), says—"If any felon or other offender against the king's peace, &c., shall be within any liberty or franchise, and the justices of the peace, &c., shall direct their warrant or process to the sheriff for the apprehending of such offender, the sheriff is to enter such franchise, and to execute the process or warrant, and not to write to the bailiff of the franchise, for that here the king is a party." These authorities appear to shew, that the attachment of pleas of the Crown, although principally it may have been in the coroner since the statute of 3 Edw. 1, which undoubtedly makes him the party to attach pleas upon inquests held before him, yet at common law, and down to a later period than is now the subject of inquiry, was by no means exclusively the duty of the coroner. If that be so, the grant of attachments of pleas of the Crown, with a clause excluding sheriffs and bailiffs, may be fully satisfied by applying it to those attachments which the sheriffs and other officers were authorized to make; the words being construed merely as an extension of the previous words "retorna brevium," &c., and as giving the power to make arrests and attachments upon the writs and summonses before mentioned. And "if the king's grant can enure to two intents, it shall be taken to the intent that makes most for the king's benefit:" Com. Dig., Grant, (G. 12).

Further, it is distinctly laid down that the king cannot grant away that which is a part of his prerogative, and that the appointment of *judicial* officers is a part of his prerogative. Now a coroner is undoubtedly, to this day, a judicial officer in some sense of the word; and he was anciently a judge of very high degree. In Dalton's Sheriff, 443, it is said—" The coroners are judges of the outlawries, and are to sit with the sheriff at every county court. They are to give judgments upon the outlawries, and they are to give and pronounce the judgment, and to make a short memorandum thereof in the book: but the coroners are not to make return of the outlawry, for the custody of the record itself does not appertain to the coroners, but the sheriff." In Lord Coke's Commentary on the Statute of Westminster the First, (2 Inst. 176), he observes upon the passage, "Que les coroners loialment attachent et representent les ples del coron," &c. " By this it appeareth that the coroner is judge of the cause, and not the sheriff, and this agreeth with our old and latter books; only the sheriffs have counter-rolls with the coroners by force of this act, and therefore a certiorari may be directed to the sheriff and coroner, to remove an appeal by bill before the coroner, because the sheriff hath a counter-roll: but if the certiorari be directed to the sheriff only, in case of appeal or indictment of death, it is not sufficient to remove the record, because he is not judge of the cause, but hath only a counter-roll." The coroner's is a Court of Record, and he may commit for contempt: *Garnett* v. *Ferrand* (a). It is stated to be so in the 4 Inst. 271, and Com. Dig., Officer, (G. 5): where also it is said that the coroner has jurisdiction to take an appeal of robbery or other felony, and that upon such appeal he alone is judge,

(a) 6 B. & Cr. 611; 9 D. & R. 657.

though by the Statute of Westminster the sheriff has the

counter-rolls of appeals and inquests with the coroner.

Even, however, if the office of coroner be not of a strictly judicial nature, it was one of great importance and dignity, and a grant in terms so vague and general as this ought not to be considered as conveying it. The question ought to be construed as if it had arisen at the time the grant was made : all that the subsequent *parliamentary* charters purported to do was, to confirm what was granted by the original charter of Edw. 3. It is therefore to be construed like any other grant to an ordinary subject of the Crown, and as if the Duke of Lancaster were now a party unconnected with the Crown, claiming, on the one hand, against the Crown's prerogative, and on the other, against the general rights of the commonalty, as they originally existed at common law, and were afterwards confirmed by statute. Now it is submitted, that the true rule for the construction of grants by the Crown is, that they are to be construed *strictly*, in reference to the question whether the Crown has parted with any portion of its prerogative. When that is made clear, then the grant is to be taken in the most ample and abundant sense, and to be construed liberally, for the purpose of giving that ascertained intention its fullest effect. The strongest words against the Crown, according to the authorities, are, " ex certâ scientiâ ;" the next strong, " ex mero motu ;" the third, those which are found in this case,— " ex speciali gratiâ ;" and the weakest where it professes to be granted " ex humili petitione." This is not a case, therefore, in which the charter is to be construed strongly against the Crown, but one in which the intention ought to be certain upon the face of it.

The finding of the jury in this case can be made use of only to this extent :—the jury find what has been the usage, and the Court are to put their construction upon the charter, assisted by the finding of the jury. But the con-

struction of an ancient charter of this kind is not a matter
in pais, and cannot be properly left to the decision of a
jury. The law is, that the jury are to find the usage, and
the Court, applying that usage to the charter, may, if it
throws light upon the subject, assist itself by the usage in
construing the terms of the charter: but first the Court
are to say whether, in point of law, those terms are sufficient to convey anything with that reasonable degree of
certainty which the law requires.

Now it is laid down as a general position of law, (Vin.
Abr., Prærogative, (C.), where the authorities are collected),
that *general words* will not take away the right of the
Crown. The question is, what is the meaning of " general
words " with reference to this matter. It appears to be
this — that inasmuch as " dolus latet in generalibus,"
under general words the Court cannot see distinctly that
the Crown knew what it was granting. That principle is
the foundation also of another rule already referred to,
which, in other terms, means almost the same thing,—
that if a charter of this nature is capable of two interpre-
tations, each of which is equally favourable or unfavourable
to the Crown, it is uncertain and void. Thus, a grant of "all
mines, amerciaments, and escheats," will not pass mines
royal or escheat royal: 17 Vin. Abr. 133. So, by a grant of
" retorna omnium brevium," the grantee shall not have return of Exchequer summons: Bro. Abr., Patents, pl. 32;
17 Vin. Abr. 132. In *Parmeter* v. *Attorney-General* (a), it
was held, that where a part of the sea coast, being the
property of the Crown, was alleged to have been granted
to a subject, he must shew a specific description of the
particular place so meant to be conveyed, for he could not
avail himself of general words. In that case occurs the
following observation, attributed to Lord *Eldon* :—" The
Lord Chancellor inquired what part of the letters patent

(a) 10 Price, 378, 412; 1 Dow, P. C. 316, 323.

had described the appellant's land; because the first difficulty is, said his Lordship, whether it be possible, in point
of law, that a grant of the Crown in these general terms
can be good." Now the terms of the grant in that case
were,—" All and singular other his said Majesty's lands
commonly called the wastes of the sea, vazes and vazey lands,
&c. &c., lying, being, and abutting in or near Bewley
Haven, Porchester Haven, the haven of the town of
Lymington, Hurst Castle, the town of Yarmouth, Thorley,
and Althans, in the Isle of Wight, Yarmouth Haven,
Freshwater, and Newtonhook Point." The same doctrine
was recognized in *Alcock* v. *Cooke* (a), which was a question
whether wreck passed by a grant from the Crown. It is
said, indeed, that these are not *general words* in this sense,
but that this is a specific form of words, to which, by a
necessary implication, is attached a certain effect, viz. that
the words " attachments of pleas of the Crown" necessarily
imply the performance of the duties of coroner. But it
has already been shewn that those words are capable of
more than one construction, and that being so, the grant
is therefore either uncertain and void, or, if it is to have
any effect, it must enure to take the least out of the
Crown, and to grant only the power to make attachments
on the proceedings previously mentioned in the charter.

Cur. adv. vult.

The judgment of the Court was now delivered by

Lord ABINGER, C. B.—In the case of *Jewison* v. *Dyson*,
which was argued at great length on the motion for a new
trial, upon the construction of the charter which is supposed to create the Duchy of Lancaster, we have considered the arguments that have been offered; and although

(a) 5 Bing. 340; 2 M. & P. 625.

I cannot think the question of so much importance as it is
represented by the counsel who argued it, for it is a mere
question which of two coroners shall have the fees for
executing the duties of coroner in a certain district, (which
is of comparatively little importance to the public); yet
we are of opinion, considering the whole of the case, that
the charter has been rightly construed by the Judge and
the jury, at least by the jury, and that we ought not to
disturb the verdict.

The question is this, whether or not the words of the
charter were sufficient to convey to the Duchy of Lancaster
the right of appointing a coroner within the district of the
Honor of Pontefract. The words are "attachiamenta tam
de placitis coronæ quam de aliis quibuscumque." And the
words are followed by a declaration, that none of the king's
ministers or bailiffs shall interfere with the rights granted
to the duchy. Then, at the conclusion, " Our coroners "
are mentioned amongst others who shall not interfere.

Mr. *Cresswell*, in the very able argument which he
addressed to us upon the subject, adduced sufficient authorities to shew that the words "attachiamenta de placitis
coronæ," and the words " attachiamenta placitorum
coronæ," are used in contemporaneous charters in the
same sense; and I think they must have been so used,
because the preposition " de," which is Norman French
idiom, found its way very early into our Law Latin, and
is generally used to express the genitive case. But if
there be any distinction, the words "attachiamenta de
placitis coronæ" must be construed in a larger sense than
the words " attachiamenta placitorum coronæ," because
the one would be confined strictly to what were pleas of the
Crown, the other would apply to all matters *of and relating
to* pleas of the Crown; therefore, if there be any distinction in the words, those used in the charter are the
larger. But I think it was clearly proved by the authorities adduced by Mr. *Cresswell*, to which I need not refer

more particularly, that these words were sufficient to con-

vey, and have been rightly construed to convey, a right to
appoint a coroner, or rather the right to perform the
duties of a coroner. The arguments adduced by Mr.
Cresswell satisfied my mind, and I believe those of my
learned Brothers, that the words of the charter are sufficient to convey the right to appoint a coroner.

It was then said that the king could not by these general
words grant power to appoint a coroner; and in order to
establish that, it was contended that the coroner was a
judicial officer, and that the Crown could not delegate the
right to appoint a judicial officer. But I am surprised
that it was not seen at an earlier period of the discussion,
that those two arguments were inconsistent with each
other; because, if the king could not delegate the power
to appoint a coroner at all, because he was a judicial
officer, he could not do it by the most express words.
That argument, therefore, is really of no weight, and the
question still turns upon the point, whether these words
are sufficient to give the right to appoint a coroner. If
the king could not give the right by express words, what
is the use of the other argument? It is said that the
coroner is a judicial officer; but that argument consists in
attributing two uses to the word " judicial;" using the
popular sense of the word in order to cover an argument
that is derived from the use of the word in a strictly legal
sense. Many officers may be called judicial to a certain
extent, who are not judicial within the general meaning of
the law which says that the Crown cannot delegate to
another person its right to appoint judicial officers. Is it
to be said that the officers of this Court are judicial
officers? and yet they do much more in the character of
judicial functionaries than coroners do. There are many
other officers who, to a certain extent, in the popular sense
of the word, are called "judicial," and yet are not judicial
officers to determine causes *inter partes*; for it is to that

that the power of the Crown is limited, that it must not delegate the right of appointing to the administration of justice, to be performed by the delegate, and divest itself of the power of administering justice to all its subjects.

It has been said that the coroner's is a court of record. I am very unwilling to enter into that discussion; but I must own, if it were *res integra*, I think it would be wise to consider whether that extra-judicial opinion, delivered by the Lord Chief Justice of the Queen's Bench in the case that has been cited (a), is a sufficient authority for saying that the coroner's court is a court of record. It would be quite sufficient, in order to decide that case, to say that every person who administers a public duty has a right to preserve order in the place where it is administered, and to turn out any person who is found there for improper purposes.

If the coroner's is a court of record, because he makes a record to deliver to the judges of assize (or the justices in eyre, as was the ancient practice), why is not the sheriff's court a court for record? because he makes the plaint into a record, and transmits it to the superior court. It is not a court of record merely because the instrument upon which he takes the inquisition is to be reduced to parchment, and made the record of another court. If, however, there be any ancient practice to shew that there are any functions (which I am not prepared to say there are not) which the coroner is entitled to perform, of a judicial nature, as well as others which are not judicial, I see no reason to think that at least the Crown may not delegate the right to appoint an officer, whether he is called a coroner or otherwise, who may do those duties which are not of a judicial nature. Now, I cannot think that an inquisition upon a body, and assisting a jury in taking that inquisition, is in

(a) *Garnett* v. *Ferrand*, ante, p. 580.

its nature a judicial duty; and the words "attachiamenta *Exch. of Pleas,* de placitis coronæ" appear emphatically to refer to the province of the coroner's jury; because it is when an in- *Jewison* vestigation is made by a jury, which he is to assemble, and *Dyson.* to which he is to afford all the assistance he can, that, if they find a verdict for murder or manslaughter, he is to issue his warrant, which is the "attachment." I think that is the fair meaning of the words of the statute as to the appointment of coroners. If, then, the words here are sufficient to carry the right to appoint, and if the appointment is not of a judicial officer, it appears to me that the whole argument falls to the ground, which is founded upon those principles. It has been said, again, that the statute of 28th of Edward 3, which regulates the appointment of coroners, declares that they shall be appointed by the freeholders, from the proper men in the counties: and it is contended by Mr. *Wortley* that that statute precluded the Crown from exercising the power it had before, of delegating the right to appoint a coroner, inasmuch as there is no power to appoint a coroner in any other way than that which the statute recognizes. But there is a clause in that statute which saves to the king, and all lords of franchises and seigniories, the right to appoint a coroner as they have done before. And according to this construction, as the charter in question was granted before the passing of the 28th of Edward 3, the consequence is, that if by that charter this right was granted, the statute of 28th Edward 3 is not in opposition to it, but rather a recognition of it. Therefore that argument also falls to the ground.

It was alleged that the Duchy of Cornwall have never appointed a coroner. Now, supposing that were so, and supposing that the words of the charter which created the Duchy of Cornwall granted in the same terms the right to appoint a coroner, but that the Duke of Cornwall has never exercised it, would that be any argument in this case? The mere omission to use the power in the one case is not an argument upon the construction of the words. But let us look at the case, and see what it is. Mr. *Wortley* stated that there had been seventeen Dukes of Cornwall, but he omitted to state how long they continued in each case. It is well known, and any one who consults *The Prince's Case* in Coke's Reports (*a*) (one of the most learned and elaborate which is to be found in those Reports) will see, that the question there was as to the tenure and constitution of the Duchy of Cornwall; and after a long debate of all the judges, in a judgment full of learning and research, they came to the conclusion that the Duchy of Cornwall could not be created by the king's prerogative at common law, because it was constituting an honor, and a tenure inconsistent with the common law, and that it could only be legally done by statute. And in the same manner the creation of the County Palatine of Lancaster was by statute, passed at the requisition of the king and his lords in Parliament.

The Duchy of Cornwall is, indeed, a very peculiar tenure. It only exists when there is the eldest son of a king born after he becomes reigning king. He alone can enjoy it, and the moment he becomes king it ceases, and is absorbed in the Crown. What, then, is the consequence of that? The necessary consequence is, that in the Duchy of Cornwall, whenever the duchy ceases to exist, being absorbed in the Crown, the appointments of coroners are made in the same way as the appointments in any other county, by the freeholders; and if afterwards a different authority should intervene by the birth of a Prince of Wales, he cannot interfere with such existing appointments; he has no power to divest an existing officer, but only to appoint to those offices when they become vacant. Therefore it would be extremely difficult to found any argument at all upon that state of things, be-

(*a*) 8 Rep. 1, a.

cause the fact may have been that there was no instance during the existence of a Duke of Cornwall in which a coronership was vacant. Before the argument could have any weight, that fact ought to be ascertained.

With respect to the Duchy of Lancaster, I have had some opportunity of knowing that, in ancient times, a great portion of the records of the duchy were not very well kept. There is one class of documents that are very well preserved, namely, bills in equity filed in the Duchy Court; and it is very remarkable that, I believe, some of them are of more antiquity than any now existing amongst the records of the Court of Chancery: but with respect to other proceedings, such as the appointments of officers, and so on, I believe that, till a very recent period, the records of the proceedings of the Duchy of Lancaster generally were not kept in a place of deposit, so as to be traceable to any great antiquity. It was so likewise in the Duchy of Cornwall. In the case of the Duchy of Cornwall, it is almost incredible how the documents belonging to that Court were scattered about: a great many are in the Court of Exchequer—a great many in the Tower of London; and certainly till a very recent period, the accession of King George the Fourth, the records of the Duchy of Cornwall were never kept in a proper place and condition. I am therefore not at all surprised at the deficiency of early evidence, as to the appointment of a coroner, and as to his duties: it is a matter that one would naturally infer from the state of things that existed anterior to the time of Queen Elizabeth. I think, therefore, there is nothing in the state of facts, which have been carefully looked at upon the learned Judge's notes, that can be properly used to contravene the arguments which have been adduced to establish the construction that has been put upon this charter. It is not inconsistent with ancient usage. The jury had a right to presume that that usage had existed at a time

Exch. of Pleas,
1842.

JEWISON
v.
DYSON.

anterior to that at which it was proved to exist, and the mere non-existence of any record of the coroner performing the duty I consider as of the less importance, on account of the circumstance I have stated, that the records of that period were very imperfectly kept.

Under these circumstances, conceiving that these words are sufficient to delegate to the Duke of Lancaster the right to appoint a coroner, and conceiving that such a right might exist in the Crown at the time that the charter was granted ,we think that a proper construction has been put upon it by the jury, that we ought not to disturb the verdict,and that therefore the rule must be discharged.

PARKE, B.—I had not an opportunity of hearing a great part of the argument in this case. All that I can say is, that so far as I did hear it, I see no reason to dissent from the view taken by the Lord Chief Baron, that this verdict ought not to be disturbed.

ALDERSON, B.—I am of the same opinion. It appears to me that the charter is capable of the construction which the Lord Chief Baron has put upon it, and that that construction, coupled with the evidence, fully authorized the jury to come to the conclusion at which they arrived. It is not necessary to say whether by the charter a power is given to the Duke of Lancaster to create a coroner *eo nomine :* it is only necessary to say that it is in the power of the Duke of Lancaster, under that charter, to appoint an officer to perform the duties which are granted to him, of "attachiamenta de placitis coronæ;" and the duty that in this case was attempted to be performed by the defendant, the coroner for the West Riding, interfered with and was contrary to the performance of that duty under the charter. That is quite sufficient for the judgment in this case. If there are any duties of the coroner which are properly of a judicial nature, it may be that those fall within the rule laid down by Mr. *Wortley*, upon the authorities which he cited to us yesterday. But this is not a case within that rule.

GURNEY, B.—I have heard the argument on one side only, and only a portion of that; and not having heard the case on the other side, I cannot presume to give any opinion.

Rule discharged.

VACATION SITTINGS AFTER HILARY TERM.

HARRIS *v.* BIRCH, Bart.

Feb. 9.

TROVER for wine.—Pleas, first, not guilty; secondly, not possessed; on which issues were joined. At the trial before *Wightman*, J., at the last Liverpool assizes, it appeared that the defendant, the sheriff of Lancashire, had seized the wine in question under a fieri facias against Messrs. Jones, Windle, & Co. Those persons had previously pledged the wine to the plaintiff, by virtue of the following letter :—

"To Rice Harris, Esq., Birmingham.
"Liverpool, 12th January, 1840.

"Dear Sir,—Agreeably to the arrangement between the writer and yourself, we now wait on you with our draft for £500, for which we beg your acceptance, with the understanding that we shall provide for the same at maturity; and in consideration of your accepting said draft, we hand you herewith bill of lading and policy of insurance for

A firm that was negotiating to obtain an advance of money on their bill, wrote to the proposed lender, stating that, in consideration of his accepting their draft, they handed him therewith the bill of lading and policy of insurance for wines expected to arrive, which would afford him security beyond the amount of the bill, and engaging to land and warehouse the wines, to be held at his disposal :—*Held*, that this document did not require a mortgage stamp, within the 55 Geo. 3, c. 184, sched., part 1, title 'Mortgage.'

wines daily expected per 'Jason,' now discharging part of her cargo at Waterford, and particulars of other wines we have placed in your name. These together will afford you security beyond the amount of the bill. With regard to the wines to arrive, we shall land and warehouse them, to be held at your disposal. Assuring you it is our wish to place you beyond all risk, we have thus readily complied with your suggestion.

> "We remain, dear Sir,
> "Yours very truly,
> "Jones, Windle, & Co."

With this letter were transmitted the particulars of the wines, and the bill of lading, indorsed generally by Jones, Windle, & Co. The plaintiff, after some correspondence had taken place, acceded to the request of Jones, Windle, & Co., and advanced them the money. The letters were produced in evidence, and bore an agreement stamp. It was objected for the defendant that they amounted to a mortgage of the wines, and were not admissible without a mortgage stamp, under the 55 Geo. 3, c. 184, sched. 1, part 1, tit. "Mortgage (a)." The learned Judge overruled the objection, and received the evidence, and the plaintiff obtained a verdict.

(a) The following are the material clauses of the schedule:— "Mortgage, conditional surrender by way of mortgage, further charge, wadset, and heritable bond, disposition, assignation, or tack in security, and eik to a reversion, of or affecting any lands, estates, or property, real or personal, heritable or moveable whatsoever." "Also any defeazance, letter of reversion, backbond, declaration, or other deed or writing for defeating or making redeemable, or explaining or qualifying, any conveyance, disposition, assignation, or tack, of any lands, estate, or property whatsoever, which shall be apparently absolute, but intended only as a security." "Also any agreement, contract, or bond, accompanied with a deposit of title-deeds, for making a mortgage, wadset, or any such other security or conveyance as aforesaid, of any lands, estate, or property, comprised in such title-deeds, or for pledging or charging the same as a security."

In last Michaelmas term, *Cresswell* obtained a rule nisi for a new trial, on the above objection.

Baines and *Martin* now shewed cause.—The letters read in evidence do not amount to a *mortgage*, within the meaning of the Stamp Act, but merely to an agreement for a *pledge* of these wines. The distinction between a mortgage and a pledge is well known to the law, and is obvious in itself. A mortgage conveys to the mortgagee the whole property in the land or chattel, conditionally, so that as soon as the condition is broken, the property, at law, remains absolutely in the mortgagee: but in the case of a pledge, the pawnee has only a special property in the thing pledged, with power, indeed, to dispose of it in default of payment, but subject to the obligation of accounting to the pawnor for the surplus. The authorities relating to this subject are all collected in the notes to the case of *Coggs* v. *Bernard*, in Smith's Leading Cases, vol. 1, p. 100, where the legal distinction above referred to is ably illustrated. In *Smith* v. *Cator* (a), a letter whose primary object was, as here, the obtaining an advance of money on a pledge of goods expected to arrive, was held nevertheless to require only an agreement stamp. [They cited also *Tomkins* v. *Ashby* (b); *Sneezum* v. *Marshall* (c); *Jones* v. *Smith* (d); *Ratcliff* v. *Davies* (e); *Walter* v. *Smith* (f); Bac. Abr., Bailment, (B.); Story on Bailments, p. 197]. But it may be said, that though not strictly a mortgage, this is a "disposition" of "personal property," within the meaning of those words in the first clause under the title 'Mortgage' in the Stamp Act. But those words refer only to dispositions of property by way of mortgage in Scotland. This is plain from the former items in the schedule under the word 'Disposition,' where express reference is made to the title

(a) 2 B. & Ald. 778.
(b) 6 B. & Cr. 541; 9 D. & R. 543.
(c) 7 M. & W. 417.
(d) 2 Ves. jun. 378.
(e) Cro. Jac. 244.
(f) 5 B. & Ald. 439.

'Mortgage:' as "Disposition in security, in Scotland.—
See Mortgage." "Disposition of any wadset, heritable
bond, &c.—See Mortgage."

Kelly and *Crompton*, contrà.—The transaction in question was in substance a mortgage of these wines, within the provisions of the Stamp Act. A mortgage is a delivery to another of land or goods, as a security for money, to be re-delivered on repayment of the money. Suppose these parties had entered into a deed for the same purposes as are expressed in the letter of Jones, Windle, & Co.; could it have been said that that was not a mortgage security for the £500, and that a stamp accordingly would not have been necessary? It can make no real difference in the nature of the transaction, that ordinarily interest is made payable, and that the principal is not to be repaid until after a certain time. But, at all events, this is a disposition of personal property within the meaning of the Stamp Act. The word *disposition* has reference to transfers of *personal* property of this kind, as the previous words have to conveyances of real property.

PARKE, B.—The Stamp Act is to be construed strictly, and to be extended to such cases only as clearly fall within its provisions: and I am of opinion that this case does not fall within any of the clauses in question. A mortgage stamp is required only where there is a regular conveyance by way of security for money, and not where there has been merely a deposit of goods, or of some document relating to goods, as a bill of lading or a dock-warrant. This transaction, therefore, certainly does not amount to a mortgage, because that can only be by a regular instrument of conveyance. I was, however, at first disposed to think that it came within the words of the first clause of the schedule under the title 'Mortgage,' and might be considered as a "disposition" of "personal property," within the meaning of that clause; but I am now satisfied that the word " disposition" is made use of only as a term of the Scotch law, and that those words have reference to legal instruments used in Scotland. Nor do I think that this transaction can be considered to fall within the other clause of the schedule, which comprehends "any agreement, contract, or bond, accompanied with a deposit of title deeds, for making a mortgage, wadset, or any other such security or conveyance as aforesaid." A bill of lading bears no resemblance to the instruments mentioned in that clause; it is a well-known mercantile mode of transferring the property in goods. Neither can the transaction be considered as falling within the terms of a preceding clause, as a " defeasance," because that applies to deeds or writings " for defeating, or making redeemable, or explaining, or qualifying any conveyance, disposition," &c., which on the face of it appears to be absolute, but in truth is intended as a security only. The indorsement on a bill of lading does not amount to a conveyance. Upon the whole, therefore, I think the stamp in this case was sufficient, and that the rule must be discharged.

Exch. of Pleas 1842.

HARRIS
v.
BIRCH.

ALDERSON, B.—I am of the same opinion. I think it is clear that none of the first three clauses of the schedule, under the title 'Mortgage,' have any application to this case. Then the fifth refers only to the case of agreements, contracts, or bonds, to make a mortgage, accompanied by a deposit of title-deeds. Here no title-deeds were deposited. Nor do I think the preceding clause applies, for the reason which has been given. This transaction amounted to a pledge of the goods merely, and is not within the terms of this part of the act at all.

GURNEY, B., and ROLFE, B., concurred.

Rule discharged.

Exch. of Pleas,
1842.
⌣
Feb. 9.

The plaintiffs, merchants at Liverpool, were in the habit of consigning to the defendants, brokers at Montreal, goods on sale or return, and of receiving in payment bills on British houses pur-chased by the defendants with the proceeds. The plaintiffs having desired that none but undoubted bills should be sent to them, the defendants re-mitted a bill drawn by and upon parties supposed at the time to be in good credit. The plaintiffs, on receiving it, returned for answer that it had been re-fused accept-ance, and re-quested the de-fendants to do what was need-ful to procure security from the drawer, and to take all legal and necessary steps for their security. In an action brought by the plain-

HARDMAN and Others *v.* BELLHOUSE.

ASSUMPSIT for goods sold, money had and received, and on an account stated. Pleas, first, non assumpsit; secondly, payment; thirdly, as to £350, parcel &c., deli-very to the plaintiffs, and acceptance by them, of a bill of exchange for that amount, drawn by R. M'Lellan, and in-dorsed to him by the plaintiffs, in full satisfaction and discharge of the said sum of £350, parcel &c.: on which pleas issues were taken and joined. At the trial before *Wightman*, J., at the last Liverpool assizes, the facts ap-peared to be as follows:—

The plaintiffs were the surviving partners of E. Hard-man, and with him had carried on business as merchants in Liverpool. The defendant was the surviving partner of the late firm of Budden & Vennor, merchants and com-mission brokers at Montreal. Messrs. Hardman & Co. had been in the habit of sending out goods to Budden & Vennor, at Montreal, for sale or return; and with the proceeds of such consignments the latter purchased and remitted bills on British houses. Budden & Vennor had no del credere commission, either as to the sale of the goods or the purchase of the bills. On the 15th of Au-gust 1840, the plaintiffs wrote to Budden & Vennor, who had remitted to them bills drawn on a certain person therein mentioned, as follows:—"We do not wish, from what we learn, to have any more [i. e. of bills on that person]: and as there must be drawers of undoubted paper with you, such as the Robertsons and others, we

tiffs for money had and received, to recover from the defendants the proceeds of the consign-ment to which this bill had reference, the defendants pleaded the delivery to the plaintiffs, and acceptance by them, of the bill of exchange in full satisfaction. The Judge directed the jury, that if the bill was such a one as by the course of dealing between the parties the plaintiffs were bound to take, that was a taking in full satisfaction:—*Held*, that this was a misdirection; for that *acceptance* in satisfaction must be an act of the will in the party receiving.

Quære, whether money had and received was maintainable, the proceeds having been applied by the defendants to the purpose contemplated by the course of dealing between the parties.

wish you would take such, in preference to mere second-rate people, as in the present instance." Subsequently to the receipt of this letter, Budden & Vennor remitted to the plaintiffs a bill for £350 on the house of M'Lellan, which was then supposed to be in good credit. The plaintiffs acknowledged the receipt thereof in the following letter:—" The draft on M'Lellan has been refused acceptance, and we now inclose protest, requesting you to do the needful with the party. We do not know the usage of your country, but possibly you may be able to require security from the drawer of the bill, that he will take it up on its being finally returned for non-payment. You will however take all legal and necessary steps for our security."

The only question disputed between the parties at the trial was, whether the plaintiffs had accepted the bill of exchange in satisfaction of the consignment to which it related. It was contended on the one side that the count for goods sold, and on the other that the plea of payment, could not be supported: but no specific objection was taken to the count for money had and received. The learned Judge, in summing up, stated to the jury, that, if the bill in question was such a one as, by the course of dealing between the parties, the plaintiffs were bound to take, then it was taken by them in full satisfaction, and the defendant was entitled to a verdict on the third issue. The jury having found for the defendant accordingly,

Knowles, in Michaelmas Term, obtained a rule to shew cause why a new trial should not be had, on the ground of misdirection: against which

Kelly and *Atherton* now shewed cause.—In the first place, the defendant is entitled, on the facts proved in the case, and the finding of the jury thereon, to a verdict on the plea of non assumpsit; for money had and received was not maintainable in this case. The defendant's house were not del credere agents, and therefore were not liable for the insufficiency of the bills remitted by them for the proceeds of the consignments: and besides, the jury have found that this was a good bill according to the course of dealing between the parties, and therefore that the defendant's house performed their duty according to their contract with the plaintiffs. [*Parke*, B.—You say the brokers were never liable for money had and received, but that this was money entrusted to them for a special purpose, and until they had violated their duty by applying it to some other purpose, it was not had and received to the plaintiffs' use.] Yes; they never were debtors to the plaintiffs for money. The action for money had and received lies only where the money of one man is in the hands of another, under such circumstances as make it the duty of the latter to pay it over at once, and without demand, to the former. But the proceeds of these goods was money in the hands of Budden & Vennor for a special purpose, that of purchasing good bills and remitting them to the plaintiffs; which duty, as the jury have found, they have performed. The case would have been different if the plaintiffs had countermanded their previous order, and required the brokers, instead of applying the money to the purchase of bills, to remit it in cash; or if after the lapse of a reasonable time they had failed so to apply it: but no action for money had and received arises until there has been a breach of duty in the agent. [*Parke*, B.—This objection cannot prevail now; it ought to have been made at the trial, because then the plaintiffs would have had the opinion of the judge on the point, and might have tendered a bill of exceptions. If we were now to refuse a new trial on this point, we should be depriving them of that right.]

Secondly, the third issue was rightly found for the defendant. As soon as this bill, which the jury have found to be a good one according to the contract of the parties, came into the hands of the plaintiffs, it operated *in law* as a satisfaction, and they could not afterwards undo its operation. [*Alderson*, B.—The plea alleges an *acceptance* in satisfaction: that is a voluntary act, and implies *will*.] If the party agrees to take payment in bills instead of money, that payment operates as a satisfaction. Such facts being proved, it becomes a question of law; and the party receiving the bills cannot afterwards say it is not satisfaction. The terms of the plea may be satisfied by proof either of a delivery and acceptance in fact, or of a detention of the thing delivered, under circumstances from which satisfaction is to be implied. [*Alderson*, B.—An implied contract of that kind ought to be stated in the plea, in order to give the other side an opportunity of denying it.] The cases in which it has been held that a less sum cannot be received in satisfaction of a larger, shew that satisfaction may be a matter of legal inference. At all events, the correspondence afforded ample evidence for the jury that the bill was in fact accepted in satisfaction. [*Alderson*, B.—But that was not left to the jury; the learned Judge told them, that if it was a bill warranted by the course of dealing between the parties, it followed that it was accepted in satisfaction.]

Knowles and *Cowling*, in support of the rule, were stopped by the Court.

ALDERSON, B. (a)—Two questions have been raised in this case. The first is, whether the action for money had and received is maintainable. With respect to that, there is great weight in what has been urged by Mr. *Kelly*; but the point was never raised at the trial, when a bill of exceptions might have been tendered to the opinion of the Judge; and if we were to determine it against the plain-

Exch. of Pleas,
1842.

HARDMAN
v.
BELLHOUSE.

(a) *Parke*, B., had left the Court during the argument.

tiffs now, we should impliedly be taking away their bill of exceptions. On that point, then, we pronounce no judgment: and the only question, therefore, for our consideration is, whether there has been any misdirection on the issue which the learned Judge submitted to the jury. And upon that the question is, what is an acceptance in satisfaction? To constitute an acceptance, there must be an act of the will. Every *receipt* is not an *acceptance*: but if the party accepts the thing, though but for a moment, for that for which the other pays it, he cannot afterwards, by his subsequent dissatisfaction, get rid of the effect of it. And although there was abundant evidence of such being the case here, still it was not left to the jury whether there was in fact an acceptance: the only direction to them was, that if the bill in question was warranted by the course of dealing between the parties, and if it was received by the plaintiffs conformably to the terms of the contract, that was necessarily an acceptance whereby the plaintiffs would be bound, notwithstanding their dissent. In that we think the learned Judge was mistaken, and therefore the rule must be absolute for a new trial; and both parties may have liberty to amend their pleadings.

GURNEY, B., and ROLFE, B., concurred.

Rule absolute.

———◆———

JOHNSON and Another *v.* MACDONALD.

ASSUMPSIT.—The declaration stated, that on the 24th September, 1840, by a certain agreement then made be-

of nitrate of soda, at 18*s.* per cwt., *to arrive* ex Daniel Grant, to be taken from the quay at landing weights," &c.; and below the signature of the brokers there was the following memorandum: " Should the vessel be lost, this contract to be void."—*Held*, that the contract did not amount to a warranty on the part of the seller, that the nitrate of soda should arrive if the vessel arrived, but to a contract for the sale of goods at a future period, subject to the double condition, of the arrival of the vessel, with the specified cargo on board.

tween the plaintiffs and the defendant, it was agreed that *Exch. of Pleas,* 1842.
the plaintiffs should buy of the defendant, and that the
defendant should sell to the plaintiffs, a hundred tons of JOHNSON
nitrate of soda, at the rate or price of 18s. for every hun- MACDONALD.
dred weight, duty paid, *to arrive* ex a certain vessel called
the Daniel Grant, to be taken from the quay at landing
weights, with the customary allowances of tare and draft, to
be paid for by a bill of exchange, to be drawn by the defendant upon and directed to the plaintiffs, for the amount
of the said purchase-money, payable at four months after
the date of the delivery of the said nitrate of soda to the
defendant or order, and to be accepted by the plaintiffs;
and that should the said vessel, the Daniel Grant, be lost,
the said contract should be void; and that, if the said vessel should not be lost, the said hundred tons of nitrate of
soda should so arrive as aforesaid in the same vessel, when
the said vessel should arrive. It then averred mutual
promises, performance by the plaintiffs, and the arrival of
the ship; stating as a breach, that the hundred tons of
nitrate of soda did not, nor did any part of that quantity,
arrive in the said vessel, when she so arrived as aforesaid;
whereby the defendant was unable to sell, and did not sell,
the hundred tons of nitrate of soda to the plaintiffs, or any
part thereof, &c.—Plea, non assumpsit.

At the trial before *Wightman*, J., at the last Liverpool
Assizes, the bought and sold note was produced, which
was signed by Roscow, Arnold, & Leete, the defendant's
brokers, and was as follows:—

" Messrs. John & Thomas Johnson.

" Liverpool, 24th September, 1840.

" Sirs,—We have this day bought for your account, from
Messrs. A. Macdonald & Co., a hundred tons of nitrate of
soda, at 18s. per cwt., duty paid, to arrive ex ' Daniel
Grant,' to be taken from the quay at landing weights, with

the customary allowances of tare and draft; payment, four months' acceptance from date of delivery.

> " We are, Sirs, your obedient Servants,
>   " Roscow, Arnold & Leete."

" N. B.—Should the vessel be lost, this contract to be void."

The Daniel Grant arrived in due time, without any nitrate of soda on board, but a quantity sufficient to enable the defendant to complete the contract arrived subsequently by two other ships belonging to him; and the present action was brought to recover the sum of £350, the difference between the price of nitrate of soda at the time of the contract, and of the vessel's arrival. On this state of facts, it was contended by the defendant's counsel, that the contract was at an end, it being conditional on the arrival of the requisite quantity of nitrate of soda by the Daniel Grant; and a verdict was, by consent, taken for the plaintiffs for the amount claimed, with leave to the defendant to enter a nonsuit, if the Court should be of opinion in favour of that objection. *Wortley* having, in Michaelmas Term last, obtained a rule accordingly,

Martin now shewed cause.—The true construction of this agreement is, that the defendant undertook that one hundred tons of nitrate of soda should arrive, at all events, by the Daniel Grant, *unless* the vessel were lost.—[*Parke*, B. —All the difficulty that exists in the case arises from the memorandum at the bottom, which is quite useless. If it were not for that memorandum, it is clear that the contract means to imply a condition of the happening of the double event, of the arrival of the ship and her cargo. We expressed that opinion in *Stockdale* v. *Dunlop* (a)].

(a) 6 M. & W. 224.

That case is distinguishable. There the words were " oil to arrive ;" and it was proved that that was a mercantile term, and that if the oil did not arrive by the vessel, the purchaser had no right. Here there was no such usage proved. [*Alderson*, B.—Nothing is said about *usage* in the judgment of the Court. *Parke*, B.—Is it not a condition rather than a contract?] Lord *Abinger*, C. B., in *Lovatt* v. *Hamilton* (a), puts the case on the ground of its being a contract. In *Boyd* v. *Siffkin* (b), *Hawes* v. *Humble* (c), and *Idle* v. *Thornton* (d), it was impossible to put any other construction upon the agreement than was put upon it, because the parties had confined the contract to goods *on arrival.* So, in *Alewyn* v. *Pryor* (e), the words were " *on arrival.*" But here the words " to arrive " mean that the seller warrants that it shall arrive. One general rule of construction, laid down in Sheppard's Touchstone, 87, is, " that the construction be such as the whole deed and every part of it may take effect." If this contract be construed as is contended for on the other side, the effect would be to render the contract obligatory only on the double condition of the vessel not being lost, *and* the cargo arriving in her; but that inference is negatived by the memorandum at the bottom, which shews that the parties contemplated that the contract should be put an end to upon the happening of one condition only, namely, the loss of the vessel. The rule is, to give such a construction that every part of the agreement shall take effect; but if the defendant's construction were held to be correct, the last clause must be rejected. The party, by inserting the clause as to the loss of the vessel, means to protect himself against loss by the elements and the perils of the sea :—why should the Court protect him further than he has thought fit to protect himself? This is a new question, which is

---

(a) 5 M. & W. 644.   (b) 2 Camp. 326.   (c) 2 Camp. 327, n.
(d) 3 Camp. 274.   (e) Ry. & M. 406.

governed by none of the decided cases. If a man thinks proper so to contract, he must bear the loss, if he does not perform his part of it.

Wortley and *Cleasby*, in support of the rule, were stopped by the Court.

PARKE, B.—This is an action on a contract, wherein the agreement between the parties is alleged to be, that the plaintiffs should buy, and the defendant should sell to the plaintiffs, 100 tons of nitrate of soda, to arrive by a certain vessel called the Daniel Grant, to be taken from the quay at landing weights; and the declaration then goes on to state that, in case the said vessel should not be lost, the said 100 tons of nitrate of soda should so arrive as aforesaid in the same vessel, when she should arrive. To this the defendant has pleaded non assumpsit; and the question is, can we import into the contract, as given in evidence, an agreement on the part of the defendant, that, in case the vessel should not be lost, the 100 tons of nitrate of soda should arrive in her when she should come into port? And I am clearly of opinion, that no such contract can be inferred from the bought and sold note before us. First of all, suppose that the words used in the memorandum at the end were not inserted, what would be the nature of the agreement? It would then run thus:—"We have this day bought for your account from Messrs. A. Macdonald & Co., 100 tons of nitrate of soda, at 18*s.* per cwt., duty paid, to arrive ex ' Daniel Grant,' to be taken from the quay at landing weights, with the customary allowances of tare and draft, payment four months' acceptance from the date of delivery." Now I admit that, in the cases which have been referred to, with the exception of *Lovatt* v. *Hamilton*, and *Stockdale* v. *Dunlop*, the words used in the contract entered into were not simply the words " to arrive," but were, that the contract was to be completed " on arrival " of the vessel. It appears to me, however, that the meaning of both these expressions is precisely the same. This is a contract not passing any property in any existing chattel on board the vessel at the time it was entered into, but merely an agreement for the sale and delivery of a portion of her cargo at a future period, namely, when the vessel should arrive; in short, that the goods are to be delivered at the quay out of the vessel, if she should arrive; in order to fulfil which condition, a double event must take place, namely, the arrival of the vessel with the nitrate of soda on board. Such was the meaning put by the court on a similar contract in *Lovatt* v. *Hamilton*; and I must own that I, for my own part, never had the least doubt as to the meaning of these words. The word " to " does not mean that the goods " shall " arrive, but merely that they shall be sold on their arrival. I think, therefore, that, according to its true meaning, the language of this contract renders the performance of it conditional on a double event, the arrival in safety of the vessel and her cargo. That being so, the short question remaining for our consideration is this : is that construction altered or interfered with by the short memorandum inserted at the end of the bought and sold note, namely, " should the vessel be lost, this contract to be void ? " It is a very loose memorandum; and although the parties might possibly have thought that it fully expressed their meaning, I think we cannot attribute to it the efficacy of altering the original contract, and that it must be understood as confined solely to this, that if the vessel is lost, the contract is to be altogether void. It is, as I have said before, a loose memorandum, and ought not to be allowed to alter the meaning of a contract, which clearly contains within itself a double condition for its performance. This rule must therefore be made absolute.

ALDERSON, B.—The memorandum at the foot of this note is in the affirmative, not in the negative. Had it been

Exch. of Pleas,
1842.

JOHNSON
v.
MACDONALD.

the latter, it might have made a difference in the construc-. tion of this document. When goods are to be sold on a condition to take effect at some future time, I agree in thinking, that it is more rational to construe the words " to arrive " in the light of a condition, than as amounting to a warranty.

GURNEY, B., and ROLFE, B., concurred.

Rule absolute.

———◆———

Feb. 10.

TODD *v.* EMLY and Another.

A Judge at Nisi Prius is bound to accept a plea puis darrein continuance, even after the jury are sworn, provided it be tendered in due form, and accompanied with the usual affidavit, that the subject-matter of it arose within eight days of the time of its being pleaded.
Semble, that such affidavit is unnecessary, where the subject-matter of the plea arose at the trial in the presence of the Judge.

ASSUMPSIT for the price of wine supplied to the Alliance Club, brought against the defendants, who were members of the committee of the Club at the time the wine was ordered (*a*). At the trial before *Tindal,* C. J., at the last Surrey Assizes, the plaintiff, in support of his case, called a Mr. Charles Stewart, who stated on the voir dire, that he also was a member of the committee at the time the wine was ordered, and that he considered himself as much liable as the defendants. Upon this, it was objected on the part of the defendants, that the witness was incompetent; whereupon a release was executed and delivered to him.

Thesiger, for the defendants, then applied to the learned Judge for leave to plead the release puis darrein continuance, inasmuch as the release of one joint contractor operated as a discharge of all, and thus put an end to the plaintiff's claim. The plaintiff's counsel contended, that it was not competent for a defendant to plead such a plea

(*a*) See the former discussions of this case, 7 M. & W. 427, and 8 M. & W. 505.

after the jury had been sworn. The learned Judge per-

mitted the case to proceed, reserving leave to the defendants
to move to set the verdict aside, and to plead the plea nunc
pro tunc, dispensing with the usual affidavit, that the subject-matter of the plea arose within eight days previously.
No formal tender of the plea on paper, or of the affidavit,
was made.

A verdict having been found for the plaintiff, *Thesiger*, in
Michaelmas term last, obtained a rule nisi pursuant to the
leave reserved at the trial; against which

Petersdorff (*Platt* with him) now shewed cause.—The
proper mode of pleading a plea puis darrein continuance is
to tender it on paper, accompanied by an affidavit stating
that the subject-matter of the plea has arisen within eight
days. Neither of those requisites was complied with in
this case; and the Court will not interfere to relieve
the defendant from the necessity of pursuing the usual
course, in order to enable him to defeat a claim which the
jury have found to be a just one. The rule is, that the
Court will never interfere summarily with the course of
proceedings in a cause, except there be some irregularity,
or where, in the event of their not doing so, some injustice
would ensue.

Thesiger, in support of the rule, contended, that a defendant might plead a plea puis darrein continuance at any
time before the verdict had been delivered; and that the
Judge had no discretion to reject the plea; citing *Prince* v.
Nicholson (*a*), *Pearce* v. *Perkins* (*b*).

PARKE, B.—The only question in this case is, whether
the point reserved by the Lord Chief Justice has the effect
of dispensing with the necessity of a formal tender of this

(5) 5 Taunt. 333.   (*b*) Bull. N. P. 310.

plea on paper, accompanied by the proper affidavit—requisites which are indispensable to the validity of such a plea, unless it is otherwise ordered by the Court or a judge. It appears, from a communication we have had with him, that his intention was to have raised before us the question, whether, after the jury were sworn, such a plea was receivable; in which case, the defendant was to be in the same position now, as if he had formally tendered the plea at Nisi Prius. Now, as it is quite clear that a judge at Nisi Prius ought always to receive such a plea as this, when tendered in due form with the proper affidavit annexed, it follows that this rule must be made absolute.

ALDERSON, B.—There is one respect in which we cannot now be in exactly the same position as the Judge at Nisi Prius; namely, that an affidavit cannot *now* be made, that the subject-matter of the plea arose within eight days of this present time. But then it appears to me, that such an affidavit was not necessary at Nisi Prius in the present case, inasmuch as the subject-matter of the plea arose at the trial in the presence of the Judge himself, and thus became a fact coming within his own personal knowledge.

GURNEY, B., and ROLFE, B., concurred.

Rule absolute.

———————

DAVIES *v.* WATERS and Others.

A party who is
protected from
producing a
deed at Nisi
Prius, on the
ground that he
holds it as a
trustee for one
of the parties, is not compellable to disclose the contents of it.

THIS was an action of replevin, tried before *Erskine,* J., at the last assizes for Carmarthenshire. A Mr. Jeffries, the attorney of one of the defendants, was called as a witness on their behalf, and on cross-examination by the

An attorney for a party in a cause is not bound to state the contents of a deed, of which he first obtained a knowledge by having obtained and read it, at the suggestion of his counsel, at the consultation in the cause. (*Rolfe,* B., dubitante.)

plaintiff's counsel, was required to produce a certain deed.
He declined to produce it on the ground of privilege, alleging that he held it as a trustee for the defendant, his
client, and the learned Judge allowed the objection. The
plaintiff's counsel was thereupon proceeding to examine
him as to the contents of the deed, when the defendants'
counsel interposed ; and in answer to questions put by him,
the witness stated that he had not read the deed until that
morning, when, at the suggestion of his counsel in consultation, he obtained it from the defendant, and in the
presence of his counsel, and for their information, ascertained its contents. The learned Judge thereupon expressed his opinion, that the witness's knowledge of the
contents of the deed was acquired by him in his professional
character, and rejected the evidence ; and the defendants
had a verdict.

In Michaelmas Term, *E. V. Williams* obtained a rule
nisi for a new trial, on the ground of the rejection of this
evidence ; citing *Marston* v. *Downes* (a).

Chilton and *Nicholl* now shewed cause.—The evidence was
rightly rejected. It was clear that the witness did not acquire
his knowledge of the contents of this deed in his character
of trustee, but as the professional adviser of the defendant,
his client ; and therefore he could neither be compelled to
produce the deed itself, nor to state the contents of it. The
rule is laid down in *Wheatley* v. *Williams* (b), where it was
held, that an attorney, when examined as a witness, is not
bound to state whether a document, which had been shewn
to him by his client in the course of a professional interview, was then in the same state as when it was produced
at the trial ; for instance, whether it was at that time
stamped or not. Lord *Abinger*, C. B., there appears to

(a) 1 Ad. & Ell. 31 ; 3 Nev. & M. 861.   (b) 1 M. & W. 533.

consider the rule on this subject to have been stated too
broadly in Buller's Nisi Prius, p. 284, where it is said that
a professional witness is bound to state a fact " of his own
knowledge, and of which he might have had knowledge
without being counsel or attorney in the cause." [*Alderson,* B.—Perhaps the words " might have had " were intended to have no larger meaning than the word " had."]
Cocks v. *Nash* (a) will probably be cited for the plaintiff.
There it was held, that although a party who held a composition deed as trustee, was not bound to produce it, an
extract from it which had been furnished by him to the
defendant's attorney, and was by him proved to be correct,
might be given in evidence. That case, however, is distinguishable from the present. Where a party is not bound
to produce a deed in evidence, he surely cannot be compellable to state its contents; if he be, the privilege of his
client becomes wholly nugatory. *Marston* v. *Downes,* also,
is distinguishable; there the witness was not the attorney
of either of the parties to the action. Here, moreover, the
witness held the deed as trustee, and if he had not also
been attorney in the cause, might have refused to produce
it. In *Beard* v. *Ackerman* (b), it was held that an attorney
was not bound to speak as to the particulars of a bill of
exchange, his knowledge of those particulars having been
derived from the bill having been entrusted to him by his
client. That is a case quite parallel with the present.

E. V. Williams, contrà.—It is too late for the defendants
now to object that the witness might, in his character of
trustee, refuse to state the contents of the deed of his cestui
que trust; the only ground for the exclusion of the evidence
which was taken at the trial was, that the witness had obtained his knowledge of the deed in his professional capacity,
and therefore was privileged from disclosing its contents.

(a) 6 C. & P. 154.   (b) 5 Esp. 119.

Where one ground only of objection to the admission of evidence is relied on at Nisi Prius, another cannot be urged on the motion for a new trial: see per *Patteson*, J., in *Marston* v. *Downes* (a). Then the present case falls within the exception stated in Buller's Nisi Prius; the facts tendered in evidence being such as the witness might have had a knowledge of without being attorney in the cause. He was also a trustee, and in that character might have insisted on having the custody of the deed, and was bound to make himself acquainted with its contents. [*Alderson*, B.—But in this case he did not insist on receiving the deed in his character of trustee, but obtained it from his client on the ground of a knowledge of it being necessary to the client's defence; how then can he be permitted to state its contents?] In *Griffith* v. *Davies* (b), a witness who was the attorney for the defendant was permitted to state a conversation, in which the defendant proposed a compromise to the plaintiff. [*Alderson*, B.—That was not knowledge gained by the witness by reason of its being entrusted to him in his professional character, but merely by his being present at the conversation.] Neither did the witness in this case obtain his knowledge from any communication made to him, or any consultation with him, in his professional character, by his client; but from the circumstance of its being thought necessary by the counsel to be acquainted with the contents of the deed. That is not a confidential communication within the rule of law on this subject, extended as it undoubtedly has been of late years. The case of *Marston* v. *Downes* is an authority for holding that the witness was bound to state the contents of the deed, even if, on the ground of privilege, he was not compellable to produce the deed itself.

ALDERSON, B.—It seems to me that this rule should be

Exch. of Pleas,
1842.

DAVIES
v.
WATERS.

(a) 1 Ad. & Ell. 33.   (b) 5 B. & Adol. 502.

discharged, and that the evidence was properly rejected at the trial, and properly rejected upon two grounds: the one, that which the learned Judge himself adopted; and the other, one to which he appears not to have given so much attention at Nisi Prius. In the first place, Mr. Jeffries, being called upon, refused to produce the deed. The conclusion to be drawn from that is, that he refuses to give any information of the contents of the deed, by producing it to be read in Court. Now it appears to me, that it would be perfectly illusory for the law to say that a party is justified in not producing a deed, but that he is compellable to give parol evidence of its contents; that would give him, or rather his client through him, merely an illusory protection, if he happens to know the contents of the deed, and would be only a roundabout way of getting from every man an opportunity of knowing the defects there may be in the deeds and titles of his estate. I am clearly of opinion, therefore, that when a party refuses to produce a deed, and is justified in so doing, he ought not to be compelled to give parol evidence of its contents. On that ground the rejection of the evidence may well be sustained: and on the second ground also, if the learned Judge had directed the witness to give parol evidence of the contents of the deed, I think he would have done wrong, notwithstanding its afterwards appearing that the only information he had on the subject arose from his having obtained it at the suggestion of his counsel, and having read it at the consultation in the cause. I think that gave his knowledge a privileged character. To oblige him to give parol evidence of a deed under such circumstances, would be in fact seeking to have in evidence what occurs at consultation between the parties.

GURNEY, B.—I am of the same opinion. The attorney for one of the defendants was called as a witness, and asked to produce a deed, which he was possessed of

as trustee for his client, and therefore objected to its production; and the learned Judge, being appealed to, supported the witness in his objection, and I think supported
him rightly. And I agree with my brother *Alderson*, that
it would be perfectly illusory to entitle a witness to withhold the production of a deed, and yet to compel him
to divulge its contents. The same right that he has to
withhold the one, I think he has to withhold the other.
But the objection here goes further; for just an hour
before the trial, being possessed of the deed, and possessed
of it in the character of trustee, he takes it to the consultation, and there, in the character of attorney for the defendant, and for the express purpose of informing the
minds of the counsel for the defendant, he reads the deed,
and by that means acquires his knowledge of its contents. Can it be doubted that this is a knowledge acquired in the character of professional adviser of the party?
If so, it is fit and proper that knowledge so acquired
should be held sacred.

ROLFE, B.—I entirely concur with my learned Brothers
in opinion, that this rule should be discharged. Although
Mr. *Williams's* ingenuity may have occasioned some
doubt, yet I think, giving a reasonable construction to
the Judge's note, it must be taken that the witness
meant to object from the first to the production of this
deed, which he held as trustee, and to disclose nothing but
what he was bound to disclose. But it is urged, that the case
of *Marston* v. *Downes* is an authority for the position, that
although he was not compelled to produce the deed, he yet
was compellable to state the contents of it. If that had been
so, I should have acceded to that authority with great re-
luctance; but, on looking at the case, I do not find it to
be any authority for the proposition for which it is cited.
That was the case of an action against an executrix, with a
plea of plene administravit, there being evidence given of

assets, and of payments counterbalancing those assets.
The question was, whether proof could be given of further
assets; and the plaintiff gave in evidence this fact, that a
person, who was an attorney, had paid to the defendant a
large sum of money, not included in the assets, which had
been raised on a mortgage made with a client of the witness.
The witness was then called upon to produce the mortgage deed, and refused to do so; and the learned Judge
held that he was not bound to produce it. He was then
questioned as to its contents; an objection was taken to
the admission of the secondary evidence; but the Judge
overruled it; and then the attorney appealed to the Judge,
whether he was bound to state the contents of the deed.
The Judge said that he thought he ought to answer.
On the motion for a new trial, two questions arose, as
to which the Lord Chief Justice thus expresses himself:—
" We are of opinion, first, that the evidence was admissible
for the purpose for which it was produced; and secondly,
that whether or not the privilege of the mortgagee extended
to protect him from the attorney's giving parol evidence of
the contents of the deed, still, the evidence being actually
before the jury, *the defendants* were not a privileged party;
and they, therefore, had no right of objection, even on the
supposition that the learned Judge had done wrong." So that
when the case is sifted, it is plain it never could establish a
proposition so absurd, as that a person, who is privileged from
producing a deed because the party interested under it is
his client, nevertheless is to be compelled to state even
the whole contents, if he know them. To put the case in
another point of view, could it be contended that, if the
deed had been written by himself, he could be required to
hold it open before him in Court, and refresh his memory
with its contents? It appears to me, therefore, that the
learned Judge was quite right in rejecting the evidence. On
the other ground, of the witness being privileged as attorney
for one of the defendants, I confess that, as at present ad-

vised, I feel a difficulty in concurring in opinion with the rest of the Court; but it is unnecessary to say whether the witness was rightly rejected on two grounds, if one of those grounds was sufficient for the purpose.

Rule discharged (*a*).

(*a*) See *Bate* v. *Kinsey*, 1 C., M. & R. 38.

───◆───

BETTY EASTWOOD *v.* SAVILLE.

Feb. 12.

ASSUMPSIT on a promissory note, made by the defendant, dated the 6th of June 1834, whereby he promised to pay the plaintiff on demand £35, with lawful interest. There was also a count upon an account stated. Pleas, first, to the first count, that the defendant did not make the note; secondly, to the second count, non assumpsit; thirdly, to the whole declaration, actio non accrevit infra sex annos. Issues thereon.

The particulars stated, that on the indebitatus count in his declaration, the plaintiff sought to recover £28, and interest from the 4th of August 1837, being the balance due on the promissory note, after giving the defendant credit for the sum of £7 paid on account of the note, and also all interest due thereon up to the said 4th of August, 1837.

At the trial before *Rolfe*, B., at the Middlesex sittings in Hilary Term, on the note in question being produced in evidence by the plaintiff, it bore an indorsement as follows:—

"4th August, 1837.

"Received of John Saville £6.

"Betty × Eastwood."

In an action on a promissory note by the payee against the maker, the note, when produced in evidence by the plaintiff at the trial, bore upon it an indorsement as follows:—"4th Aug., 1837,—Received of J. S. £6—B. x E." The whole of this entry, except the cross, was in the handwriting of the defendant, and there was no attestation, nor any proof that the cross was the mark of B.E., nor any proof of the *fact* of payment:— *Held*, that the indorsement was no tevidence of part payment, to take the case out of the Statute of Limitations.

There was no attestation to this indorsement, nor any proof that the cross was made by the plaintiff; and the whole of it, except the cross, was proved to be in the handwriting of the defendant. There was no proof of any payment by the defendant on account of the note; but to take the case out of the stat. 9 Geo. 4. c. 14, the plaintiff relied solely on the above indorsement. For the defendant, it was contended that it was an indorsement *charging the plaintiff* with the *receipt* of the money, and not an acknowledgment or promise to *charge the defendant*, within the meaning of Lord *Tenterden's* Act; and that it was necessary to prove a payment of money in fact, to take the case out of the statute. The learned Judge directed the jury to find a verdict for the plaintiff, with liberty to the defendant to move to enter a verdict for him on the third issue, if the Court should be of opinion that the evidence was not sufficient to take the case out of the statute. In Hilary Term, *W. H. Watson* obtained a rule accordingly, against which

Hoggins now shewed cause.—The indorsement on the promissory note, in the handwriting of the defendant, coming from the possession of the plaintiff, amounted to evidence of part payment. It is admitted that a verbal acknowledgment by the debtor, within the six years, of the part payment of a debt, is not sufficient to take the case out of the Statute of Limitations, as was decided in *Willis* v. *Newham* (a), *Bayley* v. *Ashton* (b), and *Maghee* v. *O'Neill* (c); and that such an acknowledgment must be in writing, and signed by the defendant; but if part payment be by any means shewn, that is enough; and there was here evidence to shew it. In *Waters* v. *Tompkins* (d), it was held that the appropriation of part payment of principal, or of pay-

(a) 3 You. & J. 518.   (c) 7 M. & W. 531.
(b) 4 Per. & D. 204.   (d) 2 C., M. & R. 722.

ment of interest, to a particular debt, may be shewn by any medium of proof: that therefore it does not require an express declaration of the debtor at the time of the payment to establish it, but may be proved by previous or subsequent declarations made by him; although the *fact* of the payment must be proved by independent evidence. There *Parke*, B., says: "The act of 9 Geo. 4, as explained by that case (a), does not prohibit or qualify the ordinary mode of legal proof in any respect, save that it requires something more than *mere admission.*" [*Alderson*, B.—In that case the fact of payment was proved, and the acknowledgment was only used to point the payments to particular debts. What is there here to prove the fact of payment?] This is a promissory note, and the plaintiff is bound by it, and by what appears upon it; and the entry made by the defendant on the instrument in the hands of the plaintiff, is evidence against her. Upon its being produced before the jury, they would see the indorsements of part payment and payments of interest, and they must find that part of the money had been paid. The mere indorsement on the note in the handwriting of the defendant, coming from the plaintiff's possession, is sufficient to shew part payment.

Watson, contrà, was not called upon.

ALDERSON, B.—There is here no evidence of anything, but only the production of the document by the plaintiff, and proof of the indorsement being in the handwriting of the defendant. There is no proof of its being signed by "the party chargeable thereby." *Bayley* v. *Ashton* goes the whole length of this case. I dare say the jury would find what was reasonable, but the question is whether they are not prevented from doing so by law. There is no distinction in principle between *Bayley* v. *Ashton* and the

(a) *Willis* v. *Newham.*

Exch. of Pleas,
1842.

EASTWOOD
v.
SAVILLE.

present case; and we must be bound by the authorities until they are overruled by a superior court. When I reserved the case of *Bayley* v. *Ashton* for the opinion of the Court, I thought the decision would have been the other way; and I confess that I still think it ought to have been so.

GURNEY, B., and ROLFE, B., concurred.

Rule absolute.

———◆———

Feb. 12.

PEPPERCORN *v.* HOFMAN.

By a local act, 10 Geo. 3, c. lxxv., the 15th section enacted, that the rates directed by that act to be made should and might, on refusal or neglect to pay the same by any person or persons *liable*

TRESPASS for breaking and entering two rooms of the plaintiff, in and parcel of a certain house or premises situate and being No. 15, Buckingham-street, &c., and making a great noise &c., and staying and continuing therein for a long space of time &c.; and seizing and taking the plaintiff's goods.

Plea—not guilty, by statute.

thereto, be recovered in such manner as the rates made for the relief of the poor are directed to be recovered; and by the 17th section it was provided, that any person, whether landlord or tenant, who should let out his or her house in separate apartments, or ready furnished to a lodger or lodgers, should be deemed to be the *occupier* thereof, and might be rated or assessed accordingly, and should be liable to the payment of the sum so rated. And s. 18 enacted, that the goods and chattels of each and every person renting or occupying any separate part or apartment in such house or building, or renting or occupying any ready-furnished house, or any part thereof, *should be liable to be distrained and sold* for the payment of the said rates :—*Held,* first, that under that act, the goods of a lodger are liable to be distrained and sold for rates assessed upon and due from the landlord, under a warrant directing the churchwardens and overseers to take the goods of the landlord.

The warrant recited that the rates were due from D., the landlord; that they had been lawfully demanded, and refused to be paid; and that it had been fully proved to the justices on oath, that D. had been duly summoned before them to shew cause why he had refused to pay the rates: but that he had not shewn any sufficient cause :—*Held,* in an action against the constable for seizing the goods, that it was not any objection that there was no proof that the landlord had been duly summoned.

Held, also, that the action could not be maintained against the constable for anything done under the warrant, without a demand of a perusal and copy of the warrant, unless he were guilty of any excess; in which case he would be liable for such excess, without such a demand.

The constable having entered the house of D. and there distrained the goods of a lodger, placed a person in possession of the goods in the room in which they were, saying that, unless the money were paid, he should remain there five days; he remained in possession eight hours, until the lodger paid the amount to redeem the goods :—*Held,* that this was not an impounding, but that it was a question for the jury whether he had remained an unreasonable time for the removal of the goods under the warrant.

Exch. of Pleas,
1842.

PEPPERCORN
v.
HOFMAN.

At the trial before *Rolfe*, B., at the Middlesex sittings in Hilary Term, it was proved by the person who had the care of the house in question as housekeeper, that the defendant entered the house, the outer door being open, to make a seizure for rates due from Duncan, who lived in Chancery-lane, but was the landlord of the house, 15, Buckingham-street, in which house the plaintiff was a lodger; and having entered the plaintiff's room to make the distress, the plaintiff said he had nothing to do with the rates, as he paid his rent to Duncan. The defendant said he must seize the goods for the rates, and sat down and took an inventory of them. In an hour after, the defendant called in an assistant, and told him he should leave him in charge of the furniture and in possession of the place. The plaintiff said he had no right to do so, and he should seek his remedy:—that he was going out and must lock up his room, and could not allow the man's staying there. The defendant said, that if he locked the door he should break it open; and that unless the money was paid, the man must remain five days. The plaintiff then said, if the defendant wanted to take the goods he must take them, as he (the plaintiff) wanted to go out. The plaintiff went out and left the man in possession, but returned at eight o'clock, the entry having taken place at twelve o'clock. The plaintiff then said, if they would not take the furniture, he must pay the money to get rid of the man; and he accordingly sent for the defendant, and paid the amount. The defendant, in answer to this case, proved that he had acted in execution of two warrants of distress for levying poor's rates due from Duncan. The warrants were put in, and proved to be under the hands and seals of two justices; and those warrants stated, that the rates were due from Duncan; that they had been lawfully demanded, and refused to be paid; and that it had been fully proved to the justices on oath, that Duncan had *been duly summoned* before them to shew cause why he had refused to pay the rates, but that he had not shewed any sufficient cause, and therefore the warrants required the churchwardens and overseers to make distress of the goods and chattels of Duncan, and if, within the space of five days next after such distress, the said rate or sum, together with the reasonable charges of taking and keeping the said distress, should not be paid, that then they should sell the goods distrained. No evidence was given at the trial to prove the fact that Duncan had been summoned. The poor's rates were put in and proved. It was contended, on behalf of the defendant, that the plaintiff ought to be nonsuited, on the following grounds :— first, that the plaintiff should have demanded a copy of the warrant, under the stat. 24 Geo. 2, c. 44, s. 6; secondly, that the defendant was authorized by the local act of St. Martin's-in-the-Fields, 10 Geo. 3, c. lxxv., to take the goods of the plaintiff, he being a lodger in the house. The learned Judge nonsuited the plaintiff, giving him leave to move to enter a verdict for £20, the amount of damages found by the jury, and 12l. 6s., the amount received from the plaintiff under the levy. The plaintiff was also to be at liberty to move on the ground that there was no evidence that the summonses had been served on Duncan.

Platt, in Hilary Term, moved for a rule on several grounds :—first, that the defendant had no right to distrain the tenant's goods for rates due from the landlord; secondly, that the warrant did not authorize the seizure of the plaintiff's goods, but only those of Duncan; thirdly, that there was no proof that Duncan had been summoned to pay the rates, which was necessary before a distress warrant could be issued; fourthly, that it was not necessary to prove any demand of the warrant; fifthly, that the defendant had no right to put a man in possession of goods to remain upon the premises, as it was not like a distress for rent, but a species of execution. The Court having granted a rule,

Byles (*Kelly* with him) now shewed cause.—First, it is

clear that, under the stat. 10 Geo. 3, c. 75, the church-   *Exch. of Pleas,*
wardens had a right to take the lodger's goods for rates   1842.
due from the landlord of the house. The local act, inti-   PEPPERCORN
tuled " An Act for building a workhouse in the parish of St.   *v.*
Martin's-in-the-Fields" (10 Geo. 3, c. lxxv), enacts, by s. 15,   HOFMAN.
" that the rates thereby directed to be made shall and may,
on *refusal* or *neglect* to pay the same by any person or
persons liable thereto, be recovered *in such manner as the
rates made for the relief of the poor* are directed to be recovered by the 43 Eliz., and 17 Geo. 2, c. 38, s. 8." Then
the 17th section recites, that "whereas there are divers
houses and buildings in the said parish, which are let out
in separate apartments, or ready-furnished, to lodgers,
whereby the payment of the said rates or assessments may
in such cases be evaded : for prevention whereof be it
further enacted, that any person, whether landlord or
tenant, who shall let out his or her house in separate
apartments, or ready-furnished, to a lodger or lodgers,
shall, for the several purposes of this act, be deemed and
taken to be the occupier thereof, and may be rated or assessed accordingly, and shall be liable and subject to the
payment of the sum so rated or assessed." And the
18th section provides, "that the goods and chattels of each
and every person renting or occupying any separate part
or apartment in such house or building, or renting or occupying any ready-furnished house, or any part thereof,
shall be liable to be distrained and sold for the payment of
the said rates or assessments ; and that each and every
person, who shall pay such rates or assessments so charged
on his or her respective landlord or landlords, or upon
whose goods or on whose chattels the same shall be levied
in pursuance of this act, shall and may deduct the same
from and out of the rent due and payable, from time to time,
to his, her, or their respective landlord or landlords so
letting out the same." The owner is to be considered as
the occupier, and the rate is to be made upon him. The

goods, therefore, of the lodgers are liable to be seized for the rates due from the owner. The goods of the landlord, where they are in another county, cannot be seized. Then the second question is, were they liable to be seized on this warrant, directing the defendants to distrain the goods of Duncan? It is submitted that they were. It is said that the magistrate ought to state in the warrant, that the tenant's goods are to be taken; but that cannot be, for suppose there are ten or twelve lodgers in the house, how can the magistrate ascertain their names? Is he to say, if the goods of one are not sufficient to satisfy the rates, then the goods of another are to be taken? By the 15th section of the above act, the rates, on refusal or neglect to pay the same by any person liable thereto, are to be recovered *in such manner* as the rates made for the relief of the poor are directed to be recovered by the 43 Eliz., and 17 Geo. 2, c. 38. The warrant, therefore, must pursue that form. Now, by the 4th section of the 43 Eliz. c. 2, the churchwardens and overseers are " to levy the sums of money and all arrearages of every one that shall refuse to contribute according as they shall be assessed, by distress and sale of *the offender's goods;*" and by 17 Geo. 2, c. 38, " the goods of any person assessed and refusing to pay may be levied by warrant of distress." Therefore, the warrant is to seize the goods of the person refusing to pay, that is, Duncan. Not only, therefore, the convenience of the matter, but the very words of the act, require that the warrant should be against the goods of Duncan. Then, by the 18th section of the local act, the goods of the tenant are made the goods of Duncan for the purposes of the act.

Thirdly, it was unnecessary to prove that Duncan had been summoned to pay the rates, as it must be assumed that he was until the contrary were shewn, or the warrant would not have been issued. The onus of shewing that there was no summons lay upon the other side. Fourthly, there ought to have been a demand of a perusal and copy of the warrant, under 24 Geo. 2, c. 44, s. 6. A churchwarden or person acting under him in obedience to a warrant, is a person within that act. The 6th section enacts, " that no action shall be brought against any constable, &c., or against any person or persons acting by his order and in his aid, for any thing done in obedience to any warrant under the hand or seal of any justice of the peace, until demand hath been made or left at the usual place of his abode by the party or parties intending to bring such action, or by his, her, or their attorney or agent, in writing, signed by the party demanding the same, of the perusal and copy of such warrant, and the same hath been refused or neglected for the space of six days after such demand ; and in case, after such demand, and compliance therewith by shewing the said warrant to and permitting a copy to be taken thereof by the party demanding the same, any action shall be brought against such constable, &c., or against such person or persons acting in his aid, for any such cause as aforesaid, without making the justice or justices who signed or sealed the said warrant defendant or defendants, then, on producing and proving such warrant at the trial of such action, the jury shall give their verdict for the defendant or defendants, notwithstanding any defect of jurisdiction in such justice or justices." There is no doubt that this entry and seizure of the goods was in obedience to the warrant; but it will be said that the defendant has done more than he was authorized by the warrant, and therefore he is not entitled to the protection of the act; and *Bell* v. *Oakley* (a) will be relied on. There the defendants, in order to levy a poor's rate under a warrant of distress granted by two magistrates, broke and entered the house, and broke the windows, &c., and it was held that they might be sued in trespass, without a previous demand of a perusal and copy of the warrant. But

Exch. of Pleas, 1842.

PEPPERCORN
v.
HOFMAN.

(a) 2 M. & Selw. 259.

that case is distinguishable, for there the original entry and
the whole proceeding were unlawful; but here the entry was
perfectly lawful, and the objection only is, that the defendant stayed too long upon the premises. That question was
not left to the jury, and the plaintiff did not request that
it should be left to them; it is therefore not open to him to
make that complaint now. [*Rolfe*, B.—This is not, strictly
speaking, a distress: it is in the nature of an execution.]
It was contended that the goods were impounded upon the
premises, but that is not so; the staying too long is not an
impounding. It was necessary to stay some time to complete the levy. Whether the party staid an unreasonable
time is not a question now; the plaintiff should have required it to be left to the jury, whether or not the goods
were kept too long upon the premises. By 27 Geo. 2, c.
20, s. 1, it is enacted " that, in all cases where any justice
or justices of the peace is or are or shall be required
or impowered by any act or acts of Parliament now in
force, or hereafter to be made, to issue a warrant of distress for the levying of any penalty inflicted, or any sum
of money directed to be paid, by or in consequence of
such act or acts, it shall and may be lawful for the justice
or justices granting such warrant, therein to order and
direct the goods and chattels to be distrained, to be sold
and disposed of *within a certain time to be limited in*
such warrant, so as such time be not less than four days
nor more than eight days, unless the penalty or sum of
money for which such distress shall be made, together with
the reasonable charges of taking and *keeping* such distress,
be sooner paid." And the 2nd section enacts, " that the
officer making such distress shall and is hereby impowered
to deduct the reasonable charges of taking, *keeping,* and
selling such distress, out of the money arising by such sale."
Whether that act allows the goods to be kept upon the
premises may be a matter of doubt; but it may do so.
It is, however, unnecessary to decide that question, for if the

party is bound to remove them, he must have a reasonable time to do so. He might perhaps be justified in waiting till the following morning : it has not been shewn, at all events, that he stayed there an unreasonable time. He must necessarily have a reasonable time to procure a conveyance to remove the goods. If it be shewn that the original entry is unlawful, then the whole proceeding is bad; but where the majority of what is done is good, then the plaintiff is not entitled to maintain the action without a demand of a perusal and copy of the warrant. *Money* v. *Leach* (a), in which it was laid down that where the justice cannot be liable, the officer is not within the protection of the act, does not apply. [*Alderson*, B.—If no summons had been issued against Duncan, it was the fault of the magistrate in granting the warrant without it, and he would be the person liable.] The magistrate had jurisdiction to issue the warrant; but suppose there had been no summons, and he ought not to have issued the warrant; the onus of shewing that lay upon the plaintiff. Such an objection might have been made in an action against the magistrate, but not in an action against the defendant. It was incumbent on the plaintiff to shew that the warrant was improperly issued. The presumption is, that the magistrate has done everything to give him jurisdiction, rather than the contrary: *Rex* v. *Wheeton* (b); *Rex* v. *Witney* (c). It may be that, in the action against this magistrate, who has the means of knowing whether he has done all that was necessary to give him jurisdiction, the onus is on him; but it is not so in the case of the constable, who has no such means of knowledge. [*Alderson*, B.—If it were otherwise, it would be no defence that the warrant was issued. It is enough to shew general jurisdiction in the magistrate to issue the warrant.]

Exch. of Pleas,
1842.

PEPPERCORN
v.
HOFMAN.

(a) 3 Burr. 1742; 1 W. Black. 563.

(b) 4 Ad. & Ell. 607; 6 Nev. & M. 65.

(c) 5 Ad. & Ell. 191; 6 Nev. & M. 552.

Pashley (*Platt* with him) in support of the rule.—First, it was not necessary to prove any demand of a copy of the warrant. It is said that the warrant could not be executed against Duncan's goods in another county; but the 17 Geo. 2, c. 38, s. 7, expressly enacts, "that the goods of any person assessed and refusing to pay may be levied by warrant of distress, not only in the place for which such assessment was made, but in any other place within the same county or precinct; and if sufficient distress cannot be found within the said county or precinct, on oath made thereof before some justice of any other county or precinct (which oath shall be certified under the hand of such justice on the said warrant), such goods may be levied in such other county or precinct by virtue of such warrant and certificate." [*Alderson*, B.—If there is a sufficient distress within the county, then they cannot seize goods in another county. If the plaintiff's goods were seizable under this warrant, then arises the question whether a demand of the warrant was necessary.] If by the 18th section they are to take the goods of any one occupying the property rated, then the goods of the tenants were liable to be taken. But at least the tenant should have some notice of his liability before his goods are taken. [*Alderson*, B.— Against whom should the distress go, but the landlord? The act does not make the tenants liable to be rated for the premises, and therefore it could not go against them.] It is submitted, that as they are made virtually liable by the act, they should have had some notice of their liability. [*Alderson*, B.—Suppose you are right in that, these defendants are officers acting in obedience to a warrant, and you must shew a demand of the warrant, in order to render them liable. The only remaining question is, whether the defendant was guilty of any excess.] He ought to have gone as soon as he was required to go, and taken the goods with him. Whether this be considered an impounding, or a staying an unreasonable time, the defendant was guilty of

excess, and is therefore liable. But there clearly was an impounding, because the defendant said that, unless the money
were paid, he should stay there the five days. The moment
he exceeded what the warrant authorized him in doing, then
the plaintiff was entitled to maintain his action, without
proving any demand of the warrant. Here he is told to take
the goods seized away, and he refuses to do so, saying that
unless the money is paid, he shall remain the five days;
that constitutes an impounding, which was not justified by
the warrant. At common law, the only place where the
party distraining cannot stay, is the place where the goods
are found. Bro. Abr., Distress, 30, translated in Vin.
Abr., Distress, (E. 4)—"If lord or lessor distrains, he cannot make a pound in the same land for this distress."
Since the stat. 11 Geo. 2, c. 19, in the case of rent in
arrear, undoubtedly the landlord may impound on the
premises; but before it was otherwise. Co. Litt. 47. b.
clearly shews that goods are not to be impounded on the
premises—"He that distrains anything that hath life must
impound them in a lawful pound within three miles in the
same county;" and again—"If the distress be of utensils
of household, or such-like dead goods, which may take harm
by wet or weather, or be stolen away, then he must impound them in a house or other pound covert, within three
miles in the same county;" clearly shewing that they are
not to be impounded on the premises. [*Alderson*, B.—It is
perfectly clear he has a right to stay some time; the question is, whether he stayed an unreasonable time.] [*Byles.*—
That will not affect the necessity for a demand of the warrant.] [*Alderson*, B.—Yes; where the defendant has committed an excess, he must pay for that.] In *Winterbourne*
v. *Morgan* (a), where one who entered under a warrant of
distress for rent in arrear continued in possession of the
goods upon the premises for fifteen days, during the last

(a) 11 East, 395.

four of which he was removing the goods, which were afterwards sold under the distress; it was held, that at any rate
he was liable in trespass for continuing on the premises,
and disturbing the plaintiff in the possession of his house,
after the time allowed by law.

ALDERSON, B.—I think there ought to be a new trial,
for the purpose of submitting the point to the jury, whether
the defendant stayed an unreasonable time on the premises
or not. I am of opinion that, if he did, he is liable. The
act of Parliament makes the rate leviable in the same
manner as poor-rates are leviable by the statute of Elizabeth.
That applied to those persons who are rated. By the 17th
section, the owner is liable, and he is the person from whom,
by the 15th section, the rates are to be recovered. Then
the 18th section says, that "the goods and chattels of each
and every person renting or occupying any separate part
or apartment in such house or building, or renting or
occupying any ready-furnished house, or any part thereof,
shall be liable to be distrained and sold for the payment of
the said rates or assessments." The goods of all the lodgers
are therefore liable; they are to be deemed and taken to
be the goods of the person rated. Then the mere fact
for the officer to ascertain is, who is the person rated; and
having done so, he is to go to the house of the person rated,
and if he finds goods which belong to a person renting
premises under the party rated, he may take them under
the warrant, unless the warrant be informal. I think this
is a good warrant. But before he can make any objection
to it, the party must first make a demand of a copy of the
warrant. If he relies on the fact of the warrant having
been issued without a previous summons, that objection
can only be raised after a demand of the warrant, and in no
case against the officer. That makes an end of the case.

But then there is no doubt that the party can only justify
that which he *lawfully* did under the warrant. He has a

right to stay a reasonable time before he removes the goods; but here the officer said, unless the money was paid, he should stay the five days. Perhaps the excess of damage is trifling, but the case must now go to the jury, to ascertain whether there was any excess.

GURNEY, B., and ROLFE, B., concurred.

Rule absolute for a new trial.

Exch. of Pleas, 1842.

PEPPERCORN v. HOFMAN.

———◆———

SPONG v. WRIGHT.

Feb. 12.

DEBT by the drawer against the acceptor of a bill of exchange for £20, payable to the drawer's own order three months after date, with counts for money lent, and on an account stated.

Pleas, first, except as to 10l. 11s., parcel &c., a set-off for board and lodging &c. with the following averment:—"which said sum of money so due to the defendant as aforesaid exceeds the supposed debt above demanded, except as in the introductory part of this plea mentioned, and all damages by the plaintiff sustained by reason of the detention thereof, and out of which said sum he the defendant is ready and willing &c."—Verification. And as to the sum of 10l. 11s., payment into Court of that sum, and that he the defendant never was indebted to the plaintiff to a greater amount than the sum of 10l. 11s., in

Debt on a bill of exchange by payee against acceptor for £20.—Pleas, first, except as to 10l. 11s., parcel &c., a set-off for board and lodging; and as to the sum of 10l. 11s., payment of that sum into Court. —Replication, that the alleged debts and causes of set-off did not accrue within six years before the commencement of the suit, concluding to the country: to which the defendant, by his rejoinder,

added the similiter. At the trial, the plaintiff having proved his case, and the defendant his set-off, the latter put in a letter from the plaintiff to the defendant, in which the following passages were relied upon, to take the case out of the statute:—"Before closing this, I have to request you will be pleased to send me in any bill or what demand you have to make on me, and *if just*, I shall not give you the trouble of going to law. If you refer to your books, you will find the *last payment* I made you was in May, 1839; the day I have forgot. I shall leave town to-morrow, but shall be back in a few days, for a month, and if you will *bring my bill* in here to me by eleven, I shall be at your service:"—*Held*, that this was not a sufficient admission to take the case out of the Statute of Limitations.

Held, also, that the issue joined on the replication of the Statute of Limitations was no proper issue, and that there ought to be a repleader.

respect of the cause of action in the introductory part of the plea mentioned.—Verification.

Replication to the first plea, that the several alleged debts and causes of set-off in the said first plea mentioned did not, nor did any or either of them, accrue to the defendant within six years before the commencement of the suit, concluding to the country. To the second plea the plaintiff replied, taking the money out of Court in satisfaction of the causes of action, as to the said sum of 10*l.* 11*s.*

The defendant, by his rejoinder to the first replication, added the similiter.

The particulars of the plaintiff's demand were, to recover the amount of the bill of exchange for £20, set out in the declaration, with interest thereon, and for money lent; and also £2, the amount of an I. O. U. of the defendant, dated 31st July, 1841, under the account stated.

The particulars of set-off were for fifteen weeks' board and lodging, at 16*s.* per week, £12; so that, with the sum paid into Court, it exceeded the plaintiff's demand.

At the trial before *Rolfe,* B., at the Middlesex sittings in Hilary Term, the plaintiff proved his case by producing and proving the bill on which the action was brought. The defendant, in answer, proved that, in the year 1835, the plaintiff resided and boarded and lodged with him, the defendant, for nearly four months. The following letter, written in November last, from the plaintiff to the defendant, was given in evidence to take the case out of the Statute of Limitations:—

"Sir,—I have this day placed in my solicitors' hands, Messrs. Baker & Parsons, your bill, with the order on my banker for the same, for which you received twenty sovereigns, which my banker can prove; consequently I suppose there will be but little difficulty in obtaining the same by a course of law. I have now given you ample time for consideration; and you still feel disposed to oblige me to this course, my having no other way of obtaining it. I hope you will not have to regret the step you have taken, *Exch. of Pleas,* besides that of paying the money. I need not put you in 1842. mind of the threat you held out to me. I deny having tried to injure you, nor do I yet feel disposed to do so. You have SPONG *v.* my full permission to carry your threats into execution, WRIGHT. which if you can, you will, I am sure. *Before closing this, I have to request you will be pleased to send me in any bill or what demand you have to make on me; and if just, I shall not give you the trouble of going to law.*

"If you refer to your books, you will find the last payment I made you was in May, 1839; the day I have forgot, but it is on the stamp receipt with the bill, which I left this day; but I think it was the 9th or 29th—no matter the day. I shall leave town to-morrow, but shall be back in a few days, for a month, *and if you will bring my bill* in here to me by eleven, I shall be at your service, after which it will be out of my hands entirely.

"Yours obediently,

"G. A. Spong."

This letter the defendant contended was sufficient to take the case out of the statute; the learned Judge, however, was of a different opinion; and the jury, under his lordship's direction, found a verdict for the plaintiff for 9*l.* 16*s.*, leave being reserved to the defendant to move to enter a verdict for him, if the Court should be of opinion that it was sufficient. *Montague Smith* having obtained a rule accordingly, either to enter a verdict for the defendant, or for a repleader, on the ground that there was no proper issue joined on the replication of the Statute of Limitations, on the authority of *Wheatley* v. *Williams* (a),

Creasy shewed cause—The letter was insufficient to take the case out of the statute. In Starkie on Evidence,

(a) 1 M. & W. 533.

vol. 2, p. 666 (a), the following is the rule deduced from the recent cases: "From the late decisions on the effect of an acknowledgment under the provisions of the stat. 21 Jac. 1, c. 19, where all the former cases were brought under consideration, the result seems to be that, to repel the limiting power of the statute, it must either amount to an *express promise*, or to so clear an admission of a still subsisting liability, that a promise must necessarily be implied." Now here there is clearly no express promise, nor any clear admission of a liability. The plaintiff merely asks the defendant to send him in any bill or demand he has to make on him, and *if just*, he will not give him the trouble of going to law; which is nothing like a promise or admission of liability. This rule was obtained on the authority of *Colledge* v. *Horn* (b), and *Waller* v. *Lacy* (c). In *Colledge* v. *Horn*, the letter was this :—"I have received yours respecting the plaintiff's demand; it is not a just one; I am ready to settle the account whenever the plaintiff thinks proper to meet on the business; I am not in his debt £90, nor anything like that sum ; shall be happy to settle the difference by his meeting me." There is the important distinction that the party uses the terms, "shall be happy to settle the difference," which admits something due; and then, that parol evidence may be given to determine the amount, is not disputed. So in *Waller* v. *Lacy*, the defendant having a claim against the plaintiff, the latter wrote at the foot of his bill "By Mr. Lacy's bill," leaving a blank for the amount. He then wrote below: "Agreeably to your request above I send you my bill, which I will thank you to peruse, and if correct, favour me with a bill for the balance." There the word *balance* necessarily implied that something was due. But here there is nothing of the sort, and no admission of anything being due, as in those cases.

(a) 3rd Edition.   (c) 1 Man. & G. 54; 1 Scott,
(b) 3 Bing. 119; 10 Mo. 431.   N. R. 186.

There is, indeed, a condition, that *if* the demand is *just*, the plaintiff will satisfy it; but that is nothing like an admission of anything being due. He then goes on to desire the defendant to refer to his books to see what payments have been made. That may be an admission that there have been dealings between them; but that is not sufficient; there must be an admission of a subsisting debt. Then there is the allusion to his leaving town, but that he shall be back in a few days, for a month, and if the defendant will bring his bill to him, he shall be at his service. But that carries the case no further. [*Alderson*, B.—Have the cases gone further than this, that an absolute admission of some debt being due is sufficient; and that that admission may be coupled with evidence to prove the amount (a)? I had occasion to consider this matter very fully in the case of *Cheslyn* v. *Dalby* (b), and I there said that I apprehended it must be considered as fully established, that a general promise in writing to pay, not specifying any amount, but which can be made certain as to the amount by extrinsic evidence, is sufficient to take the case out of the operation of the Statute of Limitations. Here, however, the party says, *if* the demand is a just one he will pay it.] In *Morrell* v. *Frith* (c), the defendant wrote in answer to a letter from the plaintiff's attorney, as follows :—" Sir,—Since the receipt of your letter, and indeed for some time previously, I have been in almost daily expectation of being enabled to give a satisfactory reply to your first application respecting the demand of Messrs. Morrell against me. I propose being in Oxford to-morrow morning, when I will call on you upon the matter.— W. C. Frith :" and this was held an insufficient acknowledgment under the statute. He was then stopped by the Court.

Exch. of Pleas,
1842.

SPONG
v.
WRIGHT.

(a) He referred to *Lechmere* v. *Fletcher*, 1 C. & M. 623.

(b) 4 You. & Coll. 238.
(c) 3 M. & W. 402.

Montague Smith, in support of the rule.—The letter is an admission of some bill being due from the plaintiff to the defendant, and that is sufficient, coupled with proof of a demand being in fact due. It does not appear that the letter was written in answer to any application, but from a consciousness that the defendant had a demand against the writer to some amount. He says, " Before closing this, I have to request you will be pleased to send in any bill, or what demand you have to make on me." He then refers to payments, which must be payments on account of something due, and says, " if you will bring my bill to me by eleven, I shall be at your service ;" that imports that there was something due, to be then accounted for, and which the plaintiff was ready to pay. [*Alderson,* B.—He admits there is some demand upon him, but he does not admit it is a just one. It does not appear to me to be any admission of a just demand.] Then there must be a repleader. In *Wheatley* v. *Williams* (a), where there was a plea of the Statute of Limitations, concluding to the country, and the similiter added to it, it was expressly held that no sufficient issue was joined, there being no denial of the averment in the plea :—there was nothing for the jury to try. *Bodenham* v. *Hill* (b) merely decided that such a plea need not conclude with a verification : it did not decide that a conclusion to the country would be proper, or that a replication was unnecessary. That decision does not affect the mode of pleading on the other side—it was simply a declaration of what might be dispensed with in point of form, in the *conclusion* of the plea of the statute ; but did not affect the substance of the issue. Here there is *no issue.*

Creasy, contrà.—In *Smith* v. *Smith* (a), the informal conclusion of a plea was held to be no ground for arresting the

(a) 1 M. & W. 533.   (b) 7 M. & W. 274.

judgment, or for a repleader, if there has been an issue to try; for that the objection could only be taken advantage of on special demurrer. [*Alderson*,B.—There there was clearly an issue, and a fact to be proved.] Here the plaintiff has put the issue on the ground whether the set-off accrued within six years. That cannot be immaterial. It is merely an informal issue, which must be taken advantage of on a special demurrer. Where the conclusion is to the country, instead of with a verification, it is a ground of special demurrer. In Chitty on Pleading, 559, it is said, " Since this statute (4 Ann. c. 16, s. 1), a wrong or defective conclusion, either to the country or with a verification, can only be taken advantage of on special demurrer."

ALDERSON, B.—My Brother *Parke* pointed out this difficulty in *Wheatley* v. *Williams*, that there was a negative and no affirmative; nothing on the record equivalent to an averment that the cause of action arose within six years. So it is here. The plea of set-off does not contain any statement that the matter arose within six years. Then the replication states that the plaintiff was not indebted, for the causes of set-off did not accrue within six years. If you add to that by a rejoinder that they did accrue within six years, then there is a definite issue, but not before.

GURNEY, B., and ROLFE, B., concurred.

Rule absolute for a new trial, both parties to be at liberty to amend.

(*a*) 5 Dowl. P. C. 84.

IN THE EXCHEQUER CHAMBER.

———◆———

(In Error from the Court of Exchequer).

———◆———

M'CALLAN *v.* MORTIMER.

Indebitatus as-sumpsit for stock sold and caused to be transferred by the plaintiff to the defendant, and by the de-fendant duly accepted.—Plea, that the stock alleged to be caused to be transferred was so caused to be transferred by virtue of an agreement with the plaintiff for the transfer of the same, in con-sideration of £4531 5s. to be therefore paid to the plaintiff for the same; and that,

A WRIT of error having been brought on the judgment of the Court of Exchequer in this case (*a*), it was argued in this Court in the vacations after Hilary and Michaelmas Terms, 1841, by Sir *W. W. Follett,* Solicitor-General, for the plaintiff in error: and by *Cresswell,* for the defendant in error.

In addition to the authorities cited on the former argu-ment, the following were referred to, on behalf of the plaintiff in error:—Wilkinson on the Public Funds, 155; *Brown* v. *Turner* (*b*); *Steers* v. *Lashley* (*c*); *Simpson* v. *Bloss* (*d*); *Blachford* v. *Preston* (*e*); *Thomson* v. *Thomson* (*f*); *De Begnis* v. *Armistead* (*g*); and *Ewing* v. *Osbaldiston* (*h*). For the defendant in error:—*Bullock* v. *Richardson* (*i*); *Wigan* v. *Fowler* (*k*); *Crespigny* v. *Wittenoom* (*l*); *Shales* v. *Seignoret* (*m*); *Shepherd* v. *Johnson* (*n*); *Downes* v. *Back* (*o*);

at the time of making such agreement, the plaintiff was not actually possessed of or entitled to the stock in his own right, &c.; by means whereof the said contract became and was null and void:—Held, on error brought upon the judgment of the Court of Exchequer, that the plea was no answer to the action, and that the contract was not within 7 Geo. 2, c. 8, s. 8; affirm-ing the judgment of the Court below.

(*a*) See the pleadings and argu-ments in the Court below, ante, Vol. 7.

(*b*) 7 T. R. 630.

(*c*) 6 T. R. 61.

(*d*) 7 Taunt. 246.

(*e*) 8 T. R. 89.

(*f*) 7 Ves. 470.

(*g*) 10 Bing. 107; 3 M. & Sc. 511.

(*h*) 2 Myl. & Cr. 53.

(*i*) 11 Ves. 373.

(*k*) 1 Stark. N. P. C. 459.,

(*l*) 4 T. R. 790.

(*m*) 1 Ld. Raym. 440.

(*n*) 2 East, 211.

(*o*) 1 Stark. N. P. C. 318.

Rumball v. *Maddock* (a); *Dorriens* v. *Hutchinson* (b); *Cope* v. *Rowlands*(c); and *De Begnis* v. *Armistead*:—and by the Solicitor-General in reply —*Marchant* v. *Evans* (d); *Waymoll* v. *Reed* (e); and *Foster* v. *Taylor* (f).

The Court took time to consider, and now the judgment of the Court (g) was delivered by—

Lord DENMAN, C. J.—This is an action of indebitatus assumpsit, by which the plaintiff alleges that the defendant was indebted to him in the sum of £5000, for certain, to wit, £5000 interest in the joint stock of three per cent. annuities, transferable at the Bank of England, called the Consolidated Three Pounds per Cent. Annuities, *then sold and caused to be transferred* by the plaintiff to the defendant, at his special instance and request, and by the defendant then, to wit, on the same day and year aforesaid, duly accepted; and also upon an account stated; and that the defendant, in consideration of the premises, then promised the plaintiff to pay. The declaration then alleges a breach in not paying.

The defendant pleaded, 1st, that he did not promise; and 2ndly, to the first count of the declaration, that the said interest or share in the said joint stock was so caused to be transferred under and by virtue of a certain contract and agreement made with the plaintiff after the 1st of June, 1734, for the transfer by the plaintiff to the defendant of the said sum of £5000 interest or share in the said joint stock, for and in consideration of the sum of 4551l. 5s. to be therefore paid to the plaintiff for the same. And the defendant further says, that at the time of making such contract and agreement, the plaintiff was not actually

---

(a) 8 East, 304.

(b) 1 Smith, 420.

(c) 2 M. & W. 149.

(d) 8 Taunt. 142.

(e) 5 T. R. 599.

(f) 5 B. & Adol. 887.

(g) Consisting of Lord *Denman*, C. J., *Tindal*, C. J., *Patteson*, J., *Williams*, J., *Coltman*, J., and *Erskine*, J.

possessed of or entitled unto in his own right or in his own name, or in the name or names of any trustee or trustees to his use, of the said interest or share in the said joint stock or any part thereof, by means whereof the said contract and agreement, and the said promise in the said declaration mentioned, so far as the same relates to the said first count, then became and was, and from thence hitherto hath been and still is, according to the form of the statute &c., null and void: and 3rdly, the defendant pleaded that he did not accept the said stock.

Issue was taken on the first and third pleas, and the plaintiff has demurred to the second plea, and the only question which the Court has to consider is, whether the second plea contains any valid answer to the first count of the declaration.

The declaration in this case is on a promise founded on an executed consideration. It was contended in argument by the defendant's counsel, that on these pleadings it must be assumed there was no other agreement between these parties than the original executory contract; but this is, we think, a misapprehension of the true effect of the pleadings. The declaration alleges a promise, founded on an executed consideration. The defendant by his plea does not deny this, but alleges a matter quite consistent with it, that the transfer was made by virtue of a previous executory contract, which was illegal, because the plaintiff was not possessed of the stock contracted for, by means whereof the said contract and agreement, and the *said promise in the declaration* mentioned, became void.

The plea, therefore, expressly treats the promise in the declaration as being different from the contract mentioned in the plea; and the case, as disclosed by the pleadings on both sides, appears to be, that the plaintiff and the defendant contracted for the sale and delivery to the defendant of certain stock of which the plaintiff at the time was not in possession, but that fact not being alleged to have been in the knowledge of the defendant at the time; that the stock was afterwards transferred by the procurement of the plaintiff to the defendant, and that, on the occasion of the transfer, the defendant promised to pay the price which had been stipulated for; and the question arising hereupon is, whether the promise so made is one which the law will not give effect to, and by which the defendant is not bound. *Exch. Chamb.* 1842.

M'CALLAN *v.* MORTIMER.

In considering the statute on which this question turns, it appears to us that a substantial difference exists between a contract to sell, or to transfer, and an actual sale, or actual transfer. This distinction is recognised in the case of *Heckscher* v. *Gregory* (a), in reference to one of the clauses of this statute, and rests on the distinction, quite familiar in the law, between contracts executory and contracts executed.

Now assuming, for the purpose of the argument, that the original contract between the plaintiff and the defendant was void, and that it would have been illegal for the defendant to have entered into it if he had been aware that the plaintiff was not possessed of the stock which he was contracting to transfer; yet here it does not appear that he was aware of it; and on these pleadings it must be taken that the defendant was not aware of the illegality of the contract he was entering into, for illegality is not to be presumed, and the party who seeks to avoid a contract on the score of any illegality, must shew whatever is necessary to make out that illegality.

What then is the situation in which a party stands, who has contracted for the purchase of stock of which the seller is not possessed, the purchaser not being aware of that fact?

If the stock is contracted to be paid for at a future day, and it is not transferred as agreed, he falls within the

(a) 4 East, 607.

words, and is, we conceive, entitled to the remedy given by the 7th section of the act; he is a person who has bought stock to be accepted and paid for on a future day, and which has been neglected to be transferred in such case; he may go into the market and purchase the stock from any other person, and after such purchase may recover the difference from the person with whom the contract was made.

If, instead of the purchaser going into the market to purchase from a third party, the parties contracting meet together, and agree that on transferring the stock to the defendant, the defendant will pay to the plaintiff the sum originally stipulated for, such an agreement does not fall within the prohibition of the statute; it is not a contract to sell, but an actual sale; it is not a contract to transfer, but an actual transfer; such a contract is not prohibited by the words, nor does it, we think, fall within the mischief of the act.

If the contract were not for stock to be accepted and paid for on a future day, but on the very day on which the contract is made, the same reasoning would apply,— there would be no illegality in the promise, founded on a transfer then actually made, to pay the agreed sum of money.

The objection urged against this view of the subject was, that by this means effect is given to a contract which, on the part of the seller at least, was illegal; but to this objection the answer is, that it is not the illegal contract to which effect is given, but the subsequent legal contract founded on a new and sufficient consideration.

It is urged as being absurd and unreasonable, when the contract, originally made to do a certain act, is an illegal contract, that the thing itself, when done, should be held to be legal—that it should be legal to do what it is illegal to contract to do; but this difficulty disappears, if we consider the object of the act of Parliament, the provisions of which are studiously framed with a view to secure in every case an actual transfer of all stock bargained to be sold; and it may well be, that an executory contract to transfer stock which the party is not possessed of, may be void and illegal, and yet the actual transfer of the stock by such party, or by his procurement, may be deemed not to fall within the mischief, as it certainly does not within the express prohibitions, of the act.

On behalf of the defendant many cases were cited, which appear to us to be distinguishable from the one under consideration.

Cases were cited to shew, that where an act is prohibited, either by the common or statute law, the doing of it cannot form a consideration to raise any debt or duty in favour of the party by whom it has been done; as in the case of victuals supplied to an elector at the expense of a candidate; *Ribbans* v. *Crickett* (a) : books printed without the name of the printer; *Bensley* v. *Bignold* (b) : coals sent in for sale without a vendor's ticket, signed by the meter; *Little* v. *Poole* (c) : bricks sold of a less size than by law required; *Law* v. *Hodgson* (d) : paying differences contrary to the provisions of 7 Geo. 2, c. 8; *Brown* v. *Turner* (e); *Steers* v. *Lashley* (f) : payment of a sum of money for the purchase of the command of a ship in the service of the East India Company; *Blachford* v. *Preston* (g). These cases are distinguishable from the case now in judgment, there being in this case a consideration, namely, the actual transfer, not prohibited by statute, nor tainted by any illegality at common law.

Another class of cases was cited, resting on similar principles, where money had been paid or received in the prosecution of some illegal adventure, out of which payments

(a) 1 Bos. & P. 264.

(b) 5 B. & Ald. 335.

(c) 9 B. & C. 192.

(d) 11 East, 300.

(e) 7 T. R. 630.

(f) 6 T. R. 61.

(g) 8 T. R. 89.

or receipts it has been held that no debt or duty could arise; as in the case of *De Begnis* v. *Armistead* (a), where the plaintiff and defendant having engaged in a joint adventure, to bring out Italian operas at a theatre not duly licensed, the plaintiff, at the request of the defendant, paid various sums of money for dresses for the dancers, and for the expense of sending the dancers down: and it was held, that the amount could not be recovered from the defendant. So, where parties have engaged as partners in the business of marine insurance, and, in the prosecution of the adventure, one of the parties has paid more than his share of the losses, as in the cases of *Mitchell* v. *Cockburn* (b); *Aubert* v. *Maze* (c); or if one of the partners has received the whole, or more than his share, of the profits, as in the cases of *Booth* v. *Hodgson* (d); *Ex parte Bell* (e); no claim arises to the other partner capable of being enforced at law.

The case last cited, of *Ex parte Bell*, was mainly relied on as supplying an analogy for the decision of the case of *Simpson* v. *Bloss* (f). In that case an illegal wager had been laid, in which the plaintiff and the defendant were jointly interested; the money was to be paid by the loser on a future day; before that day arrived, the sum which the defendant was entitled to receive as his share of the profits of the bet, was paid over to him by the plaintiff, in anticipation of the expected payment of the bet, an expectation which, in the result, was not realized. This was, in fact, a partnership in the profits of an illegal adventure;—if the plaintiff had received the whole, the defendant could not have recovered his share; the defendant did receive a sum of money as his share of the profits, but it turned out that there were no profits: the law will not lend its assistance to adjust the

---

(a) 10 Bing. 107.   (d) 6 T. R. 405.
(b) 2 H. Bl. 379.   (e) 1 M. & Selw. 751.
(c) 2 Bos. & Pul. 371.   (f) 7 Taunt. 246.

profits of such a partnership, or to settle the claims of the parties engaged in it.

But the cases cited differ from the case now in judgment in a material point; for in those cases the transactions in which the parties were engaged at the time when the money was paid, and the consideration arose, and indeed from first to last, were illegal; in the present case it is not so; for although the original contract of sale should be deemed to be illegal on the part of the seller, yet the transfer is a legal act, and for a legal purpose. There is here, therefore, a dividing point; the transaction, if illegal in its inception, had ceased to be so : a promise to pay, in consideration of a transfer actually made, is neither prohibited by the words, nor is it, as we think, within the intent of the statute. At the time when the consideration arose on which the promise rests, the act out of which it arose was legal, and the parties were engaged in carrying into effect a lawful agreement.

On these grounds, we are of opinion that there ought to be judgment for the plaintiff.

Judgment affirmed.

Exch. Chamb.
1842.

M'CALLAN
v.
MORTIMER.

TURNER *v.* DOE *d.* BENNETT.

Feb. 21.

IN this case, a new trial having been granted on the ground of misdirection (*a*), the cause was tried again before *Gurney*, B., at the Gloucestershire Spring Assizes, 1841. The facts proved were substantially the same as on the first trial; and the learned Judge, in accordance with the

A., in 1817, let B. into possession of a farm as tenant at will, and in 1827, A. entered upon the land without B.'s consent, and cut and

carried away stone therefrom :—*Held*, on error in the Exchequer Chamber, that this entry amounted to a determination of the estate at will.

In 1829, B., being one of the assessors for the land-tax in the parish, signed an assessment, in which he was named as the occupier of the farm, and A. as the proprietor :—*Held*, that this was evidence whence the jury might infer that a new tenancy at will had been created between the parties.

(*a*) See the case reported, 7 M. & W. 226.

law laid down by the Court of Exchequer, stated to the
jury, in summing up, that the acts of the lessor of the
plaintiff amounted to a determination of the defendant's
original tenancy at will, and that it was for them to consider whether a new tenancy at will had been created by
the parties; and that if they thought it had, they must
find for the lessor of the plaintiff, because such tenancy at
will would not be determined, under any construction of
the stat. 3 & 4 Will. 4, c. 27, ss. 2 & 7, until 1821, and
this ejectment, having been commenced in Easter Term,
1840, would be within twenty years of. the determination
of such tenancy.   To this direction the defendant's counsel tendered a bill of exceptions : and a verdict having been
found for the plaintiff, a writ of error was brought, which
was argued in this Court in last Michaelmas vacation (a),
by *Kelly*, for the plaintiff in error, and by the *Solicitor-
General*, for the defendant in error.   The arguments were
in substance the same as those urged in the Court below.

Cur. adv. vult.

The judgment of the Court was now delivered by

Lord DENMAN, C. J.—In this case it appeared in evidence that the lessor of the plaintiff, being seised in fee of
the farm in question under the will of his uncle, let the
defendant into possession as tenant at will in the year
1817, the defendant having married the sister of the lessor
of the plaintiff, and being entitled in her right to an annuity
under the same will. The defendant remained in possession
till the time of this action, but never paid any rent.   In
1820, the parish authorities wished to cut a drain through
the farm, and applied to the defendant for leave, who was

_____

(a) Dec. 14th, before Lord *Den-*   *son*, J., *Williams*, J., *Coleridge*, J.,
man, C. J., *Tindal*, C. J., *Patte-*   *Coltman*, J., and *Maule*, J.

not willing that it should be done: they then applied to the lessor of the plaintiff for leave, which he gave, and it was done. In the subsequent years of 1823, 1825, and 1827, stones were dug at a quarry on the farm by the order of the lessor of the plaintiff, and trees planted by him on the farm at different times. In the year 1829, the defendant, being one of the assessors for the land-tax in the parish, signed an assessment in which he was named as the occupier of the farm in question, and the lessor of the plaintiff was named as the proprietor.

Under these circumstances, the learned Judge directed the jury that the acts of the lessor of the plaintiff amounted to a determination of the tenancy at will, and that it was for them to consider whether a new tenancy at will had been created by the parties; and that if they thought it had, they must find for the lessor of the plaintiff, because such tenancy at will would not be determined, under any construction of the stat. 3 & 4 Will. 4, c. 27, ss. 2 & 7, before 1821, and this ejectment being brought in Easter Term, 1840, would be within twenty years. A bill of exceptions was tendered, and it has been argued before us that this direction was wrong, for that the learned Judge should have put a question to the jury, whether the acts of the lessor of the plaintiff were done with intention to determine the will, in which case only they would so operate; and also that there was no evidence of a new tenancy at will, but the possession of the defendant after those acts, if the will was determined, amounted to a tenancy by sufferance only; and in either case, the time of the right of entry first accruing, according to the true construction of the 3 & 4 Will. 4, c. 27, was at the end of one year from the original taking in 1817.

We do not think it necessary to determine what is the true construction of that statute, inasmuch as we are of opinion that the direction of the learned Judge was quite correct, and as the jury found that a new tenancy at will was created after 1820, this ejectment was brought in proper time, whatever may be the true construction of the statute.

The intent of an entry is undoubtedly in many cases important, but in the case of a tenancy at will, whatever be the intent of the landlord, if he do any act upon the land, for which he would otherwise be liable to an action of trespass at the suit of the tenant, such act is a determination of the will, for so only can it be a lawful and not a wrongful act. This appears to be clear from the passages cited in argument from Co. Litt. 55 b, 57 b, and 245 b, and none of the cases cited on the other side lead to a contrary conclusion. See also the judgment in 7 M. & W. 232, after the first trial of this cause. Now it is clear in this case, that an action of trespass would have lain against the lessor of the plaintiff at the suit of the defendant, for the cutting of the drain in 1820, which was done by his permission and authority, after the defendant had refused to allow it, unless that act be referred to the right of the lessor of the plaintiff to enter and determine the will at any time. The act must therefore be referred to such right, and the tenancy at will was clearly determined. When it had been so determined, the defendant either became a mere trespasser, or a tenant by sufferance, and for our present purpose it is immaterial to decide which. If however nothing had been done after that cutting of the drain to constitute a new tenancy, it would have been necessary to construe the stat. 3 & 4 Will. 4, c. 27, whether the defendant continued a mere trespasser, or might be treated as a tenant by sufferance. But we find that in 1829 the defendant signs an assessment in a form which can hardly be reconciled to any state of things except a rightful tenancy of some sort, and none other appearing, and no rent being paid, there must be a tenancy at will. At all events, that document was evidence to go to a jury as to the creation of a new tenancy, which is sufficient to shew that the learned Judge was right in so leaving it to them.

The judgment of the Court below must therefore be affirmed.

Judgment affirmed.

HATFIELD and Another *v.* PHILLIPS and Others.

Feb. 21.

THIS was an action of assumpsit for money had and received, tried before Lord *Abinger*, C. B., at the London Sittings after Trinity Term, 1840. The pleadings and the facts of the case were in substance the same as in the case of *Phillips* v. *Huth* (a). The Lord Chief Baron, in summing up, stated, that in order to entitle the defendants below to a verdict, it was necessary that they should prove that Messrs. Warwick & Clagett, from whom they received certain dock-warrants for a cargo of tobacco belonging to the plaintiffs below, by way of pledge for advances of money, were not only *possessed of* the dock-warrants, but *intrusted with* them by the plaintiffs below, the real owners: and that whether they were so intrusted was a question of fact for them to determine upon the evidence. To this direction a bill of exceptions was tendered on the part of the defendants below; and a writ of error having been brought thereon, the case was argued in this Court in last Michaelmas vacation (b), by *Kelly* for the plaintiffs in error, and by the *Solicitor-General* for the defendants in error. It was contended for the plaintiffs in error, that the factors,

P. & Co. owners of a cargo of tobacco, on the arrival of the vessel, placed the bill of lading, indorsed in blank, in the hands of W., as their factor for sale. W. entered the goods at the Custom-House in his own name, and, before the cargo was weighed, and without the knowledge of P. & Co., obtained a dock-warrant for it in his own name, which he pledged with H. & Co as a security for money advanced by them to him:—*Held*, on error in the Exchequer Chamber, that W. was not, under the circumstances, by

reason of his being intrusted with the bill of lading, necessarily and impliedly intrusted with the dock-warrant, &c., within the meaning of the Factors' Act, 6 Geo. 4, c. 94, s. 2; but that whether he was so intrusted or not was a question of fact for the determination of the jury.

Held also, that the judge was not bound to state to the jury what was an intrusting in point of law.

(a) Dec. 13 & 14, before Lord *Denman*, C. J., *Tindal*, C. J., *Patteson*, J., *Williams*, J., *Coleridge*, J., *Coltman*, J., and *Maule*, J.

(b) 6 M. & W. 572.

being intrusted with the bills of lading, were necessarily and impliedly, in the absence of any prohibition on the taking out of dock-warrants, or of any specific instructions as to the mode of effecting a sale, intrusted also with the dock-warrants, and with all other documents which the possession of the bills of lading enabled them to obtain in the course of business, with a view to a sale; or at all events, that the learned judge ought to have stated to the jury what was an *intrusting* within the meaning of the Factors' Act, 6 Geo. 4, c. 94, s. 2.

Cur. adv. vult.

The judgment of the Court was now delivered by

Lord DENMAN, C. J.—This case turns entirely upon the second section of the 6 Geo. 4, c. 94. Lord *Abinger*, in his charge to the jury, laid it down, that in order to entitle the defendants to a verdict, it was necessary for them to shew that Messrs. Warwick & Clagett, the factors for sale, from whom they received the dock-warrants for the tobacco in question, by way of pledge for advances of money, were not only *possessed of* the dock-warrants, but *intrusted* with them by the plaintiffs, the real owners. He also told the jury, that whether they were so intrusted was a question of fact for them to determine upon the evidence laid before them. To this charge a bill of exceptions was tendered, on the ground that the question was one of law and not of fact; and that the factors, being intrusted with the bills of lading, were necessarily and impliedly intrusted with the dock-warrants; or, at all events, that the judge should have told the jury what was an intrusting in point of law.

The counsel for the defendants did not contend that the mere possession of a dock-warrant was sufficient to bring a party within the second section of the statute in question; the words of the section, " any person *intrusted with* and in possession of any bill of lading, dock-warrant, &c.," are

too plain to admit of such contention. But he insisted
that where a factor for sale is intrusted with a bill of
lading, and authorized to deposit the goods in the dock
warehouse in his own name, he is necessarily intrusted in
point of law to take out a dock-warrant in his name: and
this, although it appeared in evidence that a dock-warrant
is not only not necessary for the purpose of sale, but is
even inconvenient. We think that the answer given by
Lord *Abinger* in his charge is perfectly correct: viz., that
the intrusting a factor with the bill of lading cannot have
any such effect; the bill of lading is functus officio as soon
as the goods are landed and warehoused in the name of the
holder; that holder then becomes possessed of the goods
themselves in the eye of the law, and any power he may
have over them arises not from the bill of lading, but from
such possession. If they are received into his own warehouse, it is clear that neither by the common law nor by
the statute in question can he pledge the goods, nor will
there be any document indicative of title which can bring
him within the second section of the statute. If they
remain in the dock warehouse, and are only in his constructive possession, he will be authorized to do such acts
and to procure such documents as are necessary and proper to enable him to sell the goods. To this extent, and
no further, is he intrusted, in the absence of any specific
instructions and authority. Whether a dock-warrant be
such a document, and the taking it out in his own name
be such an act, as is necessary and proper to enable him to
sell, must depend upon the practice of each particular
trade, and frequently upon the circumstances attending
each particular transaction, and therefore cannot be a
question of law, but of fact, and ought to be submitted to
a jury. Neither is it possible to say what is an intrusting
in law, inasmuch as there may be an express intrusting by
delivering of a document by the owner to the factor, or by

desiring him expressly to procure such document, or there may be an implied intrusting, from the usual course of dealing or other circumstances, which intrusting, either express or implied, is manifestly matter of evidence. This point was determined, and we think quite rightly, in the Court of Exchequer, in the case of *Phillips* v. *Huth*, in which case the second section of the statute in question was much considered, and the necessity of a factor being intrusted with, as well as possessed of, the document pledged was fully shewn. The legislature has enabled the factor to pledge goods, not when he has the possession only of the goods, because the owner cannot earmark them, and so give the pawnee notice that they are not the property of the factor, but where he has a document shewing the title to the goods, which may be so marked as to shew whose the goods are; therefore, if the owner does so mark the document, the factor cannot pledge; if the owner does not so mark it, he holds the factor out to the world as owner, and must take the consequence. But he cannot be justly said to hold the factor out to the world as owner by such document, unless he has intrusted him with the document; and hence the legislature has made such intrusting a necessary circumstance to bring the case within the operation of the statute in question. The existence or not of that circumstance must in all cases be a question of fact, and was properly left as such in this case to the jury.

We are of opinion, therefore, that the direction and charge of the learned judge was perfectly correct, that the judgment must be affirmed.

Judgment affirmed (*a*).

(*a*) After this decision, the stat. 5 & 6 Vict. c. 39 was passed, intituled "An Act to amend the Law relating to Advances bonâ fide made to Agents intrusted with Goods;" by the first section of which it is enacted, "That any agent who shall thereafter be intrusted with the possession of goods, or of the documents of title to goods, shall be deemed and taken to be owner of such goods and documents, so far as to give validity to any contract or agreement by way of pledge, lien, or security bonâ fide made by any person with such agent so intrusted as aforesaid, as well for any original loan, advance, or payment made upon the security of such goods or documents, as also for any further or continuing advance in respect thereof; and that such contract shall be binding upon and against the owner of such goods, and all other persons interested therein, notwithstanding the person claiming such pledge or lien may have had notice that the person with whom such contract or agreement is made, is only an agent." And the 4th section enacts, " That any bill of lading, India warrant, warehouse-keeper's certificate, warrant, or order for the delivery of goods, or any other document used in the ordinary course of business, as proof of the possession or control of goods, or authorizing or purporting to authorize, either by indorsement or by delivery, the possessor of such document to transfer or receive goods thereby represented, shall be deemed and taken to be a document of title within the meaning of this act: and any agent intrusted as aforesaid, and possessed of any such document of title, whether derived immediately from the owner of such goods, or obtained by reason of such agent's having been intrusted with the possession of the goods, or of any other document of title thereto, shall be deemed and taken to have been intrusted with the possession of the goods represented by such document of title as aforesaid; and all contracts pledging or giving a lien upon such document of title as aforesaid, shall be deemed and taken to be respectively pledges of, and liens upon, the goods to which the same relates, &c. &c.. and an agent in possession as aforesaid of such goods or documents, shall be taken, for the purposes of this act, to have been intrusted therewith by the owner thereof, unless the contrary can be shewn in evidence."

Exch. Chamb.
1842.

HATFIELD
v.
PHILLIPS.

MEMORANDUM.

Mr. Justice *Bosanquet* having resigned his seat in the Court of Common Pleas, he was succeeded, in this Vacation, by *Cresswell Cresswell*, of the Inner Temple, Esq., one of her Majesty's Counsel; who was first called to the degree of Serjeant-at-law, and gave rings with the motto *Leges juraque:* and, shortly afterwards, received the honour of knighthood.

REPORTS OF CASES

ARGUED AND DETERMINED

IN

𝕿𝖍𝖊 𝕮𝖔𝖚𝖗𝖙𝖘 𝖔𝖋 𝕰𝖝𝖈𝖍𝖊𝖖𝖚𝖊𝖗

AND

𝕰𝖝𝖈𝖍𝖊𝖖𝖚𝖊𝖗 𝕮𝖍𝖆𝖒𝖇𝖊𝖗.

EASTER TERM, 6 VICT.

Exch. of Pleas,
1842.

April 16.

ROADKNIGHT *v.* GREEN.

The stat. 4 & 5 Vict. c. 28, s. 2, applies to cases in which the plaintiff had not only obtained a verdict, but had signed judgment and taxed his costs, before the passing of that act.

THIS was an action for assault and battery, which was tried at the Spring Assizes, 1837, when the plaintiff recovered a verdict, damages 1*s.*, and the judge refused to certify under the stat. 22 & 23 Car. 2, c. 9, s. 136, to give the plaintiff costs. On the 3rd July, 1840, the stat. 3 & 4 Vict. c. 24 was passed, which repealed so much of the stat. 22 & 23 Car. 2, c. 9, as related to costs in personal actions. On the 20th January, 1841, the plaintiff signed judgment; on the 23rd January, the costs were taxed in full, the defendant's attorney attending the taxation; and on the same day execution was issued. On the 28th January, a rule was obtained, calling upon the plaintiff to shew cause why the taxation should not be reviewed, which was argued in Easter Term, 1841. The Court postponed their judgment, but appeared to be of opinion that the

plaintiff was entitled to full costs (*a*), there being no statute
in operation which could deprive him of that right at the
time when the judgment was signed. On the 21st June,
1841, the stat. 4 & 5 Vict. c. 28, intituled " An Act to
prevent plaintiffs in certain frivolous actions from obtaining their full costs of suit," was passed (*b*). And in last
Hilary Term, a rule was obtained on the part of the defendant, calling upon the plaintiff to shew cause why proceedings should not be stayed, pursuant to the second
section of that statute, on such terms as the Court should
direct. Against which rule

Humfrey now shewed cause.—The right of the plaintiff,
who has obtained judgment and execution, is a vested right,
and is not affected by the stat. 4 & 5 Vict. c. 28. It may

(*a*) The following cases were
cited on the argument :—*Morgan
v. Thorne,* 7 M. & W. 310; *Char-
rington* v. *Meatheringham,* 2 M. &
W. 228; *Reg.* v. *Inhabitants of
Mawgan,* 8 Ad. & Ell. 496, 3 N.
& P. 502; *Warne* v. *Beresford,*
6 Dowl. P. C. 157.

(*b*) Sect. 1 of this act, after reciting that it is expedient to remove all doubts whether plaintiffs
in actions commenced, and wherein verdicts had been returned, before the passing of the 3 & 4 Vict.
c. 24, for less than 40*s.*, may not
be entitled to their full costs, contrary to the manifest intention of
the same; repeals the 3 & 4 Vict.
c. 24, so far as the same repeals or
may be deemed to repeal the 43
Eliz. c. 2, s. 6, or the 22 & 23 Car.
2, c. 9, s. 136, in respect to actions
wherein verdicts had been returned
before the passing of the 3 & 4 Vict.
c. 24.

Sect. 2 enacts and declares,

" That no plaintiff who had, before
the passing of the said act of the
last session, obtained a verdict for
a less amount of damages than 40*s.*
shall now be entitled to full costs,
unless he was so entitled immediately before the passing of the said
act of the last session : provided
nevertheless, that if any such plaintiff shall have proceeded, since the
passing of the said last-mentioned
act, and before the 3rd day of May,
1841, to tax his full costs on any
such verdict so obtained for less
than 40*s.*, nothing in this act contained shall deprive such plaintiff
of any remedy thereon which he
may now have for the recovery
thereof : but it shall be lawful for
such Court or Judge, on the application of any defendant in such
action, to stay all the proceedings
on such application, upon payment
of such costs as such Court or Judge
shall think fit.

now be assumed that, but for the delay of the Court, he would have had judgment in his favour before the passing of the act. At the period of his signing judgment, there was no law in force to prevent his recovering his full costs. The last branch of the second section supposes a case where the plaintiff had not yet taxed his costs, but must make some *application* to the Court or its officer for that purpose. In *Merrick* v. *Wakley* (a), there had been no taxation of costs; and the present is the only case in which this question has arisen, where judgment has been signed and execution issued. The statute cannot be retrospective upon a judgment, except by express words; but it speaks only of persons who had, before the passing of the former act, obtained a *verdict* for less than 40s. The plaintiff is now entitled to that judgment which would have been pronounced in his favour in Easter Term, 1841, had the Court then delivered judgment.

Arnold, contrà, was stopped by the Court.

PARKE, B.—The meaning of this act of Parliament appears to me to be perfectly clear. But for the proviso in the second section, the plaintiff would not have been entitled to proceed at all; if he had, the defendant would have been entitled to relief on auditâ querelâ, or by an application to the Court. Then the effect of that proviso is, that when he has incurred the expense of the taxation, the act allows him to go on, and throws it upon the defendant to make an application to stay the proceedings, he being compelled to do justice by paying the plaintiff the costs he has incurred in the taxation. There is a little redundancy of expression; but the meaning clearly is, that the Court shall stay all the proceedings of the plaintiff on such application of the defendant. The clause appears

(a) Q. B., not reported.

to have been framed to meet this very case. If the execution had been actually levied, there might have been some question; but it is not so; the writ is only in the hands of the sheriff. The defendant is therefore entitled to apply to stay the execution; and the question is, on what terms he is entitled to our interference. It certainly should be on the terms of the plaintiff's being fully indemnified the costs of the taxation, of signing judgment, and issuing execution, and also the costs of resisting the application for a review of the taxation, and of the present rule.

Exch. of Pleas,
1842.

ROADKNIGHT
v.
GREEN.

ALDERSON, B.—I am of the same opinion. It seems to me that Mr. *Humfrey* was right on the question involved in the first rule, and the plaintiff was entitled to sign judgment and tax his costs; but that the defendant is equally entitled, under the second act, to apply for a stay of the proceedings on the execution, on the terms of his paying all the costs which the plaintiff has incurred, trusting that the law would remain the same.

ROLFE, B., concurred.

Rule absolute accordingly.

The above costs having been taxed at the sum of 29*l.* 11*s.* 4*d.*, a rule was obtained, calling upon the plaintiff to shew cause why the sum of 9*l.* 11*s.* 4*d.*, being the amount of costs of the day for not proceeding to trial in the year 1837, should not be set off against the above sum. It appeared that these costs had never been demanded, and that all the proceedings subsequent to the verdict had been taken by the plaintiff's attorney at his own expense, in order to recover his costs.

Humfrey shewed cause.—These costs of the day, which *May 9.*

x x 2

have never been demanded until the present time, cannot be set off against the costs upon this rule. They ought to have been set off against the costs of the trial.

W. H. Watson, contrà.—These are interlocutory costs, which may be set off either against final or against other interlocutory costs. The attorney, who came to the Court on mere speculation, is not entitled to any extraordinary favour.

PER CURIAM.—This rule must be discharged with costs. The attorney has a lien to the amount of the costs allowed on this rule, and is entitled to retain it for that amount, and ought not to have that sum reduced by the costs of the day. These were costs specially given under an act of Parliament : the rule was discharged on equitable grounds, and the object of the Court was, to prevent the attorney from sustaining any loss ; we should, therefore, have disallowed this claim of set-off, had we been apprised of it. As the law stood at the passing of the 3 & 4 Vict. c. 24, he was clearly entitled to go on and recover his full costs; and even under the second act, he was at liberty to proceed, and would have obtained his full costs, unless the defendant had interposed by applying to the Court. He is therefore entitled to be indemnified.

Rule discharged, with costs.

Exch. of Pleas, 1842.

LOOSEMORE v. RADFORD.

April 16.

COVENANT.—The declaration stated, that whereas the defendant, before and at the time of the making of the indenture hereinafter mentioned, was indebted to H. D. and G. B. in the sum of £400, secured to them by a promissory note made by the defendant, and by the plaintiff as the defendant's surety, and in 95l. 5s. 9d. for interest thereon; and thereupon, by a certain indorsement bearing date &c., made between the defendant of the one part, and the plaintiff of the other part, the defendant covenanted with the plaintiff, that he the defendant would well and truly pay to the said H. D. and G. B. the sum of £400, with interest as aforesaid, on the 13th day of August then next. Breach, that the defendant did not pay to the said H. D. and G. B., or either of them, the said sum of £400 and interest, or any part thereof, on the said 13th day of August, or at any other time.

The defendant pleaded payment into Court of 1s. and no damages ultrà, which latter averment was traversed by the replication.

At the trial before Lord *Abinger*, C. B., at the Middlesex Sittings after Hilary Term, it appeared that the defendant being in embarrassed circumstances, the payees had informed the plaintiff that they should hold him liable upon the note, whereupon he obtained from the defendant the deed mentioned in the declaration. The note was still unpaid at the time of the trial: and it was objected that the plaintiff was therefore entitled to recover nominal damages only. The Lord Chief Baron overruled the objection, and under his direction the plaintiff had a verdict, damages £500.

Erle now moved for a new trial, on the ground of misdirection.—The plaintiff, not having actually paid any

The plaintiff and defendant being joint makers of a promissory note, the defendant as principal and the plaintiff as his surety, the defendant covenanted with the plaintiff to pay the amount to the payee of the note on a given day, but made default: —Held, in an action on this covenant, that the plaintiff was entitled, though he had not paid the note, to recover the full amount of it by way of damages.

money on the note, has suffered no substantial injury, and is entitled to nominal damages only. The money might have been paid by the defendant after the day of payment mentioned in the covenant. The action is prematurely brought. In *Hambleton* v. *Veere* (a), where the plaintiff declared for an injury in procuring his apprentice to depart from his service, and for the loss of his service for the whole residue of his term of apprenticeship, and the jury assessed the damages generally, the judgment was arrested on the ground that the term had not expired when the action was brought. Here the plaintiff had no substantial cause of action until after payment of the note by him. There is nothing to prevent the payees of the note from suing the defendant, in which case he will have to pay the money twice over.

PARKE, B.—I think there ought to be no rule. This is an absolute and positive covenant by the defendant to pay a sum of money on a day certain. The money was not paid on that day, nor has it been paid since. Under these circumstances, I think the jury were warranted in giving the plaintiff the full amount of the money due upon the covenant. If any money had been paid in respect of the note since the day fixed for the payment, that would relieve the plaintiff pro tanto from his responsibility. The defendant may perhaps have an equity that the money he may pay to the plaintiff shall be applied in discharge of his debt: but at law the plaintiff is entitled to be placed in the same situation under this agreement, as if he had paid the money to the payees of the bill.

ALDERSON, B.—The question is, to what extent has the plaintiff been injured by the defendant's default? Certainly to the amount of the money that the defendant ought to have paid according to his covenant. The case resembles that of an action of trover for title-deeds, where the jury may give the full value of the estate to which they belong by way of damages, although they are generally reduced to 40s. on the deeds being given up.

GURNEY, B., and ROLFE, B., concurred.

Rule refused.

ELKINGTON v. HOLLAND.

April 18.

THIS was an action for work and labour as an attorney. The defendant pleaded the general issue.

At the trial before Lord *Abinger*, C. B., at the last Assizes for the county of Warwick, it appeared that the plaintiff, having been applied to by the defendant to advise him as to the best mode of securing a debt due to the defendant from one Ankers, recommended that a warrant of attorney should be given by Ankers, and drew up a form for it, together with the attestation; which latter was in the following words:—" Signed, sealed and delivered by the said Joseph Ankers in my presence, and I subscribe myself as attorney for the said Joseph Ankers, expressly named by him to attest his execution of these presents." The warrant of attorney was signed by Ankers, and attested by his attorney, who subscribed himself as " John M. Underhill, attorney, No. 110, New-street, Birmingham." By an order of *Alderson*, B., this warrant of attorney was set aside, on the ground that it was defective in not containing an *express declaration* by the attesting witness of his being the attorney for the defendant, according to the provisions of 1 & 2 Vict. c. 110, s. 9: and the defendant, who had seized in execution and sold the

A warrant of attorney was attested in the following form: " Signed, sealed, and delivered by J.A., in my presence, and I subscribe myself as attorney for the said J. A., expressly named by him to attest his execution of these presents:"— *Held*, by *Alderson*, B., to be insufficient; *Parke*, B., dubitante.

But, assuming such attestation to be bad, *held*, that it was not such gross negligence as to preclude the attorney of the creditor from recovering his charges in respect of the warrant of attorney, it having been set aside as defective.

goods of Ankers under a judgment entered up on the warrant of attorney, was compelled to refund the amount to
the assignees of Ankers, who had become bankrupt. It
was contended at the trial of this cause, that the plaintiff
was not entitled to recover the costs of preparing the
warrant of attorney, on the ground that the instrument
had been so improperly and negligently drawn that it
became altogether useless to the defendant. The learned
Judge thought the plaintiff entitled to recover, as it was
not a case of gross negligence; and he accordingly directed
the jury to find for the plaintiff, giving leave to the plaintiff
to move to enter a nonsuit. A verdict having been found
for the plaintiff,

Hill now moved accordingly.—The plaintiff is not entitled to recover the charge for preparing the warrant of
attorney; for either the attestation was good, in which
case he ought to have moved to set aside the Judge's
order; or if it was defective, the instrument having been
prepared by himself, and turning out to be utterly value-
less from his own gross negligence, he cannot recover any
charge for preparing it. The stat. 1 & 2 Vict. c. 110, s. 9,
enacts " that no warrant of attorney to confess judgment
in any personal action, or cognovit actionem given by any
person, shall be of any force, unless there shall be present
some attorney of one of the superior courts on behalf of
such person, *expressly named by him*, and attending at his
request, to inform him of the nature and effect of such
warrant or cognovit, before the same is executed, which
attorney shall subscribe his name as a witness to the due
execution thereof, and *thereby declare himself* to be attorney for the person executing the same, and state that he
subscribes as such attorney." The meaning of that is, that
he shall state in precise and positive terms in the attestation, that he is the attorney of the party executing the instrument. But that was not done in the present case. In

Potter v. *Nicholson* (a), it was held that a witness to a cog-

novit must not only declare himself in the attestation to be
the attorney for the party, but also that he subscribes his
name as such. This is such a disregard of the express
words of an act of Parliament as amounts to gross negligence in an attorney, and will preclude him from recovering
for the work so done. He is required by the act to do two
things; first, to make the subscribing attorney declare,
in positive terms, that he was the defendant's attorney;
secondly, that he subscribed as such attorney : and he takes
upon himself to omit one of these requisites.

PARKE, B.—I doubt much whether the attestation is
not sufficient. The act of Parliament does not state the
precise terms that are to be used, but merely the substance. Two of the requisites of the act have been complied with; the defendant's attorney has subscribed his
name as a witness, and has stated that he subscribes
as such attorney. Does he not, by the act of subscription, declare that he is the attorney, or must he make
that statement in positive terms? My Brother *Alderson*
adheres to his former opinion, and thinks that a positive
statement is necessary, and I am far from saying that
he is wrong. But at all events, this is not a case in which
the attorney has been guilty of that crassa negligentia
which disentitles him to recover. It would be hard on so
doubtful a point as this to deprive him of his remuneration.
He has not infringed any plain rule of law or point of
practice; the utmost that can be said is, that he has mis-
construed a doubtful act of Parliament.

ALDERSON, B.—I agree in thinking that this rule ought
to be refused, on the ground that it would be most unfair
if an attorney were to be precluded from recovering his
fair remuneration, merely because he has made a mistake

(a) 8 M. & W. 294.

in construing a doubtful act of Parliament. Before I set aside this warrant of attorney, I consulted several of the Judges, which shews that I entertained a doubt about it; and they concurred in my view of the case. I still adhere to the opinion I then entertained, and think that he ought to state in positive terms that he is the attorney of the party. Every attorney who witnesses an instrument of this nature should declare in the attestation, not only that he is the attorney attending on behalf of the party executing the instrument, but that he subscribes his name thereto as such attorney.

ROLFE, B., concurred.

Rule refused.

——————•——————

DOE *d.* SOPHIA LEWIS, Administratrix of W. J. LEWIS, *v.* WILLIAM LEWIS.

Where a lessee of lands demised to him, his heirs and assigns, for lives, devised the premises for the residue of the term to W. J. L. and his assigns, who died intestate :—*Held,* that the premises did not go to the heir of W. J. L., but to his personal representative, under the Stat. of Frauds, 29 Car. 2, c. 3, s. 12.

EJECTMENT.—The cause was tried before *Maule*, J., at the last Assizes at Carmarthen, when a verdict was taken for the plaintiff by consent, with liberty to the defendant to move to enter a verdict or a nonsuit, according to the opinion of the Court upon the facts of the case, which were as follows :—William Lewis, the grandfather of the defendant, being possessed of a lease granted to him by one Nathaniel Morgan, to hold to him the said William Lewis, his heirs and assigns, for the lives of three persons named in the lease, one of whom was still living, by his will, dated the 25th of March, 1817, devised the premises in question to his son W. J. Lewis, and his assigns, during the residue of the lease, subject to the payment of the rent and the performance of the covenants. W. J. Lewis, the son, having died intestate in possession of the premises, the defendant took possession of them as his nephew and heir-at-law. This ejectment was brought by the administratrix of W. J. Lewis, and the question was whether the leasehold premises belonged to the personal respresentative or to the heir.

John Wilson now moved accordingly.—This case raises a question about which much doubt exists in the profession. The original lease to Wm. Lewis, the grandfather, having created a real estate pur autre vie in him and his heirs, the right of the heirs to take as special occupants could not be taken away without the use of technical language in the will sufficient for that purpose; but this will, so far from containing any words of that description, devises the premises to Wm. Lewis and his *assigns*,—a word which is construed to mean heir or executor according to the subject-matter of the devise; where it is real estate it goes to the heir, where personal, to the executor or administrator. This was an estate of freehold, and the defendant, being the heir, would be considered the assignee in law: *Williams* v. *Jekyl* (a). Where the designation is equivocal, it has been held that the title of the heir is preferable to that of the executor: *Atkinson* v. *Baker* (b).

PARKE, B.—It has been said that much doubt exists in the profession as to the question which has been raised in this case; but I do not see why such doubt should have existed. Originally there was a special occupant designated in the lease to William Lewis, the grandfather, his heirs and assigns; but when the grandfather devised the premises to W. J. Lewis, the son, and his assigns, he thereby defeated the title of his heirs as special occupants, and the devisee continued to hold the property to himself and his assigns for the residue of the term. The utmost that could be said is, that if W. J. Lewis the son had made an assignment of the lease, perhaps his assignee

(a) 2 Ves. sen. 681.   (b) 4 T. R. 229.

would be entitled to hold the estate as special occupant; but where, as is the case here, he makes no assignment at all, it falls within the express words of the Statute of Frauds, 29 Car. 2, c. 3, s. 12, which provides that, in case there shall be no special occupant of an estate held pur autre vie, it shall go to the executors or administrators of the party that had the estate thereof. Now here there is no special occupant, the title of the first lessee having been put an end to by the will; the land has been held under a tenancy pur autre vie to W. J. Lewis the son, and his assigns; and as he died without creating any assigns, the property goes to his personal representative. It is said, however, that although there was here no express assignment by W. J. Lewis the son, the property may go to his heir, as being the assign in law; but it must be remembered that this is a devise under the stat. 29 Car. 2, c. 3, not under the Statute of Wills, relating to an estate in fee-simple; and I do not think that "assigns" can be considered as comprised under the words "heirs, executors, or administrators," used in that statute. The word "assign" does not mean "heir;" it means a person substituted for another by an act of some kind or other; and as the devisee has not done any act to appoint any assign, the property must go to his administratrix.

ALDERSON, B., and ROLFE, B., concurred.

Rule refused.

Exch. of Pleas,
1842.

April 19.

NORTON v. SCHOLEFIELD.

CASE for an injury to the plaintiff's reversionary interest.—The declaration alleged, that before and at the time of committing the grievance, &c., the premises were in the possession of one A., as tenant thereof to the plaintiff, the reversion thereof expectant on the determination of the said tenancy belonging to the plaintiff. It then stated the right of the plaintiff and his tenants to a certain well and pump: that the defendant was possessed of premises adjoining the premises of the plaintiff, and that he, intending to injure the plaintiff, &c., erected a cesspool so near the well and pump, that the water was contaminated and rendered useless by the oozing out of the soil and filth from the cesspool. The defendant had applied to Lord *Denman*, C. J., at chambers, for leave to plead the following pleas:—first, not guilty; secondly, a traverse of the right of the plaintiff and his tenants to the use of the well and pump; thirdly, a traverse of the plaintiff's reversionary interest in the premises; and lastly, a special plea, denying that the water in the well had been contaminated by the erection of the cesspool. Lord *Denman*, C. J., refused to allow the last plea, on the ground that the subject-matter of that defence might be given in evidence under the plea of not guilty.

Waddington now applied to the Court for leave to plead the above four pleas, and submitted that the plea of not guilty put in issue only the fact of the erection of the cesspool.

PARKE, B.—I think the Lord Chief Justice was right in disallowing the last plea; not guilty puts in issue both the act complained of and its consequences. In actions for

In case for erecting a cesspool near a well, and thereby contaminating the water of the well, the plea of not guilty puts in issue both the fact of the erection of the cesspool, and that the water was thereby contaminated.

negligence, a defendant is never allowed to plead that the injury was caused by the plaintiff's own negligence.

ALDERSON, B.—By the general issue the defendant says, " I am not guilty of erecting a building which is a nuisance."

ROLFE, B., concurred.

Motion refused.

———◆———

PRITCHARD *v.* LONG.

April 19.

Trespass for breaking and entering the dwelling-house of the plaintiff, and taking away certain goods therein, *not* alleging them to be the plaintiff's goods. Plea, not guilty by statute. The learned judge at the trial having directed the jury to find a verdict for the plaintiff, with nominal damages, for the trespass to the house :—
Held, that the plaintiff was not entitled to damages also for the value of the goods, as they were not alleged to be the property of plaintiff.

TRESPASS for breaking and entering the dwelling-house of the plaintiff, and taking and carrying away certain goods and chattels therein, and converting and disposing of the same to his own use.

Plea, not guilty by statute.

At the trial before *Cresswell*, J., at the last Spring Assizes at Oxford, the trespass to the dwelling-house, and the taking the goods and selling them by auction, having been proved, it was objected by the defendant's counsel, that the plaintiff was entitled to recover damages only for the trespass to the house, as the declaration did not aver that the goods were the plaintiff's ; and the learned Judge being of that opinion, directed the jury to find for the plaintiff, with nominal damages ; but gave the plaintiff liberty to move to increase the damages by the amount which the goods produced on the sale.

Ludlow, Serjt., now moved accordingly.—The gist of the action was the trespass to the dwelling-house, and the taking away the goods was matter of aggravation, which the jury ought to have been directed to take into their consideration, although the goods were not alleged to be the property of the plaintiff. In the note to *Taylor* v. *Wells* (a), Mr. Serjeant *Williams* lays down the rule thus: —" If the declaration were for *breaking the close* as well as for taking the fish, without specifying their number or kind, it seems it would be good, even upon a special demurrer; because breaking the close is considered as the principal ground and foundation of the action, and taking the fish as matter of aggravation only :"—citing *Chambers* v. *Greenfield* (b). [*Alderson*, B.—In that case the fish were alleged to be the property of the plaintiff.] In this case the goods were stated to be in the dwelling-house, and must therefore be presumed to be the property of the plaintiff.

PARKE, B.—I am of opinion that the plaintiff is not entitled to a rule to increase the damages. He could not maintain an action for taking the goods, without proving that they were his property; but here there is no allegation that they belonged to him, nor any admission to that effect on the record. Taking the goods is not mere matter of aggravation, but of substance. If the case had gone generally to the jury, and they had found joint damages for the trespass to the house and for taking the goods, there would be no error on the face of the record; but if there had been a special plea that the goods were not the plaintiff's, and general damages had been assessed, the judgment would be arrested, according to the case of *Granvel* v. *Robotham* (c). As the record now stands, you have no right to damages for the goods separately.

ALDERSON, B., and ROLFE, B., concurred.

Rule discharged.

Exch. of Pleas,
1842.

PRITCHARD
v.
LONG.

(a) 2 Saund. 74.   (b) 3 Wils. 292.   (c) Cro. Jac. 865.

Exch. of Pleas,
1842.
~~~~~
April 20.

KIDDELL *v.* BURNARD.

The term
" sound," in a
warranty of a
horse or other
animal, im-
plies the ab-
sence of any
disease or seeds
of disease in
the animal at
the time, which
actually dimi-
nishes or in
its progress
will diminish
his natural
usefulness in
the work to
which he would
properly and
ordinarily be
applied.

ASSUMPSIT to recover damages for the breach of a warranty of the soundness of three bullocks.

The defendant pleaded two pleas, traversing the warranty and the unsoundness.

At the trial before *Erskine,* J., at the last Spring Assizes for the county of Somerset, it appeared that the bullocks in question had been sold, with a warranty of soundness, by the defendant to the plaintiff at a fair, and that the plaintiff immediately put them into a drove, and sent them on a journey of considerable length. It was proved that after the bullocks had been bought they appeared very weak, and exhibited appearances of unsoundness, in scouring more than usual, which was confirmed during the journey, as one of them died, and the other two were afterwards sold by the plaintiff at a much less price than he had paid for them. The learned Judge told the jury, that in order to entitle the plaintiff to recover, he must shew that at the time of the sale the beasts had some disease, or the seeds of some disease, in them, which would render them unfit, or in some degree less fit for the ordinary use to which they would be applied. The jury having under the above direction found a verdict for the plaintiff, with £25 damages,

Crowder now moved for a new trial, on the ground of misdirection.—The learned Judge was not correct in the mode in which he left the case to the jury. If it were held to be correct, any slight injury or disorder, which required only a little attention, and could be easily cured, would constitute an unsoundness. In *Garment* v. *Barrs* (a), it was laid down by *Eyre,* C. J., that a horse labouring

(a) 2 Esp. 673.

Exch. of Pleas,
1842.

April 22.

JONES *v.* TARLETON.

TROVER for pigs.—Pleas; first, not guilty; secondly, not possessed; on which issues were joined. At the trial before *Coltman*, J., at the last assizes for Anglesey, it appeared that the plaintiff was a pig-drover in Anglesey, and the defendant was the owner of a steam-vessel, plying between the Menai Bridge and Liverpool. The plaintiff had been in the habit of shipping pigs by the defendant's vessel for Liverpool; and on the 30th January, 1841, he sent by it a number of pigs, of which, on their arrival at Liverpool, the defendant's agent there detained three, to satisfy an alleged lien in respect of a balance which he claimed to be due from the plaintiff on the freight of former shipments. On the 19th February, the plaintiff shipped another cargo, the whole of which the defendant, by his agent, detained on the same ground. There was conflicting evidence as to whether the plaintiff had made any offer of payment of the freight of these two cargoes; but according to the evidence of the witnesses for the plaintiff, he had, on each occasion, produced a purse of sovereigns, and stated that he was ready to pay the freight for that cargo, but the defendant's agent claimed a further sum of about £5, in respect of the old balance, which the plaintiff refused to pay, denying that it was due. No precise amount was, however, actually tendered by the plaintiff. In order to bring home to the plaintiff knowledge of a usage of the defendant's trade, that all goods coming by his vessels were to be subject to his general lien, it was proposed to shew, that in the defendant's office at Liverpool, where the plaintiff had repeatedly been, a printed notice to that effect was hung up. It appeared that this notice was of small size, and was pasted on a piece of card-

In trover against a carrier, where the question was whether the goods were rightfully detained by the defendant in satisfaction of a general lien:—

Held, that parol evidence could not be given of the contents of a portable notice, hung up in the defendant's office, containing a statement that all goods carried by the defendant were to be subject to such general lien, but that the notice itself must be produced.

Held, also, that evidence of bills delivered to the plaintiff, containing a similar statement, could not be received without a notice to produce the bills.

In trover by the owner of goods against a carrier who has detained the goods under a claim of lien, it is not necessary, in order to entitle the plaintiff to recover, that he should prove an actual tender

of the carriage money, if it appear that he was ready to pay it, but that the defendant refused to deliver the goods except on payment of an alleged old balance, which the jury find not to have been really due.

board, and suspended on a nail in the office. It was objected for the plaintiff, that the notice itself ought to be produced; and the learned Judge being of that opinion, rejected the evidence. It was then proposed to shew, that bills containing a notice to the same effect had been delivered to the plaintiff. This evidence was objected to, on the ground that no notice to produce the bills had been given to the plaintiff, and was accordingly rejected. The learned Judge, in summing up, left it to the jury to say, first, whether any old balance was in fact due from the plaintiff to the defendant; and, secondly, whether the defendant had established that he had the general lien claimed by him, and that it was known to the plaintiff; and he told them, that if they thought the plaintiff was ready to pay all that was really due from him, but did not pay it because the defendant demanded something more, that was sufficient, without tender or payment of the specific sum. The jury found for the plaintiff, damages, £100.

Biggs Andrews now moved for a new trial.—First, the evidence as to the notice was wrongly rejected. In *Rex* v. *Hunt* (a), evidence was held to be receivable of inscriptions on banners, carried by the mob at the unlawful meeting at which the defendant was charged with being present, without producing the banners themselves. [*Parke,* B.— That was on a different ground: there the evidence was received as part of the res gestæ.] Here, this being a notice which the defendant must reasonably be presumed to have seen and read, evidence of its contents was admissible. Secondly, no notice to produce the bills was necessary. It is like the case of a notice to quit, or a notice of action delivered to a party, no notice to produce which is necessary. [*Parke,* B.—This is different from those cases: this notice is an intimation of terms on which

(a) 3 B. & Ald. 566.

the parties deal, as the basis of their contract; you cannot give evidence of such a document without a notice to produce.] Thirdly, there ought to have been proof of a *tender* of the amount really due to the defendant, in order to entitle the plaintiff to recover: *Scarfe* v. *Morgan* (a).

Exch. of Pleas, 1842.

JONES *v.* TARLETON.

PARKE, B.—I think no ground has been laid for this rule. With respect to the notice, it appears to have been a mere portable notice, which might have been taken off the nail and produced at the trial: and, being a document which was put forward as the basis of the contract between the parties, it ought itself to have been produced. It is different where the thing is a fixture, or where it cannot be produced on account of the public convenience. As to the notice to produce, this was not a document with respect to which no notice to produce is necessary, like a notice to quit, but was an intimation of the terms of the contract between the parties, which cannot be proved unless a notice has been given to produce it, in the ordinary way. Then, as to the tender, the direction of the learned Judge amounts to this, that if the defendant refused to deliver the pigs until payment of the old account, which he had no right to demand, that was a waiver of an express tender. I think it was a perfectly correct direction.

ALDERSON, B.—I am of the same opinion. With respect to the question as to the sufficiency of the tender, I think if the defendant absolutely refused to deliver the pigs when they were demanded, until payment by the plaintiff, not only of the freight for that particular cargo, but also of the freight due on a former account, and which, as now appears by the finding of the jury, the defendant was not entitled to demand, that must be considered as a waiver of any tender of the precise sum really due, and

(a) 4 M. & W. 270.

z z 2

which the plaintiff was ready to pay: it was equivalent to saying to the plaintiff, "Do what you will, tender what you will, it is of no use, I will not receive it unless you pay the old account also." It would have been different if the defendant had merely demanded too large a sum in respect of the same subject-matter; in that case, the plaintiff would perhaps have been bound to tender a reasonable sum, before he could have been entitled to the possession of the goods demanded.

ROLFE, B., concurred.

Rule refused (a).

(a) See *Scarfe* v. *Halifax*, 7 M. & W. 288; *Ashmole* v. *Wainwright*, 2 G. & D. 217.

——◆——

HORNER *v.* FLINTOFF.

ASSUMPSIT to recover the sum of £200, being the alleged value of tenant-right due to the plaintiff on his relinquishing certain premises to the defendant; with counts for goods sold, and on an account stated. The defendant pleaded, amongst other things, a set-off for goods sold, and also for the sum of £100, agreed to be paid by the plaintiff to the defendant, as liquidated damages for the non-performance by the plaintiff of a certain agreement made between them.—At the trial before *Parke*, B., at the last York Assizes, it appeared that the defendant had entered into a written agreement with the plaintiff for the purchase of the good-will, stock, and tenant-right

The plaintiff and defendant entered into an agreement for the purchase by the defendant of the plaintiff's good-will, stock, tenant-right, &c.; it was stipulated by the agreement that the plaintiff should give possession on a certain day, and in the meantime should pay the rates and taxes, and keep the defendant indemnified therefrom: and the defendant agreed to pay £100 for the tenant-right, and take the fixtures at a valuation, and pay all rents, rates, taxes, &c., and to indemnify the plaintiff from the same; and lastly, the parties "mutually bound themselves the one to the other in the sum of £100 as settled and liquidated damages, to be paid and forfeited without any deduction, by such of them as should make default in the premises, unto the other of them requiring the same:"—*Held*, that the sum of £100 was a penalty only, and not recoverable as liquidated damages for the breach of any of the stipulations.

of the plaintiff, who was an innkeeper and farmer. It was *Exch. of Pleas,* stipulated by the agreement, that the plaintiff should give *1842.* the defendant possession of certain premises, together with HORNER the furniture, farming-stock, &c. thereon, on a certain FLINTOFF. day; and that in the meantime he, the plaintiff, should pay all rates, taxes, &c., in respect of the premises, and should keep the defendant indemnified from all costs and expenses by reason of the non-payment thereof. The defendant on his part agreed to pay the sum of £100 for the tenant-right, to take the furniture, plate, &c., and to pay the amount of a valuation to be made thereof, and all rents, rates, and taxes, and to indemnify the plaintiff from the same. The agreement contained also the following clause :—" And lastly, the said parties do hereby, for the more effectually carrying all the said matters and things above mentioned into execution, and for the full observance and performance of all the covenants, clauses, and agreements hereinbefore contained, mutually bind themselves the one to the other of them in the sum of £100, *as liquidated and settled damages,* to be paid and *forfeited* without any deduction, by such of them as shall make default in the premises, unto the other of them requiring the same." The learned Judge expressed his opinion, that notwithstanding the terms of the above clause, the sum to be paid on breach of the agreement was to be considered as a penalty only, and not as liquidated damages, according to the authority of *Kemble* v. *Farren* (a). The plea of set-off therefore failed, and the plaintiff recovered a verdict, damages 86*l.* 19*s.* 8*d.*, leave being reserved to the defendant to move to enter a nonsuit, or a verdict for him, if the Court should think that the £100 were to be considered as liquidated damages.

Wortley now moved accordingly.—This is a stronger case than that of *Kemble* v. *Farren.* There the parties

(a) 6 Bing. 141 ; 3 Moo. & P. 425. .

were undertaking to agree to construe the law, and introduced the words "not a penalty or penal sum." They
had no right to construe the law for themselves. But here
they stipulate that the damages to be paid for breach of
the agreement (which in their nature are wholly uncertain)
shall be the sum of £100, to be paid as liquidated and
settled damages, and *without any deduction*. All the
clauses in this agreement sound in uncertain damages;
and therefore, there was nothing unreasonable in the parties thus ascertaining the amount, in order to avoid expense and litigation.

PARKE, B.—I think we are bound by the authority of
the decision of the Court of Common Pleas in *Kemble* v.
Farren. Where parties say that the same ascertained sum
shall be paid for the breach of every article of an agreement, however minute and unimportant, they must be considered as not meaning exactly what they say, and a contrary intention may be collected from the other parts of
the agreement. The rule laid down in *Kemble* v. *Farren*
was, that where an agreement contains several stipulations
of various degrees of importance and value, a sum agreed
to be paid by way of damages for the breach of any of them
shall be construed as a penalty, and not as liquidated
damages, even though the parties have in express terms
stated the contrary. And this case is rather stronger than
that of *Kemble* v. *Farren*, because the word "forfeited" is
used, which points to a penalty. The words "liquidated
and settled damages" must therefore be rejected, as being
inconsistent with the legal effect of the instrument. If the
parties intend it to be construed otherwise, they must contract, in clear and express terms, that for the breach of each
and every stipulation contained in the agreement a sum
certain is to be paid; and in that case, although the stipulations are of various degrees of importance, they must be
held to their contract. But here I think the £100 must

be taken as a penalty; and as a penalty cannot be set off, the verdict is right, and there will be no rule.

ALDERSON, B.—I think the case of *Kemble* v. *Farren* is decisive of the present. The correct principle appears to have been laid down also by *Bayley*, J., in *Davies* v. *Penton* (a):— " Where the sum which is to be a security for the performance of an agreement to do several acts, will, in case of breaches of the agreement, be, in some instances, too large and in others too small a compensation for the injury thereby occasioned, that sum is to be considered a penalty." Where, therefore, the parties do not specifically annex the penalty to each and every of the stipulations in the agreement, it must be taken that, in the case of stipulations of various degrees of importance, it is a penalty only, and not liquidated damages.

ROLFE, B., concurred.

Rule refused.

(a) 6 B. & Cr. 216; 9 D. & R. 369.

———◆———

PERRY and Others v. SMITH.

April 22.

ASSUMPSIT to recover the amount of the purchase-money of certain copyhold premises sold by the plaintiffs to the defendant, which, by the conditions of sale, were to be paid for on or before the 27th of June, 1841. The declaration averred, that the plaintiffs were ready and willing to surrender or cause to be surrendered the said hereditaments and premises, &c., and alleged as a breach, that the defendant did not, on the said 27th of June, or at any other time, pay the said purchase-money. Pleas, first, non assumpsit; secondly, that the plaintiffs were not ready and willing to surrender or cause to be surrendered the said hereditaments and premises, &c., modo et formâ: on which issues were joined.

Where, upon the sale of an estate, the same attorney was employed by the vendor and by the purchaser, a communication from the purchaser to the attorney, asking for time to pay the purchase-money, was held not to be privileged.

At the trial before *Patteson*, J., at the last Stafford
Assizes, the plaintiffs called as a witness a Mr. Stevenson,
who had acted, in the matter of the purchase, as attorney
for both parties; and who stated, that the defendant, on
being applied to by him, on the 25th of June, about the payment of the purchase-money, said that he could not be
ready with it on the 27th, and wished the payment to be
postponed to the last Thursday in July; that in consequence the witness did not prepare the surrender, but that,
had it not been for this delay on the part of the defendant,
the plaintiffs would have surrendered the premises. It
was objected for the defendant, that these communications,
having been made by him to his own attorney, were privileged, and ought not to be received in evidence. The
learned Judge, however, admitted the evidence, on the
ground that the communication was made to the witness in
his character of attorney for the vendors: and the plaintiffs
had a verdict, leave being reserved to the defendant to
move to enter a verdict for him on the second issue.

W. J. Alexander now moved to enter the verdict accordingly, or for a new trial.—This communication was made
to the witness, being the attorney of the defendant in this
transaction; and ought not, therefore, to have been admitted in evidence. *Doe* d. *Shellard* v. *Horner* (a), *Doe* d.
Peter v. *Watkins* (b). In the latter case, a party who, being
attorney both for the borrower and the lender of money
on mortgage, perused the borrower's title-deeds on behalf
of the lender, was not permitted to give evidence of their
contents. It can make no difference in the application of
the principle of law, that this is the case, not of borrower
and lender, but of vendor and purchaser. [*Parke*, B.—In
Doe v. *Watkins*, the Court thought the communication was
made by the party to the witness in the character of his

(a) 5 C. & P. 592.   (b) 3 Bing. N. C. 421; 4 Scott, 155.

own attorney, not as the attorney of the mortgagee. If

the party be consulting him as his own attorney, then the bond of secrecy is imposed upon him; if the communication be made to him in the character of the adverse attorney, it is not: and here there is no doubt whatever, that the communication was made to the witness in the character of the adverse attorney; the defendant was asking for time.] The defendant may well be considered to have communicated to him as his own attorney, that he wished him to obtain time for payment.—He cited also *Moore* v. *Terrell* (*a*), and *Clark* v. *Clark* (*b*).

PARKE, B.—I have not the least doubt in this case. If the party employs an attorney who is also employed on the other side, the privilege is confined to such communications as are clearly made to him in the character of his own attorney. It is plain this was not, but in his adverse character of attorney for the vendors. The attorney, therefore, stood in the character of an ordinary witness, and the evidence was properly received.

ALDERSON, B.—I am of the same opinion. It is clear that the communication made to this witness was made to him in his character of attorney for the vendors, on whose part he was applying for payment. If Mr. *Alexander's* argument were right, the effect would be, that wherever an attorney is employed by both parties, no communications made to him could be admitted in evidence, because they must all be made through the common attorney. The point was expressly ruled in *Baugh* v. *Cradocke* (*c*), that where one attorney only is employed, a communication made to him in his character of attorney for both parties may be used against one of them.

ROLFE, B., concurred.

Rule refused.

(*a*) 4 B. & Adol. 870.   (*b*) 1 M. & Rob. 3.   (*c*) 1 M. & Rob. 182.

Exch. of Pleas,
1842.

April 26.

Where there
are issues both
in fact and in
law in an ac-
tion, although
the plaintiff has
an option to try
either first, that
is subject to the
discretion of the
Court; and they
will, in general,
direct the issues
in law to be de-
termined first,
since the cause
may be decided
thereby, and
the trial be-
come unneces-
sary; and also
because after
verdict there
can be no
amendment on
the demurrer.

CRUCKNELL v. TRUEMAN and Another.

*E*RLE moved for a rule to shew cause why a demurrer
to one of the pleas in this cause, (a plea going to the whole
cause of action), set down for argument by the defendants,
should not be struck out of the paper, on the ground that
there were also issues in fact joined; and that the plaintiff
had the option to try them first. The venue was in London.
He cited 2 Saund. 300, n. (8), *Bird* v. *Higginson* (a). [*Parke*,
B.—The general rule is, that the plaintiff has the option;
but the Court has nevertheless a discretion: *Burdett* v.
Colman (b).]

W. H. Watson for one of the defendants, and *Peacock*
for the other, shewed cause in the first instance; and contended that either party had a right to set down the demurrer for argument, subject to the control of the Court,
if it be against convenience to have it argued first. [*Parke*,
B.—If it be a plea to the whole declaration, and held to be
good, there is no use in a trial. *Alderson*, B.—After trial
the Court cannot amend on the demurrer. The case of
Mortimer v. *M'Callan* (c) went to a Court of error, simply
because the demurrer was argued after verdict; for the declaration was clearly amendable.] The dicta relied on by
the plaintiff are no longer of any weight, since the rule of
H. T. 4 Will. 4, s. 6.

Erle.—The plaintiff would strictly have a *right* to go
down to trial, even though the judgment might be for the
defendants on the demurrer. There are material costs depending besides those on the demurrer. But, if it be the
general rule that the plaintiff has the option, the defendant

(a) 5 Ad. & E. 83.   (b) 13 East, 27.
(c) 7 M. & W. 20; 9 M. & W. 636.

ought to shew that the course proposed by him will be at- *Exch. of Pleas,* tended with some great inconvenience. [*Parke*, B.—It 1842. does seem to be very convenient in general, first to dispose CRUCKNELL of the issue in fact; but as the venue is in London, both *v.* TRUEMAN. may go on pari passu.]

It was then agreed that both proceedings should go on, the defendants undertaking, if judgment were first given for them on the demurrer, and the plaintiff would undertake to bring no writ of error, to withdraw their other pleas, and pay the costs of the issues thereon.

Rule accordingly.

GEE *v.* SWANN.

April 23.

IN this case, which was tried before *Parke*, B., at the last York Assizes, it was discovered during the trial, and objected for the defendant before the verdict was returned, that no distringas juratores had been returned by the sheriff before the trial. The trial however proceeded, and a verdict was found for the plaintiff.

The Court refused, on motion, to set aside a verdict for the plaintiff, on the ground that no distringas juratores had been returned before the trial; although the objection had been taken before verdict.

Pashley now moved for a rule to shew cause why the verdict should not be set aside and a new trial had, or why a venire facias de novo should not be awarded.—This was a mis-trial. In *Rogers* v. *Smith* (a), the Court of Queen's Bench reversed the judgment on error coram nobis, on the ground of the want of a return of a distingas juratores, and of the jury panel. The want of such a return is ground of error, and is not cured by the statutes of jeofails; and a venire de novo is grantable in such a case. In Tidd's Pr. 922, it is stated, that "a venire facias de novo is grantable in the following cases :—first, when the jury are

(a) 1 Ad. & 11. 772; 3 Nev. & M. 760.

improperly chosen, or there is any irregularity in returning them." The grant of a venire de novo is not confined
to cases of a defect which appears on the record: for
instance, it is grantable if the jury improperly eat or
drink before they deliver their verdict: Bro. Abr., Verdict,
pl. 17, 18; Process, pl. 72; Venire facias, pl. 15, 16. In
Dovey v. *Hobson* (a), the Court awarded a venire de novo
where a juryman was sworn by mistake who had not been
summoned. [*Parke*, B.—There there would be an entry
on the record according to the fact.] In *Arundel's case* (b),
a venire de novo was awarded where the jury had been
summoned from a wrong county. In *Theoballs* v. *Newton* (c), where the distingas juratores bore date on a Sun-
day, and out of term, a venire de novo was awarded. In
the cases of *Lewis* v. *Witham* (d) and *Corner* v. *Shew* (e), a
venire de novo was certainly refused for matter not apparent on the record. [*Parke*, B.—The only cases against
that are those of the jury's eating and drinking before the
verdict; and we must assume that something appeared
on the record to shew the fact, or else that the term ' venire
de novo' is used instead of a new trial.]

PER CURIAM.—The defendant need not move in the
matter. If the plaintiff chooses to proceed, the defendant
will have his writ of error. In *Rogers* v. *Smith*, the Court
had first refused to interfere on motion.

Rule refused.

(a) 6 Taunt. 460.   (d) 2 tr. 1185; 1 Wils. 55.
(b) 6 Rep. 14 a.   (e) 4 M. & W. 163.
(c) Styles, 307.

1842.

April 23.

THIS was an action of debt, brought by the plaintiff as clerk to the commissioners under a local act, 51 Geo. 3, c. xliii, "for improving the Navigation from the Hythe at Colchester to Wivenhoe, in the county of Essex, and for better paving, lighting, watching, and cleaning the town of Colchester," to recover the sum of £30 for rates and duties payable to the commissioners for coal, culm, &c. by the defendant landed at Wivenhoe and the Hythe, and other places between the same. The second count was on an account stated.

Pleas, first, nunquam indebitatus: secondly, payment into Court of 12*l.* 10*s.*, and that the defendant was not indebted to a greater amount; which was denied by the replication (*a*).

Where, by a navigation act, certain rates and duties were imposed on coals, &c., landed within a certain district, to be paid to commissioners therein named; and the commissioners were empowered to sue in the name of their clerk for the time being for " any penalty or sum of money due or payable by virtue of the act : "—*Held*, that an action of debt might be brought in the name of the clerk for arrears of rates and duties; although, by another clause, a power was given of detaining and selling the vessel and goods in case of neglect or refusal to pay the rates and duties.

The act directed, that any surplus of rates remaining in the hands of the commissioners should be annually invested in the funds until it should amount to £3000, and that after that sum should be invested they should reduce the rates, so as they should not, together with the dividends of the £3000, exceed the charges annually expended in carrying the act into execution :—*Held*, that the commissioners had impliedly a power, after so reducing the rates, also to raise them again in case of necessity.

Held, also, that after the passing of the Weights and Measures Act, 5 & 6 Will. 4, c. 63, the commissioners had power to levy the rates by the *ton* (they having been previously levied by the *chaldron*), without first applying to the sessions for an inquisition under the 14th section of that act.

(*a*) The following sections of the statute are material to the case :—

Sect. 17 enacts, that there shall be paid to the commissioners by the owners or masters having the command of vessels, who shall land any coal, culm, or cinders at Wivenhoe or at the Hythe, or in any place between, the sum of 1*s.* per chaldron for every chaldron so landed.

Sect 22 gives a power, on any neglect or refusal to pay the rates or duties to the person entitled or employed by the commissioners to collect or receive the said rates or duties, to seize and detain the ship, &c., or any goods, &c., wherewith the same shall be laden; and, if within fourteen days the rates shall not be paid, to sell such ship, &c., or so much thereof as shall be sufficient for raising and paying such rates, &c.

At the trial before *Gurney*, B., at the last Assizes for Essex, it appeared that the action was brought to recover the sum of 25*l.* 19*s.*, alleged arrears of duties payable by the defendant for coals landed out of his vessel, the Isabella, at Wivenhoe and the Hythe. It was shewn that, from the passing of the local act, in the year 1811, the duty of 1*s.* per chaldron on coal, culm, &c., landed within the district mentioned in the act, was levied by the commissioners, pursuant to the 17th section. In 1833, the accumulations in the hands of the commissioners amounted to £3000; that sum was invested by them in the funds, according to the direc-

Sect. 26 directs, that if any surplus of the rates and duties should accrue or remain in the hands of the commissioners at the time of their settling their annual accounts, the same shall be invested in the public funds, in the names of the commissioners or any five of them, until the same shall amount to the sum of £3000, to be thence drawn when necessary, for the purpose of answering any emergency through accidents, &c.; and that the dividends and interest thereof shall from time to time be received by the commissioners, and applied to the purposes aforesaid. And s. 27 requires, that after the said sum of £3000 shall be so raised and invested, the commissioners shall reduce the rates and duties, so as the same shall not, with the dividends arising from the said sum of £3000, exceed the costs and charges which they shall yearly expend in executing the several matters which by this act they are authorized and required to do. Sect. 72 provides, that the rates and assessments by the act directed to be assessed on houses, &c., shall be applied in paving, lighting, &c., the streets, &c., in the town of Colchester; and requires the commissioners, after the effecting of certain improvements therein mentioned, to reduce the rate of assessment so as that it shall not exceed 1*s.* in the pound in a year; but provides also, that in case it shall hereafter happen that the annual charges of paving, lighting, &c., shall from any cause exceed the sum which the reduced rate is intended to defray, it shall be lawful for the commissioners so to increase the rate as that it shall be sufficient to defray such annual charges, and all other incidental expenses, not exceeding 1*s.* 3*d.* in the pound. Sect. 87 enacts, that the commissioners may sue and be sued in the name of their clerk for the time being; and that all actions or suits that may be necessary or expedient to be brought for the recovery of any penalty or sum of money due or payable by virtue of this act, or for or in respect of any other matter or thing relating to this act, may be brought in the name of the said clerk.

tions of s. 26.; and, in the following year, the duties were reduced to 4d. per chaldron. In the year 1835 the Weights and Measures Act, 5 & 6 Will. 4, c. 63, was passed. In 1841, the commissioners raised the rates to 9d. per ton (which, it was admitted, was less than 1s. per chaldron) without having made any application to the justices in sessions to adjust the amount of toll payable with reference to the proportion between a chaldron and a ton. Upon these facts, it was objected for the defendant, first, that the commissioners were not empowered, under the 87th section of the local act, to sue for arrears of rates and duties in the name of their clerk; secondly, that, having once reduced the rates in question, they had no power to raise them again; thirdly, that, not having applied to the justices, pursuant to the 14th section of the Weights and Measures Act, 5 & 6 Will. 4, c. 63, to regulate by inquisition the difference of toll as between a ton and a chaldron, they could not charge the duties on the ton. The learned Judge reserved the points, and the plaintiff had a verdict, leave being given to the defendant to move to enter a nonsuit.

Channell, Serjt., now moved accordingly.—First, the commissioners had no power in this case to sue by their clerk. The 87th section entitles the clerk to sue only where, but for that provision, the commissioners themselves must and *might* have sued: it makes him the statutable representative of the commissioners. But no power is given by the act to the commissioners to sue for those rates, but only a power, by s. 22, of distress or detention of the vessel in case of nonpayment. [*Parke*, B.—To whom are the rates and duties to be paid by the act?] Undoubtedly to the commissioners. [*Parke*, B.—Then they have a parliamentary right of action, by the statutory obligation to pay the rates to them. It is clear the clerk has a right to sue for some "sums of money" not penalties; and no sums of money appear to be receivable under the act, except the rates and duties; therefore he is within the provision of the 87th section.]

Secondly, the commissioners had no authority, after they had reduced these tolls, to raise them again. After realizing the sum of £3000, they are to go on reducing the rates, so that, together with the interest on that sum, they shall not exceed the annual charges; but no express power · is given to raise them again. On the other hand, they have, by express words, a power to raise the rates on houses, &c., for watching and lighting the town, after a previous reduction of them. [*Alderson*, B.—The commissioners have to raise a sum which in one year may be lower and in another higher. What an absurdity would it be, then, if they have power only to reduce the rates! Supposing, in one year, the charges did not exceed the interest of the £3000, then they are to raise nothing; but, if in the next year the charges amounted to £500, according to your argument, they could raise nothing towards it.] Thirdly, there ought to have been an inquisition at the sessions, under the 5 & 6 Will. 4, c. 63, s. 14, in order to ascertain the proportions to be charged by the ton. [*Parke*, B.—That is only in the case of an immemorial toll; but where commissioners have power from time to time to vary the tolls, the act does not apply. *Alderson*, B.— Besides, this was a rate made after the passing of the Weights and Measures Act, and therefore was lawfully made by the ton. The 14th section applies to then existing contracts, by immemorial usage or otherwise.]

PARKE, B.—I think there is no foundation for any of the objections which have been taken. The first is, that the clerk of the commissioners has no authority to bring this action. But on looking at the act of Parliament, it appears that the clerk has authority to sue for " any penalty or sum of money due and payable by virtue of this act." The rates and duties are clearly within this description;

under a temporary injury, which is capable of being speedily cured or removed, is not an unsound horse. The rule was thus laid down by *Coleridge*, J., in *Bolden* v. *Brogden* (a), that a disease which was not calculated permanently to render the horse unfit for use, or permanently to diminish his usefulness, but which with ordinary care would soon be cured, did not amount to an unsoundness so as to constitute a breach of a warranty. That ruling would support the defendant's case. On the other hand, *Parke*, B., in *Coates* v. *Stevens* (b), lays the rule down thus—"that if at the time of the sale the horse has any disease, which either actually does diminish the natural usefulness of the animal, so as to make him less capable of work of any description, or which in its ordinary progress will diminish the natural usefulness of the animal," such a horse is unsound. [*Parke*, B.—If that is not the rule, where is the line to be drawn between temporary and permanent illness or disease?] If that rule be correct, a horse which is laid up by illness of ever so short a duration is not sound. But the learned Judge here laid down the law more strongly even than that, in saying if there were any seeds of disease, the animal was unsound. [*Parke*, B.—He said, if there were any seeds of disease which would render him unfit for use. *Alderson*, B.—That temporary unsoundness may be the commencement of permanent disease.]

PARKE, B.—I think there ought to be no rule in this case. The rule I laid down in *Coates* v. *Stevens* is correctly reported; and I am there stated to have said, " I have always considered that a man who buys a horse warranted sound, must be taken as buying him for immediate use, and has a right to expect one capable of that use, and of being immediately put to any fair work the owner chooses. The rule as to unsoundness is, that if at

Exch. of Pleas, 1842.

KIDDELL v. BURNARD.

(a) 2 M. & Rob. 113.   (b) Id. 137.

the time of the sale the horse has any disease, which either actually does diminish the natural usefulness of the animal, so as to make him less capable of work of any description, or which in its ordinary progress will diminish the natural usefulness of the animal; or if the horse has, either from disease or accident, undergone any alteration of structure, that either actually does at the time, or in its ordinary effects will diminish the natural usefulness of the horse, such horse is unsound. If the cough actually existed at the time of the sale as a disease, so as actually to diminish the natural usefulness of the horse at that time, and to make him then less capable of immediate work, he was then unsound; or if you think the cough, which in fact did afterwards diminish the usefulness of the horse, existed at all at the time of the sale, you will find for the plaintiff. I am not now delivering an opinion formed on the moment on a new subject: it is the result of a full previous consideration." That is the rule I have always adopted and acted on in cases of unsoundness: although, in so doing, I differ from the contrary doctrine laid down by my brother *Coleridge*, in the case of *Bolden* v. *Brogden*, which has been referred to. I think the word "sound" means what it expresses, namely, that the animal is sound and free from disease at the time he is warranted to be sound. If, indeed, the disease were not of a nature to impede the natural usefulness of the animal for the purpose for which he is used, as for instance, if a horse had a slight pimple on his skin, it would not amount to an unsoundness: but even if such a thing as a pimple were on some part of the body where it might have that effect, as for instance, on a part which would prevent the putting a saddle or bridle on the animal, it would be different. An argument has, however, been adduced from the slightness of the disease and facility of cure; but if we once let in considerations of that kind, where are we to draw the line? A horse may have a cold, which may be cured in a day; or a fever, which may be cured in a week or month : and it would be difficult to say where to stop. Of course, if the disease be slight, the unsoundness is proportionably so, and so also ought to be the damages : and if they were very inconsiderable, the Judge might still certify under the statute of Elizabeth to deprive the plaintiff of costs. But on the question of law, I think the direction of the Judge in this case was perfectly correct, and that this verdict ought not to be disturbed. Were this matter presented to us now for the first time, we might deem it proper to grant a rule, but the matter has been, we think, settled by previous cases : and the opinion which we now express is the result of deliberate consideration.

ALDERSON, B.—I am of the same opinion. The word "sound" means *sound*, and the only qualification of which it is susceptible, arises from the purpose for which the warranty is given. If, for instance, a horse is purchased to be used in a given way, the word "sound" means that the animal is useful for that purpose; and "unsound" means that he at the time is affected with something which will have the effect of impeding that use. If the disease be one easily cured, that will only go in mitigation of damages. It is, however, right to make to the definition of unsoundness the addition my brother *Parke* has made, namely, that the disqualification for work may arise either from disease or accident : and the doctrine laid down by him on this subject, both to-day, and in the case of *Coates* v. *Stevens*, is not new law; it is to be found recognised by Lord *Ellenborough* and other Judges in a series of cases.

GURNEY, B., and ROLFE, B., concurred.

Rule refused.

Exch. of Pleas,
1842.

April 21.

WILD and Two Others *v.* HOLT.

In trespass for breaking and entering the plaintiff's mine and taking coals, evidence of working by the plaintiff in another part of the same mine, within eighty yards of the place of the alleged trespass, coupled with a statement by the defendant, that he had got the coal, and was willing to pay such a-mount as should be settled by arbitration, was held to be evidence of the plaintiff's being in possession of the place where the trespass was committed.

In trespass for taking coals from the plaintiff's mine, where the defendant is a mere wrong-doer, the mea-sure of damages is the value of the coals at the time when they first existed as chattels, and the defendant is not entitled to any deduction for the expense of getting them, or for a rent pay-able to the mine-owner on coals got from the mine.

TRESPASS for breaking and entering a mine in the possession of the plaintiffs and one Edward Stelfox, in the lifetime of Stelfox, and taking coals therefrom. Pleas, first, not guilty ; secondly, that the plaintiffs were not possessed of the mine in the declaration mentioned : on which issues were joined. At the trial before *Rolfe,* B., at the last Liverpool Assizes, the plaintiffs claimed to be possessed as the surviving assignees of certain leases of the mine in question, granted by Lord Suffield, but failed to derive a title under those leases. The plaintiffs then proved, that at the time of the alleged trespass they were working the coals within about 80 yards of the spot where the trespass was committed ; and that the defendant had admitted that he had got the coal, and had expressed his willingness to pay such amount as should be settled by arbitration. It was proved that the expense of getting each quarter of coals amounted to 4*s.* 6*d.*, which included a payment to Lord Suffield of 2*s.* 6*d.*, under the name of quarterage. The value of the coals taken by the defendant was esti-mated at £748, being calculated at £1 per quarter. For the defendant, it was contended that there was no sufficient evidence of the joint possession of the mine by the plain-tiffs, and that they ought therefore to be nonsuited ; or, at all events, that the defendant was entitled to deduct the 4*s.* 6*d.* per quarter, the expense of getting the coals. The learned judge thought there was evidence to go to the jury of the plaintiffs' possession, and directed them, if they were satisfied of that fact, to return a verdict for £748. The jury thereupon found for the plaintiffs for that sum, and the learned judge reserved leave to the defendant to move to enter a nonsuit, or to reduce the damages to 1*s.*, or to reduce them by deducting the 4*s.* 6*d.* per quarter.

Exch. of Pleas,
1842.

WILD
v.
HOLT.

Knowles now moved accordingly.—No title having been proved by the plaintiffs under the leases granted by Lord Suffield, their case must stand on the proof of their apparent possession of the mine, and on the supposed admission of the defendant. But that statement did not admit a joint possession in the four parties in whose right the plaintiffs claimed. And the working on a part of the land so far distant from the place of the alleged trespass is no proof of their title to the land trespassed on, but only shews a possession of the part in which they actually worked. It would have been different if there had been proof of a lease giving them the whole mine, and defining its limits, as in the case of *Taylor* v. *Parry* (a). It may be that the lessees had granted them a license to work a particular part of the mine only.

At all events, the defendant was entitled to deduct the expense of getting the coal, including the quarterage rent, or at least the latter. [*Parke*, B.—The case of *Martin* v. *Porter* (b) establishes that, as against a wrong-doer, no such abatement ought to be made, but that the jury are at liberty to give as damages the full value of the coals when they first exist as chattels, in consequence of the trespass. Where there is a real disputed title, it is different.] Lord Suffield may come upon the defendant again for the quarterage, notwithstanding this verdict. [*Parke*, B.—No; the payment under it will be good evidence as against him, or any body claiming under his lease.] But the plaintiffs were only bound to pay the quarterage on the coal *they* got; the verdict, therefore, gives them more than its full value. [*Rolfe*, B.—When they have recovered the value from you, they will have got it, and will be liable to the quarterage on it.]

PARKE, B.—I think that, coupling the evidence of the

(a) 1 Man. & Gr. 605 ; 1 Scott, N. R. 576.

plaintiffs' working in different parts of the mine with the defendant's admissions, there clearly was evidence for the jury of the plaintiffs being in possession of the whole mine. Then as to the damages, the jury are at liberty to give the full value of the coals, calculated at the time when they first exist as chattels, without deducting the expense of getting them, according to the rule laid down in the case of *Martin* v. *Porter,* which is a very salutary one, because the parties must know—at least they may know by proper dialling—that they are. trespassing on their neighbours' property. And the defendant is not entitled to any deduction in respect of the rent payable to Lord Suffield, because he will be entitled to quarterage on the coals when their value has been recovered by the plaintiffs.

ALDERSON, B.—I am of the same opinion. With respect to the evidence, in the first place, the statement of the defendant is an admission that the place where he got the coals belongs to the mine which the plaintiffs are working. And I think the act of ownership exercised in one part of the mine is evidence of the plaintiffs being in possession of the other part. The effect of that act cannot be confined to the very spot from which the party is exhausting the mineral. It might as well be said, that when a man stands on the surface of a field, he is exercising an act of ownership upon that part only on which his foot rests. Coupling these two facts together, I think there was quite sufficient evidence for the jury of the plaintiffs being in possession of the spot trespassed on. As to the amount of damages, I quite concur with my brother *Parke.*

GURNEY, B., and ROLFE, B., concurred.

Rule refused.

indeed, there are no other sums of money for which the commissioners could sue by virtue of the act. Then will an action of *debt* lie in this case? Now it is laid down in Comyns's Digest, Dett, (A. 1), that "debt lies upon every contract in deed or in law;" and one instance given is this,—"Upon the stat. 28 Eliz. c. 4, which says, the sheriff shall take for his fees no more than 12*d.* for every 20*s.* under £100, and 6*d.* for every 20*s.* above £100, the sheriff shall have debt for his fees." The duties, therefore, being under this act to be paid to the commissioners, an action of debt lies by them or their clerk. Secondly, it is objected that, as the commissioners have once lowered the tolls, they cannot afterwards raise them again. But that appears to me to be quite an erroneous construction of the act. It must be implied that, in cases of exigency, the rates may be varied, the charges for which the commissioners have to provide being of an uncertain nature; and what reason can there be, because the rates have been once lowered, that, in a case of necessity, they cannot be raised again? Thirdly, I do not think it was necessary to apply to the justices to apportion the rates. The stat. 5 & 6 Will. 4, c. 63, s. 14, applies only to cases of fixed contracts or payments, which cannot be varied by the parties, and to tolls or rates payable according to the weights and measures previously in use. In such cases, the proportions are to be adjusted by the sessions. But the act does not apply to such a case as this, where the commissioners have power to vary the tolls, and where they have actually fixed the amount since the passing of the act.

ALDERSON, B., GURNEY, B., and ROLFE, B., concurred.

Rule refused.

Exch. of Pleas,
1842.

MOORE *v.* CLARKE.

April 20.

In an action on
the case, for pi-
rating an en-
graving, brought
under the stat.
17 Geo. 3,
c. 57, which
gives a right of
action against
any one who
shall copy any
print " in the
whole or in
part, by vary-
ing, adding to,
or diminishing
from, the main
design," the
judge directed
the jury to con-
sider whether
the defendant's
engraving was
substantially a
copy of the
plaintiff's :—
Held, that this
direction was
correct.

THIS was a special action on the case, under the stat. 17
Geo. 3, c. 57, for pirating an engraving of the plaintiff's.
It appeared that the plaintiff was the publisher and proprietor of an engraving of the portrait of a celebrated mare
called " Bee's-Wing," and the defendant was the printer
and publisher of a work called " Tom Spring's Life in London." The alleged piracy was by a woodcut in the defendant's publication, professing to be a " portrait of ' Corona-
tion,' winner of the Derby, 1841," which bore a strong resemblance to the plaintiff's engraving, and was alleged to
be a copy of it, varying only in the direction in which the
animal was proceeding, and a slight alteration in the dress
of the jockey. Lord *Abinger*, C. B., directed the jury to
consider whether the main design of the plaintiff's engraving had been copied, and whether the defendant's engraving was substantially a copy of the plaintiff's; and
secondly, whether the plaintiff had sustained any damage.
The jury found that the defendant's engraving was not a
copy of the plaintiff's, and that the plaintiff had not sustained any damage; and thereupon returned a verdict for
the defendant.

Knowles now moved for a new trial, on the ground of misdirection. It was not necessary, to bring the case within
the act of Parliament, that the defendant's print should be
an exact copy of the plaintiff's. The 17 Geo. 8, c. 57, enacts,
" That if any engraver, etcher, printseller, or other person,
shall, within the time limited by the recited acts of the 8
Geo. 2, and 7 Geo. 8, or either of them, engrave, etch, or
work, or cause or procure to be engraved, etched, or
worked, in mezzotinto, or chiaro oscuro, or otherwise, or
in any other manner copy in *the whole or in part*, by *varying, adding to,* or *diminishing from the main design,* or shall

print, reprint, or import for sale, or cause or procure to be printed, reprinted, or imported for sale, or shall publish, sell, or otherwise dispose of, or cause or procure to be published, sold, or otherwise disposed of, any copy or copies of any historical print or prints, or any print or prints of any portrait, conversation, landscape, or architecture, map, chart, or plan, or any print or prints whatsoever, which hath or have been, or shall be engraved, etched, drawn, or designed, in any part of Great Britain, without the express consent of the proprietor or proprietors thereof first had and obtained in writing, signed by him, her, or them respectively, with his, her, or their own hand or hands, in the presence of and attested by two or more credible witnesses, then every such proprietor or proprietors shall and may, by and in a special action upon the case, to be brought against the person or persons so offending, recover such damages as a jury on the trial of such action, or on the execution of a writ of inquiry thereon, shall give or assess, together with double costs of suit." Now it was not necessary that the piracy should be an exact copy in every respect, because the act says *in the whole or in part;* and although the jury found that the plaintiff had sustained no damage, that did not affect his title to sue. It is quite clear that it is not necessary that the whole design should be copied, to bring the case within the act. [*Parke*, B.— The act only gives a remedy by action for such damages as the plaintiff has sustained.] The plea is not guilty, and the defendant has not pleaded to the damage; and it is a question well worth considering, whether he ought not to have done so, to entitle himself to take the objection that the plaintiff has not sustained any damage. [*Parke*, B.—We will look into the act of Parliament, and consider the case.]

On the following day (April 21) the judgment of the Court was delivered by

PARKE, B.—In this case the objection to the Lord Chief

A A A 2

Baron's direction was, that he told the jury to consider whether the defendant's print was substantially a copy of the plaintiff's. We think that direction correct, and in accordance with the act of Parliament. Whether the print be an exact copy, and whether the variations are altogether immaterial, is not for us to consider; that was a question for the jury, and one which they have determined, and the motion is not made on the ground of the verdict being against the evidence. That being the case, the other point, as to the plaintiff's right of maintaining an action where he has sustained no actual damage, does not arise. Perhaps, if the piracy were established, the law would imply damage; but that point does not arise here, and therefore it is unnecessary to deliver an opinion upon it. There will be no rule.

Rule refused.

JOSHUA FIELD and Elizabeth his Wife, Executrix of JOHN STOCKDALE, deceased, *v.* ALLEN (a).

To an action of debt by husband and wife, in right of the wife as executrix, for money had and received, the defendant pleaded, as to £35, that that sum was part of the prices received by him upon the sales of two

DEBT, in the sum of £115, for money had and received by the defendant for the use of the plaintiff Joshua and his wife, as executrix, and on an account stated between them.

Pleas,—as to the several sums of money in the declaration mentioned, &c., except as to £80 parcel thereof, nunquam indebitatus; on which issue was joined. And as to the said sum of £80, payment into Court of that sum, which

horses of the testator, which were in the hands of the plaintiffs to be administered, and which, under an authority given by them to the defendant, were sold by him in his own name, and warranted sound to the respective purchasers [naming four persons]; that at the time of the sales the horses respectively were unsound; that the defendant, from the time of the receipt of the money until he paid the same as after mentioned, was indebted to the plaintiffs in the sum of £35, payable on request, for the said money so received by him for their use, and always was ready and willing to pay it to them; and that after he so became indebted, and before the commencement of the suit, he was, by reason of the breaches of the warranties as to the said horses, compelled by the said persons who so purchased them, without any fault on his part, to repay, and did necessarily repay, to them the said sum of £35, and the residue of the prices, whereby the said debt of £35 was discharged:—*Held*, on special demurrer, that the plea was no answer to the action.

(a) This case was decided in Hilary Term, Jan. 17.

was taken out by the plaintiffs. And as to the sum of £35, parcel of the money in the first count mentioned, and other than and distinct from the said sum of £80, that the said sum of £35 was part of the prices by him the defendant received for and upon the sales hereafter mentioned of certain, to wit, two horses, which were of the said John Stockdale at the time of his death, and which, at the respective times of the giving of the authority and making of the sales hereinafter mentioned, were in the hands of the said Joshua and Elizabeth his wife, as executrix as aforesaid, to be administered, and which said horses, under and by virtue of an authority before then, to wit, on the day and year in the first count mentioned, to him the defendant in that behalf by the said Joshua and Elizabeth his wife, as executrix as aforesaid, given, were by the defendant, before then also, to wit, on &c., respectively sold in his the defendant's own name as the seller thereof, and, upon those sales, and by the terms thereof respectively, warranted to the respective purchasers thereof, to wit, [naming four persons] to be sound at the respective times of the said sales thereof respectively. And the defendant further says, that, at the time of the said sales respectively, the said horses respectively were not sound, but on the contrary thereof, were then respectively unsound. And the defendant further says, that he the defendant was, from the time of the receipt of the said sum of £35 until he paid the same as hereinafter mentioned, indebted to the said Joshua and Elizabeth his wife, as executrix as aforesaid, in the said sum of £35, payable on request, for the said money so received, and which was so as aforesaid received by him for the use of the said Joshua and Elizabeth his wife, as executrix as aforesaid. And the defendant further says, that at and from the time when he the defendant so as aforesaid became and was indebted to the said Joshua and Elizabeth, as executrix as aforesaid, in the said sum of £35, until he paid the same as hereinafter mentioned, he the defendant always constantly was ready and willing to pay the said sum of £35 to the said Joshua and Elisabeth, as executrix as aforesaid; and that, after he so became indebted as last aforesaid, and before the commencement of this suit, and after the said sales, to wit, on &c., he the defendant was, by reason and in consequence of the said breaches of the said respective warranties as to the said horses respectively, compelled by the said persons who so purchased the said horses respectively, without any fault or impropriety on the behalf of him the defendant, to repay, and then did necessarily and unavoidably repay to them the said purchasers, as well the said sum of £35, part of the said prices as aforesaid, as also the residue of the said prices, whereby the said debt of £85 was discharged.—Verification.

To the last plea the plaintiffs demurred specially, assigning for causes (inter alia), that the defendant has thereby confessed that he is indebted to the plaintiffs in the sum of £35, and yet has not shewn any sufficient matter of discharge or excuse for the non-payment of the same: that the plea neither traverses, nor confesses and avoids, the matter in the declaration alleged as to the said £85. That it does not distinctly appear from the plea that the defendant had any authority from the plaintiffs to warrant the horses therein mentioned to be sound; that, although it is averred that the horses were sold in the name of the defendant by the authority of the plaintiffs, it is not stated that they were warranted sound by their authority, or with their knowledge. That the plea is uncertain, inasmuch as it is not set forth with sufficient clearness to whom each of the said horses was sold; but whereas it appears from the plea that they were sold at different times, and under different contracts, it does not appear whether they were sold to the same persons, or to different persons, or to which of the said persons one of the said horses was sold, and to which the other; and the plaintiffs cannot safely take issue as to the sale of the said horses or either of them, as averred in the plea; and it does not appear to whom the several warranties, as set forth in the plea, were given, or who the parties were, whether jointly or separately, who were entitled to enforce or sue upon the said warranty: and whereas the sale of each horse, and the warranty of each horse, and the unsoundness and return of each horse, involved an entirely distinct issue, the defendant has confounded the sale, warranty, unsoundness, and return of the two horses together, so as to make it unsafe for the plaintiff to take issue upon any of those points, with respect to either horse singly, &c. &c. That it does not appear by the plea that the money therein mentioned was repaid at the request or by the desire or consent of the plaintiffs, or that the defendant was under any legal compulsion to refund the prices of the said horses, &c. That the plea amounts to the general issue, &c. &c.—Joinder in demurrer.

O'Malley, in support of the demurrer.—The plea is bad. It does not distinguish between the sale of one horse and of the other, and gives no accurate description of the contract as to either: it does not state the price of each, or the parties to whom each was sold; so that the plaintiff cannot take a distinct issue as to the sale or warranty of the one horse for which the £35 was paid. [Lord *Abinger*, C. B.—It does not appear which horse was unsound, or to which purchaser the money was returned.] No; the plea says only that the money was returned " to the respective purchasers thereof," not distinguishing to which. Where a party proposes to set out in pleading, as a defence to an action, a contract to which he was one of the parties, he ought to state the nature and terms of it with full particularity. Here the plea sets forth two contracts and four persons, and does not shew whether either was made with the whole, or with which of those persons. [Lord *Abinger*,

C. B.—Is that material? Suppose the plea proved as it is, is it not an answer to the action?] If a party seeks to discharge himself by a contract, he ought to set it out fully.   [Lord *Abinger,* C. B.—Yes, if it be a contract with the plaintiff, because then his right is founded on the contract; but that is not so here. But the plea does not state that the horses were returned; and if so, the defendant was not bound to return the price.]   For aught that appears, it may have been repaid voluntarily : the plea, therefore, does not shew such a state of things as that the defendant was bound to return the money, the contract being rescinded. *Street* v. *Blay* (a). And even if it had, it would have amounted only to an informal plea of set-off; because the plaintiffs' right of action accrued upon the receipt of the money to their use.   On the other hand, if it be matter of discharge, it amounts to nunquam indebitatus, as shewing that the defendant received the money, not to be paid over absolutely to the plaintiffs on request, but to be held for a reasonable time, until it were ascertained whether the horses would be returned, and then to be paid over.—The Court here called on

Addison, contrà.—The plea does not amount to nunquam indebitatua, because it admits a time when the defendant was indebted to the plaintiffs in right of the wife, namely, during the interval when the money was in his hands. Nor is it strictly a plea of set-off.   It resembles the case of *Waddilove* v. *Barnett* (b), where it was held, that in answer to a count for use and occupation, the defendant might give in evidence, under non assumpsit, that the plaintiff had mortgaged the premises before the defendant came into occupation; and that the mortgagee had given notice to the defendant not to pay the plaintiff any subsequent rent. [Lord *Abinger,* C. B.—The Court do not say that the defence might have been pleaded specially.]

(a) 2 B. & Adol. 456.   (b) 2 Bing. N. C. 538; 2 Scott, 763.

This matter could not be pleaded by way of *set-off* to the action by these plaintiffs, one of them being a married woman, who could not contract a debt. The defendant could not sue them jointly on any cause of action which has accrued since the coverture, the wife being incapable of binding herself. [Lord *Abinger*, C. B.—Your argument comes to this, that as against these plaintiffs, the defendant could not discharge himself at all.] This is money which under the circumstances the plaintiffs never had a right to receive. It is not stated that the horses were ever *delivered* to the purchaser; but it is alleged that they were sold under a warranty authorized by the plaintiffs. [*Alderson*, B.—Does that sufficiently appear? (His Lordship read the terms of the plea.)] It states that the horses were sold under their authority; but if one of the terms of such sales were a warranty not authorized by the plaintiffs, the sales would not have been made under their authority. All the terms of the sales must have been taken to be authorized by the plaintiffs: and this action is an adoption of those contracts of sale, whatever they were. [Lord *Abinger*, C. B.—Suppose the money had all been paid over to the plaintiffs, and the defendant were afterwards sued by the purchaser on the warranty, and obliged to repay it; could he have recovered it back from the plaintiffs?] Perhaps not; but it does not follow that he cannot discharge himself, in order to avoid circuity of action, by setting forth circumstances which shew that they had no right of action at the commencement of the suit. [Lord *Abinger*, C. B.—How can he destroy their vested right of action by applying the money otherwise, unless he have a counter-right of action? If their right of action did not subsist at the commencement of the suit, it is only because the defendant has acquired a cross right by payment of the money on their account and for their benefit. *Alderson*, B. —The husband, if anybody, is liable personally to the defendant; how then can he set off the claim against money due from him to the husband and wife in auter droit?] If this had been money had and received to the use of the testator, the defendant might certainly have discharged himself by such a plea; and it is an action brought in right of the testator.

Lord ABINGER, C. B.—The very principle which Mr. *Addison* lays down shews that the defendant cannot sue the plaintiffs for this claim; neither can he set it off to an action by them. The plea is therefore bad.

ALDERSON, B.—The defendant says this has ceased to be money had and received to the use of the plaintiffs, because he has subsequently applied it to the payment of a sum for which he was liable for a breach of his contract. That is no answer to this action.

GURNEY, B., concurred.

                                        Judgment for the plaintiff.

Exch. of Pleas,
1842.

BAIN, registered public officer of the Commercial Bank of England, *v.* COOPER and BRASSINGTON.

April 26, 28.

COVENANT on a guarantee given to the Commercial Bank of England. The declaration set forth a guarantee signed and sealed by the defendants, whereby, after reciting that S. Mayer, J. Mawdesley, and J. Bridgwood, carrying on business under the name of S. Mayer & Co., were about to open an account with the said banking copartnership, the defendants covenanted to guarantee the copartnership from all loss or damage thereby, and from all sums due or to become due from Mayer & Co. to the copartnership. The declaration then averred that the sum of £2000 became and was due from Mayer & Co. to the copartnership, and that Mayer & Co. did not pay the same; and alleged as a breach the non-payment by the defendants of £1500, part thereof. The defendant Cooper pleaded (inter alia), sixthly, that after the making of the said deed-poll, and after the said sum of money had become due from Mayer & Co. to the copartnership as in the declaration mentioned, by an indenture made between the said Samuel Mayer, the said Joseph Mawdesley, Ralph Lees, and the said Jesse Bridgwood of the first part, Hugh Henshall Williamson, Richard Howard Haywood, and William Malpass of the second part, and the several per-

To an action of covenant by a joint-stock banking co-partnership, on a guarantee given by the defendant to secure advances made by the company to M., M., and B., carrying on business under the name of M. & Co., the defendant pleaded, that by indenture between M., M., L., and B., of the first part, W., H., and O., of the second part, and the several persons or partnership firms who should execute the said indenture, being creditors of M., M., L., and B., of the third part, H., being a member and partner in the said banking co-partnership,

released M., M., L., and B., from all actions, debts, &c. The defendant, in support of his plea, gave in evidence a composition deed, made between M., M., L., and B., of the first part, W., H., and O., of the second part, and the several persons or partnership firms, being creditors of M., M., L., and B., who should have executed or who should execute the said composition deed, of the third part. The deed, after reciting that M., M., L., and B., were indebted to W., H., and O., and to the several parties to the deed of the third part, and being unable to pay the said debts, had conveyed all their property and effects to W., H., and O., in trust for payment of their debts, stated, that in consideration thereof, each of the said creditors, parties to the said deed of the second and third parts, did for themselves, their heirs, executors, &c., and partners, release M., M., L., and B., from all actions, debts, demands, &c. At the date of this release, a separate debt of 2*l*. 16*s*. was due from M. to H., and H., at the date of the release, was a shareholder in the joint-stock banking co-partnership. H. executed the deed in his own name:—*Held,* that the plea was not proved, the release from M., M., L., and B., not including the debt due from M. & Co. to the joint-stock banking company, but applying only to debts due to such partnership firms as should execute the deed of the third part.

sons or partnership firms who should execute the said indenture, being creditors of the said S. Mayer, J. Mawdesley, R. Lees, and J. Bridgwood, of the third part, the said R. H. Haywood, then being a member of and a partner in the said banking copartnership, and a holder of 1000 shares in the said copartnership, and then being also duly authorized by the said copartnership, for himself, and for the said copartnership and his partners, did acquit, release, and for ever discharge the said S. Mayer, J. Mawdesley, R. Lees, and J. Bridgwood, from all actions, claims, and demands whatsoever, which the said R. H. Haywood, the said copartnership and his partners, then had or might have, by reason of the said debts then due from the said S. Mayer, J. Mawdesley, R. Lees, and J. Bridgwood, or any of them, to the said copartnership: And the defendant says, that the said indenture was made by the said R. H. Haywood, without the privity or consent of him the said defendant, by means whereof he became and was wholly discharged of and from all liability in respect of the said guarantee or agreement, in respect of the said debt or sum of money alleged to be so due and owing from the said S. Mayer & Co. to the said copartnership as aforesaid — Verification.

Replication, that the said R. H. Haywood, for himself and for the said copartnership, and for his partners, did not acquit, release, or discharge the said S. Mayer, J. Mawdesley, R. Lees, and J. Bridgwood, or any of them, in manner and form, &c.:—on which issue was joined.

At the trial before Lord *Abinger,* C. B., at the London sittings after last Michaelmas term, the defendant put in, in support of the above plea, a deed of composition, dated 7th March, 1840, made between Samuel Mayer, Joseph Mawdesley, Ralph Lees, and Jesse Bridgwood of the first part, Hugh Henshall Williamson, R. H. Haywood, and William Malpass of the second part, and "the several other persons or partnership firms, who by themselves or their respective attornies or agents, have executed or shall execute these presents, being creditors of the said S. Mayer, J. Mawdesley, R. Lees, and J. Bridgwood," of the third part. This deed, after reciting that S. Mayer, J. Mawdesley, R. Lees, and J. Bridgwood, had carried on business in co-partnership under the firm of Samuel Mayer & Co., and being indebted to the said H. H. Williamson, R. H. Haywood, and W. Malpass, and to the several parties thereto of the third part, in considerable sums of money, which they were unable to pay, had agreed to convey the whole of their property, except &c., to Williamson, Haywood, and Malpass, in trust to sell the same, and apply the proceeds in payment of the several sums due from Mayer, Mawdesley, Lees, and Bridgwood, to Williamson, Haywood, and Malpass, and the several other persons or firms, parties thereto of the third part, and after proceeding to convey the property accordingly, contained the following clause :—" In consideration whereof, each of these the said creditors, parties hereto of the second and third parts, doth for himself and herself, his and her heirs, executors and administrators, and partner or partners respectively, acquit, release, and for ever discharge the said S. Mayer, J. Mawdesley, R. Lees, and J. Bridgwood, and each and every of them, all and all manner of action and actions, suit and suits, cause and causes of action and suit, claims and demands whatsoever, which they the said creditors, and their partner or partners respectively, now have, or which they or any of them, or their respective heirs, executors, or administrators respectively, hereafter may, can, or might have, claim, challenge, or demand, for, upon, or by reason of the several and respective debts of them respectively, due and owing from the said S. Mayer, J. Mawdesley, J. Lees, and J. Bridgwood, or any of them, or in any relation thereto, or in any manner howsoever." This deed purported to contain also an assignment by Lees of his personal estate, by way of security for the debts of the firm; but it appeared that Lees had not executed it. At the date of the deed, a separate debt of 2l. 15s. was due from Mayer to Haywood, and the sum of £1500 was owing from Mayer & Co. to the banking company, in which Haywood was a shareholder. It was contended for the defendant, that the deed operated as a release of the partnership debt. The Lord Chief Baron, however, was of opinion that the plea was not proved, and under his direction a verdict was found for the plaintiff, with liberty to the defendant to move to enter a verdict for him upon the sixth issue.

Kelly having obtained a rule accordingly,

Erle and *Crompton* now shewed cause.—The deed produced in evidence did not prove a release of the debt due from Mayer & Co. to the banking copartnership, as alleged in the plea. In the first place, there is nothing to satisfy the Court that the other parties did not intend to withhold the operation of it until Lees's personal property had been assigned by him. [*Parke*, B.—Then it should have been delivered as an escrow.] Until all parties have executed it, where the act of any one forms a part of the consideration for the execution by the opposite party, it is no valid deed. *Soprani* v. *Skurro* (a); Com. Dig. Covenant, (F.). [*Parke*, B.—But here an interest passed by the execution by the other three]. On this point *Rose* v. *Poulton* (b), *Johnson* v. *Baker* (c), and *Dutton* v. *Morrison* (d), were also referred to.

Secondly, this is pleaded as a release to the *three* persons mentioned in the declaration, of the debts due from them; whereas the deed shews that there were *four* persons in partnership, and that the debts were due from them. The recitals of the deed clearly confine it to debts from the four

(a) Yelv. 18.   (c) 4 B. & Ald. 440.
(b) 2 B. & Adol. 822.   (d) 17 Ves. 193; 1 Rose, 213.

jointly; and the recital is to be looked to, to explain and *Exch. of Pleas,* control the language of the release itself. *Simons* v. *John-* 1842. *son* (a); *Payler* v. *Homersham* (b). Again, the recital shews that the debts intended to be released were the debts owing from the firm to Williamson, Haywood, and Malpass in their private capacity, not as members of any joint-stock banking company. And Haywood executes the deed in his character of trustee—not as releasing any debt. It does not even extend in terms to debts owing to them-selves *and others.* Who are to obtain the benefit of the composition? The three parties named, and "the several other persons or partnership firms, who by themselves or their respective attornies have executed or shall execute these presents of the third part, being creditors of Mayer, &c." Under no words of this trust could the banking company be entitled to receive anything. A banking co-partnership acts by its public officer, and it cannot be presumed that a private member of the company intended to release a debt due to the copartnership. The plea alleges, indeed, that Haywood had the authority of the bank to release the debt; but there was no proof of that fact.

BAIN
v.
COOPER.

Kelly, and *W. H. Watson,* contrà.—The question is not whether this debt was released in point of law, but whether the plea was proved in fact. The plea follows precisely the words of the releasing part of the deed. It does not say that the release was of the debt for which this action is brought, but applies the release to all the debts due to the banking copartnership. Now, in the first place, it is a clear proposition of law, that if one of several partners execute a release of a debt, that prevents any of his co-partners from afterwards suing for it. *Ruddock's case* (c). And here it is distinctly alleged in the plea, that Haywood

(a) 3 B. & Adol. 175.   (b) 4 M. & Sel. 423.
          (c) 6 Rep. 25.

had authority from the copartnership to release their debt, which is not denied in the replication.

It is said, indeed, that the release is confined to the separate debt due to Haywood, and that the general terms of the operative part of the deed are to be controlled by the recital, according to the doctrine laid down in *Payler* v. *Homersham*, and *Simons* v. *Johnson*. The principle established by those cases is not disputed. But the question here is, whether, taking the whole instrument together, there is anything in the recitals to control the release in this particular. Haywood executes the deed once only: and it is said for the plaintiff, that that must be taken to have been in his character of party of the second part, that is, as trustee and not as creditor : but there is no authority for that; if it were so, it must follow that a party under such circumstances must execute the deed twice over. His one act of execution binds him in every character in which he is described in the deed; he thereby adopts and binds himself by the whole instrument. It is urged, that the recital excludes the supposition of the release applying to debts due to Haywood jointly with others. But it was not necessary to name him specially as a joint creditor; his release operates as well as party of the third as of the second part; and the deed is very general in its terms, and conveys the whole joint and separate property of the four debtors. How can it be said they are not to have, on the other hand, an absolute and general release from the parties who thus divest them of all their property? They could never intend to get rid of a debt of 2*l.* 15*s.*, but remain liable to a demand of £1500. It is the same as if Haywood had in terms said, " I, being a party of the second, and a party of the third part, do for myself and my partners release." [Lord *Abinger*, C. B.—Those only who execute for themselves and their partners, release for their partners. Besides, a man does not usually call himself a *partner* in a banking company. *Parke*, B.—The only provision in the deed is for the satisfaction of persons who, or *Exch. of Pleas,* whose firms, have executed or shall afterwards execute 1842. the deed; the only firm which can take a provision for BAIN the payment of its debts, is one that is a party thereto *v.* of the third part; therefore, it is in consideration of the COOPER. provision to be made for payment of the firms parties thereto of the third part, that the three parties of the second part release. Each releases his own separate debt, and those who afterwards execute as partners, release for all as partners : but the payment of *firms* applies only to those who execute of the third part.] If a person, being a member of a partnership firm, executes for himself and his partners, it is not necessary to describe him as a partner, and as executing for them : if it were so, then, if the firm were misnamed, the trustees would have no power to pay that particular debt. [*Parke*, B.—It must be taken that the word "partners" means such partners as take a benefit under the deed; *i. e.* partners of such firms as shall subscribe it of the third part.] The Court will not act on any distinction between a joint-stock and any other partnership, in construing a deed; they are equally partners in law, and a release is equally operative in either case: *Brooks* v. *Stuart* (a). The release ought to be construed liberally, inasmuch as the debtors part with all their property in consideration of it.

Lord ABINGER, C. B.—I am of opinion that there is no ground for making this rule absolute. I cannot accede to much of the argument which has been urged in support of it. If there had been an execution of the deed by one person who was a partner in the ordinary sense of the word, of the third part, and it had appeared that there was a debt due to him individually, and also to the firm of which he was a member, I should have thought that it imported a release only of his individual debt. I think it

(a) 9 Ad. & Ell. 854; 1 P. & D. 615.

was meant that where parties released for firms, they should sign for their firms, and where for themselves, that they should sign as for themselves only. But this case is far stronger; because the recitals of the deed, and all the other terms of it, import that Haywood was a party to it only as an individual creditor. There is no mention of *firms* introduced until the deed is speaking of the parties of the third part. But to suppose that he signed as releasing for the joint-stock banking company is absolutely absurd. There is no evidence that he knew a word about the debt owing to them: and even if, in the case of an ordinary partnership, his release might operate on behalf of the firm, it does not follow that it would extend to the case of a joint-stock company. The members of such a company are not in ordinary parlance *partners;* and why should we construe a deed as implying by that term the members of a joint-stock bank, when we should not ordinarily so apply it? The words of a deed are to be construed like those of any other writing, according to the ordinary use and application of them. The members of such a company are *shareholders,* acting by means of directors, and having no power of disposition over the funds, as in the case of an ordinary partnership. Therefore, in order to wrest this into a release of the debt of the banking company, we must violate entirely the ordinary interpretation of words, and all the inferences of intention arising from the recitals of the deed. I am of opinion, therefore, that the plea has not been proved, and that this rule ought to be discharged.

PARKE, B.—I am also clearly of opinion that this rule ought to be discharged. This is an action on a guarantee under seal, for the payment of debts due from three persons alleged to be carrying on business under the firm of Mayer & Co., to the Commercial Bank of England: and the question is, whether the release given by Mr. Haywood, who was a member of the banking company, to Mayer & Co. has released the debt due from them to the company. The question arises on the sixth plea. [His Lordship stated the terms of the plea.] And the point is, whether that plea was supported by evidence at the trial. Several objections have been taken on behalf of the plaintiff, but I think it sufficient to refer to one. The question is, did the release operate as a discharge of the debt due to the banking company? That depends on the recitals of the deed, and on the language of the whole instrument taken together. [His Lordship read the recitals.] Perhaps, according to the strict grammatical construction, those words apply only to joint debts due from Mayer & Co.; but taking them to include the separate debts of each of the debtors, they then proceed to convey all their property to trustees, for the benefit of such of their creditors, whether individuals or partnership firms, as have executed or shall execute the deed of the third part; and then follows the release, on the terms of which the present question arises. That is in these words. [His Lordship read it.] Now, even supposing the word " partners " to be understood as applying not merely to ordinary commercial partnership, but also to joint-stock companies,—which I quite agree it ought not,—at all events it is only to be construed as applying to those firms, some partner of which should execute the deed of the third part, and so derive a benefit under the instrument. The execution by Haywood, therefore, is not a release of any partnership debt, but only of the debt due to him individually. But I agree that, even if it were made out that he expressly executed for his partners, we ought to construe that term according to the ordinary meaning of language; and unless there be some context to explain it otherwise, or there be no other joint debt, it ought not to be extended to include a joint-stock banking company, which is not in ordinary parlance a partnership, although certainly the members are in law partners. However, it is not necessary to decide that point, although I quite agree with the Lord Chief Baron in his view of it: but, on the other ground I have referred to, I am clearly of opinion that the rule ought to be discharged.

ALDERSON, B., concurred.

ROLFE, B.—I am of the same opinion. I think this case may be disposed of on this short ground,—that there is nothing on the face of the deed to shew that the parties meant to discharge any debts, except those for the payment of which provision was made by the deed. If they had so said in express terms, the release clearly could apply to no other; and I think it so appears by necessary implication. It is clear that they never intended it to apply to a case where one of the parties of the second part was a partner, whether of an ordinary partnership or of a joint-stock company.

Rule discharged.

———◆———

RAPSON v CUBITT.

The defendant, a builder, was employed by the committee of a club to execute certain alterations at the club-house, including the preparation and fixing of gas-fittings. He made a sub-contract with B., a gas-fitter, to execute this part of the work. In the course of doing it, through B.'s negligence, the gas exploded, and injured the plaintiff:—
Held, that the defendant was not liable in case for this injury.

CASE. The declaration stated, that before and at the time of the committing of the grievances, &c., the plaintiff had been and was the butler, and his wife the housekeeper, of a certain club, called the Clarence Club; that the defendant had been and was retained and employed to execute certain alterations and improvements in the club-house, and, as part thereof, to make certain alterations and improvements in the gas-apparatus and gas-lights therein: and that the defendant made the said last-mentioned alterations with such gross negligence and carelessness, that by means thereof the gas escaped and exploded with such force and violence as greatly to burn, wound, and otherwise injure the plaintiff and his wife. Pleas, first, not guilty; secondly, that the defendant was not retained and employed to execute the said alterations and improvements, and, as part thereof, to make the said alterations in the gas-apparatus and gas-lights, in manner and form, &c. : on which issues were joined.

At the trial before Lord *Abinger,* C. B., at the London sittings after the last Michaelmas term, it appeared that the defendant, a builder, had contracted with the committee of the Clarence Club to make extensive alterations and improvements in the club-house; and, amongst the rest, to prepare and fix the necessary gas-fittings. The defendant made a sub-contract with a person of the name of Bland, a gas-fitter, to execute this latter portion of the work, and it was accordingly performed by Bland. In consequence of the omission of Bland, or some of his servants, to turn off the gas from a pipe on the staircase, a large quantity of it escaped therefrom and exploded, very seriously injuring the plaintiff and his wife. It was objected for the defendant (amongst other things) that he was not liable, in an action of tort, for the negligent acts of the sub-contractor, Bland. The Lord Chief Baron inclined to this opinion, but declined to nonsuit; and in summing up, directed the jury to consider whether the injury occurred through the negligence of the defendant, or of any person employed by him; and the jury found a verdict for the plaintiff, damages £500, leave being reserved to the defendant to move to enter a nonsuit.

Biggs Andrews having obtained a rule nisi accordingly (*a*), citing *Stone* v. *Cartwright* (*b*), and *Bush* v. *Steinman* (*c*),

(*a*) He obtained a rule also for arresting the judgment, on the ground that the plaintiff, not being a member of the club with whom the defendant had contracted, and no public duty being imposed upon the defendant, had no right of action; but on this point the Court gave no judgment. *Langridge* v. *Levy,* 2 M. & W. 519, was referred to.

(*b*) 6 T. R. 411.

(*c*) 1 Bos. & P. 404.

Platt, Saunders, and Sir *J. Bayley* now shewed cause.—
The defendant is responsible for the negligence of Bland,
who was employed by him. The case falls within the principle of *Witte* v. *Hague* (a), where an engineer, who was
employed to construct a steam-engine boiler, was held
liable for the consequences of an explosion produced by
the insufficiency of the materials, the boiler being under
the management of his servants. [*Alderson*, B.—There
the engine was worked by the man who had misconstructed
it. *Parke*, B., referred to *Quarman* v. *Burnett* (b).] In
Randleson v. *Murray* (c), the defendants, who were warehousemen, engaged a master porter to lower a barrel of
flour from their warehouse; and during the process of
lowering it, the barrel fell and injured the plaintiff, owing
to the defectiveness of a rope furnished by the master
porter: the defendants were held to be liable for the injury. That was, equally with the present, the case of a
contract; and shews that the *servant,* for whose acts the
employer is liable, does not mean a menial servant, but
any one who is performing a service for another by whom he
is employed. So, in *Bush* v. *Steinman,* the owner of a
house, who had contracted with a workman for the repair
of it, was held to be responsible for an injury occasioned
by the negligence of a sub-contractor. *Heath*, J., there
says,—" I found my opinion on this single point, that
all the sub-contracting parties were in the employ of the
defendant." So also, in *Matthews* v. *The West London
Waterworks Company* (d), it was held that an action might
be maintained against the company by a person who, in
passing along the street, had been injured by reason of the
negligence of workmen employed by persons who had contracted with the company to lay down water-pipes. [Lord
Abinger, C. B.—There the defendants caused their sub-

(a) 2 Dowl. & R. 33.   P. 239.
(b) 6 M. & W. 499.   (d) 3 Campb. 403.
(c) 8 Ad. & E. 109; 3 N. &

contractor to commit a public nuisance.] In *Bates* v. *Pil-*
ling (a), the general principle was recognized, that any one
who employs another to do an act, in the course of which
he commits a trespass, is equally liable with him.

B. Andrews and *J. Henderson*, contrà, were stopped by
the Court.

Lord ABINGER, C. B.—The rule must be absolute to
enter a nonsuit. The injury was occasioned by the negligence of Bland, who did not stand in the relation of servant to the defendant, but was merely a sub-contractor
with him; and to him the plaintiff must look for redress.
I think the true principle of law, consistent with common
sense, was laid down in the case of *Quarman* v. *Burnett*, in
which all the previous cases on this subject were cited and
considered, and some distinguished and some overruled.
I have always been of the same opinion, and therefore see
no reason for departing from that decision.

PARKE, B.—I am of the same opinion. The plaintiff has
his remedy against Bland, whose negligence was the cause
of the injury; if he attempts to go further, and to fix the
defendant, it can only be on the ground of Bland's being
the servant of the defendant: but then the obvious answer
is, that Bland was only a sub-contractor to do certain of
the works, and that the relation of master and servant did
not subsist between him and the defendant. The true
rule on this subject was laid down by this Court in the
case of *Quarman* v. *Burnett*, which is directly in point, and
cannot be distinguished from the present case. The Court
there said,—" The liability by virtue of the principle of
relation of master and servant must cease when the relation itself ceases to exist; and no other person than the
master of such servant can be liable, on the simple ground

(a) 6 B. & Cr. 38; 9 D. & R. 44.

that the servant is the servant of another, and his act the act of another; consequently, a third person entering into a contract with the master, which does not raise the relation of master and servant at all, is not thereby rendered liable." And again,—" It is true that there are cases— for instance, that of *Bush* v. *Steinman*, *Sly* v. *Edgeley* (a), and others—and perhaps amongst them may be classed the recent case of *Randleson* v. *Murray*—in which the occupiers of land or buildings have been held responsible for acts of others than their servants, done upon, or near, or in respect of their property. But those cases are well distinguished by my brother *Littledale*, in his very able judgment in *Laugher* v. *Pointer* (b). In that case he says, —' The rule of law may be, that in all cases where a man is in possession of fixed property, he must take care that his property is so used and managed that other persons are not injured; and that, whether his property be managed by his own immediate servants, or by contractors or their servants. The injuries done upon land or buildings are in the nature of nuisances, for which the occupier ought to be chargeable, when occasioned by any acts of persons whom he brings upon the premises. The use of the premises is confined by the law to himself, and he should take care not to bring persons there who do any mischief to others.' " The case of *Quarman* v. *Burnett* has been approved of, in its main principles, by the Court of Queen's Bench, in the case of *Milligan* v. *Wedge* (c). There a butcher had employed a licensed drover to drive home a bullock he had bought at Smithfield market, and the drover's boy, by his negligent driving, had allowed the bullock to run into the plaintiff's show-room, where it did considerable damage; it was held that the owner of the bullock was not liable for the damage; and Lord *Denman*

(a) 6 Esp. 6.   (b) 5 B. & Cr. 547; 8 D. & R. 559.
          (c) 12 Ad. & Ell. 737; 4 P. & D. 714.

there said,—" In *Randleson* v. *Murray*, the work to be

done was necessary work done on the premises; the owner
would have been liable if he had used his own servants and
his own tackle; by hiring a porter and his tackle for a
day, he could not exempt himself from that liability."
Lord *Denman* there seems to adopt the distinction which
this Court, in *Quarman* v. *Burnett,* said ought to be taken.
If a man has anything to be done on his own premises, he
must take care to injure no man in the mode of conducting
the work. Whether he injures a passenger in the street,
or a servant employed about his work, seems to make no
difference. I think, therefore, that as Bland was a sub-
contractor, and not the servant of the defendant, the latter
is not liable, and the rule for a nonsuit must be made
absolute.

ALDERSON, B., and ROLFE, B., concurred.

Rule absolute.

IN THE EXCHEQUER CHAMBER.

————

(In Error from the Court of Exchequer).

————

Exch. Chamber,
1842.

April 26.

Sir JOHN TOBIN, Knt. *v.* CRAWFORD and Others.

Goods were shipped at Bombay on board a ship of the plaintiff, a shipowner in Liverpool, and by the bill of lading were to be delivered " unto order, or to his and their assigns, on paying freight for the same." The bill of lading was indorsed by the shipper, and forwarded to defendants, East India agents in London, who indorsed it in blank to C. & Co., their factors in Liverpool. On the arrival of the goods at Liverpool, C. & Co. presented the bill of lading to the plaintiff, and received the goods; the plaintiff debiting C. & Co. with the freight. Afterwards C. & Co. became bankrupt without having paid the freight, whereupon the defendants claimed the goods from them, and took possession of them :—*Held*, on error brought upon the judgment of the Court of Exchequer, that the defendants were not liable to the plaintiff for the unpaid freight; affirming the judgment of the Court below.

A WRIT of error having been brought on the judgment of the Court of Exchequer in this case (*a*), the case was argued in this Court in the vacation after Trinity Term, 1841, by Sir *F. Pollock* for the plaintiff, and by *Erle* for the defendants.

The Court took time to consider, and now the judgment of the Court was delivered by

TINDAL, C. J.—This was an action of indebitatus assumpsit for freight. The defendants pleaded three pleas; 1st, non assumpserunt; 2nd, a special plea, shewing that the bills of lading of the goods had been indorsed to Coupland & Duncan, that Coupland & Duncan received the goods from the plaintiff, (the ship-owner), under those bills of lading, and that the plaintiff debited them in account for the freight; 3rd, a special custom at Liverpool, which being negatived by the jury, that plea is out of the case.

To the 2nd plea the plaintiff replied, that the defendants were the consignees of one of the bills of lading and the first indorsees of the rest, and were the owners of all the

————

(*a*) See the case reported, antè, vol. 5, p. 235.

goods; that the defendants indorsed the bills of lading to Coupland & Duncan, without consideration, as their agents only; that the plaintiff, when he delivered the goods to Coupland & Duncan, was ignorant that they were agents only, and had never received the freight. The defendants rejoined, admitting that, at the time of the indorsement and delivery of the bills of lading, they were the owners of the goods, but that they indorsed the bills of lading to Coupland & Duncan as their agents for sale, but without so describing them, and for the purpose of vesting the legal ownership in them, *without this*, that they the defendants, at the time when the goods were delivered by the plaintiff to Coupland & Duncan, were the owners of the goods in manner and form, &c.

The plaintiff demurred specially. Upon this demurrer the plaintiff had judgment in the Court below.

The cause went to trial upon the issues in fact. And upon the first issue of non assumpserunt, the jury found a special verdict, stating in substance that the defendants were owners of the goods; that they had indorsed the bills of lading to Coupland & Duncan in blank, without consideration, and as their agents; that Coupland & Duncan obtained the goods as indorsees of the bills of lading; that the plaintiff debited them in account for the freight, but did not know that they were agents only; that Coupland & Duncan became bankrupts in about two months; and that the plaintiff had received no freight. Upon this special verdict the Court below has given judgment for the defendants. On the part of the plaintiff, it is now contended, that as Coupland & Duncan were mere agents for the defendants, their receipt of the goods under the bills of lading is in law a receipt by the defendants, and that an implied promise by the defendants to pay the freight arises from that receipt, and that although the plaintiff debited Coupland & Duncan for the freight at first, in ignorance of their being agents, yet that when he discovered that

they were so, he was, as in ordinary cases of agencies, at
liberty to proceed against their principals, the defendants,
it not being shewn by the special verdict, that their situation or right as against Coupland & Duncan had been in
any way affected, or that they had furnished Coupland &
Duncan with money to pay the freight. The defendants,
on the other hand, contend that as the bills of lading made
the goods deliverable to order *or assigns on paying freight
for the same,* the plaintiff should have required the payment
before he delivered the goods, and that not having so done,
he must be taken to have given credit to Coupland & Duncan only, they being the only actual indorsees and holders
of the bills of lading, from whom only the law would imply
a promise to pay the freight arising from the receipt of the
goods under the bills of lading, unless it had been shewn
by the special verdict that Coupland & Duncan had express
authority from the defendants to pledge their credit for the
freight. This was the view of the case adopted by the
Court below in giving their judgment, and we are of opinion
that it is the correct view. None of the cases cited on the
argument are directly in point—for in all of them the
agent had authority to pledge his principal's credit. A
master who sends his servant to buy goods, and gives him
no money to pay, doubtless authorizes him to -pledge his
credit. A person who employs an agent to purchase goods
on the usual terms of any particular trade doubtless gives
the like authority, and so in other instances. But it is by
no means a matter of course that credit should be given
for freight under bills of lading, which make the goods deliverable on *paying freight ;* and it is plain that where such
credit is given, it is on the responsibility of the individuals
actually receiving the goods, or in consequence of the usual
course of dealing between them and the ship-owner. Accordingly, the special verdict finds here that the plaintiff
debited Coupland & Duncan in account with the freight,
shewing that there were transactions between them of

which the defendants are not found to have any knowledge.

And as to the argument, which was so much pressed on the part of the plaintiff, of the great injustice that the defendants should receive their goods without the payment of any freight, if the fact is so, the answer is that it is the voluntary act of the plaintiff, who chose to give credit to Coupland & Duncan, the owners of the goods on the face of the bill of lading; but the fact that the goods came to the defendants' hands without payment of freight by no means appears upon the special verdict. If the plaintiff was indebted to the bankrupts to the amount of the freight, the freight will be set off against the debt, and then the assignees might recover the full amount of the freight against the defendants, subject to any cross demand. But however this may be, we think the plaintiff's demand against the defendants is completely answered at law, by the fact that the bankrupts were not the agents of the defendants in procuring the delivery of the goods on credit for the freight.

Under these circumstances, we are of opinion that the judgment of the Court below ought to be affirmed.

Nothing was said on either side upon the argument, as to the grounds on which judgment was given for the plaintiff on the second plea, and the rejoinder arising out of it; nor was any objection made to that judgment on the part of the defendants, therefore it is not necessary for us to consider that question.

Judgment affirmed.

EXCHEQUER OF PLEAS.

———◆———

Exch. of Pleas,
1842.

April 30.

LEWIN *v.* EDWARDS.

Where the drawer of a bill indorses it in blank, and delivers it to A., who passes it without a fresh indorsement to B., B. cannot maintain an action of debt on it against the drawer.

A declaration in debt contained a count on a bill of exchange by indorsee against drawer, and also counts for money paid, and on an account stated. It appeared from one of the pleas to the first count, that the plaintiff and defendant were not immediate parties to the bill, and the Court therefore held that the plaintiff could not recover on that count: and the plaintiff having at the trial obtained a verdict for the amount of the bill, with general damages, the Court awarded a venire de novo, but refused to arrest the judgment.

DEBT on a bill of exchange, drawn by the defendant on C. H. W., and alleged to have been indorsed by him to the plaintiff; with counts for money paid, and on an account stated. The defendant pleaded to the first count of the declaration, first, that he did not indorse the bill; secondly, that it was not duly presented for payment; thirdly, that he the defendant had not due notice of the presentment and dishonour; and fourthly, that after the making of the bill, the defendant indorsed and delivered it in blank to one Whitehead, who afterwards delivered it, with the defendant's said indorsement thereon, to the plaintiff, without value or consideration, which is the same supposed indorsement by the defendant to the plaintiff in the first count of the declaration mentioned; and that there never was any value or consideration passing from the plaintiff to the defendant in respect of the said bill. Verification.—Plea to the second and third counts, non assumpsit. To the fourth plea the plaintiff replied, that Whitehead did not deliver the bill to him the plaintiff without value or consideration.

At the trial before *Rolfe,* B., at the Middlesex sittings in last Hilary Term, the cause was taken as undefended, and a general verdict was found for the plaintiff for 51*l.* 1*s.*, the amount of the principal and interest on the bill.

In the same term, *W. H. Watson* obtained a rule to shew cause why the judgment should not be arrested, on the ground that an action of debt could not be maintained by the second indorsee of a bill of exchange against the drawer, there being no privity of contract between them.

Ogle now shewed cause.—First, inasmuch as the plaintiff has a right at all events to retain his verdict on the *Exch. of Pleas*,
1842. common counts of the declaration, the judgment ought not to be arrested, but the verdict should have been distributed by an application to a Judge at chambers. The defect resembles that of a misjoinder of counts, where the verdict may be amended by the Judge's notes. Tidd's Pr. 919, (9th ed.) In *Leach* v. *Thomas* (a), that course might have been adopted, but that the plaintiff could not say on which breach he was entitled to recover, and on that ground a venire de novo was awarded. Secondly, the action is maintainable. The principle to be derived from the cases of *Bishop* v. *Young* (b), *Stratton* v. *Hill* (c), *Priddy* v. *Henbrey* (d), and *Watkins* v. *Wake* (e), is, that debt will lie on a bill of exchange, wherever privity exists between the parties to the action. Such privity exists in this case, by reason of the law merchant. The defendant's indorsement being in blank, and there being no intermediate names upon the bill, the plaintiff had no remedy on it against Whitehead, and the first party against whom he could recover is the present defendant. Why is it that the plaintiff is allowed to recover upon the count for money paid, but that a privity of contract exists between him and the defendant by reason of the indorsement? In Bayley on Bills, (5th edit.), it is laid down that "a bill is primâ facie evidence of money lent by the payee to the drawer, and consequently of money had and received by the drawer to the use of the holder, and of money paid by the holder to the use of the drawer." The plaintiff and defendant are in effect immediate parties to the bill. [*Parke*, B.—Supposing for the present that you cannot recover on the first count, how can you get rid of the difficulty arising from the nominal damages being assessed generally? You cannot get your costs without the da-

LEWIN
v.
EDWARDS.

(a) 2 M. & W. 427.

(b) 2 Bos. & P. 78.

(c) 3 Price, 253.

(d) 1 B. & C. 674; 3 D. & R. 165.

(e) 7 M. & W. 488.

mages, which are general; and if you release the damages, you lose your costs, by the Statute of Gloucester. Lord *Abinger,* C. B.—There is in this case no evidence but the bill; therefore, if the verdict were set right by the Judge's notes, it would be for the plaintiff only on the count upon the bill; and if that be bad, must not the judgment be arrested? If the plaintiff had gone down to trial upon the count for money paid only, he would have been nonsuited; the bill would be no evidence on that count, as between these parties.] Mr. Justice *Bayley* lays it down generally that the bill is evidence of money paid by the holder to the use of the drawer. [*Parke*, B.—That must surely mean where the bill has been dishonoured and taken up by the plaintiff. But at all events, if the bill be evidence on the count for money paid, the plaintiff must sue on that count and no other; not upon the bill, except against an immediate party; and here, although primâ facie the declaration presents a good cause of action, yet the plea shews that the defendant was not an immediate party.]

W. H. Watson, contrà.—Assuming that the plaintiff is not entitled to recover upon the bill, the motion is properly made for an arrest of judgment. Upon this record, the plaintiff recovers the entirety of his debt, and also damages for the detention of that whole debt; that the damages are nominal can make no difference in the consideration of the pleadings. They are not always so in debt; as in debt on a mortgage deed, where interest after the day of payment is recoverable as damages. Then the damages being general, and one of the three counts of the declaration being answered, the judgment must be arrested.—[*Parke*, B.—The question is, whether a venire de novo ought not to be awarded. In case of a defective count or breach, the course is to award a venire de novo; *Leach* v. *Thomas*; is there any difference where one count is answered?] The last case on this subject is that of

Corner v. *Shew* (a), where there was a *misjoinder* of counts, the Court arrested the judgment; and this, looking at the whole record, is substantially the same case; for the plea shews that these counts have been misjoined. This is not a case for a venire de novo, there having been no fault in the jury: and if it were awarded, the issues on the first count must be tried again, as well as on the other counts. —[*Parke*, B. On a new trial, the plaintiff may sever the damages, and assess them separately on the 2nd and 3rd counts]. But the jury must also find the debt, because there are express issues upon it.—On the other point, as to the maintenance of the action, he was stopped by the Court.

Lord ABINGER, C. B.—I think the judgment in this case cannot be sustained. Here is a general verdict for the plaintiff, for the debt, and also for the damages arising from the detention of the debt. Then the first count is answered on the record, because the contract transferred by the delivery of the bill to the plaintiff, being only the contract *on the bill*, he cannot sue this defendant, with whom he has no privity of contract, in an action of debt; and therefore on that count no judgment can be entered. The rule will be absolute for a venire de novo.

PARKE, B.—I am of the same opinion. On the face of the declaration there appears a good cause of action in debt, because the plaintiff and defendant appear to be immediate parties to the bill; but when the whole of the case is disclosed on the record, no such contract appears as that which is set forth in the declaration, because the bill having been indorsed in blank by the defendant, and transferred by delivery to a third person, and by him handed over to the plaintiff, no privity of contract exists between

(a) 3 M. & W. 350.

the plaintiff and the defendant; therefore, unless the holder of a banker's cheque can sue the maker of it in debt, the present plaintiff cannot recover; but for that there is no authority. In this case, as in that, there is no privity of contract, and therefore an action of debt cannot be maintained. That being so, and there having been a general assessment of damages on the whole declaration, the question is, can we deal with the case otherwise than by arresting the judgment? Now the plaintiff is not entitled to costs otherwise than by virtue of the damages; and we cannot take notice, with reference to this question, that they are merely nominal. The judgment, therefore, cannot stand; and the only remaining question is, whether we ought to arrest the judgment, or to award a venire de novo. And I think the case is not distinguishable from that of an ordinary assessment of damages on a bad and also on a good count or breach, and therefore that, according to the authority of *Leach* v. *Thomas*, which has been confirmed by the Court of Common Pleas in *Gould* v. *Oliver* (a), a venire de novo ought to be awarded.

ALDERSON, B., and ROLFE, B., concurred.

Venire de novo awarded.

(a) 2 Scott, N. R. 241; 2 Man. & Gr. 208.

Exch. of Pleas,
1842.

HOWARD *v.* WILLIAMS.

May 3.

DEBT for goods sold, and on an account stated. Plea, nunquam indebitatus. The particulars of demand were for goods supplied by the plaintiff, who was an innkeeper, to the defendant, in the year 1836. At the trial of the cause, at Monmouth, before the under-sheriff of Monmouthshire, it was proved that in the year 1836 a bill had been delivered by the plaintiff to the defendant's wife, by whom the debt was contracted. Notice to produce this bill was given to the defendant's attorney at Newport, (twenty miles from Monmouth), where both he and the defendant lived, at eight o'clock in the evening of the day before the trial. The attorney had to set off from Newport to Monmouth between six and seven o'clock the next morning, in order to attend the trial of the cause. It was objected for the defendant, that this notice was not given in sufficient time to let in secondary evidence of the account. The under-sheriff overruled the objection, and the plaintiff's books, from which the account had been made out, were produced in evidence, and the plaintiff had a verdict for 7*l.* 3*s.*; the jury stating their opinion that the defendant had no knowledge of the debt having been contracted.

In the present term, *Gray* obtained a rule nisi for a new trial, on the ground that the evidence had been improperly admitted; and produced affidavits, stating that the attorney never had the account, and that at the time of the service of the notice, the defendant was not at home, and did not come home until twelve o'clock at night. He cited *Byrne* v. *Harvey* (a).

Whateley now shewed cause.—The notice to produce was

A notice to produce was served on the defendant's attorney at his residence, twenty miles from the place of trial, at eight p. m. on the night before the trial. The defendant resided in the same town with the attorney, but was not at home on that evening until twelve o'clock: *Held*, too late.

(a) 2 M. & Rob. 89.

c c c 2

sufficient in this case. If the account was in existence, it might have then, by the exercise of reasonable diligence, been found and produced on the trial. Here the defendant and his attorney were both living near each other in the same town, and there was ample time, after the receipt of the notice, for the latter to have communicated with his client, and obtained the document. There is no general rule of law which limits any particular *time* for the service of a notice to produce; the only question in each case is, whether the party had, under all the circumstances of the case, reasonable notice, so as to enable him to produce the document at the trial.

Gray, contrà, was not called on.

Lord ABINGER, C. B.—The sole question is, whether the service of this notice to produce was sufficient; and we think it was not. It was served upon the attorney, at eight o'clock at night, he having to leave at an early hour the next morning, in order to attend the trial of the cause. A party is not bound to abstain from his necessary business, and always to be at home ready to receive notices: and if he were, he is not bound at such a time of the night to make a search for papers. It is not necessary to lay down any general rule, but we think that in the circumstances of this case the notice was insufficient. It follows that no evidence of the contents of the document was admissible; and the rule for a new trial must therefore be made absolute.

PARKE, B., ALDERSON, B., and ROLFE, B., concurred.

Rule absolute.

Exch. of Pleas,
1842.

TURQUAND and Another, Assignees, &c., *v.* HAWTREY and Another.

May 3.

TROVER by the assignees of one Taylor, a bankrupt. Lord *Denman*, C. J., had allowed the defendant to plead the following amongst other pleas : first, a traverse of the plaintiff's property as assignees : secondly, that, after Taylor became bankrupt, and before the issuing of the fiat, the plaintiffs, as his assignees, by reason of the relation of their title to the time of his bankruptcy, although not then appointed assignees, were the owners of and entitled to the possession of the goods ; that Taylor,. subject only to the said title of the plaintiffs as assignees, was possessed of the goods, and that the defendants took the goods under an execution bonâ fide executed and levied against him, without notice of any prior act of bankruptcy.

Erle having obtained a rule to shew cause why one or the other of these pleas should not be struck out,

Thesiger now shewed cause.—There is a preliminary objection which is fatal to this application : namely, that no motion has been made to set aside the judge's order allowing the pleas. *Howen* v. *Carr* (a) is precisely in point to shew that that ought to have the form of the application to the Court. There an order to plead several matters had been obtained, and consented to by the plaintiff : and it was held by this Court, on a motion to strike out one of the pleas, that the plaintiff was concluded by the consent, and that the application should have been to set aside the order. In *Wright* v. *Elliot* (b), where a judge at chambers

A rule to strike out pleas allowed by a judge at chambers will not be entertained by the Court; the rule should be to set aside the judge's order.

To an action of trover by assignees of a bankrupt, the defendant pleaded, first, a traverse of the plaintiff's property as assignees; secondly, that after the bankruptcy, and before the fiat, the plaintiffs, as assignees, by reason of the relation of their title to the time of the bankruptcy, although not then appointed, were the owners of and entitled to the possession of the goods; that the bankrupt, subject only to their said title as assignees, was possessed of the goods, and that the defendants took them under an execu-

tion bonâ fide executed and levied against him without any notice of any prior act of bankruptcy. Semble, per Parke, B., that the latter plea amounted only to an argumentative traverse of the possession of the plaintiff's assignees, and therefore that the two pleas could not be pleaded together.

(a) 5 Dowl. P. C. 305.   (b) 5 Ad. & Ell. 818.

had refused to discharge a defendant on the ground of an irregularity in the affidavit of debt, and an application for the same purpose was afterwards made to the Court, Lord *Denman*, C. J., appears to have thought that the motion ought, in point of form, to be to discharge the judge's order. And in the case of *The South Eastern Railway Company* v. *Sprot* (a), it was expressly laid down by the Court, that where a motion is made to strike out pleas pleaded by a judge's order or rule of Court, the motion ought to be to rescind the rule or order, and not to strike out the pleas. [*Parke*, B.—There has been a recent decision on this subject, after conference among the judges (b)]. That was as to the form of a rule to *add* pleas to those already pleaded, in which case it was held not to be necessary that the rule should refer to the judge's order to plead several matters.

Lord ABINGER, C. B.—I thought at first that the Court had the power of striking out pleas, and that the new rules made no difference except in giving the same power to a judge; but it appears from the decision in this Court, which has been cited, that we have no such original power. The rule must be amended and re-served.

PARKE, B.—The case of *Smith* v. *Goldsworthy* (b) has established that a rule to *add* pleas need not refer to the judge's order; but the Masters of the Court of Queen's Bench, to whom I have sent for information on the point, do not think that rule applies to a motion to strike out pleas which have been allowed by a judge. The party must first go before a judge, and then the motion comes by way of appeal from his order.

Thesiger then waived this objection, and contended that

(a) 11 Ad. & Ell. 167; 3 P. & D. 110.   (b) *Smith* v. *Goldsworthy*, 2 G. & D. 189.

the two pleas contained distinct matters of defence. The
latter plea raises the question, what is the effect of the
stat. 2 & 3 Vict. c. 29, on the title of the assignees by relation to the act of bankruptcy? The question is, whether
the effect of the statute is altogether to destroy the title by
relation in the cases to which it applies, or to leave it as
before, but to render valid all intermediate executions, &c.,
without notice of an act of bankruptcy. [*Parke*, B.—I do
not well see how the execution can be rendered valid, except by defeating the relation in cases of bonâ fide executions without notice. If that be so, the latter of these
pleas is only an argumentative traverse of the plaintiff's
possession. Lord *Abinger*, C. B.—That is probably the
true construction of the act, but we shall not decide the
point on motion.]

PER CURIAM.—The plaintiff may demur specially to
the plea, on the ground that it is only an argumentative
traverse of the possession, and so may have the opinion of
the Court upon the point, and if necessary, that of a Court
of error also. This rule must, however, be discharged, and
with costs, as it is an appeal from the decision of a judge.

Rule discharged, with costs.

———◆———

BRISTOWE v. NEEDHAM.

DEBT for money lent, and on an account stated. Plea,
nunquam indebitatus. At the trial before Lord *Abinger*,
C. B., at the Middlesex sittings after Hilary Term, it appeared that the plaintiff, who was a trustee for the defen-

May 3.

Money advanced upon a contract to repay it on demand, or to execute a mortgage, may, after refusal to execute a mortgage, be recovered back under a count for money lent.

dant under his father's will, had at four different times advanced to him sums out of the trust-monies, amounting in the whole to £22,350, and had received from him the following memorandum :—

　　　　　　　　　　　" London, Nov. 28, 1841.

" Memorandum, that I have, at three sundry times, to this day, received of Samuel Ellis Bristowe, Esq., the sole trustee of my fortune under my late father's will, the sum of £15,000, which I promise, on demand, to repay, or to execute a mortgage on my houses, Nos. 70 and 71, Jermyn-street, as soon as it can be completed, with such further security as may be necessary.

　　　　　　　　　　　" F. H. W. Needham."

The defendant having refused, on demand made, to execute the mortgage, this action was brought. It was contended for the defendant, that the plaintiff could not recover on the count for money lent, but ought to have declared specially upon the memorandum, as upon an alternative contract. The Lord Chief Baron overruled the objection, and a verdict was found for the plaintiff.

In the present term, *Platt* obtained a rule nisi for a new trial, on the ground of misdirection, against which

Kelly and *Whitehurst* now shewed cause.—The count for money lent is maintainable. The option in this case lay with the plaintiff, not with the defendant: and as soon as the defendant made default in executing the mortgage, the right of action for money lent accrued. But even supposing the option to repay the money, or secure it by mortgage, was with the defendant, still, as he has refused to exercise that option, his right of election is now gone. In Com. Dig., Election, (A. 2), it is said, " A man by his wrong or default may lose his election, and give it to the feoffee, &c. As if a man grants so much wood, to be taken by assignment, if the grantor does not assign at the day, the grantee may take it in what part of the wood he pleases, without assignment :" citing 1 Roll. 725, b. 30. Therefore, at the time of action brought, the defendant was indebted absolutely to the plaintiff in so much money to be paid on request, and the count for money lent is sufficient.

Platt and *Bramwell,* contrà.—The defendant had, by the terms of the memorandum, the option of paying the money or executing a mortgage. The doctrine is, that the party who is to do the first act has the election. The law is stated thus in Com. Dig., Election, (A. 2) :—"If a man grants a rent or a robe, at such a feast, and does not deliver it at the day, the grantee may demand which he pleases: Co. Litt. 145. a." The general form of action deprives the defendant of this election. But in whomsoever the option was, this is an alternative contract, and ought to have been specially declared upon as such: *Penny* v. *Porter (a), Tate* v. *Wellings (b)*. If the option was in the plaintiff, he exercised it by requiring the execution of a mortgage; and after the lapse of a reasonable time, he might have declared on the contract as an alternative one, and claimed damages for the non-execution of the mortgage; but he could not at the same time have also a right of action for money to be paid on request; otherwise he might bring one action declaring his option to have been exercised by the demand of a mortgage, and another for the money, and the judgment in the one could not be pleaded in answer to the other. If a party claims under a contract, he must state it according to its terms.

Lord ABINGER, C. B.—I think the rule must be discharged. It appears to me that this is not an alternative contract, but that it is substantially the case of money lent, to be secured by a mortgage, or to be repaid on demand, unless a mortgage were given. It is a contract subject to

(a) 2 East, 2.   (b) 3 T. R. 531.

a condition to execute a mortgage; and when the condition is not complied with by the party for whose benefit it is introduced, it becomes an absolute contract to repay the money on demand. It is like a contract for the sale of goods, to be paid for in a particular manner, as by a bill of exchange in three months; if the bill be not given within that time, an implied assumpsit arises to pay for them on request, and the seller may declare for goods sold, and need not state that condition of the contract. So here, this is in the nature of a condition, to execute a mortgage, which not being fulfilled, it becomes a debt payable on demand. The plaintiff in effect declares to the defendant, that if a mortgage be executed, he will not ask for the money instanter.

ALDERSON, B.—I am of the same opinion. The whole fallacy consists in treating this as an alternative contract: it is not an alternative contract, but a contract to pay on demand, unless the defendant satisfies the plaintiff by giving a mortgage: when he fails to do so, he must pay on demand.

ROLFE, B.—I entirely concur. It clearly must be so, from the very nature of a mortgage. It is obvious that the defendant intends to hold himself liable for the payment of the money at any period of time, unless he performs the condition of giving security by mortgage.

Rule discharged.

ASSUMPSIT for money had and received, and on an account stated. Plea, non assumpsit. At the trial before Lord *Abinger*, C.B., at the Middlesex Sittings after Hilary Term, it appeared that the action was brought under the following circumstances. The plaintiff was the acceptor of a bill of exchange drawn upon him by a person of the name of Butler; and on the day when the bill fell due, he sent his son to the defendant, who represented himself to be the holder of the bill, with directions to pay the defendant the amount, and bring back the bill. The son accordingly paid the amount of the bill to the defendant, who gave him a receipt for the money, but said he could not give up the bill. The son went back to the plaintiff and informed him of this, and the plaintiff sent him again to the defendant, to bring back the bill or the money; but he returned without either. Afterwards, on the same day, the defendant sent to the plaintiff a paper in the following terms:—

"I hereby acknowledge the receipt of Mr. Strong of £17, for a bill drawn by Butler on Mr. Alexander, which I believe to have been lost at my house.

"L. M. Goddard, surgeon,

"June 16, 1841. St. John's Road.

"Further, I undertake to bear Mr. Alexander harmless for the above amount, should the bill be again presented.

"June 16, 1841. L. M. G."

The plaintiff retained this guarantee, but brought the present action. It was contended for the defendant, that the

The plaintiff, the acceptor of a bill of exchange, on the day it fell due, sent a person to the defendant, who held it, to pay the amount of the bill and bring it back. The defendant received the money and gave a receipt for it, but said he could not give up the bill. The plaintiff being informed of this, sent again to the defendant to demand the bill or the money, but he did not give up either. Afterwards, on the same day, the defendant sent to the plaintiff a paper signed by one G., acknowledging the receipt from the defendant of the amount of the bill, and undertaking to bear the plaintiff harmless for the amount, if the bill, which he stated to have been lost, should be presented. The plaintiff kept this guarantee, but nevertheless sued the defendant for money had and received:—*Held*, that his right of action vested on the defendant's refusal to repay the money or give up the bill; and therefore that the receipt by the plaintiff of G.'s guarantee was in the nature of accord and satisfaction, and was no defence to the action, unless specially pleaded.

receipt of the guarantee by the plaintiff disentitled him from recovering as for money had and received, and that this defence was open under the plea of non assumpsit; and the Lord Chief Baron being of that opinion, directed a nonsuit, reserving leave to the plaintiff to move to enter a verdict for £17.

Jervis having obtained a rule accordingly,

Platt and *Busby* now shewed cause.—The receipt of Goddard's guarantee by the plaintiff was not, as will be contended on the other side, in the nature of an accord and satisfaction, but was evidence to explain the nature of the payment which had been made by the plaintiff, and to shew that no right of action arose out of it.   The plaintiff, by his agent, pays the money in satisfaction of the bill, and that act of the agent is adopted by the plaintiff by the receipt of the guarantee.   Suppose the parties had all met, and immediately after the son had paid the money and taken the receipt, Goddard had handed over this document to him, and he had given it to the plaintiff; could this action have been afterwards maintained?   This is substantially the same case; it was all one continuing transaction, which was not completed until the receipt of the guarantee by the plaintiff.—They referred to *Hansard* v. *Robinson* (a), and *Wilson* v. *Ray* (b).

Jervis (C. *Jones* with him), contrà.—This defence clearly ought, if available at all, to have been specially pleaded. It is in effect admitted on the other side, that a right of action had vested in the plaintiff, on the re-demand of the money by him; but it is said that that vested right of action was got rid of by the subsequent giving of an in-

(a) 7 B. & Cr. 90; 9 D. & R. 860.
(b) 10 A. & E. 82; 2 P. & D. 253.

demnity. If that be so, it is a defence in the nature of *Exch. of Pleas,* accord and satisfaction, and should have been specially pleaded. It is clear that the act of the son, in taking the receipt instead of having the bill delivered up, was wholly unauthorized, and it was immediately repudiated by the plaintiff, who sent him back to demand the money.—He was then stopped by the Court.

Exch. of Pleas,
1842.

ALEXANDER
v.
STRONG.

Lord ABINGER, C. B.—I am sorry to say that I am now satisfied the nonsuit was wrong. The right of action having vested in the plaintiff, he afterwards takes Goddard's indemnity: that was in the nature of accord and satisfaction for his claim upon the defendant for not repaying the money or delivering up the bill. It ought therefore to have been specially pleaded.

ALDERSON, B.—I am of the same opinion. The plaintiff paid this money on the supposition that he was to have back the bill; then the son takes the receipt without any authority; he is then sent back for the money or the bill, and the defendant refuses to give him either. At that time a right of action vested in the plaintiff. The plaintiff then agrees, in effect, that he will give up that right of action on receiving an indemnity from Goddard, and the indemnity is accordingly given. That is in the nature of accord and satisfaction, and ought to have been specially pleaded.

ROLFE, B., concurred.

Rule absolute.

Exch. of Pleas,
1842.

JONES *v.* GOODAY.

April 27.

By a local act (6Geo.4, c. lxx), certain commissioners were empowered to cause any "present or future sewers, ditches, drains, &c. to be opened, enlarged, altered, or cleansed:" and it was enacted, that in case any action should be brought against any person for any thing done in pursuance of the act, or in relation to the matters therein contained, the plaintiff should not recover in any such action, if tender of amends should have been made to him, &c. or his attorney, by or on behalf of the defendant, &c. before such action brought; and in case no such tender should be made, that it should be lawful for the defendant, by leave of the Court, to pay money into Court; and if the matter should appear to have been done in pursuance and under the authority of the act, or after sufficient satisfaction made or tendered as aforesaid, then that the jury should find for the defendant.

TRESPASS for breaking and entering the plaintiff's close, and digging up and carrying away his soil. Plea—Not guilty (by statute). The cause was tried before *Tindal,* C. J., at the Suffolk Spring Assizes for 1841, when a verdict was found for the plaintiff, damages £5, subject to the opinion of the Court on the following case.

The plaintiff was the owner and occupier of Friar's Meadow, situate in the borough of Sudbury, and the trespass complained of was a taking by the defendant of part of the plaintiff's land, for the purpose of widening a ditch and drain adjoining Friar's Meadow. An act of Parliament (local and personal) passed in the 6th Geo. 4, (c. lxx), for paving, cleansing, improving, &c. the borough of Sudbury, under which the defendant and plaintiff were and still are commissioners. In April, 1840, at a meeting of the commissioners, it was resolved to appoint certain persons as a committee, to inspect the ditch in question, with a view to widen and deepen it, and to report to the commissioners. At a meeting of the commissioners, at which the plaintiff and defendant were present, the commit-

The commissioners, of whom the defendant was one, appointed a committee to inspect a certain ditch, with a view to widening the same, and to report thereon. The committee having reported thereon in favour of widening the ditch, the commissioners appointed a second committee, of whom the defendant was one, to confer with a surveyor respecting the work, with power to two of them to act. The defendant being afterwards told by the clerk to the commissioners that he might proceed without further instructions from the commissioners, took the plaintiff's land for the purpose of widening the drain, without having given him notice or obtained his consent. The land was taken for the bonâ fide purpose of widening the drain. The defendant, before action, tendered £10 as amends, which the plaintiff refused to accept; but no tender was pleaded, nor was the amount paid into Court. The jury found the trespass, and that the damage amounted to £5:—*Held,* first, that although neither the defendant nor the commissioners were authorised to take plaintiff's land without his consent in writing, yet the defendant was entitled to the protection of the act.

Secondly, that the defendant was not bound to plead the tender, or pay the amount tendered into Court.

tee recommended the widening and deepening of the ditch. The commissioners thereupon ordered an estimate to be obtained, and a committee of four to be appointed, of whom the defendant was one, to confer with the surveyor, and that two of them should be empowered to act. No further authority was given by the commissioners in respect of the work; no application was made by the commissioners to the plaintiff to treat for his land, and no notice given to him that his land would be required. The plaintiff's land was not within the schedule of the act of Parliament. A report having been made to the commissioners, the clerk told the defendant and the other commissioner that they might proceed without further instructions from the commissioners. The defendant accordingly caused the ditch in question to be deepened and widened, and in so doing cut into and carried away part of the plaintiff's soil. The defendant, after notice of action, tendered as amends the sum of £10, which was refused by the plaintiff, but the tender was not pleaded, nor was the amount paid into Court. The jury found specially that a trespass had been committed by the defendant, and that the damages done to the plaintiff's land amounted to £5; that the alteration was necessary for the more effectual carrying off the water and filth from the highways of the borough; and that such alteration was really and bonâ fide made for that purpose.

The questions for the opinion of the Court were, first, whether the defendant or the commissioners had any right to take the plaintiff's land for the purpose of widening the ditch in question without his consent, in writing; secondly, whether the defendant was entitled to the protection of the act; thirdly, whether the defendant could avail himself of the tender of £10, not having pleaded the same, or paid the amount into Court. The act of Parliament, 6 Geo. 4, c. lxx, was to be taken as forming part of the case, and the Court was to determine for which party the

Exch. of Pleas,
1842.

JONES
v.
GOODAY.

verdict was to be entered ; and if for the plaintiff, then for what sum (a).

Kelly, for the plaintiff.—No doubt the commissioners had power, under the 20th section, to widen the drains in question, and to go upon the adjoining land for that pur-

(a) The sections of the act material to the case are as follows : — By section 20, the commissioners, of whom five were to be present at each meeting, were authorized to "cause any of the present or future sewers, gutters, or watercourses to be stopped up, or otherwise opened, enlarged, altered, or cleansed, or the form or course thereof to be altered, turned, varied, changed, or diverted."

By another section of the act, the commissioners were authorized to take certain scheduled lands within five years after the passing of the act ; after which they could take the land only with the consent of the owners.

By section 113, it was enacted, "that no plaintiff shall recover in any action to be commenced against any person for any thing done in pursuance of this act, unless notice in writing shall be given to the defendant or defendants, twenty-eight days before such action shall be commenced, &c. &c. Nor shall the plaintiff or plaintiffs recover in any such action, if tender of amends shall have been made to him, her, or them, or to his, her, or their attorney, by or on behalf of the defendant or defendants, before such action brought ; *and in case no such tender shall be made,* it shall be lawful for the defendant or defendants, in any such action, by leave of the Court, at any time before issue joined, to pay into Court such sum of money as he, she, or they shall think proper, whereupon such proceedings, order, and judgment shall be made and given in and by such Court, as in other actions where the defendant is allowed to pay money into Court."

By section 114, it was enacted, that "no action or suit shall be brought against any person or persons for any thing done in pursuance of this act, or in relation to the matters therein contained, after three calendar months from the fact committed ; and the defendant or defendants in every such action or suit shall and may at his or their election plead specially, or the general issue, and give this act, or the special matter, in evidence at any trial, and that the same was done in pursuance of and under the authority of this act ; and if the same shall appear to have been so done, or if such action or suit shall have been brought before the expiration of twenty-eight days next after such notice shall have been given as aforesaid, or after sufficient satisfaction made or tendered as aforesaid, or, &c., then and in any of the said cases, the jury shall find a verdict for the defendant or defendants."

pose, but they had no power to take the plaintiff's or any other person's lands for that purpose, without giving notice, and obtaining his consent. They had no authority under the act to deprive him of the possession of it without such notice; and the plaintiff might have maintained ejectment against them to recover possession of the land they so took. If the commissioners thought proper to take the plaintiff's land for the purpose of widening the drains, they should have given him notice in writing, and asked him to give his consent, and if he refused, they should have resorted to the compulsory proceedings under the act.

Secondly, the defendant is not within the protection of the act. Whatever might have been the case if this act had been done by the commissioners, the defendant, who in doing it was not acting as a commissioner, had no authority to widen the ditch; he was a mere stranger, not authorized to do any act at all. Where a person is authorized to do the act, but in doing it goes beyond his authority, he is within the protection of such a clause as this; but where he has no authority to do the act at all, he is not protected. Thus, where a magistrate, who has an authority to commit, under a summary jurisdiction, for six months, commits for twelve months, he is within the protection, because he has merely exceeded his jurisdiction. There are several cases to shew that the party's bonâ fide believing himself to have authority to do the act, and acting on that belief, is not sufficient to bring him within the protection of an act of Parliament. In *Cook* v. *Leonard* (a), the protection to which a party was entitled, under an act of this description, was held not to depend upon bona fides, but upon the question whether he had reasonable ground for supposing that the thing done by him was done in execution or under the authority of the act. *Bayley*, J., there says: "Where a statute gives protection to persons acting in execution or

Each. of Pleas, 1842.

JONES
v.
GOODAY.

(a) 6 B. & C. 351; 9 D. & R. 339.

in pursuance of it, all persons acting under its provisions are entitled to that protection, although they exceed their authority by so doing. There must, however, be some limits to that rule, and it seems to me that there are cases which warrant this distinction. If an officer does any act, part of which is, and part of which is not, authorised by the statute; or if a magistrate act in a case which his general character authorizes him to do, the mere excess of authority in either case does not deprive the officer or magistrate of that protection which is conferred upon those who act in execution of it; but where there is a total absence of authority to do any part of that which has been done, the party doing the act is not entitled to that protection." The same principle was recognised in *Hopkins* v. *Crowe* (a). Here the defendant did an act which no one authorized him to do; and although he was in fact a commissioner, it was not an act done under the authority of the commissioners, but altogether without authority, even for the purpose of entering upon the lands, and he is therefore not within the protection of the statute.

Thirdly, although the defendant tendered the sum of £10 before action brought, he has not pleaded it, nor brought it into Court, which he ought to have done. It was essentially necessary, if he had pleaded it, to have brought the money into Court, in order to give the plaintiff an opportunity of taking it out if he chose to do so. The 114th section may relieve the defendant from the necessity of pleading it specially, but he must pay the money into Court under the general issue. If he is not bound to do so, the plaintiff may altogether lose the benefit of the money tendered, whatever be the result of the action. If it were not for that clause, the defendant must have pleaded it, and he ought therefore to have paid the money into Court, because the legislature only intended to relieve him from the necessity of pleading it.

(a) 4 Ad. & Ell. 774.

Byles, contrà, was stopped by the Court.

Lord ABINGER, C. B.—I am of opinion that this case is clearly within the provisions of this act of Parliament, and that the defendant is entitled to the verdict. There are two points of view in which cases of this class may be looked at; one, as against a party who has been authorized to proceed, and the other, as in the case of an act done which was not authorized by the act of Parliament at all. Those are two very different cases, and should not be confounded together. Suppose the case of an act authorized by the act of Parliament to be done, but that the party who performs the act is not invested with the exact authority in the form which the act of Parliament prescribes; for example, suppose the commissioners were bound to make all their orders in writing, but instead of doing so they make an order verbally, and direct their clerk to communicate it to the defendant, who is one of their own body, and to authorize him to proceed;—that would be a case, according to Mr. *Kelly's* argument, in which the action would have been maintainable; and so doubtless it would be, strictly speaking, because he was not authorized modo et formâ as the act required; but Mr. *Kelly* must go the length of saying, that though proceeding strictly in pursuance of the act, in performing the act authorized to be done, yet because he was not the person authorized to do it, he would be without protection, even if he entertained a bonâ fide supposition that he was acting in pursuance of the act of Parliament, and that he had due authority. Another point of view is, supposing the act of Parliament itself in no respect authorized the doing of the act,—as if it were the proceeding to make a bridge, which is not mentioned in the act at all:—in such case, a party has no authority to do the act himself, or to authorize others to do it; nevertheless, if there were a case where the commissioners, acting bonâ fide on a doubt as to the meaning of the words of the act of Parliament, did such an act, I am far from supposing that they might not have a defence under this clause. Now here is a case where it is admitted that the commissioners are authorized under the act of Parliament, only they have not used their authority modo et formâ; they are authorized by the clause which has been read, " to enlarge, alter, and cleanse the sewers, drains, &c." Can it be said that those are words that are not affected by, or that these powers have no relation to, the clause "that no action or suit shall be brought against any person or persons for anything done in pursuance of this act, or in relation to the matters herein contained?" Who can doubt that widening of sewers is a thing relating to the matters therein contained? This is an action for doing a thing in respect of the matters therein contained, though not executed modo et formâ, and therefore the plaintiff is entitled, strictly speaking, to an action of trespass, which can be maintained against the doer of the act, unless a tender is made before the action is brought. Here the jury have found that satisfaction was tendered before the action was brought; and the commissioners, and the defendant, were acting under the bonâ fide supposition, and no other, that the latter was performing an act in relation to the matters therein contained. It seems to me, therefore, that in any view of the case this clause affords a complete protection, the jury having found the satisfaction and tender to have been made. I do not think it necessary to consider whether an ejectment could be maintained by the plaintiff; it will be time enough to determine that question when such an action is brought. Here the plaintiff has brought an action of trespass for that which, although authorized to be done, has not been done in the exact form which it ought to have been, but that trespass has been compensated by the tender of amends.

The last point is this, whether the tender of amends should have been pleaded, or the money paid into Court. I think not. Here tender of amends was made, but the plaintiff chooses to renounce it, and prefers the chance of what he may gain by a verdict; it turns out that he has received a sufficient tender of amends, and the verdict is against him. It is not the case, therefore, where a party is required to pay money into Court, or to plead a tender.

PARKE, B.—In this case several questions are submitted for the opinion of the Court. I am of opinion that these questions are all to be answered so as to entitle the defendant to our judgment.

The first question is, whether the commissioners have any right to take this land without the consent of the owner in writing. I am of opinion that neither the defendant nor the commissioners had any power to take or use the land without the owner's consent in writing, because it is land not mentioned in the schedule, and all other land is not to be taken without the consent of the owner. The next question is, whether the defendant is entitled to protection for this act that he has done; and I am clearly of opinion that he is. In the first place, he is a person within the meaning of the protecting clause, which extends to all the commissioners, and all those who have the authority of the commissioners for acting : now he was a commissioner himself. And it is clear that he bonâ fide supposed he was acting in pursuance of the act, and that he had the authority of the commissioners, as he appealed to their clerk, and the clerk said he was to go on. It is very true that even five of the commissioners had no power to take land under these circumstances; but if they acted upon the bonâ fide supposition that they had authority to do so, they would be protected under the clause in question. If the rule laid down in *Cook* v. *Leonard* were strictly interpreted and acted upon, it might be the occasion of much mischief. Clauses of this nature were meant for the protection of honest persons, who bonâ fide meant to discharge their duty. The case is distinguishable from *Hopkins* v. *Crowe,* for there two persons only were authorized to act, or to do any thing under the act of Parliament, the constable, and the owner of the animal, and the defendant there was neither the one nor the other. In this case the clause was clearly intended to benefit the commissioners, who act under a bonâ fide belief that they have authority for what they are doing. The next question it is not strictly necessary to give an opinion upon, because I think the defendant is entitled to our judgment on these two grounds. That question, as to the tender, depends on the wording of that clause of the act of Parliament which gives the power of pleading the general issue. The words are—" and the defendant or defendants in every such action or suit shall or may, at his or their election, plead specially or the general issue, and give this act and the special matter in evidence at any trial, and that the same was done in pursuance of and under the authority of this act." If the clause had stopped there, and had not proceeded to allow the tender of amends, there might have been a question; but it goes on—" and if the same shall appear to have been so done, or if such action or suit shall have been brought before the expiration of twenty-eight days next after such notice shall have been given as aforesaid, or after sufficient satisfaction made and tendered as aforesaid, or after the time limited for bringing the same, or shall be brought in any other county or place than as aforesaid, then and in any of the said cases the jury shall find a verdict for the defendant or defendants." What does that mean? It clearly means that they shall find a verdict for the defendant *upon that plea*, whether it be a special plea or the general issue. It is said this is a great hardship upon the plaintiff, because in that case he loses the sum of money tendered as amends; but the sum tendered is not a *debt*; it is a sort of defence which the law gives to a man for doing inadvertently an improper act: the law allows him to do justice by tendering amends, and if the plaintiff refuses the sum offered at the time it is tendered, he has no claim to call upon the de-

fendant to pay it into court. There is a case referred to
in Bacon's Abridgment, tit. "Tender," pl. 6, of *Lawrence* v.
Cox, where it was held that it was not necessary for a party
who *pleads* a tender of amends, to pay the money into court.
That is a precedent for pursuing the course the defendant
has taken here; indeed, it goes beyond the present case,
because it is an authority that even on a plea of tender it
was unnecessary to pay the money into court. The sum
tendered is not a debt, but the tender is a matter collateral
to the defence, and I think it imposed no obligation on the
defendant to pay the money into court. It seems to me,
therefore, that there is a good bar to the action, and that
the verdict must be entered for the defendant.

Exch. of Pleas,
1842.

JONES
v.
GOODAY.

ALDERSON, B.—I am of the same opinion. It seems
to me that if a party is acting bonâ fide in what he considers to be the execution of the authority vested in him,
he is entitled to notice of action, and to tender amends,
and then the only question is, has he tendered sufficient
amends? If the law, as laid down in the case cited by
Mr. *Kelly*, were to be strictly acted upon, I concur entirely
with my brother *Parke* in thinking it would take away the
protection the legislature intended to give to officers acting
in the execution of their duty, because it would impose on
third persons the task of deciding, in every case, whether
they had acted reasonably or not. If the act done was such
that no reasonble man could, in doing it, be supposed to
have acted bonâ fide, that would be another question. In the
case of *Cook* v. *Leonard*, the Court must have considered that
no reasonable man could have acted as the defendant did;
that it was not merely gross ignorance on his part, but
amounted to mala fides. The law on this subject is well laid
down by Lord *Ellenborough*, and *Bayley*, J., in *Theobald* v.
Crichmore (a). There it appeared the defendant acted in
ignorance; but what does Lord *Ellenborough* say? that the

(a) 1 B. & Ald. 227.

sole question was, not whether he acted illegally, but whether, in so acting, he did it with a bonâ fide intention of carrying out the act of Parliament: and *Bayley*, J., at the conclusion of his judgment, says, "It appears to me that the officer acted illegally, but in the supposed bonâ fide execution of his duty, and that he is therefore entitled to the protection of the statute." So here, I should say this defendant acted illegally, but in the supposed bonâ fide execution of his duty, as one of the commissioners, carrying into effect the act of all the commissioners, under the authority of this act of Parliament, and he is therefore within the protection of the statute. Then has he tendered sufficient amends for what he has done? The jury have found that he has. But then it is said, that he ought to have brought the money into court; I do not think so. Suppose this case, that before the act was done, it had been required that he should make an offer to pay so much to the other party; he does make the offer, and does the act. In that case he is authorized, and it could not be necessary to bring the money into court: here he has done the act without authority, but he tenders the amount before the action is brought. It is said that inflicts great hardship, and that if a party were to tender £10,000 for amends, the plaintiff may lose it all, because a jury might happen to say that £9,999 was sufficient. I do not think that follows at all: a party to whom amends are tendered may take it, and yet say, "This is not sufficient," and may go on notwithstanding. I am putting the case where one party thinks the sum tendered is sufficient, and the other party alleges that it is not enough; but if the latter chooses to go on, according to the words in the clause, " after *sufficient* satisfaction made or tendered," there is no hardship in his being deprived of it altogether.

ROLFE, B.—I entirely concur, and the only observation I shall make is this, that this statute is merely a local one, and there is no reason for supposing there ever will be a case like the extreme one that has been put; it is not like a provision applying generally to all times and all places; and the only injury a party can sustain in trifling matters of this sort will be, that if sufficient amends have been tendered, then he cannot maintain his action.

Judgment for the defendant.

———◆———

HUTCHINGS *v.* REEVES and BOXALL.

TRESPASS for breaking and entering the plaintiff's shop, and taking and carrying away three pewter pots. Plea, not guilty (by statute). At the trial before *Gurney*, B., at the Middlesex Sittings after Hilary Term, it appeared that the defendant Reeves, in his capacity of inspector of weights and measures for the county of Middlesex, appointed by the justices in sessions, under the stat. 5 & 6 Will. 4, c. 63, s. 17, on the 30th August, 1841, entered the premises of the plaintiff, who kept a beershop, and proceeded to try by the imperial standard the beer measures he found there; and the three pots in question being in his judgment deficient in measure, he seized them, and gave them to the other defendant, who accompanied him with a basket for that purpose, and carried them away. The warrant under which the defendant Reeves acted, dated 2nd December, 1840, was put in and read. It recited that it had been granted in pursuance of an application made by him for that purpose to the magistrate by whom it was signed, and empowered him, at all seasonable times, to enter all shops, houses, &c., whatsoever " within his jurisdiction," wherein goods should be exposed or kept for sale, &c., and to require the production of all weights, measures, steelyards, &c., and to compare and try the same with

An inspector of weights and measures, appointed by the sessions under the 5 & 6 Will. 4, c. 63, s. 17, and having a general warrant from a magistrate, under s. 28, to act as such within his jurisdiction, may, by virtue of such appointment and warrant, enter any shop, &c., within his district, at all seasonable times, to examine and seize false weights and measures, and need not have a special warrant from a justice in each individual case.

the imperial standard weights and measures, &c. Upon
this evidence, it was objected for the plaintiff, first, that
this warrant, being in general terms, and not containing
any authority to enter and search the premises of the
plaintiff by name, was insufficient, and afforded no justification to the defendants: and secondly, that the defendant
Boxall, who had no warrant or appointment under the
statute, but merely accompanied Reeves as his servant, was
not entitled to plead the general issue and give the special
matter in evidence, under the 39th section of the act,
which enacts that "in all actions brought against any
person for any thing done in pursuance of the act, or in
the execution of the powers or authorities thereof, the defendant or defendants may plead the general issue, and
give this act and the special matter in evidence, at any
trial to be had thereon, and that the acts were done in
pursuance or by the authority of the act(*a*)." The learned
Judge reserved the points for the opinion of the Court,
and the plaintiff had a verdict, damages 2*l.* 6*s.*, leave being
reserved to the defendants to move to enter a verdict for
them or either of them.

In this Term, *R. V. Richards* obtained a rule accordingly, against which

Platt and *Bovill* now shewed cause.—It is clear that the
inspector of weights and measures has not the power contended for in this case,—to enter any shop and seize the
measures which he may deem deficient in weight, under a
general warrant such as this,—unless it be given him by
the 28th section of the stat. 5 & 6 Will. 4, c. 63. The
17th section, which relates to the original appointment of
inspectors by the justices in sessions, certainly gives no
such authority. It merely enacts, that in England, at the
general or quarter sessions of the peace, the justices shall

_____

(*a*) The latter objection was abandoned on the argument of the rule.

determine the number of copies of the imperial standard *Exch. of Pleas,*
1842.
weights and measures, which they shall deem requisite for
the comparison of all weights and measures in use within HUTCHINGS
their respective jurisdictions, and shall direct that such *v.*
REEVES.
copies, verified and stamped at the Exchequer, shall be
provided for the use of the same, and shall fix the places
at which such copies shall be deposited, and shall appoint
a sufficient number of inspectors of weights and measures
for the safe custody of such copies, and for the discharge
of the other duties thereinafter mentioned; and shall
allot to each inspector a separate district. The question,
therefore, turns altogether upon the 28th section, by
which it is enacted, " that in England and Ireland it shall
be lawful for every justice of the peace of any county, &c.,
and in Scotland for every sheriff, &c., or for any inspector
authorized in writing under the hand of any justice of the
peace &c., at all seasonable times, to enter any shop &c.
whatever ' within his jurisdiction,' wherein goods shall be
exposed or kept for sale,&c., and there to examine all weights,
measures, steelyards, or other weighing machines, and to
compare and try the same with the copies of the imperial
standard weights and measures required or authorized to
be provided under this act; and if upon such examination
it shall appear that the said weights or measures are light
or otherwise unjust, the same shall be liable to be seized
and forfeited, &c. &c." And if the defendant did not
well justify his entry under this section, he did not bring
himself within the protection of the 39th section. Now the
warrant put in evidence gave the defendant no specific
authority to enter the plaintiff's shop. The statute requires that the inspector shall be armed with the warrant
of a magistrate, authorizing the act which would otherwise
be a trespass. The *appointment* and the *warrant* are two
entirely different things; the former is a general nomination of the party to the office, to be made by the sessions; the latter is a particular authority, to be given by

one magistrate, to enter and seize if necessary. It will be said that this construction will tend to defeat the object of the statute, because, in that case, there must be a previous summons, which will give the party notice to remove all evidence of the fraud: but that is not so; this is in the nature of a search-warrant, and therefore no previous summons would be necessary; but, on the other hand, it ought to be granted upon reasonable information given to the magistrate with reference to the specific shop or place. There can be no difference in principle as to the insufficiency of a general warrant, whether granted against the person or the goods. Now it is laid down distinctly in 4 Bl. Comm. 291, that "a general warrant to apprehend all persons suspected, without naming or particularly describing any person in special, is illegal and void for its uncertainty; for it is the duty of the magistrate, and ought not to be left to the officer, to judge of the ground of suspicion." If it had been intended that such a general warrant should be an authority, the act would have said in express terms, that it should be lawful for the inspector *so appointed as aforesaid*, at all seasonable times, to enter &c.; but the words used in sect. 28 shew that *he* is not considered by the legislature as an officer of sufficient dignity to exercise the discretion himself, although the justice or sheriff is. He ought, therefore, to have their special authority for the particular act. [Lord *Abinger*, C. B.—If that be so, what becomes of the words "at all seasonable times?" The inspector is already appointed, and is a known officer; and the question is, whether, if a justice or sheriff give him such authority in writing, he is not thereby put in the same position with them.] So also is a constable a known officer; yet no such general authority is vested in him. There can be no inconvenience in having the authority of a justice before the inspector enters the premises, while much danger to the rights of the subject must necessarily arise from reposing the discretion in an inferior officer such as this.

But, further, upon the true construction of the 28th section, this power is only given to the inspector within his jurisdiction, that is, within the district to which he is assigned by the sessions, under the 17th section; and it could not have been intended that the justice should have power to enlarge the inspector's jurisdiction to the full extent of his own. The power of entering, &c., is *within the jurisdiction of the justice*—the words "*within his jurisdiction*," mean the jurisdiction of the justice, and the warrant here is made out in the same terms; but the inspector has no authority, by the statute, to act out of his own limits; he cannot know the extent of the jurisdiction of the justice who signs the warrant. If this general warrant, co-extensive with the jurisdiction of the justice, be valid, *every* justice might authorize *every* inspector, though with a limited jurisdiction, to enter *every* house throughout the whole county. The true construction of the 28th section is, that the justice within his jurisdiction must exercise his own discretion, and from time to time, and in each particular instance, authorize the inspector acting within the limits of his appointment, to enter, &c., and that the justice has no power to delegate the whole of his discretion, throughout the whole of his own extended jurisdiction, to a subordinate officer, who is to act only within certain limits and under his authority.

R. V. Richards and *Whitehurst*, in support of the rule. —The inspector, when authorized by the justice in writing, has thereafter the same power that by the act is given to the justice himself; that is, *at all seasonable times* to enter *any* shop, &c. If there be any restriction upon the inspector, when so authorized, so is there also upon the justice. It is said this is a large power to be conferred on such an officer; but it is less extensive than that of the leet jury (for whom the inspector is substituted by this act), who had authority, though altogether unknown to the party, to enter into any shop and seize measures they deemed deficient. The object of the act was to give additional remedies for the prevention of frauds of this kind. It is admitted that this power is given to the justice or sheriff; and it is clear that the inspector, when authorized by their warrant, is to all intents their deputy for these purposes. There is good reason for the warrant being required, because the inspector has no appointment except by the resolution of the sessions, filed at the sessions; and it was expedient that, before he entered any house, he should have an instrument to produce, shewing his authority and character. And it is very possible that the legislature might not think it fit that *every* inspector should be intrusted with this power, but only such as from time to time were deemed by a magistrate proper persons to execute it. This is no question as to the validity of general warrants, but merely as to the meaning of the legislature in this particular case. If it were necessary first to obtain a search-warrant in each case, there must, for that purpose, be an information on oath. Then how is such information to be obtained? not by entry of the officer on the premises, because the argument supposes that the entry for such a purpose renders him liable to an action; and if it is to be given on the oath of a third party, the tradesman would thereby be subjected to a particular and perhaps wholly unjust suspicion; while, on the other hand, an opportunity would be given to fraudulent persons to remove all their defective measures. The justice clearly might grant several warrants, applicable to every house in the district; why may he not then do the same thing by one general warrant?

Lord ABINGER, C. B.—I am of opinion, upon the main point which has been discussed, that this was a good warrant. It is very true that general warrants are considered bad by the common law; but if an act of Parliament chooses to

give a justice the power of making a general warrant, then
the act of Parliament so far repeals the common law. The
question therefore turns on the construction of this particular clause; and it appears to me that the sound construction of the clause is, that the legislature intended to give to
the inspector, acting under the general authority derived
from the quarter sessions, and under the particular authority of the justice who gives him the authority in writing,
the same power exactly as it gives to the justice. It is given
in the same words, and there is no distinction pointed out
between the one and the other—each is to enter at all
seasonable times into any shop, &c. The warrant must
contain those words; and whether the justice puts a number of particular persons into the same warrant, or gives a
general warrant such as this is, it is the same in effect. I
think, therefore, the clear construction of the clause is,
that when the justice chooses, within the jurisdiction in
which he acts, to depute to the inspector the power of
entering at seasonable times into any house, he may do so
by the sort of warrant which has been read, and that such
authority is sufficient, although it be in general terms.
The inspector is appointed at the quarter sessions of the
county, by the authority of all the justices there assembled;
the district is limited within which he is to act; then the
magistrate, in order to entitle him to do what the magistrate himself may do, is to give him an authority in writing,
and that authority is to enable him to enter at all seasonable times. Those very words imply that the power is not
limited to any particular time; and I do not see why it
should be limited to any particular house. It was intended to give him the same authority and supervision that the
leet jury had before: and they did not require any specific
authority to enter into any particular house, but entered
into all houses at all seasonable times.

It appears to me, therefore, that this warrant was suffi-

Exch. of Pleas,
1842.

HUTCHINGS
v.
REEVES.

cient to justify the act done by the defendants, and that this rule must be made absolute.

PARKE, B.—I am of the same opinion. In this case the only point which we have now to dispose of is, whether the authority which was given in this general form to the inspector, to enter any house, and to search and examine the weights and measures there found, is an authority within the meaning of the 28th section. If it was an authority warranted by the 28th section, there is no doubt that it need not in terms go on to authorize the officer to carry away the measures that he found defective: the act of Parliament itself justifies that. The act gives the power to any person authorized under that section, that is, authorized to enter the house and to examine the weights and measures therein, to carry them away if they are found to be light or otherwise unjust.

The question, therefore, to which I shall confine my attention, is this; whether under the 28th section, according to the true construction of it, the general authority given by a justice of the peace for the county of Middlesex to an inspector, appointed to act for a particular district within the county of Middlesex, within which district the shop lies, is sufficient to justify his entering, at any seasonable time, into any shop, for the purpose of seizing weights and measures he may find to be deficient. I think the true construction, and that which alone is consistent with the ordinary meaning of the language of this clause, is, that such general authority was sufficient. There is some obscurity, no doubt, with respect to the meaning of the terms "within his jurisdiction;" whether that applies to the jurisdiction of the justice, or whether it applies to the jurisdiction of the inspector appointed by the justice; but it is not necessary to determine the precise meaning of that term in the present case, because we learn from the evidence, that the jurisdiction of the magistrate, and the jurisdiction of the inspector, both coincide; and the only question would be, whether any weight is to be attributed to the ingenious argument of Mr. *Bovill* on this subject, that it is not likely the legislature would have contemplated a general authority to be given, because the person who was to act under the authority might be presumed not to know the extent of the jurisdiction of the justice. That argument, however, does not appear to me to be entitled to much weight, when brought into contrast with the other words of the section, and the extreme inconvenience there is in adopting any other construction than that which my Lord has put upon it, and in which I entirely concur. The words are—"It shall be lawful for every sheriff, justice, or magistrate of any borough or town, or for any inspector authorized in writing under the hand of any justice of the peace in England and Ireland, or of any sheriff, justice, or magistrate in Scotland, at all seasonable times to enter any shop, store, warehouse, stall, yard, or place whatsoever *within his jurisdiction.*" Now I apprehend that the term "within his jurisdiction" is to be referred to all the persons previously mentioned: that is, the sheriff may enter within his jurisdiction, the justice may enter within his jurisdiction, the magistrate for the borough or town may enter within his jurisdiction, and persons authorized in writing by the justice, &c., (although the use of the term *jurisdiction* is not very proper with reference to an inspector, who does not act judicially, and who has not, properly speaking, jurisdiction), have thereby a general authority at all seasonable times to enter into all shops, &c., within the limits of the authority so given to them, for the purpose of ascertaining whether the weights and measures are correct.

It seems to me, therefore, that whatever authority the justice has, a person authorized by him in writing must have; and that being a general authority to enter at all

Exch. of Pleas, 1842.

HUTCHINGS *v.* REEVES.

seasonable times, it follows that he may in a general form transfer the same authority to the inspector.

Let us look at the opposite side of the question, and consider what inconvenience there would be in putting upon the act the construction contended for by Mr. *Platt*. According to that construction, there must be a summons—the shopkeeper must be called before a magistrate, to shew cause why there should not be an entry into his shop, and seizure of false weights in the shop, which would certainly be a signal to defeat the ends of justice, because it is quite clear no false weights would then be found there :—Mr. *Platt* does not, however, press the matter so far as that; but he says there ought to be something in the nature of a search-warrant. But in order to obtain a search-warrant, there must be an affidavit of some person who will make oath that he believes that the party has false weights, the same as there must be to authorize a search in a dwelling-house where stolen goods are alleged to be;—a species of evidence which it would be very difficult to obtain in cases within the mischief of the act; and it is not easy to see how it could in general be procured, unless the inspector went first into the shop to buy some article, to ascertain whether the weights were false; for of course he would not be able to make the oath on the mere statement of a third party. The probability therefore is, that if it were required that there should be a special authority in each case, the act of Parliament would almost become a dead letter, and no search would be made in the different shops. The object no doubt is, that these examinations shall take place at a time when the shopkeeper does not expect such an inquiry, so that he may be likely to be detected, if he be in the habit of making use of false weights and measures.

According, therefore, to the ordinary construction of the terms of the 28th section, and the reason and convenience of the case, it appears to me that it was not intended there should be a particular warrant on each occasion, but that every inspector who has been appointed at the quarter sessions, and who is thought a trustworthy person, may be authorized by any justice, within the limits of his jurisdiction, to make a search whenever, at seasonable times, he thinks the interest of the public requires such search should be made. I am of opinion, therefore, that this is a proper warrant within the meaning of the act of Parliament, and that the rule ought to be made absolute.

Exch. of Pleas,
1842.

HUTCHINGS
v.
REEVES.

ALDERSON, B.—I am of the same opinion. It seems to me quite clear that the power to be given to the inspector was to be a general power, and that the legislature intended to intrust it to the discretion of the inspector, authorized in writing under the hand of any justice of the peace. I apprehend that it is a mere description of the individual who was to be substituted by warrant for the justice, and was to have authority to do the same thing as the justice was empowered to do. That power is, to enter at all seasonable times into any shop within his jurisdiction, for the purpose of inspecting the measures and weights: so an inspector, appointed by the sessions, and being also authorized in writing by the justices, was to have a power precisely similar. And when we look at the older act of Parliament on this subject (the statute of the 35 Geo. 3, c. 102), it seems to me to throw a considerable light upon the construction which the Court ought to put on this section. By that act, inspectors were to be appointed by the quarter sessions, who were first to take an oath, which was to be administered to them by the justices of the peace; and they were then at certain periods, that is to say, once in every month at the least, (but not at any fixed time, so that the party would know when they were coming), to enter into shops and stalls, and examine and seize all false weights and measures. Is it likely, therefore, that an act of Parliament subsequently passed would require a specific warrant on every particular occasion, when the state of the law, as it existed before, empowered that same class of persons, on an oath which they took to execute their duties properly, to enter once a month at least without giving notice, and without any information laid before any magistrate whatever, into premises of this nature? The two acts are in pari materiâ, and each proceeds upon the same ground, that of the examination being made without any previous notice given to the individual whose weights are supposed to be fraudulent, or whose weights it is desirable to examine for the purpose of seeing whether they be just or not. It seems to me, therefore, that these two acts of Parliament throw great light on each other, and that inasmuch as the old inspector was to enter at least once a month, but oftener if he should think fit, in the day-time, so here the justices of the peace give him an authority to do the like; namely, to enter at all seasonable times, for the purpose of making the same inspection. It does not require, as it seems to me—it would be a monstrous proposition if it did—that the magistrate should only grant power to enter when he has had information upon oath; that would be to require what in the vast majority of cases he could never have.

On these grounds, I am of opinion that this general warrant was a sufficient justification for the present defendant, and that he was authorised under it to enter and examine, and to carry away, the measures in question.

ROLFE, B.—I am of the same opinion; and I fully concur in the force of the observations just made by my Brother *Alderson*, as to the light thrown on this case by the prior act of the 35th of Geo. 3, c. 102. The 2nd section enacts, that it shall be lawful for the examiners, (as they were then called), and they are thereby required, once in every month at the least, in the day-time, to enter into shops or other premises of every person whose sales be material, for the purpose of inspecting the weights and measures: so that under that act they had no discretion, but were bound to enter into every shop for that purpose.

Then by a subsequent act, intermediate between that and the present statute, (the 5 Geo. 4, c. 74), that provision was mitigated, I suppose by reason of its being found too inconvenient to the public and to the parties that this process should take place once in every month; and therefore it was cut down to this extent, that it should only be done at such times periodically as the justices should direct. The doctrine of general warrants, on which so much comment has been made, has nothing to do with the present question; and to require a special one, in cases like the present, would be to render the statute a mere dead letter, which could never be acted on at all.

There was one observation which struck me in the course of the argument, which however, on consideration, seems to be capable of an obvious explanation. It was contended by Mr. *Platt*, If you do not require a specific authority for each case, why require any warrant from the magistrate in writing at all?—the inspector has already been appointed by the magistrates, and therefore any subsequent appointment is altogether redundant. The force of that observation is entirely removed by considering what it is that the body of justices in sessions do when they appoint, and what it is the magistrate afterwards does. The justices in sessions, under the 17th section, appoint an inspector: but that appointment does not give him a title, quà inspector, to enter into shops. An inspector has many duties to perform: amongst other things, I see, by section 24, in England the justices, and in Scotland the justices at a meeting called by the sheriff, and in Ireland the grand jury of each county, county of a city, or county of a town, are to determine on what day or days each and every such inspector shall attend with the stamps and copies of the imperial standard weights and measures in his custody, at each of the several market towns, to have the originals and copies compared, and to take charge of them. There are other duties also to be performed; and it would be very fit that the magistrates at sessions should make the appointment, and still that something further should be required before the party could be considered as authorized to enter and search: and if that is necessary in England, it is still more necessary when we come to see by whom the original appointment is made in Ireland, namely, by the grand jury, an irresponsible body, and a body that has no existence after they are once discharged: it was therefore very fit, that before the party should be authorized to enter into another's house, and seize his weights and measures, he should have the sanction of some magistrate, or some responsible person, who should, as it were, vouch for the respectability of the officer. I see very good reason for requiring this: at all events this, and no more, is required, and it is sufficient to say that ita lex scripta est; the legislature has given the power, and we are bound to uphold it. The rule must therefore be absolute to enter the verdict for the defendants.

Rule absolute.

REGINA *v.* RAY and Others.

THIS was an information at the suit of the Crown, filed in Easter Term 1838, against the defendants, as executors of one Ray, deceased, for breaches of covenants contained in a lease granted by the Crown to the testator, which expired in 1836. The defendants pleaded in the same term, and in the following Trinity Term issue was joined, and notice of trial given, which was afterwards countermanded. No further proceedings were taken until July 1841, when a bill was filed in the Court of Chancery for taking the deposition, de bene esse, of a witness on the part of the Crown; and his evidence was accordingly taken, but he was not cross-examined by the defendants.

In last Hilary Term, *Swann* moved for a rule to shew cause why the information should not be dismissed for want of prosecution, or why judgment of a nonsuit should not be entered. The Court refused that application, but granted a rule to shew cause why the defendants should not be at liberty to set down the cause for trial at the sittings after the present term.

The *Attorney-General* now shewed cause, and contended that the rule must be discharged, as the Crown had the power of withdrawing the record at any period, even after the commencement of the trial. He offered, however, to proceed to trial, if the defendants would consent to the reading of the deposition in evidence; but this was objected to.

PER CURIAM.—We cannot supersede the prerogative of the Crown. The rule must therefore be discharged.

Rule discharged.

————————

BIRD *v.* HOLMAN.

THIS was an action of debt for non-payment of money pursuant to a covenant contained in a deed of apprenticeship. The declaration described the instrument throughout as a " deed," and " deed of apprenticeship." The defendant pleaded, that " the said indenture of apprenticeship in the declaration mentioned is not his deed." The plaintiff having demurred specially to this plea, on the ground that no *indenture* of apprenticeship was mentioned in the declaration, by an order of Lord *Denman*, C. J., at chambers, the demurrer was set aside as frivolous.

May 5.

To a declaration in debt for non-payment of money pursuant to a covenant in a " deed of apprenticeship," (so describing the instrument throughout the declaration), the defendant pleaded, " that the said *indenture* in the declaration mentioned is not his deed."

On special demurrer to the plea, the Court refused to set aside the demurrer as frivolous, and intimated their opinion that the plea was bad.

Bere having obtained a rule to shew cause why this order should not be rescinded,

Warren now shewed cause. This instrument is sufficiently shewn on the face of the declaration to be an *indenture*, because it appears that it contains covenants on both sides: for the plaintiff avers, in the usual form, performance of the covenants on his part. Further, this is a deed of apprenticeship, to which there must be three parties. The defendant in effect says, by his plea, " Whatever you (the plaintiff) call the instrument, I did not execute it." *Risdale* v. *Kelly* (a) is a case like the present. There the declaration, in debt, demanded £60, and contained six counts, each of which was for £10, parcel, &c.; the defendant pleaded that he did not owe the said sum of £10 above demanded; and the plaintiff having treated the plea as a nullity, and signed judgment, the Court set the judgment aside, holding that the words "of £10," being inapplicable to the declaration, might be rejected. So here, the plea may be read as if it had been "the said instrument" or " writing" in the declaration mentioned, &c.—He cited also *Innes* v. *Colquhon* (b).

Bere, contrà, was not called upon.

Lord ABINGER, C. B.—I think the rule must be made absolute. Is it a proper description of a *deed* to call it an *indenture?* Would it not be a bad plea, that the promissory note in the declaration mentioned was not the defendant's deed?

PARKE, B.—I also think this order must be set aside. The plaintiff in his declaration does not aver that the instrument is an indenture, but the plea calls it so: so that

(a) 1 C. & J. 410; 1 Tyrw. 337.   (b) 7 Bing. 265; 5 M. & P. 63.

there is no negative in the plea of any affirmative proposition contained in the declaration. A deed-poll may contain many conditions precedent to be performed by the other party.

ALDERSON, B.—The plea does not contain any negative of a given affirmative. It should be a very clear proposition indeed, that is to give the Court a right to take away the subject's writ of error.

> Rule absolute without costs, with liberty to the defendant to amend his plea.

BLYTH and Another *v.* SHEPHERD and Another.

ASSUMPSIT on a policy of insurance against the defendants, as directors of the Marine Insurance Company. The declaration contained two counts; the first alleging a loss by perils of the sea, the second a loss by barratry of the master. *Rolfe*, B., having made an order that one of these counts should be struck out, on the ground that they did not establish a distinct subject-matter of complaint within the meaning of the rule of H. T., 4 Will. 4,

May 5.

Two counts on the same policy of insurance, one alleging a loss by perils of the sea, and the other a loss by barratry, cannot be pleaded together.

R. V. Richards obtained a rule to shew cause why the order should not be set aside, on affidavits which stated, that the settlement of the loss was resisted on the alleged ground that the ship had been wilfully lost (off the island of Borneo) by arrangement and conspiracy between the master and the supercargo; that owing to the absence of witnesses abroad, the plaintiffs were unable to ascertain whether such was the case or not; and that, if they were limited to one count, they might be nonsuited by proof either of barratry, or of loss by perils of the seas, as the case might be.

Butt, who appeared to shew cause, objected that the rule was not drawn up on reading the declaration, without which the Court could not judge of the propriety of the order; and cited *South Eastern Railway Company* v. *Sprot* (a). He contended also, that the two counts were pleaded together in express violation of the rule, which prohibited two counts on the same policy.

The Court called upon

R. V. Richards, contrà.—It cannot be necessary to draw up the rule on reading a long declaration, if it appear by affidavit, as it does here, what the two counts are. And under the circumstances of this case, unless both counts are allowed, or the plaintiffs are at liberty, under the count for a loss by perils of the sea, to prove barratry, or the defendants are precluded from insisting on barratry as a defence, the plaintiffs will be under great hardship, because they cannot fully know the facts until they have sent out a commission to examine witnesses at Borneo, and after it has been returned, they cannot amend their declaration, because the witnesses are examined to the particular issue joined. The case of *Guest* v. *Elwes* (b) is an exemplification of the difficulty a plaintiff may be liable to by the strict application of this rule. It can hardly be held to apply strictly to a case of foreign loss, where there are no means of ascertaining the facts in the first instance.

Lord ABINGER, C.B.—I think the perils of the sea would be properly alleged as the cause of the loss, although there were previous barratry, and therefore that there will be no prejudice to the plaintiffs by this rule being discharged; but even if there is, it is clear that the rule of Court applies in terms to the case.

(a) 11 Ad. & E. 167; 3 P. & D. 110.   (b) 5 Ad. & E. 118; 2 N. & P. 230.

PARKE, B.—The rule must be discharged with costs.

The declaration is framed in open violation of the new rules: and as to the alleged hardship of not allowing two counts in a case like the present—which, however, I believe to be really imaginary, because the plaintiffs may describe the loss as caused by perils of the sea, notwithstanding previous barratry—yet if there be any, it is by no means equal to the evil of allowing a multitude of counts on the same policy. The plaintiffs must delay commencing their action until they obtain information sufficient to enable them to state the facts correctly.

ALDERSON, B.—*Heyman* v. *Parish* (a) is an authority to shew that, if the declaration allege a loss by perils of the sea, the plaintiff may recover on proof that the ship was wrecked, although that was occasioned by the barratry of the crew (b).

ROLFE, B., concurred.

Rule discharged, with costs.

———————

TROTT v. SMITH, Executor.

THIS was an action of covenant against the defendant as executor, on a covenant contained in a mortgage deed made by his testator, to pay the mortgage money to W. J. W., for whom the plaintiff was by the deed named a trustee: breach, non-payment thereof to the plaintiff or to W. J. W. The defendant, being under terms of pleading issuably, pleaded, first, non est factum, and secondly, a plea setting forth the bankruptcy of the plaintiff before the commencement of the suit. The plaintiff, after having obtained time to reply, signed judgment as for want of a plea. A rule having been obtained to set aside this judgment, and the subsequent proceedings thereon, for irregularity,

(a) 2 Campb. 149.   (b) See also *Walker* v. *Maitland*, 5 B. & Ald. 171.

Ogle now shewed cause, and contended that the second plea was not an issuable one, inasmuch as assignees of a bankrupt take only property wherein he is beneficially interested, not that in which he has an interest only as a trustee. [*Parke*, B.—Have you not waived the objection by obtaining time to reply, thereby admitting that there is something to reply to?] The question is, whether the party can waive a *nullity*, though he may a mere irregularity. It has been held that a plea in abatement, delivered without a sufficient affidavit of verification, is such an absolute nullity that the defect cannot be waived: *Garrett* v. *Hooper* (a). So, where a defendant is charged in custody on a writ of execution which is a nullity, the lapse of time does not waive his right to apply for his discharge: *Mortimer* v. *Piggott* (b).

Lord ABINGER, C. B.—The rule must be absolute. In the case of a plea in abatement, the act of Parliament expressly requires that it should be accompanied by a sufficient affidavit of verification. Here the plea is voidable by the agreement of the parties, but not absolutely void on the face of it. The plaintiff might at once treat it as a nullity; but surely he could not do so at the moment before trial, after he had replied, and issue was joined.

PARKE, B.—If the plaintiff had replied to this plea, he certainly could not afterwards have signed judgment: then does he not, by applying for time to reply, admit that there is something to reply to?—whereas his case now is, that the plea ought not to be upon the file at all, by reason of the non-compliance with the judge's order.

ALDERSON, B., and ROLFE, B., concurred.

Rule absolute, with costs; no action
to be brought.

(a) 1 Dowl. P. C. 28.　　　　　(b) 2 Dowl. P. C. 615.

Exch. of Pleas,
1842.

MATCHETT v. PARKES.

May 5.

IN this case the defendant had employed Messrs. J. K. Beswick and George Beswick as his attorneys, to conduct for him certain prosecutions for perjury, as well as on other business. It appeared that between the 28th of May, 1838, and the 15th of November, 1839, (within which period a great part of the business was done), George Beswick was not an attorney, but his name had been permitted, before his actual admission, to appear as the partner of his brother, J. K. Beswick, at the desire of their friends. The indictments for perjury were ultimately quashed. Messrs. Beswick delivered a bill to the defendant in the names of both of them, amounting to 694*l.* 0*s.* 9*d.*, and it was referred to the Master for taxation. The defendant objected, before the Master, that the sum of 474*l.* 0*s.* 3*d.* should be struck out of the bill, on the ground that it consisted of items for business done while George Beswick was not certificated as an attorney; and that the sum of 167*l.* 13*s.* 10*d.* should also be disallowed, on the ground that it was incurred in respect of the indictments, which, by the alleged negligence of the attorneys in preparing them, had been wholly useless to the defendant. The attorneys denied the negligence, and produced affidavits to shew that the indictments had been quashed by arrangement with the defendant. The Master, however, disallowed both the above sums, and thereby, after giving the defendant credit for sums received on his account, a balance was found to be due to him from Messrs. Beswick.

Welsby had obtained a rule to shew cause why the taxation should not be reviewed, and why Mr. I. K. Beswick should not be at liberty to deliver a fresh bill of costs in his own name only, in respect of the sum of 474*l.* 0*s.* 3*d.*;

On taxation of an attorney's bill, the Master has no jurisdiction to disallow items on the ground that in respect of the business to which they refer, the attorney was guilty of negligence.

Where A. & B. delivered a bill in their joint names for business done as attorneys, and the Master, on taxation, disallowed part of the bill, on the ground that B. was not a certificated attorney during a portion of the time to which the bill referred, the Court, on affidavit that B.'s name was used at the request of friends, but that he was really not a partner with A., allowed A. to deliver a fresh bill in his own name only for the items so disallowed.

and cited *Jones* v. *Roberts* (*a*), as an authority to shew that the Master had no jurisdiction to entertain the question of negligence.

Petersdorff now shewed cause, and contended that the Master had jurisdiction to enter into the matters brought before him by the parties; that the attorney's services having been, as to the indictments, altogether useless, he had no right to charge anything for them; *Hill* v. *Featherstonhaugh* (*b*); and that, as to the o her business done while the brothers were in partnership, it was clear one of them only could have no right to recover.

Welsby, contrà, was stopped by the Court.

Lord ABINGER, C. B.—The rule must be made absolute; the Master has clearly exceeded his jurisdiction.

PARKE, B.—The Master had certainly no authority to entertain the question of negligence; that is a matter for the consideration of a jury. Then, as to the other point, the object of the attorney who makes this application is to shew that he alone was the real party with whom the contract was made, and for that purpose he wishes to deliver a bill in his own name, so as to be in a situation to establish that fact before a jury. If the brothers were really partners, and the contract was made with both of them, the defendant may avail himself of that as a defence.

ALDERSON, B.—I am of the same opinion. The Master has exceeded his authority in this case. His duty is to moderate the charges of attornies, not to determine the question of negligence. He has no power to subpœna witnesses, or to compel the production of affidavits. On the other point, also, I concur with the rest of the Court.

Rule absolute.

(*a*) 4 Tyrw. 310; 2 Dowl. P. C. 656.   (*b*) 7 Bing. 569; 5 M. & P. 541.

Exch. of Pleas,
1842.

BAILY v. BAKER.

May 7.

IN this case, the defendant, having obtained an order to plead several matters, pleaded a plea to the whole declaration, and also delivered a demurrer to one count. No mention was made of the intended demurrer at the time of obtaining the order. The plaintiff signed judgment as for want of a plea, and *Rolfe*, B., made an order for setting the judgment aside.

On a former day in this term, *W. H. Watson* obtained a rule to shew cause why this order should not be rescinded.

Bere now shewed cause.—The judgment was irregular. A party need not obtain the leave of a judge in order to demur; the defendant, therefore, when obtaining the order to plead several matters, was not bound to inform the judge that he intended also to demur. Even if the pleas are irregular, the plaintiff had no right to treat them as a nullity and sign judgment; he ought to have applied to set the demurrer aside.

Watson, contrà, was stopped by the Court.

PARKE, B.—I think the defendant ought, on obtaining a rule to plead several matters, to inform the judge what he purposes doing in respect to the whole declaration; and that the intended demurrer, as well as the pleas, ought to be before the judge, that he may determine in what manner his discretion ought to be exercised. The judgment may be set aside on the defendant's striking out the demurrer, and paying all the costs occasioned by his defective pleading, except the costs of this application.

The other Barons concurred.

Rule accordingly.

A defendant having obtained an order to plead several matters, pleaded a plea to the whole declaration, and delivered also a demurrer to one count, whereupon the plaintiff signed judgment as for want of a plea. The Court refused to set aside the judgment, except on the terms of the defendant's striking out the demurrer, and paying the costs of his defective pleading.

Exch. of Pleas,
1842.

April 30.

To an action for use and occupation, for a quarter's rent from Lady-day to Midsummer 1841, the defendant pleaded, that by an agreement made between the plaintiffs, executors of T., and the defendant, the defendant agreed to take of the plaintiffs, executors as aforesaid, the premises in question; that it was afterwards agreed between them and W., that W. should become tenant to the plaintiffs from Lady-day 1841, and that the defendant should be discharged from all liability to subsequent rent; that the defendant accordingly gave up possession to W., and the plaintiffs accepted him as tenant:—*Held*, that this plea was not proved by evidence that *one* of the plaintiffs had so agreed to accept W. as tenant in lieu of the defendant.

M. TURNER, H. J. TURNER, and LAYTON *v.* HARDEY.

ASSUMPSIT for use and occupation. Pleas, first, non assumpsit; secondly, that the plaintiffs were by this action claiming to recover the amount of a quarter's rent, due from the 25th day of March to Midsummer-Day, 1841, by virtue of a certain memorandum of agreement made between the plaintiffs, *executrix and executors* of H. H. Turner, deceased, of the one part, and the defendant of the other part, whereby the said plaintiffs agreed to let to the defendant, and the defendant agreed to take of the plaintiffs, *executrix and executors as aforesaid*, the premises in the declaration mentioned; that it was afterwards, to wit, on &c., agreed by and between the plaintiffs, the defendant, and one W. Wasbrough, that the said W. Wasbrough should hold and occupy the said premises as tenant thereof to the plaintiffs, from the 25th day of March, 1841, and that the defendant should be discharged from all liability to pay any rent accruing subsequently to the said 25th day of March, 1841. The plea then averred, that the defendant, on that day, delivered up possession of the premises to Wasbrough, who held and occupied them until the Midsummer-Day following, on the terms of the said agreement, and that the plaintiffs accepted Wasbrough as their tenant, and in discharge of the liability of the defendant to the said rent, &c. Verification.—Replication, de injuriâ.

At the trial before Lord *Abinger*, C.B., at the Middlesex sittings after Hilary Term, the plaintiffs gave in evidence a memorandum of agreement made between the plaintiffs, " executrix and executors " of H. H. Turner, deceased, of the one part, and the defendant of the other part, whereby " the said executrix and executors " agreed to let to the defendant the premises in question, and the defendant agreed " with the said executrix and executors " to pay

them rent for the same. The defendant called a witness
to prove, that in September 1840, Wasbrough applied to
one of the plaintiffs, H. J. Turner, to be allowed to become
tenant of the premises for a year from the 25th March,
1841, and that the latter accepted him as such tenant.
The jury, upon this evidence, found a verdict for the defendant on the second issue.

In the present term, *Thesiger* obtained a rule to shew
cause why this verdict should not be set aside, and a verdict entered for the plaintiffs, pursuant to leave reserved
at the trial, or for a new trial, on the ground that the plea
was not proved.

Hurlstone (with whom was *Crowder*) now shewed cause.
—This was a demise by the plaintiffs in their character of
executors, and therefore they cannot allege that one of
them had no authority to bind the other by his acceptance
of Wasbrough as the tenant. The release of a debt, or the
grant of a term, by one executor, is valid, and binds the
rest : Williams on Executors, 730. *Gore* v. *Wright* (a) is
in point. There the defendant pleaded, to debt for rent
due under a demise, that before the rent became due, it
was agreed between the plaintiff and defendant, that in
consideration of his giving up possession, he should be discharged from any further rent, and that he had given up
possession accordingly, and the tenancy was thereby surrendered : and it was held that the plea, although it did
not shew a surrender properly so called, afforded a valid
excuse for non-payment of the rent, by shewing the agreement, and the giving up of possession pursuant to it. So
here, one of the parties who demised has excused the debt
of the defendant, and that operates as a discharge as against
all : *Wallace* v. *Kelsall* (b). And it is properly so pleaded.
Where an instrument operates differently from its lan-

Exch. of Pleas, 1842.

TURNER
v.
HARDEY.

(a) 8 Ad. & Ell. 118 ; 3 N. & P. 243.   (b) 7 M. & W. 264.

guage, it ought to be pleaded according to its legal operation, not according to its strict terms : Stephen on Pleading, 419. [Lord *Abinger*, C. B.—Pleading a deed according to its *legal effect*, does not mean according to its legal
consequences, as derived from extrinsic facts; the *legal
effect* must be collected from the deed itself]. A contract
or debt of one of several partners might be stated as
the contract or debt of all. If therefore this agreement
operates by way of discharge as against all the executors,
it is correctly so pleaded.—He cited also Sheppard's
Touchstone, 484, 2 Saund. 97, and *Thomas* v. *Cook* (*a*).

Ogle (with whom was *Thesiger*), contrà.—This action is
brought by the plaintiffs in their individual capacity, and
not as executors; and if it had not appeared on the face
of the agreement put in evidence that they were executors, it would have been impossible to contend that the
plea was proved; because in the case of several ordinary
persons, it is clear that such an agreement by one of them
would not bind the rest. Now, first, it does not appear
that they demised as executors : all that appears from the
agreement is that they *were* executors, and there is nothing to shew that the defendant contracted with them as
such. It is not stated either in the plea or in the agreement
that they were parties to it *as executors*. They might have
assented to the vesting of the estate in them as trustees, and
so they would become joint lessors, and as such could demise
each in his individual capacity. But even if they did demise
in their representative capacity, the agreement of one of
them to excuse the defendant from the rent is not properly pleaded as a discharge by all. It is not like the case
of a *release* by deed. The plea alleges a discharge by the
three executors, and the proof is of a discharge by one only.

Lord ABINGER, C. B.—I think the plea is not sustained.
It is alleged that the three plaintiffs agreed to accept an-

(*a*) 2 B. & Ald. 119.

other person as tenant in the place of the defendant, and discharged him from the rent; but that allegation is not proved by such an agreement with one of the plaintiffs. Even if the legal consequence were that it should bind the three, it is not properly stated. But I think there is no pretence for saying that the plaintiff Turner, by a contract made with himself only, could bind the other two. Where executors join in a personal contract, they are bound in the same way as other persons in whom the property is vested; and though one may dispose of the assets so as to bind the others, they cannot severally make a new contract so as to bind each other. The issue, therefore, was not proved, and the rule must be absolute for a new trial.

PARKE, B.—I am also of opinion that the plea in this case was not proved. Though there appears to have been no distinct evidence of that fact, yet from the agreement with the defendant having been in the names of the plaintiffs, describing them to be executors, it is probable that the testator was entitled to a term, which devolved on them as executors, and that they made an underlease to the defendant. If so, the reversion on this demise belonged to the executors *as such*, and was assets (although the right to sue on the contract for rent may have belonged to them in their individual character), and the reversion might have been sold, or a new interest in it created, by one of the executors; and if one demised to Wasbrough with the consent of the defendant, I am not prepared to say whether there might not have been a defence to this action, on a proper plea, on the ground that such a transaction between Turner, one of the plaintiffs, Wasbrough, and the defendant, amounted to a surrender by operation of law, on the principle laid down in the case of *Thomas* v. *Cook*, and within which this case is attempted to be brought. But the present plea is not supported by the evidence; for it is founded on an alleged *agreement* of *all* the plaintiffs with the defendant and Wasbrough, and there is no proof of such an agreement, as Turner alone agreed in point of fact, and one executor is not the agent of another, to bind him by contract. The agreement, therefore, which is alleged in the plea was not proved. For this reason, I think the rule must be absolute.

ALDERSON, B.—I am of the same opinion. The plea sets up one contract, and the proof is of a different one.

ROLFE, B., concurred.

Rule absolute for a new trial.

———◆———

GREENSHIELDS *v.* HARRIS.

May 7.

Where, the venue being in Surrey, final judgment was signed on the 2nd April 1840, and a testatum ca. sa. of the same date issued into Yorkshire, on which the defendant was arrested; an original ca. sa. into Surrey, also dated the 2nd April 1840, with a general return of non est inventus thereon, was held sufficient to warrant the testatum.

A writ of ca. sa. may be executed more than a year after its date.

IN this case, the venue being in Surrey, final judgment was signed on the 2nd April, 1840, and a testatum ca. sa. of the same date was issued to the sheriff of Oxfordshire, under which the defendant was taken into custody on the 19th June, 1841. *Pigott* had obtained a rule calling on the plaintiff to shew cause why the defendant should not be discharged out of custody, on two grounds; first, on an affidavit stating that, on search in the office, there appeared to be no original writ of ca. sa. issued into Surrey on which to found the testatum ca. sa. into Oxfordshire; and although this might have been amended under the old practice, when writs of execution were made returnable as of the term, this was otherwise since the statute 3 & 4 Will. 4, c. 67, whereby they were made returnable immediately on execution; for which *Towers* v. *Newton* (a) was cited as an authority : and secondly, that the testatum ca. sa. had lost its force at the time of the arrest, not having been executed within a year from the day on which it bore date.

(a) 1 Ad. & E. (N. s.) 319; 4 P. & D. 625.

Barstow (with whom was *Byles*) now shewed cause on an affidavit, verifying an original writ of ca. sa. issued into Surrey, tested the same day as the testatum ca. sa., and returned generally "non est inventus," without any date. This, he contended, clearly distinguished the present case from *Towers* v. *Newton*, where there was no writ into the original county; and the circumstance of the two writs bearing date the same day could make no difference. He cited also *Newnham* v. *Law* (a), as an authority that the Court would, if necessary, allow the plaintiff to amend by suing out an original ca. sa. to support a testatum; and urged that the alteration in the form of the writ introduced by the stat. 3 & 4 Will. 4, c. 67, made no difference in the practice in this respect. As to the other point, he referred to *Simpson* v. *Heath* (b) as a conclusive authority against the application.—The Court called on

Pigott, contrà.—This being a judgment obtained in Surrey, the plaintiff was bound to have his execution into that county in the first instance; and there can be no testatum into another county, until the first writ has been returned non est inventus, and filed. Under the old practice, indeed, where the writs were dated as of the term, no irregularity would appear on the roll, and on this principle it was that an amendment was permitted: but now that writs of execution are tested on the day when they are issued, the irregularity cannot be cured by bringing in a writ returned after the testatum issued. [Lord *Abinger*, C. B.—Here both are dated on the same day, and non constat that the ca. sa. was not tested before the issuing of the testatum.] In *Shaw* v. *Maxwell* (c), where the Court allowed a testatum ca. sa. to be amended agreeably to the judgment, and an original ca. sa. to be sealed to warrant it, it was on the ground that no irregularity would appear upon the roll when produced in

(a) 5 T. R. 577.   (b) 5 M. & W. 631.   (c) 6 T. R. 450.

Exch. of Pleas,
1842.

GREENSHIELDS
v.
HARRIS.

Court. [Lord *Abinger*, C. B.—So a regular roll may now be produced here.] As to the other point, where more than a year has elapsed after the last act of record, a presumption of law arises in favour of the defendant, that the plaintiff's claim has been satisfied or otherwise put an end to, and it can only be revived by scire facias: Bac. Abr., Execution (H.); *Sir W. Waller's case* (a). In *Simpson* v. *Heath,* according to the report, the defendant was arrested within a year after the issuing of the ca. sa. [*Parke*, B.— No; the date 1838 is a mistake for 1839. The Court fully intended to decide that the party might be arrested after the expiration of the year.]

PARKE, B.—The rule must be discharged. With respect to the first point which has been made, that the testatum ca. sa. is void for want of an original ca. sa. to support it, we ought not to interpose difficulties to invalidate writs of this nature, but should endeavour to assimilate the new practice as far as possible to the old; and here we can hold this writ to be good without doing violence to any principle, inasmuch as we have produced before us an original writ of ca. sa. issued into the proper county, bearing date the same day with the judgment and testatum, to which there is a general return of non est inventus, which we may therefore presume to have been made on the same day: and therefore the plaintiff has now the materials for making up the roll in the most regular manner, by stating the issuing of a ca. sa. into Surrey, the return of non est inventus to that writ, and the subsequent award of the testatum into Oxfordshire, all of which is perfectly possible. In *Towers* v. *Newton* this could not be done, because there the testatum bore date on an earlier day than the original writ on which it professed to be founded. With regard to the other point, I have referred to my own note of the case

(a) 2 Leon. 77; 3 Leon. 259; 4 Leon. 44.

of *Simpson* v. *Heath*, and find that the point was expressly decided in that case. A writ of ca. sa., unlike those writs the duration of which is limited by the legislature, runs until it is executed; and it is a mistake to suppose, that if it be not executed within twelve months, the law makes any presumption in favour of the defendant. Where, indeed, the plaintiff has neglected to take a step in the cause for twelve months, it is otherwise; but where he has done everything necessary to the issuing of a valid writ of execution, the only inference, if any, from the writ's not being returned, is, that the sheriff has been unable to find the defendant in order to make the arrest.

Lord ABINGER, C. B., and ROLFE, B., concurred.

Rule discharged, without costs.

Exch. of Pleas, 1842.

GREENSHIELDS
v.
HARRIS.

DAKINS, Clerk, *v.* SEAMAN, Clerk.

DEBT.—The declaration stated, that whereas, after the death of John Dakins, clerk, who at the time of his death was incumbent of the parsonage and parish church of St. James, Colchester, the same being a benefice and spiritual promotion, with cure of souls, within the diocese of London, to wit, &c., the said spiritual promotion being then vacant, from the time of the death of the said J. Dakins, and from thence during such vacation, and until the defendant was instituted parson of and into the parish of the said spiritual promotion, the plaintiff, being a clerk in holy orders and ordained by the Archbishop of York, did during all that time duly serve and keep the cure of the said spiritual promotion, at the request of G. R. and G. H. C.,

April 27.

Where a curate is appointed by the special sequestrators of the bishop of the diocese, to serve the cure of a benefice during the vacation between the death of the last and the appointment of the next incumbent, he may, although not licensed by the bishop, and notwithstanding the stat. 1 & 2 Vict. c. 106, recover his reasonable stipend in an

action of debt under 28 Hen. 8, c. 11, from the next incumbent; the tithes which accrued during the interval not being sufficient to pay him a reasonable stipend.

being special sequestrators, ordained and appointed by the Bishop of London to ask for and sequester all the tithes, &c., and to cause the said cure of the said spiritual promotion to be served; and whereas the tithes, &c., growing and arising during the said vacation, were not sufficient to pay the said plaintiff a reasonable stipend for keeping the said cure; and whereas the defendant was the next incumbent; and whereas, by an act passed in the reign of Henry 8, it was provided, that if the fruits, &c., of the vacation of the spiritual promotions were not sufficient to pay the curate's stipend for serving the cure during such vacation, the same were to be borne by the next incumbent, within fourteen days next after he had possession of any of the promotions spiritual; whereupon, and by reason of the premises, the defendant has become liable, &c.

To this declaration the defendant pleaded, 4thly, That the death of J. Dakins, and the vacation of the said spiritual promotion, and the serving and keeping of the same, took place after the passing of the 1 & 2 Vict. c. 106, &c. Verification.

The fifth plea was, That the plaintiff, during the said vacation, was curate of the said spiritual promotion, and was not duly licensed by the Bishop or Ordinary of London.

Seventh plea.—That the death of John Dakins, and the vacation of the said spiritual promotion, happened after the passing of the statute 1 & 2 Vict. c. 106, and that the Bishop of London alone had jurisdiction to enforce the payment of the plaintiff's stipend, by monition and sequestration of the profits of the said spiritual promotion.

Demurrer to the fourth plea, assigning for cause that that plea did not shew with sufficient certainty how the statute 1 & 2 Vict. c. 106, prevented the plaintiff from having his said action.

Demurrer to the fifth plea:—the cause assigned, among others, being, that the plea did not shew, with sufficient certainty how a license from the Bishop or Ordinary was re- quisite or material.—To the 7th plea also there was a demurrer, the principal cause being, that it did not appear with sufficient certainty why the Bishop of London alone had jurisdiction to enforce by monition and sequestration the said payment in that plea mentioned.

The following were the defendant's points :—

That the payment of a curate performing the ecclesiastical duties of any benefice, during the vacancy of such benefice upon the avoidance of the same by death, being expressly provided for and regulated by the stat. 1 & 2 Vict. c. 106, ss. 100, 101, (and other sections), no action is now maintainable on the stat. 28 Hen. 8, c. 11 :

That the stat. 28 Hen. 8, c. 11, admitting it to be still in force, so far as its provisions extend, provides no form of remedy, and that from the nature of the demand, and otherwise, in the absence of any express provision, the remedy is not by action at law :

That the effect of the stat. 1 & 2 Vict. c. 106, is that no curate since the passing of that statute can have any legal claim or demand for or in respect of the performance of the ecclesiastical duties of a benefice during the vacancy thereof by death, except he be appointed by the bishop of the diocese, and have a stipend assigned to him under the provisions of the said act :

That the right set up by the declaration is stated therein to be founded upon the plaintiff having served as curate at the request of the sequestrators, but the authority given to the sequestrators is also set out in the declaration, and from that it appears that they had no authority in this respect, except to cause the cure to be served out of the profits of the benefice collected, sequestrated, and recovered by them and their authority : being so expressly limited, it follows that they are not shewn to have had the power, by employing a curate, to charge the succeeding incumbent, or to employ the said curate otherwise than on the credit

of the profits so to be collected and received by themselves :

That the declaration expressly states that the plaintiff
was ordained by the Archbishop of York, and the benefice
in question not being averred to be in the diocese or ecclesiastical jurisdiction of the said Archbishop, or even in the
province of York, but, on the contrary thereof, being expressly averred to be in the diocese of London, and province of Canterbury, it the more plainly appears that the
plaintiff's orders of priesthood, although they may have
put him in a capacity to be licensed, did not of themselves
dispense with a license from the bishop of the diocese, under the 36th & 37th canons of the year 1603 :

That the declaration is bad, for stating the cause of action to be for the whole amount of the stipend and wages
for the entire period of the vacancy, without negativing
the receipt by the defendant of any part of such amount
out of the profits of the benefice during such vacancy, or
from any other source, so that, according to the said declaration, if the fruits of the vacation are insufficient, by
however small an amount, and notwithstanding (except as
to such amount) they may have been actually received by
the curate, or even though such curate may have been
otherwise paid in full, nevertheless such curate has a right
of action against the succeeding incumbent for the stipend
and wages of the entire vacation, including what he may
have already received ; whereas the defendant will contend
that the right of action of the plaintiff against the defendant (if it exists at all) is only as to so much, and no
more, as the fruits of the vacation may have been deficient
in amount, and that the amount of such deficiency
ought to have been shewn, and the action limited to that
amount :

That the declaration is bad, and shews no title in the
plaintiff to maintain the present action, it not being stated
or shewn that the plaintiff was appointed or admitted by

the Bishop and Ordinary of the diocese to serve and keep the cure in the declaration mentioned.

Cowling, in support of the demurrer.—The pleas are bad in substance, as well as for the reasons assigned. The action is founded on the stat. 28 Hen. 8, c. 11, s. 10, which enacts, "that if the fruits of the vacation of the said spiritual promotions be not sufficient to pay the curate's stipend and wages for serving the cure the vacation time, that then the same be borne and paid by the next incumbent, within fourteen days next after that he hath possession of any of the said promotions spiritual." The fourth and seventh pleas are pleaded for the purpose of shewing that the stat. 1 & 2 Vict. c. 106, either impliedly repeals that section, or takes away the jurisdiction of the common law courts. Before this last-mentioned statute, it is clear, notwithstanding the doubt in 2 Gibs. Cod. tit. 32, c. 2, note (t), that the only remedy upon s. 10 was by action in the courts of law : Com. Dig. Prohibition, (F. 5) ; *Birch* v. *Wood* (a). Now, though the 99th section of the stat. 1 & 2 Vict. c. 106, provides that where any benefice shall be under sequestration, "it shall be lawful to the bishop, and he is hereby required, *if the incumbent shall not perform the duties of the said benefice,* to appoint and license a curate thereto, and to assign to him a stipend not exceeding &c.," it would seem, from referring to the title of the act and some prior passages, that the language was intended to be confined to cases where there was an incumbent in existence, who, for some reason, did not discharge the duties of his benefice. At all events it would not repeal the stat. 28 Hen. 8, nor the power which sequestrators always previously had of appointing clergymen to serve the cure ; for the language of s. 99 is in the affirmative, without any negative either express or implied: 7 Bac. Abr. tit. Statute, (G.); *Rex* v. *Pinney* (b). Hence

(a) 2 Salk. 506.   (b) 2 B. & Cr. 322.

sequestrators may appoint as formerly, at least until the bishop exercises his power of appointing : and indeed, if it were otherwise, the mischief might arise that, in case from any accident the bishop omitted to appoint a curate, the parish might be altogether without Divine service. As to the objection that the plaintiff is either, by virtue of s. 100, restricted to the profits which the sequestrators may receive, or, if they are not sufficient, the bishop, under s. 101, is to enforce payment from the succeeding incumbent, it is an answer, that those sections are confined to cases of curates appointed by the bishop. A similar answer may be given to the objection, that the jurisdiction of this court is taken away by s. 109, which enacts that, " in every case in which jurisdiction is given to the bishop, &c., under the provisions of this act, and for the purposes thereof, and the enforcing the due execution of the provisions thereof, all other and concurrent jurisdiction in respect thereof shall, except as herein otherwise provided, wholly cease," &c.; for this refers to s. 83, and relates only to " licenses granted and salaries assigned in some way in conformity to the act," as was decided in *Rex* v. *The Bishop of Peterborough* (a), upon a similar clause in the stat. 57 Geo. 3, c. 99. The legislature merely meant that, where the bishop appointed the curate and fixed his stipend, he should have the whole jurisdiction over any disputes relating to it. In *West* v. *Turner* (b), where the plaintiff was barred, the bishop had appointed under the statute. As to the fifth plea, which alleges that the plaintiff was not duly licensed; a license is not requisite for a priest, but only for deacons, and preachers or lecturers. Previously to the Act of Uniformity, 13 Car. 2, c. 4, perhaps a license might have been required for priests, for in ancient times preaching formed no part of the ordinary celebration of Divine service; and the form used in ordaining a priest was, " Take thou power to read the Gospel in

(a) 3 B. & C. 47.   (b) 6 Ad. & Ell. 614.

the Church of God, as well for the living as the dead. In the name of the Father," &c.: Nelson's Rights of the Clergy, p. 431, 2nd ed. But the form in the Rubric since that statute has been, "Take thou authority to preach the word of God, and to minister the holy sacraments in the congregation where thou shalt be lawfully *appointed* thereunto:" whilst that of a deacon is, "Take thou authority to read the Gospel in the Church of God, and to preach the same, if thou be thereto *licensed* by the bishop himself." So that a priest is at once qualified to discharge everything requisite for the service of the cure. This objection was made, but abandoned, in *Powell* v. *Milburn* (a), *De Grey*, C. J., saying, that "no such license is required, or necessary to be had, but only for lecturers." Perhaps the 48th canon of the canons of 1603 will be referred to, but that does not require a "license." The 36th and 37th canons are referred to by the defendant's points; but, though the plea would seem to have reference to one of them, they are subject to several exceptions enumerated in them, which are not negatived in the plea; and therefore it is bad, even if they are not only valid rules of law, but cognizable by a court of law as a defence to the action. But they are in fact not noticeable here, not being binding on the laity, *Middleton* v. *Croft* (b); and cannot affect the plaintiff, who was licensed by the Archbishop of York, whilst the canons purport to have been passed only by a convocation of the province of Canterbury, and it is not clear that they are all binding even in that province. Even if noticeable here, the punishment for a breach of them ought not to be the forfeiture of the plaintiff's salary. Indeed, the plea admits that there was a license, but denies that it was a due license, and the validity of it must at all events be for the decision of the ecclesiastical courts, and cannot be investigated here: *Matingley* v. *Martyn* (c); *Martyn* v.

Exch. of Pleas, 1842.

DAKINS
v.
SEAMAN.

(a) 3 Wils. 355, 361.
(b) 2 Stra. 1057.

(c) Sir W. Jones, 259, 2nd and 3rd Resolutions.

Hind (a). In addition, this plea is bad in form, because it does not state in what respects the plaintiff was not duly licensed: *Hume* v. *Liversidge* (b).

E. V. Williams, contrà.—The declaration is bad, and the pleas are good. The fifth plea is a good answer to the action; for the plaintiff cannot recover unless he is licensed by the bishop. In Watson's Clergyman's Law, which is a book of great authority, it is said (c): "A priest, by his ordination, receives authority to preach the word, and administer the holy Sacraments in the congregation where he shall be lawfully appointed thereunto: Rubr., Stat. 1 Mar. c. 3. Yet, notwithstanding, he may not preach without the license either of the King, or his respective archbishop, bishop, or other lawful ordinary, or one of the universities of Oxford or Cambridge: Stat. 1 Mar. c. 3; 14 Car. 2, c. 4; 13 Eliz. c. 12. But a license by the bishop of any diocese is sufficient, although it be only to preach within his diocese, the statute not requiring any license by the bishop of the diocese where the church is: Pasch., 15 Car. 2, B. R.: *Brown* v. *Spence*, 1 Keble, 503. But this is only to be intended so as to satisfy the words of the statutes, as not to be punished by them for want of a license to preach; for I take it, a preacher by the canons is obliged to procure a license from the bishop of the diocese in which his church is, notwithstanding any former license obtained by him from another bishop." It is said that the canons do not bind the laity; but in investigating an ecclesiastical matter, it is the constant practice to cite the canons. Thus the canons were recognized in *Creswick* v. *Rooksby* (d). So Lord Mansfield, C. J., in *Martyn* v. *Hind* (e), says, "The second objection is, that the plaintiff is not licensed by the incumbent. Within the true intent and meaning

(a) 2 Cowp. 437.	(d) 2 Bulstr. 47.
(b) 1 Cr. & M. 332.	(e) 2 Cowp. 443.
(c) Vol. 1, p. 260, 2nd ed.	

of the *canon law* he is licensed by the bishop; for he has or-

dained him on his title;" thereby recognizing that law, but
getting rid of the objection by saying that the clerk was properly licensed. A person is not a curate unless he is admitted according to the laws of the land. In *Gates* v. *Chambers* (a), Sir *John Nicholl*, after stating the 48th canon,
that " no curate or minister shall be permitted to serve in
any place without examination and admission of the bishop
of the diocese" &c., says, " and the canon is headed, ' None
to be curates, but allowed by the bishop.' Now the object
of this canon seems at least to be, that curates .who are engaged to take charge of parishes, either altogether or in
part, for a continued time, shall be *examined* and *admitted*
by the diocesan." The plaintiff would not be legally in
the office, unless he were admitted and appointed by
the ordinary. In Watson's Clergyman's Law (b), it is
likewise said, " Also if such person as did attend the
cure was only appointed by the churchwardens or other
person, and not duly licensed and admitted thereunto by
the ordinary, or did not duly qualify himself according to
the statute 14 Car. 2, c. 4, I conceive neither the ordinary
nor his minister may detain any part of the profits in respect thereof, for that his license (he not being duly qualified) is void; stat. 13 Eliz. c. 12, and stat. 14 Car. 2, c. 4;
and his serving the cure an unlawful act. And if the
bishop's commission doth employ some neighbouring ministers that have cures of their own, to serve such cure for
the time, without admission as aforesaid by the ordinary,
I suppose that their case is the same, although that they
performed the legal acts aforesaid to settle them in their
own churches." And in Burn's Eccles. Law, tit. Vacation (c), it is said, " And Dr. Gibson says, such curate
ought to be duly licensed by the ordinary for serving of the

(a) 2 Addams's Eccles. Rep.   (c) Vol. 4, p. 4, last edition, by
189, 191.   Dr. R. Phillimore.
   (b) Vol. 2, p. 758.

cure; otherwise, if he proceeds without such license, he can have no title to any stipend or salary, nor can any be legally reserved and deducted for him;" citing Gibson's Codex, 750. The plaintiff should therefore have shewn, on the face of his declaration, as part of his title, that he was appointed by the bishop. Then as to the new act, 1 & 2 Vict. c. 106, the 99th section was intended to apply to all cases of sequestered benefices; it contemplates every case where a benefice is under sequestration. The first case it applies to is, where the incumbent is alive, and shall not perform the duties himself; the second, where there is a sequestration in consequence of death or resignation. The statute assumes (as all the authorities cited demonstrate), that the curate will be appointed and licensed by the bishop. It then provides that the sequestrators are to pay such stipend as the bishop shall order to be paid, and that alone. Then the 101st section provides for what is to be done if the proceeds are not sufficient, and gives a remedy by monition. This statute provides for and regulates this very case, and no action is maintainable on the former statute. By section 109, in every case where jurisdiction is given to the bishop, all other jurisdictions are to cease. By sections 100 and 101, he has power conferred on him to name the stipend and compel its payment; therefore, as neither this nor any other Court or person has jurisdiction to say what is a reasonable stipend, or to compel the payment of it, it is a case within the mischief which the act intended to provide against, and the remedy given by it. The sequestrators are merely the bishop's bailiffs, and have no power to appoint. Even if authority were given to them by the bishop to appoint, it would be void, because he had no right to delegate his authority. But he does not do so. The object of the act was, that the bishop should have authority to assign the amount of the salary, and to enforce payment by monition; and the common-law courts are ousted of their jurisdiction. The fifth plea is therefore good, inasmuch as the plaintiff had no authority to perform the office of curate; and the other pleas are good, because no other person had authority to appoint a curate but the bishop. With respect to the technical objection to the fifth plea, that it is a negative pregnant, if if there be anything in that objection, perhaps the Court will allow the defendant to amend. If the issue went down to be tried, it would be just the same, whether the word *duly* was there or not.

Then the declaration is bad, for stating the cause of action to be for the whole amount of the stipend and wages for the entire period of the vacancy. The statute did not mean that if one shilling short of a reasonable stipend were unpaid, an action was to be had for the whole amount. The plaintiff should have negatived the receipt of any portion of the profits, or stated what the amount received was, and averred further, that the action was merely to compel a reasonable stipend. It is not sufficient to follow the exact words of a statute, where it is clear that by reasonable intendment a larger sense must be given to them than the exact words express. The true meaning of the statute is, that the deficiency may be claimed.

Cowling, in reply.—With regard to the objection to the declaration, that it ought to have stated what the plaintiff had received, and that he was going for the balance, that is matter of defence. The plaintiff could only recover what he was entitled to, after deducting what he had received. The extracts respecting the necessity of a license, which have been cited, appear all to have been based on the one first cited from Watson's Clergyman's Law, and that would seem to have been hastily written, without considering the alteration produced by the Act of Uniformity, coupled with the Rubric. As to the power of the sequestrators, it has always been taken as clear that they had power, and also that it was the most important part of their duty, by virtue of the writ from the bishop appointing them, to provide for the serving of the cure. *Whinfield* v. *Watkins* (a); *Hubbard* v. *Beckford* (b). *Gates* v. *Chambers* (c) shews that even in the ecclesiastical court a license is not necessary for the temporary supplying a cure; and such may have been the case here: indeed, from the apprehension of a lapse taking place, it is very unlikely that the services of a person in the situation of the plaintiff would be wanted for a long space of time.

Lord ABINGER, C.B.—I am of opinion that the plaintiff is entitled to the judgment of the Court. It is not necessary to say how far the canons are obligatory upon the clergy, but it is clear that modern canons do not bind the laity. Nor need we, in the present case, determine whether a license from the bishop is requisite or not. Without doubt, sequestrators cannot appoint a curate permanently, but they may appoint him from week to week, and he will have a claim upon the incumbent for his stipend, fourteen days after the latter has been inducted; and I think this appointment was one of the latter description. The statute of Hen. 8 is not affected, in this respect, by the act of Victoria, which does not contain negative words; and as there is no inconsistency in the two acts, they may well stand together. The plaintiff was duly appointed by the sequestrators, who derived their authority from the bishop. It does not appear for what time the appointment was made, but there is nothing to lead us to suppose that it was of a permanent character. I think, therefore, that the plaintiff is entitled to recover. I have looked into the case of *Middleton* v. *Croft*, as it is reported in Cas. temp. Hardw. 326; it was a case of prohibition, argued by eminent civilians, and involved an elaborate discussion upon the autho-

(a) 2 Phillim. 1.   (b) Id. 5, note.   (c) 2 Addams, 177.

rity of the canons. Lord *Hardwicke* there says, " Sub-
quent acts of Parliament in the affirmative only, although
giving new penalties, are never taken to be a repeal of
former acts, unless there be negative words, or a plain con-
trariety between the two acts, so as there is a plain indi-
cation in the latter of an intention to repeal the former."
In the present case, I can see no intention that the late
act should repeal the former, and therefore, on this and
other grounds, our judgment must be for the plaintiff.

PARKE, B.—I am of the same opinion, and think the
plaintiff may maintain an action for his stipend. The
main question is, whether the statute of Hen. 8 is repealed by the statute of Victoria, and whether the curate
can recover in a court of common law. It is to be observed, that as the words of the latter act are affirmative,
both statutes are compatible, and may well stand together.
The language of the statute of Victoria affords strong
ground for the argument, that as the courts of common
law cannot determine what salary the curate is to receive,
so neither can they assist him in recovering it; and undoubtedly that argument applies, where the curate is appointed under that act; but if the curate is not appointed
by the bishop, the statute of Hen. 8 remains in full force
and effect. It is said that the canon law requires the
curate to be licensed, but I should have great difficulty in
determining that the effect of the statute of Hen. 8 is taken
away by the canons of 1603; that question, however, need
not be considered here; for I am not satisfied that the
plaintiff need be licensed under the 48th canon. A license applies to the case where the appointment is permanent, but here the plaintiff is employed by the sequestrators, and is not appointed for any specified time. The
sequestrators are to see that the duties of the parish are
performed by somebody, and accordingly they appoint the

plaintiff for a short period; it may not, perhaps, be necessary for them to provide for more than two Sundays. Under the circumstances of the present case, I think the plaintiff is entitled to our judgment.

ALDERSON, B., and GURNEY, B., concurred.

Judgment for the plaintiff.

CHAMBERLAYNE v. GREEN.

April 30.

The plaintiff, having obtained final judgment in a cause in the Court of Exchequer, afterwards proceeded for the same cause of action by foreign attachment in the Lord Mayor's Court in London, against the defendant's goods; the defendant surrendered himself into custody in discharge of the attachment; and on the following day, whilst he was so in custody, the plaintiff issued a ca. sa., under which the defendant was detained:—
Held, that the ca. sa. was not irregular; and that, the plaintiff having

HUMFREY had obtained a rule calling upon the plaintiff to shew cause why the ca. sa. issued against the defendant should not be set aside, and the defendant discharged out of custody. It appeared from the affidavits, that the plaintiff, after having obtained judgment against the defendant in this Court, proceeded against him by foreign attachment in London. On the 14th of March, the defendant surrendered himself into custody, in discharge of the attachment. On the 15th, this ca. sa. was sued out against him, by virtue of which the defendant was detained in custody. On the 19th of March, judgment of nonpros for not declaring was signed in the Mayor's Court: it being stated that the mode of abandoning proceedings in the Mayor's Court was not to discontinue the action, but to allow the defendant to sign judgment of nonpros for want of a declaration.

W. H. Watson shewed cause.—The ca. sa. is not irregular, and as the judgment is unsatisfied, there is nothing to prevent the plaintiff from issuing execution. [*Parke*, B.—

abandoned his proceedings in the Lord Mayor's Court, and the defendant having in consequence obtained judgment of nonpros thereon, there was no ground for his discharge under the equitable jurisdiction of the Court.

Mr. *Humfrey*, on moving for the rule, relied upon *Burdus*
v. *Satchwell* (a), as an authority to shew that, there being
an action pending in the Mayor's Court, which had not
been discontinued, it was irregular to issue a ca. sa. in this
court.] The case of *Burdus* v. *Satchwell*, if it can be supported at all, is distinguishable. There, after a writ of
error, the plaintiff brought an action on the judgment;
afterwards the writ of error was nonprossed for want of
transcribing the record, and the plaintiff, without discon-
tinuing his action on the judgment, took the defendant's
goods in execution by testatum fieri facias, which was held
irregular. But there both proceedings were in the same
Court, and that Court had jurisdiction over both. [*Alderson*, B.—And both proceedings were being continued at
the same time.] Here, notwithstanding the proceeding
in the Mayor's Court, the judgment is unsatisfied. That
was a proceeding against the goods of the defendant, and
the defendant has voluntarily surrendered himself to release
his goods from the attachment. One of the proceedings
has been put an end to by the judgment of nonpros; but
in *Burdus* v. *Satchwell* they were both continuing. In
Wood v. *Thompson* (b), the Court of Common Pleas held,
on the authority of *Bromley* v. *Peck* (c), that a defendant
may be arrested in an action in a Court at Westminster,
after having surrendered in discharge of a foreign attachment in the Mayor's Court of London, for the same
cause.

Humfrey, in support of the rule.—The ca. sa. was clearly
irregular. The plaintiff having obtained his judgment in
this Court, pursued another remedy by attachment in the
Mayor's Court, on which the defendant surrendered; and
then the plaintiff proceeds by ca. sa. on the judgment in this

(a) Barnes, 208.   (b) 5 Taunt. 851.   (c) Ibid. 852, n.

Court, on which the defendant is detained; he is therefore twice detained in prison for the same cause of action. *Burdus* v. *Satchwell* is an authority in favour of the defendant, and it makes no difference that there the proceedings were in the same Court; it is equally irregular whether they be in the same Court or another. [Lord *Abinger*, C. B.—We have no jurisdiction where the proceeding is in another Court.] *Burdus* v. *Satchwell* went upon the general principle, that two writs of execution against the person cannot issue at the same time for the same cause of action.

PARKE, B.—It seems to me that there is no irregularity in this case, but that the circumstances merely afford ground for an application to the discretion of the Court, to relieve the defendant from the consequences of two remedies for the same debt being pursued at the same time. It is analogous to the case of a person bringing two actions for the same debt, where it is the practice of the Court to relieve the defendant on motion, instead of leaving him to plead the pendency of the former action. This ca. sa. cannot be said to be irregular, inasmuch as the judgment is regular, and all proper steps have been taken in respect of the execution founded on that judgment. The objection that another proceeding is taken at the same time is merely a collateral matter, and does not make the ca. sa. irregular. Whether the case in Barnes was rightly decided or not, it is unnecessary to discuss; it may have been an application to the equitable jurisdiction of the Court, and the word "irregular" may have slipt into the report by accident. But admitting it to be irregular to commence a second proceeding on the same judgment in the same Court, here the proceeding is in a different Court, and that does not constitute an irregularity, whatever ground it may afford for the exercise of the equitable ju-

risdiction of the Court. In the present case that is unne- Exch. of Pleas,
cessary, as the proceeding in the Mayor's Court has been   1842.
put an end to by a nonpros.

CHAMBERLAYNE
v.
GREEN.

ALDERSON, B.—I agree in thinking that this is properly
the subject of an application to the equitable jurisdiction of
the Court. In the case in Barnes, both proceedings were
pending at the same time, and that was one ground for
setting aside the execution.

ROLFE, B., concurred.

Rule discharged.

———◆———

FORD v. NASSAU.   *April 29.*

C. C. JONES moved (April 15) for a writ of habeas   The Court
corpus, to be directed to the sheriff of Middlesex, com-   will not grant
manding him to bring up the body of the plaintiff, in   a habeas corpus to bring
order that he might be enabled to move in person to set   up a party in
aside two writs of attachment for non-payment of costs,   custody under
under which he was in custody. The affidavit of the plain-   an attachment,
to enable him
tiff stated, that he had been informed and believed that he   to move in per-
had good ground, upon the merits, for his application to   son to set it
the Court to set aside the attachments.   aside.

PARKE, B.—I am not aware of any precedent for such
an application. In the *Attorney-General* v. *Hunt* (a), this
Court refused to grant a habeas corpus to enable a defendant in an information, who was confined in a county gaol
under sentence of another Court for libel, to attend in
Court at Westminster, and conduct his defence in person;
and in *Rex* v. *Parkyns* (b), the Court of King's Bench refused a similar application, where the object was to shew

(a) 9 Price, 147.   (b) 3 B. & Ald. 679.

cause against a rule for a criminal information. You had better look into the authorities, and apply again.

Jones now renewed his application, and said the only authority he could find was the case of the *Attorney-General* v. *Cleave* (a), where this Court granted a writ of habeas corpus to bring the defendant into Court, for the purpose of enabling him to defend an information filed against him for selling unstamped papers.

PARKE, B.—The difficulty is to see in what form the writ is to be. A writ of habeas corpus is issued for some specified purpose, either ad testificandum, or ad respondendum, as the case may be. There is no general form for a writ of habeas corpus; and as there is no authority for doing this, we cannot grant the application.

The rest of the Court concurred.

Rule refused.

(a) 2 Dowl. P. C. 668.

Exch. of Pleas,
1842.

LAWTON v. SUTTON and Others.

April 29.

COVENANT. The declaration stated, that by a certain indenture, William Lawton demised to the defendants certain mines of coal, cannel, and slack; that the defendants covenanted with Lawton and the parties who, for the time being, should be entitled to the mines, that he and the parties entitled should, when they should think fit, employ a proper person at each machine, set up for weighing coals, &c., to weigh the same and keep the accounts, the person so weighing and keeping the accounts to be paid by the defendants; but in case such person should not duly attend at the same machine, and duly keep the necessary accounts, the defendants were authorized to discharge such person. The declaration then stated, that the plaintiff, being the person entitled to the mine, employed one John Hargreaves at a machine in the mine, for the purpose of weighing coals, &c., and of keeping the accounts thereof. Breach, that although Hargreaves had done the usual work at the machine, and had duly attended thereto, and had regularly kept the necessary accounts, yet the defendants had refused to pay him any wages, whereby the plaintiff had been compelled to pay him the necessary wages, amounting to a large sum, to wit, &c. Plea, that the said John Hargreaves was not a fit and proper person; that he had not done the usual work at the machine, nor had duly attended thereto, nor had duly kept the necessary accounts:—on which issue was taken.

At the trial before *Coltman*, J., at the last Chester Assizes, it appeared that Hargreaves had been appointed by the plaintiff, and had been in attendance at the machine for three months; that the defendants had then dismissed

In covenant, the declaration stated, that it was covenanted and agreed between the plaintiff as lessor, and the defendants as lessees, of certain coal mines, that the plaintiff should, when he thought fit, employ a fit and proper person at each machine for weighing the coals, who should weigh the same and keep the accounts, and that his wa^{ge}s should be paid by the defendants; but that in case such person should not duly attend at the machine, and duly keep the necessary accounts, the defendants were author^{1}sed to discharge him. It then averred that the plaintiff appointed J.H., being a fit and proper person, and alleged as a breach, that the defendants refused to pay him his wages. The defendants pleaded, that J. H. was not a fit and proper person, that he had not duly

attended to the machine, and had not duly kept the necessary accounts. At the trial, it was proved that J. H. had been appointed, and had attended for three months, after which period he was dismissed as incompetent by the defendants:—*Held*, that the plaintiff was not entitled to judgment non obstante veredicto: the appointment of a fit and proper person being a condition precedent to the defendants' liability to pay wages.

him without notice, on the ground of incompetency, and refused to pay him any wages. The jury found that Hargreaves was not a proper or competent person, and returned a verdict in favour of the defendants.

On a former day in this term (April 18),

Jervis moved for a rule to shew cause why there should not be a new trial, or why there should not be judgment for the plaintiff non obstante veredicto.—Hargreaves never having been properly dismissed, and no notice having been given, he was entitled to be paid wages for the time he was actually employed. The plaintiff is to appoint a proper person to weigh coals and keep the accounts; if he does not duly attend and duly keep the accounts, then the defendants may discharge him; but until they do so they are bound to pay him. All that the plaintiff is to do, is to select a proper person. The learned Judge treated it as a dry question of law, and ruled that the conduct of the plaintiff, in not appointing a proper person, was an answer to the action, as that was a condition precedent. But by the terms of the contract, the lessees are bound to pay him until they dismiss him, and the plaintiff would presume that he was capable, unless they gave him notice to the contrary. Secondly, this is not a plea which is severable, and it was necessary to establish the whole of it. The plea is, that Hargreaves was not a fit and proper person, that he had not done the usual work at the machine, nor had duly attended thereto, nor duly kept the necessary accounts. Now it was not pretended that Hargreaves had not attended every day, and kept the accounts until he was dismissed. Suppose that he was a fit and proper person, but that he did not properly keep the accounts; the defendants are bound to pay him unless they dismiss him, and give the plaintiff notice of it. The plaintiff is not supposed to be upon the premises, but the defendants are.

Exch. of Pleas,
1842.

LAWTON
v.
SUTTON.

Consistently with this plea, the jury may have found that he was a fit and proper person, but that he did not properly keep the accounts. [*Parke,* B.—We will consult my Brother *Coltman.*]

Cur. adv. vult.

On this day,

PARKE, B., said:—In this case Mr. *Jervis* moved for a new trial, and also for judgment for the plaintiff non obstante veredicto. By the covenant made between the plaintiff and the defendants, the former was to employ a fit and proper person to attend the machine and keep the accounts, the defendants covenanting to pay his wages. The declaration averred, that the plaintiff did appoint a person, and that such person was a fit and proper person, and that he attended at the machine, did the usual work, and kept the necessary accounts. Whether this was the case or not, was a question for the jury. They had ground for thinking that Hargreaves was not a fit and proper person, and we cannot say that their verdict was wrong. Nor do we see any ground for entering judgment for the plaintiff non obstante veredicto. The appointment of a fit and proper person is a condition precedent to the defendants' liability to pay such person his wages. It is argued, that the defendants had the use of his services; that they had the power of dismissing him in case of incompetency, but that if they did not dismiss him, they were bound to pay him his wages. We do not, however, think that the power of dismissal qualifies the rest of the covenants to this extent. If the person appointed was incompetent, the defendants were not bound to pay his wages, although they had also in their hands the other remedy of dismissal. There will therefore be no rule.

Rule refused.

Exch. of Pleas,
1842.

April 29.

An action
being brought
against Wil-
liam Hender-
son for neg-
ligently navi-
gating a ves-
sel, and the cir-
cumstances
under which
the collision
took place
having been
proved, it was
objected that
no evidence
had been given
that the defend-
ant was the
pilot in charge
of the vessel,
whereupon the
plaintiff's coun-
sel called out,
" Mr. Hender-
son !" upon
which a person
in Court answer-
ed "here;" and
said, " I am
the pilot." It
was proved by
one of the wit-
nesses who had
gone on board
the vessel at the
time of the ac-
cident, that he
had seen that
person then act-
ing as pilot :—
Held, that this
was sufficient
evidence of the
identity of the
defendant with
the pilot.

SMITH and Another v. WILLIAM HENDERSON.

CASE against the defendant, for negligence in navigating
a vessel on the River Thames, whereby she ran foul of and
damaged a vessel of the plaintiffs.

At the trial before *Rolfe*, B., at the Middlesex sittings
in Hilary Term last, it appeared that the action was
brought against the defendant as the pilot having the
management and direction of the vessel in question. The
plaintiffs having given evidence to shew that the circumstances under which the collision and the negligence imputed took place, it was objected that no evidence had
been given that the defendant was the pilot who had the
charge of the vessel at the time the accident occurred :
whereupon the plaintiffs' counsel called out " Mr. Henderson !" intending to call the defendant's son as a witness to prove that fact. A person in Court answered
" here," and, coming forward, said, " I am the pilot."
He was not sworn; but one of the plaintiffs' witnesses,
who had gone on board at the time of the accident, proved
that he had seen this person then acting as pilot. The
learned Judge being of opinion that there was no evidence
for the jury of the identity of the defendant, directed a
nonsuit to be entered, giving leave to the plaintiffs to move
to set that nonsuit aside, and to enter a verdict for the
sum of 20l. 14s., the amount of the damage found by the
jury.

Martin having, in Hilary Term last, obtained a rule accordingly,

Montagu Chambers now shewed cause.—Assuming that
the negligence was proved, the identity of the defendant
was not made out by proper evidence. The defendant
ought not to be bound by the statement of a party not

upon oath. The question is, whether the pilot is the present defendant; and there ought to be evidence on oath to the person of the defendant; a person's merely answering to the name of Henderson amounts to nothing, unless it be shewn that he is William Henderson the defendant. In actions on bonds and promissory notes, it is not enough to shew that they bear the signature of a person of the same name, but the plaintiff must identify the defendant with that person. Thus, in *Whitelocke* v. *Musgrove* (a), it was held, that in an action upon an instrument, the subscribing witness to which is dead or resides abroad, it is necessary, besides proving the handwriting of the subscribing witness, to give some evidence of the identity of the party sued with the party who appears to have executed the instrument. So here, there ought to have been something besides the name to connect the defendant with the pilot. [*Parke*, B.—Similarity of name and residence, or similarity of name and trade, will do. This is an action against William Henderson, who is a pilot; then a man gets up in court, who is a pilot, and answers to the name of Henderson.] The answer given by the man is not upon oath. A statement or admission of a stranger cannot be used to affect the defendant. If at the time he was at the helm he had been asked his name, and he had said "William Henderson," that declaration might have been admissible, as it would have been part of the res gestæ. In *Middleton* v. *Sandford* (b), where issue was joined on non est factum, it was held that some evidence must be given of the identity of the party executing the deed, which was not to be presumed from its having been executed by a person in his name, in the presence of the attesting witness, who was unacquainted with him. *Dampier*, J., there held that some evidence of identity was indispensably

(a) 1 Cr. & M. 511.　　　　(b) 4 Camp. 34.

necessary; and he said, " Even presuming that the name of the person who executed the bond was Thomas Sandford, how did it appear that this was the Thomas Sandford sued in the present action ?" So here, there is nothing but the similarity of name. Again, in *Parkins* v. *Hawkshaw* (a), it was held by *Holroyd*, J., that on non est factum pleaded to a bond, it was not sufficient to prove the execution by a person who executed in the name of the defendant, without proof of identity. A person's appearing in court, and bearing the name of Henderson, and sworn to be the pilot, was not enough; his identity with the defendant ought to have been shewn. *Hennell* v. *Lyon* (b) may perhaps be relied upon on the other side, but that case is distinguishable, because there the identity of the defendant was made out by character and description, as well as by name.

Martin, in support of the rule, was stopped by the Court.

Lord ABINGER, C. B.—It appears to me that this rule ought to be made absolute. The action was brought against William Henderson, a pilot, and a person in court answers to the name of Henderson, and is proved to be a pilot, and to have been the pilot on board the vessel in question. That is evidence from which the jury might assume him to be the defendant. But then Mr. *Chambers* objects that the statement is not made upon oath. As to that, there are many things which are incapable of strict legal proof. A man's name is a mere matter of reputation; that which is termed in Scotch law the status of a man, is matter of reputation : and if precise evidence of the relationship of one man to another, or other matters of that nature, were always required, no fact of that kind could ever be proved in practice. Here, there was evidence of the identity

(a) 2 Stark. N. P. C. 239.   (b) 1 B. & Ald. 182.

of the defendant, although it was not proved directly that the name of the party who answered in court was "William." There was evidence that he was a pilot; that he was the pilot on board the vessel; and he answered to the name of Henderson. I think that is sufficient.

PARKE, B.—I think there was some evidence of identity. The defendant is sued on the face of the declaration as William Henderson, a pilot. A man in court answers to the name of Henderson, is a pilot, and was proved to be the pilot acting on board the vessel. He therefore fulfils the description in the declaration in two respects, at least, that his name and calling resemble those of the alleged defendant.

ALDERSON, B.—I am of the same opinion. If the very strict proof required by Mr. *Chambers* were necessary, it would be almost impossible to try any cause whatever.

ROLFE, B., concurred.

Rule absolute.

April 29.

THORNTON and Another *v.* CHARLES.

Assumpsit for
goods sold and
delivered. It
appeared at the
trial that a
broker, em-
ployed by the
plaintiffs to sell
200 casks of
tallow, sold 50
to the defend-
ant, and the
remainder to
two other par-
ties, to be de-
livered some
months subse-
quently to the
sale. In the
bought note he
described the
transaction as
a purchase of
50 casks for
"his prin-
cipals," i. e.
the buyers; and
in the sold note,
as a sale of 200
casks sold to
his principals.
In his book he
stated the de-
fendant as the
purchaser of
50 casks, and
the two other
parties as pur-
chasers of the
remainder.
There was no

ASSUMPSIT for goods sold and delivered, and on an
account stated.

Plea, non assumpsit.

At the trial before Lord *Abinger,* C. B., at the London
sittings after last Michaelmas Term, it appeared that the
action was brought for the price of 50 casks of tallow, alleged to have been sold and delivered by the plaintiffs to
the defendant. On the 20th of February 1841, the plaintiffs instructed their brokers, Messrs. Smith & Marshall,
to sell for them 200 casks of tallow, to be delivered between the 1st of September and the 31st of December
following, and on the same day received from the brokers
a sold note, in the following terms :—" London, 20th Feb.
1841.—Sold for Messrs. B. & R. Thornton & West, to our
principals, 200 casks of St. Petersburgh first sort of yellow
candle tallow," &c. The bought note was in the same
terms, except that it stated the purchase to be of 50 casks,
" for our principals." The entry in the brokers' book was
as follows :—" London, 20th Feb. 1841.—Sold for Messrs.
R. Thornton & West, (Messrs. Paton & Charles, 50; Mr. John
Smith, 50; Messrs. Cattley & Stephenson, 100), 200 of St.
Petersburgh first sort of yellow candle tallow," &c. All
the above documents were put in evidence at the trial.

disclosure of the principals on either side. About the time appointed for the delivery, the broker
urged the defendant to buy 100 other casks of a third person, and on the latter objecting to do so,
on the ground that the 50 casks already contracted for by him would soon be delivered, offered to
" put off " those casks. The 50 casks were never actually delivered to the defendant. It was objected, on this evidence, that the plaintiff ought to be nonsuited, on two grounds : first, that inasmuch as there was a variance between the bought and sold notes, the broker's book not being evidence of the contract, there was no valid contract; secondly, that there was nothing to shew
any delivery of the 50 casks to the defendant. The learned Judge being of that opinion, nonsuited the plaintiffs :—*Held,* that the nonsuit was wrong on the second ground, it being a question for the jury, whether the words " put off " meant a sale of the goods to a third person by
the broker on account of the defendant, or a postponement of the delivery with or without the
consent of the plaintiffs.

Quære, whether the memorandum of a sale in the broker's book, signed by him, is admissible as evidence of the contract, to satisfy the Statute of Frauds, in cases where there is no other
written contract, or where the bought and sold notes disagree.

The names of the principals on either side were not disclosed. On the 14th September, the plaintiffs delivered to the brokers, in fulfilment of their contract, 75 casks of tallow, and on the 22nd of the same month, the remaining 125 casks. On the 14th September, the broker Marshall applied to the defendant to buy 100 casks of tallow from another party, and on the defendant's objecting, on the ground that the 50 casks already contracted for by him would be delivered between September and December, stated that he would undertake to " put off" the 50 casks. It did not appear clearly whether the words " put off" meant a sale of the 50 casks to a third party by the broker, on account of the defendant, or whether it meant a postponement of the delivery, with or without the consent of the plaintiffs. No actual delivery of the 50 casks ever took place. At the trial, it was objected for the defendant that the plaintiffs ought to be nonsuited, on two grounds: first, that there being a variance between the bought and sold notes, and the entry in the broker's book not being admissible, no valid contract had been proved; and secondly, that there was no evidence to shew the *delivery* of the 50 casks to the defendant. The learned Judge being of that opinion, nonsuited the plaintiffs, giving them leave to move to enter a verdict, if the Court should be of a contrary opinion.

R. V. Richards, in Hilary Term last, obtained a rule accordingly, or for a new trial.

Crowder and *C. A. Wood* now shewed cause.—First, there was no legal contract entered into with the plaintiffs, inasmuch as there was a variance between the bought and sold notes with respect to the number of the casks. The bought and sold notes are the only legal evidence of the contract: *Thornton* v. *Kempster* (a). It is clear, from *Hawes* v. *Forster* (b), that the bought and sold notes constitute the con-

(a) 5 Taunt. 786.   (b) 1 M. & Rob. 368.

tract, and therefore the broker's book is not admissible to prove it. [*Parke*, B.—I always thought it was, because the broker is the agent of both parties; he is sworn to do his duty, and bound by his bond to enter the terms properly. May not the entry in his book, therefore, be evidence of the contract between the parties?] In *Thornton* v. *Meux* (a), *Abbott*, C. J., says, "I used to think, at one time, that the broker's book was the proper evidence of the contract; but I afterwards changed my opinion, and held, conformably to the opinion of the rest of the Court, that the copies delivered to the parties were evidence of the contract they entered into, still feeling it to be a duty in the broker to take care that the copies should correspond." And in *Hawes* v. *Forster* it was held, that where a contract is made through a broker, the bought and sold notes delivered to the parties constitute the contract; not the entry made by the broker in his book. That case, it is submitted, settled the law on this subject. [*Parke*, B.—This is not a case like *Hawes* v. *Forster;* here the bought and sold notes do not agree, and therefore there is no contract on the face of them. The case of *Hawes* v. *Forster* is not an authority against the reception of such evidence; it only shews, that although there be a contract in the broker's book, the parties may by their own act constitute the bought and sold notes the contract. The difficulty with me is, why is a broker called upon to sign his books, and obliged by his bond to do so, if they are not to have a binding effect?] In *Thornton* v. *Meux*, the notes did not agree: so also in *Thornton* v. *Kempster*. Secondly, there has been no delivery of the 50 casks. There was no contract between these plaintiffs and this defendant at all,—neither a sale nor delivery; but assuming that there was a contract, there was, at all events, nothing like a delivery. What took place between the defendant and the broker was nothing but a postponement of the delivery to a future period.

(a) Moo. & Malk. 44.

R. V. Richards and *Martin*, contrà.—The real contract

between the parties is that which takes place verbally; but
the statute requires that the contract should be in writing,
and if any memorandum of that contract is in writing, it is
sufficient. The bought and sold notes may constitute such
memorandum; but if there be none, or none which are
valid, then the contract in the broker's book is the real evidence of the contract; that being an entry signed by an
agent for both parties, lawfully authorized so to do. What
was said by *Abbott*, C. J., in *Thornton* v. *Meux*, has been
misunderstood. In *Heyman* v. *Neale* (a), Lord *Ellenborough*
says, "After the broker has entered the contract in his
book, I am of opinion that neither party can recede from
it. The *bought and sold note* is not sent on approbation,
nor does it constitute the contract. The entry made and
signed by the broker, who is the agent of both parties, is
alone the binding contract. What is called the *bought and
sold note* is only a copy of the other, which would be valid
and binding, although no *bought or sold note* was ever sent
to the vendor or purchaser." [Lord *Abinger*, C. B.—That
was a case where the bought and sold notes agreed; but
I have this experience, that when they differed, Lord *Ellenborough* nonsuited the plaintiff. If the notes differ, it shews
there is no contract at all. *Parke*, B.—*Goom* v. *Aflalo* (b)
was the first case in which it was held that the bought and
sold notes were sufficient evidence of the contract.] In
Grant v. *Fletcher* (c), the broker's note was held not to be
binding, because it was not signed; but there *Abbott*, C. J.,
says, "The broker is the agent of both parties, and, as
such, may bind them, by signing the same contract on behalf of buyer and seller. But if he does not sign the *same*
contract for both parties, neither will be bound. The entry in the broker's book is, properly speaking, the original,
and ought to be signed by him. The bought and sold

(a) 2 Camp. 337.   (c) 5 B. & C. 436; 8 D. & R.
(b) 6 B. & C. 117; 9 D. & R. 148.   59.

notes delivered to the parties ought to be copies of it.   A
valid contract may probably be made, by perfect notes
signed by the broker, and delivered to the parties, although
the book be not signed; but if the notes are imperfect, as
in the present case, an *unsigned* entry in the book will not
supply the defect." Does it not follow from what he there
says, that if the book had been signed, it would have been
in his opinion sufficient? It does not appear from the report
of *Thornton* v. *Meux*, whether the broker's entry in that case
was signed or not. In *Goom* v. *Aflalo, Abbott*, C. J., says—
" The entry in the book has been called the original, and the
notes copies, but there is not any actual decision that a valid
contract would not be made by notes duly signed, if the entry
in the book be *unsigned*." That case does not decide that if
the book were signed it would not be good evidence of the
contract, but rather the contrary. In *Henderson* v. *Barne-
wall(a), Hullock*, B., says—" Bought and *sale* notes are not
essential to the validity of the contract; the entry signed by
the broker is alone the binding contract, said Lord *Ellenborough*, in the case of *Heyman* v. *Neale*, which doctrine is
confirmed by the decision in *Grant* v. *Fletcher*."

Secondly, the plaintiffs ought not to have been nonsuited,
for it was a question for the jury whether the facts proved did
not amount to a delivery to the defendant. The agreement
that the broker should " put off" the goods, was an agreement that he should receive them for the defendant, and
sell them to a third party on his behalf; it meant, not that
he should postpone the delivery, but that he should *dispose
of* the goods. If that was the true construction of the
transaction, then the delivery of the goods by the plaintiffs to the broker was a delivery on behalf of the defendant. Here the principals being unknown, the plaintiffs
had no other means of delivering the goods to the defendant than through the medium of the broker; and the effect

(*a*) 1 Y. & J. 387.

of the transaction was the same as if the tallow had ac- *Exch. of Pleas,*
1842.
tually been delivered to and received by the defendant.

THORNTON
v.
CHARLES.

Lord ABINGER, C. B.—As there appears to be some
doubt about the meaning of the term " put off," although
I thought all parties understood it in the same sense
at the trial, and as some questions may arise respecting
the arrangement between the broker and the defendant,
the rule for a new trial had better be made absolute.

PARKE, B.—It appears to me that, after all, this is a
question of fact, to be determined by the jury. Whether
enough has been done to satisfy the Statute of Frauds, is
a point that we need not discuss at present. But I apprehend it has never been decided, that the note entered
by the broker in his book, and signed by him, would not
be good evidence of the contract so as to satisfy the Statute of Frauds, there being no other. The case of *Hawes*
v. *Forster* underwent much discussion in the Court of
King's Bench, when I was a member of that Court, and
there was some difference of opinion amongst the Judges;
but ultimately it went down to a new trial, in order to ascertain whether there was any usage or custom of trade
which makes the broker's note evidence of the contract.
In that case there was a signed entry in the book, which
incorporated the terms of making the contract void in the
event of the non-arrival of the goods within a certain time.
The bought and sold notes, which were delivered to the
parties, omitted that clause. Certainly it was the impression of part of the Court, that the contract entered in the
book was the original contract, and that the bought and
sold notes did not constitute the contract. The jury found
that the bought and sold notes were evidence of the contract, but on the ground that those documents, having been
delivered to each of the parties after signing the entry in
the book, constituted evidence of a *new* contract made be-

tween the parties, on the footing of those notes. That
case may be perfectly correct; but it does not decide, that
if the bought and sold notes disagree, or there be a memorandum in the book made according to the intention
of the parties, that memorandum, signed by the broker,
would not be good evidence to satisfy the Statute of
Frauds. However, it is not necessary to pronounce a decided opinion on that part of the case, because I think, if
there has been a delivery, it is clear it was a delivery in
pursuance of the contract of the broker, and then it would
bind the parties within the statute. Then comes the question, whether there was a delivery or not? That appears
to me to be a pure question of fact, to be decided by the
jury, and it turns upon the meaning of the arrangement
made between the broker and the defendant, as to *putting
off* the tallow. If the meaning of the term " put off " be,
that it was to be put off on the defendant's account, that
is, that a new customer was to be obtained, then the moment the tallow was received by the broker, it was received
by him as the agent of the defendant, and the defendant
was liable on the contract as for goods sold and delivered.
But if it merely means that the broker was to postpone
the delivery, then there would be this further question,
whether it means that he should make an arrangement with
the unknown principal to postpone it, and not consider it
as a delivery; and if that be so, then the plaintiffs must
fail, because there has been no delivery. If it means, that
the broker, without consulting his principal, although the
broker had received the goods to deliver to the defendant,
was to postpone them contrary to his duty to his principal,
I am strongly impressed with the opinion that that would
amount to a dealing with the goods so as to make it a delivery, and render the defendant liable for them as goods
sold and delivered. All these are questions of fact, which,
from a misunderstanding at the trial, appear not to have
been submitted to the jury. The case is one of consider-

able importance to the parties, and it seems to me to be Exch. of Pleas, 1842.
right that the matter should undergo further investiga-
tion, when those points will be presented for the consi- THORNTON
deration of the jury; for, after all, this is a pure question *v.* CHARLES.
of fact.

ALDERSON, B.—I also think there ought to be a new trial.
It seems to me that this is a question of fact; but, as at
present advised, I do not entertain much doubt as to the
meaning of the words "put off." Another point which
presses on my mind is, whether an arrangement to postpone the delivery of the goods, without consulting the interest of the plaintiffs, can be considered a delivery to the
defendant. On that point I entertain great doubt.

ROLFE, B.—I concur in thinking there ought to be a new
trial. I must confess, if I were a juryman, I should have
little doubt what was the meaning of the term "put off."
Judging from the context, the meaning appears to be, that
the delivery from Thornton should be postponed. At the
same time, I think it is a question of fact, and therefore there cannot properly be a nonsuit. I inferred from
the notes of the trial, that all the parties proceeded on the
ground of this being the true construction of it, but that
does not appear to have been the case, and I think, therefore, there should be a new trial.

Lord ABINGER, C.B.—I have purposely avoided giving
any opinion about the question of the bought and sold
notes, but I desire it to be understood that I adhere to
the opinion given by me, that when the bought and sold
notes differ materially from each other, there is no contract, unless it be shewn that the broker's book was known
to the parties. With respect to the other point, I did not
imagine that any doubt existed as to the witness's explanation of the phrase "put off," after I had pointed out to

him the distinction between the delivery of the goods by the broker, or the holding of them by him as the agent of the defendant, and the undertaking not to deliver them to the defendant. I thought nobody doubted that the witness's explanation was that which I put upon it, namely, that the broker undertook not to deliver the goods. I thought that as he was the agent to deliver, and was dealing with unknown principals on both sides, he had a discretion as to when or whether he would deliver the goods; that if he delivered them to other persons, expecting to get the price for them, then he complied with the undertaking not to deliver them to the defendant. I thought the point intended to be raised was, whether, when he, being the middleman, and the agent of both parties, received the whole of the 200 casks, which included the 50 bought by the defendant, his mere reception of them was the reception of the defendant. I think that the delivery of the bill of parcels was a delivery to him as agent of the plaintiffs, which he might deliver to the buyer. The rule for a new trial will however be made absolute.

Rule absolute.

May 2.

RUSSELL and WIFE *v.* SMYTH.

An action of assumpsit or debt may be maintained against a defendant resident in this country, for costs awarded against him, after appearance, by a decreet of the Court of Session in Scotland, in a suit for a divorce.

ASSUMPSIT to recover the sum of 93*l.* 5*s.* 8*d.*, for costs due to the plaintiffs by virtue of a decreet made by the Lords of Council and Session in Edinburgh, whereby they divorced the plaintiff, Elizabeth, from the defendant, and found the defendant liable to the said Elizabeth in the costs and expenses. The defendant pleaded, first, non assumpsit; secondly, that the defendant was not in Scotland at the time of the summons and action or proceedings, or at the time of pronouncing the decreet, within the jurisdiction of the said Court; that he had not been summoned to appear, and had not any heritable property in Scotland. This plea was struck out, on the understanding that the defendant should be at liberty to give the facts stated therein in evidence under the general issue. The cause came on for trial at the Liverpool Summer Assizes, 1840, before *Rolfe*, B., when a verdict was found for the plaintiffs, damages 93*l*. 5*s*. 8*d*., subject to the opinion of the Court on the following case:—Examined copies of the summons, proceedings, and decreet, in an action of divorce in the Scotch courts, prosecuted by the female plaintiff, by her then name of E. N., against William Gray Smith, or Smyth, were proved at the trial, and copies thereof are contained in the appendix to this case, and may be referred to by either party as part thereof.

At the trial, the plaintiffs proved, by the evidence of an advocate at the Scotch bar, that the practice of the Scotch courts as to entering appearances is as follows: The process being in the custody of the clerk of the court, the procurator or agent of the defendant applies to the clerk of the court in the name of an advocate, to borrow the process out for the purpose of taking it to the advocate's chambers, to examine it on the part of the defender, in order to see whether any defence can be made. The clerk on this sends the process to the party so applying, and at the time of so doing, makes a marking in the margin according to the following form, " alt. Thomson, to see," which he signs by his, the clerk's, initials, Robt. Welsh. It appears by the appendix, that the examined copy of the summons proved in the evidence was so marked, and the witness explained the meaning of such marking to be, that Robert Welsh, as agent of the other side or defender, had, in the name of Thomson, an advocate, obtained the process, to see it on behalf of the defender. The word "act." immediately preceding, in the margin, means *actor* (the pursuer), and " alt." means *alter*, i. e., the party who is to appear on the other side.

The agent then takes the process to the advocate's chambers, to consult whether it is a case to be defended or not. This is a regular method of entering appearances according to the practice of the Scotch courts. It would not be consistent with the duty of the clerk of the court to make such a marking on the margin, unless Welsh had in fact applied as agent of the defender, and unless in pursuance of such application the clerk in court had in fact lent him the process, in order to its being taken to Thomson as the advocate, to consider; and if by any mistake an erroneous marking were made, it would be the duty of the clerk in court to amend it; and such marking, according to the practice of the Scotch courts, shews that an appearance has been entered. If the advocate does not think it a case in which a defence should be made, the case is not defended, and the process is returned to the clerk. The inquiry then proceeds, not in respect to the defendant's absence, but in respect that no defences are given in. The marking on the margin of the said proceedings in the Scotch court at the suit of Elizabeth Smith against William Gray Smith, indicates that an appearance was entered for the defender, but that no defence was made in the above action, and the proofs were taken and lent, and the decreet in question made, as in a case in which there were no defences, and not in absence or for want of appearance; and the said proceedings and decreet produced appeared to be perfectly regular according to the Scotch law. The same witness (the Scotch advocate) proved that there is no rule of Court which would prevent an advocate who happened to know that proceedings had been instituted against a friend absent from the kingdom, from applying to the clerk in court to see the summons, even though he (the advocate) had no authority to appear for the absent party; but the clerk in court would not be warranted in lending the summons for any purpose except that of enabling the party applying for it to appear in regular form; and if, after it is returned, the clerk should discover that it had

been obtained not in the ordinary course, it would be his duty to make an entry in the margin accordingly, so as to correct the mistake. No proof was given to shew that the person who lent the process, and made the marking, was a clerk authorized to enter appearances; or that either Thomson or Welsh had any authority from William Gray Smith or Smyth to appear for him; but it was proved that there was, at the time of the proceedings in question, a writer to the signet of the name of Welsh. It was proved by the same Scotch advocate, that by the Scotch law a wife may institute proceedings in the Court of Session, called a summons and action of divorce, against her husband, to obtain a divorce, and, on proof of his adultery, may obtain a divorce à vinculo matrimonii from her husband, and may lawfully marry again; that if the husband be a Scotchman, and have left the realm of Scotland, the wife may lawfully institute such proceedings in the absence of the husband, although the husband be not personally served with notice of such proceedings, and have no property within the realm of Scotland; and the wife may in such case proceed, and on competent proof of the husband's adultery, obtain a divorce from her husband, in the absence of the said husband; but the husband may, if he so please, appear by his procurator in the manner before stated, and may, if he so please, defend the action by his procurator, though personally absent.

It was proved at the trial that the plaintiff, Elizabeth Russell, was formerly the wife of William Gray Smyth, the defender in the said action of divorce, and it was also proved that he had lived at Dumfries, where his parents and the family resided, that he was a medical man, and reputed to have obtained his diploma as a surgeon, but that he never practised his profession at Dumfries, and that he is now about thirty-six years of age. The plaintiffs, in order to identify him with the defendant in this action, called Henry Jenneret, the clerk to the defendant's attorney, and proved by him that he had known William Gray Smyth, the defendant in the present action, three or four years in London; that the witness did not know of his own knowledge that the now defendant was a Scotchman, nor had he heard it from him, but that the defendant had told him that he had been in Scotland, and had lived at Dumfries; that the defendant is now a medical man, apparently forty years of age.

The questions for the opinion of the Court are—first, whether the present action is maintainable against the defendant on the said decreet; and secondly, whether there was evidence from which the jury ought to have inferred that the defendant in this action is the same person as the defender in the action in the Court of Session; the Court to be at liberty to draw any inference which a jury might have drawn. If the Court are of opinion in the affirmative, the verdict is to stand, otherwise a nonsuit is to be entered.

The copies of the proceedings in the Court of Session contained the summons, with the above marginal marking; the return of the summoning officer, that he had summoned the defendant; the appointment to the pursuer of fourteen days to appear and remit her oath of calumny; her appearance and deposition; the allowance of proof to the pursuer; a petition by the pursuer for a commission to examine a witness, "alt. not compearing or objecting;" the grant of the commission; the appointment for the proof to proceed; the following entry :—

" 9th March, 1833.

" Lo. Mackenzie.   Act. Pyper.   Alt. absent.   Advisandum.   With the proof adduced, and whole process.

" J. H. Mackenzie."

" And lastly, the judgment finding the defendant guilty of adultery, and liable to the pursuer in expenses."

Crompton for the plaintiffs.—An action is maintainable in the Courts of this country, for costs awarded by a Scotch Court. It appears, in this case, that a regular appearance was entered on the roll, and that no defences were made to the suit. The defendant appears to have allowed a judgment similar to that of nil dicit to be signed against him. It is suggested in the case that there might have been some deception, but credence must be given to the judgment-roll in this respect, there being nothing on the face of it, or anything stated in the case, to shew that it was not regular. The proceedings were therefore valid. In *Cowan* v. *Braidwood* (a), all these questions were very much discussed, and there it was held that it must be shewn that there was something wrong in the mode of proceeding. *Maule*, J., there says,—" The Courts of Westminster, in sustaining decrees of foreign courts against absent persons, have decided that, in their judgment, a decree may not be contrary to natural justice, although made against a party who is absent, for absence alone is not sufficient to invalidate the proceedings.—He also referred to *Douglas* v̇. *Forrest* (b), and *Becquet* v. *M‘Carthy* (c)."—Secondly, it was thrown out on the trial, that an action could not lie on a decreet of this kind, and *Carpenter* v. *Thornton* (d) will be relied upon. It was there held, that an action at law is not maintainable upon a decree of a court of equity for a specific sum of money, founded on equitable considerations only: but the argument to be deduced from that case is answered by that of *Henley* v. *Soper* (e). It was there held, that debt lies on the decree of a colonial Court, made for payment of a balance due on a partnership account. And Lord *Tenterden* says,—"There is a great difference between a decree of a colonial court, and of a court of equity in this country. The colonial

(a) 1 Man. & Gr. 882; 2 Scott, N. R. 138.

(b) 4 Bing. 686 ; 1 M. & P. 663.

(c) 2 B. & Adol. 951.

(d) 3 B. & Ald. 52.

(e) 8 B. & Cr. 16; 2 Man. & R. 153.

court cannot enforce its decrees here—a court of equity in this country may; and therefore, in the latter case, there is no occasion for the interference of a court of law; in the former there is, to prevent a failure of justice." Thirdly, there is abundant evidence of the identity of the present defendant, and of the party named in the proceedings in the Court of Session. There is not only the double name, but the profession, and the place of residence.—On this point he cited *Simpson* v. *Dismore* (a).

W. H. Watson, contrà.—This Court will not give effect to this decreet, on the ground that all the proceedings took place in the absence of the defendant,—as appears from the entries, "alt. not compearing or objecting;" "alt. absent;" —and are, therefore, contrary to natural justice. It might be different if it had appeared that the defendant had property in Scotland, or resided there, so as to be within its jurisdiction. It is clear, according to a variety of authorities, that the Courts of this country will not give effect to judgments obtained in the absence of the party : *Obicini* v. *Bligh* (b); *Houlditch* v. *Marquis of Donegal* (c); *Buchanan* v. *Rucker* (d); *Ferguson* v. *Mahon* (e); *Smith* v. *Nicholls* (f). The case of *Douglas* v. *Forrest* is distinguishable, for that case proceeded on the ground of the defendant being a Scotchman born, having heritable property in Scotland. Here it appears, very indistinctly indeed, that the defendant was a Scotchman born, but he has no domicile or property there. *Cowan* v. *Braidwood* does not affect this argument at all, because in that case it did not appear on the plea that the defendant was not accessible to the jurisdiction of the Court; he might have been a Scotchman born, and possessed of heritable property in that country. Secondly, no action can be maintained in this country for costs awarded

(a) Antè, 47.

(b) 8 Bing. 335; 1 M. & Scott, 477.

(c) 8 Bligh, N. S. 301.

(d) 1 Camp. 63; S. C. 9 East, 192.

(e) 11 Ad. & Ell. 179; 3 P. & D. 143.

(f) 5 Bing. N. C. 208; 7 Scott, 147.

by a foreign Court. Costs are accessary to a judgment, and although an action might be brought for them in Scotland, it does not follow that it can be maintained in this country. Costs are awarded against a party by way of punishment, for having made a false charge; and there is no implied promise that a party residing in England will pay such as have been awarded by a foreign Court.—He also contended that the suit being for a divorce, which was matter of ecclesiastical cognizance, this Court could not entertain it; and that, on the face of the proceedings, there did not appear to be any valid judgment of divorce. As to these points, he cited *Carpenter* v. *Thornton*, *Henley* v. *Soper*, *Sadler* v. *Robins* (a), 11 Geo. 4 & 1 Will. 4, c. 69, s. 31, *Warrender* v. *Warrender* (b), *Coot* v. *Lynch* (c), Bac. Abr. " Prohibition," (L.) 5, Fitz. N. B. 52, *Emerson* v. *Lashley* (d), *Fry* v. *Malcolm* (e).

Exch. of Pleas, 1842.

RUSSELL *v.* SMYTH.

Crompton, in reply, was stopped by the Court,

Lord ABINGER, C. B.—I cannot assent to the argument of Mr. *Watson*, that this is a matter of ecclesiastical jurisdiction, and that therefore we are precluded from entertaining it. The question arises in Scotland, and the decree of the Court of Session creates a duty in the party to pay a debt, and does not give rise to the question of jurisdiction. It is plain that this is not a decree of an ecclesiastical Court, but of a Court of competent jurisdiction awarding costs, and not having the power by its own process of enforcing the payment of them in this country. An action of assumpsit, or debt, therefore, lies for the recovery of them. I think we must assume the process and decree to have been perfectly regular; the examination of the advocate shews them to be so, and the decree is made, not against a party who does not appear, but against one

(a) 1 Campb. 253.
(b) 9 Bligh, 89.
(c) 5 Mod. 421.

(d) 2 H. Bl. 248.
(e) 4 Taunt. 705.

who does appear, and afterwards abandons his defence. The defendant might have offered some defence, but he quits Scotland, so that the plaintiffs had no remedy against him in that country. The action may be sustained on the ground of morality and justice. The maxim of the English law is to amplify its remedies, and, without usurping jurisdiction, to apply its rules to the advancement of substantial justice. Foreign judgments are enforced in these Courts, because the parties liable are bound in duty to satisfy them. The principles relating to this subject are well laid down by Lord *Mansfield*, in his judgment in *Robinson* v. *Bland* (a). Mr. *Watson* urges, that no action for costs has ever been brought on a foreign judgment. I cannot quite assent to that; but supposing it were so, I must own I should be disposed to set an example of such an action. Suppose litigation arises in France relating to real property, and costs are given against a party who comes to this country:—if the English law gives no remedy, the debt would be lost. In such a case, I should be disposed to say that an action for those costs may be maintained in this country. I assume this decree to be regular in all its parts; and I do not enter upon the question, how far judgment may be pronounced against a party in his absence, so as to give another the right of enforcing it against him in this country. As to the main question in this case I entertain no doubt, and think that it is governed by the principles that were laid down in *Emerson* v. *Lashley*. As to the question of identity, there is ample evidence on which the jury would have found that point against the defendant. The name, residence, and profession were the same, and the party defending the action must have known that his identity would be disputed, and yet he called no witnesses to shew that he was not the party who was alleged to have married the female plaintiff. Our judgment will therefore be for the plaintiffs.

(a) 2 Burr. 1077.

PARKE, B.—I am of the same opinion. There appears *Exch. of Pleas,* 1842.

RUSSELL
v.
SMYTH. to me to be ample evidence of identity. The defendant in the present action bore the same Christian and surname with the defendant in the Scotch suit: both had resided at Dumfries; and there was a correspondence in their ages and professions. As to the second point, it is unnecessary to deliver an opinion as to the effect of a judgment upon a party who is absent, and has no property in the country where the judgment is pronounced. Here we must assume that the defendant entered an appearance, and that the agent who took that step for him had authority for that purpose. If this had not been the case, the appearance might have been set aside in Scotland, and the party would have had a remedy against his attorney. But then it is said, that divorce is matter of ecclesiastical jurisdiction, and that the Courts of this country will not enforce a decree made by the Court of Session in Scotland in such a matter. This was a Scotch marriage; and assuming, as we must, that this decree was regular, I agree with Lord *Abinger* in thinking that an action will lie for the recovery of costs awarded by a foreign Court of competent jurisdiction. Where the Court of a foreign country imposes a duty to pay a sum certain, there arises an obligation to pay, which may be enforced in this country. The case of *Carpenter* v. *Thornton* is distinguishable, because Courts of equity have the power of enforcing their decrees by a process of their own. Whether the decree be final or not, it is unnecessary to determine; nor need we say how far the judgment of a Court of competent jurisdiction, in the absence of all fraud, is conclusive upon the parties. It is enough to determine that the present action may be maintained, and that our judgment must be for the plaintiffs.

ALDERSON, B.—I think there was ample evidence of identity, founded upon the resemblance between the names, professions, places of abode, and ages of the parties. Secondly, this was not a decree made in the absence of the defender, but a judgment by default, and I think an action can be maintained upon it in this country, on the grounds stated in the case of *Emerson* v. *Lashley*. The defendant was bound, by the decision of a Court of competent jurisdiction, to pay a sum of money, and therefore an action will lie to recover it. In *Carpenter* v. *Thornton* the decree was founded on equitable considerations only, and might have been enforced by process out of Chancery.

ROLFE, B.—The doubt created in my mind by Mr. *Watson's* argument was, how far an action for the same subject matter might be maintained in Scotland; but that is out of the question when the defendant is in this country. Here there is an obligation to pay the costs, which may be made the foundation of an action.

Verdict to be entered for the plaintiffs.

———◆———

DE MEDINA *v.* NORMAN.

THE declaration stated, that whereas the plaintiff, before and at the time of the making of the agreement as thereinafter mentioned, was lawfully possessed, for the residue of a term, whereof twenty-one years from the 24th June, 1841, were then unexpired, of a certain dwelling-house; and thereupon, on the 21st March, 1841, by an agreement made between the plaintiff and defendant, it was agreed that the plaintiff should, on or before the 24th June, 1841, let the same to the defendant, by a lease to be granted to the defendant for twenty-one years, the said term to commence from the 24th June, 1841. The declaration then stated general performance by the plaintiff, and that he was ready and willing to let the house to the defendant, and to grant and execute a lease; yet that the defendant did not nor would not become his tenant, or accept the lease. Pleas, first, that the plaintiff was not lawfully possessed of the house, for the residue of the said term, modo et formâ: secondly, that the plaintiff, at the time of the agreement, had not a good title to, and could not, on the 24th June, legally let the house to the defendant, or grant a lease for the said term:— *Held*, on special demurrer, that the first plea was bad, as containing an immaterial traverse; and that the traverse in the second plea was too large, as it included the title of the plaintiff at the time of the contract, as well as at the time when the lease was to be granted. *Held*, also, that on general demurrer, the averment of the plaintiff's readiness and willingness to grant the lease was equivalent to an averment of his having a title to grant it.

due of a term of years, whereof 21 years and upwards from the 24th of June, 1841, were then to come and unexpired, of a certain dwelling-house and premises; and thereupon, to wit, on the 31st of March, 1841, by a certain agreement made between the plaintiff and the defendant, it was agreed that the plaintiff should, on or before the 24th of June, 1841, let to the defendant, and that the defendant should become tenant to the plaintiff, and the defendant then agreed to become tenant to the plaintiff, of the said house and premises, upon the following terms; viz. that the letting should be by a lease to be executed and granted by the plaintiff to the defendant for 21 years, the said term to commence from the 24th of June, 1841, when the plaintiff was to execute such lease. The declaration then stated, that although the plaintiff *had performed and fulfilled all things* in the agreement contained on his part to be performed, and although he was within a reasonable time after the making of the said agreement, and on the 24th June, 1841, *ready and willing to let* to the defendant the said house and premises, and to grant and execute to the defendant the said lease, yet the defendant did not nor would, at any time on or before the 24th June, 1841, become tenant to the said plaintiff of the said house and premises upon the terms aforesaid, or otherwise, and on the day and year last aforesaid wholly refused to become such tenant, or to accept such lease. To this declaration the defendant pleaded, secondly, that the plaintiff was not lawfully possessed for the residue of the said term of years of the said dwelling-house and premises in the declaration mentioned, modo et formâ. Thirdly, that the plaintiff, at the time of the agreement, had not a good title to, and could not, nor could he on the 24th of June, 1841, legally let to the defendant, or grant and execute to her a lease of the dwelling-house for the said term of twenty-one years.

Special demurrer. The causes of demurrer to the se-

Exch. of Pleas,
1842.

DE MEDINA
v.
NORMAN.

cond plea were, that the traverse was immaterial, as it merely denied that the plaintiff was possessed of the term before and at the time of the agreement, whereas it would be sufficient for the plaintiff to shew that he was possessed of the term on or before the 24th of June, so as to be able on that day to complete the agreement; and that it is inconsistent with that allegation, that the plaintiff was possessed of the residue of the said term on or before the 24th of June.

The causes of demurrer to the third plea were, that it either introduces new matter, in which it should have concluded with a verification, or it is an informal traverse of the plaintiff's averment of his readiness and willingness to let the house and execute the lease; and that it put in issue more than was alleged in the averment, to wit, that at the time of the making of the agreement the plaintiff had not a good title to let the dwelling-house, or execute the lease, &c.

The following points were marked for argument on the part of the defendant:—That the declaration itself is insufficient, for that if the title set out in the declaration is to be considered as mere inducement to the action, the declaration is bad, for not alleging that the plaintiff had a legal title to the premises on the 24th of June 1841, but merely that he was on that day ready and willing to let the premises to the defendant.

Martin, in support of the demurrer. The objection to the declaration is, that it is bad for not alleging that the plaintiff had a legal title to the premises on the 24th of June; but when he states that he was ready and willing to perform the contract, it is not necessary to go on and shew that he had title, as it must be assumed that he had capacity to do so. The defendant contends that the plaintiff ought to have averred that he was able to do so; but that was not necessary, nor is there any precedent for such an

averment. It is only necessary for the plaintiff to aver
that he was ready and willing to execute the lease.

Then as to the pleas. The second is bad, as it is a traverse of immaterial matter, for it is sufficient if the plaintiff, on the 24th of June, was in a condition to grant a
lease, or if he had had a power in him to grant a
lease. The third plea is also bad, for the reasons assigned. It is true it was held in *Souter* v. *Drake* (a), that
in a contract for the sale of an existing lease, there is an
implied undertaking by the seller to make out the lessor's
title to demise; but in *George* v. *Pritchard* (b), *Abbott,* C.J.,
expressed a different opinion. He there says,—" On looking to the agreement, I do not find a syllable to warrant
the averment in the declaration, that the defendant undertook to make out a good title to the lease. Without such
a stipulation, a party selling a lease is not bound to produce his landlord's title, a thing which in most cases would
be utterly impossible." [*Parke,* B.—My doubt is, whether
the averment of readiness and willingness is sufficient. In
Martin v. *Smith* (c), there was a general allegation of title
in the plaintiff, as well as the averment of readiness and
willingness. He must have a good title to convey. If,
however, he has a good title when he is called upon to perform his agreement, it is enough. Where it is necessary
for a party to make out a title, it is necessary to state on
the pleadings that he did make out such title. The question is, whether the averment of the plaintiff's readiness and
willingness is sufficient, without an averment of his ability
to make such title.] On general demurrer, the allegation
amounts to an averment that the plaintiff was in a situation
to do that which he contracted to do. If not, the question mentioned in Sugden on Vendors, pp. 225, 226, never
could have arisen. It is there said,—" To entitle a vendor

(a) 5 B. & Ad. 992; 3 Nev.   (b) 1 Ry. & M. 417.
& M. 40.   (c) 6 East, 555.

to sustain an action for breach of contract, it has been said that he must shew what title he has; it not being sufficient to plead that he has been always ready and willing, and frequently offered to make a title to the estate (*a*). In a late case (*b*), however, where a vendor averred *that he was seised in fee*, and made a good and *satisfactory* title to the purchaser of the estate, by the time specified in the conditions of sale, it was held sufficient, and that it was not necessary for him to shew how he deduced his title to the fee. And the Court seemed of opinion, in opposition to the prior cases, that a vendor need not display his whole title on the record." If it were a material averment to shew that he had a title to grant the lease, it would be traversed in every case. At all events, this allegation is sufficient on general demurrer. If it be sufficient that he has a good title when called upon, according to the contract, to execute the lease, that shews that the third plea is bad, because it states that the plaintiff *at the time of the agreement* had not a good title to grant the lease. The traverse is too large; it puts in issue that which it is unnecessary to prove, which it ought not to do. In *Regil* v. *Green* (*c*), *Parke*, B., says,—"The plaintiff has no right to include several matters in his replication, so as to embarrass the trial." It is also bad, for saying that the plaintiff could not *legally* let to the defendant; that might be because the defendant was incapable of accepting a lease, he being an alien.—He cited also *Jevens* v. *Harridge* (*d*).

G. *T. White*, contrà.—The declaration is bad. It was incumbent on the plaintiff, in suing on an agreement for the sale of the lease, to aver that he had title to sell. The

(*a*) *Phillips* v. *Fielding*, 2 H. Black. 123.

(*b*) *Martin* v. *Smith*, 6 East,

555; 2 Smith, 543.

(*c*) 1 M. & W. 332.

(*d*) 1 Saund. 1.

case of *Souter* v. *Drake* goes even further than this. Lord
Denman, C. J., in delivering the judgment of the Court, says,
" For the reasons above given, we come to the conclusion,
that, unless there be a stipulation to the contrary, there is,
in every contract for the sale of a lease, an implied undertaking to make out the lessor's title to demise, as well as
that of the vendor to the lease itself, which implied undertaking is available at law as well as in equity; and we cannot adopt the distinction acted upon in *George* v. *Pritchard*."
In *Luxton* v. *Robinson* (a), it was held that the party who
sues for a forfeiture on an agreement by him to deliver up
possession, must shew in his declaration a possessory title
in himself. *Buller*, J., there says, " The plaintiff was to
deliver possession, and therefore he ought to have shewn
that he had a right so to do." In this case he is to grant
a lease, and he ought therefore to shew his right to do so.
That cannot be collected from this declaration. In *Lay-
thoarp* v. *Bryant* (b), which was an action for not completing a purchase of a lease, it was held that the plaintiff, who
had alleged his possession of the lease, was bound to prove
the execution of the original lease, and of the mesne assignments to him. The authorities shew that the inducement may be traversed: Com. Dig. Pleader (G), 14; *Ki-
mersly* v. *Cooper* (c); *Carvick* v. *Blagrave* (d). The case of
Poole v. *Hill* (e) is not an authority for the plaintiff, because
although it is the purchaser's duty to prepare the conveyance, the lessor is to prepare the lease. Besides, the plaintiff ought to have averred that he offered to execute a lease.
Jones v. *Barkley* (f).

Martin in reply.—The declaration is good. The plaintiff was bound to aver the performance of all conditions

(a) 2 Dougl. 620.
(b) 1 Bing. N. C. 421; 1 Scott,
327.
(c) Cro. Eliz. 168.

(d) 1 Brod. & B. 531.
(e) 6 M. & W. 835.
(f) 2 Doug. 684.

precedent, or that he has been ready and willing to perform them. Here he has averred that he has performed all things on his part to be performed, and that he was on the 24th June ready and willing to let, and to grant and execute the said lease. A traverse of the readiness and willingness would have put the title in issue. A person cannot be said to be ready to do a thing if he is not in a condition to do it. In *Lawrence* v. *Knowles* (a), which was an action by the assignees of a bankrupt against the defendant, for not delivering railway shares pursuant to a contract made with the bankrupt, the plaintiffs having in their declaration averred that the bankrupt before his bankruptcy, and the plaintiffs as his assignees since, were always ready and willing to accept and to pay for the shares, and the defendant having taken issue upon that averment, it was held that the plea was sustained by proof that before the time fixed for the performance of the contract, the bankrupt was in a state of total incapacity to pay the price agreed on, and that his effects produced no assets to the assignees. *Bosanquet*, J., there says, "The party must not only be willing, but he must be ready also; and when he is shewn to be utterly incapable, he is shewn to be not ready to do that which he has engaged to do." This averment necessarily involves in it the condition that he has power to do what he contracts to do. [*Rolfe*, B.—Et hoc paratus est verificare, means that he is in a condition to verify it.] *Jones* v. *Barkley* has to some extent been overruled by *Poole* v. *Hill.*

Lord ABINGER, C. B.—I am of opinion that the second plea is bad, as containing an immaterial traverse of the plaintiff's title. It may be that the plaintiff was not possessed of the term on the day of the agreement being entered into, but that is unimportant, if he was possessed of

(a) 5 Bing. N C. 399; 7 Scott, 381.

it on the day when he was to execute the lease to the de-

fendant. The defendant then objects to the declaration,
that it does not state that the plaintiff had a right at the
time to grant the lease in question. The contract, however, will bind the defendant, if the plaintiff was ready and
willing to grant the lease before the 24th June. The declaration is not bad on general demurrer for want of this
statement. If the defendant had traversed the averment
of the plaintiff's readiness and willingness to perform the
contract, he would have put in issue his *ability* to perform
it; for the words " ready and willing" imply not only the
disposition, but the capacity to do the act. The defendant,
therefore, ought to have traversed the readiness and willingness. The plaintiff is consequently entitled to our judgment.

PARKE, B.—I think the second plea is bad, as containing an immaterial traverse. The averment in the declaration is, that the plaintiff was possessed of the term at the
time of his agreement with the defendant, not that he contracted that he had the term on the 24th of June. The
traverse of that averment is immaterial. I doubted at
first whether it did not mean that the plaintiff was possessed of the term at the completion of the contract, in
which case the traverse would have been good. The third
plea is also bad, as being too large, since it includes the
title of the plaintiff at the time of the contract, and also at
the time of the demise. The next question is, whether the
declaration is good? The meaning of a contract to demise is, not only that a certain form of words shall be put
on paper, but that the party assuming to demise shall have
title to demise. The lessee bargains for a good lease, and
the lessor cannot maintain an action against him, unless
he had power to make a lease. It is, therefore, essential
to aver in such a case that the landlord had authority to
make a good lease. But then the objection to this decla-

ration must be considered as taken on general demurrer. That being so, it is substantially averred that the plaintiff had title to demise. The declaration states, for instance, that the plaintiff had performed all things on his part to be performed; and, if I mistake not, there is a case in Carthew's Reports (a) which decides that that averment would be sufficient for the present purpose. But supposing that averment to be insufficient, still the allegation of the plaintiff's readiness and willingness to let the premises is equivalent, on general demurrer, to an averment of his being able to execute such lease; for on the issue of readiness and willingness, the plaintiff might have proved that he was in a condition to make a valid demise. This was the opinion of *Tindal,* C. J., and the other Judges of the Court of Common Pleas, in *Lawrence* v. *Knowles,* and this Court laid down the same doctrine in *Hibblewhite* v. *M'Morine* (b). —[His Lordship here stated the facts and pleadings in that case.]—We there thought the plaintiff's title to the shares arose " on the traverse of the readiness to convey, which must involve the capacity to do so." I think, therefore, that the declaration is good on general demurrer, and that our judgment must be for the plaintiff.

Alderson, B.—I am of opinion that the pleas are bad. The second plea takes issue on an immaterial averment. The declaration states, that before and at the time of the agreement, the plaintiff was legally possessed for the residue of a term of a certain dwelling-house; now it is clearly immaterial to the right of the plaintiff to recover, that he should prove that he had a title to the lease before the demise to the defendant. The term might be merged in the fee, and so he might not be possessed of it, but still he would be able to grant a lease. There are many other suppositions in which the same result would arise. The

(a) Quære, *Knight* v. *Keech,*   (b) 6 M. & W. 200.
Carth. 271.

averment in the declaration is therefore immaterial, and *Exch. of Pleas,* the traverse insufficient. The third plea is also bad. Then, 1842. is the declaration good? I think it is. The averment of De Medina readiness and willingness to let to the defendant includes *v.* the capacity to do so. Norman.

Rolfe, B.—Whether the plaintiff be bound or not to aver that he had a title to demise, or that he tendered a lease, still the declaration is good on general demurrer. The allegation of readiness and willingness is in substance an allegation that he had done all that was necessary, and that he had the power to grant a lease to the defendant.

Judgment for the plaintiff.

Thomas *v.* Evans.

May 7.

A RULE had been obtained to rescind an order of Lord *Denman*, C. J., at chambers, made on the 11th March, for staying the proceedings in this action. An application had been made to his Lordship at chambers, on the 14th of March, to rescind the order, which he had refused. In the affidavit in support of the present rule, no mention was made of that application.

Bovill, who shewed cause, objected that the application so made at chambers should have been disclosed on the face of the affidavit, and cited *Goren* v. *Tute* (a).

Lord Abinger, C. B.—The plaintiff has brought before the Court the only order that has been made: no alteration took place in the state of facts on the second hearing at

An affidavit in support of a rule to rescind a Judge's order need not take notice of a previous application for the same purpose made at chambers, and refused; unless it be necessary to do so in order to account for apparent delay in making the application to the Court.

(a) 7 M. & W. 142.

chambers. What the Judge has done must be brought before the Court, but surely not what he has omitted to do.

PARKE, B.—In *Goren* v. *Tute,* it was necessary to state the previous proceedings at chambers, in order to account for the delay in making the application to the Court.

The rule was then dismissed on the merits.

———•———

PATRICK *v.* STUBBS.

May 4.

An owner pur autre vie of a common may approve under the statutes 20 H. 3, c. 4, and 13 Ed. 1, st. 1, c. 46.

The owner of a common may erect thereon a house necessary for the habitation of beast-keepers, for the care of the cattle of himself and the other persons having rights of common there. So he may erect a house necessary for the habitation of a woodward to protect the woods and underwoods on the common.

A plea justifying the erection of a house

CASE for disturbance of common. The declaration stated, that whereas the plaintiff was possessed of a certain messuage, and by reason thereof was entitled to common of pasture in a certain place or common, called Richard's Castle Woods, yet the defendant erected two cottages thereon, and kept them so erected, so that the plaintiff could not enjoy his right of common in as ample a manner as he otherwise would have enjoyed it.

The defendant pleaded, thirdly, that Richard's Castle Woods was a waste; that E. Salwey was seised in fee of part of it; that the Bishop of Worcester, being seised in fee of the remainder, enfeoffed E. Salwey of the remainder, during the lives of three persons, still living; that the said two parts were planted with woods and underwood; that other persons than the plaintiff had right of common over the said Richard's Castle Woods, for their cattle to browse the underwoods; that because the underwood was destroyed

for such beast-keepers need not state the names of the other commoners, nor that they assented to the appointment of beast-keepers.

To an action on the case for a continuing disturbance of common, the defendant pleaded an approvement of the locus in quo, "leaving sufficient common of pasture for the said plaintiff and all other persons entitled thereto, together with sufficient ingress and egress to and from the same, according to the form of the statute, &c.:"—*Held,* that the plea sufficiently shewed that enough of common was left at the time of the approvement, and in the place where the plaintiff was entitled to enjoy it.

by trespassers, and could not be preserved without wood-wards resident on the common, the defendant, as servant of E. Salwey, built the said cottages on the first mentioned part of the said common, for the habitation of two wood-wards of E. Salwey, who were appointed by him to preserve the woods, and were necessary for that purpose. The fourth plea was similar to the foregoing, except that it justified the erection of the cottages as habitations for beast-keepers, who were necessary for the safe custody of the cattle of the plaintiff, of E. Salwey, and of the other parties who were entitled to the rights of common. The fifth plea stated, that the said place on which the defendant so erected and continued the said cottages, as in the declaration mentioned, was part and parcel of a certain waste situate in the manor of Richard's Castle, of which said waste E. Salwey was, at &c., seised in his demesne as of fee; that the defendant, as the servant of E. Salwey, and by his command, erected the said cottages, and inclosed the same from the residue of the said waste, and approved the same, and kept and continued them so erected as in the declaration mentioned, leaving sufficient common of pasture for the said plaintiff, and all other persons entitled thereto, together with sufficient ingress and egress to and from the same, according to the form of the statute &c., as he lawfully might &c. Verification.

To these pleas there were special demurrers, the grounds of which appear by the argument.

Joinder in demurrer.

Willes, in support of the demurrers.—The third and fourth pleas contain no allegation that sufficient common was left for the commoners, and therefore are not founded on the statute of Merton, 20 Hen. 3, c. 4, which requires that when any improvements are made by the lord, sufficient common shall be left for the commoners. Those pleas therefore must stand upon the clause of the statute of Westminster 2nd, 13 Edw. 1, st. 1, c. 46, which enacts, that

"by occasion of a windmill, sheepcote, cowhouse, enlarging
of a court necessary, or curtilage, from henceforth no man
shall be grieved by assize of novel disseisin for common of
pasture." Upon this statute Lord Coke observes, 3 Inst.
476, "here be five kinds of improvements expressed, that
both between lord and tenant, and neighbour and neighbour, may be done, without leaving sufficient common to
them that have it, (anything either herein, or in the statute of Merton, to the contrary notwithstanding), and
these five are put but for examples; for the lord may
erect a house for the dwelling of a beast-keeper, for the
safe custody of the beasts, as well of the lord as the
commoners, depasturing them in that soil; and yet it is
not within the letter of this law." The third plea is bad,
for a woodward does not resemble a beast-keeper, nor
does he fall within the provisions of the clause of the statute Westminster 2nd, which was intended only to promote
buildings for agricultural purposes, and for the habitation
of the lord. 32 Lib. Ass. p. 195, pl. 5. In *Nevill* v. *Hancerton* (a), which was an action wherein the plaintiff declared
that he had common in three acres, and the defendant had
inclosed two of them, the defendant pleaded that he had
a house there, and he made the inclosure for the enlargement of the curtilage: and upon demurrer, the plea was
held ill, because it was not said that the messuage was for
his own habitation, or of his shepherd; for he might perhaps build a great messuage to lease to a nobleman, which
might require a greater curtilage than the lord himself, or
his herdsman. So, where a man justifies, as in the fourth
plea, the erection of houses for beast-keepers, he must
shew that they were necessary for his own beasts, and it is
not sufficient to shew that they were necessary for the
beasts of other people. The fourth plea is bad for another
reason, because the statute of Westminster 2nd does not
authorize the erection of a house for a beast-keeper, and

(a) 1 Lev. 62; Sid. 70, nom. *Nevell* v. *Hamerton.*

the authority in the Year Book, 7 Hen. 4, p. 38, pl. 9,

which is referred to in the third Institute, as the authority
for the position already mentioned, does not support the
dictum of Lord Coke. That was an action against a commoner for pulling down a house built by the lord upon
the common, and the defendant justified on the ground
that the house was built in disturbance of his common.
The plaintiff replied that the house was built for a beast-
keeper. No judgment was given, but the defendant's counsel being asked by the Court whether he would demur, says,
" Nous voillomus emparler, &c."; this case is mentioned
in Bro. Abr. 'Commoner,' pl. 19, and the compiler, after
saying that, by the judgment of Hull, J., the case might
be within the equity of the statute, adds a "quære."
At all events, that case is not an authority that a man
may appoint beast-keepers for the cattle of others; there is
no mention of any such power in the report, and such an
appointment, if good at all, ought to be made in the court
of the manor, where the commoners may be presumed to
have had a voice in the appointment. Without their concurrence, it is absurd to suppose that the lord could have
the power of appointing a herdsman for their cattle.
Nevill v. *Hancerton* shews that an approvement for the benefit of a stranger would be unjustifiable. Besides, the
commoners for whom the appointment was made ought to
have been named. Again, a party cannot approve unless
he is seised in fee, or is lord of the manor: *Glover* v.
Lane (a): but here the approver was merely tenant pur
autre vie of part of the common. The fifth plea is also
bad; it is founded partly upon the statute of Merton, and
partly on that of Westminster 2nd; but it is consistent
with this plea, that the "waste" therein mentioned is
larger than the place mentioned in the declaration, and as
the defendant has not stated, according to the precedents
in Rast. Entr. 'Trespass,' 626 b, and 9 Wentw. 206, that

(a) 3 T. R. 445.

he left a sufficiency of common in the residue of the common, it is consistent with the plea that the common left
by him was left in lands where the plaintiff had no right
of common. The plea is also bad, for omitting to state
the time at which the common was left. The sufficiency
must be left at the time of the approvement: Vin. Abr.
' Common.' It is uncertain to what time the expression
"leaving" refers.   [Lord *Abinger*, C. B.—It sufficiently
appears· that the common was left at the time when the
inclosure took place.]

    W. H. Watson, contrà.—The third and fourth pleas are
good, and are founded upon the statute of Westminster
2nd. That statute refers to the statute of Merton. Lord
Coke says, that the statute in terms mentions five species
of building only, but he observes, that those buildings are
merely put by way of example: for that the lord may
erect a house for the dwelling of a beast-keeper, for the
safe custody of the beasts, as well of the lord as of the
commoners, depasturing there. That construction of the
statute has never yet been objected to. In *Strother* v.
Hutchinson (a), *Tindal*, C. J., alluding to Lord Coke's commentary on this statute, says, " we must look, however,
not only to the statute, but to the commentary of Lord
Coke, which has been uncontradicted to the present day."
But the authority of Lord Coke is supported by the case
in the Year Book, for there the counsel, by refusing to raise
the question on demurrer, in fact assented to the law as
laid down by the judge in that case. And this construction of the statute is conformable to reason, for in the
present case a woodward and beast-keeper stand in the
same situation, being both necessary to preserve that which
is the subject-matter of the common. The case of *Nevill*
v. *Hancerton* is not in point, the question having been there
decided on the want of an averment that the house was

        (a) 4 Bing. N. C. 83; 5 Scott, 346.

built for the habitation of the lord, or his shepherd. Secondly, a man may erect the necessary buildings on a common, without being seised in fee. The statutes of Merton and Westminster 2nd do not mention the interest that the party making such erections must have; and it was held in *Glover* v. *Lane,* that the owner of the fee, as well as the lord of the manor, might approve the common. In principle there can be no distinction between the owner of the fee, and a tenant pur autre vie, or for a long term of years. Besides, E. Salwey was a tenant in fee of the spot where the buildings were erected. The last plea is also good, and is founded upon the statute of Merton. It is sufficiently averred therein that enough common was left for the plaintiff in the place where he was entitled to common. In *Arlett* v. *Ellis* (a), it was held that a custom to inclose parcels of the waste, leaving a sufficiency of common, was good. The last objection is, that the defendant ought to have set out the names of the parties entitled to common of pasture; but that is not necessary, and would lead to endless prolixity; the defendant is not bound to know their names; it is a matter which lies in the equal knowledge of both parties. Indeed, the plaintiff himself has a direct interest to know who the parties are who use the common. [As to this point he was stopped by the court].

Willes, in reply.—*Arlett* v. *Ellis* has no bearing upon the case, except so far as it supports the general principle that sufficient common must be left in the place from which the inclosure is made. No precedent has been referred to in which the loose mode of statement, adopted in the fifth plea, has been upheld. Lord Coke, in the 3rd Inst., does not intimate that the concurrence of the commoners to the appointment of a beast-keeper for their cattle, as well

(a) 7 B. & Cr. 346.

as of the owner of the soil, is unnecessary. Without their concurrence such an appointment would be idle, because it cannot be contended that a beast-keeper appointed by A. B. could meddle with C. D.'s cattle without his consent. This is material, because the erections complained of may be reasonable for the habitation of beast-keepers for all the cattle, but unreasonably large for the beast-keepers of the lord only.

Lord ABINGER, C. B.—I am of opinion that all the pleas are good. With respect to the last plea, the fair meaning of it is, that sufficient common of pasture was left where the plaintiff has the right of common; and although a laborious argument has been founded on the strict grammatical meaning of the words of the plea, the clear meaning is, that the plaintiff's rights have not been abridged, and that enough common has been left him in the spot where he claims his right. We may conceive cases of inclosure by one lord of a manor, by which the rights of an adjoining lord may be affected; but if enough common is left for the tenants of the manor, they at least have no right to complain. I also think that the third and fourth pleas are good. They depend upon the statute of Westminster 2nd. I never doubted that Lord Coke was right where he says, that the five buildings enumerated are put by way of example; and his observations apply to several ancient statutes, the framers of which were not so prolific in words as the authors of modern acts of Parliament. In the present day, in framing a statute, the course is to employ all the rhetoric of conveyancers and special pleaders, and to provide for every case that suggests itself to the imagination of the person who draws the act. Formerly it was otherwise, and courts of law were left to interpret the meaning of the legislature. And the case in the Year Book is far from impeaching the authority of Lord Coke; for, as Mr. *Watson* has suggested, the counsel for the defendant being invited by the Judge to demur, and thus raise the question as to the lord's right to build a house for a beast-keeper, declines to do so, saying that he would rather imparl. The object of this part of the statute of Westminster 2nd is the benefit of the commoners. The erection of a cowhouse is within the very terms of the act; and I think that a house, erected by the owner of the soil for his own advantage and that of the other commoners, falls within the principle of the statute. Our judgment must therefore be for the defendant.

PARKE, B.—I am of the same opinion. The justification in the first two pleas is, that the defendant, being owner in fee of part of the soil, and tenant pur autre vie of the remainder, built the cottages in question to protect the woods and pasture in which he and others had a right of common; and the question is, whether that is a case falling within the Statute of Westminster 2nd. The act in terms mentions only wind-mills, sheep-houses, cow-houses, and the enlargement of the necessary court or curtilage. But then Lord Coke, in his Commentary, says those instances are put merely by way of example. The principle that governs the former of those cases is the joint benefit to all the commoners from the erections, and therefore the building of a cottage for a woodward or a beast-keeper falls within the same principle. Indeed, the building of a house for a beast-keeper is expressly said by Lord Coke to be within the spirit of the act. With respect to inclosing common for a curtilage, that means that the lord has a right of inclosing so much common only as is necessary for his own mansion-house, and that explains the case of *Nevill* v. *Hancerton*, reported in 1 Lev. 62, and Sid. 79. *Windham*, J., there says, it is necessary to aver that sufficient common was left " only where the inclosure is for the improvement of the land, not where it is for the enlargement of the curtilage."

With regard to the defendant not being owner in fee of

Exch. of Pleas,
1842.

PATRICK
v.
STUBBS.

all the land, I think that makes no difference in this case, as the bishop, who is seised in fee of part of the common in question, had granted him his rights over the common. I have entertained some doubts as to the last plea, whether "leaving sufficient common of pasture" means leaving it in that place where the plaintiff was entitled to enjoy it ; but as the defendant is entitled to our judgment on the other pleas, which dispose of the substantial questions in the case, our judgment as to this plea is not of so great consequence; and I concur with the rest of the Court, that on the whole record our judgment must be for the defendant.

ROLFE, B.—The Statute of Merton says nothing as to the nature or extent of the interest that the lord is to have in the soil; and it must be quite indifferent to the commoner, if enough common of pasture is left to him, whether the lord of the manor incloses in his own right, or as the grantee of another.

Judgment for the defendant.

May 6.

A plea of the Statute of Limitations, though it need not conclude with a verification, must nevertheless be signed by counsel.

ROBERTS *v.* HOWARD.

To an action of assumpsit the defendant pleaded, first, non assumpsit ; secondly, that he " the defendant did not at any time within six years next before the commencement of this suit, promise in manner and form &c., whereof the defendant prays judgment," &c. The plea not being signed by counsel, the plaintiff signed judgment. *Knowles,* on a former day, obtained a rule calling upon the plaintiff to shew cause why that judgment should not be set aside for irregularity.

E. V. Williams shewed cause.—A plea of the Statute of Limitations, being a special plea, requires to be signed by

counsel. That was never doubted until the case of *Boden-*
ham v. *Hill* (a), which decided that such a plea, being in
the negative, required no verification. But that case has
nothing to do with this question; a plea is equally special,
although in the negative; and although it need not be
averred, it is nevertheless a special plea. In *Millner* v.
Crowdall (b), which was an action on an attorney's bill, it
was held that a plea, under the stat. 1 Jac. 1, c. 7, s. 1,
that no bill was delivered under his hand; need not be
averred, as it was needless, it being a negative plea; but
it cannot be doubted that such a plea requires counsel's
signature. By a rule of the Court of Queen's Bench, E.
T. 18 Car. 2, all special pleas were required to be signed
by counsel before they could be filed. In Vin. Abr.,
Plea and Pleading (K.) 1, it is said, " If there be a special
plea, replication, rejoinder, or demurrer, there must be
counsel's hand to it, because it is supposed to be advised
by counsel, who is to maintain it to be good if it be disputed." In *Macher* v. *Billing* (c) this Court expressly held
that a plea of the Statute of Limitations required counsel's
signature; and the decision in *Bodenham* v. *Hill* has nothing to do with it.

Knowles, contrà.—It is not true that every special plea
requires counsel's signature, for there are many which do
not; as, for instance, the plea of plene administravit and
riens per discent. Until the argument of Mr. Serjt. *Manning* in *Bodenham* v. *Hill*, it had been usual to conclude a
plea of the Statute of Limitations with a verification; and
that was the ground on which it was thought it required
counsel's signature. [*Parke*, B.—What is the reason why
a plea of son assault demesne or solvit ad diem require to
be signed, which they do? It is a mere arbitrary matter.]
It is submitted that *Bodenham* v. *Hill* having decided that

(a) 7 M. & W. 274.   (b) 1 Show. 338.

(c) 1 C., M. & R. 577.

this plea need not conclude with a verification, it does not require counsel's signature.

PARKE, B.—The general rule is, that all special pleas must be signed by counsel, although undoubtedly there are many exceptions that have been arbitrarily introduced into practice. This very point was decided in *Macher* v. *Billing*, that such a plea as this did require counsel's signature; and that was not on the ground that the plea was averred. The rule for setting aside the judgment must therefore be discharged.

The other Barons concurred.

Rule discharged.

————————

May 9.

CETTI *v.* BARTLETT.

A party entitled to costs under an interpleader order, is not bound to take out execution under the Interpleader Act, 1 & 2 Will. 4, c. 58, s. 7, but may make the order a rule of Court, and take out execution under 1 & 2 Vict. c. 110, s. 18.

THIS was a rule calling on the plaintiff to shew cause why a ca. sa. issued against one Johnson should not be set aside, and why he should not be discharged out of custody. It appeared from the affidavits, that the plaintiff had issued a fieri facias against the goods of the defendant Bartlett, and that upon the sheriff proceeding to levy, Johnson claimed the same; an application was in consequence made to a Judge at Chambers under the Interpleader Act, when Johnson appeared upon the summons, and an order was made that, upon his giving security for 21*l.* 0*s.* 4*d.*, and for such further sums for costs as the Master should think reasonable, an issue should be tried to ascertain the property in the goods. Johnson being unable to give the required security, an order was made discharging the former order with costs. This latter order having been made a rule of Court, and the costs taxed at 14*l.* 2*s.* 2*d.*, a ca. sa. was issued upon it, in pursuance of the 1 & 2 Vict. c. 110, s. 18. The present rule was obtained on the ground that the execution ought to have

been issued under the Interpleader Act, 1 & 2 Will. 4, *Exch. of Pleas,*
1842.
c. 58, s. 7, by which orders may be entered of record, and
execution issued for the costs within fifteen days after CETTI
v.
BARTLETT.
notice of taxation.

Jervis shewed cause.—The 1 & 2 Vict. c. 110, s. 18,
which gives to rules of Court the effect of judgments, applies to all rules. The plaintiff was not compelled to proceed under the 1 & 2 Will. 4, c. 58, but might pursue the
other remedy. The words of that act are not compulsory;
they are, "that rules and orders *may* be entered of record;" there is nothing to restrict a party to that course.

Humfrey, in support of the rule.—The Court will, if
possible, give effect to both the acts of Parliament. As
the proceedings were commenced under the Interpleader
Act, the execution should have been in accordance with its
provisions, and the order entered of record.

Lord ABINGER, C. B.—I think the rule ought to
be discharged. Where a party entitled to costs under
the Interpleader Act chooses to proceed for their recovery under that act, he must, doubtless, pursue the
course there prescribed, and enter the order of record.
But if he chooses to proceed under the 1 & 2 Vict. c. 110,
s. 18, he may make the order a rule of Court, and issue
execution upon it.

PARKE, B.—I also think that the plaintiff was not
obliged to proceed under the Interpleader Act. Although
the order was made under that act, it has been made a
rule of Court, and that entitles the plaintiff to have execution upon it under the 1 & 2 Vict. c. 110, s. 18.

ALDERSON, B.—I am of the same opinion. An order
under the Interpleader Act, when entered of record, may

be made the foundation of judgment and execution; but if the party proceeds under the 1 & 2 Vict. c. 110, s. 18, there is no occasion to enter the rule of record. If it were otherwise, it would be in effect repealing the latter act, by engrafting upon it the provisions of the former.

ROLFE, B., concurred.

Rule discharged.

MEMORANDA.

THE following rule, as to the taxation of the costs of witnesses on several issues, has been promulgated by the Judges :—

"In case of several issues on the record, some found for the plaintiff, and others for the defendant, the Master is to allow the costs, on the issues found for the plaintiff, of such witnesses as were bonâ fide subpœnaed for the purpose of proving such issues, and would have been so subpœnaed if the issues found for the defendant had not been on the record, and vice versâ.

"He is to allow the defendant, on the issues found for him, the costs of such witnesses as were bonâ fide subpœnaed for the purpose of proving those issues, and would have been so subpœnaed if the issues found for the plaintiff were not on the record."

In the Vacation before this Term, *Francis Stack Murphy*, of Lincoln's-Inn, Esq., was called to the degree of the coif, and gave rings with the motto *Incidere Ludum*.

AN

INDEX

PRINCIPAL MATTERS.

———•———

ACCORD AND SATISFACTION.

1. *What amounts to.*

The plaintiff, the acceptor of a bill of exchange, on the day it fell due, sent a person to the defendant, who held it, to pay the amount of the bill and bring it back. The defendant received the money and gave a receipt for it, but said he could not give up the bill. The plaintiff being informed of this, sent again to the defendant to demand the bill or the money, but he did not give up either. Afterwards, on the same day, the defendant sent to the plaintiff a paper signed by one G., acknowledging the receipt from the defendant of the amount of the bill, and undertaking to bear the plaintiff harmless for the amount, if the bill, which he stated to have been lost, should be presented. The plaintiff kept this guarantee, but nevertheless sued the defendant for money had and received:—*Held,* that his right of action vested on the defendant's refusal to repay the money or give up the bill; and therefore that the receipt by the plaintiff of G.'s guarantee was in the nature of accord and satisfaction, and was no defence to the action, unless specially pleaded. *Alexander* v. *Strong,*   733

2. *Acceptance in Satisfaction, what is.*

The plaintiffs, merchants at Liverpool, were in the habit of consigning to the defendants, brokers at Montreal, goods on sale or return, and of receiving in payment bills on British houses purchased by the defendants with the proceeds. The plaintiffs having desired that none but undoubted bills should be sent to them, the defendants remitted a bill drawn by and upon parties supposed at the time to be in good credit. The plaintiffs, on receiving it, returned for answer that it had been refused acceptance, and requested the defendants to do what was needful to procure security from the drawer, and to take all legal and necessary steps for their security. In an action brought by the plaintiffs for money had and received, to recover from the defendants the proceeds of the consignment to which this bill had reference, the defendants pleaded the delivery to the plaintiffs, and acceptance by them, of the bill of exchange in full satisfaction. The Judge directed the jury, that if the bill was such a one as by the course of dealing between the parties the plaintiffs were bound to take, that was a taking in full satisfaction:—*Held,* that this was a misdirection; for that *acceptance* in satisfaction must be an act of the will in the party receiving.

Quære, whether money had and received was maintainable, the proceeds having been applied by the defendants to the purpose contemplated by the course of dealing between the parties. *Hardman* v. *Bellhouse*,   596

ACTION ON THE CASE.

When maintainable.—Evidence of Malice.

Where, in a suit in equity, an order was made that one G. should pay into the name of the Accountant-General, in trust in the cause, a certain sum admitted by his answer to have been the amount of the sale of a trust fund; and the solicitor for the plaintiff in the suit registered it under 1 & 2 Vict. c. 110, s. 19, and G. was in consequence prevented from disposing of his lands:—*Held*, that the registering of the order was not of itself a wrongful act, and that no action could be maintained for it without proof of malice.

Semble, that such an order is within the equity of the stat. 1 & 2 Vict. c. 110, s. 19. *Gibbs* v. *Pike*,   351

AFFIDAVIT.

See LANCASTER COURT OF COMMON PLEAS.

(1). *Title.*

An affidavit on which a rule for judgment as in case of a nonsuit was founded, was intitled "Between J. S., plaintiff, and G. J., defendant." The affidavit in answer to the rule stated, that there were two G. J.'s, and that all former proceedings in the cause were intitled "J. S. *v.* G. J. *the elder:*"—*Held*, that the affidavit was sufficient. *Singleton* v. *Johnson*,   67

(2). *Jurat.*

An affidavit, intitled in the proper Court, and purporting to be sworn before A. B , " a commissioner, &c.," is sufficient: the jurat need not state that he is a commissioner for taking affidavits in that Court. *Burdekin* v. *Potter.*   13

(3). *Filed on former Rule, right of using.*

A party shewing cause against a rule has a right to read an affidavit of his filed in Court, which was made in support of a former application for a rule involving the same question, and of which the other side took an office copy. *Ryan* v. *Smith*,   223

(4). *To hold to bail, when sufficiently states a Debt.*

An affidavit to hold to bail, stating the defendant to be indebted to the plaintiff in £22 " on the balance of an account for goods sold and delivered by the plaintiff to the defendant:"—*Held* sufficient, without stating that it was an account stated between the parties. *Kenrick* v. *Davies*,   22

AMENDMENT.

Of Pleadings, Time for.

An application to the Court to amend pleadings does not fall within the rule respecting the setting aside proceedings for irregularity, with regard to the promptness of the application. *Welsh* v. *Hall*,   14

APPROVEMENT.

See COMMON.

APPROPRIATION OF PAYMENTS.

See MONEY HAD AND RECEIVED, (1).

ARBITRATION.

See Costs, (4).

(1). *Authority of Arbitrator to examine Parties.*

Where a cause is referred to arbitration, with power to the arbitrator to settle all matters in difference between the parties, the submission providing also that the parties respectively are to be examined on oath, if thought necessary by him, it is in the discretion of the arbitrator to examine the parties, each in support of his own case, if he think fit. *Wells* v. *Benskin*, 45

(2). *Award.*

1. *When final.*

1. A cause and all matters in difference between the parties (there being no matters in difference except in the cause) were referred by order of Nisi Prius to the award, order, arbitrament, final end, and determination of A. B.; the order providing, that the verdict should be entered for the plaintiff for the damages in the declaration, subject to be reduced or vacated, or instead thereof a verdict for the defendant *or a nonsuit* entered according to his award. The arbitrator, by his award, directed that the verdict entered for the plaintiff should be vacated, and a nonsuit entered:—*Held*, (*Parke*, B., dissentiente), that the award was bad, as not finally determining the matters in difference in the cause. *Wild* v. *Holt*, 161

2. A declaration on an agreement to supply timber and slates to the plaintiff for the building of a house, alleged as a breach the non-supply of the timber only. The defendant pleaded—1st, non assumpsit; 2nd, that he did supply timber; 3rd, part payment. The cause and all matters in difference were referred, and the arbitrator, by his award, after reciting that he had heard the evidence produced "touching the matters in difference," stated that he made his award "of and concerning the premises," and then proceeded to find specially on each of the issues in the action:—*Held*, that the award was sufficient, although it appeared that there was a matter in difference submitted to the arbitrator as to the non-supply of *slates*. *Dunn* v. *Warlters*, 293

2. *When final—Ascertainment of Costs of Reference.*

By the terms of an order of reference at Nisi Prius, the costs of the cause were to abide the event, " the costs of the reference and award to be in the arbitrator, *who shall ascertain the same:*"—*Held*, that the arbitrator was bound to ascertain and determine the costs of the reference and award. *Morgan* v. *Smith*, 427

3. *When uncertain or inconsistent.*

Assumpsit on an agreement to build a house according to certain drawings, plans, and specifications, and to the satisfaction of the plaintiff, and with the best materials: alleging as breaches that the defendant did not build the house to the satisfaction of the plaintiff; and that he did not perform the work with the best materials. Pleas, 1st, non assumpsit; 2ndly, that the defendant did the works to the satisfaction of the plaintiff; 3rd, that before the breach the contract was rescinded; 4th, leave and license; 5th, that the defendant deviated from the drawings by the direction of the plaintiff's architect; 6th, a plea stating an agreement between plaintiff and defendant to build a stone wall in lieu of the wall mentioned in the original agreement; 7th, that the defendant, by command of the plaintiff, erected a stone wall instead of a brick wall. The plaintiff took issue on the two first pleas, traversed the 3rd, 6th, and 7th, replied de injuriâ to the 4th, and demurred to the 5th. The cause was at the assizes referred to an arbitrator, the costs of the cause and reference to abide the event; and he awarded a general verdict to be entered for the defendant.

Held, that the award was not uncertain, inconsistent, or repugnant; and that it was not necessary for the arbitrator to assess contingent damages on the demurrer, neither party having requested him to do so, but acted as if the matter had not been submitted to him.

Held, also, that the 5th plea was bad on general demurrer, the architect not being shewn to be the plaintiff's agent to bind him by any deviation from the drawings. *Cooper* v. *Langdon*, 60

4. *Setting aside.—Statement of Objections in Rule.*

In a rule nisi for setting aside an award, an objection "that the arbitrator has not awarded on a matter in difference submitted to him" is sufficiently specific. *Dunn* v. *Warlters*, 293

ARREST.

See INSOLVENT DEBTORS' ACT. PROCESS.

ASSUMPSIT.

Consideration.

The reputed father of an illegitimate child promised to pay the mother an annuity if she would maintain the child, and keep secret their connection:—*Held*, that the maintenance of the child was a sufficient consideration to sustain assumpsit. *Jennings* v. *Brown*, 496

ATTACHMENT.

See SHERIFF.

For Non-payment of Money pursuant to Allocatur.

How waived.

An arbitrator having by his award ordered the defendant to pay to the plaintiff a sum of money, the plaintiff filed an affidavit of debt in the Court of Bankruptcy, under stat. 1 & 2 Vict. c. 110, and the defendant gave a bond, with sureties, conditioned for payment of the money, but omitting the alternative in the statute, of rendering himself to custody:—*Held*, that the plaintiff's having adopted this proceeding did not preclude him from applying for an attachment for non-performance of the award and rule of Court thereon. *Mendell* v. *Tyrrell*, 217

ATTORNEY.

See TITHE COMMUTATION ACT, (2).

(1). *Communication to, when privileged.*

Where, upon the sale of an estate, the same attorney was employed by the vendor and by the purchaser, a communication from the purchaser to the attorney, asking for time to pay the purchase-money, was held not to be privileged. *Perry* v. *Smith*, 681

(2). *When privileged from disclosing Client's Deed.*

A party who is protected from producing a deed at Nisi Prius, on the ground that he holds it as a trustee for one of the parties, is not compellable to disclose the contents of it.

An attorney for a party in a cause is not bound to state the contents of a deed, of which he first obtained a knowledge by having obtained and read it, at the suggestion of his counsel, at the consultation in the cause. (*Rolfe*, B., dubitante.) *Davies* v. *Waters*, 608

(3). *Taxation of Bill.*

Jurisdiction of Master as to Negligence.

On taxation of an attorney's bill the Master has no jurisdiction to disallow items on the ground that in respect of the business to which they refer, the attorney was guilty of negligence.

Where A. and B. delivered a bill in their joint names for business done as attornies, and the Master on taxation disallowed part of the bill, on the ground that B. was not a certificated attorney during a portion of the time to which the bill referred, the Court, on affidavit that B.'s name was used at the request of friends, but that he was really not a partner with A., allowed A. to deliver a fresh bill in his own name only for the items so disallowed. *Matchett v. Parkes,* 767

BAIL.

Exception to, how waived.

A plaintiff does not waive his right of exception to bail put in under the stat. 1 & 2 Vict. c. 110, s. 4, by delivering a declaration in chief, and consenting to further time to plead. *Regina v. The Sheriff of Montgomeryshire,* 448

BANKRUPTCY.

(1). *Operation of 2 & 3 Vict. c. 29.*

To an action of trover by assignees of a bankrupt, the defendant pleaded, first, a traverse of the plaintiffs' property as assignees; secondly, that after the bankruptcy, and before the fiat, the plaintiffs, as assignees, by reason of the relation of their title to the time of the bankruptcy, although not then appointed, were the owners of and entitled to the possession of the goods; that the bankrupt, subject only to their said title as assignees, was possessed of the goods, and that the defendants took them under an execution bonâ fide executed and levied against him without any notice of any prior act of bankruptcy. *Semble,* per *Parke,* B., that the latter plea amounted only to an argumentative traverse of the possession of the plaintiffs' assignees, and therefore that the two pleas could not be pleaded together. *Turquand v. Hawtrey,* 727

(2). *Effect of Certificate on Landlord's right of Distress.*

A landlord distrained the goods of A. on his tenant's premises, for rent; the tenant afterwards became bankrupt, and obtained his certificate:—*Held,* that the certificate did not operate as a release of the rent, and therefore that the landlord had a right, in replevin at the suit of A., to avow for a return of the goods. *Newton v. Scott,* 434

(3). *Right of Bankrupt to set aside Verdict.*

A defendant who has become bankrupt and obtained his certificate after trial and verdict against him, has a right to set it aside for the want of a sufficient notice of trial, although his estate is insolvent, and his assignees are no parties to the application. *Shepherd v. Thompson,* 110

BEAST-KEEPER.

See COMMON.

BEER ACTS.

Penalties on Retailers of Beer.

The keeper of a beer-shop, licensed under 1 Will. 4, c. 64, and 4 & 5 Will. 4, c. 84, is liable to the penalties imposed by 56 Geo. 3, c. 58, s. 2, for having in his possession any of the prohibited articles therein specified, or any other article or preparation to be used as a substitute for malt or hops.

In order to render such a person liable to those penalties, for having in his possession any of the articles *enumerated* in the 56 Geo. 3, c. 58, s. 2, it is unnecessary to aver or prove, either that the party had them in his possession to be used as a substitute for malt or hops, or that he had them in his possession with any criminal intention. But where the information is, for having in his possession any article *not designated by name* in that section, it is necessary to shew that it was intended to be used as a substitute for malt and hops in the making of beer. *The Attorney-General* v. *Lockwood*, 378

BENEFICE.

See CURATE.
DILAPIDATIONS.

BILLS AND NOTES.

See LIMITATIONS, STATUTE OF, (1).
PLEADING, III. (2), (10); IV.

I. *Promissory Note payable on demand, Negotiability of.*

A promissory note, payable on demand, cannot be treated as over-due, so as to affect an indorsee with any equities against the indorser, merely because it is indorsed a number of years after its date, and no interest had been paid on it for several years before such indorsement. *Brooks* v. *Mitchell,* 15

II. *Acceptance by Partner, when it binds the Firm.*

A partner has no implied authority by law to bind his co-partners by his acceptance of a bill of exchange, except by an acceptance in the true style of the partnership.

Therefore, where a firm consisted of J. B. & C. H., the partnership name being " J. B." only, and C. H. accepted a bill in the name of " J. B. & Co.," it was held that J. B. was

not bound thereby. *Kirk* v. *Blurton,* 284

III. *Right of Action against Drawer on Non-acceptance.*

The holder of a bill of exchange, on *non-acceptance,* and protest and notice thereon, has an immediate right of action against the drawer, and does not acquire a fresh right of action on the *non-payment* of the bill when due. The Statute of Limitations, therefore, runs against him from the former and not from the latter period. *Whitehead* v. *Walker,* 506

IV. *Actions on.*

(1). *Debt, when maintainable on Bill of Exchange.*

Where the drawer of a bill indorses it in blank, and delivers it to A., who passes it without a fresh indorsement to B., B. cannot maintain an action of debt on it against the drawer. *Lewin* v. *Edwards,* 720

(2). *Pleadings.*

1. *Allegation of Promise to pay.*

In an action by the indorsee against the drawer of a bill of exchange, the omission of a promise by the drawer to pay is at most merely matter of form, which can only be taken advantage of on special demurrer.

And *semble,* the allegation of a promise is in such a case altogether unnecessary. *Stericker* v. *Barker,* 321

2. *Statement of Bill drawn by Firm.*

1. Declaration by indorsee against acceptor of a bill of exchange, stated it to be drawn by " certain persons using the name, style, and firm of M. & Co.," and that " the said M. & Co." indorsed it. *Semble,* that this was not a sufficient description, as it did not shew that M. & Co. drew or indorsed the bill *in that name. Ball* v. *Gordon,* 345

2. Declaration by indorsee against

acceptor of a bill of exchange, stated it to be drawn " by certain persons, by and under the name, style, and firm of G. & Son," and that " the said persons, by and under the said name, style, and firm of G. & Son," indorsed it:—*Held*, on special demurrer, that this was a sufficient description of the drawers and indorsers. *Tigar* v. *Gordon*,   347

(3). *When Plaintiff bound to prove Consideration.*

Where a material fact alleged in pleading is not traversed by the subsequent pleading, it is not therefore admitted *as a fact*, so as to dispense with proof of it before the jury.

To a declaration in assumpsit by indorsee against maker of a promissory note, the defendant pleaded, that the note was indorsed and delivered to the plaintiff by his indorser, in violation of good faith, and in fraud and contempt of an order for referring the claim of that indorser to arbitration; and that the plaintiff took the note with full knowledge of the premises. The plaintiff replied that he had not, when he took the note, any knowledge of the premises in the plea mentioned. Issue thereon:—*Held*, that upon these pleadings the defendant was bound to begin at the trial, and to prove the plaintiff's knowledge of the fraud; and that the plaintiff was not bound in the first instance to prove consideration given for the indorsement to him. *Smith* v. *Martin*,   304

BOND.

See PRINCIPAL AND SURETY, (2).

(1). *Construction of Condition.*

The condition of a bond, after reciting that one A. B. had filed a bill in Chancery against several persons (naming them) and the now defendant, as defendants, was, that the now defendant should pay all such costs as the Court of Chancery should award to *all* the said defendants:—*Held*, that the construction of this condition was, that the defendant should pay the costs awarded to all or any of the defendants except himself. *Vesey* v. *Mantell*,   323

(2). *Payment into Court in Action on, not pleadable.*

Payment of money into Court, under the 4 & 5 Anne, c. 16, s. 13, in discharge of principal and interest on a bond, and costs, cannot be *pleaded* to an action on the bond. *England* v. *Watson*,   333

(3). *Liability of Devisee on Bond of Testator.*

Where the obligor of a bond, having devised his land, died before the passing of the stat. 1 Will. 4, c. 47:—*Held*, that the specialty creditor could not maintain an action against the devisee alone, there being no heir, under 3 W. & M. c. 14, s. 3. *Hunting* v. *Sheldrake*,   256

CARRIER.

See STOPPAGE IN TRANSITU.
TENDER.

CHARTER.

See CORONER.

CHEQUE.

Post-dated, Admissibility of.

A post-dated cheque is altogether void, and cannot be received in evidence for any purpose. Therefore, the plaintiff cannot, in an action on such an instrument, resort to the count for money paid, because he cannot prove it without producing the cheque. *Serle* v. *Norton*,   309

COMMON.

Approvement.— Erection of Houses for Beast-keeper and Woodward.

An owner pur autre vie of a common may approve under the statutes 20 H. 3, c. 4, and 13 Ed. 1, st. 1, c. 46.

The owner of a common may erect thereon a house necessary for the habitation of beast-keepers for the care of the cattle, of himself and the other persons having rights of common there. So he may erect a house necessary for the habitation of a woodward, to protect the woods and the underwoods on the common.

A plea justifying the erection of a house for such beast-keepers need not state the names of the other commoners, nor that they assented to the appointment of beast-keepers.

To an action on the case for a continuing disturbance of common, the defendant pleaded an apportionment of the locus in quo, " leaving sufficient common of pasture for the said plaintiff and all other persons entitled thereto, together with sufficient ingress and egress to and from the same, according to the form of the statute, &c.:"—*Held*, that the plea sufficiently shewed that enough of common was left at the time of the approvement, and in the place where the plaintiff was entitled to enjoy it. *Patrick* v. *Stubbs*, 830

COMPOSITION DEED.

See DEBTOR AND CREDITOR.

CONTRACT OF SALE.

See FRAUDS, STATUTE OF, (1).
PLEADING, III., (9).

(1). *Of Goods.*

1. *Right of Purchaser to shew Defects in Quality of.*

The plaintiffs agreed with the defendants to manufacture for them certain locomotive engines, under the

following contract: " Each engine and tender to be subject to a performance of a distance of 1,000 miles, with proper loads; during which trial Messrs. S. & Co. (the plaintiffs) are to be liable to any breakage which may occur, if arising from defective materials or workmanship; but they are not to be responsible for nor liable to the repair of any breakage or damage, whether resulting from collision, neglect, or mismanagement of any of the company's servants, or any other circumstances, save and except defective materials or workmanship. The performance to which each engine is to be subjected, to take place within one month from the day on which the engine is reported ready to start; in default of which, Messrs. S. & Co. shall forthwith be released from any responsibility in respect of the said engine; the balance to be paid on the satisfactory completion of the trial, and release of Messrs. S. & Co. from further responsibility in respect of such engine." It was also agreed, that the fire-boxes should be made of copper, of the thickness of 7-16ths of an inch (and they were accordingly so made); and that the best materials and workmanship were to be used. The engines were accordingly delivered to the defendants, and performed the distance of 1,000 miles within the month of trial, but nine months afterwards the fire-box of one of them burst, when it was discovered that the copper had been considerably reduced in thickness:—*Held*, in an action against the defendants for the balance due from them, that they could not give evidence of an inherent defect in the copper (no fraud being alleged), since, by the terms of the contract, the month's trial, if satisfactory, was to release the plaintiffs from all responsibility in respect of bad materials and bad workmanship. *Sharp* v. *The Great Western Railway Company*, 7

2. " To arrive," Construction of.

The defendant, by a bought and sold note, agreed to sell the plaintiffs " 100 tons of nitrate of soda, at 18*s*. per cwt., *to arrive* ex Daniel Grant, to be taken from the quay at landing weights," &c.; and below the signature of the brokers there was the following memorandum : " Should the vessel be lost, this contract to be void:" —*Held*, that the contract did not amount to a warranty on the part of the seller, that the nitrate of soda should arrive if the vessel arrived, but to a contract for the sale of goods at a future period, subject to the double condition, of the arrival of the vessel, with the specified cargo on board. *Johnson* v. *Macdonald*,   600

3. *Memorandum in Broker's Book, when Evidence of.*

Assumpsit for goods sold and delivered. It appeared at the trial that a broker, employed by the plaintiffs to sell 200 casks of tallow, sold 50 to the defendant, and the remainder to two other parties to be delivered some months subsequently to the sale. In the bought note he described the transaction as a purchase of 50 casks for "his principals," i. e. the buyers; and in the sold note, as a sale of 200 casks sold to his principals. In his book he stated the defendant as the purchaser of 50 casks, and the two other parties as purchasers of the remainder. There was no disclosure of the principals on either side. About the time appointed for the delivery, the broker urged the defendant to buy 100 other casks of a third person, and on the latter objecting to do so, on the ground that the 50 casks already contracted for by him would soon be delivered, offered to "put off" those casks. The 50 casks were never actually delivered to the defendant.

It was objected, on this evidence, that the plaintiffs ought to be nonsuited on two grounds: first, that inasmuch as there was a variance between the bought and sold notes, the broker's book not being evidence of the contract, there was no valid contract; secondly, that there was nothing to shew any delivery of the 50 casks to the defendant. The learned Judge being of that opinion nonsuited the plaintiffs:—*Held*, that the nonsuit was wrong on the second ground, it being a question for the jury, whether the words "put off" meant a sale of the goods to a third person by the broker on account of the defendant, or a postponement of the delivery with or without the consent of the plaintiff.

Quære, whether the memorandum of a sale in the broker's book, signed by him, is admissible as evidence of the contract, to satisfy the Statute of Frauds, in cases where there is no other contract, or where the bought and sold notes disagree. *Thornton* v. *Charles*,   802

COPYRIGHT.

Of Engraving.

In an action on the case, for pirating an engraving, brought under the stat. 17 Geo. 3, c. 57, which gives a right of action against any one who shall copy any print "in the whole or in part, by varying, adding to, or diminishing from, the main design," the judge directed the jury to consider whether the defendant's engraving was substantially a copy of the plaintiff's:—*Held*, that this direction was correct. *Moore* v. *Clarke*,   692

CORONER.

Office of, by what Words granted— Construction of Charter—Evidence.

By charter of the 23 Edw. 3, the

King granted to the Earl (afterwards Duke) of Lancaster (inter alia), that he might have the return of all writs of the King and his heirs, and summons of the Exchequer, and *the attachment* as well *of pleas of the Crown* [attachiamenta de placitis coronæ] as of other pleas whatsoever, in all his lands and fees, so that no sheriff or other bailiff or minister of the King, or his heirs, might enter those lands or fees to execute the same writs and summons, or to make attachment of pleas of the Crown, or other pleas aforesaid, or to do any other office there, unless in default of the same Earl and his bailiffs and ministers in his lands and fees aforesaid:—*Held*, that thereby the right to appoint coroners within the Duchy of Lancaster was granted, and that such right was an exclusive one : that, therefore, notwithstanding modern usage to the contrary, the county coroner had no authority to exercise the office within any of the possessions of the duchy, concurrently with the duchy coroners, nor unless in default of their performance of the office.

Upon a question whether the Crown, in right of the Duchy of Lancaster, had the exclusive right, under the above grant, of appointing a coroner within the honour of Pontefract, evidence of appointments of coroners, and of their acting, in other parts of the duchy, out of the honour of Pontefract, was held admissible.

By an order made in 1670, by the Chancellor and Council of the Duchy of Lancaster, after reciting that the Court was informed that the coroner within the honour of Pontefract, parcel of the duchy, had usually returned their inquests to the Crown Office, without taking notice therein that they arose within the liberties of the duchy, it was ordered that the coroners should thenceforward specify in their

returns when and where the inquests were held:—*Held* admissible in evidence, although no proof was given of any thing done under it.   *Jewison* v. *Dyson,*   540

COSTS.

See ARBITRATION, (2), 3.
   FOREIGN JUDGMENT.
   INTERPLEADER ACTS.

(1). *Of several Issues.*

1. Where several pleas are pleaded, and one of them, which amounts to an answer to the whole cause of action, is found for the defendant, and others for the plaintiff, the latter is entitled to the costs of the issues found for him, including a portion of the briefs and counsel's fees. *Hazlewood* v. *Back,*   1

2. Memorandum,   842

(2). *Of Proof of Document.*

A party who proposes to adduce in evidence a document at the trial, is bound in every case, in order to entitle himself to the costs of proving it, to give a notice to admit, under R. 20 of H. T. 4 Will. 4, to afford the other party an opportunity of admitting it, notwithstanding the document is put in issue on the pleadings, and although, on application to the attorney on the other side, he had refused to make the admission on the ground that the document was a forgery. *Spencer* v. *Barough,*   425

(3). *Double Costs under* 11 *Geo.* 2, *c.* 19.

Where a defendant pays money into Court, in an action for an illegal distress, and the plaintiff replies damages ultra, on which issue the defendant succeeds, he is not entitled to double costs under stat. 11 Geo. 2, c. 10, s. 21.   *Handcock* v. *Foulkes,*   431

(4). *On Reference, after new Trial granted.*

After a verdict for the plaintiff, the defendant obtained a rule for a new trial, which was made absolute, no mention being made of costs. The parties then agreed to a reference, and the order of reference stipulated that the costs were to abide the event. The arbitrator having decided the cause in favour of the defendant:— *Held*, that the defendant was not entitled to the costs of the trial. *Thomas* v. *Hawkes*, 53

(5). *In Trespass.*

Operation of 4 & 5 *Vict. c.* 28.

The stat. 4 & 5 Vict. c. 28, s. 2, applies to cases in which the plaintiff had not only obtained a verdict, but had signed judgment and taxed his costs, before the passing of that act. *Roadknight* v. *Green*, 652

(6). *When taxable on higher Scale.*

In an action of debt, in which the writ of summons was indorsed for £57, the defendant pleaded, as to all but £19, payment; as to the £19, payment into Court. At the trial he proved payment to the plaintiff of all the debt beyond the £19; but it appeared that a sum of £13 was paid after action brought. The verdict was thereupon entered for £13, the plaintiff undertaking to sue out execution for the costs only:—*Held*, that the plaintiff was entitled to costs to be taxed on the scale applicable to a recovery of a sum above £20. *Fewster* v. *Boggett*, 20

(7). *Under Court of Requests' Act.*

Where an action was brought for a sum of 5*l.* 12*s.*, and the defendant paid into Court the sum of 4*l.* 18*s.* 6*d.*, which the plaintiff took out in full satisfaction of his demand, and entered a nolle prosequi as to the resi-

due:—*Held*, that the acceptance by the plaintiff of the smaller sum was not of itself sufficient evidence that no more was due, so as to entitle the defendant to enter a suggestion under a Court of Requests' Act, giving jurisdiction over debts to the amount of £5.

The form of the plea of payment of money into Court does not preclude a defendant from applying to enter a suggestion to deprive the plaintiff of costs. *Jorden* v. *Berwick*, 3

COURT OF REQUESTS.

See Costs, (7).
    Municipal Corporation Act.

The sheriff or other inferior judge to whom a writ of trial is directed out of a superior court has no authority to certify, under the Tower Hamlets Court of Requests' Act, 23 Geo. 2, c. 30, s. 8, that there was a probable and reasonable cause of action for 40*s.* or more.

A party who sues in a superior court a defendant residing within the jurisdiction of the Tower Hamlets Court of Requests' Act, for a debt being the balance of account on a demand originally exceeding £5, but reduced below that amount by payments before action brought, is not liable to costs, though he recover less than 40*s.* *Elsley* v. *Kirby*, 536

COVENANT.

Construction of— Condition—Precedent.

In covenant, the declaration stated, that it was covenanted and agreed between the plaintiff as lessor, and the defendants as lessees, of certain coal mines, that the plaintiff should, when he thought fit, employ a fit and proper person at each machine for weighing the coals, who should weigh the same and keep the accounts, and that his wages should be paid by the defendants ; but that in case such person should not duly attend at the machine, and duly keep the necessary accounts, the defendants were authorized to discharge him. It then averred that the plaintiff appointed J. H., being a fit and proper person, and alleged as a breach, that the defendants refused to pay him his wages. The defendants pleaded, that J. H. was not a fit and proper person, that he had not duly attended to the machine, and had not duly kept the necessary accounts. At the trial, it was proved that J. H. had been appointed, and had attended for three months, after which period he was dismissed as incompetent by the defendants :—*Held*, that the plaintiff was not entitled to judgment non obstante veredicto: the appointment of a fit and proper person being a condition precedent to the defendants' liability to pay wages. *Lawton* v. *Sutton*, 795

COVENANT TO REPAIR.

Liability of Occupier under Agreement for Lease.

By agreement, dated 20th October, 1824, reciting a former agreement in 1819, for the grant of a lease of copyhold premises to A. B. for twenty-one years, from the 25th of March, 1820, and that A. B. had requested, and the plaintiff had agreed, that the defendant should be accepted as tenant, and a lease should be granted to him instead of to A. B., on the same terms; and that the plaintiff was desirous to let the premises to the defendant so soon as a good license for that purpose should be granted to him by the lord of the manor, but not before : the plaintiff, in consideration of the covenants and agreements thereinafter contained on the part of the defendant,

covenanted that he would, so soon as a good license for that purpose should have been procured by him from the lord, at the defendant's expense, lease the premises to the defendant for all the residue then unexpired of the term of twenty-one years from the 25th of March, 1820, &c.: and the defendant thereby covenanted, from thenceforth yearly during the remainder to come of the said term, to pay the plaintiff the rent, and also that he would *from time to time during the term to be granted as aforesaid*, keep the premises in repair, &c. &c. The agreement contained also a covenant by the plaintiff for quiet enjoyment during the remainder of the term, on payment of the rent and performance of the covenants. The defendant entered upon the premises, and occupied them until the expiration of twenty-one years from the 25th of March, 1820 :— *Held*, that he was liable on the covenant for repair, although no lease had ever been made to him pursuant to the agreement, nor any license obtained from the lord for that purpose. *Pistor* v. *Cater*, 315

CURATE.

Appointed during Vacancy of Benefice, Payment of.

Where a curate is appointed by the special sequestrators of the bishop of the diocese, to serve the cure of a benefice during the vacation between the death of the last and the appointment of the next incumbent, he may, although not licensed by the bishop, and notwithstanding the stat. 1 & 2 Vict. c. 106, recover his reasonable stipend in an action of debt under 28 Hen. 8, c. 11, from the next incumbent; the tithes which accrued during the interval not being sufficient to pay him a reasonable stipend. *Dakins* v. *Seaman*, 777

DAMAGES.

See PRINCIPAL AND SURETY, (1).
TRESPASS, (2), (3).

DEBTOR AND CREDITOR.

*Liability of favoured Creditor under
Composition Deed.*

The plaintiff, being insolvent, proposed to his creditors to pay them a composition of 10s. in the pound, to be secured by his acceptances. All the creditors agreed to the arrangement except the defendant, who refused to execute the agreement unless he were paid the additional sum of 2s. in the pound on his debt. A cheque for that amount was accordingly given him by a relation of the plaintiff, without the plaintiff's knowledge, and he then signed the agreement, and received from the plaintiff his acceptances for the 10s. composition. *Semble*, that, under these circumstances, the plaintiff, if he were compelled to pay the bills at maturity to bonâ fide indorsees, to whom they had been transferred by the defendant for value, might recover back from the defendant the excess received by him beyond the amount of the composition. *Bradshaw* v. *Bradshaw*, 29

DEED.

Construction of Release in.

To an action of covenant by a joint-stock banking copartnership, on a guarantee given by the defendant to secure advances made by the company to M., M., and B., carrying on business under the name of M. & Co., the defendant pleaded, that, by indenture between M., M., L., and B., of the first part, W., H., and O., of the second part, and the several persons or partnership firms who should execute the said indenture, being creditors of M., M., L., and B., of the third part, H. being a member and partner in the said banking copartnership, released M., M., L., and B., from all actions, debts, &c. The defendant, in support of his plea, gave in evidence a composition deed, made between M., M., L., and B., of the first part, W., H., and O., of the second part, and the several persons or partnership firms, being creditors of M., M., L., and B., who should have executed or who should execute the said composition deed, of the third part. The deed, after reciting that M., M., L., and B., were indebted to W., H., and O., and to the several parties to the deed of the third part, and being unable to pay the said debts, had conveyed all their property and effects to W., H., and O., in trust for payment of their debts, stated, that in consideration thereof, each of the said creditors, parties to the said deed of the second and third parts, did for themselves, their heirs, executors, &c., and partners, release M., M., L., and B., from all actions, debts, demands, &c. At the date of this release, a separate debt of 2l. 15s. was due from M. to H., and H., at the date of the release, was a shareholder in the joint-stock banking copartnership. H. executed the deed in his own name:—*Held*, that the plea was not proved, the release from M., M., L., and B., not including the debt due from M. & Co. to the joint-stock banking company, but applying only to debts due to such partnership firms as should execute the deed of the third part. *Bain* v. *Cooper*, 701

DETINUE.

See PLEADING, III., 7.

DEVISE.

(1). *Estate in Fee by Implication.*

A testator, being possessed of estates in the counties of L. and H., bequeathed certain legacies and annuities to his two sons and two daughters. The will then proceeded thus: "That my wife, M. C., may be left in as comfortable a situation as possible, I bequeath to her for her natural life, the possession of my house in Stanley-place, Chester, together with the use of the plate, linen, &c., and all the joint property in houses in Liverpool, and likewise of interest of money as often as due, arising from the £3 and £4 per cents., and to have and to hold the same during her natural life, save and except the clauses in favour of my daughters, as already mentioned; at her decease, it is my will and pleasure that M. N., and C. C., (his daughters), shall divide equally between them, *as residuary legatees, whatever I may die possessed of*, ex-except what is already mentioned in favour of others." The will, after giving the executors the power of selling certain leasehold houses in Liverpool, concluded thus : " But the house in Chester must not be sold as long as my wife lives:"—*Held*, that the residuary legatees took the estates in L. and H. for an estate in fee-simple, commencing at the death of the wife, and that they took the Stanley-place house in fee-simple in remainder, expectant on the death of the wife. *Held*, also, that the wife did not take any interest for life by implication, in the estates in L. and H. *Davenport* v. *Coltman*,   481

(2). *Of Estate pur autre Vie.*

Where a lessee of lands demised to him, his heirs and assigns, for lives, devised the premises for the residue of the term to W. J. L. and his assigns, who died intestate :—*Held*, that the premises did not go to the heir of W. J. L., but to his personal representative, under the Statute of Frauds, 29 Car. 2, c. 3, s. 12.   *Doe* d. *Lewis* v. *Lewis*,   662

DILAPIDATIONS.

On Exchange of Livings, Liability for.

Two clergymen being possessed of livings, agreed to exchange the one for the other, with the consent of their respective patrons, and the livings were accordingly resigned into the hands of the bishop, and each party respectively was inducted into the other of them. There was no specific agreement entered into upon the subject of dilapidations, but it was found that neither party at the time contemplated any claim for dilapidations:—*Held*, in an action by one of the incumbents against the other, as his successor, for dilapidations, that the plaintiff was entitled to recover. *Downes* v. *Craig*,   166

DISTRESS.

See BANKRUPTCY, (2).
COSTS, (3).

DUCHY OF LANCASTER.

See CORONER.

EJECTMENT.

Judgment against Casual Ejector.

It is not too late to move for judgment against the casual ejector, in the term following that in which the tenants have had notice to appear; whether the cause be a town or country cause. *Doe* d. *Walker* v. *Roe*,
426

ESTATE AT WILL.

See LANDLORD AND TENANT, (1).

ESTATE PUR AUTRE VIE.

See DEVISE, (2).

EVIDENCE.

See ATTORNEY, (1), (2).
CORONER.
WITNESS.

(1). *Secondary Evidence—Notice to produce.*

1. In trover against a carrier, where the question was whether the goods were rightfully detained by the defendant in satisfaction of a general lien: — *Held,* that parol evidence could not be given of the contents of a portable notice, hung up in the defendant's office, containing a statement that all goods carried by the defendant were to be subject to such general lien, but that the notice itself must be produced.

Held, also, that evidence of bills delivered to the plaintiff, containing a similar statement, could not be received without a notice to produce the bills. *Jones* v. *Tarleton,* 675

2. A notice to produce was served on the defendant's attorney at his residence, twenty miles from the place of trial, at eight p. m. on the night before the trial. The defendant resided in the same town with the attorney, but was not at home on that evening until twelve o'clock:—*Held,* too late. *Howard* v. *Williams,* 725

(2). *Rejection of at Nisi Prius.*

Where evidence is rejected by a judge at *Nisi Prius,* the counsel proposing it ought to make a formal tender of it to the judge, and request him to take a note of it, or he will not be allowed to raise before the Court any questions arising out of such evidence, if the judge's note does not shew the point to have been raised at the trial. *Gibbs* v. *Pike,* 351

(3). *Erasure—Subscribing Witness.*

The defendant became tenant to the plaintiff of a farm from year to year, by parol, but afterwards signed an agreement containing certain stipulations as to the mode of tillage. In an action by the landlord for breaches of these stipulations, the agreement, on being produced, contained an erasure in the term of years mentioned in the habendum, which was altered from seven to fourteen:—*Held,* that in this action the agreement might be received in evidence without any explanation of the erasure, the term of years being immaterial to the parol contract between the parties, to hold from year to year, subject only to the terms of the agreement as to the cultivation of the land.

The agreement was attested by the landlord's steward, who, after having been apprehended for embezzlement, had absconded, and could not be found after search at his house, and at the inns he was in the habit of frequenting: — *Held,* that evidence of his handwriting was properly received. *The Earl of Falmouth* v. *Roberts,* 469

(4). *Judgment in former Action.*

A judgment obtained by A. in an action of use and occupation, against B. and C., is no evidence to charge B. in a subsequent action brought by A. against him alone, for the use and occupation of the same premises for a subsequent period. *Christy* v. *Tancred,* 438

(5). *Of Identity of Party to Suit.*

1. In an action for medicine and attendances by the plaintiff as an apothecary, the plaintiff put in evidence a license from the Apothecaries' Company to practise as such, granted to a person bearing the same christian and surname:—*Held,* that this was sufficient primâ facie evidence to shew the identity of the plaintiff with the person named in the license. *Simpson* v. *Dismore,* 47

2. In an action by indorsee against maker of a promissory note, the defendant pleaded, first, that he did not make the note; secondly, that he made it for the accommodation of the plain-

tiff. There was an attesting witness to the note, who, on being called at the trial, stated that he saw the signature (Hugh Jones) to the note written by a party whose occupation and residence he described, but that he had had no communication with him since, and that this was a common name in the neighbourhood where the note was made:—*Held*, there was no evidence to go to the jury of the identity of the defendant with the maker of the note, and that the second plea could not be called in aid for that purpose. *Thomas Jones* v. *Hugh Jones,*   75

3. In an action by indorsee against acceptor of a bill of exchange, it appeared that the bill was directed to " Charles Banner Crawford, East India House," and accepted " C. B. Crawford." It was proved that this signature was the handwriting of a gentleman of that name, formerly a clerk in the East India House, who had left it five years ago:—*Held*, that this was sufficient evidence of the identity of the defendant with the person whose handwriting was proved. *Greenshields* v. *Crawford,*   314

4. An action having been brought against William Henderson for negligently navigating a vessel, and the circumstances under which the collision took place having been proved, it was objected that no evidence had been given that the defendant was the pilot in charge of the vessel, whereupon the plaintiff's counsel called out, " Mr. Henderson!" upon which a person in Court answered " here;" and said, " I am the pilot." It was proved by one of the witnesses who had gone on board the vessel at the time of the accident, that he had seen that person then acting as pilot:— *Held*, that this was sufficient evidence of the identity of the defendant with ·the pilot. *Smith* v. *Henderson,* 798

EXCISE ACTS.

See BEER ACTS.

Permit, in whose Name to be made out.

Where G. the licensed keeper of a public-house, sold the lease of it to N., who entered into the occupation of it, the license still remaining in the name of G.; and a quantity of spirits, which required a permit for its removal under 2 Will. 4, c. 16, was supplied by a distiller on the order of N., and delivered on the premises in question:—*Held*, that a permit made out in the name of G. was a valid permit under the statute. *Nicholson* v. *Hood,*   365

EXECUTION.

(1). *Capias ad satisfaciendum.*

1. *Duration of.*

A writ of ca. sa. may be executed more than a year after its date. *Greenshields* v. *Harris,*   774

2. *When irregular for pendency of other Process.*

The plaintiff having obtained final judgment in a cause in the Court of Exchequer, afterwards proceeded for the same cause of action, by foreign attachment in the Lord Mayor's Court in London, against the defendant's goods; the defendant surrendered himself into custody in discharge of the attachment; and on the following day, whilst he was so in custody, the plaintiff issued a ca. sa., under which the defendant was detained:—*Held*, that the ca. sa. was not irregular; and that, the plaintiff having abandoned his proceedings in the Lord Mayor's Court, and the defendant having in consequence obtained judgment of nonpros thereon, there was no ground for his discharge under the equitable jurisdiction of the Court. *Chamberlayne* v. *Green,*   790

3. *Testatum, when warranted by original Writ.*

Where, the venue being in Surrey, final judgment was signed on the 2nd April, 1840, and a testatum ca. sa. of the same date issued into Yorkshire, on which the defendant was arrested; an original ca. sa. into Surrey, also dated the 2nd April, 1840, with a general return of non est inventus thereon, was held sufficient to warrant the testatum. *Greenshields* v. *Harris*,　　　　774

(2). *Fieri facias.*

1. *Against Defendant discharged under Insolvent Debtors' Act.*

Where one of several defendants, having been arrested on a ca. sa., has been discharged under the Insolvent Debtors' Act, his goods cannot be afterwards seized under a fi. fa. issued against him and the other defendants. *Raynes* v. *Jones*,　　　104

2. *Assignment of Term under.*

Where the sheriff sells a term taken in execution under a fi. fa. to the execution creditor, but executes no assignment in writing of the term, the estate remains in the debtor, and the execution creditor has no defence to an ejectment at his suit. *Doe* d. *Hughes* v. *Jones*,　　　372

3. *Expenses of Execution, what are.*

The costs of an interpleader rule obtained by a sheriff or other similar officer, cannot be considered as "expenses of the execution," which may be levied under the stat. 43 Geo. 3, c. 46, s. 5. *Hammond* v. *Nairn*, 221

EXECUTOR AND ADMINISTRATOR.

(1). *Assent to Legacy, how proved.*

A testator bequeathed to his two sons his two carriage manufactories, with all fixtures, implements, tools, *stock*, job-carriages, harness, and every thing appertaining to his trade in the said manufactories. At the time of his death, a carriage was in one of the manufactories, unfinished, which was being built to the order of a purchaser. A question arose between the executors and the sons, whether this carriage fell within the above bequest; and the executors paid the legacy duty on the whole, but annexed the following memorandum to the legacy receipt:—"A disagreement arising between the sons of S. and T. and the executors, as to whether the whole of this item belongs to the said sons, or part to the residue, the executors desire to pay the duty on the whole, leaving it for them to settle with the legatees the proportion of duty, when the matter in dispute shall be determined." The sons retained possession of and finished the carriage, delivered it to the purchaser, and received the price. In an action by the executors against them for money had and received, commenced two years afterwards:—*Held*, that there was no evidence to go to the jury of assent by the executors to the legacy of the carriage to the defendants. *Elliott* v. *Elliott*,　　　23

(2). *Authority to bind Co-executor by Contract.*

To an action for use and occupation, for a quarter's rent from Lady-day to Midsummer 1841, the defendant pleaded, that by an agreement made between the plaintiffs, executors of T., and the defendant, the defendant agreed to take of the plaintiffs, executors as aforesaid, the premises in question; that it was afterwards agreed between them and W., that W. should become tenant to the plaintiffs from Lady-day 1841, and that the defendant should be discharged from all liability to subsequent rent; that the defendant accordingly gave up .possession to W., and the plaintiffs accepted him as tenant:—*Held*, that this plea was not proved by evidence that *one* of the plaintiffs had so agreed to accept W. as tenant in lieu of the defendant. *Turner* v. *Hardey,*   770

EXTENT.

Inquisition to find Debts, Evidence on.

In the case of an immediate extent, on an inquisition to find debts, the jury may find the fact of a debt being due to the Crown, on the sole evidence of an affidavit that the debt is due. *Regina* v. *Ryle,*   227

FACTORS' ACT.

P. & Co., owners of a cargo of tobacco, on the arrival of the vessel, placed the bill of lading, indorsed in blank, in the hands of W., as their factor for sale. W. entered the goods at the Custom-House in his own name, and, before the cargo was weighed, and without the knowledge of P. & Co., obtained a dock warrant for it in his own name, which he pledged with H. & Co. as a security for money advanced by them to him: —*Held*, on error in the Exchequer Chamber, that W. was not, under the circumstances, by reason of his being intrusted with the bill of lading, necessarily and impliedly intrusted with the dock-warrant, &c., within the meaning of the Factors' Act, 6 Geo. 4, c. 94, s. 2; but that whether he was so intrusted or not was a question of fact for the determination of the jury.

Held also, that the judge was not bound to state to the jury what was an intrusting in point of law. *Hatfield* v. *Phillips,*   647

FEIGNED ISSUE.

See NAVIGATION ACT, 2.

FOREIGN JUDGMENT.

Costs upon, Action for.

An action of assumpsit or debt may be maintained against a defendant resident in this country, for costs awarded against him. after appearance, by a decreet of the Court of Session in Scotland, in a suit for a divorce. *Russell* v. *Smyth,*   810

FRAUDS, STATUTE OF.

See CONTRACT OF SALE, 3.

(1). *Sale of Interest in Land.*

An agreement for the sale of growing fruit is an agreement for the sale of an interest in land, and if of the value of £20 requires a stamp. *Rodwell* v. *Phillips,*   501

(2). *Delivery and Acceptance.*

Memorandum in Writing, when to be made.

The defendant ordered goods of H., the del credere agent of the plaintiff, at a stipulated price, to be paid for on delivery; and on receiving notice that the goods had arrived at H.'s warehouse, went there, and directed a boy whom he saw there to put a certain mark on the goods. On the defendant's refusal to receive the goods by reason of a dispute about the price, an action was commenced against him by the plaintiff; after which, at H.'s request, the defendant wrote in H.'s ledger, at the bottom of a page, containing the statement of the goods in question, and headed with the plaintiff's name, the words " Received the above," which he signed:—*Held*, that there was no evidence to go to the jury of a delivery and acceptance, sufficient to satisfy the Statute of Frauds.

A memorandum in writing of a contract, to satisfy the Statute of Frauds, must have been made before action brought. *Bill* v. *Bament.*   36

FREIGHT.

Goods were shipped at Bombay on board a ship of the plaintiff, a shipowner in Liverpool, and by the bill of lading were to be delivered "unto order, or to his and their assigns, on paying freight for the same." The bill of lading was indorsed by the shipper, and forwarded to defendants, East India agents in London, who indorsed it in blank to C. & Co., their factors in Liverpool. On the arrival of the goods at Liverpool, C. & Co. presented the bill of lading to the plaintiff, and received the goods; the plaintiff debiting C. & Co. with the freight. Afterwards C. & Co. became bankrupt without having paid the freight, whereupon the defendants claimed the goods from them, and took possession of them:—*Held*, on error brought upon the judgment of the Court of Exchequer, that the defendants were not liable to the plaintid for the unpaid freight; affirming the judgment of the Court below. *Tobin* v. *Crawford*, 716

GOODS SOLD & DELIVERED.

See FRAUDS, STATUTE OF, 2.

HABEAS CORPUS.

For what Purpose grantable.

The Court will not grant a habeas corpus to bring up a party in custody under an attachment, to enable him to move in person to set it aside. *Ford* v. *Nassau*, 793

HUSBAND AND WIFE.

See PLEADING, II. (1).
PRACTICE, (8), 1.

IDENTITY OF DEFENDANT.

See EVIDENCE, (5).

ILLEGAL CONTRACT.

See STOCKJOBBING ACT.

INFERIOR COURT.

See WRIT OF TRIAL, (1).

INFORMATION.

Right of Crown to delay Proceedings in.

In an information at the suit of the Crown, notice of trial was given in Trinity Term, 1838, but afterwards countermanded. The Court discharged a rule obtained by the defendants in Hilary Term, 1842, to set down the cause for trial at the sittings after Easter Term. *Regina* v. *Ray*, 760

INSOLVENT DEBTORS' ACT.

See EXECUTION, (2), 1.
PLEADING, III. (8), 2.

Arrest of remanded Insolvent.

Where a defendant has been conditionally discharged under the Insolvent Debtors' Act, 1 & 2 Vict. c. 110, s. 84, and is again arrested under a writ of capias, issued pursuant to the 85th sect. of the same act, it is not necessary that a judge's order should have been taken out for the defendant's arrest under the 3rd section of the act. *Bilton* v. *Clapperton*, 473

INSURANCE.

See PLEADING, I. (1), 2.

INTERPLEADER ACTS.

See EXECUTION, (2), 3.

(1). *Costs.*

1. *Jurisdiction as to.*

Where an application for an interpleader rule is made to a judge at chambers, pursuant to the stat. 1 & 2 Vict. c. 45, s. 2, a judge at chambers only, and not the Court, has authority as to the costs of the proceedings. *Burgh* v. *Scholefield,*   478

2. *Execution for.*

A party entitled to costs under an interpleader order is not bound to take out execution under the Interpleader Act, 1 & 2 Will. 4, c. 58, s. 7, but may make the order a rule of Court and take out execution under 1 & 2 Vict. c. 110, s. 18.   *Cetti* v. *Bartlett,*   840

JOINT STOCK BANKING COMPANY.

(1). *Action by.*

Description of Co-partnership in Declaration.

A declaration described the plaintiff as "one of the present public officers of certain persons united in co-partnership *for the purpose of* carrying on the trade and business of banking in England, according to the stat. 7 Geo. 4, c. 46:"—*Held* bad on special demurrer, for not stating that the co-partnership was carrying on the trade and business of bankers, or had carried on such trade. *Fletcher* v. *Crosbie,*   252

JUDGMENT.

Jurisdiction under 1 & 2 Vict. c. 110, s. 14.

A judge at chambers only, and not the Court, has authority, under the stat. 1 & 2 Vict. c. 110, s. 14, to make an order to charge a fund with the payment of money recovered by a judgment: if he makes an absolute order, the Court has jurisdiction to set it aside if wrongly made; but if he only makes an order nisi, the Court has no authority to entertain the question, although the judge expresses his desire to refer it to the Court. *Brown* v. *Bamford,*   42

JUDGMENT AS IN CASE OF NONSUIT.

See PRACTICE, (8).

JURY.

See WRIT OF TRIAL, (1).

Defective Jury Process, effect of.

The Court refused, on motion, to set aside a verdict for the plaintiff, on the ground that no distringas juratores had been returned before the trial, although the objection had been taken before verdict.   *Gee* v. *Swann,*   685

LANCASTER COURT OF COMMON PLEAS.

Executions on Judgment in—Form of Affidavits.

On an application under the stat. 4 & 5 Will. 4, c. 62, s. 31, for leave to issue execution on a judgment in the Court of Common Pleas at Lancaster, the affidavit must state distinctly that the defendant was a resident within the jurisdiction of that Court at the time of the judgment or of action brought, and then had goods and chattels there, which he has since removed out of the jurisdiction. It is not sufficient to state that he is not now a resident in the county of Lancaster, and has not any goods or chattels within the jurisdiction; or, that he is not now a resident there, and has removed all his goods and chattels out of the jurisdiction since the judgment.

The affidavit must be intitled in the superior Court.   *Wigden* v. *Birt,*   50

LANDLORD AND TENANT.

See COSTS, (3).

COVENANT TO REPAIR.

(1). *Tenancy at Will, how determined.*

A., in 1817, let B. into possession of a farm as tenant at will, and in 1827, A. entered upon the land without B.'s consent, and cut and carried away stone therefrom:—*Held*, on error in the Exchequer Chamber, that this entry amounted to a determination of the estate at will.

In 1829, B., being one of the assessors for the land-tax in the parish, signed an assessment, in which he was named as the occupier of the farm, and A. as the proprietor:—*Held*, that this was evidence whence the jury might infer that a new tenancy at will had been created between the parties. *Turner* v. *Doe* d. *Bennett*, 643

(2). *Notice to quit—Disclaimer.*

Lands being held by G. as tenant from year to year to D., D., who died in 1837, devised the same to trustees for the term of 140 years, upon trust (inter alia) to permit his wife E. D. to take the rents and profits thereof during her life. G. paid the rent to E. D. the widow, after D.'s death, from 1837 to 1840, and on receiving a notice to quit from her in March 1840, stated that he did not think she would turn him out of possession, as she had promised he should continue on as tenant from year to year:—*Held*, in an action of ejectment brought by the trustees for the recovery of the premises, that this was sufficient evidence of a disclaimer by G. of the title of the trustees, to warrant the jury in finding a verdict for the plaintiff. *Doe* d. *Davies* v. *Evans*, 48

LEASE.

See Covenant to Repair.

LEGACY.

See Executor and Administrator, (1).

LIEN.

See Tender.

LIMITATION ACT.

To what Rents it applies.

The stat. 3 & 4 Will. 4, c. 27, s. 2, does not apply to rent reserved on a demise. *Grant* v. *Ellis*, 113

LIMITATIONS, STATUTE OF.

See Pleading, III., (2).

(1). *Part Payment.*

In an action on a promissory note by the payee against the maker, the note, when produced in evidence by the plaintiff at the trial, bore upon it an indorsement as follows:—"4th Aug. 1837,—Received of J. S. £6— B. × E." The whole of this entry, except the cross, was in the handwriting of the defendant, and there was no attestation, nor any proof that the cross was the mark of B. E., nor any proof of the *fact* of payment:— *Held*, that the indorsement was not evidence of part payment, to take the case out of the Statute of Limitations. *Eastwood* v. *Saville*, 615

(2). *Acknowledgment.*

Debt on a bill of exchange by payee against acceptor for 20*l*.— Pleas, first, except as to 10*l*. 11*s*., parcel &c., a set-off for board and lodging; and as to the sum of 10*l*. 11*s*., payment of that sum into Court. —Replication, that the alleged debts and causes of set-off did not accrue within six years before the commencement of the suit, concluding *to the country:* to which the defendant, by his rejoinder, added the similiter. At the trial, the plaintiff having proved his case, and the defendant his set-off, the latter put in a letter from the plaintiff to the defendant, in which the following passages were relied upon, to take the case out of the statute:—"Before closing this, I have to request you will be pleased to send me in any bill or what demand you have to make on me, and *if just*, I shall not give you the trouble of going to law. If you refer to your books, you will find the *last payment* I made you was in May 1839; the day I have forgot. I shall leave town to-morrow, but shall be back in a few days, for a month, and if you will *bring my bill* in here to me by eleven, I shall be at your service:"—*Held*, that this was not a sufficient admission to take the case out of the Statute of Limitations. *Held*, also, that the issue joined on the replication of the Statute of Limitations was no proper issue, and that there ought to be a repleader. *Spong* v. *Wright*,   629

LIQUIDATED DAMAGES.

See PENALTY.

MASTER AND SERVANT.

The defendant, a builder, was employed by the committee of a club to execute certain alterations at the club-house, including the preparation and fixing of gas-fittings. He made a sub-contract with B., a gas-fitter, to execute this part of the work. In the course of doing it, through B.'s negligence, the gas exploded, and injured the plaintiff:—*Held*, that the defendant was not liable in case for this injury. *Rapson* v. *Cubitt*,   710

MINE.

Proof of Possession of.

In trespass for breaking and entering the plaintiff's mine and taking coals, evidence of working by the plaintiff in another part of the same mine, within eighty yards of the place of the alleged trespass, coupled with a statement by the defendant, that he had got the coal, and was

willing to pay such amount as should be settled by arbitration, was held to be evidence of the plaintiff's being in possession of the place where the trespass was committed. *Wild* v. *Holt*,   672

MISTRIAL.

See JURY.

MODUS.

See TITHE COMMUTATION ACT, 1.

MONEY HAD AND RECEIVED.

See ACCORD AND SATISFACTION, 1.

(1). *Appropriation of Payments.*

The plaintiff sold goods to B., taking his acceptances for the price, and sent them to the defendant as B.'s agent, who consigned them to his partners abroad for sale. While the acceptances were running, the plaintiff, doubting B.'s solvency, required further security; whereupon it was agreed between the plaintiff, B., and the defendant, that B. should write and deliver to the defendant a letter authorizing him, out of any remittances he might receive against the net proceeds of the above consignments, to pay the acceptances as they became due, if not honoured by him, B., previously to the receipt of such net proceeds. The letter was accordingly delivered to the defendant, and he assented to the terms of it. Before the bills were due, B. became bankrupt, and the defendant, having received the net proceeds of the goods, refused to pay any part thereof to the plaintiff, but handed them over to B.'s assignees:—*Held*, that the plaintiff was entitled to recover the amount of the acceptances from the defendant in an action for money had and received; this being an appropriation irrevocable except by the consent of all parties, for which the existing debt, although not then payable, was a good consideration.

Held, also, that the letter did not require a stamp, either as an inland bill or as an agreement. *Walker* v. *Rostron*,   411

(2). *Payment under mistake of Fact.*

Money paid by the plaintiff to the defendant under a bonâ fide *forgetfulness* of facts which disentitled the defendant to receive it, may be recovered back in an action for money had and received.

It is not sufficient to preclude a party from recovering money paid by him under a mistake of fact, that he had the *means of* knowledge of the fact; unless he paid it intentionally, not choosing to investigate the fact. *Kelly* v. *Solari*,   54

MONEY LENT.

When maintainable—Alternative Contract.

Money advanced upon a contract to repay it on demand, or to execute a mortgage, may, after refusal to execute a mortgage, be recovered back under a count for money lent. *Bristowe* v. *Needham*,   729

MORTGAGE.

See STAMP.

MUNICIPAL CORPORATION ACT.

Right of Election of Clerk of Court of Requests in Borough.

By an act of Parliament creating a Court of Requests for the borough of Boston, it was enacted, that the mayor, recorder, deputy recorder, aldermen, and common councilmen for the time being of the borough, the justices of the peace for a certain district, together with other persons therein mentioned, should be the commissioners thereof; and that in case of a vacancy in the situation of clerk of the court, &c., the mayor and aldermen of the borough for the time being, or the major part of them, should appoint a successor, and that until such appointment should be made, the commissioners, or any three or more of them, should nominate officers to do the business of the Court. At a meeting of the town council of B., specially summoned for the purpose of electing a clerk, the plaintiff, who was a member of the council, was elected by the council, and before the end of the election he tendered to the mayor his resignation of the office of town councillor, together with the sum of £50 as a fine on resignation, under 5 & 6 Will. 4, c. 76, s. 51. No bye-law had been made to enforce a fine on resignation, and therefore the mayor returned the £50, in the presence of the council, after the election. The plaintiff's seat in the council was afterwards filled by the election of another person, and at a quarterly meeting of the town council, held on the 7th of May, 1840, of which no notice had been given, the plaintiff was again elected by the town council:—*Held*, first, that neither the 73rd section of 5 & 6 Will. 4, c. 76, nor the 8th section of 6 & 7 Will. 4, c. 105, was applicable to this case.

Secondly, that the case was within the 72nd section of 5 & 6 Will. 4, c. 76; the true construction of which was, that the body corporate, under that act, should be trustees or commissioners for executing, by the town council, the *powers and provisions* of all acts of Parliament, of which *powers and provisions* the old body corporate, or any of the members thereof, in their corporate capacity, were sole commissioners or trustees before the election of the town council: and as the mayor and aldermen were, by the local act, sole trustees or commissioners for the purpose of appointing the clerk, that their powers devolved upon the town council, and that the plaintiff was duly elected at the first meeting; that, under all the circumstances of the case, the plaintiff's resignation of the office of town councillor was sufficient; but that if it was not, his election to the office of clerk had the effect of vacating his office of town councillor. *Staniland* v. *Hopkins*, 178

NAVIGATION ACT.

(1). *Construction of.*

Where, by a navigation act, certain rates and duties were imposed on coals, &c., landed within a certain district, to be paid to commissioners therein named; and the commissioners were empowered to sue in the name of their clerk for the time being for " any penalty or sum of money due or payable by virtue of the act:"—*Held*, that an action of debt might be brought in the name of the clerk for arrears of rates and duties; although, by another clause, a power was given of detaining and selling the vessel and goods in case of neglect or refusal to pay the rates and duties.

The act directed, that any surplus of rates remaining in the hands of the commissioners should be annually invested in the funds until it should amount to £3000, and that after that sum should be invested they should reduce the rates, so as they should not, together with the dividends of the £3000, exceed the charges annually expended in carrying the act into execution:—*Held*, that the commissioners had impliedly a power, after so reducing the rates, also to raise them again in case of necessity.

Held, also, that after the passing of the Weights and Measures' Act, 5 & 6 Will. 4, c. 63, the commissioners had power to levy the rates by the *ton* (they having been previously levied

by the *chaldron*), without first applying to the sessions for an inquisition under the 14th section of that act. *Goody* v. *Penny*, 687

(2). *Construction of—feigned Issue under.*

By a local act, 1 Will. 4, c. 55, the Trent and Mersey Navigation Company were empowered to take lands for the purposes of the navigation; and by sect. 118 and other sections, provision was made for ascertaining, by a sheriff's jury, the sum to be paid for the land, and for any damage occasioned by the company in carrying the provisions of the act into effect. And in order to protect the company from injury to arise from working any mines near two tunnels by which the canal passed under a certain hill, the act provided, by section 170, that no mine owner should work any mine in or under any land within forty yards of the tunnels, without leave of the company; and by section 171, that if the company, instead of insisting on their full right of having forty yards left unworked, should require less than thirty yards to be so left, then the mine owner might insist on the necessity of leaving, for his security, any greater quantity unworked not exceeding thirty yards, and the question so in dispute as to the quantity necessary to be left for the security of the mine owners was to be tried, settled, and determined, *by an issue at law*. And by section 172 it was provided, that whenever any mine became workable in ordinary course, within forty yards of the tunnels, the mine owner should give notice to the company, and thereupon the company should pay to the mine owner for so much of the mine within the forty yards as they should require to be left unworked for security of their works; or (as the case might be) for so much of the mines as, under the provisions of section 171, it might be ascertained to be necessary to leave unworked, for security of the mines. Provided, that no mines should in any case be worked under the tunnels; but whenever any such last-mentioned mines should become workable, satisfaction should be made by the company for the same, "*such satisfaction to be settled by an issue at law.*"

By the 178th section, the course to be taken in trying any feigned issue was pointed out; and it enacted, that after trial and verdict in such issue, the Court was to give judgment for the sum of money to be awarded by the jury:—*Held*, that by the express terms of the 172nd section, the owner of a mine which had become workable within the space of forty yards of the tunnels mentioned in the act, was entitled to be paid for the value of the forty yards of mine left unworked for the security of the navigation, the whole having been by the company required to be so left unworked; but that the only remedy open to him to enforce his right was by a feigned issue, and consequently that he was not entitled to proceed by an action on the case. *Fenton* v. *The Trent and Mersey Navigation Company*,   203

NOTICE TO PRODUCE.

See EVIDENCE, (1).

NUL TIEL RECORD.

See PRACTICE, (5).

PARTNERSHIP.

See BILLS AND NOTES, II.

(1). *By what Agreement constituted.*

In May, 1839, A., a creditor of the firm of B. & S., proposed to become a partner with them, the terms of the intended partnership being, that A. should bring in £1000 in money and £1000 in goods, and should be enti-

titled to one-third of the profits, and be a dormant partner; the name of the firm was to be changed to B. S. & Co., and the partnership was to date from the 1st April, 1839, but A. reserved to himself the option of determining, at any period within twelve months from that day, whether he would become a partner. The name of the firm was altered accordingly, and a new banking account was opened in the name of B. S. & Co.; and A. advanced the £2000 to the firm; but within the twelve months he declared his determination not to enter into the partnership:—*Held*, that A. was not liable for goods supplied to the firm after May, 1839, for that he never became a complete partner. *Gabriel* v. *Evill*,   297

(2). *Liability of dormant Partner under written Agreement made by his Co-partners.*

A., B., & C. being in partnership together as type founders (C. as a dormant partner), an agreement was entered into between A. and B. of the one part, and the plaintiff of the other part, by which, after reciting that the plaintiff had been in the employment of A. and B., as foreman in carrying on the said trade of type-founders, the plaintiff covenanted and agreed with A. and B., and the survivor of them, to serve them and the survivor of them in their said trade for the term of seven years; and they covenanted and agreed to employ him as their foreman for the term of seven years, if they or either of them should so long live, and to pay him three guineas per week; and it was mutually agreed, that if either party should not perform the covenants on their respective parts, the party so failing or making default should pay to the other £500, by way of specific damages. At the time the agreement was entered into it was unknown to the plaintiff that C. was a partner in the business:—*Held*, that an action was maintainable by the plaintiff against A., B., & C., for a breach of this agreement, although C. was not a party named in it or signing it. *Beckham* v. *Drake*,   79

PATENT.
Novelty.

The "public use and exercise" of an invention, which prevents it from being considered a novelty, is a use *in public*, so as to come to the knowledge of others than the inventor, as contradistinguished from the use of it by himself in private; and does not mean a use *by the public generally.*

Therefore, where an improved lock, for which the plaintiff had a patent, had previously been used by an individual on a gate adjoining a public road, for several years; and several dozens of a similar lock had been made at Birmingham from a pattern received from America, and sent abroad; it was held that this constituted such a public use and exercise of the invention as to avoid the patent. *Carpenter* v. *Smith*,   300

PAUPER.
Admission of, pendente Lite.

A plaintiff may be admitted to sue in formâ pauperis after the commencement of the suit. *Doe* d. *Ellis* v. *Owens*,   455

PAYMENT.
See PLEADING, III., (5).

PAYMENT INTO COURT.
See BOND, (2).
       COSTS, (6), (7).
       TENDER OF AMENDS.

PAYMENT UNDER MISTAKE.
See MONEY HAD AND RECEIVED, (2).

PENALTY.
Penalty of liquidated Damages.

The plaintiff and defendant entered into an agreement for the purchase by the defendant of the plaintiff's goodwill, stock, tenant-right, &c.: it was stipulated by the agreement that the plaintiff should give possession on a certain day, and in the meantime should pay the rates and taxes, and keep the defendant indemnified therefrom: and the defendant agreed to pay £100 for the tenant-right, and take the fixtures at a valuation, and pay all rents, rates, taxes, &c., and to indemnify the plaintiff from the same; and lastly, the parties " mutually bound themselves, the one to the other, in the sum of £100 as settled and liquidated damages, to be paid and forfeited, without any deduction, by such of them as should make default in the premises, unto the other of them requiring the same:"—*Held*, that the sum of £100 was a penalty only, and not recoverable as liquidated damages for the breach of any of the stipulations. *Horner* v. *Flintoff*, 678

PEREMPTORY UNDERTAKING.
See PRACTICE, (8).

PLEADING.
See ARBITRATION, (2), 3.
    BILLS AND NOTES, II., (2).
    BOND, (2).
    LIMITATIONS, STATUTE OF, (2).
    PRACTICE, (3), (4), (7).
    PRINCIPAL AND SURETY, (2).
    TRESPASS, (1).

I. *Declaration.*
(1). *Several Counts.*

1. Where the defendant took possession of premises under a demise for three years from Christmas, 1839, and continued to occupy them until the 27th of July, 1841, when he quitted

them, having paid rent to the Midsummer previous:—*Held*, in an action brought to recover the rent which subsequently accrued due, that the plaintiff was not entitled to have a count on the demise and also a count for use and occupation, but that he must make his election. *Arden* v. *Pullen*,　　　　　　　　　　430

2. Two counts on the same policy of insurance, one alleging a loss by perils of the sea, and the other a loss by barratry, cannot be pleaded together. *Blyth* v. *Shepherd*,　　　763

(2). *Averment of Title to demise, when sufficient.*

The declaration stated, that the plaintiff, before and at the time of the agreement thereinafter mentioned, was lawfully possessed for the residue of a term, whereof twenty-one years from the 24th June, 1841, were then unexpired, of a certain dwelling-house; and thereupon, on the 21st March, 1841, by an agreement made between the plaintiff and defendant, it was agreed that the plaintiff should, on or before the 24th June, 1841, let the same to the defendant, by a lease to be granted to the defendant for twenty-one years, the said term to commence from the 24th June, 1841. The declaration then stated general performance by the plaintiff, and that he was ready and willing to let the house to the defendant, and to grant and execute a lease; but that the defendant did not nor would not become his tenant, or accept the lease. Pleas, first, that the plaintiff was not lawfully possessed of the said house, for the residue of the said term, modo et formâ: secondly, that the plaintiff, at the time of the agreement, had not a good title to, and could not, on the 24th June, legally let the house to the defendant, or grant a lease for the said term:—*Held*, on special demurrer, that the first plea was bad, as containing an immaterial traverse; and that the traverse in the second plea was too large, as it included the title of the plaintiff at the time of the contract, as well as at the time when the lease was to be good. *Held*, also, that on general demurrer, the averment of the plaintiff's readiness and willingness to grant the lease was equivalent to an averment of his having a title to grant it. *De Medina* v. *Norman*,　　　820

II. *Pleas in abatement.*

(1). *Coverture.*

Verification by Affidavit.

A plea in abatement, to an action of debt, of the defendant's coverture, is a dilatory plea requiring an affidavit of verification under the stat. 4 Anne, c. 16, s. 11: and if there be no such affidavit, the plaintiff is entitled to sign judgment as for want of a plea, although part of the cause of action accrued after the coverture. *Lovell* v. *Walker*,　　　　　　　　　299

III. *Pleas in bar.*

(1). *Rule to plead several Matters.*

A defendant having obtained an order to plead several matters, pleaded a plea to the whole declaration, and delivered also a demurrer to one count, whereupon the plaintiff signed judgment as for want of a plea. The Court refused to set aside the judgment, except on the terms of the defendant's striking out the demurrer, and paying the costs of his defective pleading. *Baily* v. *Baker*,　769

(2). *Signature.*

A plea of the Statute of Limitations, though it need not conclude with a verification, must nevertheless be signed by counsel. *Roberts* v. *Howard*, 838

(3). *Puis darrein continuance, when pleadable.*

A judge at Nisi Prius is bound to accept a plea puis darrein continuance, even after the jury are sworn, provided it be tendered in due form, and accompanied with the usual affidavit, that the subject-matter of it arose within eight days of the time of its being pleaded.

Semble, that such affidavit is unnecessary, where the subject-matter of the appeal arose at the trial in the presence of the judge. *Todd* v. *Emly,* 606

(4). *Plea of Judgment recovered, what is.*

To an action of assumpsit for money lent, the defendant pleaded, that in an action in which the now defendant was plaintiff, and the now plaintiff was defendant, the now plaintiff set off the same debt for which the present action was brought, and in that action the now defendant obtained a verdict:—*Held,* that this was not a plea of judgment recovered, within the meaning of the rule of H. T. 4 Will. 4, r. 8, and that the plaintiff could not sign judgment as for want of a plea. *Brokenshir* v. *Monger,* 111

(5). *Payment, when proveable under General Issue.*

Where goods are sold for ready money and payment is made accordingly, no *debt* arises, and such payment is therefore proveable under the general issue. *Bussey* v. *Barnett,* 312

(6). *Not Guilty, in Case.*

In case for erecting a cesspool near a well, and thereby contaminating the water of the well, the plea of not guilty puts in issue both the fact of the erection of the cesspool, and that the water was thereby contaminated. *Norton* v. *Scholefield,* 665

(7). *Non detinet.*

Under the plea of non detinet, the plaintiff is entitled to a verdict on proof that the defendant has not returned the chattel to the plaintiff on demand, having previously delivered it, under a supposed contract of sale, to a third party. *Jones* v. *Dowle,* 19

(8). *Issuable Pleas.*

1. Where, to an action of covenant on an indenture of apprenticeship against the father, for breaches by the apprentice, the defendant, being under terms of pleading issuably, pleaded that the plaintiffs carried on the business of engineers as copartners, that the covenants were made with them as such copartners; and that before any breach of duty, they dissolved partnership:—*Held,* that the plea was an issuable one, and ought not to be set aside. *Lloyd* v. *Blackburn,* 363

2. To an action by the indorsee against the acceptor of a bill of exchange, the defendant pleaded, first, that before and at the time of the indorsing of the bill by the drawer, he, the drawer, was indebted to the defendant in a sum of money exceeding the amount of the bill: and that after the bill became due, in order to deprive the defendant of his right of set-off in respect of the debt, he fraudulently indorsed the bill, to enable the plaintiff to sue the defendant on the bill, and without any consideration for the indorsement. The defendant pleaded, secondly, that the drawer, before he indorsed the bill, petitioned for relief under the Insolvent Debtors' Act, whereby the right and title to the bill vested in his assignees:—*Held,* that both were issuable pleas. *Watkins* v. *Bensusan,* 422

3. To a declaration in debt against

executors, containing a count for non-payment of money due on a covenant of the testator, with counts for money paid, and on an account stated, the defendants, being under terms of pleading issuably, pleaded, 1. that "the writing in *the declaration* mentioned" was not the deed of the testator; 2. that "the said writing in the declaration mentioned" was executed for an immoral consideration : — *Held*, that these were not issuable pleas, being in form pleaded to the whole declaration, whereas they applied to the first count only. *Parratt* v. *Goddard*, 458

(9). *Immaterial Traverse.*

Declaration in assumpsit stated, that the defendants bought of the plaintiff a quantity of linseed, to be worked by the buyers in fourteen days from the ship's arrival in the river, the price to be paid in ready money, less 2¼ per cent. discount, or by the defendants' acceptance at two months. Averment, that the linseed arrived and was ready for delivery; that the fourteen days had elapsed; and although the plaintiff tendered it to the defendants for their acceptance, and would have received their acceptance at two months for the price, and although the defendants were requested to pay in ready money, or to give their acceptance, and refused to do the latter, and discharged the plaintiff from tendering a bill for their acceptance, yet they did not accept or work the linseed, or pay for it in ready money.—Pleas, first, that the defendants were not requested to pay for the linseed in ready money, or to give their acceptance: second, that they did not refuse to give their acceptance, or discharge the plaintiff from tendering a bill for their acceptance: — *Held*, that both pleas were bad, as traversing averments which were immaterial to the maintenance of the action. *Spaeth* v. *Hare*, 326

(10). *Duplicity.*

Assumpsit on a bill of exchange drawn by one S. B. upon and accepted by the defendant, for £25, payable three months after date. Plea, that after the bill became due, and before the commencement of the suit, to wit, &c., the said S. B. paid to the plaintiff divers monies, to the amount of £17, and did for the plaintiff work and labour to the value of £8, in full satisfaction and discharge of the sum of money in the bill specified, and of all damages sustained by the non-payment thereof, which were then accepted and received by the plaintiff in such full satisfaction and discharge; and further, that he the defendant accepted the bill at the request and for the accommodation of the said S. B., and not otherwise, and that there never was any consideration or value for the payment by the defendant of the said bill, or any part thereof, and that the plaintiff, at the time of the commencement of the suit, held and now holds the said bill without any consideration or value whatever: — *Held*, that the plea was bad for duplicity. *Purssord* v. *Peek*, 196

(11). *Duplicity—Argumentative Traverse.*

Declaration in assumpsit, stating that the plaintiff had recovered in an action against R. S. the sum of £3000, and had sued out a ca. sa. under which R. S. had been taken in execution, alleged, that in consideration that the plaintiff would procure the release of R. S. from custody, the defendant promised to pay him £500. Averment, that the plaintiff did procure the release of R. S. from custody. Breach, in non-payment of the £500.

The defendant pleaded as follows: —1st. That R. S. was a member of the House of Commons, and entitled to privilege of Parliament, and freedom from arrest; that his release from custody was only on the ground of his being so privileged; that he afterwards ceased to be a member of the House, and became and still is liable to be taken in execution at the suit of the plaintiff; that the promise of the defendant was a promise to answer for the debt of another, and that there was no memorandum in writing thereof.

2nd. That R. S., at the time of his becoming indebted to the plaintiff, was a member of the Commons House of Parliament, and that whilst he continued such member, the plaintiff recovered judgment and issued a ca. sa., under which he was taken into custody; that R. S. was as such member entitled to his discharge from arrest, and that during the continuance of his privilege, a judge ordered his discharge out of custody, and he was discharged accordingly; and that, save as aforesaid, there never was any consideration for the defendant's promise:—*Held*, on special demurrer, that the first plea was bad for duplicity, and the second, as being an argumentative traverse of the allegation in the declaration, that the plaintiff had procured the release of R. S. from custody. *Butcher* v. *Stewart*, 405

(12). *Other Cases.*

To an action of debt by husband and wife, in right of the wife as executrix, for money had and received, the defendant pleaded, as to £35, that that sum was part of the prices received by him upon the sales of two horses of the testator, which were in the hands of the plaintiffs to be administered, and which, under an authority given by them to the defendant, were sold by him in his own name, and warranted sound to the respective purchasers [naming four persons]; that at the time of the sales the horses respectively were unsound;

that the defendant, from the time of the receipt of the money until he paid the same as after mentioned, was indebted to the plaintiffs in the sum of £35, payable on request, for the said money so received by him for their use, and always was ready and willing to pay it to them; and that after he so became indebted, and before the commencement of the suit, he was, by reason of the breaches of the warranties as to the said horses, compelled by the said persons who so purchased them, without any fault on his part, to repay, and did necessarily repay, to them the said sum of £35, and the residue of the prices, whereby the said debt of £35 was discharged: —*Held*, on special demurrer, that the plea was no answer to the action. *Field* v. *Allen*,   694

IV. *Replication.*

(1). *De Injuriâ.*

To an action of assumpsit by the fourth indorsee of a foreign bill of exchange against the first indorser, alleging for breach non-payment by the drawee, the defendant pleaded, that before the bill became due, and after the indorsement to the third indorsee, and before the indorsement to the plaintiff, the bill was refused acceptance, and was protested; that the third indorsee and the plaintiff, at the time of the indorsement to the latter, had notice of the non-acceptance and protest; and that the defendant had not due notice of the non-acceptance or of the protest:—*Held*, on special demurrer, that a replication de injuriâ to this plea was good. *Whitehead* v. *Walker*,   506

(2). *Of prior Demand, to Plea of Tender.*

Assumpsit for work and labour, money paid, and on an account stated.

Plea, as to 4l. 16s., parcel &c., that, after the making of the defendant's promises, to wit, on &c., the defendant tendered to the plaintiff 4l. 16s., and, as to that sum, he has always been ready to pay the said sum of 4l. 16s. to the plaintiff, and now brings the same into Court, &c.—Replication, that before the making of the tender in the plea mentioned, and before and at the time of the demand and refusal hereinafter mentioned, a larger sum than 4l. 16s., to wit, 7l. 12s., that sum including the 4l. 16s., was due from the defendant to the plaintiff on account of divers of the causes of action in the declaration; and that before the making of the said tender, to wit, on &c., the plaintiff demanded of the defendant payment of the said sum of 7l.12s., which so included the said sum of 4l. 16s.; yet the defendant did not pay the said sum of 7l. 12s., or any part thereof, but refused to pay the same and every part thereof, and that no set-off or other just cause then existed for the non-payment:—*Held*, on special demurrer, that the replication was good. *Tyler* v. *Bland*, 338

V. *Frivolous Demurrer.*

To a declaration in debt for non-payment of money pursuant to a covenant in a " deed of apprenticeship," (so describing the instrument throughout the declaration), the defendant pleaded, " that the said *indenture* in the declaration mentioned is not his deed." On special demurrer to the plea, the Court refused to set aside the demurrer as frivolous, and intimated their opinion that the plea was bad. *Bird* v. *Holman*, 761

VI. *Arrest of Judgment, or Venire de Novo.*

A declaration in debt contained a count on a bill of exchange by indorsee against drawer, and also counts for money paid, and on an account stated. It appeared from one of the pleas to the first count, that the plaintiff and defendant were not immediate parties to the bill, and the Court therefore held that the plaintiff could not recover on that count: and the plaintiff having at the trial obtained a verdict for the amount of the bill, with general damages, the Court awarded a venire de novo, but refused to arrest the judgment. *Lewin* v. *Edwards,* 720

POOR RATE.

Distress on Tenant for Rates due from Landlord. Construction of Local Act.

By a local act, 10 Geo. 3, c. lxxv., the 15th section enacted, that the rates directed by that act to be made should and might, on refusal or neglect to pay the same by any person or persons *liable thereto,* be recovered in such manner as the rates made for the relief of the poor are directed to be recovered; and by the 17th section it was provided, that any person, whether landlord or tenant, who should let his or her house in separate apartments, or ready furnished to a lodger or lodgers, should be deemed to be the *occupier* thereof, and might be rated or assessed accordingly, and should be liable to the payment of the sum so rated. And s. 18 enacted, that the goods and chattels of each and every person renting or occupying any separate part or apartment in such house or building, or renting or occupying any ready-furnished house, or any part thereof, *should be liable to be distrained and sold* for the payment of the said rates:—*Held*, first, that under that act, the goods of a lodger are liable to be distrained and sold for rates assessed upon and due from the landlord, under a warrant directing the churchwardens and overseers to take the goods of the landlord.

The warrant recited that the rates were due from D., the landlord; that they had been lawfully demanded, and refused to be paid; and that it had been fully proved to the justices on oath, that D. had been duly summoned before them to shew cause why he had refused to pay the rates; but that he had not shewn any sufficient cause:—*Held*, in an action against the constable for seizing the goods, that it was not any objection that there was no proof that the landlord had been duly summoned.

Held, also, that the action could not be maintained against the constable for any thing done under the warrant, without a demand of a perusal and copy of the warrant, unless he were guilty of any excess; in which case he would be liable for such excess, without such a demand.

The constable having entered the house of D. and there distrained the goods of a lodger, placed a person in possession of the goods in the room in which they were, saying that, unless the money were paid, he should remain there five days; he remained in possession eight hours, until the lodger paid the amount to redeem the goods:—*Held*, that this was not an impounding, but that it was a question for the jury whether he had remained an unreasonable time for the removal of the goods under the warrant. *Peppercorn* v. *Hofman*,   618

POWER.

Execution of—Attestation.

A power to demise premises with the consent of A. B., in writing, *duly attested*, is not well executed by a demise which professes to be made with the consent of A. B., "testified by his being a party to those presents;" the meaning is, that the written consent shall be signed in the presence of a witness. *Freshfield* v. *Reed*,   404

PRACTICE.

(1). *On moving to rescind Judge's Order.*

An affidavit in support of a rule to rescind a Judge's order, need not take notice of a previous application for the same purpose made at chambers, and refused; unless it be necessary to do so in order to account for apparent delay in making the application to the Court. *Thomas* v. *Evans*,   829

(2). *Service of Rule.*

An affidavit of service of a rule nisi stated that the deponents served "the above-named defendant with a true copy of the rule, by delivering and leaving with one H., at the defendant's residence, situate &c., a true copy of the said rule, and at the same time shewing the original thereof, and that the said H. promised to deliver the said copy to the defendant:"—*Held* to be insufficient, as it did not shew a service on any person connected with the defendant's residence. *Taylor* v. *Whitworth*,   478

(3). *Rule to strike out Pleas.*

Rule to strike out pleas allowed by a judge at chambers will not be entertained by the Court; the rule should be to set aside the judge's order. *Turquand* v. *Hawtrey*,   727

(4). *Non issuable Plea, how waived.*

Obtaining time to reply is a waiver of an objection that the plea is not an issuable one, the defendant having been under terms to plead issuably. *Trott* v. *Smith*,   765

(5). *Rule to produce Record.*

Where, on an issue on nul tiel record, the record is to be produced by the defendant, a four-day side-bar rule to produce it is necessary, and a notice to the defendant to produce it is not sufficient. *Swinburn* v. *Taylor,* 43

(6). *Notice of Trial.*

A notice of trial in an inferior court of record is insufficient, unless it specify the day of trial. Such defect is waived by the defendant's taking out a summons to set aside the notice, and insisting, on the hearing of the summons, on a different objection only, which is overruled by the judge. *Farmer* v. *Mountfort,* 100

(7). *Issues in Law and Fact, Order of Determination of.*

Where there are issues both in fact and in law in an action, although the plaintiff has an option to try either first, that is subject to the discretion of the Court; and they will, in general, direct the issues in law to be determined first, since the cause may be decided thereby, and the trial become unnecessary; and also because after verdict there can be no amendment on the demurrer. *Crucknell* v. *Trueman,* 684

(8). *Judgment as in case of Nonsuit.*

1. *Peremptory Undertaking given by Husband and Wife.*

Where in an action by husband and wife, in right of the wife as executrix, a peremptory undertaking was given to try at a specified time; and the husband afterwards died:—*Held,* that the undertaking was not binding on the wife. *Lee* v. *Armstrong,* 14

2. *Service of Rule containing Peremptory Undertaking.*

Where a rule nisi for judgment as in case of a nonsuit, is discharged on a peremptory undertaking, either party may draw up the rule containing the undertaking, and if the defendant does so he must serve the plaintiff with it, to enable him to try according to the undertaking; and where the plaintiff gave a peremptory undertaking to try at the sittings after term, and on default a rule absolute was obtained for judgment as in case of a nonsuit, the Court set aside that rule and all proceedings thereon for irregularity, the defendant not having served the plaintiff with the rule containing the undertaking until the first day of the sittings. *Sawyer* v. *Thompson,* 248

PRINCIPAL AND AGENT.

See MONEY HAD AND RECEIVED, (1).

PRINCIPAL AND SURETY.

(1). *Liability of Principal on Covenant with Surety.*

The plaintiff and defendant being joint makers of a promissory note, the defendant as principal and the plaintiff as his surety, the defendant covenanted with the plaintiff to pay the amount to the payee of the note on a given day, but made default:—*Held,* in an action on this covenant, that the plaintiff was entitled, though he had not paid the note, to recover the full amount of it by way of damages. *Loosemore* v. *Radford,* 657

(2). *Liability of Surety on Agreement to join Principal in Bond.*

To a declaration stating that T. was the lessee of certain tolls, and that S. and the defendants agreed to join with T. in a bond conditioned for payment of the rent under the lease; and alleging as a breach that the defendant refused to join T. in the bond: the defendant pleaded, first, that at the time of tendering the bond to him, S.

had not executed the same, nor was he present ready to execute it jointly with the defendant: 2nd, that S. died before the commencement of the suit, and that before his death the bond was not tendered to the defendant for execution, nor was he requested to execute it:—*Held,* that the pleas were bad. *Horne* v. *Ramsdale,*   329

PROCESS.

(1). *Amendment of.*

A judge made an order for the arrest of the defendant for £422. The capias was indorsed for 422*l.* 13*s.* 4*d.*, (the real amount of the debt). The Court refused to discharge the defendant out of custody, and directed the writ to be amended on payment by the plaintiff of the costs of the application for the defendant's discharge. *Plock* v. *Pacheco,*   342

(2). *Variance of Writ from Affidavit to hold to Bail.*

1. The affidavit in support of a capias described the plaintiff as "J.R. one of the public officers of the Western District Banking Company *for Devon and Cornwall:*" in the writ these last words were omitted. The Court discharged, without costs, a rule for discharging the defendant out of custody on the ground of the variance, upon the plaintiff's filing a fresh affidavit, omitting those words in the title. *Richards* v. *Dispraile,*   459

2. Where an affidavit of debt described the plaintiff as "W. B. the younger," but in the capias he was called "W. B." only, his father bearing the same name and residing in the same town as himself:—*Held,* that the writ was bad, but the Court allowed the plaintiff to amend it on payment of costs, on the ground that the plaintiff might suffer a detriment if the defendant were discharged out

of custody, and it not being a mere question of costs. *Bilton* v. *Clapperton,*   473

RELEASE.

See DEED.
    PLEADING, III., (3).
    WITNESS, (1), (1).

RENT.

See LIMITATION ACT.

REPLEADER.

See LIMITATIONS, STATUTE OF, (2).

SHERIFF.

(1). *Attachment against.*

1. *For not returning Writ returnable in Term.*

The rule of M. T., 3 Will. 4, r. 13, applies only to the case of writs issued *and returnable* in vacation; in the case of a fi. fa. issued in vacation, but returnable, under a judge's order obtained in vacation, on a day in term, the plaintiff must still pursue the old practice, and cannot bring the sheriff into contempt after the writ has been actually returned, although after the day on which it was returnable. *Williamson* v. *Harrison,*   225

2. *How waived.*

A plaintiff does not waive his right to an attachment against the sheriff for not duly returning a writ of fi. fa., by directing him, after the expiration of the rule to return the writ, to proceed with the execution, which had been suspended by an adverse claim. *Howitt* v. *Rickaby,*   52

STAMP.

See FRAUDS, STATUTE OF, (1).
    MONEY HAD AND RECEIVED, 1.

On mortgage.

A firm that was negotiating to obtain an advance of money on their bill, wrote to the proposed lender, stating that, in consideration of his accepting their draft, they handed him therewith the bill of lading and policy of insurance for wines expected to arrive, which would afford him security beyond the amount of the bill, and engaging to land and warehouse the wines, to be held at his disposal: —*Held,* that this document did not require a mortgage stamp, within the 55 Geo. 3, c. 184, sched, part 1, title ' Mortgage.' *Harris* v. *Birch,* 591

STATUTE.

See NAVIGATION ACT.
     POOR RATE.
     TENDER OF AMENDS.

Construction of.

By a local act, for raising the sum of £21,000 to pay the amount of damages recovered of the hundred of B. for the partial destruction of Nottingham Castle by rioters, the justices of the peace for the county of N. were empowered to borrow the required sum by mortgage, or a sale of annuities secured on the proportion of the county rate chargeable on the inhabitants of the hundred of B. And by sect. 5, the justices were required to charge the proportion of the county rate to be raised upon the inhabitants of the hundred (except as thereinafter mentioned) not only with the interest of the money borrowed, but also with the payment of such further sum as should insure the payment of the sum borrowed within seven years, or with the payment of such annuities for the like period, as should be agreed to be paid or granted in respect of any part of the money so borrowed; and such sums should be assessed and recovered on the hundred in such manner as county rates are directed to be assessed and recovered;

and should be paid and applied under the direction of the justices in discharge of the interest, and so many of the principal sums secured, or of such annuities, as such money would extend to discharge in each year, until the whole of the money should be paid. The 8th sect. provided a method for each parish to exempt itself from the operation of the act, by paying its proportionate quota in the first instance, and for that purpose directed the justices, after ascertaining the amount of the sum to be borrowed, to specify and declare the sum to be paid or contributed by each parish as the proportionate quota or share of the whole sum so ascertained; and also to appoint a day on or before which the churchwardens or overseers of the poor of any such parish, desirous of paying the full amount of its proportionate quota, might pay the same to the person appointed as receiver under the act; and upon payment thereof, such parish should be discharged from all future payments relating to the integral sum whereof such quota should have been so paid, and from the interest thereof, and also from any share of the expenses, &c. And the 9th sect. enabled the churchwardens and overseers in every such parish, to raise the sum required as the quota of such parish, by loan on the security of their parochial rates, to be repaid within seven years.

In pursuance of the 8th sect. the justices fixed the quota of each parish in the hundred. Four availed themselves of the option of paying their quota. The parish of R., and thirty more, did not; and the justices raised the required sum, after allowing for these payments, by granting annuities of £3600 per annum, for seven years.

Held, that the effect of the 8th and 9th sections was to exempt from the operation of the 5th section those pa-

rishes only who paid their ascertained quota; that the annuities granted by the justices to pay the remainder were to be secured upon the portion of the county rate raised upon the hundred of B., with the exception of those parishes which had paid; and that the county rate, with those exceptions, was liable in the aggregate to the incumbrance, which was to be raised, in addition to the ordinary county rate, by order of the justices, in the same way in all respects as the other county rate is levied. *Walker* v. *Sherwin,*
266

STOCK-JOBBING ACT.

Indebitatus assumpsit for stock sold and caused to be transferred by the plaintiff to the defendant, and by the defendant duly accepted.—Plea, that the stock alleged to be caused to be transferred was so caused to be transferred by virtue of an agreement with the plaintiff for the transfer of the same, in consideration of 4531*l.* 5*s.* to be therefore paid to the plaintiff for the same; and that, at the time of making such agreement, the plaintiff *was not actually possessed of or entitled to the stock* in his own right, &c.; by means whereof the said contract became and was null and void:—*Held,* on error brought upon the judgment of the Court of Exchequer, that the plea was no answer to the action, and that the contract was not within 7 Geo. 2, c. 8, s. 8; affirming the judgment of the Court below. *M'Callan* v. *Mortimer,*
636

STOPPAGE IN TRANSITU.

A notice of stoppage in transitu, to be effectual, must be given either to the person who has the immediate custody of the goods, or to the principal whose servant has the custody, at such a time, and under such circumstances as that he may by the

exercise of reasonable diligence communicate it to his servant in time to prevent the delivery to the consignee. Therefore, where timber was sent from Quebec, to be delivered at Port Fleetwood in Lancashire, a notice of stoppage given to the shipowner at Montrose, while the goods were on their voyage, whereupon he sent a letter to await the arrival of the captain at Fleetwood, directing him to deliver the cargo to the agents of the vendor—was held not to be a sufficient notice of stoppage in transitu.

The vessel arrived in port on the 8th of August, on which day, before the captain had received his owner's letter, the agent of the assignees of the vendee (who had become bankrupt) went on board, and told the captain he had come to take possession of the cargo. He went into the cabin, into which the ends of timber projected, and saw and touched the timber. When the agent first stated that he came to take possession the captain made no reply, but subsequently, at the same interview, told him that he would deliver him the cargo when he was satisfied about his freight. They then went on shore together. Shortly afterwards the agent of the vendor came on board, and served a notice of stoppage in transitu upon the mate, who had charge of the cargo; and a few days afterwards received possession of the cargo from the captain:—*Held,* that, under these circumstances, there was no *actual* possession taken of the goods by the assignees; and that, as there was no contract by the captain to hold the goods as their agent, the circumstances did not amount to a *constructive* possession of the goods by them.

Quære, whether the act of marking, or taking samples, or the like, without any removal of any part of the goods from the possession of the carrier, even though done with the intention of taking possession, will amount to a *constructive* possession, unless accompanied by circumstances denoting that the carrier was intended to keep, and assented to keep, possession of the goods as the agent of the vendee.

Before the consignor knew of the bankruptcy of the consignee, he had sent three letters to the manager of a bank in Liverpool, inclosing bills drawn by himself upon certain parties, and he referred therein to the defendants as persons who would settle any irregularity that might occur respecting the acceptances. These letters were communicated to the defendants, and assented to by them. Another letter to the same party inclosed a bill drawn upon the consignee for the price of the timber in question:—*Held,* that the letters were admissible in evidence, and were some evidence to shew an authority in the defendants to stop the cargo in transitu.

The consignor, *before* the stoppage in transitu, wrote a letter to the defendants, in which he assumed that they had stopped the cargo, and gave directions as to the sale of it. This letter did not reach the defendants until *after* the stoppage. *Quære,* whether it gave authority to them to stop the cargo at the time of the stoppage, or amounted to a valid ratification of that act. *Whitehead* v. *Anderson,*　　　　　518

TENDER.

See PLEADING, IV. (2).

When necessary before Action of Trover.

In trover by the owner of goods against a carrier who has detained the goods under a claim of lien, it is not necessary, in order to entitle the plaintiff to recover, that he should prove an actual tender of the carriage money, if it appear that he was ready to pay it, but that the defendant refused to deliver the goods except on payment of an alleged old balance, which the jury find not to have been really due. *Jones* v. *Tarleton,*　675

TENDER OF AMENDS.

By Party acting in execution of Statute.

By a local Act (6 Geo. 4, c. lxx.), certain commissioners were empowered to cause any "present or future sewers, ditches, drains, &c. to be opened, enlarged, altered, or cleansed:" and it was enacted, that in case any action should be brought against any person for any thing done in pursuance of the act, or in relation to the matters therein contained, the plaintiff should not recover in any such action, if tender of amends should have been made to him, &c., or his attorney, by or on behalf of the defendant, &c. before such action brought; and in case no such tender should be made, that it should be lawful for the defendant, by leave of the Court, to pay money into Court; and if the matter should appear to have been done in pursuance and under the authority of the act, and after sufficient satisfaction made or tendered as aforesaid, then that the jury should find for the defendant.

The commissioners, of whom the defendant was one, appointed a committee to inspect a certain ditch, with a view to widening the same, and to report thereon. The committee having reported thereon in favour of widening the ditch, the commissioners appointed a second committee, of whom the defendant was one, to confer with a surveyor respecting the work, with power to two of them to act. The defendant being afterwards told by the clerk to the commissioners that he might proceed without further instructions from the commissioners, took the plaintiff's land for the purpose of widening the drain, without having given him notice or obtained his consent. The land was taken for the bonâ fide purpose of widening the drain. The defendant, before action, tendered £10 as amends, which the plaintiff refused to accept; but no tender was pleaded, nor was the amount paid into Court. The jury found the trespass, and that the damage amounted to £5:—*Held*, first, that although neither the defendant nor the commissioners were authorized to take plaintiff's land without his consent in writing, yet the defendant was entitled to the protection of the act.

Secondly, that the defendant was not bound to plead the tender, or pay the amount tendered into Court. *Jones* v. *Gooday*,   736

TITHE COMMUTATION ACT.

(1). *Right of Commissioners to entertain successive Claims of Modus.*

Where a claim of a modus or other exemption from tithe is preferred before the tithe commissioners appointed under 6 & 7 Will. 4, c. 71, who decide against the claim set up, the party is not precluded from setting up a claim to a different modus on the same lands, unless the commissioners have made their final award under the act; even though a feigned issue, delivered under the 46th section, be pending to try the validity of the first modus. *Barker* v. *Birch*,   129

(2). *Expenses of Apportionment, what are.*

Expenses incurred by the employment of an attorney by the landowners of a parish, to conduct the proceedings towards a commutation of the tithes of the parish, under the stat. 6 & 7 Will. 4, c. 71, are not "expenses of or incident to making the apportionment," within the 75th section of that act: and the attorney may therefore recover the amount of his bill for such services, in an action against the landowners who were parties to employing him. *Hinckcliffe* v. *Armitstead*,   155

TOWER HAMLETS COURT OF REQUESTS' ACT.

See COURT OF REQUESTS' ACT.

TRESPASS.

(1). *To Real Property.*

1. *Statement of Abuttals.*

In trespass qu. cl. fr., a description of a close by two abuttals only is a sufficient compliance with the rule of H. T. 4 Will. 4, trespass, 1. *North* v. *Ingamells*,   249

(2). *De bonis asportatis.*

1. *Damages in.*

Trespass for breaking and entering the dwelling-house of the plaintiff, and taking away certain goods therein, *not* alleging them to be the plaintiff's goods. Plea, not guilty by statute. The learned judge at the trial having directed the jury to find a verdict for the plaintiff, with nominal damages, for the trespass to the house:—*Held*, that the plaintiff was not entitled to damages also for the value of the goods, as they were not alleged to be the property of the plaintiff. *Pritchard* v. *Long*,   666

(3). *By taking Minerals.*

1. *Damages in.*

In trespass for taking coals from the plaintiff's mine, where the defendant is a mere wrong-doer, the measure of damages is the value of the coals at the time when they first existed as chattels, and the defendant is not entitled to any deduction for the expense of getting them, or for a rent payable to the mine-owner on coals got from the mine. *Wild* v. *Holt,*   672

TROVER.
See TENDER.

USE AND OCCUPATION.
Liability of Tenants holding over.

Where premises are let for a certain term to A. & B., and A. holds over after the expiration of the term, with B.'s assent, both are liable in an action for use and occupation, for so long as A. continues actually to occupy, but no longer.

Quære, whether both are so liable where A. holds over without B.'s consent. *Christy* v. *Tancred,*   438

VENIRE DE NOVO.
See PLEADING, VI.

WARRANT OF ATTORNEY.
Attestation.

A warrant of attorney was attested in the following form: " Signed, sealed, and delivered by J. A., in my presence, and I subscribe myself as attorney for the said J. A., expressly named by him to attest his execution of these presents:"—*Held,* by *Alderson,* B., to be insufficient; *Parke,* B., dubitante.

But assuming such attestation to be bad, *held,* that it was not such gross negligence as to preclude the attorney of the creditor from recovering his charges in respect of the warrant of attorney, it having been set aside as defective. *Elkington* v. *Holland,* 659

WARRANTY.
Of Horse—Unsoundness, what is.

The term " sound," in a warranty of a horse or other animal, implies the absence of any disease or seeds of disease in the animal at the time, which actually diminishes or in its progress will diminish his natural usefulness in the work to which he would properly and ordinarily be applied. *Kiddell* v. *Burnard,* ·   668

WEIGHTS AND MEASURES' ACT.
See NAVIGATION ACT, 1.
Authority of Inspector.

An inspector of weights and measures, appointed by the sessions under the 5 & 6 Will. 4, c. 63, s. 17, and having a general warrant from a magistrate, under s. 28, to act as such within his jurisdiction, may, by virtue of such appointment and warrant, enter any shop, &c., within his district, at all seasonable times, to examine and seize false weights and measures, and need not have a special warrant from a justice in each individual case. *Hutchings* v. *Reeves,*   747

WITNESS.
(1). *Competency.*
1. *Of Next of Kin.*

In an action against an administrator for taking the plaintiff's goods, to which he pleaded that they were his goods as administrator:—*Held,* that one of the next of kin of the intestate was a competent witness for the defendant, without a release.

Quære, whether a release by *two* of the next of kin to the administrator, of their respective interests in the goods the subject of the action, required more than one stamp?

Such a release (if necessary) would have been sufficient, without extending also to the costs of the action; inasmuch as they would not necessarily be allowed to the administrator as a charge on the estate, in case of a verdict for the plaintiff. *Thomas* v. *Bird*, 68

2. *Of Co-contractor.*

In an action against one of several joint contractors, the other co-contractors are competent witnesses for the defendant, since the stat. 3 & 4 Will. 4, c. 42, ss. 26, 27. *Poole* v. *Palmer*, 71

3. *Of Copyholder to prove Custom.*

In an action by the lord of a manor against a copyholder, for taking stones, where the defendant justifies under an alleged custom of the manor, entitling the copyholders to take the stones to be used on premises within the manor, any other copyholder is a competent witness for the defendant since the stat. 3 & 4 Will. 4, c. 42, ss. 26, 27. *Hoyle* v. *Coupe*, 450

WRIT, AMENDMENT OF.

See PROCESS, (1).

WRIT OF TRIAL.

See COURT OF REQUESTS' ACTS.

(1). *Jury to be summoned under.*

A writ of trial was directed to the recorder of a borough, directing him to summon a jury of the borough, duly qualified according to law:—*Held* regular, and that it was not necessary, under the stat. 3 & 4 Will. 4, c. 42, s. 17, that the jury should be taken from the county. *Farmer* v. *Mountfort*, 100

(2). *Amendment of informalities in.*

Where the issue and writ of trial were informal in the following respects:—1. that the date of the writ of summons did not appear in the writ of trial; 2. that the issue did not recite any writ of summons or award of venire; 3. that the award of venire, in the writ of trial, stated the debt to be above £20; 4. that the writ of trial bore no date; and 5. that it did not recite when and out of what Court it issued: the defendant having appeared at the trial without objection, and a verdict having been found for the plaintiff, the Court refused to set aside the proceedings, but directed that the writ of trial should be amended, the plaintiff paying the costs of the amendment and of the application to set aside the proceedings. *Emery* v. *Howard*, 108

(3). *When set aside for Informalities in Issue.*

Where the date of the writ of summons, and the recital of the writ itself, were omitted in the issue, but the writ of trial was correct in these particulars, and the defendant, at the trial, protested against the irregularity, and refused to take any part in the proceedings; a rule afterwards obtained to set aside the issue and all subsequent proceedings was discharged with costs, on the ground that the defendant ought to have returned the issue when delivered, or applied before the trial to set it aside. *Coose* v. *Neumegen*, 290

END OF VOL. IX.

W. M'DOWALL, PRINTER, PEMBERTON-ROW, GOUGH-SQUARE.